DESTROYING DEMOCRACY

DESTROYING DEMOCRACY

How Government Funds Partisan Politics

James T. Bennett · Thomas J. DiLorenzo

CATO INSTITUTE

Library of Congress Cataloging in Publication Data

Bennett, James T.
    Destroying democracy.

    Bibliography: p. 505
    Includes index.
    1. Pressure groups—United States—Finance.
2. Campaign funds—United States. 3. Government
spending policy—United States. 4. United States—
Social policy—1980–   . I. DiLorenzo, Thomas J.
II. Title.
JK1118.B393   1985   322.4'3'0973   85-25486
ISBN 0-932790-53-4
ISBN 0-932790-54-2 (pbk.)

Printed in the United States of America.

CATO INSTITUTE
224 Second Street SE
Washington, D.C. 20003

Contents

Tables

TEXT

APPENDIX

Preface

As practitioners of public choice, the subdiscipline of economics that studies politics, we have long had an active interest in public policy. The development of public choice theory has opened many windows to that often murky and confusing world of politics, but there are still many questions about governmental programs that have never been satisfactorily answered. Why, for example, does government spend tens of billions of dollars each year on a bewildering array of social programs when there is abundant evidence that these programs are ineffective and often counterproductive? Despite massive spending over a period of more than two decades to combat poverty, hunger, unemployment, and many other social problems, little and often no real progress has been made. The documented failures of these efforts have been used primarily as excuses to increase the appropriations for existing programs and to initiate new programs. It is clear that the poor, the hungry, and the unemployed do not seem to have benefited greatly from these expenditures. One may reasonably ask, then, who does benefit from these programs, and where does the taxpayers' money go?

A central tenet of public choice theory is that all individuals, whether in the public sector or the private sector, act in their own self-interest. Politicians and bureaucrats, therefore, can be expected to allocate the taxpayers' dollars in ways that benefit them personally. In effect, politicians view social programs as a way of directing political benefits to themselves, often regardless of whether the intended beneficiaries of the programs are helped. This book demonstrates how tax funds appropriated for social and other programs have been diverted on a massive scale to support political advocacy, that is, to help in the reelection campaigns of those who hold office and to expand the bureaucratic empires of public employees. This process constitutes tax-funded politics.

Some evidence of tax-funded politics has appeared from time to time, usually in scattered newspaper accounts of the political activities of groups that receive taxpayer funding. It occurred to us, however, that there was no comprehensive documentation of the allocation of tax funds to groups that actively pursued political goals, so it was not clear whether these scattered reports of political misdeeds were indicative of a major problem or were merely isolated instances. Using taxpayers' money for political purposes has long been illegal, but little attention has ever been given to the problem. Our goal was to investigate the phenomenon of tax-funded politics, offer an explanation for it, and explore the economic consequences. This book is the result.

Our research has provided us with insight into and understanding about how government operates—and how the government often fails to serve the taxpayers' interests. In our view, tax-funded politics represents a national scandal, which, unfortunately, the Reagan administration has done little to correct. Taxpayers deserve better treatment, and it is our hope that this book will focus attention on the serious and illegal misuse of tax dollars and will contribute to ending this practice.

The reader may conclude from the tone of our writing that we have become jaded about tax-funded politics. The conclusion is warranted. We spent months going through piles of computer output, congressional testimony, General Accounting Office audits, studies and reports from dozens of public and private sources, newspaper clippings, books, and monographs, as well as brochures, annual reports, newsletters, pamphlets, press releases, training manuals, and proposals produced by advocacy groups. In doing so, we were amazed at the size and scope of activities financed with tax dollars, the number of organizations involved, the callous treatment accorded the unfortunate members of society in whose name the funds were obtained, and the degree to which these organizations cooperate in promoting their common goals. We trust that others will find the information useful and revealing and that it will encourage further research in this area. There is still much to be done, for we have only scratched the surface of the problem.

Many individuals and organizations have contributed to our efforts, and our work would have been impossible without their assistance. Howard Phillips of the Conservative Caucus Research, Analysis & Education Foundation permitted us to use his organization's extensive research files on grants and contracts to political groups. Access to such a rich data base greatly facilitated our efforts. Eric Busch, a Scaife Summer Research Fellow in the Department of Economics at George Mason University, spent months gathering, organizing, and analyzing data obtained from these files. Other Scaife fellows who participated in the project were Robert Kneuper, Diek Carlson, Arthur Fleisher, Samson Kimenyi, and Debbie Walker. Marianne Keddington edited the entire manuscript and can be credited with making sense of occasional nonsense. The staff of the Cato Institute made many valuable comments and suggestions. We are especially grateful to William Niskanen, chairman of the Cato Institute, and to Ed Crane, the institute's president, for their extensive comments. The assistance of all these individuals and others with whom we have discussed our work has been indispensable. We absolve them entirely for any shortcomings; any mistakes are entirely ours.

We also gratefully acknowledge the generous research support that enabled us to undertake this work over a period of more than two years. Grants were provided by the John M. Olin Foundation, the J. M. Foundation, the Earhart Foundation, the Sarah Scaife Foundation, the Sunmark Foundation, and D. Tennant Bryan.

I. Introduction

> To compel a man to furnish contributions of money for the propagation of opinions which he disbelieves is sinful and tyrannical.
>
> —Thomas Jefferson
> *Virginia Statute of Religious Liberty*

If one accepts Jefferson's view, stated in 1786, there is a great deal of sin and more than a little tyranny in the United States today. This book demonstrates that federal, state, and local governments give hundreds of millions of taxpayer dollars each year to organizations that use the money for political advocacy, including lobbying, campaigning, and grass-roots organizing. Given a choice, many taxpayers would not support the political agendas of these recipients of governmental largesse. Indeed, an important reason advocacy groups seek tax funding is that they cannot obtain resources from voluntary contributions.

There is no way to know precisely how many tax dollars are diverted for political purposes, for it is impossible to analyze and investigate the tens of thousands of grants and contracts issued each year through hundreds of governmental programs. There is no doubt, however, that the potential for abuse is enormous. In 1982 one researcher noted that at the federal level alone there were "some 1,000 programs that annually give over $190 billion in loans and loan guarantees and $287 billion in grants and direct payments. Individuals are eligible for 519 programs, nonprofit organizations for 496 programs, and state and local governments for 796 programs." Even this accounting, however, is incomplete, because it is "close to impossible to include every program that is currently available."[1]

It is not only reprehensible to force individuals to contribute to causes they oppose, it is also illegal. Congress has repeatedly prohibited the use of federal funds for political activities and has made it a criminal offense for federal officials to spend appropriated funds to encourage grass-roots lobbying:

1

No part of the money appropriated by any enactment of Congress shall, in the absence of express authorization by Congress, be used directly or indirectly to pay for any personal service, advertisement, telegram, telephone, letter, printed or written matter, or other device, intended or designed to influence in any manner a member of Congress, to favor or oppose, by vote or otherwise, any legislation or appropriation by Congress, whether before or after the introduction of any bill or resolution proposing such legislation or appropriation.[2]

In addition, many appropriation bills contain riders that also ban the use of tax dollars for political purposes. Even the Supreme Court has ruled that a person cannot be required "to contribute to the support of an ideological cause he may oppose."[3]

Some people have claimed that regulations and laws against the use of tax dollars for political advocacy are unconstitutional because they limit the right of free speech.[4] But such claims have no merit. The relevant issue is the taxpayer subsidy of political speech and activity. Political speech by those who receive their livelihood from the federal government has long been restricted by the Hatch Act, which prohibits any officer or employee in the executive branch of the federal government, or any agency or department, from taking any active part in political management or in political campaigns. The courts have upheld extending the restrictions in the act to include an "officer or employee of any state or local agency whose principal employment is in connection with any activity which is financed in whole or in part [by the federal government]."[5]

Extending the restrictions further to include employees of private organizations that are funded by the federal government would not be a drastic step. If political advocacy can be legally restricted for public employees, it is difficult to argue that constitutional issues suddenly surface when the same restriction is applied to individuals who are different only because they are employed by organizations that claim to be private, but which often obtain their revenues from the taxpayer.[6]

The legal and moral strictures against tax-funded politics have done nothing to curb this misuse of taxpayers' money. The laws and regulations have not been enforced, and there is evidence to indicate that they are widely ignored and openly flaunted. Even flagrant and widely publicized violations are generally tolerated. Although Congress has mandated against the use of taxpayers' funds for political activity, no real attempt has been made to enforce the law, and alternative means have not been sought to curb the abuses. This is not surprising, for members of Congress are the major beneficiaries of tax-funded politics; tax revenues are used to bolster support for the expansion of their powers and to increase their chances for reelection.

One important reason Congress has made little effort to control the use of tax funds for political purposes is that there has been almost no pressure from taxpayers to address the problem. Few taxpayers are even aware of the size and scope of tax-funded political advocacy. Our first objective in this book, therefore, is to remedy this deficiency by documenting the political use of tax funds that advocacy groups obtain through grants and contracts from federal, state, and local government agencies. Requests for information made to various federal agencies (under the Freedom of Information Act) revealed that hundreds of grants and contracts have been awarded to organizations that routinely engage in lobbying, campaigning, and grass-roots organizing. These activities are summarized throughout the book, but time and resources did not permit us to investigate every agency, and the reports provided were often incomplete. Many federal programs channel federal tax funds to state and local government agencies, and we were unable to trace their subsequent allocation to interest groups. It was also impossible to ascertain the amount of state and local government revenue diverted to political advocacy.

It is important to stress that the listings of grants and contracts presented in the book are incomplete, even though they are extensive and show that hundreds of millions of tax dollars are distributed each year to hundreds of groups. Thus, although our analysis indicates that the amount of taxpayers' money used for political advocacy is enormous and far in excess of the reported spending on federal elections, the true total is far greater. If anything, our estimates are much too low.

Our second objective is to show how political advocacy groups obtain tax dollars for their activities. Because it is illegal to use federal funds for political purposes, advocacy organizations obtain their support under the guise of either helping the less fortunate—the poor, the hungry, the elderly, the unemployed—or of advancing the "public interest" by "protecting" the consumer, the environment, or minorities. The less-fortunate people in society, however, often do not benefit from the funds that Congress appropriates to assist them because the money is siphoned off for political pur-

3

poses. In effect, the leaders of political advocacy groups use tax funds to further their own interests rather than the interests of the constituencies they purportedly represent. Social programs and the so-called public-interest activities of the federal government are sometimes little more than funding vehicles for a wide variety of lobbying, campaigning, and grass-roots organizing activities. This partly explains why the billions of dollars ostensibly spent each year to alleviate the plight of the poor, the hungry, the elderly, and the unemployed have had so little effect.

Our third objective is to reveal the goals and political ambitions of political advocacy groups that receive tax funds. We collected enormous amounts of information from the newsletters, books, monographs, training manuals, brochures, press releases, and other materials of numerous organizations. We have extensively quoted these original sources so that the political goals of these groups could be described in their own words. Virtually without exception, the recipients of government grants and contracts advocate greater governmental control over and intervention in the private sector, greater limitations on rights to private property, more planning by government, income redistribution, and political rather than private decision making. Most of the tax dollars used for political advocacy are obtained by groups that are on the left of the political spectrum. One would hardly expect government to support groups on the right, since such groups often question the efficacy of many public-sector programs and advocate a reduction in the size and scope of the public sector.

In the course of our study, we discovered some disturbing patterns. For example, the programs pursued by advocacy groups often do more harm than good for the individuals whom the groups are supposedly assisting. In addition, many of these programs actually slow the rate of economic growth, create unemployment, exacerbate inflation, reduce the level of output, and make U.S. products less competitive in world markets. Congressional incumbents, public employees, and the leaders of the advocacy organizations are the ones who prosper from the plight of the less fortunate.

Our fourth objective is to explain how politicians, bureaucrats, and leaders of advocacy groups benefit from tax-funded politics and how they work together to disguise the use of federal funds for such purposes. Once the mechanics of tax-funded politics are revealed, it is possible to offer a simple solution that has conven-

4

iently eluded Congress for decades. Advocacy organizations obtain tax funds under the guise of doing good for others in society. If those in need were given the money directly, rather than having it diverted to people who claim to be their champions, the opportunity for misuse of tax dollars would be greatly reduced. In short, the middlemen should be eliminated and, through such devices as vouchers or a negative income tax, those in need could be aided directly.

The analysis of tax-funded politics is presented in 14 chapters. Chapter 2 explores the myth that the groups that receive tax funding are independent organizations motivated solely by concerns over a specific social problem. In reality, there is a well-orchestrated and carefully oiled network, or coalition, of groups that have the same political goals. The network's activities are coordinated through interlocking directorates, and the leaders are often drawn from the same training programs, thereby ensuring a consistency in policies and approaches. On the left, a few major think tanks dominate political activism, setting the agenda for leftists involved in grassroots organizing. Thus there is widespread cooperation in obtaining tax funds and in determining how they should be allocated to achieve specific political objectives.

Chapters 3 through 7 develop a common theme: the antibusiness bias of tax-funded political advocacy groups is pursued under the rubric of the public interest. Although private enterprise has brought unprecedented prosperity to Americans, left-wing activists seek to cripple the system through regulation, national economic planning, governmental allocation of capital, worker control of industry, and the redistribution of wealth. Their tactics and objectives are illustrated by the Campaign for Economic Democracy, which is discussed in chapters 3 and 4. Chapter 5 explores the tax-funded and so-called consumer movement and reveals that its ultimate goal is to advance the political agenda of the movement's leaders rather than to protect consumers. The energy industry has long been a prime target of the left, and chapter 6 reviews in detail the anti-energy bias. Chapter 7 is devoted to the tax-funded environmental movement, which has consistently opposed economic growth. In each of these five chapters, we identify the groups involved, their sources of tax funding, and their publicly stated goals, and we evaluate the economic consequences of their activities.

Chapters 8 through 13 also treat a common theme: the activities of political advocacy organizations that receive tax funding under

5

the guise of helping the less fortunate. Chapters 8 and 9 examine the so-called apostles of the poor, that is, the interest groups that obtain their funds from programs designed ostensibly to alleviate poverty. Substantial amounts of this funding, however, are diverted from the poor, the hungry, and the unemployed to advocacy groups that constantly lobby for greater spending on behalf of the poor and then use the funds to enrich themselves and to pursue their own political agendas. The apostles of the poor have a vested interest in increasing rather than reducing poverty in the United States, for if poverty were to disappear, their sources of funding would be in jeopardy. Chapter 10 summarizes the activities of the tax-funded civil rights movement. Chapter 11 is devoted to the senior citizen lobby. Chapter 12 reviews the Legal Services Corporation and its use of the courts and the legislative branch to advance the social agenda of activist lawyers. Chapter 13 covers labor unions as political entities that receive vast sums of taxpayers' funds under the ruse of helping the unemployed and bringing culture to workers.

As shown in chapter 14, the evidence indicates that advocacy groups on the right of the political spectrum have received only minuscule amounts of tax funds to support their activities, in comparison with the hundreds of millions of dollars routinely given to liberal groups. Explanations are offered for why right-wing advocacy groups hesitate to seek tax funding and why they are unsuccessful in obtaining grants and contracts from government when support is sought.

Chapter 15 summarizes the study's findings, attempts to explain the widespread existence of tax-funded political advocacy despite the legal prohibitions against it, and offers a solution for ending this misuse of taxpayers' money.

The study is important because it challenges and destroys myths that have been cultivated for years and presented as truth to the taxpayer. The idea that those in the public sector are concerned only about the public interest and are motivated only by compassion for the less fortunate in society is shown to be false, in that taxpayers' funds have been used to advance the careers of those in government at the expense of the less fortunate. The claim that spending for social programs has been cut to the bone by the Reagan administration is not valid because, among other reasons, little has been done to reduce the use of taxpayers' funds for political advocacy. The notion that public interest groups and poverty groups are advancing the cause of the nations' citizens and the less fortunate is belied by the fact that political activists are enriching themselves and promoting their own agendas at the expense of taxpayers, the poor, the hungry, the unemployed, minorities, and others.

More fundamentally, we believe that tax-funded politics is indeed "destroying democracy," as the title of this book asserts. James Madison wrote in the *Federalist Papers*, no. 10, that "among the numerous advantages promised by a well-constructed union, none deserves to be more accurately developed than its tendency to break and control the violence of faction."[7] Throughout history, governments that failed to do this introduced "instability, injustice and confusion" into public life, which are "the mortal diseases under which popular governments have everywhere perished." By a "faction" Madison meant a special-interest group that, "whether amounting to a majority or minority of the whole," had interests "adverse to the rights of other citizens, or to the permanent and aggregate interests of the community." From this perspective the nation's founders created a system of checks and balances within the Constitution that would restrain the "violence of faction." This was essential to arrest the "prevailing and increasing distrust" of the new government about which "complaints [were] everywhere heard" because of a widespread sense of injustice. The cause of the injustice, according to Madison, was that governmental measures "are too often decided, not according to the rules of justice and the rights of the minor party, but by the superior force of an interested and overbearing majority." Moreover, the reason for writing the *Federalist Papers*, an intellectual defense of the Constitution, was clearly stated by Madison: "To secure the public good and private rights against the danger of . . . faction . . . is then the great object to which our inquiries are directed."

Unfortunately, government long ago relinquished its role as a regulator of factions and a protector of private rights by ignoring or openly subverting the safeguards of liberty that Madison and the other founders incorporated into the Constitution.[8] Rather than *restraining* the power of special-interest groups, government at all levels *nourishes* them through tax-funded politics, thereby destroying democracy, as Madison warned. As shown in this book, tax-funded politics has intensified the "instability, injustice and confusion" that Madison feared and has rendered government more authoritarian and less democratic.

Tax-funded politics is destructive from an economic perspective as well. Interest groups that seek governmental empowerments and wealth transfers engage in what is at best a "zero-sum game": What one group receives can only come out of the pockets of other taxpayers and consumers. With the growth of government and the expansion of interest-group politics, more and more resources are used trying to influence government to obtain wealth transfers. The "cost" of these resources can be seen as the forgone goods and services that would have been produced had the same resources been directed at *producing* rather than *transferring* wealth through governmental aegis. Interest-group politics is not a zero-sum but a negative-sum game. By encouraging interest-group behavior, tax-funded politics reduces the wealth of nations.[9]

Every taxpayer should be interested in this research, for our findings reveal nothing less than a national scandal that taxpayers have been forced to finance through coercive taxation. If tax-funded politics continues on the same scale as in the past, it is inevitable that the welfare state will continue to expand, rights to private property will continue to be eroded, and the economic system that has been the envy of the world and has brought such abundance will eventually be replaced by policies that will impoverish us all.

II. The Tax-Funded Political Network

> As the surfacing of similar movements in Europe, Japan, and even the Soviet bloc nations makes clear—the citizen movement in the United States is a world-wide phenomenon, part of a vast, often inchoate popular resistance to the ravaging power of multinational corporations . . . and the logic of the marketplace. To prevail over the long run against such forces will require cooperative action on the part of . . . movements all around the world.
>
> —Harry C. Boyte
> *The Backyard Revolution*

There is a well-organized, taxpayer-funded network of special-interest groups in the United States—a network that contains thousands of groups of different sizes and with different functions. Organizations belonging to this political network focus on a wide variety of policy issues, such as those involving the environment, consumer protection regulation, energy, poverty and welfare, civil rights, social security, unions, and monetary and fiscal matters. When a segment of the network decides to lobby on a particular issue, it can usually count on the support of dozens of other special-interest groups. These groups may not necessarily be concerned about the issue at hand, but cooperation is the price they pay for support on other issues from those other groups.

As shown in this book, interlocking directorates abound in the tax-funded political network, and the members of some organizations are on the boards of directors of dozens of others. One reason such political cooperation is possible is that these special-interest groups share common political perspectives: They are usually anti-free-market and anticapitalist, often oppose private property, are sometimes even Marxist in their orientation, and favor a governmentally imposed redistribution of wealth, both domestically and internationally.

As long as the media ignore this tax-funded political network, their portrayals of the governmental process will be incomplete and somewhat misleading. When one sees a news story about environ-

9

mental policy, for example, one obtains the impression that a few environmentalist interest groups advocate one position while corporations or government officials advocate another and that the news story usually focuses on the conflict between the environmental groups and the other parties. This impression, however, is far from being the entire story. One reason the media portray a handful of environmental interest groups as being so powerful (such groups, for example, have been given credit for forcing out of office Secretary of the Interior James Watt and Environmental Protection Agency Director Anne Burford) is that they are part of a large network that routinely opposes reduced government control of the economy. The network is composed of environmentalist interest groups, together with labor unions, consumer groups, feminists, welfare rights organizations, civil rights lobbyists, and many others. In short, taxpayer funds are being used to support a well-organized network of special-interest groups that promote an expansion of the size, scope, and power of government and a corresponding contraction of the private sector.

This chapter focuses only on the organizational mechanics of the tax-funded political network, which contains four major elements: think tanks, training centers for professional political activists, grassroots lobbying organizations, and labor unions. The following chapters describe how this network uses tax dollars to promote its political objectives.

Think Tanks of the Left

Several public policy research centers (think tanks) serve as organizational vehicles for the tax-funded political coalition. The Institute for Policy Studies (IPS) is the most prominent and serves as a prototype for other centers, such as the Foundation for National Progress, a former IPS affiliate; the National Center for Economic Alternatives, founded by leftist economist Gar Alperovitz; the National Center for Policy Alternatives; the Conference on Alternative State and Local Policies; the Industrial States Center, in Cleveland; the California Policy Center, in Los Angeles; the Institute for Community Economics, in Cambridge, Massachusetts; Community Economics, in Oakland, California; and the Planners' Network, in San Francisco. Many of these centers are offshoots of IPS, and all of them share a common ideological perspective and perform similar functions. They hold conferences; support researchers; publish newsletters, books, magazines, and monographs; distribute newspaper op-ed articles; and collect and disburse funds from and to other nonprofit foundations.

A closer look at IPS, which the *New York Times* once called "the preeminent think tank of the left," will illustrate the role it and similar organizations play in the tax-funded political network (although IPS itself receives little or no government funding).

IPS is a "radical" institution, and one of its objectives is to promote socialism in America. Saul Landau, the director of the Transnational Institute, an IPS affiliate, said in 1980:

> I think that at age 40 the time has come to dedicate myself to narrower pursuits, namely, making propaganda for American Socialism. . . . We cannot any longer just help out third world movements and revolutions, although obviously we shouldn't turn our backs on them, but get down to the more difficult job of bringing the message home.[1]

IPS was founded in 1963 by two former government bureaucrats, Richard J. Barnet and Marcus G. Raskin, who still direct the organization. Barnet's view of the U.S. economy provides a perspective on the type of research produced at IPS and disseminated through the news media. Barnet believes that citizens are "held hostage" in a "plantation colony" where they "work at meaningless and unreal jobs to obtain things that they are led to want but which do not satisfy human needs."[2] According to this perspective, people do not know what they want, but in some preferred state of affairs, they would presumably be forced to pay for (through taxes) and consume those things that Barnet and his associates believe satisfy human needs.

From its inception, IPS has served as a source of radical ideas to be implanted in the nation's colleges and universities by IPS fellows. In a publication issued in 1963, for example, IPS made this assertion:

> The Institute for Policy Studies has recently been established in Washington, D.C. It will bring university scholars and other creative thinkers to the Capitol [*sic*] to carry on research on key problems of public policy and American civilization under conditions permitting close contact with the policy making process. The Institute will also train younger scholars to carry on research in these areas.[3]

IPS also has encouraged and supported "a growing corps of teachers, researchers, and scholars, who will return to their respective

11

universities with a more sophisticated and realistic awareness of how government really operates," and it has developed a "new curriculum" that encourages students to be "more policy and solution minded."[4] IPS openly shuns the role of objective academic scholarship, saying that "efforts will be made to avoid research which is primarily of value to the development of particular academic disciplines."[5] Instead, it hopes to "produce a body of new knowledge in the field of political and social science . . . to point to the *how* as well as the *what* of solutions to difficult public problems."[6] IPS Fellow Arthur Waskow, who claims to "have a gut preference for disorder,"[7] stated that "the Institute [for Policy Studies] is not just an ordinary research center because it's committed to . . . social action and social experiment" that "creates tension."[8] The hoped-for result of this tension, according to Waskow, is "creative disorder." For example, Waskow is concerned with whether "the underclass of the world is going to be able to create an effective . . . rebellion. The possibility exists; that *is* clear. Whether it works, whether it becomes real is not clear."[9] The role of IPS is to try to "make it [rebellion] work." Moreover, "if one has identified an end goal which one considers desirable, then . . . one has avoided the problem of judging whether certain means are legitimate to achieve certain ends."[10]

Among IPS's most important developments has been the creation of the National Conference on Alternative State and Local Public Policies in 1975. Although still closely linked to IPS, the conference is now independent and is called the Conference on Alternative State and Local Policies (CASLP). The basic function of CASLP is to build a nationwide leftist political network. A useful description of CASLP's function is provided by Martin Carnoy and Derek Shearer, who are writers affiliated with IPS and the authors of *Economic Democracy*, which IPS and a large part of the tax-funded political network consider to be economic gospel. According to Carnoy and Shearer:

> In 1974, the Institute for Policy Studies in Washington realized that many 1960s activists were running for and winning public office at the state and local levels. It seemed that substantial political change could occur only if a base of support could be built in local communities where people actually live and work, not in Washington, a town of bureaucrats and lobbyists. A network was formed called the National Conference on Alternative State and Local Public Policy [sic], which publishes a regular newsletter,

produces readers on public policy and model legislation, and sponsors annual gatherings where progressive public officials, community organizers, and labor leaders meet to exchange experience and discuss political programs and strategy. The conference provides a vital link for reform efforts in different cities and states.[11]

The national director of CASLP is Lee Webb, a former national secretary of Students for a Democratic Society (SDS), Washington, D.C., past bureau chief for the *Guardian* (a communist weekly newspaper), and once an assistant to former Senator George McGovern. According to *Public Interest Profiles*, CASLP's steering committee is co-chaired by Ira Arlook, director of the Ohio Public Interest Campaign, and Marion Barry, mayor of Washington, D.C.[12] Other members of the steering committee include Robert Borosage, director of IPS; Ivanhoe Donaldson, a former aide to Mayor Barry and (like Barry) a former leader in the violence-prone Student Nonviolent Coordinating Committee during the 1960s; and Derek Shearer, coauthor of *Economic Democracy*, a former fellow at IPS, and a participant in several other related groups, including the California-based Campaign for Economic Democracy (see chapter 4) headed by former campus radical Tom Hayden. The steering committee plans and organizes the annual conferences:

> One of CASLP's primary activities is organizing an annual national conference for state and local activists. These conferences represent the only major national gathering of local public officials, community leaders, and political activists, and provide an important opportunity for the exchange of innovative ideas and strategies.[13]

Many of the public officials, community leaders, and political activists who attend these conferences are part of the tax-funded political network. One of the objectives of these conferences, according to *Public Interest Profiles*, is to work through state and local governments to expand government ownership of natural resources and capital. As conference participant Lori Hancock, a member of the Berkeley, California, city council, has stated, one of the aims of the conferences is to "turn the unthinkable into the inevitable."[14] As a more specific example of the policies that CASLP promotes, Carnoy and Shearer, who describe the CASLP as "the first conference on alternative economic policy from a leftist perspective," point to the Humphrey-Hawkins full-employment bill

13

(eventually passed in a watered-down version), which they identify as "merely one of the significant outgrowths of this effort."[15] Another specific example: Conference participants Gar Alperovitz and Jeff Faux formed the National Center for Economic Alternatives and received a $300,000 grant from the Department of Housing and Urban Development to study the possibility of community ownership of closed-down steel facilities in Youngstown, Ohio.[16] This exemplifies how individuals affiliated with IPS can form spinoff groups to obtain government grants while IPS can claim to be independent of government influence and avoid forfeiting its antiestablishment image.

Other CASLP activities include establishing a "planners' network," which links left-wing government employees who work in urban planning; drafting model rent-control laws; giving advice on how to ward off tax-limitation movements, how to use public pension funds in a more socially responsible manner; how to impose additional regulation of the banking industry; how to advance government ownership of land; and constructing alternative federal budgets. In addition to its annual conference, CASLP holds issue-specific conferences throughout the country, such as its conferences on energy policy held in 1981 in Michigan, Washington, Idaho, New Hampshire, New Mexico, Texas, New York, West Virginia, Mississippi, North Carolina, Missouri, Nebraska, and California.

CASLP's publications guide those who wish to implement various leftist policies at the local level of government—policies that range from tax reform to land-use planning and housing policy. *America's Cities and Counties: A Citizen's Agenda,*[17] for example, addresses dozens of such issues in articles written by members of special-interest groups affiliated with IPS and CASLP, including the New Jersey Tenants Organization, the Association of Community Organizations for Reform Now (ACORN), Ralph Nader's Public Citizen, the Children's Defense Fund, the AFL-CIO, the National Consumer Law Center, and the American Federation of State, County and Municipal Employees (AFSCME).

The Amsterdam-based Transnational Institute, another important IPS spin-off, has as its stated purpose to "investigate the operations of different multinational corporations."[18] Basically, it directs anticorporate propaganda at multinationals. It works with the Corporate Data Exchange, another IPS affiliate, which provides a more comprehensive store of data on all major industries. IPS's Institute for Southern Studies also uses these data to evaluate the operations

14

of southern corporations. All the data collected are used in well-organized media campaigns against corporations in particular and the market system in general. IPS has been very successful in this effort; its views have been presented by some major media outlets, such as the *New York Times*, and it has its own outlets, such as *Mother Jones* magazine, the Center for Investigative Reporting, and the Pacific News Service, which are operated in California as part of the West Coast branch of IPS.

The radical perspective that permeates IPS can perhaps best be illustrated by its approach to foreign policy. Although IPS sometimes claims to favor a noninterventionist foreign policy, its nonintervention often seems simply a defense of leftist or Marxist-Leninist regimes. In January 1984, for example, IPS Director Robert Borosage, ardently defended the communist government of Nicaragua. When it was pointed out that there were severe shortages of goods and services in that country, an inevitability in any socialist economy, Borosage replied, "When supplies are limited and prices rise . . . then the poor cannot buy any. So the price was fixed at a low price and the rationing was instituted to prevent the wealthy from buying it all."[19] When asked about the abolition of freedom of the press, Borosage excused the Nicaraguan government's censorship: "In Nicaragua you probably have as great a degree of freedom of the press and personal freedom as you find in any similar revolution."[20] Borosage then noted that "the Sandinistas have done with their economy exactly what most of us . . . social democrats would like to do with ours."[21]

Although IPS in the United States is often described as a liberal organization, its European affiliate, the Transnational Institute, takes positions that are far to the left of most American liberals. The Transnational Institute publishes *Race and Class*, a journal that routinely supports the Palestine Liberation Organization, the Communist party of the Philippines, the Thai Communist party, and the Burmese, Malaysian, and Indonesian Communist parties.[22] Tariq Ali, head of the British section of the Trotskyite Fourth International and a fellow of the Transnational Institute, is so radical (and possibly dangerous) that he has been legally barred from the United States, France, India, Japan, Turkey, Thailand, Hong Kong, and Bolivia.[23]

IPS rightly criticizes the excesses of authoritarian right-wing governments in Latin America but then praises Marxist dictatorships that are often even more brutal and oppressive. For example, it has joined with the North American Congress on Latin America, the

15

Council on Hemispheric Affairs, the Washington Office on Latin America, the Center for Cuban Studies, the Cuban Resource Center, and other organizations to work "in solidarity" with the so-called national liberation movements in countries ranging from Chile to El Salvador and Guatemala.

In summary, IPS and its affiliates act as clearinghouses of ideas for radical American leftists who would like the United States to move far to the left politically. The organization's financial support comes from the sale of its books and monographs; from the government, to the extent that IPS affiliates have received government funding; and from several private foundations, especially the Samuel Rubin Foundation. (The late Samuel Rubin was born in Russia in 1901, was a member of the Communist Party, U.S.A. during the 1930s, and made his fortune through Fabergé cosmetics. The foundation is now run by his daughter, former Vietnam War protester Cora Weiss. Her husband, Peter Weiss, is on the IPS board of directors.)

IPS is far more radical than the U.S. media often suggest, especially if one considers its foreign operations. The organization routinely works with other special-interest groups that are considered to be liberal, such as Ralph Nader's various organizations; the public employee division of the AFL-CIO, AFSCME; and various other environmentalist, civil rights, and women's organizations. These groups all share a common objective—increased government control of the economy—although they may have different uses of that control in mind and different ultimate objectives for American society.

IPS and other think tanks of the left provide conferences, ideas, strategy sessions, publications, and other information for the tax-funded political network. Another important part of the network is a nationwide collection of training centers where network members can attend seminars, workshops, and classes to learn about the various techniques used to implement the political agendas promoted by the think tanks. These techniques range from putting together petitions to throwing garbage on the steps of city hall, and they are an important and effective element of the tax-funded political network's successes.

Training Political Activists

There are at least a dozen training centers around the nation (see Table A2.1, in appendix), including the Midwest Academy, in Chi-

16

cago; The Institute, in New Orleans; the Center for Urban Encounter, in Minneapolis; the New England Training Center for Community Organizers, in Providence, Rhode Island; the Laurel Springs Institute run by Tom Hayden and Jane Fonda, in Santa Monica, California (see chapter 4); and the Pacific Institute for Community Organization, in Oakland, California. These centers work together and with individuals affiliated with IPS, CASLP, and other IPS spinoffs, and they share common organizing techniques. Most of these groups claim to carry on their activities in the spirit of the late Saul Alinsky, who first used such organizing techniques to influence city politics in Chicago. According to Heather Booth, president of the Midwest Academy, "Alinsky is to community organizing as Freud is to psychoanalysis."[24] An examination of the Midwest Academy and another training center illustrates Alinsky's techniques and the role of the training centers in the tax-funded political network.

The Midwest Academy

A recent but undated Midwest Academy brochure reports that the institution's president, Heather Booth, is "the leading social action trainer in the United States" and that she has "previously worked as a civil rights and labor union organizer." Booth was an activist in Students for a Democratic Society during the 1960s and also helped found the Citizen/Labor Energy Coalition (see chapter 6) with Michael Harrington, president of the Democratic Socialists of America, and William Winpisinger, president of the International Association of Machinists and a self-described "seat-of-the-pants socialist." Booth describes her organization as "a place that could serve as a link between different groups—between community organizers, labor unionists, environmentalists, feminists."[25] The Youth Project, a funding source for many radical political organizations, describes the Midwest Academy as

> a national training center for community leaders and organizers. Based in Chicago and staffed by experienced organizers and researchers, the Academy holds two-week training sessions in organizing and weekend workshops in fundraising and research. In addition, the Academy conducts over 50 on-site consultations and training sessions each year. Since it was founded in 1973, over 6,000 leaders and organizers have participated in these training sessions, including representatives of Massachusetts Fair Share, Carolina Action, the Vermont Alliance, the East Tennessee Research Group, Environmental Action, the Gray Panthers, the National

17

Organization for Women and many other citizen action, labor and women's organizations.[26]

A 1982 brochure published by the academy contains several organizations listed as "Midwest Academy Alumni," that is, organizations that have sent staff members through Midwest Academy training sessions (see Table A2.2), and includes some well-known special-interest groups, such as AFSCME, Ralph Nader's public interest research groups (see chapter 5), the United Auto Workers, the National Education Association, the American Federation of Teachers, and Nine to Five (a labor union representing primarily female clerical workers). These and other members of the tax-funded political network rely heavily on the academy as a resource and many of the trainers come from these very groups. For example, a recent, but undated, brochure entitled "Administration and Management" lists as "resource people" Paul Booth, Heather Booth's husband and a director of AFSCME; Mary Jean Collins, president of the Chicago chapter of the National Organization for Women; Robert Creamer, executive director of Illinois Public Action Council; and Henry Scheff, an organizer for the United Textile Workers of America and research director for Citizen Action (located in Chicago). This brochure also cites the lavish praise accorded the Midwest Academy by some of its alumni. For example, Jerry Wurf, late president of AFSCME, stated:

> The Midwest Academy provides an invaluable service for many labor, community, consumer and feminist organizations. You have been training leaders, activists and staff in our organizations in the techniques that enable people to organize effectively. . . . I know about how good your program is because many people from AFSCME have attended the Midwest Academy's training sessions.

Day Creamer, executive director of a labor union called Women Employed, noted that "There can be no better model for women to aspire to than the Academy's director, Heather Booth."

Apparently, some people within the federal government have also held these views, for during the 1978–79 period the Midwest Academy received $595,846 in federal grants, which it used to train political activists.[27] Some insight into Booth's perspective on such training and on the uses to which this tax money was put can be gleaned from her remarks to the 1979 CASLP conference:

18

The anti-business message [of the conference] was taken up at the opening session by Heather Tobis Booth, director of the . . . Midwest Academy and of the Citizen-Labor Energy Coalition. Booth forecast a "new level of political activities distinct from the 60's and 70's." She characterized the 1960s as a time of "multi-sector movements inspired by a new analysis," and the 1970s as a period of local "digging in" amidst "popular disillusionment and disunion caused by economic decline." Stating that the new economic crisis was creating a new unity of effort, Booth said that a coalition of labor, citizens groups, women, minorities and environmentalists—which sounded very much like the Citizen-Labor Energy Coalition . . . which she leads—would contest national policies, "organize across sectors," and focus on anti-corporate issues.[28]

According to a Midwest Academy brochure, the academy's objective is to create a "majority movement," defined as a "campaign where our collective stength wins concrete improvements and begins the job of redistributing social wealth."[29] To achieve this, says Booth, activists must "destroy corporate control over . . . [their] lives, politically and economically."[30]

In These Times, a magazine sponsored by IPS, reported that in establishing the Midwest Academy,

Booth set out to combine Alinsky's methods with some of the goals of the '60's left. The students not only learned how to write a leaflet, organize a press conference and stage a dramatic protest, but also were encouraged to read Sheila Rowbotham's *Women, Resistance, and Revolution*, and articles on workers' control of industry by British socialist Michael Barratt Brown. . . . [T]he Academy alumni constitute an informal network of political organizers that span the concerns of the post-'60's left.[31]

To mold these interest groups into what Booth calls "a common anticorporate political program,"[32] the academy runs a series of two-week basic courses, as well as special sessions on such topics as fundraising and research. Harry C. Boyte, author of *The Backyard Revolution*, describes the basic course:

In the two-week course, students learn histories of grassroots organizations, techniques of meetings, press relations, leaflet making, and methods for holding effective demonstrations and doing research. . . . Steve Max, the main Academy teacher, who himself helped found the Students for a Democratic Society, adds

19

a wealth of practical detail from years of experience in election campaigns, union battles, and community fights. . . . The students sing songs from the range of people's struggles in the century—"Solidarity Forever," "Union Maids," "We Shall Overcome," "Gonna Study War No More," "I Am Woman." They go out with groups like the Illinois Public Action Council on demonstrations or show up at press conferences of senior citizen groups. They plan skits for confronting city officials.[33]

The type of organizing and direct-action methods taught at the Midwest Academy are found in a number of its training manuals:[34]

"[1] The Third Principle of Direct Action organizing is that it attempts to alter the relations of power between people's organizations and their real enemies. The enemies are often unresponsive politicians, tax assessors, utilities, landlords, government agencies, large corporations or banks.

"[2] Give people a 'taste of blood.' Push your opponents so hard you can see them squirm.

"[3] You may want to assign some people to be 'inciters' and move about to heat up the action getting people angrier and encouraging them to show their anger. You may at other times want some 'calmers' to stand near people who may be disruptive to the focus of the action.

"[4] Make what the opposition is doing or not doing sound scandalous. . . . [T]he edge may have been dulled by the routine manner in which it is normally treated.

"[5] Your power is your ability to hurt the target or withhold something the target wants. The hurt can be immediate, as in a strike or boycott, or it can be potential, as when bad publicity will cause a politician to be unseated.

"[6] Stunts can help. . . . If, for example, a politician won't meet with you, tape a sign across his office which says, 'This Office Closed to the Public.' If someone won't come into a debate, put a dummy in the chair and debate that for dramatic effect.

"[7] Be ever on the lookout to play targets off against each other, Republican vs. Democrat, Up-State vs. Down-State, In-Group vs. Out-Group. Your enemy's enemy may be your ally.

"[8] Civil disobedience . . . is not generally a good mass recruitment tactic. There are some exceptions. A community group . . . found that by having several hundred people cross a strategic street corner at rush hour, cars could be prevented from making a right turn on a red signal and traffic would be backed up for miles. The leadership was unjustly arrested."

Another role of the academy, in addition to direct-action organizing, is the training of campaign workers. Booth has established a subsidiary, the State and Local Leadership Project, as a training school for campaign workers. She is assisted by Paul Tully, who has worked on the presidential campaigns of George McGovern, Edward Kennedy, and Walter Mondale.[35] In preparing for the 1982 and 1984 national elections, the project set up statewide political action committees, selected congressional and legislative districts "where Reagan Republicans could be defeated,"[36] and sent campaign workers door to door to promote issues and candidates who supported a leftist agenda. *In These Times* reported in 1982 that a national advisory committee has been established to coordinate the project's efforts and that $30,000 had been donated by the International Association of Machinists. Other financial support was expected from the National Education Association, AFSCME, Ralph Nader's organizations, and senior citizen groups,[37] all of them being part of the tax-funded political network (as shown in later chapters). Thus, by unknowingly supporting these groups financially, U.S. taxpayers are indirectly supporting the Midwest Academy.

According to the March–April 1978 issue of *Working Papers for a New Society*, another IPS project, the Midwest Academy distributed some of the grant money it received from the federal government to its numerous affiliates around the nation:

> The academy gave five VISTA volunteers each [provided in addition to the grant money] to a black, Latino, and consumer group in Illinois to help develop the individual organizations and to strengthen their ties with the Illinois Public Action Council. . . . The Academy also placed VISTA volunteers with . . . six . . . new women's organizations on the East Coast and two established ones in Cleveland and Boston. Another group went to the Carolina Brown Lung Association, which organizes . . . textile workers. Yet another went to the New Jersey Senior Citizens Coalition. . . . It also conducted two weeks of training.[38]

Volunteers in Service to America (VISTA), the government agency responsible for the Midwest Academy grants, eventually audited the use of the grants and found that the "VISTA volunteers" whose salaries were paid by Midwest Academy grant money were often employees of existing lobbying organizations for which salaries were also covered by VISTA grants. The government investigators also found that even though VISTA is a poverty program and its funds are intended by law to help alleviate the problem of poverty, "[a] number of the organizations [funded through the Midwest Academy] were not serving poverty constituencies, and . . . were not working with poor people."[39] With respect to the funds given to "working women's organizations," the investigators found that "it had not been established that the working women were poor or the proposed VISTA assignments poverty related."[40] In Rhode Island the investigators found that employees funded by the Midwest Academy "were engaged substantially full time in . . . union organizing related activity." In short, these taxpayers' funds were being used to promote the Midwest Academy's political agenda. At a tenth anniversary celebration held by the Midwest Academy in July 1983, Heather Booth stated this agenda in broad terms: "The goal during the next five years is to build a movement that will manifest itself in a noticeable shift in public opinion and emergence of national leaders with progressive tendencies. . . . What we represent is part of the infrastructure of this new movement."[41]

The National Training and Information Center

There are many other training centers that aid the tax-funded political network. One in particular—the National Training and Information Center (NTIC)—illustrates tactics that are common to all of these centers. NTIC, which is part of National People's Action (NPA), claims an annual budget in excess of $500,000 and sees its purpose as being "a national center for training, information, consultation, technical assistance, and research."[42] NTIC breaks down its activities into seven categories:

1. State and local activities are carried out by "more than 300 member organizations" but are "coordinated and publicized by NPA and NTIC." NTIC members are kept informed of the efforts of other affiliates through their newsletter, *Disclosure.*

2. Corporate "negotiations" are a major activity. To induce corporate managers to give in to their demands, NTIC members usually hold demonstrations or protest marches. After one series of demonstrations, NTIC boasted: "In 1980 Aetna Life and Casualty announced a major commitment to neighborhood reinvestment following meetings with NPA . . . and awarded NTIC a $225,000 grant for that purpose."[43]

3. Demonstrations are perhaps the major focus of NTIC's efforts.

According to *Public Interest Profiles*, "NPA often organizes demonstrations when corporations or associations refuse to consider NPA proposals." NPA's annual conference is usually followed by demonstrations in Washington, D.C., to draw attention to NPA's demands. After a March 1981 convention in Baltimore, for example, the group organized protests at the Washington offices of the Business Roundtable, the National Association of Manufacturers, and the American Petroleum Institute; these protests, NPA claims, eventually led to an agreement with the three groups. In May 1981, NPA organized protests at corporate headquarters in nine major cities. On the cover of a brochure advertising its 1983 conference, NTIC boasted:

> The actions shown here in our "NPA Hit Parade" [pictures of demonstrations] were key steps in winning victories over the years. [The pictures are of demonstrations at] Senate Banking Committee hearings . . . in 1975 . . . the home of Garth Marston, then head of the Federal Home Loan Bank Board, in '76, James Schlesinger's house (Secretary of the Department of Energy) in '77 through the halls of HUD and into the office of Secretary Pat Harris in '78 . . . spilling into the plush boardroom of the American Bankers Association in '79 . . . the American Petroleum Institute's headquarters in '81 . . . and the home of Charles Butler, Chairman of the Federal Energy Regulatory Commission, in '82. We'll be in Washington for 3 action-packed days this September, time enough to create a new "1983 NPA HIT PARADE"—on all issues, from heating costs to budget cuts and everything in between.[44]

4. NTIC holds conferences and seminars that usually focus on specific issues, such as energy policy, government jobs programs, and government-subsidized housing. Some of these meetings are supported by U.S. taxpayers: "During 1980–81 NTIC and the Department of Energy co-sponsored a series of 10 regional hearings on energy issues. Meetings were held in Brainerd, Minnesota; Columbus, Ohio; Des Moines, Iowa; Chicago, Illinois; Portland, Oregon; New York; Denver; Knoxville; Providence; and Atlanta."[45]

5. NTIC provides training and "technical assistance": "During 1981 NTIC conducted one-week training sessions for community organizers in . . . February, June, and October. NTIC also held one-day sessions in 23 cities during 1981."[46]

6. NTIC publishes books and monographs on such issues as insurance red-lining, rent-control legislation, and how-to manuals on community organizing, demonstrating, and protesting.

7. NTIC and NPA staff members testify before congressional committees, engage in other forms of direct lobbying, and instruct their affiliates to do the same. For example, the November–December 1982 issue of *Disclosure* declared the theme of that year's conference to be "The Days of Lobbying"[47] because "NPA leaders met with more members of Congress and regulators than ever before."

The types of policies that are advocated by NTIC and are the focus of its training efforts involve increased government expenditure on a variety of programs, such as housing subsidies, jobs programs, and welfare payments, and on support for increased regulation of industry, especially the energy and banking industries. For example, after "ten bus loads of NPA conference participants went into the AMA [American Medical Association] meeting" to harass the medical profession at its annual conference in 1983, an NTIC spokesman said, "This experience [was a way of dealing] with the many economic problems being experienced by the American people as a result of domestic [budget] cuts and a high military budget."[48]

NTIC has been very effective in teaching its affiliates the techniques of coalition politics. In 1982, for example, it sponsored "Reclaim America Week," a series of well-organized demonstrations around the nation. Participants included Ralph Nader; Maggie Kuhn, president of the Gray Panthers (see chapter 11); Heather Booth of the Midwest Academy; John Jacob of the National Urban League (see chapter 10); and representatives of several unions, including the International Association of Machinists, the United Auto Workers, AFSCME, and the Amalgamated Clothing and Textile Workers Union.[49] In Chicago, groups involved represented "not only community groups but senior citizen organizations, church organizations, peace groups, and labor unions."[50] Similar events were held in Cleveland, Philadelphia, Washington, D.C., and New York City. According to Gale Gincotta, president of NTIC:

> [In 1980] we thought Reagan would win . . . so we wanted to pull together. . . . We thought we should invite unions, seniors and women's groups. We had to start pulling together the community organizing network—ACORN [Association of Community Organizations for Reform Now (see chapter 8)], National People's Action, the training centers, the statewide networks. . . . One of the first successes was Big Oil Day with Citizen/Labor Energy Coalition and NPA.[51]

24

Gincotta continues: "We're . . . targeting companies and using publicity for leverage on them. We're getting support from unions, like the Machinists, AFSCME, Food and Commercial Workers, Clothing and Textile Workers. . . . This is the beginning of a national organizing drive to put . . . corporate America on notice. We cannot let corporations . . . continue to set anti-people policies."[52]

The above examples show that the tax-funded political network is well organized, and they help to explain the effectiveness of this network (as discussed in chapters 3 through 13).

"Grass Roots" Coalitions of the Left

"Throughout the country," according to the *New York Times*, "activist organizations on the left are developing sophisticated candidate support systems and broadening their horizons from local issues to national politics."[53] These groups both lobby for specific local policies, such as plant-closing laws, rent-control laws, and regulation of energy prices, and provide local liaison for national politicians, pressure groups, and other political organizers. For example, Ralph Nader has established scores of "Congress Watch Districts" that work to publicize, lobby for, and get out the vote for various national policies and politicians favored by Nader's organization and its allies in Congress. Regardless of their approaches to national or international policy, congressmen depend heavily on political organizations in their home districts, and these grass-roots organizations are an important part of the local political support provided to congressmen. Local groups have developed links to national organizations and to politicians who are involved in many public policy areas, such as energy policy, welfare, regulation of business, social security, farm policy, and public policies toward labor unions. The following examples illustrate these linkages.

The Illinois Public Action Council

The *New York Times* has cited the Illinois Public Action Council (IPAC), a coalition of about 130 organizations in Illinois, as being typical of these groups. Groups affiliated with IPAC include the Champaign-Urbana Tenants Union, which lobbies for rent-control laws; Citizens Against the Rate Increase, which lobbies against all utility rate increases by investor-owned utilities; the Illinois Public Interest Research Group, a Ralph Nader affiliate; and Metro Seniors in Action. Labor unions, including the International Association of

Machinists, the United Auto Workers, and the Illinois Farm Alliance, are also affiliated with IPAC.

IPAC claims to "provide ongoing research and information to local community organizations; develop and train local leadership in skills of research, problem analysis and strategy development."[54] For example, it organized a demonstration against President Reagan in 1981 when he appeared in Chicago. The demonstration effort was called the Illinois Coalition Against Reagan Economics (ICARE) and was a coalition organized to block cuts in the federal budget proposed by President Reagan and to advance "a new political program supported by a new political movement."[55]

IPAC is directed by Robert B. Creamer, who at one time worked for Saul Alinsky. With an annual budget of approximately $1.5 million, IPAC operates offices in six cities and spends much of its time organizing teenagers and college students to solicit money from approximately 7,000 homes each day:

> Every day at 2 P.M., IPAC canvassers gather in scattered locations across the state. In Rockford, Nell Lancaster, a veteran activist and a canvass supervisor, is giving a pep talk on the issues to a dozen or so workers. . . . Utility rates have increased . . . and Miss Lancaster predicts more hikes if President Reagan's bill to deregulate natural gas passes. . . . There is no pretense of objectivity . . . [and] the issue is black and white: the people versus big business.[56]

IPAC also operates a political action committee that provides both personnel and research for leftist candidates for local government, the state legislature, and Congress, and it maintains a full-time lobbying office in Springfield. For example, IPAC workers went door-to-door campaigning for Chicago mayoral candidate Harold Washington and in 1984 targeted five conservative congressmen for defeat. The political candidates favored by IPAC are often chosen by the AFL-CIO: "Organized labor has become such an important element in the [IPAC] coalition that its members have decided its choice would have to coincide with that of the AFL-CIO."[57]

The policies advocated by the IPAC coalition are, not surprisingly, thoroughly interventionist. IPAC favors some form of national industrial policy, including greater government control over credit allocation so as to channel credit into "more productive areas," such as manufacturing plants (as long as they are unionized), and less into mergers and acquisitions. It also seeks greater consumer-product regulation, bans on mortgage foreclosures, price controls on energy, more progressive income taxation, stricter occupational safety regulation, and more government spending on welfare programs, especially jobs programs.

The Association of Community Organizations for Reform Now

In addition to statewide efforts such as IPAC, many organizations have developed a national network of like-minded pressure groups. One such group, the Association of Community Organizations for Reform Now (ACORN), is what author Harry C. Boyte calls "the preeminent example of such mass-based, multi-issue citizen organizations."[58] It claims to have affiliates in 25 states, and its activities are nearly identical to the Midwest Academy, NTIC, and the NPA. Its "principal activity is organizing, and all other functions are designed to enhance this capability."[59] ACORN's campaigns usually involve demonstrations, confrontations with industry and government officials, and significant media coverage.

ACORN has established a political action committee to work for or against certain political candidates, and it has participated in several state and local initiative campaigns. It has also joined with other members of the tax-funded political network to become part of a national political coalition (see chapter 8). In this role, ACORN has written a "People's Platform," which is anti-free-enterprise and generally favors a larger welfare state. On energy policy, for example, it uses the slogan, "Put people before profits" as its first priority.[60] On the issue of conservation, it opts for a government takeover of the utility industry, the abolition of the nuclear power industry, and government subsidization of such alternative sources of energy as windmills. On health care issues, ACORN basically favors replacing private health care administrators with ACORN representatives: "Throw doctors and hospital administrators off the boards of directors, and replace them with a low and moderate income majority." The organization's ultimate goal is nationalized health care. ACORN also advocates greater government subsidization of public housing, government jobs programs, nationalization of the railroad industry, more welfare spending, higher taxation, and the provision of "citizens' rights" that are essentially demands for taxpayer-financed day care, housing, and so on.

ACORN has had some success with these policies. For example, it convinced Rep. Mickey Leland (D-Tex.) to try to incorporate the policies into the Democratic party's platform in 1984. It has also successfully fought utility rate hikes, participated in union organizing, and supported striking farm workers. Because of its size, the organization serves as a model for dozens of other pressure groups, and it claims that there is one overriding purpose at the root of all it hopes to achieve: "Behind the organization's concern . . . is a basic understanding which says that all these [public policy] issues are mere manifestations of a much more fundamental issue: the distribution of power in this country." ACORN's "Organizing Manual" goes on to claim that people are getting "nailed" because "a bunch of corporate directors and New York bankers have the power to unilaterally make decisions that affect the lives of ACORN members."[61]

National Coalitions

The think tanks, training centers, and grass-roots lobbying groups that make up the tax-funded political network frequently come together to form national coalitions to promote various policies. These coalitions include the National Anti-Hunger Coalition (see chapter 8), which was formed in 1979 to lobby for expanded welfare payments; the National Low-Income Housing Coalition, which lobbies for more government-subsidized housing; the Citizen/Labor Energy Coalition; the National Rural Housing Coalition; the Coalition on Block Grants and Human Needs; the Save our [Social] Security Coalition; and the Coalition to Save Legal Services. These coalitions are organized on a national level and maintain offices in Washington, D.C., where much of their time is spent lobbying members of Congress. The national coalitions also establish local affiliates, such as the Illinois Coalition Against Reagan Economics, which publicize a particular point of view in the local media and which confer with congressmen when they visit their home districts.

It is useful to briefly discuss two examples of national coalitions that are part of the tax-funded political network. The examples selected are the Fair Budget Action Campaign and the Citizen/Labor Energy Coalition.

The Fair Budget Action Campaign was established in 1983. As shown in Table A2.3, the organizations belonging to the campaign are quite diverse. They include labor unions, such as the United Steelworkers, AFSCME, and the American Federation of Government Employees; Ralph Nader's affiliates, such as Congress Watch and the Consumer Federation of America; environmentalist groups, such as Environmental Action (see chapter 7); welfare lobbyists, such as the Food Research and Action Center (see chapter 8), ACORN, and the National Association of Social Workers; civil rights organizations, such as the National Urban League and Wider Opportunities for Women; social security lobbyists, such as the Gray Panthers; and some of the more radical left-wing organizations, such as the Democratic Socialists of America and the Cuban Planning Council. The coalition was quite successful at harshly and relentlessly criticizing President Reagan's budget proposals during his first term. The *National Journal* reported that once the smoke had cleared over the "budget battles" of 1981 and 1982, "the lobbyists for labor, civil rights, education, health, welfare, religious, urban and community organizations are beginning to smile again. Many social program budgets have held their own for fiscal 1983 . . . [and] no major structural changes have been made in social programs for 1983."[62] One reason these pressure groups have been so successful (as demonstrated in later chapters) is that their political activities are supported by hundreds of millions of taxpayers' dollars.

The Citizen/Labor Energy Coalition (C/LEC) was founded by Heather Booth of the Midwest Academy; William Winpisinger, president of the International Association of Machinists; and Michael Harrington, president of the Democratic Socialists of America (see chapter 5). C/LEC's board of directors consists mostly of representatives of labor unions, such as the Amalgamated Clothing and Textile Workers Union; AFSCME; the National Education Association; the Oil, Chemical and Atomic Workers International Union; the Service Employees International Union; the United Auto Workers; and the machinists union. The Midwest Academy's State and Local Leadership Project is a participant, as are various Ralph Nader affiliates and environmentalist groups.

C/LEC's political agenda focuses on greater government control, through regulation and government ownership, of the energy industry. Since 1975 there has rarely been a news report on national energy policy in the *New York Times*, the *Washington Post*, or the *Los Angeles Times* that has not said something to the effect that the proconsumer viewpoint is represented by the Citizen/Labor Energy Coalition. But C/LEC's views are rarely in the consumers' best interests, although the organization has been extraordinarily successful at having the media make the case that they are (see chapter 6), again with the help of government subsidies. C/LEC is just one

29

example of the role that labor unions play in the tax-funded political network—a role that deserves closer scrutiny.

The Role of Labor Unions

One reason that many labor unions have become affiliated with members of the tax-funded political network is that as their membership has declined in the private sector over the past 40 years, the unions have determined that the practice of "business unionism" (in which the unions' major efforts are at the bargaining table) is not paying off. Instead, unions have turned to politics as a way of bolstering their membership by advocating laws that promote unionization and that isolate unionized industries from competition. To achieve their ends, they have joined with a variety of leftist groups to form political coalitions that are being subsidized by hundreds of millions of dollars in taxpayers' funds.

Members of each coalition gain strength by supporting each other's causes. For example, unions have reversed their long-standing opposition to hiring quotas based on racial preference to cooperate with civil rights lobbyists. Unions, especially those in the public sector, are major advocates of equal-pay-for-comparable-worth legislation (see chapter 10), which would severely restrict their ability to negotiate wage increases. In addition (as shown in chapter 5), labor union executives sit on the boards of directors of many consumer groups. They frequently support self-described socialists such as William Winpisinger in harsh anticorporate campaigns against the energy industry. Unions have become an important part of what is called the anti-industry coalition (see chapter 3), which generally seeks greater government regulation or ownership of industry. It is easy to understand why union leaders are interested in these causes. Unions may be happy to contribute to the negative public image of corporations fostered by the consumer groups, because such an image helps sustain the notion that workers are more likely to be exploited by employers when there are no unions.

Unions are also major supporters of the welfare state. As the *Congressional Quarterly* observed in 1981: "In recent budget battles, the master coalition-builder has been the AFL-CIO. Its current National Budget Coalition is an impressive directory of 157 disparate groups, generally in agreement that President Reagan's budget gouges the poor and spares the rich."[63] By organizing coalitions to oppose reductions in government spending, the AFL-CIO is pro-

30

tecting a major source of union dues, namely, the wages of public employees, as well as government grants to unions.

Unions are also behind many senior citizen organizations. The board of directors of the National Council of Senior Citizens is almost entirely composed of union presidents (see chapter 11). By being so involved, unions are in a position to organize senior citizens into effective support and lobbying groups for the unions' political objectives, such as public housing construction, which is a source of lucrative construction jobs and union dues.

In short, unions are involved in almost every aspect of national politics and are an important part of the infrastructure of the tax-funded political network. Although union political activity is well publicized on such issues as plant-closing laws, protectionism, and occupational health and safety regulation, it is less well known on many other issues, such as social security, housing policy, energy policy, and welfare.

Many unions have become radicalized in their political perspective because many individuals in the groups that make up the tax-funded political network have found employment in union organizations. Once so employed, they naturally work with their colleagues and acquaintances at IPS, the Midwest Academy, ACORN, and other organizations in the network. In 1981, the 750,000-member American Federation of Government Employees (AFGE), a member of the AFL-CIO, hired as its legislative director Jane McMichael, who was formerly an IPS fellow.[64] After accepting the job, one of the first things McMichael did was to issue a public warning to President Reagan: "Public employees are not as passive as they used to be. . . . Making government change is going to be more difficult than it was four years ago, or 10 years ago."[65]

McMichael apparently arranged for AFGE and IPS to work together on some issues. For example, IPS held a series of lectures for AFGE personnel on April 16, 1982, to instruct federal employees how to "disrupt the Reagan administration's plans to reduce the size of the federal work force by making attempts at cutting back so tedious and confrontational that agencies would be forced to give up."[66] Tactics mentioned included burying agencies with Freedom of Information Act requests and then charging the agencies with "improper motives"—under the guise of "whistleblowing"—if they were slow in responding. Seminar instructions advised getting a sympathetic congressman to hold well-publicized hearings to harass agency personnel and, ultimately, the president. A legislative

31

assistant to Rep. Michael D. Barnes (D-Md.), who held such hearings, attended the IPS seminar and said, "We're hoping it will become so tedious for the agencies to provide all the documentation . . . that they will seek alternatives to RIF's [reductions in force, or layoffs]."[67]

Summary and Conclusions

The tax-funded political network has one overriding purpose: to expand the size and scope of government at the expense of the market economy. The think tanks of the left produce a steady flow of anti-free-enterprise and anticorporate literature that routinely finds its way into the major media outlets. Their basic objective is to influence public opinion, and there is evidence that they have been quite successful. The dozens of training centers instruct members of pressure groups in how to lobby for interventionist policies at the local and national levels. The efforts usually produce results, for every congressman must rely on his home district to perpetuate his tenure in office. Interestingly, if government responsibilities are shifted more to state and local governments, as the Reagan administration has proposed, it is likely that the tax-funded political network, which is quite active at the local government level, will become even stronger. CASLP, for instance, would surely welcome such a shift, because one of its purposes is to pursue leftist policies at the local level.

Coalition building among those in the tax-funded political network is likely to be effective in the future because the large fixed costs of establishing dozens of large, national coalitions have already been borne (sometimes at taxpayers' expense) and the network keeps its hand on the nation's political pulse so it is prepared to fight any attempts to reduce the size and scope of government.

Conservatives are often derided for believing in conspiracy theories about the activities of the left, and they are ridiculed in an effort to diminish their criticism of interventionist government policies. After all, as it is so often said, anyone who believes in such conspiracy theories is obviously a "crank." Conspiracy, however, is a loaded term and does not accurately reflect conservatives' positions—positions that are supported by a considerable amount of evidence.

As has been demonstrated in this chapter, the tax-funded political network is a well-oiled political machine, not an ad hoc collection of special-interest groups that rallies for a particular cause and then disbands when the legislative battle is over. The network is a permanent fixture of the political landscape and is so well organized that it even publishes books and directories on networking. In 1982, for example, Jessica Lipnack and Jeffrey Stamps published *Networking: The First Report and Directory*, a directory that is meant to be used by network members as a guide to thousands of organizations, which are listed alphabetically and by region.[68] *Networking* also lists the issues tackled by the various organizations and provides lists of publications and materials they have produced. The authors have written that their volume was "fueled in large part by the sweat equity of the survivors of the 1960s" and describe networks as "stages on which dissonance is not only tolerated but encouraged."[69] The policy issues laid out by Lipnack and Stamps in the introductory chapter are almost identical to the positions held by the tax-funded political network as described throughout our book. A major theme of *Networking* is that there does indeed exist a leftist network (some may prefer to call it a conspiracy) that transcends single issues; for example: "Although a utility rate-reform network might not feel it has any similarity to a home-birth group, both networks are posing similar challenges to monopolistic institutions—in one case power companies, in the other case to hospitals."[70] This fundamental theme runs throughout the entire book, and the authors give instructions on networking techniques used by a wide range of groups, including environmentalists, welfare lobbyists, and teachers' unions.

The permanency and diversity of the tax-funded political network can also be seen in the creation of the so-called OMB Watch, which is based in Washington, D.C. In the early 1980s, the federal government's Office of Management and Budget (OMB) made an effort to enforce the federal laws against tax-funded politics, and the tax-funded political network predictably responded with a roar of opposition that pressured OMB to ease up on its enforcement measures. As reported in the *Washington Post*, "OMB Watch was . . . started by a coalition of anxiety-ridden nonprofit groups concerned about an OMB proposal to ensure that government-funded organizations did not lobby with government funds."[71] Reportedly, OMB Watch has over 1,000 member organizations; according to its technical coordinator, Terry Bass, "If not 100 percent, at least 90 percent of our members are federal grantees."[72] Moreover, "We operate as a network. Community groups feed us the information they're hearing [about OMB policy proposals and federal grant opportunities] and we check it out. Our network also includes . . . professionals who are civil servants within OMB. . . . This is the same work we were trying to do before. This is the way we sustain ourselves."[73]

Finally, although the U.S. labor movement has not formed a formal political party as have its European counterparts, it does operate as an integral part of the tax-funded political network by providing it with funding, personnel, and training. In this capacity it has probably been even more influential than the British Labour party over the past several years. The remainder of this book examines in more detail the political agenda of the tax-funded political network, the extent to which that agenda has been implemented in the United States, its economic consequences, and the role of tax-funded politics.

III. The Anti-Industry Coalition

The . . . system of capitalism is such a society in which merit and achievements determine . . . success or failure. . . . In such a society each member whose ambitions have not been fully satisfied resents the fortune of all those who succeeded better. . . . They sublimate their hatred into a philosophy, the philosophy of anti-capitalism, in order to render inaudible the inner voice that tells them that their failure is entirely their own fault.

—Ludwig von Mises
The Anti-Capitalist Mentality

"I was just a housewife and blamed all my troubles on blacks, Puerto Ricans and other victims. . . . Now I know it's the corporations that are keeping people down."

—Midwest Academy brochure

Chapters 4 through 7 are closely related, for they focus on the use of tax funds by various advocacy groups that together form what in broad terms may be called the anti-industry coalition. Their overall objective is greater government control over the private sector. As shown in these four chapters, the political activities of these groups reflect a number of common economic objectives that the groups refer to collectively as economic democracy. It is useful, at the outset, to outline the composition of the anti-industry coalition, its objectives, and the likely economic consequences of its policies. The tax-funded political activities of specific groups within the anti-industry coalition are explored in detail in chapters 4 through 7.

The U.S. corporation is being attacked by a coalition of groups that espouses the idea that corporations in particular and the free enterprise system in general is the root cause of nearly all that is presumed to be wrong in U.S. society, both politically and economically. As William T. Poole has written, "To these people, the corporation manipulates our foreign policy in its own selfish interests; it squanders our resources; and it exploits our people in its uncaring pursuit of profit."[1] Poole quotes Ralph Nader, a major participant in this coalition, as stating that "the powers of giant corporations in the United States . . . erode the rule of law and ethical precepts." Richard Barnet, director of the Institute for Policy Studies, has proclaimed: "The corporation's excessive power . . . over the political and economic life of the country has all but destroyed the system of checks and balances in our economy."[2] Built on perspectives such as these is a well-orchestrated attack on private enterprise.

An important group within this anti-industry coalition is the Interfaith Center on Corporate Responsibility, an affiliate of the National Council of Churches (NCC). NCC is involved in publishing a harshly biased newsletter, *The Corporate Examiner;* it finances the leftist North American Congress on Latin America; and it directs the Corporate Data Exchange, which provides information and propaganda to other coalition members. The Institute for Policy Studies (IPS) is the preeminent think tank for the anti-industry movement, and its affiliate, the Transnational Institute, with centers in London and Amsterdam, "addresses the fundamental disparity between the rich and poor peoples and nations of the world, investigates its causes and develops alternatives for its remedy."[3]

These groups, and many others like them, have formed a very effective coalition through which "activists for one cause often help out campaigners for another."[4] Many of their political activities are funded by taxes (as discussed in the next four chapters). The coalition comes together periodically at the Conference on Alternative State and Local Policies (CASLP).[5] The ideological thread that binds these groups together is "economic democracy," a term popularized by activist Tom Hayden, who heads the California-based Campaign for Economic Democracy (see chapter 4).

Economic democracy is a major part of the political agenda that is being actively pursued by all segments of the anti-industry movement, including the IPS and NCC networks (see chapter 2), some labor unions, Tom Hayden's Campaign for Economic Democracy, the Citizen/Labor Energy Coalition, and dozens of so-called consumer groups. A basic complaint of the advocates of economic democracy is that corporate managers have too much influence over production decisions in the economy, to the detriment of workers and consumers.

Although the details of what is meant by economic democracy differ from group to group, the principal participants all agree on one basic point: The free enterprise system is the source of most of the nation's problems. In their view the market system is inefficient

36

and inequitable and should be replaced by more centralized government control. Members of the anti-industry coalition see themselves ultimately as being in the best position to begin making decisions that are now overly influenced by naive consumers who are easily manipulated by corporate management. This chapter discusses what the anti-industry coalition means by economic democracy, why the coalition believes it would be superior to a free enterprise economy, and the economic consequences of economic democracy. Subsequent chapters show how taxpayers' funds are being used to finance the political activities of this coalition.

What Is Economic Democracy?

Derek Shearer, coauthor of *Economic Democracy*, a book that lays much of the theoretical groundwork for the anti-industry coalition, has described the essential nature of the coalition's political agenda: "Socialism has a bad name in America, and no amount of wishful thinking on the part of the left is going to change that in our lifetimes. . . . The words Economic Democracy are an adequate and effective replacement."[6] Other members of the coalition also carefully avoid the term "socialism" and generally heed Shearer's advice. Shearer is personally involved in many of their organizations as a board member, conference participant, and organizer. Regarding the political strategy used to achieve economic democracy, Shearer has stated that the economic democracy movement

> is, and should be, decentralized and pluralist, with a focus on winning state and local elections, not a third party or a national left organization; and on founding and running democratic enterprises, schools, and publications. Only once such a base is built will we be in a position to run a candidate for the presidency or in any other way challenge for national power.[7]

That this political movement is capable of achieving some of its goals is evidenced by the coalition's strength and breadth. Journalist Justin Raimondo has observed that

> a loose coalition is beginning to take shape around the country; Massachusetts Fair Share [a so-called welfare rights organization], ACORN [Association of Community Organizations for Reform Now], International Association of Machinists' president William Winpisinger with the Citizen/Labor Energy Coalition, the Progressive Alliance headed by UAW's Douglas Fraser, as well as Michael Harrington's DSOC [Democratic Socialist Organizing

37

Committee] and groups like the New American Movement, all share a somewhat common political perspective.[8]

In *Economic Democracy*, Shearer and his coauthor Martin Carnoy have offered some perspectives on their basic strategy: "The two essential elements of any strategy of fundamental reform in the United States today are: (1) The shift of investment control from corporate domination to the public; and (2) The reconstruction of economic decision making through democratic worker—and worker/consumer—controlled production."[9] This position has evolved from the authors' personal disdain for private corporations. They have written that the means of production should be controlled by government (which Shearer calls "the public"), not by private corporations, for

> these corporations are impersonal and powerful; in their relations with another set of large corporations—the banks—they govern the capital accumulating process and, with it, employment technology, income distribution, work organization, consumption patterns, and, in large part, our relations with other nations. Any alternative economic and social strategy must start by dismantling, or at least restricting, the power of these corporations. They are the antithesis of democracy. But we are not proposing a return to the competitive capitalism of the past. America is no longer a nation of farmers and artisans. Today we are a nation of employees; that is our reality. Nor do we think that the best way to work is necessarily to compete individually one against another for bread and status. Employees can produce cooperatively; their wages can be largely the direct fruit of their labor, and they themselves can decide the best way to produce and how much to produce in a democratically planned economy. A strategy of reform must transfer capital from the corporations to the public, so that the people who work and consume can collectively and democratically decide what to do with it. The logical vehicle for that process should be the government.[10]

Thus, the economic democracy movement seeks the politicization of the production process by building "a mass political movement on the basis of a program such as ours and to win a majority of local, state, and national governing bodies."[11] Carnoy and Shearer also have emphasized the importance of the anti-industry coalition:

> [T]he struggle in the United States has been waged by minorities and women seeking greater equality and, in the sixties, by

38

youth . . . against the Vietnam War, although consumer groups and environmentalists have directly challenged corporate power. . . . In the absence of forces to unite these movements into a coherent whole, however, they also tend to fractionalize a broader movement for social change.[12]

This "broader movement" is the pursuit of elected and appointed positions in government, especially at the state and local levels, by individuals who can use the powers of government (and tax revenues) to pursue their political agenda. CASLP, for example, claims to be an "important new force in American political life" and has enlisted the assistance of such groups as Nader's Public Citizen, ACORN, the New Jersey Tenants Organization, the Children's Defense Fund, the American Federation of State, County and Municipal Employees, the AFL-CIO, and many other nonprofit special-interest groups.[13]

To implement this program, a number of specific policy goals have been established. They include the formation of a government-owned "holding company," a government-owned energy corporation, government radio and television stations, greater government control over pension fund assets, the promotion of "worker co-ops" or codetermination, the mandatory use of "appropriate technology," price controls, and more centralized economic planning.

The Policy Goals of the Anti-Industry Coalition

Holding-Company Strategy

A government "holding company" would purchase "from ten to twenty percent of the shares in at least one major firm in each major industry dominated by a few companies." The board of directors would consist of representatives of "consumers, labor, and government itself." In other words, using the holding company strategy, the anti-industry coalition would slowly nationalize the nation's major industries and would "help finance and encourage new public enterprises at the municipal, state, and regional levels."[14] The holding company would also be a "source of financial support and consulting talent for major experiments in worker-owned and worker/community-owned enterprises," and it would establish a school to train bureaucrats in "democratic management."[15] There already is such a school in San Francisco, established by Shearer and others, that is largely financed by the Foundation for National Progress, an arm of IPS. The school also receives taxpayer subsidies (as described in chapter 5).

According to Shearer the objective of such a holding company is to serve as "a vehicle for selective and, in many cases, partial public ownership without the immediate financial and ideological burdens that large-scale nationalization efforts would entail."[16] Supporters hope that this plan will be a way to nationalize industry, bit by bit, without widespread public awareness. This is hardly a democratic attitude.

To facilitate the process of nationalization, Carnoy and Shearer have prescribed that greater government control first be exerted over the use of investment assets, such as pension funds. According to Carnoy and Shearer:

> The basic elements of our strategy for democratizing investment are: the creation, from both private and public employee funds, of city- and state-owned banks staffed with trust departments competent to handle large pension fund accounts; the establishment by the labor movement itself of a national pension fund investment advisory service to assist unions in fashioning strategies for using this "pension power"; federal purchase of at least one healthy national bank holding company and one nationally active insurance company . . . giving the government a stronger position from which to influence the activities of the remaining private banks.[17]

Compulsory Codetermination

Shearer considers the nationalization of industry as a necessary, but not sufficient, condition to achieve economic democracy. What is also needed is "worker control" over how work is to be allocated and how much workers are to be paid. It is basic to Carnoy and Shearer's argument that "in the capitalist production process . . . the ownership of property carries with it legal control over its use."[18] Thus, given their view that "economic power and rights" determine political power, they believe that "direct employee ownership . . . would seem to be the most far-reaching of . . . reforms, since ownership should give the employees the right to govern their own work organization and the nature of the work situation." Further, "the governmental promotion of cooperatives should be an explicit part of strategy for democratizing the economy. Even a handful of worker-owned and democratically run companies can serve as models of what a democratic economy would be like."[19]

Because private banks have deemed most cooperatives to be

uncreditworthy, Carnoy and Shearer naturally have viewed the government as a means of financing, through taxation, what may be called compulsory codetermination. This strategy has become a reality. In 1978, after a fierce lobbying campaign led by Ralph Nader and his associates, Congress created the National Consumer Co-op Bank (see chapter 5). In a particularly revealing statement, Carnoy and Shearer have said of the campaign for the National Consumer Co-op Bank:

> [This legislation] is a top-down strategy: organizers and intellectuals push a particular idea, progressive elements in the government come to accept its validity and promote it and, finally, under this stimulus workers respond. . . . Government in a democratic society can pass legislation that opens new political and social opportunities for citizens. Enactment of the legislation is often made possible by the lobbying and organizing efforts of a mass movement [the anti-industry coalition]; the new legislation in turn helps the movement to grow by legitimizing the movement's goals and providing new legal, and financial resources to it.[20]

It is clear that the anti-industry coalition views the National Consumer Co-op Bank and other similar organizations as a means of getting taxpayers to finance its political agenda.

National Economic Planning

Essential to the success of any plan of the economic democracy movement is government control of production. Until nationalization of some industries can be achieved, the strategy is to control corporate behavior through antitrust laws, regulation, collective bargaining laws weighted in favor of so-called progressive labor unions, and "subsidies and incentives" to selected firms. As Carnoy and Shearer have stated:

> The government must have the means at hand to carry out economic development in the event that private enterprise refuses to enter into planning agreements—in other words, there must be a core of publicly-owned firms more responsive to government requests than private ones—and real sanctions must be levied against private firms that choose not to bargain. These could include denial of tax advantages and other subsidies, denial of export licenses, threat of antitrust suits, and so on.[21]

The political agenda set forth by the anti-industry coalition is inherently incompatible with a free enterprise system. The empha-

41

sis varies among the different segments of the coalition, but these groups form a remarkably close alliance when they address one common goal: "organizers and intellectuals" exerting government control over activities that are currently being carried on by corporate management on behalf of shareholders and consumers. Government ownership of at least some industries is urged by all members of the coalition, as is greater government regulation of economic activity. All members of the anti-industry coalition attempt to at least limit price determination through use of the market process and to replace it with a system of wage and price controls. Some of these efforts have been successful, especially in the area of rent control and in regulations governing the prices charged by public utilities.

The economic consequences of such campaigns should be of serious concern to those who value economic growth and prosperity in the United States and who are unknowingly paying taxes to support these activities.

The Anti-Industry Coalition: Rhetoric and Reality

A principal source of animosity toward private enterprise in the United States is so-called industrial concentration, which is generally measured in terms of the total market share enjoyed by a few firms in an industry. Nader, the Corporate Data Exchange, IPS, and many others are continually warning of the dangers of increasing industrial concentration. The danger, they assert, arises because in those industries where only a few firms control the majority of sales, there is no competition and consumers are at the mercy of monopolists. Richard Barnet, a senior fellow of IPS, has argued that the "myth of free enterprise" is not "legitimate," for "the most important development" challenging it has been the "concentration of economic power" that has led to "the age of oligopoly," wherein products are shaped not according to public need but to "the requirements of corporate growth." Most important, according to Barnet, "the concentration of economic power in the hands of a few hundred corporate managers and stockholders is inevitably translated into political power which destroys the myth of democracy."[22]

A closer examination of the relation between industrial concentration and economic and political power, however, reveals that these claims are misguided and often erroneous. One well-known example is John Kenneth Galbraith's assertion that half of all economic activity in the United States is controlled by the 500 largest industrial corporations (the Fortune 500).[23] Galbraith's work serves as a foundation for much of the work of the anti-industry coalition, but his data are misleading. Galbraith failed to mention that half of all *manufacturing* employment occurs in the Fortune 500 and that manufacturing accounts for less than one-fourth of all employment in the United States. Thus, the 500 largest industrial corporations are responsible for at most one-eighth of all employment—a 300 percent error on Galbraith's part. Similar abuses of statistical information are common and have been especially well documented in the critiques of Nader's organizations.[24] The Corporate Data Exchange and many other organizations discussed in chapters 4 through 7 specialize in such delusions.

Even if the data were not doctored, however, warnings about excessive concentration are misguided because of a fundamental misunderstanding of how markets function. It has long been recognized that businessmen, given any opportunity, would like to conspire to raise prices and exert other forms of monopoly power. In his *Wealth of Nations*, Adam Smith observed that "people of the same trade seldom meet together, even for merriment and diversion, but the conversation ends in a conspiracy against the public, or in some contrivance to raise prices."[25] However, Smith knew that there was a vast difference between the willingness and the ability to "conspire against the public." Historically, market forces have broken up cartel arrangements that were privately concocted and that did not enjoy government protection from competition. As long as competitors or potential competitors are not legally barred from entering an industry, above-normal economic profits will soon be dissipated by competition and the cartel will be destroyed. Talk of an "age of oligopoly" in the manufacturing sector is especially misleading because it ignores the impact of foreign competition. It may be true that the U.S. steel and automobile industries, for example, are characterized by relatively few firms, but can we seriously believe that these firms have monopoly power in light of the fierce competition from West Germany, Japan, and many of the so-called developing nations?

Excessive reliance on concentration ratios is further flawed because such data say nothing about the existence of substitutes and their ability to prohibit the long-term success of any cartel arrangement. Du Pont, for example, was once sued for violating antitrust laws because it allegedly monopolized the cellophane industry. Du Pont invented cellophane and was for a time a "pure monopolist," for no one else had yet learned how to produce it. This was a case of industrial concentration par excellence—only one producer with 100 percent of the sales. The Supreme Court ruled that despite its apparent monopoly, Du Pont exercised no monopoly power in its pricing practices. Not that the company would not have liked to; rather, it was unable to. Any increase in price above that paid for available substitute food coverings would have resulted in a sharp decline in sales and profits. Du Pont simply perceived a market for cellophane and, to the great advantage of consumers, invented a remarkably useful product. This is only one of hundreds of examples of how emotional claims about industry concentration have led to destructive government policies.[26]

Yale Brozen has closely examined the data on profit trends in manufacturing industries to determine whether, as many claim, they are monopolized. According to Brozen, "If [accounting] returns remain high in high-return industries and low in low-return industries . . . then we can at least say that we have failed to show that manufacturing is not monopolized. . . . If, however, high rates of return erode and low returns improve, with returns converging on the average rate, then we may . . . suspect that the market is competitive."[27]

Using data for leading corporations grouped by industry, Brozen analyzed the top earning industries of 1948, a year in which the business cycle was at a peak. He then looked at their ranks in 1956, the next year in which a cyclical peak occurred, and he concluded

> that the top 20 of our 40 industries ranked by earnings in 1948 fell in average rank in the next eight years. They ended in 1956 with a random distribution among the 40 ranks, ranging from fourth to bottom rank instead of top to middle rank. The average earnings rank among the 1948 top 20 dropped to very near the average for all 40 industries. . . . Similarly, the average industry in the bottom half did not remain in the middle of the bottom half. Its rate of return rank rose from the average for the bottom half to very near the average for all industries. This is exactly what is supposed not to occur in monopolized markets. What happened is what we would expect in a group of competitive industries.[28]

Brozen repeated the experiment for the years 1966 to 1978, demonstrating that his initial finding is not peculiar to any particular period of time. He found that "the average industry in the 1966 top 20 dropped from a 10.5 rank in 1966 to 18.1 in 1978. The average

44

industry in the 1966 bottom 20 rose from a 30.5 rank in 1966 to 22.9 in 1978."[29] Thus, if the data are carefully examined, one finds that the manufacturing sector is very competitive, despite the emotional rhetoric of the critics. Even more important, it is now well-established that there is no necessary relationship between industrial concentration and profitability, and that no such link has ever been found.[30] In fact, it is more likely that the main cause of industrial concentration is superior economic performance, not collusion. In 1950 Benjamin Fairless made this point:

> The size of any company depends . . . upon the product it intends to manufacture—upon the amount of money it is going to take to buy the plants, machines and tools that will be necessary to produce that product efficiently and competitively. From that point on, the growth of the company depends on its customers. If they like the product and want to buy more of it, the company will have to expand to meet their demands. If they don't like the product there is no way on earth that the company can force them to buy, no matter how big . . . it may be. That is why today's giant must be useful, helpful, and necessary or he simply goes out of business because he failed to serve his customers to their satisfaction. [W]hen the top companies in any industry win the highest percentage of the customers, they naturally are going to have the highest percentage of the business.[31]

More recent research has confirmed this observation. It is now recognized that concentration is caused by numerous factors, such as accumulated experience in individual firms, superior management, economies of scale, reductions in less-than-optimum-sized plants, and capital-intensive technology. All of these factors enable larger firms to provide better and cheaper service to customers.

In light of this, government policies that attempt to penalize large-scale business enterprises are bound to harm both competition and consumers. This, however, is precisely the type of policy pursued by lobbyists for the anti-industry coalition.

The Separation of Ownership from Control

A second reason why the anti-industry coalition agitates for greater government control or ownership of private industry stems from a thesis first expounded by Adolf A. Berle and Gardiner C. Means in their 1932 book, *The Modern Corporation and Private Property*. According to Berle and Means and their disciples, during the twentieth century the increase in the number of corporate shareholders, each

45

owning relatively few shares, has enabled corporate management to usurp control of wealth they do not personally own. According to Galbraith, perhaps the most prominent economic spokesman for the anti-industry coalition,

> The case for private ownership through equity capital disappears whenever the stockholder ceases to have power—when he or she or it becomes a purely passive recipient of income. The management is a self-governing, self-perpetuating bureaucracy. It can make no claim to the traditional immunity associated with property ownership. The logical course is for the state to replace the helpless stockholder as a supervisory and policy-setting body; the forthright way to accomplish this is to have a public holding company take over the common stock.[32]

This popular theme is a part of Shearer's economic democracy platform and of Ralph Nader's objectives. The so-called public policy solutions to this alleged problem vary in detail, but they all hinge on government, rather than market, allocation of resources.[33] According to this view, large corporations are indistinguishable from governments because they wield great power over customers, employees, and communities. They are said to be private governments, but they are undemocratic and despotic. From this viewpoint, it is deduced that corporate management is led to expose customers to injury and death due to faulty products, hazardous working conditions, and dangerous chemical wastes which they recklessly discard. Corporations are said to crush their smaller competitors and then shamelessly charge monopoly prices. On top of that, they withhold dividends from their shareholders.

In their campaign to condemn corporate management, anti-industry advocates ignore how markets function. Consider the claim that corporate management is unresponsive to the owners of business firms, the shareholders. This view ignores some very important economic institutions that discipline corporate management in ways that favor shareholders and consumers. The market for corporate control is one such phenomenon. As Henry Manne has pointed out, the management teams that do not try to maximize the profits of shareholders will cause investors to sell some of their shares in favor of more lucrative investments.[34] Consequently, the price of the firm's stock will be depressed, inviting the possibility of a takeover bid. There are always enterprising entrepeneurs who discern profit opportunities by taking over poorly managed companies. Even Nader would not accuse businessmen of not pursuing profits. Through the market for corporate control, a poorly managed firm runs the risk of having another firm purchase a controlling interest, replace existing management, and turn a higher profit. The surest way to fend off a takeover bid is to act in the interests of shareholders, and corporate managers can be expected to act in this way, in that their own salaries, positions, and job tenure depend on it.

Salaries of corporate managers are also often directly tied to profitability through bonus or stock-option plans so that it is in the managers' self-interest to act in the interest of shareholders. High rates of turnover among top corporate management attest to the fact that the bottom line—profits—is a convenient and simple way to monitor managerial performance. Even if a manager does not significantly increase his salary by reducing costs and increasing profits, a demonstrated ability to do so may earn him a superior position (and salary) at another firm.[35] Thus, maximizing shareholder wealth is in the best interest of corporate management, for it tends to increase both pecuniary income and the marketable human capital of management.

In addition, what Eugene Fama[36] called the "inside labor market" reduces the divergence between shareholder and managerial interests. The inside managerial labor market works in two ways. First, upper-level managers monitor the behavior of middle- and lower-level managers to ensure that shareholder wealth is protected. Upper-level managers do this because their own tenure and salary depend on it. Second, lower-level managers monitor the behavior of upper management as it strives to replace managers who are considered less competent, but higher paid, than they are. Thus, managerial salaries depend not on abusing but on protecting shareholder interests.

Both economic reasoning and evidence indicate that the claims of the anti-industry coalition regarding the separation of ownership from control are unsubstantiated. Common sense indicates that firms that produce ostensibly silly or useless products will not survive for very long, nor will those that exploit their employees, because in a competitive labor market, employees are free to seek work elsewhere. For decades, critics have complained that capitalism grants disproportionate power to corporate management in making day-to-day production decisions. Managers do have control over such decisions, but consumers are the ultimate decision makers in a capitalist economy. In claiming that private businesses exert too much power, the anti-industry coalition blurs the distinction between political and market allocation of resources. Only governments, which can compel obedience to their laws, can exploit people by taking from them and offering nothing in exchange. Private business can only survive, in the absence of government subsidization, by offering consumers and workers items of value to them in a voluntary exchange. No business, however large, can coerce anyone to buy its product. But government can and does do this, and it is the expansion of this coercion that the anti-industry coalition seeks. To the extent that private businesses are protected from competition as a matter of government policy, the appropriate policy is to eliminate, not expand, the role of government in regulating industry. Corporate power is to be most feared when it is aided by government sanction.

The anti-industry coalition is concerned not only about the concentration of political and economic power but also about the distribution of that power. More specifically, members of the coalition are dissatisfied that the market allocates resources in ways that may meet consumers' demands but are inconsistent with their own personal preferences. For example, Nader once stated his philosophical objectives as follows: "We are going to rediscover smallness. If people get back to the earth, they can grow their own gardens, they can listen to the birds, they can feel the wind caress their cheek, and they can watch the sun come up."[37] To realize this vision, Nader said, corporations must be abolished and replaced by small "consumer co-ops." Nader described a "lost age of competition" wherein, during pre–Civil War times, "business firms tended to be small, and bought their raw materials and sold their goods locally."[38] This system was less competitive than the current system, because technology, especially in the area of transportation, has allowed more efficient, large-scale enterprises to compete nationally and internationally. Consumers now enjoy a wide array of products produced at home and abroad, rather than those provided by a single, small, local firm. Not only has large-scale production and big business produced a vast array of products, but as even Nader once admitted, it has been "a major reason why our real per capita income has tripled in the past forty years."[39]

Public-Enterprise Strategy

It is unlikely that many are pleased that tax dollars are routinely used to finance the lobbying efforts of those who wish to replace those enterprises that provide us with the highest quality products, namely, private firms, with those that have the reputation of providing services that are mediocre at best, namely, public enterprises. If there is any doubt about this assertion, ask which products are least satisfactory and which have shown the least improvement over time? Postal services and elementary and secondary schools would surely be high on the list. The most satisfactory products could include home appliances, televisions, radio sets, stereo equipment, and home computers. It is no accident that the former group is produced by government and the latter is the domain of private enterprise in which there is little government involvement.

Conventional wisdom has long held that government is grossly inefficient. An indication of this sentiment is found in the terms "bureaucrat" and "bureaucracy," which, as Ludwig von Mises noted in his classic work on the subject, are always used with an opprobrious connotation.[40] Bureaucracy conjures visions of paperwork, excessive regulation, and institutional rigidity—the opposite of the dynamic and efficient organization. Public employees as individuals cannot be blamed for the widely accepted view that government is wasteful. Whether in the public or the private sector, workers are the same in that they seek to enhance their self-interest: They seek rewards and attempt to avoid punishment. The structure of rewards and punishment is vastly different in the public sector than it is in the private sector. The rank of a public employee determines his salary, perquisites, and prestige, and it is determined by the number of subordinates under his control.[41] Thus, every civil servant has an incentive to expand his organization, which implies obtaining ever-greater appropriations to hire more employees and undertake more tasks.

In the public sector there are no real incentives to reduce costs because a civil servant cannot increase his salary by increasing the efficiency of the organization. Furthermore, if the bureau's appropriation is not spent by the end of the year, it may be difficult to justify a larger budget for the following year. In addition, cutting waste is often a thankless task, and part of bureaucratic life is a relaxed operating style.

By legislative fiat, public enterprises are granted a monopoly franchise so that competitive pressures are not present. Even if alternative sources of supply do exist, the taxpayers still must support the bureaucratic enterprise. For example, there are both public and private universities, and if a student elects to go to a private institution, taxes must still be paid to support the public counter-part. Thus, incentives for efficiency are virtually nonexistent in the public sector. Moreover, it is all but impossible to terminate the employment of a government worker, and punishment for inadequate performance is also largely absent.

The incentive structure is vastly different in the private sector than it is in the public sector. Private managers are more likely to get promoted if they are able to come in under budget consistently. It is also a common practice in private industry to give bonuses based on cost savings achieved by the manager; that is, if costs can be reduced, the manager's income rises. Moreover, individuals can be and often are terminated for poor performance. Even if managers were to become lax and careless, they could escape the repercussions for only a short time. Competition is a fact of life for the private firm, and the ever-present threat of loss of market share (if prices are increased to cover increased costs) or declining profits (if the cost increases are absorbed internally) forces managers to make continuing efforts to lower production costs.

Municipal governments throughout the world provide an almost bewildering array of services, including refuse collection, fire and police protection, ambulance and transit services, health care and hospitalization, education, debt collection, road and building maintenance, parking lot operations, and (in some cases) power generation and provision of other utilities. In many instances, public enterprise directly displaces private firms; in other instances, one may legitimately question whether the goods and services produced conform to the accepted definition of public goods.

A great deal of research has been devoted to cost comparisons between the public and private sectors to determine their relative efficiency so as to test the hypothesis that differing structures of incentives or property rights influence economic behavior.[42] Regardless of the service analyzed, the findings support the same conclusion: The private sector can produce the same or a better quality of goods and services at much lower cost than can the public sector. So consistent has been this empirical result that the "Bureaucratic Rule of Two" has been proposed: Transfer of a service from the private to the public sector doubles the unit cost of production.[43]

Government ownership of industry has and will increase the cost of providing goods and services, thereby rendering U.S.-made products less competitive in world markets. This trend would only enable us to imitate British industry, for example, where government ownership is more common and industrial performance is lethargic. Historically, once an industry or firm is taken over by government and becomes uncompetitive, the managers, workers, and some customers form a powerful political coalition that can pressure the legislature to bail it out with taxpayers' funds. Industrial dinosaurs such as British Steel and British Leyland are a strain on the British taxpayers' pocketbooks and provide costly and inferior products, but as subsidized industries they are politically difficult to eliminate.

Government ownership tends to produce a vicious circle in which inefficient enterprises are subsidized at taxpayer expense, which provides even less incentive for efficiency, which leads to more political plans for even greater subsidies, and so on. These well-known facts are ignored by the anti-industry coalition, which continues to claim that government-owned enterprises are more responsive to consumers than is private industry. In contrast to private markets, where consumers are the ultimate decision makers, government-operated enterprises allocate resources in a way that rewards those who can provide the most political support for the government.

Do Workers Want Worker Ownership?

Recognizing that the outright nationalization of industry may not be politically possible, at least in the near future, all segments of the anti-industry coalition have promoted another substitute for the corporation: the cooperative. Because the anti-industry coalition views the corporation as a political rather than as a private entity, it views codetermination as a way of restructuring society in conformance with its own perceptions of justice and democracy. As Carnoy and Shearer have stated, "The promotion of cooperatives should be an explicit part of the strategy for democratizing the economy. Even a handful of worker-owned and democratically run companies can serve as models of what a democratic economy would be like."[44] Similarly, worker-owned cooperatives have been a major part of Nader's lobbying efforts in his return-to-smallness campaign. Worker ownership may sound attractive, but where it does exist it generally has come about by government fiat, implying that it is not an efficient form of business organization.

There has been surprisingly little work done on the economic effects of codetermination, perhaps because of its novelty. Organizational psychologists, however, have paid a lot of attention to the

51

issue, and, even though it generally contains no economic analysis, they often assume that codetermination is desirable.[45]

As Michael Jensen and William Meckling have pointed out, one significant problem is how to reconcile the supposed desirability of codetermination with the fact that laws are generally needed to force codetermination on the owners of business firms. If codetermination were truly beneficial to all the parties involved and not just a means of transferring wealth, it should develop voluntarily. If it must be mandated by government, there is evidence that it is inefficient. Jensen and Meckling have asserted that

> labor can start, and in rare cases has started, firms of its own. Moreover, firms are free to write any kind of contracts they wish with their employees. If they choose to, they can offer no-dismissal, no-layoff contracts (tenure at universities). If they choose to, they can establish worker councils and agree not to change production methods without worker approval. Moreover, employers would establish such practices if the benefits exceeded the costs. Furthermore, if laborers value the security and "self realization" which such participatory arrangements afford them at more than their costs to the employer, they are in a position to offer voluntary changes which it will pay the employer to take. . . . Since (with minor exceptions) these arrangements are not observed, we infer that workers do not value the security, management participation, "self realization," etc. at more than the cost of providing them.[46]

There have been only preliminary investigations of the economic effects of codetermination.[47] Nevertheless, there is an economic framework for analyzing codetermination, which is neatly summarized by Svetozar Pejovich.[48]

First, codetermination violates two of the foundations of a free enterprise, private property economy: the freedom of contract and the right of ownership. The right of ownership gives individuals incentives to seek to put resources to their most highly valued uses, and freedom of contract allows mutually advantageous trade to take place to achieve that task. Forced codetermination by government fiat (which is what the anti-industry coalition seeks) abridges both of these rights and, therefore, reduces the domain of mutually advantageous trade.

Second, forced codetermination interferes with the rights of the owners of capital to claim and dispose of profits, thereby ignoring (if not subverting) the role of profits in allocating resources to the uses most highly valued by consumers. Advocates of codetermination make arguments that are based on the erroneous view that profits emerge from the exploitation of labor and for that reason are the legitimate object of redistribution.

Third, codetermination severs the link between decision making and risk bearing. Under a system of private property rights, owners and managers can benefit from increases in the value of the firm's assets, which creates incentives to make the best use of those assets. By attenuating the right of ownership, codetermination reduces the quality of business decisions. In particular, the codetermined firm has fewer incentives to seek the most profitable uses of resources. For example, because of workers' short-term time horizon, labor (union) representatives may have incentives to pursue policies that raise current wages as much as possible and that postpone costs. As Pejovich has explained:

> [C]onsider two investment alternatives of equal costs. The expected present value of one alternative is $1000 while the other yields only $750. However, if the returns from the first alternative are discounted over a period of 20 years and those of the second over only five years, workers could easily push the management in the direction of choosing the less profitable one. Even in the absence of sharing in the firm's profits, wage negotiations and their perception of job security would provide workers with incentives to prefer business policies that promise larger annual earnings over a limited time period . . . to those policies that maximize the firm's present worth.[49]

Finally, codetermination is most forcefully defended on the grounds that labor productivity will increase in response to a more satisfied work force. Even if work effort is positively related to workers' utility, however, it is not clear that such productivity gains would outweigh increased labor costs. According to Pejovich,

> If codetermination means a transfer of wealth from the shareholders to labor we can conjecture the following chain of events. The rate of return from capital invested in labor participatory firms (mostly corporations) will fall. The resulting flight of capital into the other (non-participatory) alternatives such as small firms, human capital, bonds, and foreign investment will change investment patterns in the economy. The rate will be smaller and in other areas greater than it would otherwise be. The rate of return in non-participatory investments will fall while the marginal pro-

ductivity of labor will fall. In equilibrium, corporate firms will produce smaller outputs and charge higher prices than they would otherwise. Conversely, prices will be lower and outputs greater in non-participatory sectors of the economy. If this simple scenario is predictive of the general effects of codetermination, labor participation in the management of business firms will result in the reallocation of resources away from the most efficient, technically advanced and productive sectors of the economy and toward less efficient, technically less capable and less productive alternatives. A general decline of the level and character of the economy could then be predicted.[50]

In sum, it stands to reason that the mandatory codetermination advocated by the anti-industry coalition is simply a means of redistributing wealth and power. The result is likely to be an overall reduction in economic growth and a further deterioration of the market economy. This is exactly what is openly hoped for by some proponents of codetermination.

Should the subsidization of cooperatives occur on a wide scale, as the anti-industry coalition plans, Jensen and Meckling have offered a rather gloomy, but realistic scenario:

> This state of affairs will lead to unfavorable international comparisons, outcries of outdated technology, foreign exchange problems, and a general clamor for state subsidies to capital accumulation to augment the "failures" of the private markets. As the state provides capital loans to firms it will impose additional controls to prevent the workers from simply transforming the new resources into consumption. . . . The final result will be fairly complete, if not total, state ownership of the productive assets of the economy.[51]

Is Consumer Protection Hazardous to Your Health?

Although the size and scope of government activity has been steadily expanding for decades, there has been a veritable explosion in federal government regulatory activity since the mid-1960s. This growth in regulation has been strongly supported by the anti-industry coalition and permits government agents to regulate the environment, the production and distribution of almost all goods and services, product safety, occupational safety, ad infinitum. In addition to reflecting an ostensible concern for consumers' pocketbooks, regulation allegedly offers protection from exploitation by sellers and also from consumers themselves by banning certain products that the regulators decide should not be produced or sold.

Government exenditures on regulatory agencies ballooned from less than $1 billion annually in 1970 to more than $5 billion in 1979. The number of bureaucrats employed by regulatory agencies tripled, from 28,000 in 1970 to 81,000 in 1979, and the number of pages of regulations in the *Federal Register* rose from 20,000 in 1970 to over 77,000 in 1979.[52] Regulatory agencies have become a primary source of employment for members of the anti-industry coalition. During the same time, economic growth in the United States slowed dramatically. From 1949 to 1969, output per man-hour in the private nonagricultural sector rose at an annual rate of about 3 percent. In the 1970s, labor productivity rose at about half that rate and had even declined by the end of that decade.

These two developments—regulation and economic stagnation—are not unrelated. Regulations have imposed heavy costs on private industries by preventing some products from being sold, requiring capital to be used for nonproductive purposes, and strangling the industries with red tape and paperwork. The prices paid for goods and services have risen dramatically in many cases because of the regulatory activities of government. For example, it is estimated that because of federal regulations imposed between 1968 and 1978, the average cost of a new car increased by $665.87. As approximately 10 million new cars and trucks are purchased each year, government regulations cost car purchasers about $6.7 billion annually.[53] The federal government has dictated the shape of toilet seats, the size of knotholes in wood ladders, and the way that stepladders may be climbed. Although the contents of many regulations seem comical, the price tags for U.S. consumers are not. One carefully developed, conservative estimate placed the cost of federal regulation of businesses at over $102 billion in 1979— approximately $500 per capita.[54] A similar expansion of regulatory activity has also taken place at the state and local levels of government and, combined with federal regulation, has severely impaired the vitality of U.S. industry and contributed to unemployment.

Regulation has traditionally been justified as a means of protecting the public interest, however that may be defined. Despite these claims, however, a large number of economic studies have shown that many regulations are not only costly but also ineffective. For example, many of the automobile regulations are related to safety, yet a study conducted at the University of Chicago showed that

55

these safety devices have no effect in reducing death rates from automobile accidents, because they fail to take into account the principal cause of automobile fatalities—the drunk driver. The Occupational Safety and Health Administration supposedly was established to reduce hazards to workers on the job. Yet one study reported that the agency's enforcement policies have not had any direct impact on job hazards.[55] The regulation of new drugs has sharply reduced the rates of innovation and the introduction of effective new drugs in the United States; in contrast, in Great Britain and other countries where the environment is less restrictive, there have been marked benefits from new drugs that have not been introduced in the United States.[56] These studies are just a few among hundreds conducted during the past two decades, and they indicate why so many economists and taxpayers are critical of government regulation. Many of these studies have been published in the *Journal of Law and Economics*, whose editor, Ronald Coase, has said that

> there have been more serious studies made of government regulation of industry in the last fifteen years or so, particularly in the United States, than in the whole preceding period. These studies have been both quantitative and nonquantitative. . . . The main lesson to be drawn from these studies is clear: they all tend to suggest that the regulation is either ineffective or that when it has a noticeable impact, on balance the effect is bad, so that consumers obtain a worse product or a higher-priced product or both as a result of the regulation. Indeed, this result is found so uniformly as to create a puzzle: one would expect to find, in all these studies, at least some government programs that do more good than harm.[57]

Despite the public interest rhetoric, it is evident that much economic regulation serves various special interests at the expense of the general public. Trucking regulation has maintained cartel pricing arrangements for the benefit of trucking firms and the teamsters union; airline regulation restricted entry into the airline industry; and occupational licensing restricts entry into various professions ranging from fortune telling to hairdressing.

Another indirect cost of regulation is government red tape. As of June 1972 the Office of Management and Budget reported that federal agencies (excluding the Internal Revenue Service) used 5,567 forms that generated 418 million responses—about two for every person in the country.[58] The costs and frustrations involved in federal paperwork are enormous. Consider a statement from the U.S. Commission on Federal Paperwork's *Final Summary Report*, issued in October 1977:

> The total costs of federal paperwork are difficult to determine; but, as best we can estimate, more than $100 billion a year, or about $500 for each person in this country, is spent on federal paperwork. Our estimates of costs to some major segments of society are:
>
> | | |
> |---|---|
> | The federal government: | $43 billion per year |
> | Private industry: | $25 to 32 billion per year |
> | State and local government: | $5 to 9 billion per year |
> | Individuals: | $8.7 billion per year |
> | Farmers: | $350 million per year |
> | Labor organizations: | $75 million per year |

The paperwork burden imposes particularly onerous costs on small businesses, which can ill afford to spend the time, effort, and money required to comply with the bureaucracy's seemingly insatiable desire for forms, many of which are redundant or ignored by the bureaucracy.

Economic growth has been severely stifled by what has been called the "new regulation" resulting from the regulatory agencies formed since the mid-1960s—such as the Environmental Protection Agency, the Occupational Safety and Health Administration, and the Consumer Product Safety Commission—which are distinctly different from older agencies, such as the Interstate Commerce Commission and the Civil Aeronautics Board. These older agencies were either created at the insistence of regulated industries or they were in effect captured by those industries, which then staffed them with many of their own personnel and used them to reduce competition in their particular industry. As these circumstances have become more widely known, the deregulation of the trucking and airline industries, although not yet complete, has enjoyed wide popular support.

By contrast, the newer regulatory agencies are not staffed by industry representatives or even by people who are very knowledgeable about the industry. Instead, they are the domain of people who are indifferent or even hostile toward private corporations. Consequently, these agencies routinely issue directives and orders without considering the economic consequences to be borne by the owners, workers, and consumers of the regulated industries, even though a large body of research has shown that regulatory directives and orders rarely achieve their stated objectives. It has been known for centuries that the market system is the best protector of consumers and workers, but the market places little value on elitist groups of social engineers charged with the duty of protecting the public.

Subverting the Price System

Members of the anti-industry coalition are very dissatisfied with how the price system allocates resources, and they have successfully lobbied for government restrictions—namely, price controls—on the use of the price system. Because resource allocation by way of the price system is the key to the success of any capitalistic economy, the coalition has chosen this system as its main target. Some members of the coalition simply do not appreciate the importance of the price system; others do, but they are intent upon subverting it.

Perhaps the most important attribute of the price system, one that the anti-industry coalition rejects, is that the complex information on consumer preferences is embodied in one element—prices. Changes in consumer demand are registered through price fluctuations. Without a smoothly functioning price system, consumers cannot effectively control what is produced, as they can in an unregulated regime. Changes in relative prices send a signal to profit-maximizing entrepreneurs that consumer preferences have shifted. Those who fail to make use of the information provided by prices simply will not survive in the long run. By permitting politicians to control prices by legislative fiat, price controls severely reduce consumers' ability to voice their preferences (and have them satisfied) in the marketplace. From a supply-side perspective, price controls on factors of production distort the information needed to minimize the costs of production. Higher production costs mean higher prices, which is hardly in the interest of consumers—the people purportedly protected by the anti-industry coalition.

It has been demonstrated that government regulation of wages and prices has never been anything but impoverishing in that it distorts the effectiveness with which the price system conveys information. Minimum-wage laws, rent control, and price controls in general are known to be major causes of unemployment, shortages, and diminished product quality.

58

Summary

The anti-industry coalition is undertaking a well-organized attack on the basic institutions of a free-enterprise, private-property economy. Its philosophy of economic democracy, according to Derek Shearer, is not substantially different from socialism. Most professional economists acknowledge that such policies as the government ownership of industry, price controls, government-mandated codetermination, and strict regulation can only reduce the wealth of nations. It is precisely this result, however, that would provide the anti-industry coalition with opportunities to take control politically at the federal, state, and local levels of government. As discussed in the next four chapters, U.S. taxpayers are unwittingly contributing to the coalition's campaign.

IV. The Campaign for Economic Democracy: Socializing the State and Local Sectors

> We want to get hundreds or thousands of CED activists into the Democratic Party. Then we'll get the party involved in local elections and at the precinct and assembly district levels. If we can do that, we'll elect mayors, county supervisors and city councils. . . . After we do that, we can elect members of the legislature.
>
> —Tom Hayden

The agenda for so-called economic democracy is being actively pursued, partly at taxpayers' expense, at the state and local levels of government all over the nation. As journalist John Herbers has stated in the *New York Times:*

> A multitude of citizen-action groups on the left, which sprang up in the 1970s to secure specific but frequently narrow goals on the state and local level, are now seeking to organize the discontent nationally. . . . Many leaders of this movement were the angry youth of the 1960s who disrupted American society. . . . Compared with other groups, the evolving and emerging groups on the left have received less attention even though their influence, both actual and potential, may be greater.[1]

The Conference on Alternative State and Local Policies (CASLP) serves a major organizational function in this effort, and it has claimed that what it does "is spread the conviction that state and local government will be the major area of progressive change in the 1980s."[2]

The most prominent state-level organization aimed at pursuing the anti-industry agenda is Tom Hayden's Campaign for Economic Democracy (CED), located in California. Hayden is a former student radical and a defendant in the Chicago Seven trial; he is also the husband of actress Jane Fonda, who works closely with him on

61

CED projects. CED is a prototype for dozens of similar organizations (see Table A4.2, in appendix).

CED and those similar organizations claim to have broad grass-roots support for their views and policies. This chapter presents a case study of how CED has diverted taxpayers' funds to pursue its own political agenda throughout California. As Hayden's neighbor and CED activist Derek Shearer has candidly admitted, one of CED's objectives in his home town of Santa Monica, California, is "to use the power of the city government to control the wealth of the city."[3]

Tax-Funded Socialism: The Campaign for Economic Democracy

In 1982, journalist Justin Raimondo provided an informative account of CED's origins and activities:

> The Campaign for Economic Democracy was founded, by Hayden and [Jane] Fonda, in 1977, after Hayden's defeat in his attempt to win John Tunney's Senate seat. The group is run by a steering committee elected from local chapters; no public convention has ever been held. Hayden claims that membership has doubled in two years, to a current total of 8000. Of these, approximately 500 to 1000 are activists who can be depended on to come to weekly meetings, integrate CED work into daily life, and travel for the organization if necessary. Founding members include left wing Congressman Ron Dellums and Cesar Chavez. It has a budget of about $300,000 per year and a paid staff of twenty-one. The super-structure of affiliated organizations is all tax exempt. The California Public Policy Center researches issues like rent control and solar energy. The Organizer Training Institute does exactly what it says it does. There is even a ranch in the hills overlooking Santa Barbara for staff retreats and a children's summer camp.

> A host of CED associates have been appointed by Governor [Jerry] Brown to various positions with the growing solar power bureau-cracy; Hayden himself was appointed by Brown to the State SolarCal Council, a CED idea that Brown championed as California's "soft technology" answer to the energy crisis. Presidential candidate Brown also made Hayden a "special counsel" to his administration, and appointed him to the Southwest Border Regional Commission. In recent months, Brown has appointed two CED members to county supervisor positions, one in Santa Cruz, and one in Orange County.

> But the measure of CED's initial success is more than the measure of Brown's trendy opportunism. Within the last 18 months, CED

members and CED-backed initiatives and candidates for public office have won elections around the state; rural Yolo and Butte counties, Chico, Berkeley, Bakersfield, Santa Monica and Los Angeles are all scenes of CED victories. CED has been the backbone of the rent control movement in California, which Hayden initially saw as a losing issue, until the victory of Proposition 13 made landlords who did not pass along tax savings to renters an easy target.

CED claims 17 electoral victories in California, so far—and the Democratic Party leadership is running scared. Hayden's recent tour is an indication that soon the panic will achieve national proportions.[4]

Currently, CED's primary objective is the election of local and state officials who are sympathetic to Hayden's political agenda. Because CED has achieved some acceptance within the Democratic party, it must be taken seriously. Some insight into Hayden's basic philosophical position is found in his statement in a CED promotional brochure:

We all know about the stagnant thing in our midst. And we've all fallen in—one way or another. We suffer its racism and sexism and joblessness and wars and inflation and its sugar-coated poisonings of our minds and bodies. It has a name, this source of our ills. An x-rated word—rarely spoken in polite company. Or in schools. Or in the media. Or in the workplace, especially. We think it's time to name—and publicly challenge the foul thing out loud. The stink in our midst is called corporate capitalism—and who says we have to live with it forever? Enough's enough.[5]

Hayden has every right to make such statements. What is objectionable is that these statements underpin a political agenda that is partly financed by taxes, as shown below. While Hayden and other so-called economic democrats decry the allegedly coercive nature of corporate capitalism, they compel taxpayers to pay for their campaign by receiving hundreds of thousands of dollars in federal grants. This practice appears to be consistent with the rather authoritarian perspectives of the economic democracy movement. Shearer has stated that "activists should avoid using the word socialism. We have found in the greatest tradition of American advertising that the word 'economic democracy' sells. You can take it door to door like Fuller Brushes and the door will not be slammed in your face."[6] It appears that Shearer and others are indignant over false advertising in the private sector, but they view it as acceptable and even necessary to further their own personal ambitions.

Hayden, Shearer, and others know that economic growth would be severely stifled by the array of interventions they have suggested, but they do not seem to care much. In a 1979 interview in *Barron's* magazine, Hayden was asked about inefficiencies that could arise under his scheme. He responded: "Inefficiencies will arise in a democracy. What I'm looking for is a process of accountability."[7] It is not convincing to argue that accountability can be achieved by increasing the size of the governmental bureaucracy. Hayden is apparently more interested in power than accountability. This is evident if one considers his personal history, beginning with his antiwar activities during the 1960s and 1970s. Political scientist John Bunzel has written a book on Hayden's political career in which he concludes:

> Hayden's career is more than a series of changes from student to radical to revolutionary to politician. It is intimately involved with social movements of the era. His basic strategy has been to become identified with several of them, move into the media spotlight, and promote his particular cause. He began with the civil rights movement, abandoning it when it became obvious that white, middle class radicals were not needed or welcomed in the ghetto. Hayden and others attempted to use the antiwar movement as a vehicle for large-scale social change in American society. Although many young men flocked to antidraft rallies, some of the evidence suggests that many were attracted not for the . . . ideology, but for a more personal reason—ending the draft. The Nixon administration's support of a volunteer army removed from the revolutionaries the one issue they had been able to use to mobilize young men. . . . Hayden's latest tactic—the championing of solar power, environmental protection, and opposition to nuclear power—follows a similar pattern. . . . He apparently hopes to use the rather inchoate environmental ideology that most Americans support as a basis for electoral victory. Hayden's newest venture . . . revolves around recognizing the external limits to economic growth. . . . It comes down, he says, to moving from a "wasteful, privately oriented, self-indulgent existence to a more conserving, caring, and disciplined lifestyle."[8]

Hayden, of course, became famous for his antiwar activities. In 1968, at the age of 29, he worked closely with North Vietnamese communists in producing propaganda and wrote to a Colonel Van

Lau "We hope that the current Paris discussions go well for you. The news from South Vietnam seems very good. We hope to see you this summer in Paris," and he signed the letter, "Good fortune! Victory! Tom Hayden." As recently as 1975, one year before he ran for the U.S. Senate, Hayden was quoted in the *New York Times* as commenting on the final communist takeover of South Vietnam, Cambodia, and Laos: "This is a result of something we've been working toward a long time. Indochina has not fallen—it has risen. . . . Communism is one of the options that can improve people's lives."[9]

It is true that CED has had only limited success in California, but such successes are reason for at least some general concern, in that CED's politics are used as a role model by other elements of the anti-industry coalition. Hayden laid out his agenda to a national audience in a November 1980 *Wall Street Journal* article entitled "An 'Activist' Agenda for Liberals." Central to this agenda, wrote Hayden, is "a new social contract . . . between government, business, labor, minorities, and the general voting public." The program specifies mandatory energy conservation; "industrial policy" that would "deal with . . . the invasion of competition from abroad"; "breaking the concentrated power of the private monopolies over necessities like food and medicine," presumably through governmental provision or regulation; governmental control of employee pension funds; prohibitions on plant closings; and the government takeover of some industries.[10]

Campaign Financing

One source of funds for CED is the various business interests of Hayden's wife, Jane Fonda. The U.S. taxpayers are also paying part of the bill. In light of Hayden's radical philosophy and objectives, it should not be surprising that his campaign does not have the broad appeal he claims it does and that he must rely on diverting taxpayers' funds to support his causes. The data on such tax-funded politics are scattered and very difficult to obtain, but Table A4.1 lists some recent federal funding of CED.

In 1978, a grant for $126,000 from the Department of Labor was given to the Center for New Corporate Priorities, the activist training arm of CED. The director of the center was the wife of Derek Shearer, Ruth Yannatta Goldway, a former city council member and one-time mayor of Santa Monica, California, who was elected to those posts with financial support from CED. Her salary at the center was paid from the Department of Labor grant. Much of the remainder of the grant was used for the salaries of other CED-affiliated community lobbying groups whose members were formally listed as participating in the federal Comprehensive Employment and Training Act (CETA) program. Much of those members' time was spent campaigning for rent-control laws in 1979. As a result, the Inspector General's Office of the U.S. Department of Labor determined that there was "prosecutive merit" in allegations that CETA funds had been used to subsidize CED-related political activities.

CED has also used federal funds to finance its political activities by seizing another issue, crime. In 1978 a crime-prevention program called Communitas was established in Santa Monica, and it received $334,761 from the U.S. Department of Justice that year. The project was under the direction of CED member Jim Conn. Although the group purportedly existed to aid in crime prevention, particularly among women, the elderly, and minorities, it has focused on other political issues, such as rent control. This is not surprising, for Conn was the treasurer of another CED affiliate, Santa Monicans for Renters' Rights, which lobbied for rent control. Among the "crime-prevention" projects undertaken by Communitas were block organizing and precinct work for a rent-control referendum and hosting "information nights" on the CED-backed rent-control measure. In one of Communitas' publications, "A Short History of Ocean Park" (Ocean Park is part of Santa Monica), a story was told of how the organization has "come to the rescue" of citizens by creating an organization that would "deal not only with crime, but with all areas of community concern." It described its efforts to secure land use regulation to reduce development, the forced relocation of various businesses, "eviction protections" for those who did not pay their rent, and stricter rent-control laws, to list just a few examples. In short, the operation run by Conn was a front. The problem of crime was just an excuse to raise funds in the name of the victims of crime so as to be able to pursue a largely unrelated political agenda.

Thus, in 1979, through these two grants, CED received nearly $500,000 in taxpayers' funds that was used at least in part to build up Hayden's political base in Santa Monica. This is an unusually large sum to be spent on local politics, exceeding the amounts spent by most U.S. congressmen for their reelection campaigns. Hayden has pointed out that his organization has nothing to say to the rest of the country if it cannot win in California, and Santa Monica was one of CED's first (tax-financed) testing grounds.[11] He chose the issue of rent control as a vehicle for electing a handpicked slate of candidates—in this case the rent-control board and the mayor (Goldway) of Santa Monica. Many of the CED members on the CETA payroll and employees of Communitas were "community organizers" for Hayden's affiliate, Santa Monicans for Renters' Rights, which eventually helped to pass one of the strictest rent-control laws in the nation. In the words of one California legislator who investigated CED, "We've dug up so many suspicious contracts of theirs it's incredible. There's a pattern of CED using government money for [things] like seminars on rent control."[12]

The CED activists organized the rent-control campaign on a house-by-house basis. Their objective was to mobilize tenants, particularly older and lower-income people, who would be expected to support CED in the future on other issues of so-called "corporate control," namely, the economic democracy agenda. Because many lower-income people spend a relatively large portion of their incomes on rent, the rhetoric of rent control is often appealing to them. In 1980, Derek Shearer once explained CED's rent-control strategy:

> Political campaigns are not educational vehicles. What you do is play on feelings and sentiments. . . . We sent out a postcard of an elderly family, somewhat haggard—they looked a little bit like an Auschwitz picture. Stamped across their chest was the word EVICTED. We found a senior citizen who was dying of cancer who was being evicted. We reprinted an article [about him in the local paper]; the headline was "Before I Die I'm Going to Vote for Ruth Yannatta and Rent Control." We distributed that on the door of every tenant in the city two days before the election. . . . We considered techniques that played on people's feelings and emotions around a very simple idea: that housing is a basic human right, that it comes before the need to profit.[13]

The strategy worked, and two years later CED scored another electoral victory in Santa Monica when CED candidates won five of the seven city council seats and Shearer's wife, Ruth Yannatta Goldway, was elected mayor. Goldway then appointed Shearer to the city planning commission and filled other posts with CED activists.

The Costs of CED Activism

The approximately $500,000 of taxpayers' funds channeled to CED's rent-control campaign in fiscal year 1979 represents only a minor, although strategically important, share of the "cost" of the campaign. By stating that rent control is a way of "putting people before profit," CED appealed to emotion to persuade citizens to allow CED activists to take control of the rent-control board. In that capacity, the activists substituted their own personal preferences for those of consumers, whose preferences would otherwise prevail through the market allocation of housing. The market allocation of housing serves the interests of the people precisely because of the profit motive, not in spite of it. It has long been recognized that rent control artificially stimulates demand while reducing the supply of rental housing by making it less profitable. Consequently, there are housing shortages and a deterioration in the quality of housing because the cost of housing improvements cannot be passed on in the form of higher rental prices.

The effects of rent control on the housing market are vividly portrayed in New York City, where rent controls have been in effect since 1943. Robert Bleiberg has described the effects of more than 40 years of rent control:

> Vast stretches of real estate in at least three of five boroughs have decayed beyond the point of no return. Ancient tenements and (until recently) quite habitable buildings alike stand empty, boarded up and stripped, vandalized and blackened by fire. Some no longer stand at all except in piles of broken brick and rubble. Whole blocks of Brooklyn and the Bronx have been compared by expert witnesses to the bombed-out ruins of London and Berlin.[14]

The U.S. Senate Committee on Banking, Housing, and Urban Affairs has found that rent control in New York City causes an average loss of 30,000 housing units per year.[15] In Washington, D.C., applications for multifamily building permits fell from 5,000 in 1974, the year rent controls were first imposed there, to virtually zero during subsequent years.[16] As Roger Starr, former head of the New York City Housing and Development Administration has concluded, "Rent control discourages investment in older housing, hastens the deterioration of existing buildings, and keeps the housing supply permanently inadequate."[17]

The poor and minorities, whose cause CED claims to champion, are simply used as pawns in CED's attempt to seize political power. The poor do not necessarily benefit from rent control. As economist Eric Hemel has stated:

68

For the poor and minorities who are looking for housing and are not in a rent-controlled apartment, the same characteristics that make them poor in the first place—physical handicaps, lack of education, racial discrimination, and the like—ensure that they will have the roughest time getting access to the [rent-controlled] apartments. . . . The reason is that with a housing shortage caused by controls, landlords will tend to choose only people with "favored characteristics," i.e., middle class whites, and avoid those suffering most now—welfare mothers, blacks, and large families.[18]

Although the poor are at a disadvantage in competing in the market for housing (that disadvantage, after all, is one of the things that identifies the poor), they at least can *find* housing they can afford. With rent controls, many of the poor are shut out altogether and must resort to such alternatives as doubling up with relatives or friends, or they must devote an even larger share of their income to more expensive housing elsewhere. Moreover, it is the middle- and upper-income groups that often benefit from rent control, at least in the short run.

To mitigate housing shortages, many rent-control laws permit decontrol when long-time tenants move out and new ones move in. Tenants who stay in one place benefit from this system, while those who are more mobile lose, for they must pay higher rents— rents that are even higher than if there had never been rent control. Because the poor have volatile income streams, they tend to move often to better or worse apartments, depending on their income. Middle- and upper-income tenants can often rent large, spacious apartments for the same price the poor pay for smaller apartments. Evidence indicates that rent control transfers income from the poor to the better off, although the rhetoric and propaganda put out by CED and other rent-control advocates counteracts this truth. In New York City, for example, many minorities, such as lower-income blacks and Puerto Ricans, live in crowded and expensive housing, while the city's mayor pays $250 per month for an apartment with a market rental value that is at least double that. The president of the American Stock Exchange pays $660 a month for an eight-room Upper East Side apartment with an estimated market value of as much as $1,200.[19]

It is no secret that the poor and minorities are made to suffer from rent control, despite CED propaganda. Nobel Laureate Gunnar Myrdal, an architect of the Swedish Socialist Labor party's welfare state, has said that rent control "has . . . constituted what may be the worst example of poor planning by governments."[20] New York's leading black-run newspaper, the *Amsterdam News*, has announced: "We in minority areas are forced to live in rat infested apartments that resemble bombed-out war areas, [which are] . . . rapidly increasing, instead of decreasing . . . solely because of rent control."[21]

If rent control is such a disaster, why do such laws persist? Part of the answer lies in the fact that rent control benefits a small but often well-organized special-interest group—middle- and upper-income tenants and political authorities whose power is enhanced by regulating the housing market rather than allowing the market process to do the job. Among the losers are a large but often politically impotent group, the poor. For this type of charade to continue, the losers must be kept ignorant of rent control's actual effects, or they will be motivated to rebel at the ballot box. This is why propaganda campaigns, such as those conducted by CED, are so important to the advocates of rent control. Such campaigns help to keep the public unaware of the effects of rent control so that the advocates can continue to control the housing market for political gain.

CED's tax-financed campaign for rent control in California has dire implications for housing consumers nationwide. First, CED serves as a prototype for dozens of other anti-industry organizations around the country that may try to imitate CED's apparent success. Second, CED has already begun to help organize a national tenants' rights lobby consisting of other members of the anti-industry coalition. In the January 26, 1980, edition of the *Washington Star*, for example, an article headlined "Tenant Association Trying to Form National Lobby" described CED's role in this effort: "[O]rganizations around the country are attempting to form a national renters' lobby." It also cited Cary Lowe, a "tenants' rights specialist" for CED, as saying, "We see it as high time that political pressure was brought on behalf of tenants. . . . If all goes well . . . tenants' groups will . . . campaign in the 1980 elections."[22]

Other evidence of how CED has used taxpayers' funds to finance its political programs is found in a series of articles by California journalist Bill Wallace in the *Berkeley Barb* from October 4 to October 17, 1979. After a six-month investigation, the *Barb* stated that Hayden's appointment by then-governor Jerry Brown to the board of directors of SolarCal, a California government energy corporation, had enabled Hayden to build a personal political machine with government funds. Brown also had helped Hayden become the director of Western SUN, a project of the U.S. Department of Energy. According to the *Barb*, Hayden "put as many political allies as possible on Western SUN's payroll." Mark Vandervelen, a lobbyist for the environmentalist interest group called Friends of the Earth, was quoted in the *Barb* article as saying, "It's just a big solar pork barrel. . . . Tom [Hayden] would be the first one to scream if some right-wing Republican put all of his cronies on the payroll of a federally-funded program, then used them to do precinct work for his own reelection campaign." The *Barb* referred to the California branch of Western SUN as "Hayden's baby." His administrative budget for the first year of operation was $82,000—which Hayden reportedly called "really nothing but start-up money."

CED has also channeled taxpayers' funds to community action groups. As reported in the *Barb*:

> For example, no sooner had Berkeley Citizen's Action succeeded in winning defacto control of the Berkeley City Council, last April [1979], than members of the heavily CED-dominated group touched base with Western SUN representative Larry Levin in an effort to win a federal "planning grant" for their own . . . program. In addition . . . Levin has met with CED backed office holders in Berkeley and Oakland to discuss implementing a solar power development program . . . and has spoken to local CED activists as part of series of lectures called "The Battle Against Corporate Power" in Berkeley's LaPena restaurant.

Some insight into just who Hayden has been channeling taxpayers' funds to through Western SUN is gleaned by considering that when Hayden was lobbying for the establishment of Western SUN, he was accompanied by Alvin Duskin, director of the Pacific Alliance, and Fred Braufman of the California Public Policy Center. Both of these organizations are affiliated with the Institute for Policy Studies and have received funds from it.[23]

In sum, Hayden all but expropriated the federally-funded solar power program in California to achieve his own political goals. For example, the *Berkeley Barb* investigation revealed that Larry Levin, Western SUN's field representative, is a CED member and the former public relations manager for Hayden's unsuccessful Senate campaign; Judy Corbett, a paid Western SUN "consultant," used her home for CED fundraisers; much of the subcontracting through Western SUN went to CED members; and many of Western SUN's

71

staff and consultants had no expertise in solar energy, but were simply CED "party faithfuls."

What are the end uses of the money that passes from the federal treasury, through Western SUN, and eventually to CED-affiliated community groups? The money cannot be traced precisely, but the following list of activities indicates what these groups hope to accomplish:[24]

> CED is active in lobbying for rent control and other forms of land use regulation, and has organized a group called CHAIN—California Housing Action and Information Network, to fight for tenants' rights.
>
> CED "task forces" lobby for funding for "bilingual education" and against the U.S. Supreme Court Bakke decision, which ruled against reverse discrimination.
>
> CED has joined with the United Farmworkers Union in lobbying to stop state funding of research at state universities that improves agricultural technology (making it less labor intensive).
>
> CED is actively involved in trying to place "economic democrats" into political office at the state and local level. The major success here was the election of Ruth Yannatta Goldway as Mayor of Santa Monica.
>
> CED activists have organized boycotts against Coors beer and J. P. Stevens textile products, since they are produced by non-union labor.
>
> CED has sponsored "confrontations" with the management of nuclear power facilities.
>
> CED has lobbied for a government-funded "state bank," and against "outrageous housing speculation."

This short list illustrates that what taxpayers' dollars are paying for is an attempt to get the economic democracy agenda adopted in California.

Tax-Financed Training in Left-Wing Activism

The strategy of building a political power base at the state and local levels of government serves at least two purposes for CED. First, it puts CED's foot in the door of mainstream, Democratic party politics. Second, it provides CED with experience in politics—a human capital investment for Hayden and other CED members who may wish to influence national politics.

An even longer-range strategy is the training of future CED activists at the Laurel Springs Institute, located about 10 miles north of Santa Barbara. As reported in the May 26, 1977, edition of the *San Francisco Examiner*, Jane Fonda gave the following reason for establishing the institute: "We're building a political power base. . . . To be able to do this you need to bring your people together. We needed a land base for that." As seen in Table A4.1, the institute received more than $200,000 from the federal government during the 1979–81 period. This grant was obtained to purportedly train VISTA volunteers in California. The background of this grant is established in the following correspondence between Hayden and Marge Tabankin, at that time the acting deputy associate director of VISTA[25] (she later became director of VISTA).

> May 5, 1977
>
> Dear Marge,
>
> I'm sorry we didn't have more time to talk the other day.
>
> The CED will view the new Administration by several concrete standards, including how VISTA-type programs work. Either they will go back to effective community organizing, or they should be shut down.
>
> We want a voice in the training of VISTAs in California and the definition of their work. This should not be farmed out to individuals without a base or to traditional agencies.
>
> Sam [Brown, formerly director of ACTION] indicated his agreement with this approach, though I sensed a need to pursue the implications further.
>
> Therefore, I am proposing a) that we in California will brainstorm about VISTA possibilities and b) you should be directly in touch with Bonnie Ladin of our organization, who was once a very effective VISTA organizer in Long Island (before she ran afoul of the Nixon group).
>
> Specifically I would hope she will be invited to any national brainstorming sessions you might be having. . . .
>
> I know you are on a tight schedule between now and August. Let me know how fast we should move, and we will not fail you.
>
> Let's get it together again.
>
> Love,
>
> Tom

Dear Tom:

I too am sorry we couldn't talk longer when you were here with Sam.

I took this job because I believe VISTA should be redirected to volunteers working for grassroots community organizations, especially as organizers. However, as you point out, training is very important, as is placement.

You are correct that Sam also agrees with this emphasis on community organizing and training, and I believe that is why I was hired for this job.

I will have [name indistinct], who is dealing with national VISTA programming, contact Bonnie Ladin of your organization to talk about organizational concerns, and to hopefully figure out a direction to move in.

If I can be in California between now and the summer, I'd love to sit down with you folks.

My love to Jane [Fonda].

Warm regards,

/s/
Marge Tabankin
Acting Deputy Associate Director for VISTA and AEP

In August 1979, a contract was awarded to the Laurel Springs Institute for $201,238.

In addition to this kind of direct grant, support for the CED training institute has been obtained from other members of the tax-funded political network. For example, in the June-July issue of *CED News*, an appeal for new members was made by Hayden, Fonda, Rep. Ronald V. Dellums (D-Calif.), and United Farmworkers of America President Cesar Chavez. They cited the advantages of an "opportunity to meet and get to know political activists from all over the state in . . . organizer workshops . . . where you can increase your skills in the fields of electoral campaigning and community organizing or learn more about the way our economic and political systems operate and what CED's alternatives are." Thus, labor unions such as the United Farmworkers of America, as well as many other tax-receiving groups in the anti-industry coalition, indirectly aid the Campaign for Economic Democracy. Hayden makes little attempt to conceal this. As reported in the Summer 1977 issue of *Santa Barbara Tomorrow:*

Although Hayden promised to hold no large political gatherings at the site, he did not attempt to disguise his plans for regular strategy meetings by organizers of the Campaign for Economic Democracy. Nor did he rule out creation of a "training institute" . . . to be financed in part by taxpayers' funds. The institute would be designed to impart organizational skills to CED activists, but also to publicly supported groups. "We might contract also with community or government agencies or unions," Hayden announced.

The institute also has a children's camp that focuses on crafts, hiking, horseback riding, animal husbandry, gardening, and games. The camp is administered by a CED affiliate, the Center for Public Policy. Even though the camp's advertising brochures emphasize youth activities, there is evidence that it is also used for political education. As reported in the August 29, 1979, issue of *Time* magazine, the camp was serving "150 youngsters from 7 to 14. Mostly the offspring of minorities and veteran left-wing activists, the children are schooled in such weighty issues as why farm-workers should be unionized or why gas companies should not be allowed to construct a liquefied natural gas terminal on sacred Indian land along the California coast."

The training materials issued by the Laurel Springs Institute reflect the orientation of CED. For example, its "Pre-Service Training Organizing Manual" for 1980 reproduces in full a manual, "Direct Action Organizing," by the Midwest Academy, which at one point states that "it is important that the membership be reminded that it is the institution [i.e., the free enterprise system], not the person, which is the real cause of the problem, and that we are about structural changes, not just getting nicer bureaucrats to confront."[26]

Another Laurel Springs Institute manual, "Resource List and Bibliography on Public Interest Research," instructs apprentice activists on how to use the resources of other CED affiliates, such as the California Public Policy Center and the North American Congress on Latin America. The Congress, an offshoot of Students for a Democratic Society (SDS), describes itself as seeking the support of those "who not only favor revolutionary change in Latin America, but also take a revolutionary position toward their own society."[27]

There is evidence that Hayden has used his positions in state government to channel even more resources into CED, in addition to federal funds. For example, then-Governor Brown nominated

Hayden to head the Regional Border Commission, a state-funded agency that has the stated purpose of "helping communities near the Mexican/U.S. border work out common problems." Hayden packed the commission with CED members, and the "common problems" that it will probably address include rent control, regulation, and general legislative restrictions on private business activity in border towns.

Summary and Conclusions

The Campaign for Economic Democracy may be considered a prototype for scores of other anti-industry lobbying groups at the state and local levels of government. It is run by a man who believes that "communism is one option that can improve people's lives" and who has co-opted hundreds of thousands of taxpayers' dollars to pursue his own political agenda. CED has scored some political successes in California and is beginning to get involved in national politics, particularly by organizing a national tenants' rights lobby. The sums advanced to the CED, courtesy of unknowing U.S. taxpayers, are strategically important, for hard cash is the lifeblood of any political organization. More importantly, however, the social costs of the policies pursued by CED are much greater. Rent control, for example, creates housing shortages, lowers housing quality, and often harms the poor, but benefits the more affluent.

Other policies pursued as part of the CED agenda are sure to have effects that are equally as detrimental. Ironically, these policies sometimes cause resentment toward the market system rather than toward the ways in which government controls interfere with the market. This is an outcome about which CED takes a casual attitude—or perhaps even endorses and promotes. Resentment toward the market system is an objective openly admitted by CED, and much of CED's political propaganda is intended to foster such resentment. How else can one interpret Hayden's statement that corporate capitalism is "a stink in our midst" and his question, "Who says we have to live it forever?" The CED agenda, if adopted, would damage California's economy, but it would enhance the political clout of Hayden and his organization. Moreover, there are many other groups nationwide that pursue similar agendas (see chapters 5 and 6, and Table A4.2).

V. Consumer Activists and the "Public Interest" Hoax

> By pursuing his own interest [an individual] frequently promotes that of the society more effectually than when he really intends to promote it. I have never known much good done by those who affected to trade for the public good. . . . [E]very individual, it is evident, can, in his local situation, judge much better than any statesman or lawgiver can do for him. The statesman, who should attempt to direct private people in what manner they ought to employ their capitals, would not only load himself with a most unnecessary attention, but assume an authority which could safely be trusted, not only to no single person, but to no council or senate whatever, and which would nowhere be so dangerous as in the hands of a man who had folly and presumption enough to fancy himself fit to exercise it.
>
> —Adam Smith
> *The Wealth of Nations*

Just as the term "economic democracy" obscures the true preferences of economic democrats, so do such terms as "public interest" and "consumer advocate." The "public interest" is indefinable, at best, although it has been part of political rhetoric for centuries. We all have different tastes, preferences, opinions, and definitions concerning the public interest, and it is nonsensical to use that term as though there were unanimous consent. Despite much evidence to the contrary, it is part of the American political culture that good motives, that is, public spiritedness, are thought to lead to good results and that bad motives, that is, the profit motive, often lead to bad results. As political pundit H. L. Mencken noted nearly 70 years ago, there is an assumption that has "corrupted our thinking" about politics. The assumption, said Mencken, is that

> politicians are divided into two classes, and that one of those classes is made up of good ones. . . . This assumption is almost universally held among us. Our whole politics, indeed, is based upon it, and has been based since the earliest days. What is any

77

political campaign save a concerted effort to turn out a set of politicians who are admittedly bad and put in a set who are thought to be better? The former assumption, I believe is always sound; the latter is just as certainly false.[1]

In addition to the public interest rhetoric, the term "consumer advocate" also has a connotation that many find appealing. After all, as we are all consumers, who would object to someone who advocates "our" interests?

These terms—"public interest" and "consumer advocate"—have been adopted as slogans by a coalition of special-interest groups commonly known as the public interest movement. The public interest movement brings together two groups: organized consumer advocates and public interest law firms. These groups make up a major element of the anti-industry coalition and are often allied with labor unions. In an attempt to convey the image that they are selfless protectors of the public interest, they have adopted such names as Public Interest Research Group, Common Cause, Public Citizen, Consumer Federation of America (CFA), and Americans for Democratic Action. Their interests and objectives, however, are often sharply at odds with the interests of most citizens. The public interest rhetoric serves as a smoke screen that allows these self-appointed protectors of the consumer to conduct their political crusades without the popular indignation that is usually directed toward other groups that are more openly viewed as special interests. Moreover, because the public is not nearly as supportive of the public interest groups as the groups claim, the groups have resorted to tax-funded politics to achieve their political ends. It is ironic that those who claim to protect consumers have forced consumers, without their direct knowledge or consent, to pay for these activities, many of which harm them.

Tax-Funded Politics and the Public Interest Lobby

The public interest movement has co-opted millions of taxpayers' dollars to pursue its own political agenda, an agenda that the average taxpayer would probably not support voluntarily, as evidenced by data collected by Robert Lichter of George Washington University and Stanley Rothman of Smith College.[2] Lichter and Rothman surveyed a random sample of 157 leaders or top staff members of 74 different public interest organizations. They found that the personal backgrounds and political views of the "public interest elite"

78

are often dramatically different from those of the average American. Most (97 percent) are highly educated, well-paid, white males. For example, 35 percent of those surveyed earn over $50,000 annually, and 58 percent have family incomes of over $50,000. Ninety percent of the public-interest elite describe themselves as political liberals; 41 percent currently practice no religion; and 89 percent hold postgraduate degrees. Their voting records reveal that they are politically far to the left of the average citizen whose interests they purport to protect. No Republican presidential candidate has received more than 4 percent of their vote since 1968 (see Table 5.1). Their strongest support went to George McGovern, who won 96 percent of their votes in the 1972 Nixon landslide. In the other three elections, they supported third-party candidates more than Republicans. In their ideological self-evaluation, 90 percent placed themselves left of center, 8 percent in the middle of the road, and 2 percent to the right of center. By contrast, a 1982 Gallup poll of the general public found that only 21 percent described themselves as left of center, 43 percent as in the center, and 36 percent as to the right of center.

Regarding the attitudes of the public interest elite on social issues, Lichter and Rothman found that they "reject traditional . . . values, cultural norms, and older codes of behavior," and they support "a new morality" and "alternative" life styles and "seek government action in the service of social change."[3] For example, 80 percent of

---

Table 5.1

PRESIDENTIAL VOTING RECORD OF THE PUBLIC INTEREST ELITE
1968–80 (%)

1968	Humphrey	90
	Nixon	2
1972	McGovern	96
	Nixon	4
1976	Carter	93
	Ford	3
1980	Carter	80
	Anderson	12
	Reagan	2

SOURCE: S. R. Lichter and S. Rothman, "What Interests the Public and What Interests the Public Interests," *Public Opinion* (April/May 1983): 46.

the public interest lobby believe government should "guarantee" jobs; 37 percent believe that government should nationalize large corporations; 51 percent think that the United States should move toward socialism; more than 75 percent believe that women and blacks should be given preferential treatment in hiring; only 18 percent think that less regulation of business is good for the United States; and 68 percent would like to halt completely the development of nuclear power.

To obtain further evidence of the preferences of the public interest lobby, Lichter and Rothman asked the survey participants to rank a number of prominent people. The rankings, shown in Table 5.2 reveal that Ralph Nader is the most respected personality, and the Nicaraguan communists got ten times more respect than did President Reagan. Even Cuban dictator Fidel Castro was ranked seven times higher than the president of the United States.

In sum, the public interest movement is arguably not very interested in what interests the public. Its political preferences are vastly different from those of the average American, and it disdains many American traditions and institutions, not the least of which is the free enterprise system. That these people are working to selflessly

---

Table 5.2
APPROVAL RATING OF PUBLIC FIGURES AND GROUPS BY THE PUBLIC INTEREST ELITE

Person or Group	Rating (%)
Ralph Nader	93
Edward Kennedy	93
John Kenneth Galbraith	90
Gloria Steinem	89
Andrew Young	86
Sandinistas	50
Fidel Castro	34
Milton Friedman	15
Margaret Thatcher	14
Jeane Kirkpatrick	14
Ronald Reagan	5
Moral Majority	2

SOURCE: S. R. Lichter and S. Rothman, "What Interests the Public and What Interests the Public Interests," *Public Opinion* (April/May 1983): 48.

promote the welfare of those with whom they have profound ideological, religious, and philosophical differences is highly unlikely. Their livelihoods are earned through the offices of well-organized political interest groups, indicating that their careers are devoted to attempts to impose their will on the American public, not to protect it.

Tax-Funded Consumer Protection

Ralph Nader has been at the forefront of the anti-industry coalition ever since his attack on the Corvair automobile during the early 1960s. His major aim has been increased government control over private enterprise, and he has been quite successful, even though his claim that the Corvair is "unsafe at any speed" turned out to be unsubstantiated. The National Highway Transportation Safety Administration (NHTSA), one of the federal agencies established in response to Nader's claims, finally got around to studying the Covair 10 years after Nader condemned it; NHTSA concluded: "The 1960–63 Corvair compared favorably with the other contemporary vehicles used in the tests."[4]

By continuing his attack on private enterprise, Nader has had a major impact on the huge volume of consumer-protection legislation passed during the late 1960s and the 1970s. The political activists that Nader has trained or inspired now staff many of the regulatory agencies that they lobbied for in the first place. Much of the punitive business regulation discussed in chapter 3 has been implemented by Naderites who exhibit a hostile attitude toward private enterprise. For example, a Consumer Product Safety Commission member once said, "Any time consumer safety is threatened we're going to go for the company's throat."[5] And former Nader aide Michael Pertschuk, once a member of the Federal Trade Commission, stated that his staff "carried on a vendetta against certain industries."[6]

Given attitudes like these, it is little wonder that consumer protection regulation has drowned the private sector in red tape and regulatory mandates and has severely hindered economic growth, all to the detriment of the U.S. consumers, who must ultimately pay the bill. Furthermore (as discussed in chapter 3), this regulation has done little to protect the consumer. Nader's objective seems to be the imposition of his own small-is-beautiful, utopian vision on the rest of society. For example, he envisions an ideal society in which all large-scale business organizations are abolished and people live in small, self-sufficient communities where "within a five or six block perimeter, they find they have their stores, their schools. They have their parks, they have their libraries . . . compared to a big city where all of these things are miles away."[7] Once private corporations were abolished, Nader would transform plants and factories into customer-owned cooperatives so that workers would not be in a position to pursue their own self-interests. Banks and insurance companies would also become cooperatives, resulting in what Nader calls the "consumer-owned economy."

Nader's objective seems to be to save us from the tyranny of corporations that provide such "undesirables" as grocery stores, sports cars, stereos, cameras, calculators, home computers, and other tools of material enslavement. Instead, he urges a return to the economy and lifestyle of the mid-eighteenth century, when businesses were smaller and, consequently, standards of living were much lower.

Tuition Taxation without Representation

In 1970, Nader began to set up a series of organizations called public interest research groups (PIRGs). There are now PIRGs located on college campuses in about 30 states. Their purpose is to train student activists, and they pay for their activities by taxing students. The PIRGs take advantage of the fact that most students either do not bother to or are unaware that they can refuse to pay their PIRG dues, which are automatically added to their tuition bills along with other student fees. In short, Nader is literally banking on the fact that most students will not even know that part of their student fees support litigation and lobbying on social issues that the students may oppose. The amount of money involved in these PIRG taxes is difficult, if not impossible, to estimate, but there is some evidence available. For example, it has been reported that the Minnesota Public Interest Research Group (MPIRG) collects 70 to 80 percent of its annual $200,000 budget from student fees at the state's university campuses.[8] If these proportions were typical of the 30 states in which PIRGs exist, PIRGs would collect as much as $4.8 million annually in "student taxes," or roughly 80 percent of their entire annual budget. There have been some attempts to alter the so-called negative checkoff system in New Jersey and Minnesota, but there has been little success. A group of dissident students took over the local chapter of MPIRG and tried to change the way the organization collected taxes from students, but the national officers of PIRG responded by ejecting the elected student representatives from the organization.

In addition to taxing college students to finance PIRG activities, PIRGs also receive direct grants from the federal government and from some state and local governments as well. As shown in Table A5.1, in appendix, various federal agencies have funded PIRGs both with cash grants and by paying the salaries of PIRG staff members by classifying them as VISTA volunteers. It is difficult to obtain complete information, but one agency alone, ACTION, claims to have given about $1,287,000 to PIRG in the period 1979–81.[9] Adding direct federal grants to student taxes means that taxpayers were probably responsible for close to 90 percent of all PIRG revenues during those years, according to our estimates.

Just what are students and other taxpayers getting for their tax dollars? The training of political activists is one thing. For example, the December 1980 newsletter of the California Public Interest Research Group (CalPIRG) contained an advertisement for a 10-week training seminar for "housing advocates." CalPIRG did not conceal that this seminar was tax-funded, stating, "The Housing Project Training For Advocates is made possible by a grant from the Office of Consumer Education." Among the topics scheduled for discussion were "Raising the Roof: Building a Strong Tenants Union," "Strategies for Tenant Advocacy," and "Putting the Tenant Back in Landlord/Tenant Law."

Litigation and lobbying for more stringent regulation of private business activity is another PIRG activity that is directed at nearly every major industry. Even though many of the Naderites' claims of poor quality or dangerous products have been proven false, they nevertheless continue to crusade against private enterprise and the U.S. consumers, who must ultimately pay the bill. For example, the 1982 Annual Report of Public Citizen, Nader's umbrella organization, boasted of the following accomplishments:

> Petitioned the FDA to require warning labels on all aspirin.
>
> Published a consumers' information guide called "Stopping Valium, Ativan, Centrax, Dalmane, Librium, Paxipam, Restoril, Serax, Tranxene, Xanax."
>
> Protested State Department pressure on Bangladesh to rescind a ruling that banned over 1700 drugs from use there.
>
> Petitioned the Department of Health and Human Services to remove anti-morning sickness drug, Benedictin, from the market.

83

Sued the FDA for allegedly violating the Infant Formula Act of 1980 that establishes regulatory controls over infant formula manufacturers.

Lobbied for the banning of food dye FD&C Blue 2.

Lobbied against a bill in the House of Representatives that would have allowed the Office of Management and Budget to assess health and safety regulation.

Helped block attempts to alter the Clean Air Act.

Lobbied for the $300 billion tax increase embodied in the 1982 "tax reform" bill.

Local organizations "organized letter writing campaigns, accountability sessions, candidates forums, press conferences, and other media events."

In at least a dozen instances, the federal government was sued in attempts to alter regulatory policy.

Lobbied for "plant-closing" legislation that would hinder or prohibit corporations from closing down unprofitable plants.

Some insight into how Nader pursues this political agenda was also provided in Public Citizen's 1983 Annual Report:

> [A]ctivism played a pivotal role in the successful resolution of major consumer issues during the 2nd session of the 97th Congress. Focusing its efforts on Regulatory Reform, . . . Congress Watch took its issue campaigns to 15 new congressional districts in the past year. Hundreds of citizens from the existing 41 Congress Watch locals joined with those in the newly formed coalitions to effectively publicize national consumer issues on the local level. Congress Watch activists organized letter writing campaigns, accountability sessions, candidates forums, press conferences, and other media events.

The political activities of the Nader organization have one thing in common: They are aimed at either banning or increasing the cost of various products or business activities. As discussed in chapter 3, many researchers have found that federal regulation rarely if ever has the effects claimed for it, but that it does cost consumers billions of dollars. Consider, for example, the two types of regulation in which the Nader organizations are most heavily involved: drug regulation and regulation of consumer product safety.

One of the chief targets of the Nader organization has been the pharmaceutical industry. Having lobbied successfully for expanded regulatory powers for the Food and Drug Administration, the Nader organization has lent support to one of the most counterproductive forms of regulation. FDA regulation has probably done more harm by retarding the production and distribution of new and valuable drugs than it has done good by keeping harmful drugs off the market. The number of new drugs introduced each year has fallen by more than 50 percent since 1962, and it now takes much longer for any drug to be approved by the FDA, which increases the cost of drugs.[10] According to one estimate, in the 1950s and early 1960s it cost about $500,000 and took about two years to develop and market a new drug. By 1978 it cost about $5.4 million and took over eight years to get a new drug to market. William Wardell of the Center for the Study of Drug Development at the University of Rochester has written as follows:

> If you examine the therapeutic significance of drugs that haven't arrived in the U.S. but are available somewhere in the rest of the world, such as in Britain, you can come across numerous examples where the patient has suffered. For example, there are one or two drugs called Beta blockers, which it now appears can prevent death after a heart attack—we call this secondary prevention of coronary death after myocardial infarction—which, if available here, could be saving about ten thousand lives a year in the United States. In the ten years after the 1962 amendments, no drug was approved for hypertension—that's for the control of blood pressure—in the United States, whereas several were approved in Britain. In the entire cardiovascular area, only one drug was approved in the five year period from '67 to '72. And this can be correlated with known organizational problems at F.D.A. . . .
>
> The implications for the patient are that therapeutic decisions that used to be the preserve of the doctor and the patient are increasingly being made at a national level, by committees and the agency for which they are acting—the F.D.A.—are highly skewed towards avoiding risks so there's a tendency for us to have drugs that are safer but not to have drugs that are effective. Now I've heard some remarkable statements from some of these advisory committees where in considering drugs one has seen the statement "there are not enough patients with a disease with this severity to warrant marketing this drug for general use." Now that's fine if what you are trying to do is minimize drug toxicity for the whole population,

85

but if you happen to be one of those "not enough patients," and you have a disease that is of high severity or a disease that's very rare, then that's just tough luck for you.[11]

Unfortunately, when pharmaceutical drugs are regulated these outcomes are inevitable because of the incentives facing the regulators. If FDA approves a drug that turns out to have harmful side effects, it will be written up in every newspaper in the country, resulting in negative publicity for the public official who approved it. If a drug that is capable of improving health or saving lives is banned, however, it will attract little attention. People have no way of knowing how much better off they could have been, and the pharmaceutical firms promoting the drug will be dismissed as greedy businessmen willing to sell the public anything for a profit. Thus, drug regulation is sure to impose costs that far outweigh any benefits. Moreover, there is little that any regulatory agency can do that the market system will not do to protect the public from useless or harmful drugs. Producing a drug that turns out to have harmful side effects is the ultimate disaster for a pharaceutical firm, for the firm stands to lose millions of dollars in sales and legal sanctions and may be driven out of business. The market allocation of drugs is likely to be every bit as safe as allocation by bureaucratic fiat, and it would reduce the problem of so-called drug lag. To the extent that Nader's political activists have helped strengthen the government's grip over the market for drugs, it has imposed costs on society that are far in excess of any benefits.[12]

Product Safety: Market Incentives or Bureaucratic Decree?

Although competitive markets are the only reliable mechanism that can increase product safety, a major form of regulation urged by Nader and others is so-called consumer product safety regulation as administered by the Consumer Product Safety Commission (CPSC). CPSC is charged with a task that it cannot possibly achieve: "to protect the public against unreasonable risks of injury from consumer products." The goal is a good one, but no bureaucrat at CPSC can ever know how much income individuals are willing to give up for more safety or how much risk is "unreasonable." Consumer product safety regulation is simply a means of forcefully imposing the views of self-appointed consumer protectors on the public.

Regulators inevitably make mistakes, which are often of major proportions. In 1973, just three months after beginning its operations, CPSC banned certain aerosol sprays because the preliminary findings of a researcher suggested that they caused birth defects. Additional research failed to corroborate the report, so the ban was lifted in 1974, but "at least nine pregnant women who had used the spray adhesives reacted to the news of the commission's initial decision by undergoing abortions. They decided not to carry through their pregnancies for fear of producing babies with birth defects."[13]

An even more serious example occurred in 1973, when CPSC ruled that the chemical Tris was to be applied to all children's sleepwear to render it flame retardant. It was later discovered that Tris is a carcinogen, so that millions of children were exposed to the risks of cancer because of that regulation. The chemical was eventually banned in 1977.[14]

CPSC is certain to produce similar results in many other industries, for its "authority" covers "any article . . . produced or distributed (i) for sale to a consumer . . . or (ii) for the personal use, consumption or enjoyment of a consumer."[15] Product safety regulation tends to be counterproductive at best, and U.S. consumers must pay twice for the dubious privilege of being harmed by regulation! The consumers ultimately pay in the form of higher product prices and of products forgone, and they also pay, through taxation, for the political activities of the only ones who unequivocally benefit from the regulation, the public interest professionals. Being a public interest professional is not an easy task, however, for few people are willing to voluntarily pay for such services. But the members of the public interest elite have devised other ways of using taxpayers' funds to support themselves.

The National Consumer Co-op Bank and the Public Interest Dole

One of the major legislative accomplishments of the public interest elite has been the establishment of the National Consumer Co-op Bank (NCCB), which has been hailed as the first step toward "a new social order in America."[16] In 1978 Congress approved $300 million in seed money for the bank and authorized it to borrow $3 billion by selling its own bonds. In lobbying for the NCCB legislation, Nader stated that his objective was to replace the existing capitalist economy with a "cooperative economy." When asked whether this was possible, Nader replied:

> Yes, the time is ripe. More and more co-ops will be beneficiaries of people's growing awareness of the inability of giant corpora-

tions to deliver adequate employment, restrain inflation, alleviate poverty. These are failures, economic failures. It is time for a dramatic restructuring of the consumer economy so consumers can begin to disconnect from big business and develop an economy based on co-ops.[17]

Another element of the consumer movement that advocates what are called new wave co-ops seeks funding for these entities through NCCB. The new wave advocates are explicit in their desire to use NCCB as a source of tax-funded politics and to finance cooperative grocery stores, furniture outlets, and so on:

> While the blood of cooperatives is economic gain and justice, their soul is their broad sense of a better way of life. At best, cooperatives possess a vision which recognizes the necessity of community cooperation in achieving economic goals, and furthermore, it logically extends this community vision into political and social realms. . . . Because a co-op is people joining together democratically in order to satisfy their common needs, *the co-op is an explicitly political institution as well as an economic one* [emphasis added].[18]

Journalist James Rowen, writing in *Progressive* magazine, referred to NCCB as "one of several features of the 'public capital' movement intended to bring about a new banking system to finance a new social order."[19] Lee Webb, director of the Conference on Alternative State and Local Policies, was very enthusiastic about the establishment of the bank, praising it as "the start of something big." The conference has established a co-op bank "monitoring project" to help its affiliates make better use of NCCB.

All those who lobbied for NCCB have openly stated that they hope to use it to finance their political careers and agendas. One indication of this is that Nader has started up a new organization to help consumer activists establish cooperative television stations. The Cooperative Telecommunications Project would seek financing from NCCB and would be used to promote Nader's political views. Many others affiliated with the consumer activists have co-opted the financial resources of NCCB for their own personal political uses. Derek Shearer was appointed to the NCCB board of directors. Sen. Alan Cranston (D-Calif.) had glowing praise for Shearer during Senate hearings over the bank:

> I first got to know Derek when we worked together during the last Congress on the legislation establishing the National Con-

sumer Co-op Bank. . . . His leadership . . . , knowledge . . . , and his tough, persuasive intelligence were invaluable to the success of our efforts. . . . Derek is now teaching among the few courses in the country on cooperative enterprise. . . . He helped found and direct the New School for Democratic Management, which is the first alternative business school in the United States.[20]

From his position on the NCCB board, Shearer secured an $80,000 "technical assistance" contract in 1981 for his new school, which has close ties to the Institute for Policy Studies.[21] An example of what U.S. taxpayers are getting for their investment in Derek Shearer is provided by his description of the school's activities:

> Our Alternative Business School is not just about learning better skills. It is an ideological challenge to the rest of society. It is not just the models we are building, but the questions we are asking about why there are not workers and consumers on corporate boards of directors, or why workers do not run their own firms. My premise is that it is impossible for a left political movement . . . to accomplish its goals without a parallel alternative economic movement.[22]

There is evidence that many of the NCCB's technical assistance contracts are put to similar use. For example, some of the $75 million originally appropriated for these contracts has gone to the Federation of Southern Cooperatives, a "service, resource and advocacy training center" that used NCCB funds to pay tuition fees for some of its training seminars. The federation has also received grants from the Department of Labor, VISTA, and the Department of Education.

The federal government investigated some of the questionable uses to which NCCB's technical assistance funds have been put. The General Accounting Office (GAO) performed an audit of NCCB in 1983 and found that the bank's management violated the competitive bidding requirements of the technical assistance contracts.[23] According to GAO,

> the bank . . . limited competition through its reliance on sole-source contracting. It awarded at least half of the contracts sole-source and for the majority of those contracts it did not complete the required supporting justification to explain the lack of competition. These actions were contrary to stated bank policy. . . . Of the nontechnical assistance contracts, the bank could provide

some form of evidence that only . . . 6 percent were awarded competitively.[24]

GAO also found that the bank "did not fulfill its . . . responsibilities in monitoring compliance with contract terms."[25] For example, NCCB modified one contract nine months after its expiration date "in order to extend the contract and increase the program budget." GAO also found that 81 percent of the contract holders failed to file written reports on their performance, which led the agency to conclude that such practices raise "a greater concern of whether the Bank paid for services never received."[26] Apparently, the bank's practices were even more slipshod than what the GAO examiners reported. Ed Kirshner, who headed NCCB's subsidized loan division, stated that upon learning of the impending GAO audit, "it was announced as a top priority to fix up the loan files to have them ready for audit. . . . Unauthorized signatures were changed to authorized signatures. In some cases documents were backdated."[27]

We can only guess how all this unaccounted-for money has been spent, but it is possible that much of it has been used to support professional political activists in the consumer movement. One Nader associate stated that he hoped NCCB would be a way of allowing consumer activists to carry on their crusades without having to worry about earning a living. As a paid consultant to NCCB, Philip Kreitner said:

> Throughout the U.S., co-op professionalization is being given a sharp boost with the advent of the National Consumer Co-op Bank. Cooperators are captivated by the vision of a new way to capitalize the movement and their careers. The NCCB is the first solid indication to the New Wavers that they might be able to make a living doing co-op work.[28]

As a consultant, Kreitner strongly "advised" that the bank's funds be used to finance the political activities of "the movement":

> The key to the NCCB's influence on the movement will not be to whom it lends business development resources. The key will be what portion of its money, expertise, and ideology it commits to developing the noncommercial half of the cooperation: the side of co-ops which makes them education organizations, facilitators of community organizing, community institution building, community self-reliance, instruments for developing community intelligence. . . . *The New Wave cooperators have said it so well: "Bargains are the bait; collective consciousness is the hook."*[29]

One Nader associate who has done very well for herself through NCCB funding is Carol S. Greenwald, the bank's former president. While president of the bank, Greenwald attended the "Big Business Day" protest organized by the anti-industry coalition and held in Washington, D.C., on April 17, 1980. She spoke on "alternatives to the business corporation," stating that the cooperative lobby was the "prime consumer movement of the 1980s."[30] As NCCB president, Greenwald had a salary of $75,000 per year, plus benefits. Even after she went on a sabbatical to the Brookings Institution after a critical bank examiner's report, she became a consultant to NCCB and was paid $6,000 a month for 18 months—$108,000 in total—to head a financial advisory committee. According to bank officials, however, the committee never met.[31] Moreover, the NCCB staff thought that a financial consultant who had resigned the presidency because of allegations of financial mismanagement and who offered no advice anyway was worth more than $108,000 per year. Greenwald's contract also included the use of a secretary, free office space, and a $25,000 lump-sum payment. She made more as a consultant to the bank than she did as the bank's president. In addition, another $64,000 was paid to two Washington law firms to negotiate Greenwald's contract.

In addition to the use of NCCB funds to support political activities, more mischief has been carried out by the bank's granting loans to unprofitable businesses (cooperatives). As mentioned in chapter 3, the existence of cooperatives is consistent with a free enterprise economy, and many of them have thrived for decades. However, many cooperatives cannot compete in the open market with ordinary business firms that have the advantages of more specialized management and large-scale production. Consequently, one of NCCB's main purposes is to subsidize failing businesses and to give them a tax-financed advantage over other businesses, many of which are relatively small. In short, the bank will inevitably make portions of the economy less productive. For example, at one point the bank was considering a family farm cooperative project, initiated by the Southern Cooperative Development Fund, headed by an NCCB director, A. J. McKnight. The project proposed setting up a *moshav* or cooperative farm that would emphasize labor-intensive operations, despite the availability and productive superiority of more capital-intensive methods. Such a project would subsidize the type of unproductive agricultural production process that perpetuates hunger in so many Third World or underdeveloped nations. Capital-intensive production is one of the reasons U.S. agriculture is the most productive in the world, but it does not fit the utopian visions of the cooperative movement.

There is additional evidence that NCCB is in the business of perpetuating economic failures. Federal bank examiners found that 54 percent of the bank's loans were poor credit risks and that 25 percent were not even earning interest. An audit by the Farm Credit Administration revealed that several housing cooperatives with middle-class owners, such as the TownCenter Co-op in Washington, D.C., had defaulted on their NCCB loans and that the bank stood to lose approximately $3 million on other loans. With this type of performance, a private bank could not survive for long, but David Jameson, a former vice president for lending and credit, defended NCCB in the following way: "We were trying to start a bank from scratch. . . . We had a cadre of political types without banking experience. They were bright and dedicated, but were trying to set up a government bureaucracy that didn't relate to making loans."[32]

NCCB is just one recent example of how the anti-industry coalition uses taxpayers' funds to finance its political activities. NCCB, however, is only a small part of the entire picture: There are dozens of well-organized consumer groups that prosper from the public purse.

Consumer Activists: Hiding behind the Public Interest

In addition to the Nader organizations, there is an entire industry composed of so-called consumer protection professionals who use tax revenues to advance their political causes. There are hundreds of local consumer organizations around the country, and there are many well-financed and well-organized national groups as well. Among the better-known and more politically active groups are the National Consumers League (NCL), Consumer Federation of America (CFA), Consumers Union (CU), Community Nutrition Institute, and the National Council of Senior Citizens. To pursue their agendas, these groups form effective coalitions with other tax-funded organizations, such as labor unions, environmentalists, and welfare rights lobbyists. The interlocking nature of these organizations is revealed by their boards of directors, which include representatives of many of the above-mentioned groups. For example, on the NCL board of directors are Glenn E. Watts, president of the Communications Workers of America; Robert A. Georgine of the AFL-CIO; former Nader aide Esther Peterson; and radical economist Gar Alperovitz.

Consumer groups have been among the harshest critics of the Reagan administration's economic policies and have used tax revenues to voice their criticisms. NCL, for example, reportedly received about half of its $500,000 budget from the federal government in the period 1981–83.[33] CFA also has a history of tax-funded (USDA) political advocacy. For example, in 1978 the U.S. Department of Agriculture conducted an investigation that revealed that shortly after she was appointed assistant secretary of agriculture, Carol Foreman granted $23,536 to CFA.[34] Her previous position as executive director of CFA helped get her the federal position in the first place. The USDA investigation was very critical of the CFA grant because (1) it was more than twice as large as the maximum allowed under USDA guidelines; (2) the only other bid for the "consumer impact study" was immediately rejected; (3) CFA had already published its opinion on what the study should conclude before the grant was made to do the study; and (4) the head of USDA's Food Safety and Quality Service advised against the grant on ethical grounds.

CFA has also benefited from other government grants, including one for $85,000 from the Department of Energy in May 1978. CFA received the DOE funds weeks before even asking for them so that it could state its position on the decontrol of heating oil at DOE hearings.[35] When several congressmen objected to these questionable uses of funds, DOE responded by giving CFA another $49,500 to develop standards by which CFA and other consumer groups could receive grants in the future.

These examples of tax-funded consumer activism illustrate how the game is played. The special-interest groups lobby for the creation or expanded budgets of various government agencies. The agencies, often staffed by public interest lobbyists, then provide grants to the groups to lobby for even greater powers and revenues to be granted to the agencies. CFA, for example, lists as one of its major legislative accomplishments that "the CFA was an important influence on the creation of the Consumer Product Safety Commission and the National Consumer Cooperative Bank."[36] Furthermore, according to CFA, "As part of its new strategy, CFA formed the Coalition for Consumer Education in response to plans to 'zero out' the $3.6 million federal Office of Consumers' Education. The

93

result of the campaign was the restoration of $1.35 million in consumer education funds."

"Consumer education" is a euphemism for political advocacy, and it allows the public interest elite to pretend that it is merely interested in educating the public, not in forcing its political views on the public. For example, an NCL publication entitled *A Look at the Current Consumer Activists Movement* states that it was "supported by the Office of Consumers' Education, Department of Education, Grant Number G008006840."[37] There is little of educational value in the publication, however, for it is essentially a reference book on how to get in touch with other members of the public interest lobby. An appendix lists the names and addresses of "contact persons" at 145 different consumer activist lobbying organizations, including Public Citizen, the Telecommunications Cooperative Network, and the Federation of Southern Cooperatives.

Another consumer education project undertaken by a coalition consisting of NCL, Nader's Center for Science in the Public Interest, the Community Nutrition Institute, Congress Watch, CFA, Consumers Union, and the National Council of Senior Citizens reveals even more clearly how taxpayers' funds are being used for blatantly political purposes. The project, announced in January 1982, was one in which the coalition "targeted twelve issues for lobbying in the coming year."[38] The issues were laid out in a booklet entitled *Warning! Reaganomics is Harmful to Consumers.*[39] The National Council of Senior Citizens is likely to have been particularly helpful to the coalition on this project, for it received at least $212.6 million from the federal government in the period 1979–81.[40] The report is a shrill attack on any policy suggestions made by the Reagan administration regarding food, health, energy, housing, credit, transportation, product safety, "business practices," antitrust, and communications. The theme of the report is stated on page 3: "President Ronald Reagan's actions in the past year are a clear break from the 95 year history of progress. From massive budget cuts and wholesale deregulation, to lack of enforcement of existing statutes, the Reagan administration is harming consumers." The doctrinaire nature of the report is revealed on page 12, where President Reagan's energy policy is condemned for "accelerating oil decontrol." According to the report,

> the Administration has taken major steps [i.e., decontrol of oil prices] which will increase the burden on the average American.

> On January 28, 1981, eight days after taking office, President
> Reagan abruptly ordered the *immediate decontrol of crude oil*. . . .
> Estimates of the resulting costs to consumers . . . over the [next]
> ten month period range as high as $10 billion.

Although some of President Reagan's economic policies can be
validly criticized, it is very evident that the consequences of the
decontrol of oil prices have been nothing like the gloomy scenario
outlined by the consumer activists. Decontrol of crude oil prices
promoted stronger incentives to step up production. After decontrol the U.S. oil industry experienced one of the largest production
booms in its history, which caused a decline in the price of crude
oil and crude oil products. Opposing the decontrol of oil prices is
unequivocally an anticonsumer position.

In the area of antitrust, the report accepts as an article of faith
that antitrust enforcement "helps consumers buy the greatest variety of goods and services at the lowest possible cost" and promises
to lead an effort to deter any changes in antitrust practices. It is
now generally recognized that industrial mergers most often enhance
efficiency, not monopoly. By opposing more liberal merger policies,
the consumer activists are helping to stifle economic efficiency, to
the detriment of both producers and consumers.

One criticism illustrates particularly well why consumer activists
are so harshly critical of the Reagan administration. On page 43 of
the report, it is pointed out that

> since 1976, the Office of Consumers' Education in the Department
> of Education had received approximately $3.6 million per year to
> provide grants . . . to non-profit organizations for consumer education programs for students and citizens. During its five years of
> operation, this program was extremely popular. [But] the fiscal
> 1982 program monies were reduced by approximately 25 percent
> and folded into . . . block grants.

The report then complains that "community organizations [i.e.,
consumer activists] outside the school system have provided consumer education to . . . low income, elderly and minority groups. . . .
[T]hese groups no longer have access to federal funding to continue
outreach and educational programs."

Thus, consumer activists are particularly upset because the Reagan administration has proposed cutting back on their own funding
for educational programs, although they also claim concern for the

95

poor and minorities. If the report on Reaganomics is an indication of the type of education the consumer activists are offering to school children and other citizens, the elimination of all such funding would probably improve the overall quality of education. Teaching that destructive economic policies such as price controls, expansionary (and therefore inflationary) monetary policies, and stricter regulation of private business activities are in the public interest is sheer political indoctrination.

Direct lobbying is perhaps the most important aspect of what consumer groups hope to accomplish. NCL, which claims to have received over $200,000 annually in federal grants from 1981 to 1983 from such sources as CPSC, the National Bureau of Standards, the Department of Health and Human Services, and the Department of Education, boasts of numerous legislative accomplishments that have imposed severe costs on consumers and workers.[41] For example, in *Public Interest Profiles,* CFA boasts of having "opposed an attempt by the Reagan administration to eliminate regulations banning home work in certain industries."[42] In the state of Vermont, individuals have been earning extra money by knitting ski caps, sweaters, and so forth at home and selling them in nearby stores and ski resorts. Most of the workers involved are the elderly or married women who have chosen to stay home with their children and to earn extra income. At the insistence of labor unions, with which the women compete in the labor market, the U.S. Department of Labor had implemented regulations prohibiting the women from working in their homes. The issue is clear cut: Entrenched labor unions want to restrict the economic opportunities available to those people—primarily the elderly and married women—who prefer not to join the unions. What NCL lobbied against were attempts to ease or eliminate such restrictions. For example, Sen. Orrin G. Hatch (R-Utah) introduced a bill, the proposed freedom of workplace act, that would have repealed the restrictions on home work.[43] The bill was introduced because the effects of the restrictions are to help monopolize the market for garment workers: Some union members benefit, but at the expense of other workers, that is, those engaged in home work; consumers are also made worse off, for the higher, monopolistic wages will eventually lead to higher prices. These are hardly the kinds of results to be expected from a consumer protection organization, especially one that professes a concern for the elderly, women, and minorities. But they are understandable once it is realized that NCL receives money from labor unions and has several union leaders on its board of directors.[44]

NCL lists other pro-union, anticonsumer legislation among its accomplishments, including minimum-wage and child labor laws.[45] It is well known that the minimum-wage law prices the least-skilled, least-educated workers out of the market and that it benefits relatively skilled, unionized labor. That is why labor unions and their coalition partners, the public interest groups, constantly lobby for increases in the minimum wage. So-called child labor (usually meaning teenagers) is also a substitute for unionized labor, so that laws that prohibit child labor, like those that prohibit home work, help labor unions monopolize the labor market.

As with NCL, the legislative agenda pursued by the lobbyists for CFA can hardly be described as one that would benefit the average consumer, whom CFA claims to protect. The CFA lobbyists rate each congressman according to how his voting record satisfies CFA's preferences. In 1980 "the only law makers scoring 100 percent in the rankings were Representatives Ronald Dellums, D-Calif., Don Edwards, D-Calif., and Sidney Yates, D-Ill."[46] Any organization that lionizes someone such as Rep. Dellums is clearly far to the left politically of the average consumer.

On energy issues, one of its major areas of activity, CFA takes the extreme position that "its role is to combat the 'Big Oil' propaganda machine by reporting to the public the true extent of energy company profits, and by exposing the contrived nature of industry-manipulated shortages."[47] Thus, CFA lobbies for price controls that inevitably create shortages and then attempts to pass the blame for the shortages to oil companies. The type of lobbying and educational activities the taxpayers are getting for their support of organizations such as CFA is anything but in their best interest as consumers. Much of the lobbying is for destructive policies such as price controls, and the educational activities are aimed at giving consumers false information regarding the source of economic problems.[48] It is hard to imagine a more direct way to cripple the free enterprise system and impoverish the population. Consumer activists are lobbying to impose distortive regulations on U.S. business, the sole source of wealth creation and entrepreneurship. After the regulations cause shortages, product deterioration, and higher prices, the activists then wage a propaganda campaign to blame the entrepreneurs, not the regulations (and by implication, the activists), for the problems. This strategy has recently been summarized by Harry C. Boyte: "Radical economists have demonstrated how market pressures cause . . . housing shortages, shoddy merchandise, skyrocketing energy costs, and, indirectly, deteriorating services—in short, the conditions against which much of the citizen action arises."[49]

This brief survey of some of the activities of a few of the larger consumer activist organizations is meant only to illustrate the types of activities being carried on by hundreds of similar organizations. The two major activities of the activists—lobbying and education, or media relations—are likely to undermine the confidence citizens have in the free enterprise system by distorting the system with regulation and then blaming the distortions on the system. These propaganda campaigns are well financed by U.S. taxpayers, who unknowingly support not only the consumer groups but also their coalition partners, such as labor unions, welfare rights lobbyists, environmentalists, and even religious organizations.

Ironically, even though public interest groups such as Common Cause and Americans for Democratic Action constantly plead for a strict separation of church and state, they have benefited from their affiliation with a tax-financed religious organization, the National Council of Churches. Apparently, the separation of church and state is not so important if state-supported religion aids the cause of the public interest elite.

State-Sponsored Religion: The National Council of Churches and the Nestlé Boycott

An important element of the anti-industry coalition is the National Council of Churches (NCC), an affiliate of the World Council of Churches. The resources of NCC have provided an organizational framework for many of the anti-industry coalition's attacks on private corporations and the free enterprise system.

NCC's New York–based affiliate, the Interfaith Center on Corporate Responsibility, coordinates the NCC's anticorporate campaigns. There are also other affiliates, such as Clergy and Laity Concerned, which has dedicated itself to "join those who are angry and hate corporate power which the U.S. presently represents."[50] The Corporate Data Exchange gathers data on corporate activities to be used by various anti-industry coalition partners, including the Institute for Policy Studies. There is even a professional advertising agency, the Public Media Center (in San Francisco), that provides media exposure for NCC's causes. NCC is also closely intertwined with other members of the consumer activist movement. Timothy Smith, the director of the interfaith center, served on Ralph Nader's Big Business Day advisory board, and many of the consumer groups mentioned above have joined NCC in its boycott of Nestlé products (discussed below).

NCC's basic philosophy and objectives can be gleaned from some of its publications. A 1975 statement issued by NCC declared that "there is a basic contradiction between capitalism and the Biblical values of justice, mercy, stewardship, service, community and self-giving love."[51] By contrast, NCC apparently idolizes Third World Marxist dictatorships, even though freedom of religion is all but absent in such countries. In 1977, for example, NCC sent a 10-man delegation to Cuba. The delegation reported that it had been "challenged and inspired repeatedly by the determination and the success of the Cuban people to build, against great odds, a society characterized by economic equity, justice, and human dignity."[52]

NCC also has a very novel approach to the problem of crime. Instead of incarceration, it urges "a constructive social relationship" between victims and criminals whereby the victims and criminals sit down and "negotiate the resolution to their conflict."[53] One can imagine an 80-year-old burglary victim in New York City negotiating for the return of her television set. The true criminals, according to NCC, are the institutions that "oppress" people. Accordingly, NCC uses much of its resources to lobby for criminal sanctions or penalties for corporate executives whom they hold responsible for unsafe toys, cars, and so forth. For example, NCC gave $10,000 to the radical United Church of Christ to search out "evidence likely to lead to the arrest and imprisonment of the chief executive officer of a Fortune 500 company."[54] The church was also promised another $15,000 if an executive actually went to jail.

NCC, its affiliates, and its coalition partners have exploited the religious connection to promote the view that the goals of the anti-industry coalition are the will of God. Like other consumer activists and anti-industry organizations, NCC claims that it is financed primarily through voluntary contributions. There is evidence, however, that NCC has received millions of the taxpayers' dollars in the past several years to finance its religious crusades. In the period from 1978 to 1980 alone, NCC received at least $1,388,775 from various federal agencies, including the Department of Labor, the Department of Energy, and the National Endowment for the Arts.[55]

A 1980 grant by the Department of Labor, which followed up on a $500,000 award made in 1978, was to "develop and coordinate incarcerated veterans outreach projects." The Department of Energy granted NCC $438,000 during the 1979–81 period to "mobilize mass action in energy." With these taxpayers' funds, NCC promised that it would "be active participants . . . in the Citizen/Labor Energy Coalition" (see chapter 6). As one final example, a $15,000 grant from the National Endowment for the Arts was used to produce a film sympathetic to the social change that occurred recently in Marxist Zimbabwe (previously Rhodesia).[56]

The international boycott of Nestlé products illustrates the kind of activities that U.S. taxpayers are helping to fund under the auspices of NCC. The boycott was called during the late 1970s when Nestlé, the world's largest producer of baby formula, was charged with being responsible for the deaths of babies in Third World countries where mothers had mixed the formula with contaminated water. The Interfaith Center on Corporate Responsibility organized the Infant Formula Action Coalition (INFACT), which was made up of over 100 consumer activist organizations, many of which are also tax funded. One particularly active member of the coalition, the League of United Latin American Citizens, for example, received at least $2,906,847 from the federal departments of labor, education, and energy in the period 1979–81, the time during which the boycott took place.[57]

The Nestlé boycott and the media campaign surrounding it were part of an extraordinary propaganda campaign filled with terrible distortions and anticorporate rhetoric. The charge was that Nestlé (and its competitors) were hooking mothers on infant formula by giving free samples to doctors and hospitals. According to Mark Ritchie, an INFACT activist, the purpose of such stories was to link "the capitalist system—and the way it organizes our lives—to people's very personal experiences."[58] The infant formula campaign gained the sympathetic ears of many major newspapers and even the U.S. Congress, even though many of INFACT's claims turned out to be baseless. For example, in a 1979 fundraising letter, INFACT claimed that "ten million Third World babies are starving because of the heartless, money-hungry activities of powerful multinational companies."[59] However, Derick B. Aellife, the founder of the anti-formula movement, later conceded to *Newsweek* magazine that the figure of 10 million was only "symbolic" and not a scientific assessment. Another participant in the coalition,[60] James Grant, executive director of UNICEF, offered a much lower figure—1 million—but later admitted that this too was only a guess.[61] Along with such erratic estimates came publications with pictures of starving babies: "I want to tell you briefly how Nestles [sic] markets their formula so that you can understand not only how uncaring they are but also how crucial INFACT is in stopping what may become a global Jonestown where instead of Kool-Aid, formula milk is the agent of death."[62]

The major claims of the INFACT coalition were that (1) corporate advertising and promotional practices contributed significantly to a mother's decision to bottle-feed, (2) there had been a dramatic decline in breast-feeding in developing countries, (3) bottle-fed babies come largely from the poorest families, and (4) bottle-fed babies have higher disease rates than those who are breast-fed. The evidence, however, never supported these claims, and much of it was even contradictory. The few studies that do exist of patterns of breast-feeding over time show little change in developing countries. Furthermore, when asked at congressional hearings about the percentage of bottle-feeding in developing countries, INFACT witnesses simply did not know.[63] Similarly, the few studies that exist on the topic of whether breast-feeding occurs more among the poor than the rich show that the poor rely more heavily on breast-feeding while the wealthier, who can better afford infant formula, rely more heavily on the formula—precisely the opposite of INFACT's claims. The coalition's major claim, that promotion led to increased bottle-feeding, also turned out to be unfounded. As Carol Adelman concluded after surveying the evidence,

> of the four studies most frequently cited to support the key assumption . . . two had . . . nothing to do with the assumption. Of the remaining two studies, one did not scientifically examine the question and demonstrated results that conflicted with the author's opinions. The other did show an increase in breastfeeding but [did not prove] that formula advertising was the single or even the major cause.[64]

There is other contradictory evidence as well. The use of infant formula apparently has increased sharply in the Soviet Union, where promotion is prohibited, but breast-feeding has experienced a strong resurgence in the United States.[65] In light of this evidence (or lack thereof), all three U.S. pediatric organizations stated that there is

101

no support for the claim that samples of formula provided to mothers in hospitals will influence their feeding choice.[66]

Nevertheless, INFACT was quite successful in promoting its campaign against infant formula. Journalist Bill Moyers was persuaded to produce *Into the Mouths of Babes,* which won an award from the American Film Festival, and NCC financed (with taxpayers' help) a movie called *Guess Who's Coming to Breakfast.* Both movies were characterized by heart-rending footage of malnourished babies and distraught mothers stating that they had become hooked on a product they could not afford.

Various government agencies also lent a hand to the campaign. The Agency for International Development, for example, awarded a $1.2 million grant to Michael Latham of Cornell University, one of the most vociferous proponents of the Nestlé boycott, who claimed that Nestlé was "guilty of for-profit infanticide."[67] The grant, which was to be used to research the determinants of infant feeding patterns, was peculiar because Latham was the highest bidder—he bid twice the sum originally budgeted—and a technical panel judged his proposal as being inferior to others. Sensitive to the charge that his results would be biased, Latham contracted out the marketing component of the study to James Post of Boston University. But Post was not exactly an unbiased spectator—he had previously led an INFACT workshop in Washington, D.C., on "demarketing" infant formula.[68]

"Demarketing" was INFACT's stated objective. Just what demarketing is was explained to Rep. Jonathan B. Bingham's subcommittee on foreign trade in 1979 by Edward Baer of the Interfaith Center on Corporate Responsibility (and INFACT board member). Baer cited as a role model Marxist Algeria, where the importation and sale of infant formula is in the hands of a state-funded monopoly and all brand competition has been eliminated. When it was pointed out that there had been a steep rise in the importation of baby formula in Algeria, from 2.5 million half-pound cans in 1976 to 12 million in 1979, Baer replied that it did not bother him because it was taking place under government aegis. This gives the controversy the revealing and absurd proposition that capitalist infant formula allegedly kills babies but that socialist formula does not.

Ideology is clearly behind the infant formula coalition, although there are undoubtedly many genuinely concerned participants who were simply misled by the INFACT activists. One such activist is

Leah Margulies, the director of the Infant Formula Campaign for the Interfaith Center for Corporate Responsibility. An English major from Boston University, Margulies had done some reading on multinational corporations and, although an atheist, landed a job with NCC. In a conversation with a fellow employee who later resigned, Margulies reportedly said, "But . . . [businessmen are] all bastards. If they weren't they'd be living like we live and doing what we're doing."[69]

Once the dust settled, INFACT succeeded in bringing the United Nations (UN) into the campaign. In 1981 the UN voted, with the United States as the lone dissenting vote, to adopt a "code" that would limit the marketing of infant formula by private businesses in underdeveloped countries. The code places no prohibitions on the ability of government-run monopolies to engage in such practices. The Nestlé company has begun a voluntary effort to put the code into effect, after spending huge sums to pay legal fees and other expenses.

There are at least three clear-cut conclusions that can be drawn from the Nestlé boycott and the UN action. First, we now know that many of INFACT's claims were completely unjustified. Second, governments of underdeveloped countries have gained greater control over the production and distribution of infant formula, and they are likely to push for even greater controls. They are likely to have the help of the U.S. consumer activist movement in these efforts, for as INFACT board member Edward Baer has commented, "We want to see further changes and activities in the field fulfilled. Then we will call off the [Nestlé] boycott and turn to other American companies."[70] Third, because infant formula is a source of nutrition and mothers in Third World countries and elsewhere purchase it voluntarily, cutting off sales will possibly have harmful effects on the health of Third World babies.

Intervenor Funding: Biting the Hand That Feeds You

In March 1981 Ralph Nader announced that "we will be using the courts more and more to challenge regulatory action or nonaction."[71] Thus, the consumer movement will be protecting the public interest in the one branch of government that is most isolated from the public, and the public will once again be paying for these actions.

Intervenor funding, the use of tax dollars to pay public interest lawyers to sue the government, is one of the most lucrative sources of income for the consumer activist movement. The federal government is paying attorneys' fees—in some cases more than $125 per hour—to public interest lawyers who sue the government, even when they lose their cases. There are over 100 laws, ranging from the Age Discrimination Act of 1975 to the Noise Control Act of 1972, that require the government to pay the legal fees of parties that sue the government.[72] No one knows precisely how much money is involved, but the federal government's Office of Management and Budget has estimated that attorneys' fees may amount to about $146 million in 1984.[73] Intervenor funding is so pervasive that there are now dozens of Washington law firms that specialize in advising public interest lawyers on how to obtain attorneys' fees by suing the government. A bimonthly newsletter entitled *Federal Attorney Fee Awards Reporter*, and a book, *Federal Court Awards of Attorneys' Fees: How to Get $ From the Government*, have been published.[74] Sen. John C. Danforth (R-Mo.) calls this "a new cottage industry" that "seeks more regulation before which it can practice, claiming that it does so on behalf of the public interest."[75] The following examples illustrate how the public interest elite has convinced federal judges to support it with taxpayers' funds.

In *Sierra Club* v. *Gorsuch*, the court turned down the club's claims in a Clean Air Act case along with the claims of a coplaintiff, the Environmental Defense Fund. Nevertheless, both parties asked for and received nearly $100,000 for about 1,000 hours of work.[76] In *Copeland* v. *Marshall*, a group of female employees of the U.S. Department of Labor charged that sex discrimination had barred them from training programs and promotions. Before the circuit court ruled, the department agreed to a settlement in which the workers were paid more than $31,000. The court then awarded legal fees to the attorneys amounting to $171,000—nearly five times what the women received.

In a case against the Environmental Protection Agency regarding the Toxic Substances Control Act, the court ruled against the Environmental Defense Fund on 11 issues and in its favor on 2 issues. The court decided that the lawyers should be paid for time spent on all 13 issues and awarded them $99,500.

The public interest elite is also finding state and local governments to be a source of financial support. In a March 1981 survey by the National Association of Attorneys General, Florida was found to have paid $778,090 in attorneys' fees since 1976; of the 22 states responding to the survey, Washington state had paid more than

$400,000 and ranked highest, with $4.5 million in pending fee requests.[77] In New Hampshire a lawyer actually started emptying cash registers in state liquor stores—with the approval of local police officers—before persuading the state to pay a $25,000 attorney's fee.[78]

These few selected examples are not comprehensive and serve only to illustrate how public interest lawyers are using the court system, at taxpayers' expense, to pursue the anti-industry coalition's agenda. The argument made in defense of intervenor funding is that such litigation is in the public interest and therefore the public should be forced to pay for it. Otherwise, an inadequate supply of this public good would be provided. But regulation benefits only some—especially regulators and regulatory lobbyists—at great expense to the rest of the population. To those who must bear the costs of regulation, intervenor funding finances the provision of a public *bad*, not a public good, and it should, if anything, be curtailed or eliminated. Tony Roisman of the National Resources Defense Council, testifying before the President's Commission on the Accident at Three Mile Island, boasted that if he "or several other lawyers I know" were armed with federal intervenor funding, "there would never be another nuclear reactor licensed in the country, and the ones that are now operating would slowly be shut down."[79] One could think that Roisman had the public interest in mind when he made this statement. But when questioned about the topic, he replied, "I haven't the slightest idea whether nuclear power is safe."[80] This is quite remarkable admission from an attorney who has probably heard as much testimony on nuclear safety as anyone in the world and who once stated, "On the basis of the record established to date, there are no grounds to conclude anything, one way or the other."[81]

In addition to funds secured by suing various government agencies, public interest lawyers are also funded directly through several government entities, such as the Legal Services Corporation (LSC). LSC is worth mentioning here because it is a major source of taxpayers' revenue for the public interest elite (for a more detailed discussion, see chapter 12). LSC has an annual budget of more than $300 million and supports a satellite litigation center called the National Consumer Law Center. The center receives approximately $500,000 annually from LSC. LSC also supports scores of other anti-industry groups, such as the Legal Aid Society of Albany, which in turn directs the Public Utility Law Project. The project seeks to "develop and implement a model, replicable in other states," that would help stop the development of investor-owned electric utilities.[82]

Consumer activist groups and government agencies are not necessarily adversaries in these proceedings. Quite often they are allies. Many government agencies, such as CPSC and the Federal Trade Commission (FTC), are partly staffed by former consumer activists who use their access to taxpayers' funds to subsidize their former fellow activists. This appears to be true throughout the federal government, and the FTC's intervenor funding program during the late 1970s provides a good example.

The FTC staff essentially used intervenor funds to enlist the support of various consumer activist groups in expanding the reach of FTC regulation. They paid "witness fees" to consumer activists who provided testimony at FTC hearings and who helped publicize the FTC's position. More than 90 percent of the so-called expert witnesses funded by the FTC in the period from 1975 to 1979 supported the proposed regulations issued by the FTC staff.[83] This practice drew sharp criticism from some members of Congress. As reported by the Bureau of National Affairs in 1979:

> Senator Danforth blasted the FTC for funding groups friendly to agency positions, and he questioned selection procedures. "How much of your money goes to people who tell the Commission you're all wet?" he demanded of the four commissioners and the dozen FTC staff members seated before him. His line of questioning was joined in by Subcommittee Chairman Wendell Ford (D-Ky.), who has authorized his staff to undertake a very close look at the program.[84]

Although the FTC's regulatory decisions affect nearly every consumer in the country, the special-interest groups funded were a small, elite group consisting of the professional public interest lobby (see Table A5.2). Fifty-five percent of the funding went to groups located in San Francisco and Washington, D.C., and approximately 65 percent of all funds—over 1 million dollars—went to only eight groups: the California Citizen Action Group; Americans for Democratic Action; the Council on Children, Media and Merchandizing; the National Consumer Law Center; the National Council of Senior Citizens; Consumers Union; NCL; and Consumer Action–San Francisco.[85]

Many of the groups were simply offshoots of larger organizations that were formed specifically to procure FTC funds to subsidize the activities of the larger organizations. For example, Americans for Democratic Action established a separate Consumer Affairs Committee when it learned of the funding program. Prior to becoming involved in FTC rule making, the committee operated on an annual budget of approximately $2,000; during the 1976–79 period, however, it received more than $200,000 from the FTC.[86] It is clear that not all the funds received were spent on preparing expert testimony for FTC hearings, for according to FTC data, only 37 percent of all funds expended as of February 1, 1979, went for attorneys' fees and only 45 percent went to "attorneys' fees and related costs."[87]

That the groups testifying at FTC hearings represented their own special interests and not, as they consistently claimed, the public interest, was brought out in the following exchange between Mr. Markey, an attorney, and Ms. Schletter, a witness from Consumer Action–San Francisco:

> MR. MARKEY: What consumers do you represent?
>
> MS. SCHLETTER: You want their names?
>
> MR. MARKEY: How many consumers do you represent? That was the question.
>
> MS. SCHLETTER: Thirty-two hundred.
>
> MR. MARKEY: What are they, paid members?
>
> MS. SCHLETTER: Yes.
>
> MR. MARKEY: Thirty-two hundred consumers. What is the population—is this the Bay area, of just San Francisco?
>
> MS. SCHLETTER: I think this is in the record.
>
> MR. MARKEY: Can anybody be a consumer advocate or are there certain special requirements attendant to being a consumer advocate?
>
> MS. SCHLETTER: By the FTC requirements or what?
>
> MR. MARKEY: In this area.
>
> MS. SCHLETTER: I don't know.
>
> MR. MARKEY: Is [your testimony] the position of the thirty-two hundred people you represent? In other words, how many people participated in this and came to the conclusion that this is what is good for consumers and this is what is in the public interest?
>
> MS. SCHLETTER: It was a study team. We didn't have an election on it.

MR. MARKEY: How many people?

MS. SCHLETTER: Approximately twenty.

MR. MARKEY: Did you take a vote?

MS. SCHLETTER: A vote? Everybody has read it and has acceded to the results and had input and conversations before we debated and argued and came to these conclusions in a very open way.

Because the anti-industry agenda is rarely in the public's best interest, the public interest elite must use coercively obtained tax revenues to pursue it. Furthermore, the additional regulation sought by the public interest lobby is most often quite harmful to consumers, as the above proceeding illustrates. The hearing in which Markey and Schletter participated involved a proposed rule to eliminate bans on the advertising of eyeglasses. Such rules have been imposed by numerous state governments or private organizations of ophthalmologists. Consumer Action–San Francisco was arguing that "price was not a motivating factor in eyeglass purchases," a counterintuitive claim at best. It further claimed that the advertising of eyeglasses was "distasteful" and that it "could lead to market dominance by large multi-state corporations that would be less responsive to consumer complaints and less susceptible to effective supervision by state regulatory agencies."[88] Such emotional claims conflict with the known evidence of advertising's effects, especially in the eyeglass industry, where several important studies have been published. It is precisely the bans on advertising that result in higher prices, for advertising is a major vehicle through which firms compete.

In a study of the effect of advertising on the price of eyeglasses, Lee Benham of Washington University–St. Louis compared the prices paid for eyeglasses in states with differing restrictions on advertising.[89] Benham found prices nearly $20 higher for the year 1963 in the states that banned advertising. Other statistical studies have corroborated Benham's results for other goods.[90] Nevertheless, the anti-industry ideology claims that advertising is a monopolizing device that should be strictly controlled by state regulatory agencies. Ironically, it is these very agencies that have been captured by the eyeglass industry to enforce monopolizing bans on advertising. The sums spent on lawyers' fees and other related expenses are only a drop in the bucket compared to the effects of regulation on the price of eyeglasses and on thousands of other products as well.

When he took office in 1981, James C. Miller III, President Reagan's appointee as chairman of the FTC, eliminated intervenor funding from the FTC's budget. But attempts will surely be made in future years to reinstate intervenor funding at the FTC, given the political clout of the consumer activist movement. Even if intervenor funding is not available from the FTC, it is readily available elsewhere in the federal government. In 1980 Congress passed the Equal Access to Justice Act, authorizing government payment of lawyers' fees and "other court costs" to parties that win legal disputes with the government.[91] This law even permits the payment of fees to law students who may be assisting their professors on cases or working as interns for law firms. Because the fees are paid out of the budgets of the agencies that are taken to court, not from general funds appropriated by Congress, this system provides quite a boost to the consumer activist movement. Even if the activists do not receive funding, the agencies are now less likely to pursue policies that are looked upon unfavorably by the public interest elite for fear of being sued and losing part of their annual appropriation. As Stephen Babcock of the Administration Conference of the United States has stated, "I've gotten lots of calls from agencies expressing great concern about the possibility of bankrupting themselves."[92]

Summary and Conclusions

The wisdom of Adam Smith is captured in his statement: "I have never known much good done by those who affected to trade for the public good." Smith knew that when one is in the company of those who speak of acting in the public interest, it is always prudent to hold on to one's wallet. The ideology and preferences of the public interest elite are often very different from those of the average consumer, and the public interest elite has sought and obtained millions of dollars in taxpayers' funds to finance the anti-industry agenda. In the name of consumer protection, the consumers' hard-earned tax dollars are being spent to finance a political crusade that destabilizes the free enterprise system through regulation, the attempted nationalization of industry, and plain harassment. Ultimately, it is the consumers who must pay the bill for this effort.

VI. The Anti-Energy Industry

I think we have to develop a political dream that will sound at first like pie-in-the-sky, but which has the potential to capture the imagination of people as their patience with the [free enterprise] system begins to wind down and we get closer to the revolution.

—William Winpisinger

[W]e need to build a political machine. . . . This is one reason why the Citizen/Labor Energy Coalition is especially important—not just on the issue of energy, but to see how to build coalitions with the major institutions that are permanent, well-funded, and have memberships . . . in millions.

—Heather Booth

There are a number of reasons why the anti-industry coalition has singled out the energy industry as a target. First, the energy crisis during the 1970s, perpetuated by the federal government's own regulatory programs, provided an opportunity for the coalition to direct the public's anxieties toward the industry. As William R. Hutton, secretary-treasurer of the Citizen/Labor Energy Coalition (C/LEC) and executive director of the affiliated National Council of Senior Citizens, has stated: "Energy policy must be regarded as an avenue to broader national goals. . . . We can tap the widespread anger at the oil companies and channel it toward effective political action. . . . New crises spawn new opportunities."[1] Second, the coalition has a professed concern about the health of the environment. Third, the crusade against nuclear power is linked to opposition to the development of nuclear weaponry. Nuclear power has taken on a rather demonic character because of the anti-nuclear media campaign. Fourth, the energy industry is a natural ideological target for the anti-industry coalition, which, as Petr Beckmann has written, believes that "economic growth, free enterprise and technology are the culprits who have committed this sin [economic development], and they must be stopped in their tracks. And they can be stopped by denying them their lifeblood, energy."[2]

The anti-energy industry has been quite successful in halting the development of various energy sources. This chapter demonstrates how, with the use of taxpayers' funds, the anti-energy industry has reduced the availability and increased the price of several forms of energy. Despite its proconsumer rhetoric, the anti-energy industry has harmed consumers.

Citizen/Labor Energy Coalition

C/LEC, with branches in many states, is one of the anti-energy industry's chief organizational vehicles. The coalition was formed in 1978 by William Winpisinger, president of the International Association of Machinists; Heather Booth, executive director of the Midwest Academy; and Michael Harrington, founder of the Democratic Socialist Organizing Committee. From the beginning the organizers made it clear that its purpose was to use energy policy as a tool to move the Democratic party and, eventually, the country to the left politically. Winpisinger and Booth issued this statement at the organizing conference in April 1978: "Energy policy must be regarded as an avenue to broader national goals. The policies and programs which are adopted in order to resolve . . . energy issues . . . will in large part determine the economic and political direction of the country in the next decade and beyond."[3]

Winpisinger, who described himself as a "seat-of-the-pants socialist," was explicit in his expectations of C/LEC by stating C/LEC's basic perspective: "Energy supplies and prices are too important to leave in corporate hands. Both must be controlled by the government."[4] Cofounder Harrington concurred: "As socialists of the democratic left, we stand for fundamental change, for socialism, and for every immediate gain which can be achieved by the . . . movement in which we . . . participate, the unions, minority and women's organizations, the student movement, the liberal wing of the Democratic party among them."[5] Booth, the other coalition cofounder, echoed a similar view by saying: "The challenge of this decade is to develop a . . . movement . . . to unite people in step-by-step campaigns where our collective strength wins concrete improvements and begins the job of redistributing social wealth and power."[6]

Despite the well-cultivated image that C/LEC is merely a consumerist organization, its leaders have made open, unambiguous statements regarding their overriding radical objective: government control of the means of production, starting with the energy industry. A government takeover of the energy industry is seen only as "an

112

avenue for broader national goals"—for example, government control of other industries as well. Several facts lead one to question C/LEC's image as a consumer advocate organization. First, the regulatory harassment that it lobbies for has unequivocally harmed consumers, who bear the costs of regulation and taxation. Second, C/LEC's image as the little guy fighting against the special interests cannot withstand close examination given its affiliation with many of the largest and most powerful lobbying organizations in the nation, including the AFL-CIO, the National Council of Senior Citizens (see chapter 11), the International Association of Machinists, and the United Auto Workers. Third, C/LEC and its affiliates have received hundreds of millions of taxpayers' dollars over the past few years, and these revenues have been used in efforts to compel taxpayers to comply with a legislative agenda with which they often disagree.

C/LEC claims to represent more than 220 "trade union, senior, consumer, citizen, environmental, neighborhood, housing, religious, and minority organizations."[7] It lists its board of directors in terms of institutions rather than as individuals (see Table A6.1, in appendix). Labor unions, or at least union leaders, play a prominent role in C/LEC, as evidenced by the eight unions represented on the board of directors. Unions also provide much of the financial support for C/LEC activities. As Ira Arlook, director of the Ohio Public Interest Campaign and a C/LEC board member, recently stated, C/LEC's future activities "will require money, which mainly will come from the unions."[8] And the unions, in turn, are heavily subsidized by the U.S. taxpayers (see chapter 13), as are many other C/LEC affiliates.

Tax-Funding of the C/LEC

The data on recent federal funding of C/LEC affiliates are incomplete (see Table A6.2), but they do reveal that in the five-year period from 1977 to 1982, the C/LEC affiliates listed in Table A6.2 received more than $270 million in taxpayer subsidies. The U.S. taxpayers are unknowingly contributing to C/LEC's campaign "for fundamental change, for socialism," as C/LEC cofounder Michael Harrington put it. A few brief examples will illustrate what the taxpayers are getting in return for their financial support.

C/LEC itself received over $288,000 in federal grants in the period from 1979 to 1981. One such grant was provided by the Department of Energy in 1980 for "Citizen Participation in the Implementation

113

of PURPA." PURPA, or the Public Utility Regulatory Policies Act, is "intended to develop a national utility data base to allow comparison of utilities on a continuing basis."[9] PURPA requires utilities to maintain extensive records on the cost of serving each class of customer, daily kilowatt demands for all consumer classes, costs of purchased power, and so on. In short, the act imposes a huge paperwork burden on the utilities' customers, who must ultimately pay for all this red tape, so that government authorities can exert greater control over the affairs of the utilities. By subsidizing C/LEC's efforts to lobby for this legislation, the Department of Energy expanded its control over the utilities. A similar grant was awarded in 1981 for C/LEC's Petroleum Data Consortium, and another VISTA project was funded in 1979 "to organize 300–500 low-income consumers into energy activists."[10] Thus, federal grants have apparently been used to organize support for C/LEC's political agenda.

Many C/LEC affiliates have also received federal grants to help pursue their anti-energy agenda. Among these is the Conference on Alternative State and Local Policies, which in 1981 received $68,000 from the Community Services Administration for an "Energy Project" that "sponsored a series of community action training skills workshops in Colorado, Arkansas, Kentucky, Minnesota, South Dakota, and Montana."[11] The project involved conferences, "training sessions," and the publication of *Energy Planning and Education: A Handbook for Community Leaders and Organizations.* The preface to the handbook states that the federal government's expenditure of billions of dollars annually on low-income energy assistance is inadequate, because "[r]ather than treating the causes of high energy prices and inconsistent supplies, income assistance programs . . . ameliorate the effects, while subsidizing the current energy pricing and delivery structures." The book states that the Community Services Administration recognizes this "dilemma" and recommends that the "only long-term solution is a comprehensive program of conservation, alternative energy sources, adoption of energy conserving life-styles and *continued advocacy on behalf of their needs and interests*" (emphasis added). In a section entitled "Community Mobilization," the book states that the Colorado Energy Advocacy Project, funded by local community action agencies, has trained the Community Service Administration's Energy Crisis Intervention Program coordinators and has used the Colorado advocacy project as a prototype of what other anti-energy industry organizations should be doing.

The Colorado Energy Advocacy Project is one of many such projects that was funded by the Community Services Administration and other federal agencies during the late 1970s through their so-called energy advocacy programs. What these tax-funded advocates were supporting can be gleaned from some of their statements. For example, Dan Newman, executive director of one of the regional programs, stated at a Department of Energy rule-making hearing that "expanding utility [company] involvement in . . . conservation programs will perpetuate and increase their [the companies'] social, economic and political power. This would undermine a major motivation of the alternative energy/conservation movement."[12] Newman also feared that companies were investing "in solar technology that is too durable, that is excessively efficient in converting sunlight to usable energy, and that requires . . . little maintenance. These strategies increase the capital use [thus] exploiting the technology."[13] Newman's message is clear: No matter how efficient and beneficial it may be, the involvement of private enterprise in the energy business is politically unacceptable. As an aside, it is important that even though the anti-energy industry criticizes private utilities, electric utilities are not a legitimate example of private enterprise; rather, they are heavily regulated and controlled by government. A critique of the electric utility industry is not a critique of private enterprise, although it is often labeled as such.

Further insight into the Colorado energy advocates' alleged concern for the poor is gained from William Schroer of the Colorado Energy Advocacy Office. When asked why more than half of the federal revenues earmarked for the poor was not distributed in 1980, Schroer replied that such expenditures would be "harmful" because the money would end up in the coffers of the utility companies, which of course, is what Congress intended. According to Schroer, the money would be better spent in political advocacy efforts. When asked why he and his group had not done more to see that the poor received the money (the group's proper function), he responded, "We don't like having to deal with welfare programs that have to satisfy the needs of the low income with utilities."[14] To this, Schroer's supervisor, Jim Smith, added, "We are on the cutting edge of a movement for economic social change."[15] Thus, despite all the rhetoric about helping the poor pay their utility bills, the

115

Colorado Energy Advocacy program was used to promote the anti-energy industry's political agenda and to financially support the anti-energy activists.

The League of Women Voters, also an active affiliate of C/LEC, received at least $2.47 million in federal grants in the period from 1977 to 1982 and used those funds to do much more than sponsor presidential debates. The league has announced that it seeks to "bring about a significant and progressive reduction in the U.S. energy growth rate."[16] Armed with grants from the Department of Commerce, the Community Services Administration, the Department of Energy, the Environmental Protection Agency, the Department of Housing and Urban Development, the National Endowment for the Humanities, and the International Communications Agency, the league listed in its 1980 Annual Report lobbying "for specific government action" as one of its main functions.[17] It listed among its lobbying objectives and accomplishments the passage of the "windfall profits tax" on the production of oil, stricter environmental regulation, and forced conservation of energy.

The National Council of Churches (NCC), another C/LEC affiliate, received $438,000 in federal funds during 1979–81 to "mobilize mass action on energy." The NCC staff even promised that with these funds they would "be active participants . . . in the Citizen/Labor Energy Coalition."[18]

This brief listing of how taxpayers have financed C/LEC projects is anything but comprehensive; it is meant only to illustrate the types of activities engaged in by dozens of C/LEC affiliates partly at the taxpayers' expense. More important than specific examples is the broad program upon which the taxpayers' resources are brought to bear. Although price controls are C/LEC's main priority, its agenda is much broader. A 1980 C/LEC publication stated: "We reject the idea that the only initiative we should push is one aimed at recontrolling domestic prices. Such an initiative is part of a larger agenda, one of expanded [government] control over our workplace and our resources."[19] With this overriding objective in mind and with the assistance of Sen. Howard Metzenbaum (D-Ohio) and Rep. Toby Moffett (D-Conn.), in 1979 C/LEC had a measure known as the Citizen's Energy Act formally submitted to Congress. This proposed act outlines C/LEC's broader anti-energy industry agenda by providing for:

- a federal energy company responsible for developing oil and gas resources, which would be used as a yardstick by which private companies would be measured and judged;
- horizontal and vertical divestiture of the privately owned oil and gas companies;
- mandatory energy conservation;
- federal funding of a "solar development bank" to sharply increase federal funding for the development of solar power;
- increased subsidies for low-income energy assistance;
- lifeline rates on electric and natural gas utility companies.

Another of C/LEC's broad objectives is the passage of the corporate democracy act, which was introduced in Congress in 1980. The chief provisions of this measure are:[20]

- communities are to be given 24-month notices of plant closings, with "hearings on request" and reimbursement to employees and local governments if plants are closed;
- by law, corporate boards of directors would include "independents," such as union leaders, governmental officials, and consumer activists;
- corporations would be forced to disclose their "social performance" and provide environmental impact statements on their annual reports, to be audited by government regulatory officials;
- civil and criminal violations would lead to heavy fines and imprisonment for corporations directly or indirectly involved.

C/LEC affiliates have also been very active at the state and local levels. They have launched local campaigns against the deregulation of natural gas prices; waged campaigns in at least 25 states to prevent utilities from stopping services to those unwilling to pay their utility bills (which led to legislation being enacted in 16 states); fought for "lifetime rates" and against fuel price adjustment clauses; lobbied for "unitary taxation" of oil companies, whereby states could tax the companies on all profits earned worldwide, rather than just intrastate; lobbied (successfully in some states) for "divorcement" laws that prevent refiners from operating retail gasoline stations; promoted "citizen's utility boards," state-funded entities that are staffed by consumer activists and oppose all utility rate increases; and called for the imposition of new "excess profits" taxes on oil companies.[21]

C/LEC, which claims that its "canvassers" speak to 50,000 citizens each evening, seeks to dramatically increase the cost of producing oil, natural gas, and other energy sources through regulation and taxation, while legally prohibiting these cost increases from being passed on to consumers. If successful, this strategy would drive many privately-owned oil, natural gas, and electric utility companies out of business. Increased regulation and taxation is detrimental to consumers, stockholders, and the companies. Consumers are made worse off, for they must pay the lion's share of the increased regulatory costs; stockholders (mostly pension funds, banks, insurance companies, and universities) suffer from reduced dividends; and the companies themselves become less profitable. The irony is that the costs of taxation and regulatory harassment are usually passed on in the form of higher utility bills, so that the average citizen is led to believe that it is the private firms, not the regulators, politicians, and anti-energy lobbyists, that are at fault.

Economic Implications of the C/LEC

C/LEC's agenda is similar to that pursued by other elements of the anti-industry coalition in that it seeks to destroy two essential elements of our economic system: (1) the system of contract rights, and (2) the large corporation. The system of contract rights, enforced by law, permits individuals to use their assets in ways they deem most beneficial, as long as they do not interfere with the rights of others. As long as these rights are respected, businesses will coincidentally further the interests of society in their search to maximize profits. The energy industry, however, is heavily regulated so that many of these rights are already abridged. C/LEC would make matters even worse through greater regulation. The regulatory restrictions advocated by C/LEC and other members of the anti-industry coalition abridge the contractual property rights of individuals in the private sector and transfer these rights to various political authorities. These political authorities respond to well-organized special-interest groups, such as C/LEC, rather than to the mass of consumers and stockholders, who are generally not well organized. Moreover, once a regulatory apparatus is established, it is often captured by the regulated industry so that C/LEC's efforts, even if successful, may eventually backfire. Regulation is a way of denying one group of citizens (stockholders) their rights to use their legally obtained property and of transferring those rights to other, more politically active citizens. Increased government control over private business decision making will lead only to higher costs, higher prices, bankruptcy, and a loss of individual freedom. A closer look at C/LEC's agenda illustrates this point.

A Federal Energy Company? A federal energy company used as a yardstick by which other companies are judged would simply be a first step toward a government takeover of the energy industry. Like all other government-owned enterprises, such an entity would not bear the burdens of taxation and regulation that other companies do and would also receive preferential treatment in the credit markets (given its government affiliation). It would hardly be fair to compare private oil companies, for example, that are struggling to comply with federal directives costing over $60 million per year in paperwork[22] to a federal energy company that is free from such costly harassment. All the other regulatory restrictions promoted by the anti-energy industry would make this comparison even more unbalanced but would serve the propaganda efforts of the anti-energy coalition, which would use such unfair and lopsided comparisons to argue for even more regulation or nationalization of those "inferior" private energy companies.

Divestiture. Forced divestiture would also be detrimental to economic efficiency and, consequently, to the consumers. There are currently more than 10,000 oil refiners in the United States, so it is ludicrous to believe that the oil industry is overly concentrated and monopolistic. Dozens of large firms have entered the industry over the past several decades, and the oil industry is less concentrated than the rest of the manufacturing industry in the United States. Moreover, industrial concentration does not necessarily have anything to do with monopoly power; it is most often the result of superior efficiency on the part of one firm or a few firms. Forced divestiture would also risk the loss of the benefits of large-scale production.

A Free Lunch in Energy. C/LEC claims partial responsibility for laws that have been passed in 16 states to prevent utilities from shutting off power to those customers who do not pay their bills for extended periods of time. Anyone familiar with the industry knows that utilities usually go out of their way to arrange for partial or extended payments of bills owed by those consumers who have

119

financial problems. With the help of the anti-energy industry, however, it is now legal in several states to simply refuse to pay one's bills on time without having to worry about losing any service. Aside from encouraging a lot of freeloading, the major impact of this legislation is that utility revenues from services rendered will be curtailed, and the financial viability of the utilities will be impaired. Everyone feels compassion for those who have trouble paying their utility bills, which is why the federal government spends billions of dollars annually subsidizing low-income energy consumers. The problem of poverty, however, is not likely to be solved by driving privately owned electric utilities out of business. It will only make all Americans poorer by driving up the price of energy.

Excess Profits Taxation. Punitive "excess profits" and "unitary" taxation is one of the most blatant examples of how C/LEC has attempted, with some success, to have the government force up the price of energy and then to blame the higher prices on the energy companies. Ultimately, consumers must pay the taxes imposed on energy companies; the companies only serve as tax collectors for the government authorities, who benefit politically from the increased taxes. Irving Kristol of New York University described this phenomenon in a discussion of the financial problems of Consolidated Edison, a major utility serving New York City:

> [A]pproximately one third of Con Ed's billings represent a tax on the consumer which the company surreptitiously collects for the city. (This is distinct from, and in addition to, the taxes Con Ed pays on its own property.) This consumer tax is not specified as such on one's electric bill—it is simply hidden in the total. That practice, of permitting the city to tax its citizens while making it appear that Con Ed was charging them for service was instituted by the company long ago, as part of its strategy to pacify revenue-hungry politicians by quietly appeasing them. The strategy did not work. Those high electricity bills naturally caused Con Ed to be unpopular with its customers and consequently made it a target of opportunity for every political candidate who wished to posture as a defender of "the people" against "the interests."[23]

One can only estimate the additional burden such taxation would impose on consumers, but one recent C/LEC effort—the enactment of unitary taxation in Florida (i.e., state taxation of all profits, regardless of where the profits are earned)—is expected to cost Florida consumers $100 million annually in additional utility fees.[24]

120

This hidden tax is likely to stir up even more resentment toward Florida-based energy companies, not toward the real culprits, the state's legislators and their C/LEC-affiliated special-interest allies. How ironic it would be if this resentment were used as a lever to impose even greater levels of taxation on the state's energy providers and consumers.

Citizen Utility Boards. Should the animosity toward energy companies lead to the adoption of another C/LEC proposal, known as "citizen utility boards," more problems can be anticipated. There are already several such utility boards, including the People's Council in Washington, D.C., and the boards established in 1982 in New York, Arkansas, California, Illinois, and South Carolina. These boards are groups of government-funded political activists (usually lawyers), whose purpose is to participate in rate hearings to oppose all utility rate increases. Such boards would serve as a means for C/LEC spokesmen to gain prominence and respectability as friends of the consumer, all at the expense of the taxpayers. They would cause further deterioration in the financial viability of utilities, however, by inhibiting legitimate rate increases that are necessary to cover the costs of increased wages, higher fuel prices, capital expenditures, regulatory requirements, and so on.

Divorcement. Owing largely to C/LEC's efforts, legislation has been introduced in at least seven states that would enact so-called divorcement legislation to prevent oil refiners from operating retail gasoline stations. There is also an effort afoot to enact a national divorcement law. The impetus for divorcement legislation arose because of the decline between 1972 and 1981 in the number of lessee-operated gasoline stations (that is, stations leased from suppliers but operated independently) and the simultaneous increase in the number of refiner-operated stations. During that period the lessee group declined by 59 percent while refiner group increased by 14 percent.[25]

C/LEC and the lessee operators have attributed these changes to attempts by refiners to drive lessees out of business through predatory pricing, that is, temporarily dropping prices below average cost to drive competitors out of business. According to this view, refiners' upstream profits are being used to subsidize refiner-operated stations, with the ultimate objective of monopolizing the retail gasoline market. Both theoretical and empirical evidence, however,

121

contradicts this claim. There is fierce competition in the gasoline marketing business, and predatory pricing is not likely to be profitable. Even if a lessee operator is driven out of business, the money spent subsidizing the refiner's operation will be wasted if other stations enter the market (attracted by the refiner's high profits) after the previous lessee has gone. Given that there is virtual free entry into this market, any monopoly prices would quickly be eliminated. Further, lessee operators—the supposed target of predatory pricing—operate 50 percent of all service stations and 78 percent of all refiner-owned stations.[26] It is not plausible that refiners would try to destroy the value of four-fifths of their own retail asset base. Moreover, complaints about refiner subsidization and predatory pricing have been heard since the early 1970s. If, after more than 10 years, refiners still engage in predatory pricing (and lose money at it), such efforts would appear irrational.

Empirical evidence gathered by economists John Barron and John Umbeck reveals that refiner-operated stations have been successful because they are more efficient than many of the lessee-operated stations, not because they are monopolies. Refiner operated stations averaged sales of 86,000 gallons per month in 1981, twice the average of lessee operators.[27] Because of declining average cost, this disparity in volume gives the refiner-operated stations a cost advantage. Divorcement legislation would prohibit consumers from taking advantage of such efficiencies and would most likely result in higher prices because of diminished competition from the larger, more-efficient refiner operators. In fact, there is empirical evidence that divorcement would cause higher prices.

Maryland has had a divorcement law since 1974, and Barron and Umbeck have conducted a careful statistical study of the effects of divorcement on gasoline prices in that state. They found that after divorcement, stations that had been refiner-operated raised their prices by an average of 2.1 cents per gallon for self-service and 5.8 cents per gallon for full service. In contrast, after divorcement, competitors in the area around divorced stations increased their prices by an average of 0.7 cent per gallon for self-service and 2.9 cents per gallon for full service.

Assuming that these results can be applied to the national market, Barron and Umbeck estimated that a national retail gasoline divorcement law could cost consumers approximately $1 billion per year. Several other studies have corroborated these results.[28] Theoretical and empirical evidence suggests that C/LEC's continued promotion of the divorcement issue will punish oil refiners and gasoline customers, but will benefit the higher-cost lessee operators by isolating them from competition. Ironically, the majority of refiner-operated stations are owned by nonintegrated and smaller integrated refiners, not by the "giant oil companies" about which C/LEC purportedly is so concerned.[29] Thus, divorcement will not even satisfy the political biases of the anti-energy activists.

Blocking Deregulation of Natural Gas Prices. C/LEC's major legislative involvement is the regulation of natural gas. In January 1982 C/LEC joined forces with another anti-energy group, Energy Action, to oppose the Reagan administration's proposed legislation to deregulate the price of natural gas. C/LEC launched an all-out campaign to prevent deregulation and to impose even further regulation on the natural gas industry. Its affiliates have hired mostly teenagers and college students to go door-to-door in dozens of states to inform citizens of the merits of continued regulation. They have also obtained pledges from members of Congress to oppose decontrol legislation. C/LEC has also organized rallies, such as the September 24, 1983, "Gas Protest Day," when "citizens will urge their neighbors, their co-workers, and local leaders to lobby Congress to end the human suffering . . . caused by escalating gas prices."[30] *Congressional Quarterly* noted C/LEC's success by stating that "CLEC was responsible for drafting the major legislative alternative (S 996, HR 2154) to the [Reagan] administration's deregulation bill."[31] The bills were introduced by Rep. Richard A. Gephardt (D-Mo.) and Sen. Nancy L. Kassebaum (R-Kans.) and have more than 100 cosponsors in the House and at least 15 in the Senate. How C/LEC drums up political support in Congress for these issues has been noted in one of its recent publications:

> A case in point is one of our most impressive victories, which occurred in Ohio. . . . In March of 1982 the Ohio Public Interest Campaign, a CLEC affiliate, presented [Republican Representative Del] Latta with petitions containing 5,600 signatures urging him to co-sponsor the Dingell Resolution, a statement opposing decontrol. . . . Representative Latta agreed to co-sponsor that resolution. . . . In Kansas, over 400 people from . . . organizations working with CLEC attended a town meeting with several members of the Kansas and Missouri Congressional delegations. All of them, including Senator Bob Dole (R-KS), rebuffed the Reagan Administration's program. . . . Door-to-door canvass-generated letters and phone calls protesting rising gas prices have been a

key factor in developing the broad coalition of politicians sponsoring HR 2154.[32]

C/LEC and its affiliates are doing the legwork—getting out the vote for those politicians and aiding bureaucrats who wish to impose further regulatory controls on the natural gas industry—with taxpayers' funds.

C/LEC's well-organized and well-financed natural gas campaign has taken advantage of a crisis in the natural gas industry that was created by federal regulation of the industry, not by corporate greed. One of C/LEC's most consistent and effective strategies is to concentrate on whatever problems exist in the energy industry, regardless of the source, and to wage a well-publicized media campaign aimed at the excesses of big business. C/LEC's secretary-treasurer, William R. Hutton, has openly admitted as much in saying that C/LEC's basic mission is "a fight against corporate greed" and that "the natural gas campaign is a critical component of an overall progressive strategy in the 1980s. . . . New crises spawn new opportunities."[33] The crisis referred to by Hutton is the rapid increase in the average price of natural gas between 1979 and 1981 that was spawned by the Natural Gas Policy Act of 1978. To understand how this regulation-induced crisis provided new opportunities for C/LEC to promote its agenda, it is useful to briefly review some recent events in the natural gas industry.

For decades, there have been price controls on natural gas sold in interstate markets. Like all price controls, the controls in this market have created shortages. Attempts have always been made to compensate for the regulation-induced shortages by stepping up production in the nonregulated intrastate market and by importing natural gas. However, the Arab oil embargo of 1973, which led to greatly increased U.S. oil prices, stimulated the demand for natural gas as a substitute for oil. Along with especially harsh winters in 1977 and 1978, this development exacerbated the shortages of natural gas even though the interstate market and the volume of imports were increasing. The crisis, which could have been avoided by deregulation, gave rise to President Carter's Natural Gas Policy Act of 1978. Although the act was originally designed to eliminate federal price controls, the effect was to extend federal price controls to the intrastate market. The act also established an extremely complex system of categories for classifying gas wells, with provision for controlling all wells (except for "deep wells") and for the phased deregulation of so-called new gas by 1985. Energy analyst Nolan Clark has explained how this system led to the rapid increases of natural gas prices during the late 1970s and early 1980s:

> At the time of the passage of the Natural Gas Policy Act, all of the interstate pipelines . . . faced some degree of actual or potential shortage. . . . [T]hey were, accordingly, anxious to purchase gas, wherever it was available. . . . [T]hey were, indeed, overanxious to establish claims to reserves and future supplies, going far afield to nail down imported gas from Mexico and Canada, manufactured gas, and liquefied natural gas (LNG) from North Africa (cooled, compressed and shipped across the Atlantic in cryogenic tankers). Needlessly expensive facilities were built to handle LNG and needlessly expensive commitments were made to purchase unregulated gas. . . . The misbegotten product of this mating of government direction and market direction was above-market-clearing prices for unregulated gas. Remember that prices for "old" and "new" gas were not set by competition. Rather, they were set by the government at a below-market-clearing level. This provided a so-called "cushion." High-priced unregulated gas could be "rolled in" with the low-priced regulated gas. Given the excess demand resulting from government-mandated, below-market-clearing prices, market equilibrium could only be achieved by driving the price for the unregulated gas above (way above) the competitive, market-clearing price. . . . In order to satisfy their projected needs . . . the pipelines contracted for reserves, buying, as a rule, the lowest-priced gas available. Since wellhead gas prices . . . varied—because of government regulation—the pipelines most in need of added reserves purchased the largest amounts of the marginal, high-cost, unregulated gas.[34]

It was the owners of these pipelines who were forced by regulation to charge sharply higher prices, even though there were gas surpluses in some areas of the market. The *Wall Street Journal* also has recognized how consumers have been hurt by this regulatory debacle:

> A too-low federal lid on "old" gas has discouraged production, forcing users to rely on gas from deep formations and foreign sources that are not subject to controls. The resulting sharp price rise has prompted many industries to switch to other fuels, leaving home consumers to pay not only for the expensive gas but also for a larger share of pipeline overhead.[35]

Professional economists know that removing price controls from the natural gas market would both eliminate the shortages and reduce prices, as happened when the petroleum market was deregulated. C/LEC, however, has maintained the opposite—that more stringent controls are needed and that the Reagan administration's proposed decontrol should be stopped. C/LEC's ideological blindness and disregard for fact was revealed in one of its studies that concluded that gas consumers in the Washington, D.C., area would face a 20 percent increase in their bills during the winter of 1983–84.[36] Interestingly, this particular C/LEC study agreed with another study, conducted by the Natural Gas Supply Association, the gas industry's decontrol lobby. When it was pointed out that its study inadvertently admitted that existing controls led to higher prices, C/LEC immediately withdrew the study from circulation for "revision." C/LEC is able to carry on this charade because of another of its top priorities: providing disinformation on energy issues.

Disinformation and the Anti-Energy Industry

Generally, the media respond sympathetically to claims made by self-proclaimed consumer-protection organizations, and C/LEC is no exception in the media's response to its claims.[37] C/LEC has become somewhat of an authority on energy issues, and it is common to read or listen to news reports on energy issues that cite only one source of information, the Citizen/Labor Energy Coalition. The results of C/LEC's studies are also widely reported as facts in the major media and by the *AFL-CIO News*, the *Senior Citizens News* (the monthly newsletter of the 4-million-member National Council of Senior Citizens), *In These Times*, (sponsored by the Institute for Policy Studies), and the communist paper *Daily World*. This exposure has helped perpetuate a great deal of misinformation in the minds of the public. Economists have done a poor job in educating the public about the benefits of the free market allocation of energy, and counterclaims by the energy industry are usually ignored as being self-serving. As a result, C/LEC has had a disproportionate influence on public opinion.

An example of this misinformation is C/LEC's reports on oil decontrol. In 1979, before oil was fully decontrolled, C/LEC issued a press release entitled "Price Decontrol Brings Oil at 'Astounding' Costs of $56–$870 per Barrel."[38] This was contrary to what economists were saying would happen, and we now know that decontrol led to a decline in oil prices, from a peak of $37.48 per barrel in

March 1981 to less than $30 per barrel by 1984.[39] Despite C/LEC's claims, the laws of supply and demand have not been repealed.

Ed Rothschild, director of C/LEC's Energy Action Project (which produces studies of energy issues), has given some insight into why C/LEC's studies ignore the lessons of both economics and history. In a recent interview, Rothschild questioned the right of producers to keep the profits created by their production. He asked: "Why should the economic rents [that is, profits] be kept by producers of that gas?"[40] In other words, Rothschild questions whether individuals had the right to own private property and to make use of and benefit from that property. Instead, he apparently views natural gas as a commons—something that belongs to everyone. With the exception of Marxist theory, there is no widely accepted discipline that would support Energy Action's implicit assumption regarding the role of profits in the economic system. Energy Action has generally ignored the incentive effects of the profit-and-loss system and, apparently, sees private property as illegitimate, at least when owned by corporate shareholders. Rothschild exhibited further disregard for private property and individual freedom in his open admiration for Canadian government bureaucrats who have the ability to seize a private firm's records. As Rothschild approvingly stated, "They don't have to go through the process of getting subpoenas. . . . They can just walk in and get the files."[41]

In its zeal to grab headlines, C/LEC appears to have often ignored facts. For example, a June 1981 Energy Action report, "Where Have All the Dollars Gone?" claimed to show that the oil and gas companies "are accumulating cash faster than they are able, or willing, to spend on the legitimate search for oil and gas."[42] The facts, however, are quite different. In 1979 investment in domestic exploration exceeded domestic net income by 47 percent; in 1980 it was by 44 percent, and in 1981 by almost 100 percent. In recent years the oil industry has invested about $1.50 for each $1.00 in profit.[43]

C/LEC has been criticized from various quarters for its incorrect and misleading analyses, and the organization has even acknowledged many of its mistakes. Nevertheless, it has failed to issue any corrections, and its original, sensational stories remain part of the public record. And the headline hunting continues. At a December 1981 press conference, William Winpisinger announced that had natural gas been decontrolled earlier that year, "every American household would have ended up paying $50–$100 per month more in their gas bills"; a 1981 Energy Action study predicted that if gas were decontrolled, industries would be crippled and many small businesses would be bankrupted; a 1982 study, "Pipeline to Disaster," claimed that if gas had been decontrolled in 1981, the economy would have lost almost 3.5 million jobs in the subsequent four years; and in "Gas Prices Out of Control," C/LEC claimed that if the Reagan administration succeeds in decontrolling the price of natural gas, it will cost consumers $50 billion over the next four years.[44] There is no question that C/LEC is not likely to let facts stand in the way of its anti–energy-industry agenda.

In summary, C/LEC and its affiliates have received hundreds of millions of taxpayers' dollars during the past several years to help finance their relentless campaign to reduce the economic viability of private energy production. The major beneficiaries of this political game are legislators who benefit politically by crusading against the alleged excesses of the big energy companies and special-interest groups whose members often gain prominence and income as state-supported career activists or government regulators. The parties being plundered by this political process are the consumers, who must suffer the consequences of regulation and taxation, and the shareholders and managers, whose wealth is confiscated by increased government controls. Politicians are experts in benefiting personally from abridging the rights of some taxpayers to grant special privileges to more politically active groups, and their dispensation of taxpayers' funds facilitates this transfer process. The end result is that consumers are all poorer because of the detrimental effects that government controls have on production. We are killing the goose that lays the golden eggs. Michael Jensen and William Meckling of the University of Rochester have stated why energy companies in particular and large corporations in general are especially vulnerable to the attacks of politicians who promote the views of special-interest groups:

> Corporations are particularly vulnerable to the attacks of politicians promoting special interest groups because their ownership, which should represent their special interests, is often invisible. Corporate stockholders and creditors are a widely dispersed and incohesive group. The financial claims on the assets of corporations are often held by intermediaries—banks, insurance companies, pension funds, college endowments—so that many of the beneficiaries (depositors, insured individuals, students) are not even aware that they are the beneficiaries. Moreover, the market for these claims is both volatile and complex, so that even if the

"owners" are aware of their ownership, they cannot easily identify any decline in the value of their claims with the actions of government. People are often led to believe by the press, politicians and a variety of social activists that costs can be imposed on corporations without harming individuals. . . . The costs . . . imposed on the corporation are in fact imposed on . . . the corporation's stockholders and bondholders, consumers and workers.[45]

It is not certain where this process will lead, but it is likely that when investors become convinced that the rights of managers to use their corporations' assets in the interests of stockholders and creditors are very tenuous or when they become convinced that the contractual rights represented by their shares of stock or bonds are likely to be abrogated because of regulation, they will simply stop investing in corporations. This has already happened in the energy industry, as indicated by a recent *Washington Times* article entitled "Utilities No Longer a Safe Haven for Investors in Stocks."[46] The article discusses the regulatory restrictions imposed on utilities regarding plant siting and construction, environmental controls, and so on, as well as the accompanying decline in the value of electric utility stocks over the past several years. Jensen and Meckling have predicted a particularly gloomy future for private industry, one that seems very possible, especially in the energy industry:

The effect of the erosion of private rights [because of regulation] will show up first as a reduction in the capitalized values of the claims on assets of firms. What has happened to equity values in the last decade is thus consistent with the hypothesis that private rights are deteriorating at an increasing rate. The total return on Standard & Poor's 500 (adjusted for inflation) over the period 1965–75 was minus 20 percent (for 1964–74 it was minus 31 percent). Since 1926, no other 10-year periods—even those that include the market crash and the Great Depression—show such low returns as these two. . . . Many corporations will be able to remain in business only to the extent that they can finance their operations out of internally generated cash flows or through financing or subsidies from the public sector. Some firms will simply go out of business, selling off those assets that have value in other uses and abandoning those that don't. Other firms will take different organizational forms. Some will be nationalized, some will become labor managed. Large corporations will become more like Conrail, Amtrak and the Post Office. One likely scenario begins with the creation of a crisis by the politicians and the press. In some cases, the crisis will be blamed on the "bad" things corporations do or might do.

The remedy will be more and more controls on corporations (something like what has been happening in the transportation and oil industries). When the controls endanger the financial structure of the corporations, the corporations will be subsidized by the public sector, at the cost of more controls. When the controls bring the industry to the brink of collapse, the government will take over. The details of the scenario will no doubt vary. Some firms, for example, will be driven out of business simply because of regulatory costs. Although we believe that our forecasts have a high probability of being realized, their realization is not a certainty. Indeed, we hope that bringing the problem to the attention of the public will generate a solution. Moreover, even if our predictions are realized, it won't happen tomorrow, and it won't mean the end of humanity. It will mean only that we will be much poorer and—to the extent that the role of government expands— much less free.[47]

Jensen and Meckling have noted that this type of scenario is already being played out in the transportation and oil industries (with the government takeover of Penn Central and the expanded regulation of the oil industry). The costs of regulation and other government controls are nowhere more prevalent than in the nuclear power industry, which has been besieged by the anti-energy coalition for more than a decade.

The Antinuclear Power Industry

The groups formally affiliated with C/LEC, along with many others in the anti-industry coalition, have chosen the nuclear power industry as one of their major targets. Even before C/LEC was put together, many of its allies were working to stop the private development of nuclear power. Among these groups were Ralph Nader's "Critical Mass" Energy Project, the Sierra Club, Friends of the Earth, the Environmental Defense Fund, the National Center for Appropriate Technology, the Natural Resources Defense Council, Environmental Action, the Institute for Policy Studies, and dozens of local groups such as the Clamshell Alliance, in New England. Taxpayer funding of these groups has been substantial, including $359,000 for Environmental Action during 1979–81; $76,133 for the Environmental Defense Fund during 1980–81; $3,822,000 for the National Center for Appropriate Technology during 1978–81; $871,947 for the National Wildlife Federation during 1980–82; $1,367,945 for the Natural Resources Defense Council during 1979–82; $795,946 for the Sierra Club during 1979–82; and $30,000 for Friends of the Earth in 1980.[48]

Amory Lovins, who is something of a guru for the antinuclear movement, has explained what is apparently its basic philosophical stance: "Even if nuclear power were clean, safe, economic, assured of ample fuel, and benign per se, it would still be unattractive because of its political implications."[49] In *Groundswell*, a newsletter of the antinuclear movement, a brief history of the movement states that its antecedents are "the anti-war movement [that] set a precedent for citizen challenge of . . . corporate power," the "consumer movement" that "encouraged average citizens to be more skeptical of the safety and price of the products they buy," and the "public power" movement that advocates government control of power production in the United States.[50] Moreover, the newsletter states that "for the majority of these groups nuclear power represented more than just a dangerous technology—it was a symbol of growing political and economic centralization and corporate dominance of community life."[51] Thus, the nuclear power industry has become a symbol of what anti-industry advocates dislike about corporations.

The effect of the media campaign waged by the antinuclear industry is that the public and Congress are more likely to acquiesce in the extreme regulatory costs imposed on the industry—and, therefore, on consumers—and lobbied for by the antinuclear activists. One particularly costly tactic has been regulatory delay and long, costly litigation. Barry Commoner, a leader of the antinuclear movement, gave up his scientific career as a biologist to pursue a political career, promoting what he says are "the basic ideas . . . first put forward by Karl Marx."[52] Explaining the movement's tactics in an interview with the *Wall Street Journal*, Commoner boasted that they "would succeed through harassment tactics that would delay nuclear plants, escalate their costs and make them uneconomical to build."[53] This strategy has worked remarkably well, maybe even better than Commoner and his colleagues thought possible. The activists have used the courts to tie up nuclear plant construction with such absurdities as convincing a federal regulator to block construction of a plant in Boston because of allegations that the plant, which had already cost $2 billion, may damage some clam larvae.[54] In other instances, they conducted filibusters by standing up and reading newspapers in court and asking such questions as "What would happen if Cuban gunships attacked the Long Island coast?"[55]

131

There is a maze of regulations and laws regarding nuclear power plant construction, and the antinuclear activists have used them to delay plant construction. The delays have been very costly to the consumers of electricity, which is hardly an outcome a consumer activist would boast about. It now takes as long as 14 years to go through the licensing process to build a nuclear power plant, compared with less than a year in the mid-1960s.[56] This is double the time it takes in other countries. Because construction costs become inflated as delays occur, electricity bills are much higher than they would be otherwise. As M. Stanton Evans has reported:

> In a typical hassle over construction of a nuclear plant, an electric utility may have to deal with state public service, environmental, or other agencies; the Federal Nuclear Regulatory Commission; the Environmental Protection Agency; and various state and federal courts. Protests can be lodged with any of these entities—resulting in an order to suspend operations until the question is resolved—and frequently issues settled at one level can be opened again at another. This procedure can drag on for years (and has done so), resulting in an enormous increase in construction costs and interest charges. These increased costs are then invoked by the opponents as decisive evidence that nuclear power is too expensive. It is estimated, for example, that construction of the proposed nuclear plant at Seabrook, New Hampshire, has been delayed at least two years by regulatory intervention [as of 1979], at an added cost of $419 million in construction outlays, plus many other millions in losses to the state economy. The American Council on Nuclear Energy calculates that regulatory constraints extend the period from contract award to completion of a nuclear project by almost three years on the average, at an increased cost of $200 million per project.[57]

In addition to delaying construction through its licensing requirements, the Federal Nuclear Regulatory Commission now sometimes denies licenses even after companies have spent a dozen years complying with all prior licensing requirements and even have completed construction of the plant. In January 1984 the commission denied Commonwealth Edison a license to operate its new Byron, Illinois, plant, which had cost about $3.7 billion, because the commission's bureaucrats (many of them former antinuclear activists) had "no confidence" in some of the quality-control procedures that had been used during construction.[58] Is there any wonder why U.S. utilities have not placed an order for a new nuclear plant since 1978?

As a result of regulation-induced cost overruns, several electric utilities are faced with possible bankruptcy—an event that has not occurred in the United States since the Great Depression. The Consumers Power Company of Michigan, the Public Service Company of New Hampshire, the Public Service Company of Indiana, and the Long Island Lighting Company were all said to have been teetering on the brink of bankruptcy by mid-1984. The Public Service Company of Indiana was forced to abandon its Marble Hill plant after spending $2.3 billion.[59] The Consumers Power Company of Michigan is running out of money to pay its bills and says that if its critics (that is, the antinuclear activists) do not drop their opposition, it will have to declare bankruptcy. Consumers Power halted construction of its Midland plant in July 1984 while state politicians debated whether to save the plant, which at that time was $3.25 billion over budget. The Public Service Company of New Hampshire has already spent nearly $6 billion on its hopelessly delayed Seabrook nuclear plant. The Long Island Lighting Company, by 1984, was paying $1 million per day on loans for its Shoreham plant (completed in 1975, but inoperative since then because of lawsuits over safety and emergency-evacuation plans) and losing $1.5 million for every day that construction was delayed. Cincinnati Gas and Electric announced in early 1984 that it was halting further construction of its William H. Zimmer plant in Moscow, Ohio. It is planning on converting the facility, 97 percent finished at a cost of $1.7 billion, to a coal-burning installation. Government officials often seem rather indifferent or even hostile toward the plight of these companies. For example, New York governor Mario Cuomo said of Long Island Lighting, "Let them take a bath. . . . They're a private corporation."[60] In New Hampshire, Michael Holmes, a member of the state's "citizen utility board," said that "It may be in the best interests of the ratepayers that the company [Public Service Company of New Hampshire] go bankrupt."[61]

Consumers and investors are beginning to feel the effects of the antinuclear crusade. Moody's Investor's Services has dropped the ratings on bonds issued by several of the utilities, which has hampered their ability to raise capital and keep their projects going. Utility investors have become so reluctant to loan funds that between 1976 and 1981 alone 80 nuclear plants were canceled owing to lack

133

of financing. Stockholders have also seen the value of their investments shrink. The price of Long Island Lighting stock dropped from $17 to $10.13 per share during 1983, costing the company's 181,127 stockholders an estimated $70 million.[62] Long Island consumers, who already have among the highest electric bills in the nation, are expected to pay up to 50 percent more to help cover the costs of the Shoreham plant. The Public Service Company of New Hampshire foresees a 40–50 percent rate increase if its Seabrook 2 plant is ever finished. Other utilities are faced with similar prospects—and the antinuclear activists continue to tout themselves as protectors of the consumers.

There are, however, legitimate reasons for protesting the relationship between the nuclear power industry and government, as the antinuclear movement does. The industry, for example, has long been subsidized through government sponsorship of research, enrichment of fuels, and disposal of nuclear waste. A particularly important subsidy was created by the federal Price-Anderson Act of 1957.[63] Under this act, maximum liability for any facility licensed by the federal government's Atomic Energy Commission was fixed at approximately $560 million. In short, the effect of the act is to socialize the risk facing the nuclear power industry. If a free market in insurance were permitted to operate, the market could more accurately reflect the true risk involved in nuclear power generation. If this were the case, insurance rates would probably be much higher, which would leave fewer funds available for nuclear power plant construction. It is even possible that the industry could not survive on its own. The Price-Anderson Act leads to an overallocation of resources to nuclear power generation at the expense of other energy sources. Furthermore, it benefits the electric utility companies, their suppliers, power plant producers such as Babcock and Wilcox and the Bechtel Corporation, construction unions and electrical workers unions, architects, and others affiliated with the industry. This all comes at the expense of consumers and taxpayers generally. Whether the nuclear power industry is to survive is best left up to the free market, which means the abolition of the Price-Anderson Act and other subsidies.

Unfortunately, the U.S. antinuclear movement, although giving lip service to the idea of letting the market work now that some electric utilities are threatened with bankruptcy, is apparently not interested in resource allocation by way of the free market. Rather, it favors extreme regulatory restrictions that, according to the movement itself, are specifically designed to drive the nuclear power industry into extinction. The interests of energy consumers are best served by a free market allocation of energy, not a governmentally planned and subsidized industry or one regulated by spokesmen for the anti-energy industry whose influence is exerted largely through the courts and the regulatory commissions.

Summary and Conclusions

Because of regulation-induced crises in the energy industry, the anti-industry coalition has chosen this industry as a target for its disinformation and lobbying activities. One of the best organized and financed coalitions ever put together by the far left in U.S. politics, C/LEC has devoted most of its resources toward these ends. C/LEC has used millions of taxpayers' dollars to finance its campaign to promote greater government control over the energy industry, all in the guise of protecting consumers. Far from protecting the consumers, however, the policies that C/LEC promotes have caused energy shortages and higher prices.

Nowhere has the anti-energy industry been more effective than in the nuclear power industry, where regulation has sharply increased the cost of producing electricity and the rates that consumers must pay. The anti-energy coalition seeks to force its will on the public through a vast array of proposed and existing government controls over the use of private property. Wherever the next regulation-induced industrial crisis crops up, it is likely that the well-honed resources of C/LEC will meet the challenge.

VII. Politics and the Environment

> For the first time, it has become vital to inquire into the cost of unrestricted material growth and to consider alternatives to its continuation. . . . [S]hort of a world effort, today's already explosive gaps and inequalities [of income] will continue to grow larger: The outcome can only be disaster.
>
> —Donella Meadows et al.
> *The Limits to Growth*

> [I]t may be time to view the faults of the U.S. capitalist economic system from the vantage point of a socialist alternative.
>
> —Barry Commoner
> *The Poverty of Power*

> For over a hundred years we have been exhorted to embrace socialism because it would give us more goods. Since it has so lamentably failed to achieve this where it has been tried, we are now urged to adopt it because more goods after all are not important. The aim is still progressively to increase the share of the resources whose use is determined by political authority and the coercion of any dissenting minority.
>
> —Friedrich Hayek
> *Southern Economic Journal*

Crises, real or imagined, have always given interventionists an opportunity to make a case for expanded government control of the means of production and the redistribution of wealth. This has been true of the energy crisis, the health care crisis, and even the so-called crisis of confidence. Like clockwork, every time the economy enters a recession, there are calls for national economic planning (usually disguised as industrial policy or a similar euphemism). When the economy is healthy, there are calls for intervention to combat the alleged ill effects of economic growth (for example, pollution and inequalities of incomes). No matter what happens to the U.S. standard of living, attempts are always being made to improve the situation by granting greater powers to the central government. An important example of this phenomenon is the

137

environmental crisis. For years we have heard that unless greater power to regulate private industry and redistribute wealth is given to the central government, industrial pollution may lead to disastrous consequences. There are clearly a great many environmental problems in the United States, but (as shown below) they have been caused primarily by government intervention, not by the allegedly faulty workings of the market system.[1]

Americans are clearly concerned about the environment. Throughout the 1970s public opinion polls consistently showed that about 90 percent of all Americans surveyed were concerned with environmental degradation.[2] There is a strong preference to do something about the environmental problems we face, but the key question is, what should be done? As shown in this chapter, free markets and private property are essential if we are to solve many of our problems. In fact, many of the problems discussed have arisen precisely because of government intervention that has attenuated private property rights and interfered in other ways with how markets help protect the environment. This is where tax-funded politics fits in. This chapter discusses taxpayer funding of several so-called environmentalist interest groups and illustrates how the political efforts of these groups have often been harmful to the environment by encouraging greater government control over natural resources.

It is important to note that in referring to "environmentalist interest groups" we do not lump all such groups into one overall category. What is said here refers only to the specific cases mentioned. Furthermore, there is a vast difference of opinion between the attitudes of the political activists within many environmentalist organizations and many of the citizens who are their dues-paying members. For instance, the leadership of the National Wildlife Federation often espouses interventionist or even radical approaches to environmental problems, although nearly three-fourths of the membership considers itself conservative enough to have voted for Ronald Reagan in 1980.[3] In sum, many—perhaps most—citizens who call themselves environmentalists support the concepts of private property and free enterprise, that is, the economic philosophy that President Reagan espouses. Many (though not all) of the special-interest groups that claim to represent them, however, do not support these concepts. And as is usually the case, the non-support group, which is relatively small and well organized, has had a far greater impact on environmental policy. A closer look at the intellectual roots of modern environmental interventionism will help explain this situation.

The Intellectual Roots of Environmental Interventionism

There are dozens of environmentalist interest groups, including the National Wildlife Federation, the National Audubon Society, the Sierra Club, the Natural Resources Defense Council, the Environmental Defense Fund, Friends of the Earth, the Wilderness Society, and Environmental Action. For more than 20 years, segments of this movement have pursued a political agenda inspired by several well-known writers whose works have become part of the gospel of the modern environmentalist movement. Most of these writers have also been deeply involved in the political activities of the special-interest groups as trustees, directors of regional offices, advisers, and so on. A closer examination of their writings will help us to understand what these special-interest groups hope to accomplish and why they have so often turned to interventionist approaches to environmental policy.

One of the first major spokespersons for the environmental movement was Rachel Carson, who published *Silent Spring* in 1962.[4] The theme of Carson's enormously popular book was: "Man has lost the capacity to foresee and to forestall. He will end by destroying the earth."[5] The book is a fable about how man's use of pesticides had interfered with the food chain and destroyed the birds, fish, livestock, insects, and almost every other living thing. Unless drastic action is taken, wrote Carson, the fable could become a reality. Carson had a strong political perspective in her writing, attributing the potential catastrophe to the free enterprise system and criticizing salesmanship as "the soft sell and the hidden persuaders" who allegedly manipulated people into purchasing dangerous poisons. Carson also held industry accountable for the careless use of pesticides and other poisons and the way people neglect to read warning labels. She was especially concerned about DDT and what she thought was a poisoning of the U.S. food supply by pesticides. Her basic prescription was more regulation of industry to harness the evils of modern industrial technology.

Despite an almost complete lack of evidence, Carson's views became extraordinarily popular and are considered to be the basis of much environmental legislation, from the banning of DDT to the Toxic Substances Control Act of 1976. The political response to such books can be described as hysterical and was often lacking in logic or evidence. A case in point was the banning of DDT, which was apparently a purely political decision. The Environmental Protection Agency (EPA) appointed a hearing examiner who listened to evidence for and against the banning of DDT from 125 witnesses over about three months of hearings. The examiner concluded:

> DDT as offered under the registrations involved herein is not misbranded. DDT is not a carcinogenic hazard to man. The uses of DDT under the registrations involved here do not have a deleterious effect on fresh-water fish, estuarine organisms, wild birds or other wildlife. . . . [I]n my opinion, the evidence in this proceeding supports the conclusion that there is a present need for the essential uses of DDT.[6]

Less than two months later, William D. Ruckelshaus, then administrator of the EPA, banned DDT from use in the United States even though he had never attended any of the hearings and later admitted that he had not even read the transcripts of the hearings.[7] The 1972 banning of DDT was a political victory for the National Audubon Society, the Sierra Club, and the Environmental Defense Fund, which had spearheaded the campaign for the ban.

Another writer to have a powerful effect on the environmentalist movement was entomologist Paul Ehrlich, who published *The Population Bomb: Population Control or Race to Oblivion* in 1968.[8] The book was copublished by Ballantine Books and the Sierra Club. One of the book's major themes was the neo-Malthusian notion that population growth would lead to starvation and death throughout the world. The fatal flaw in Ehrlich's predictions, however, was that he assumed that for the first time in human history, technology would remain constant, so that high-technology, capital-intensive agriculture would not be able to produce larger amounts of food. Ehrlich has ignored this flaw, though, and he still believes that the root of the world's problems is too many factories, too many machines, and "too many people."[9]

From this perspective, Ehrlich repeated Carson's message that the earth was becoming poisoned, and he declared that a solution required "many apparently brutal and heartless decisions."[10] For example, he proposed the creation of a "powerful government agency" that would research and impose such solutions as "compulsory birth regulation," the addition of temporary sterilants to public water supplies, and financial rewards and penalties designed to "discourage reproduction." These policies have been imple-

140

mented—not in the United States, but in China. Ehrlich has also become known as the foremost proponent of "zero economic growth," and he believes that wealth should be forcefully taken from some to give to others so that it is equally distributed worldwide. Because of this compendium of views, Ehrlich's politics have been described as "ecological totalitarianism," which seems appropriate.[11]

Barry Commoner has also been very influential and has been described as "one of the most visible scientists in the country."[12] Commoner, who was trained as a biologist, first entered public life at the Senate hearings on environmental problems held by Sen. Edmund Muskie (D–Maine) in 1969. At the widely publicized hearings, Commoner warned that "nothing less than a change in the political and social system, including revision of the Constitution, was necessary to save the country from destroying its natural environment."[13] He argued that modern technology was destroying the nation's "capital" of land, water, and other resources: "Our present system of technology is not merely consuming this capital, but threatening—probably within the next 50 years—to destroy it irreparably."[14] To deal with this problem, Commoner suggested that the Constitution be revised to allow such unconstitutional governmental empowerments as a two-year ban on all technological research and innovation, the creation of a new international governmental body to ban all pollution of the oceans, and a new "ecological authority" to supervise all construction projects.

In addition to putting aside many of the economic and civil liberties embodied in the Constitution, Commoner urged revisions in our current system of production: "If, as I believe, environmental pollution is a sign of major incompatibilities between our system of production and the environment that supports it, then, if we are to survive, we must successfully confront these economic obligations."[15] The way to "confront these economic obligations," according to Commoner, is through socialism.[16] But socialism as a cure for environmental problems defies reality, for the socialization of natural resources is a major cause of environmental despoilation, and some of the most severe pollution in the world is found in socialist countries. In 1979 Commoner abandoned his career as a scientist, founded a new political party, called the Citizens Party, and in 1980 ran for president. His major position was that there should be greater government control of industry in the name of the environment.

141

Several other writers have repeated the theme that modern industrialized society is leading to an environmental apocalypse and have prescribed halting economic growth and redistributing wealth. Microbiologist René Dubos and Barbara Ward (also known as Lady Jackson), professor of international economic development at Columbia University, gained prominence during the mid-1970s for their own doomsday scenario. They prepared a widely discussed report for the United Nations Conference on the Human Environment in 1972, predicting that if economic growth persisted, "then we cannot rate very highly the chances of reaching the year 2000 with our planet still functioning safely and our humanity securely preserved."[17] Their political prescription denounced the industrial revolution and its "vile slums" and "urban degradation" and criticized the free enterprise system as producing "private affluence and public squalor." The essential "solution," according to Dubos and Ward, was the redistribution of wealth domestically and also from western, industrialized nations to less-developed, Third World nations.

Perhaps the most widely publicized and influential group of modern environmentalist writers is 17 people affiliated with the Massachusetts Institute of Technology (MIT) and with the Club of Rome. The Club of Rome was founded by Aurelio Peccei, an Italian businessman, and was made up mostly of intellectuals from many countries who shared the belief that existing institutions could not effectively deal with many of the world's problems, particularly those affecting the environment. The MIT group (which included 10 Americans) was commissioned by the Club of Rome to do a study that was published under the title, *The Limits to Growth*.[18] The book caused an instant international furor and sold an incredible 4 million copies in just a few years. The principal predictions of the book were hard-hitting but deliberately understated:

> If the present growth trends in world population, industrialization, pollution, food production, and resource depletion continue unchanged, the limits to growth on this planet will be reached sometime within the next one hundred years. The most probable result will be a rather sudden and uncontrollable decline in both population and industrial capacity.[19]

The prescription called for by the Club of Rome was an immediate halt to economic growth, since all our resources were assumed to be "finite," and a redistribution of "world wealth" to Third World governments to avoid potential "conflicts" caused by the impending apocalypse.

The unsubstantiated claims made by the MIT scholars in *The Limits to Growth* were so outrageous that they drew immediate and sharp criticism. The fatal flaw in the study, as analysts quickly pointed out, was that it assumed that there would be no human response and no change in technology in the foreseeable future that would address the environmental problems considered in the study. Nobel laureate and economist Gunnar Myrdal was outraged by the "inexcusably careless" nature of the study, which he referred to as "quasi-learnedness."[20] Anatomist Lord Zuckerman, chief scientific adviser to the British government, claimed that the study had been praised only by the "scientifically uninitiated"; he remarked that "the only kind of exponential growth with which the book does not deal . . . is the growth of human knowledge," and he asked, "What are we—ants, lemmings, or rational human beings?"[21]

Not only did *The Limits to Growth* ignore how environmental problems have historically spawned human inventiveness and technological advance, but it also ignored the role of the price system in resource allocation. One example of this monumental blunder is the way in which oil shortages were predicted. The world demand for oil, which had been increasing, and oil supply were extrapolated along current trends. A chart showed that in just a few decades oil demand would outstrip known supplies of oil, thereby creating a crisis. The report made no mention of the role that oil prices played in altering supply and demand. An accurate discussion would have mentioned how, if demand exceeded supply, the price of oil would rise, providing incentives for consumers to cut back or conserve and for producers to discover and produce more oil. Price also provides incentives to search for and market substitute sources of energy, such as natural gas, coal, and nuclear power. The history of the energy industry reveals that when one dominant source of energy or light (for example, whale oil during the late nineteenth century) becomes relatively scarce and therefore higher priced, the development of substitutes is stimulated as well as the exploration for and development of additional sources of the scarce resource.

In light of these glaring omissions, *The Limits to Growth* has been discredited. Even the Club of Rome repudiated the book. Four years after publication, the Club of Rome reversed its position and advocated "more growth," but this development received little attention. The club's explanation of its reversal, as reported in *Time* magazine, is what Julian Simon of the University of Maryland has called a "masterpiece of facesaving double-talk":

> The Club's founder, Italian industrialist Aurelio Peccei, says that *Limits* was intended to jolt people from the comfortable idea that present growth trends could continue indefinitely. That done, he says, the Club could then seek ways to close the widening gap between rich and poor nations—inequities that, if they continue, could all too easily lead to famine, pollution and war. The Club's startling shift, Peccei says, is thus not so much a turnabout as part of an evolving strategy.[22]

In an exceptionally candid statement, Peccei conceded to the *New York Times* that "the limits to growth report had served its purpose of getting the world's attention focused on the ecological *dangers of unplanned and uncontrolled population and industrial expansion*" (emphasis added).[23]

The truth about the *The Limits to Growth* is out, but not before it and similar studies caused what environmentalist René Dubos called "public hysteria." These studies probably enabled Congress to exert much greater influence over the affairs of private industry, through environmental regulation, than it would have otherwise. Moreover, the criticisms and repudiation of *The Limits to Growth* did not receive nearly the media attention that the original study did, so that despite the study's failure as a legitimate piece of public policy research, it was a great success for its authors and supporters. The environmentalist movement has clearly recognized this, for it has continued to promote the same kinds of falsehoods and wild projections in hopes of scaring us into accepting its redistributionist policies. For example, in 1980 a government-funded report, *The Global 2000 Report to the President*, was published that contained projections nearly identical to those in *The Limits to Growth:*

> If present trends continue, the world in 2000 will be more crowded, more polluted, less stable ecologically, and more vulnerable to disruption than the world we live in now. Serious stresses involving population, resources, and environment are clearly visible ahead. . . . Barring revolutionary advances in technology, life for most people on earth will be more precarious in 2000 than it is now . . . unless the nations of the world act decisively to alter current trends.[24]

144

The *Global 2000 Report* was a joint project of the Department of State, the Council on Environmental Quality, the Department of Agriculture, the Department of Energy, the Department of the Interior, the Agency for International Development, the Central Intelligence Agency, the EPA, the Federal Emergency Management Agency, the National Aeronautics and Space Administration, the National Science Foundation, and the National Oceanic and Atmospheric Administration.[25] That so many federal agencies were involved in this project is testimony to the political clout of some of the environmentalist interest groups. Even some of the very same people who helped prepare *The Limits to Growth* were involved with the *Global 2000 Report;* they included Anne Ehrlich (wife of Paul Ehrlich); Dennis and Donella Meadows, among the coauthors of *The Limits to Growth;* Jay Forrester, the intellectual father of the Club of Rome studies; and several other members of the Club of Rome.[26] The organizations identified with these individuals in the *Global 2000* study also included many major environmentalist interest groups, including the Natural Resources Defense Council, Friends of the Earth, the WorldWatch Institute, Environmental Action, the National Wildlife Federation, the Club of Rome, the National Audubon Society, and the Population Council. These groups used this report, funded by taxpayers, to legitimize their political agenda. It also helped the government agencies sponsoring it to argue for even bigger budgets to solve this alleged series of crises.

The *Global 2000 Report* turned out to be another wildly inaccurate headline grabber. In a meticulous study of whether or not the study's claims had any validity, Julian Simon concluded: "The facts . . . point in quite the opposite direction on every single important aspect of their prediction for which I could find any data at all."[27] Simon laid out the data, but his work is likely to have much less impact on public opinion than the study itself, which had the aura of an official government report. Such reports are likely to be judged correct regardless of their contents, and they are usually widely publicized as the latest direction in government policy.

In summary, these purported scientists seem to consistently shun the scientific method. In all of the works discussed here, there is a serious lack of data, and when data do exist, they are severely distorted. This has even been acknowledged by many of these authors. As Paul Ehrlich admitted, "One of the major drawbacks of systems ecology [that is, *The Limits to Growth*–type studies] is the relative paucity of data available with which to develop and test models."[28] The MIT group that worked on *The Limits to Growth* also stated, "Data on important physical, chemical, and ecological phenomena and parameters are . . . inadequate for providing the foundation for definitive statements about environmental effects."[29]

The power of government has been enhanced by segments of the environmentalist lobby, although it is questionable whether environmental problems are less or more severe than before the movement gained so much momentum. The federal government has funded many of the activities of the environmentalist interventionists, which is one reason why these people are among the most effective lobbyists in the nation.

Tax Funding of Environmental Interventionism

The well-publicized ideas of the above writers and their allies in the environmentalist interest groups have led to the adoption of dozens of new laws and thousands of regulations that affect the organization of industry (see Table A7.1, in appendix). The conduit through which these ideas are transformed into legislation is the leadership of special-interest groups such as the National Wildlife Federation, the Sierra Club, the Environmental Defense Fund, and Environmental Action. These professional lobbying organizations have promoted a no-growth agenda in the halls of Congress, and many politicians and bureaucrats sympathetic to these goals have given the groups millions of taxpayers' dollars to help them carry on their lobbying campaigns. Table A7.1 lists recent, selected federal grants to environmentalist interest groups, including $915,377 to the National Wildlife Federation during 1976–82; $790,746 to the Sierra Club during 1978–81; $221,483 to the National Audubon Society during 1977–81; $96,131 to the Environmental Defense Fund during 1978–82; $1,309,540 to the Center for Renewable Resources during 1979–81; $3,828,885 to the National Center for Appropriate Technology during 1978–81; $538,466 to Environmental Action during 1979–81; and more than $1 million to the Natural Resources Defense Council during 1978–82. A brief discussion of some of these groups will help explain the uses to which these tax dollars have been put—uses with which many of the groups' members would disagree.

Environmental Action

Environmental Action has claimed that in 1981 its major efforts were "directed toward helping dedicated grassroots environmen-

146

talists fight the pro-pollution policies of President Reagan and Environmental Protection Agency administrator Anne Gorsuch."[30] It has also established the Environmental Action Foundation, which "is a separate, nonmembership organization which provides technical and organizing expertise on complex environmental issues."[31]

Environmental Action was founded in 1970, when it served as coordinator for Earth Day, a series of organized teach-ins and protests. Its recent lobbying activities have included support for establishing a federal solar bank; helping secure the passage of the Superfund bill; advocacy of a national "bottle bill" requiring deposits on returnable bottles; opposition to budget cuts for Amtrak; and extensive lobbying for greater regulation of the nuclear power industry. Two of the organization's long-term efforts are the Dirty Dozen Campaign and the Filthy Five Campaign, which promote the view that the source of environmental problems is the profit motive and the free enterprise system. The Dirty Dozen Campaign focuses on "12 of the most obvious anti-environment bad guys in Congress"—for example, those who disagree most frequently with Environmental Action.[32] The Filthy Five Campaign is intended "to make voters—and politicians—aware of the large polluting corporations that contribute lavishly to candidates all around the country."[33]

Environmental Action's anticorporate bias shows up in its literature in such statements as "we have successfully analyzed, criticized, and challenged one major source of our nation's energy problems—the . . . electric utility industry" and "the reason for all this [the energy crisis], and the real villain (you're right!) is the oil industry and its greedy manipulation of a small energy crunch into a full-blown disaster."[34] The oil companies, says this literature, are "determined to keep America hooked on high energy use, conservation be damned. . . . Nothing that stands in their way is sacred— fresh air, safe drinking water, wilderness."[35] Thus, Environmental Action, which lists such people as Heather Booth of the Midwest Academy (see chapter 2) as members of its advisory board, has as one of its primary functions the spread of its anticorporate biases through its publications and the news media.

There is no doubt that the organization and its allies were quite successful in perpetuating the myth that the energy crisis of the 1970s was caused by "corporate greed," instead of the government's own price control and entitlement programs. In its 1983 Annual Report, Environmental Action boasted of "extensive coverage of our legislative and research work in the broadcast and print media," and it listed coverage in the *New York Times, Parade, USA Today,* the *Los Angeles Times,* the *Washington Post,* the *St. Louis Globe Democrat, Family Circle,* and *Woman's Day,* along with staff appearances on "Good Morning America," the Cable News Network, and "a host of local shows."[36] The annual report also discussed how Environmental Action is involved in many other segments of the anti-industry coalition, such as "the Washington, D.C. Coalition for Occupational Safety and Health, The National Coalition Against the Misuse of Pesticides, the Safe Energy Communication Council, the Citizen/Labor Energy Coalition, the Committee for Full Employment, Citizens Against Nuclear War, and several other working coalitions that formed around issues when the need arose."

The Sierra Club

The *New York Times* recently described the Sierra Club as the most influential environmentalist group in the nation and "the strongest of the environmental groups which lobby."[37] In a recent listing of its priorities, the club stated that it "is now involved in a major, ongoing effort to influence funding for environmental agencies and programs."[38] It said that it is mainly involved in lobbying the House and Senate appropriations committees to increase the budgets of the Department of the Interior and EPA. This seems a sensible goal in that these agencies have in turn given the Sierra Club hundreds of thousands of taxpayers' dollars. In addition to helping bureaucrats in these two agencies to lobby Congress for more appropriations for their agencies, the Sierra Club claimed that "our" public lands and their protection are top priorities.[39] In a publication refuting the Sierra Club's opposition to attempts to reestablish private ownership of previously nationalized land, John Hooper has stated that we "own" 740 million acres of "public lands," so that

> at present, about one third of the land in this country is owned by its citizens. A common misperception is that these lands belong to some distant landlord called the "federal government." While it is true that federal agencies *administer* this land on behalf of the citizens of the United States, *we,* in fact, are the true owners. . . . At present, federal lands are protected from overexploitation and abuse by a great number of regulations and a set of key land-use policies. . . . Privatization would remove such restrictions—and would make lands vulnerable to the sort of short-term profit taking that many corporations practice in time of economic stress.[40]

148

The one true statement here is that the federal government owns and controls more than one-third of the land in the country. As shown below, however, it is this one-third—not the land that is held privately—that has been grossly mismanaged and overexploited. The "public lands" that "we all own" actually belong to no one. The true test of whether you own something or not is an affirmative answer to the question: Can I sell it? Because no citizen can sell "his or her share" of the public lands, the concept of public ownership is misleading. The resources no one really owns, such as public grazing lands or parks, tend to be overused and run down, for there is no strong incentive to preserve them for future use. By contrast, private owners have incentives to preserve their resources for future use. Corporate landowners, if they are profit maximizers, must do this to maximize long-run profits. By contrast, government bureaucrats have no such incentives and usually act in response to the political pressures of the day, as exerted by special interests. Government decision makers generally have much shorter time horizons than do private businessmen—usually about as long as the next election—which is why government-owned resources tend to be overused relative to privately owned resources.

Another legislative priority of the Sierra Club, and of some other environmentalist groups, is to stop the private development of nuclear power. In a publication entitled *Nuclear Power and the Sierra Club,* the club stated that it opposes the licensing, construction, and operation of new nuclear fission plants and the systematic reduction of society's dependence on nuclear fission as a source of electric power by a phased closure and decommissioning of operating commercial electric power reactors. In taking this philosophical stance, the Sierra Club joined with other members of the anti-energy coalition to delay and hinder the development of nuclear power in the United States.

Although the Sierra Club lobbies Congress on dozens of different issues from atomic energy to wetlands preservation, its one overriding objective is to oppose economic growth. This is why it opposes not only nuclear power but also other forms of energy, such as coal, hydropower, and natural gas. One 1983 Sierra Club publication written by George Alderson even criticized Congress for not being sufficiently sympathetic to the club's antigrowth views by failing to eliminate the internal combustion engine from automobiles by 1975 and by not legally banning the supersonic transport. David Brower, a member of the club's board of directors, has written, "We've got to search back to our last known safe landmark. I can't say exactly where it is, but I think it's back there about a century when, at the start of the Industrial Revolution, we began applying energy in vast amounts to tools with which we began tearing the environment apart."[41] Thus, to approach the Sierra Club's "safe landmark" would require turning back the U.S. standard of living to where it was more than a century ago. It is not comforting to read that in attempts to achieve this objective, the Sierra Club

> has been remarkably successful since the early '70s. We've been instrumental in causing a huge amount of federal legislation to be enacted. The Sierra Club alone has been in the leadership position in persuading the Congress to enact well over 70 environmental measures that are now law. I might add that this is probably the most distinguished record of accomplishment of any environmental group. Indeed, since the beginning of the '70s, the environmental movement has probably showed more staying power and vitality than any other public movement.[42]

The Friends of the Earth

Friends of the Earth, founded in 1971, is a tax-funded environmentalist organization that is similar to the Sierra Club in both its outlook and activities. In a promotional letter, Friends of the Earth's president, Rafe Pomerance, wrote that

> Friends of the Earth is an environmental lobby that operates all over the country. Volunteers in FOE branches mount campaigns to control the spraying of dangerous chemicals on forest land in Wisconsin. They mobilize people in Maine to resist the expansion of nuclear power. They go to battle against the drilling of oil wells off the . . . California coast.[43]

The chairman of the board of directors of Friends of the Earth is David Brower (who is also on the Sierra Club's board). Friends of the Earth is a major participant in the no-growth movement in the United States, as evidenced by its advisory council, which includes Paul Ehrlich and Aurelio Peccei. Anne Ehrlich is listed as a vice-president. In a publication entitled *Progress As If Survival Mattered*, the group's position is clearly stated: "The only really good technology is no technology at all. . . . Technology . . . is taxation without representation imposed by an elitist species [humans] upon the rest of the natural world."[44] The organization also apparently denies the legitimacy of private property, for it believes that all

150

"wealth should be passed from generation to generation, each using what it needs and prudently conserving resources for future generations."[45] Government ownership of the land, according to this view, is necessary to ensure that "wealth" is wisely passed "from generation to generation."

Friends of the Earth is involved in hundreds of different political issues, and some of its major efforts appear to be aimed at supporting the anti–nuclear-power campaign, continuing Rachel Carson's crusade against the use of pesticides, stopping economic development, and adopting government-mandated population control. Although its publications do not usually make statements as extreme as those written by Paul Ehrlich, it has been lobbying for "a national population policy, eventual population stabilization, and the establishment of a foresight capability [that is, population forecasting by the government] for the nation, which would enable the federal government to systematically plan for population growth and demographic change in the U.S."[46] In the April 1984 issue of *Not Man Apart*, the group lamented that there is "no plan, and no effort at the federal level to . . . coordinate long-range national needs," and it called for a policy of "population stabilization." The group proposed to empower the federal government to bring the group itself into the federal bureaucracy to make "official" its pronouncements that population growth is necessarily a bad thing and to implement policies designed to reduce population growth through some form of government coercion.

The blatantly political nature of this tax-funded group is further evidenced by the group's 1984 endorsement of presidential candidate Walter Mondale. The April 1984 edition of *Not Man Apart* editorialized, "The Mondale endorsement begins a new chapter in the history of FOE, as the organization enters a presidential race for the first time. Through FOE PAC, FOE members and staff now will have money and other organizational backing needed to make significant contributions toward the defeat of Ronald Reagan."[47]

The National Wildlife Federation

The National Wildlife Federation is one of the largest tax-funded environmentalist groups, claiming over 4 million members and having a 1982 budget of $37.1 million.[48] Although in its 1983 Annual Report the federation claimed that it "places a special priority on achieving its . . . goals through cooperation rather than confrontation," most of its list of achievements includes legislation that prohibits individuals from owning and using private property. For example, the federation's "noteworthy accomplishments" include passage of the Coastal Barrier Resources Act, which banned various areas from private ownership and development; passage of major funding reductions for the Reagan administration's proposal to privatize portions of previously nationalized lands; the forced resignation of Anne Burford (formerly Gorsuch), head of the EPA; a court decision upholding the right of the government of North Dakota to acquire wetlands; and a court decision invalidating a permit for an oil refinery in Maryland. As in the case of many other similar groups, much of the federation's effort is spent trying to block the use of coal, nuclear power, natural gas, and hydroelectric power. One begins to wonder just what type of energy these individuals think is safe.

The Natural Resources Defense Council

A principal tactic of all these special-interest groups is to lock up economic development in the courts by suing coal producers, natural gas pipeline companies, oil companies, electric utilities, developers of shale oil, real estate developers, and almost every other type of business for failing to pay adequate attention to the hundreds of environmental laws and regulations for which the groups have lobbied successfully. Such groups as the Sierra Club have separate legal defense funds that serve this purpose, but there are other groups, such as the Natural Resources Defense Council (NRDC), that specialize in this type of activity. NRDC has opposed every form of conventional energy use through a variety of imaginative legal tactics, which is one reason why the nuclear power industry has been stymied by the courts (see chapter 6). In its crusade against the nuclear power industry, NRDC sometimes sues to forbid the operation of nuclear plants because of a professed concern for public safety, but the group's tactics are often less direct. For example, NRDC contested the ability of Duke Power to ship its spent nuclear fuel between its own plants for storage, even though that practice is perfectly normal under federal regulations.[49] NRDC was unable to prohibit Duke Power from operating, so it chose to try to block one of the utility's essential operations. NRDC's professed concern over public safety should be met with skepticism. As one of its most experienced attorneys, Tony Roisman, openly admitted, he "didn't have the slightest idea whether nuclear power is safe."[50]

NRDC has also been instrumental in all but closing down much

152

of the U.S. coal industry, making the country much more dependent on imported petroleum and eliminating thousands of employment opportunities. The group's favorite tactic is to sue the federal government. In 1977, for example, in *NRDC* v. *Hughes,* the group sued the Department of the Interior.[51] The department was forced to greatly expand its prepared environmental impact statement on coal leasing, thereby freezing any new coal leases on federal lands until the lengthy new requirements were met (which took more than four years). The case began in 1975 when John Leshy of NRDC filed a suit against the Department of the Interior because NRDC was dissatisfied with Interior's environmental impact statement and the direction of coal-leasing policy implied by that statement. In 1977 Leshy was appointed to the Department of the Interior and was assigned to defend the same case that he had brought against his new employer two years earlier. Apparently, Leshy was not very effective in his conflicting role. Peter Metzger has summarized the results of this adversary proceeding:

> Using the excuse of the sure delay which would have been caused by a lengthy appeal, and the fact that NRDC was willing to "compromise," the U.S. Departments of Interior and Justice, now staffed with several key people ideologically associated with the plaintiffs, signed away the government's rights of appeal in this case in return for plaintiff NRDC agreeing that a very limited amount of coal leasing could commence. But in part of that agreement, signed on February 25, 1978, government lawyers actually gave NRDC an absolute veto on certain future coal leasing permitted by Interior. . . . When the federal judge was presented with this amazing proposal he disallowed the most flagrant abuse of public trust, which was NRDC's veto privilege, but kept the rest of the restrictions on federal coal leasing which were demanded by NRDC as the "winner" of the lawsuit. . . . Utah Power and Light, the only non-environmentalist party to the case, was excluded from the negotiations between NRDC and Interior. In vain, Utah Power and Light petitioned the appeals court to bar District Judge Pratt from accepting the NRDC-Interior private agreement, but its request was denied. The final result of the negotiated settlement . . . was accepted by the court on June 14, 1978. It "favors" deep mining rather than surface mining, looks with "disfavor" on operations that are "environmentally sensitive," like valley floors, and favors operations that don't require "additional transportation facilities, industrial development or water storage or supply systems." Mining, one is left to believe, is permitted wherever it can't be done.[52]

This is just one example of the tactics that NRDC has used to forestall economic development.

Another law that is used (and abused) by NRDC and other environmental groups is the Endangered Species Act of 1973. In its 1981–82 Annual Report, NRDC stated that it "leads the 80-member Biological Diversity Task Force, affiliated with the Global Tomorrow Coalition [promoters of the discredited *Global 2000 Report*], which seeks to incorporate measures to conserve wild species." The Endangered Species Act was passed because of an understandable concern for dwindling numbers of American bison, whooping cranes, and other rare animals, but it has been exploited to stop energy and other projects. The most famous example is how the snail darter, a small fish, delayed for years the completion of the Tellico Dam in Tennessee. The dam was almost finished when a University of Tennessee ichthyologist who opposed the dam purportedly discovered the snail darter in the Little Tennessee River and claimed that it was an endangered species. Years later, after endless court hearings, it took a special act of Congress to enable the project to proceed—after snail darter populations were found in streams throughout Tennessee and other areas of the country.

Even though the snail darter was never truly endangered, environmentalist attorneys have continued to pursue their strategy with a vengeance, even applying the Endangered Species Act to obscure plants. For instance, the proposed Dickey-Lincoln Dam in Maine was delayed because the Furbish lousewort was threatened, and a wealthy beach community in Antioch, California, stopped development proposals that would allegedly endanger a rare butterfly, two lizards, ten varieties of insects, and a few other local plants.[53] In short, because there are more than a million animal species and thousands of plants, the opportunities to abuse the Endangered Species Act are unlimited, and it will continue to be exploited by NRDC and its allies to stop economic progress.

As revealed in its 1981–82 Annual Report, NRDC has been busy suing the federal government in dozens of different areas, including securing a court order directing EPA to develop controls on all discharges from offshore oil drilling operations; winning a legal challenge under the Toxic Substances Control Act of 1976 and forcing EPA to test 39 categories of chemicals; suing the Department of Energy for its failure to promulgate standards regarding "efficiency of consumer appliances"; suing President Reagan for his failure to use the Solar and Conservation Bank "adequately"; defending the

154

right to sunlight of a residential owner of a solar energy system; and successfully suing Secretary James Watt of the Department of the Interior to block the sale of oil leases. NRDC lawyers undoubtedly find this litigation to be satisfying, but it is also quite profitable. There are at least 23 environmental laws that authorize government payment of fees to attorneys who sue the government, even when they lose (see Table A7.3). An industry newsletter, *Federal Attorney Fee Awards Reporter*, has cited several recent examples of such payments, as follows. In three cases decided by the District of Columbia Circuit Court in February 1982, the court awarded fees to nonprevailing parties on the ground that even though they lost, they "conferred public benefits" in their lawsuit. In a case brought to stop offshore oil leasing in Alaska, the D.C. circuit court ruled that the government had complied with all regulations regarding offshore leasing, but it still awarded environmentalist lawyers $230,000. The Energy Action Educational Foundation (a Citizen/Labor Energy Coalition affiliate) sued to force the Department of the Interior to use alternative bidding systems on Outer Continental Shelf lease sales; the foundation lost but still filed for attorneys' fees. The Sierra Club was awarded $101,895 in April 1982 for having sued EPA, and it is also asking for $300,000 in another case. The Foundation for North American Wild Sheep received $55,000 for its unsuccessful attempt to sue the Department of Agriculture. These are just a few selected examples of just how profitable this business has become.

The Environmental Defense Fund

Another group, the Environmental Defense Fund (EDF), claimed in its 1984 Annual Report to have been awarded $282,066 in attorneys' fees in 1983. EDF's activities are almost identical to those of NRDC, but its 1983 Annual Report provides a particularly interesting and informative look at one element of the environmental interventionism: the politicization of science. As discussed earlier, the federal government banned DDT in 1972 even though the EPA hearing examiner concluded quite forcefully that DDT was safe. These conclusions have been corroborated by scientists George Claus and Karen Bolander in their book *Ecological Sanity*, which shows in painstaking detail how the studies that led to the banning of DDT failed to provide any evidence that DDT was carcinogenic or that it harmed wildlife.[54] Nevertheless, William D. Ruckelshaus, then the EPA administrator, banned DDT even though he was unfamiliar with the evidence. Interestingly, EDF's 1983 Annual

155

Report boasts that this type of action is "the backbone of EDF's efforts." The report states that the organization was born when "a small group of scientists and conservationists teamed up with a skilled attorney [and] presented evidence that DDT was harming ospreys and other wildlife. Their evidence eventually resulted in the elimination of DDT." The document then stated "As EDF built its staff, it soon became known as 'the legal arm of the environmental science community' . . . [which] ultimately spurred . . . regulation of all pesticides." And, moreover, "scientific and economic evidence teamed with skilled legal representation, is a powerful and effective force." While this may be true, it is not clear by any means that society benefits from it.

The National Center for Appropriate Technology

The National Center for Appropriate Technology (NCAT) received nearly $4 million in taxpayers' funds from 1978 to 1981 (see Table A7.1). A 1981 NCAT publication, *NCAT's Best*, stated that "principal funding for the National Center for Appropriate Technology . . . is provided by the U.S. Community Services Administration. . . . NCAT's goal is to encourage widespread use of appropriate technologies that help alleviate problems of low-income Americans."[55] The phrase "appropriate technology" is an appealing one, for who would advocate inappropriate technology? But it is not a very informative phrase unless one digs deeper into the history and literature of this organization.

"Appropriate technology" is meant to imply that existing technology, especially industrial production, is inappropriate for a host of reasons, which have been laid out by the man who has been called the father of appropriate technology, self-described "Buddhist economist," the late E. F. Schumacher. A major point in Schumacher's book, *Small is Beautiful*,[56] is that people would supposedly be much happier if they spent more time performing manual labor: "People who work in this way do not know the difference between work and leisure."[57] The division of labor that has led to large-scale production, technological innovation, and mass marketing of goods and services has deprived people of this "happiness," all to provide many goods that are "inappropriate." According to Schumacher, "Karl Marx appears to have foreseen much of this when he wrote: 'They want production to be limited to useful things, but they forget that the production of too many useful things results in too many useless people.' " Schumacher added that

156

"modern technology . . . is showing an increasingly inhuman face. . . . The technology of mass production is inherently violent, ecologically damaging, self-defeating in terms of non-renewable resources, and stultifying for the human person."[58] The most famous line in the book is "Man is small, therefore, small is beautiful."[59] Following this logic, Schumacher stipulated that man can produce all that he needs to consume from beginning to end or jointly with others only if he resides in a small community. In short, Schumacher urged a return to a Robinson Crusoe economy in which people allegedly enjoyed hard work so much that they did not "differentiate between labor and leisure."

Schumacher, then, provided a rather authoritarian definition of appropriate technology. What he felt was appropriate was his own personal utopian vision, regardless of the views of nearly everyone else. Proponents of this vision are certainly free to express their ideas, but to force them on others through government financing would be totally inappropriate in a free society. In a free market, the technology that evolves exists because entrepreneurs have borne the risks and expended the effort to create it to better serve others in society. This does not mean that entrepreneurs are necessarily altruistic. For example, Henry Ford, by inventing the assembly line, benefited thousands of consumers who could not otherwise have afforded automobiles, and he also became independently wealthy at the same time. Like other critics of capitalism, Schumacher made many derisive remarks about the role of profits in the economic system, but he offered no evidence that he understood it. The type of technology that exists can only be successful (without government subsidization) if it benefits others in society—consumers— and therefore generates profits. Appropriate technology is that which best serves human needs and which facilitates individual cooperation through market exchange.

Part of Schumacher's book argued for greater use of solar energy, and one of the purposes of NCAT is to promote government subsidization of solar energy. *NCAT's Best* is a collection of examples of how "since 1977 . . . more than 17 million dollars in [federal government] grants" has been spent[60] and shows how much of this money has been used to help people buy solar collectors for their homes. For example, NCAT directed government funds to the Iron River Solar Senior Citizens Center in Michigan; funded a "national impetus greenhouse grants program" to help people buy greenhouses; funded the New Mexico Solar Energy Institute; provided

157

funds for Herbert Lakins of Farmington, Maine, to build a four-bedroom solar home as "a highly visible demonstration of low-cost solar construction" in that community; and financed the San Luis Valley Solar Energy Association in Colorado. Other examples of NCAT financing of appropriate technology include thermal shades on windows of houses in New Hampshire; a $27,500 grant to the Passamaquoddy Indian tribe of northern Maine for a "lunar power station"; $1,500 for the Ozark Institute slide show that "demonstrates what the people of the Ozarks are doing in their backyards to beat the energy crisis"; building window-box greenhouses and establishing an "aquaculture demonstration project" in New York City; funding a radio station at Ohio University that "encourages popular dialogue centered on appropriate technology" in its programming; and granting two men in Maine $24,000 to "demonstrate a . . . two-man mussel culturing operation . . . to separate, wash and sort cultured mussels. . . . From this . . . a thorough aquaculture manual entitled *Growing Oysters and Mussels in Maine* was produced."[61]

What all these expenditures illustrate is that the technology that is being subsidized is, in fact, inappropriate. That is, if these activities served consumers better than the more centralized alternatives, there would certainly be a market for them; and if entrepreneurs were as profit hungry as Schumacher's followers insist, they would produce and sell this technology. Moreover, individual consumers would be eager to use this technology if it were superior to the alternatives. The fact that the technology has not been able to persist without the support of millions of dollars in taxpayer subsidies is evidence that it does not serve the interests of consumers better than modern technology. After all, modern technology replaced many of these labor-intensive techniques decades—or in some cases, centuries—ago because consumers found it to be superior. This point has been missed or ignored by the appropriate technology utopians, who have maintained the untenable position that such technology benefits everyone. For example, Amory Lovins, who has popularized Schumacher's work in articles in such major publications as *Foreign Affairs* and the *New Yorker*, has said that "appropriate technology"

> gives us jobs for the unemployed, capital for business people, opportunities for big business to recycle itself, and for small business to innovate, environmental protection for conservationists, better national security for the military, exciting technologies for

the secular, a rebirth of religious values for the religious, world order and equity for the globalists, energy independence for isolationists, radical reforms for the young, traditional virtues of thrift and craftsmanship for the old, civil rights for political liberals, and local autonomy for political conservatives.[62]

Surely if reverting back to eighteenth-century (or earlier) technology were so beneficial to so many people (just about everyone, according to Lovins), it would have appeared spontaneously. But it is neither beneficial nor appropriate; that is why the federal government, with NCAT's assistance, must force taxpayers to pay for it. No matter how many demonstration projects the federal government finances, consumers are not going to invest in solar energy until it is economically viable on the open market. It is now several times more expensive than conventional energy, so that forcing taxpayers to pay for it makes them worse off and uses more resources (including energy) than would be used otherwise. This is hardly a conservationist strategy.

The Nature of Environmental Interventionism

It is clear that the above-mentioned groups are very well organized politically and belong to one of the most effective political coalitions in existence. Environmental problems are often a tool used to pursue what these groups claim to be their overriding objectives: greater government control over private industry, either through regulation or nationalization; nationalization of the land; government-mandated population planning; and a redistribution of domestic and international wealth.

In 1981 and 1982 the environmentalist coalition mobilized like never before to seek the ouster of Anne Burford, the administrator of EPA, and James Watt, the secretary of the Department of the Interior. Although the criticisms of Burford and Watt were typically exaggerated and rather apoplectic (laced with accusations of "raping the environment" among other sins), it is not clear that the coalition's primary motivation was a sincere concern for the health of the environment. During her tenure, Burford had virtually cut off these special-interest groups from taxpayers' funds. For example, the Natural Resources Defense Council received more than $360,000 from EPA in 1980 and $816,382 on January 21, 1981—the day before Burford took office. After she was in office, the NRDC received only $178 from EPA during 1981.[63] This helps clarify what

159

these groups mean when they list as one of their top priorities the restoration of EPA funding.

The National Wildlife Federation also suffered during the Burford administration, having its EPA subsidy cut from $498,167 in 1981 before Burford took over to less than one-fourth of that for the remainder of the year. The Sierra Club and Environmental Action were in a similar position, having also been cut off by the Burford administration. Environmental Action, however, did receive $179,644 from the Department of Energy on July 17, 1981.[64]

The Environmental Costs of Government Intervention

Perhaps the one distinguishing characteristic of the interventionist environmentalist movement is its condemnation of private property, especially with respect to the ownership of natural resources. An important part of this approach is that parklands, grazing lands, rivers and streams, and other resources will become despoiled if private ownership and development of those resources are permitted. As mentioned above, a top priority of many of these special-interest groups is further nationalization of the land, and they consider the nationalization of 46 percent of all land in Alaska in 1979 to be one of their greatest victories. But the root cause of environmental problems is emphatically not the profit motive, free markets, and private property. Rather, it is the lack of private property rights. The two property rights systems—government ownership (or common property) and private property—produce strikingly different sets of incentives and different methods of resource management and use. As biologist and environmentalist Garrett Hardin has written, common property (that is, government ownership) can have tragic effects on the environment:

> The tragedy of the commons develops in this way. Picture a pasture open to all. It is to be expected that each herdsman will try to keep as many cattle as possible on the commons. . . . As a rational being, each herdsman seeks to maximize his gain. Explicitly or implicitly, more or less consciously, he asks, "What is the utility *to me* of adding one more animal to my herd?" The utility has one negative and one positive component. . . . The positive component is a function of the increment of one animal. Since the herdsman receives all the proceeds from the sale of the additional animal, the positive utility is nearly +1. . . . The negative component is a function of the additional overgrazing created by one more animal. Since, however, the effects of overgrazing are shared

160

by all the herdsmen, the negative utility for any particular deci-sion-making herdsman is only a fraction of -1. Adding together the component partial utilities, the rational herdsman concludes that the only sensible course for him to pursue is to add another animal to his herd. And another. . . . But this is the conclusion reached by each and every rational herdsman sharing a commons. Therein is the tragedy. Each man is locked into a system that compels him to increase his herd without limit—in a world that is limited. Ruin is the destination toward which all men rush, each pursuing his own best interest in a society that believes in the freedom of the commons. Freedom in a commons [government ownership] brings ruin to all.[65]

By contrast, private ownership provides incentives for the care and preservation of natural resources and allows owners to capture the full capital value of their resources. Thus, self-interest and the profit motive drive the owners to maintain the long-term capital value of their resources. The owner of a particular resource, whether it is a fishery or a forest, will want to benefit from it now, tomorrow, and in the indefinite future. Thus, according to Robert J. Smith, "we can see why the buffalo nearly vanished, but not the Hereford; why the greater prairie chicken is endangered, but not the red grouse of Great Britain; why the common salmon fisheries of the United States are overfished, but not the private salmon streams of Europe or the private trout farms in many American states."[66] Smith has made this point even more forcefully in the following series of questions:

Why do people litter public parks and streets, but not their own yards? Why do people dump old refrigerators and rubber tires in the public or common streams, rivers, and swamps, but not in their farm ponds or their swimming pools? Who is most likely to carefully clean the leaves out of a gutter, a homeowner or someone who is renting the house? Is private housing or public housing better maintained? Why do cattle and sheep ranchers overgraze the public lands, but maintain lush pastures on their own prop-erty? Why are the national forests so carelessly logged and over-harvested, while private forests are carefully managed, cut on a sustained-yield basis, and reforested with "super trees" grown on costly nursery tree farms? Why are many of the most beautiful national parks suffering severe overuse to the point of the near destruction of their recreational values, but many private parks are maintained in far better condition?[67]

161

The answer to these questions is that common ownership inevitably leads to the "tragedy of the commons," and private ownership induces conservation.

The poor condition of many of the national parks is one example of the tragedy of the commons, but instead of acknowledging the roots of the problem, many environmentalist interest groups urge only that the government nationalize more land for more parks. One of the most famous examples of the ill effects of common ownership is the Dust Bowl that was created in the Midwest and Great Plains during the depression years. When the country was being settled, most of the public domain was distributed to private homesteaders in 160-acre plots. But in areas where the land was not too fertile, not much could be done with 160 acres. The federal government's refusal to expand the size of the homesteads forced people to treat the land as a commons, which led not only to overgrazing but also to range wars. Amidst this turmoil and overuse of the land, the prairie eventually turned to dust. There is little evidence that this calamity has influenced the decisions made by the federal bureaucracy, however, for approximately 63 percent of all land in the 13 western states is now owned, controlled, or regulated by the federal government.[68] The possibility of future dust bowls is very real.

Whenever there is government ownership of land, bureaucratic incentives replace the incentives of private entrepreneurs in using and maintaining the land. Private landowners have a direct and immediate incentive for wise and careful use of their resources—profits if they take good care of the land, losses if they do not. By contrast, utility-maximizing bureaucrats do not bear the consequences of their decisions. They do not benefit directly from making wise decisions; nor do they bear the cost of making poor decisions. If they cut the cost of forest management, for example, neither they nor their agency benefits, for the savings go to the U.S. treasury, which is itself a common pool.

Bureaucrats generally benefit if their agencies' budgets increase. Whether they went to advance the public interest or expand their private perquisites, they require greater appropriations. Regardless of the bureaucrats' motives, in pursuing their self-interest they will opt to expand the size of their agencies' budgets. To do this, bureaucrats have to cater to the preferences of the loudest, most-active special-interest groups that can affect appropriations. In the area of federal land management, these groups include cattle and sheep ranchers, timber companies, mining companies, and environmentalists. The bureaucrats try to satisfy all of these pressure groups, regardless of the environmental costs. Consequently, cattle and sheep ranchers have been able to obtain grazing rights on the public grazing lands at bargain basement prices, causing a more rapid depletion of those lands. The Bureau of Land Management has also engaged in clear-cutting—using two 65,000-pound tractors connected by 600 feet of anchor chain driven through woodlands to clear the land of trees to provide better subsidized feeding land for livestock.[69] Other examples abound and illustrate the type of ecological problems created by common ownership.

With private property and free markets, this type of ecological destruction would not take place, but elements of the environmentalist movement ignore this fact. Even if eliminating the profit motive would solve our environmental problems, there is the problem of explaining how in those socialist countries where profit making is outlawed, environmental problems are often far worse than they are in the United States. For instance, acid rain has so corroded railroad tracks in Poland that trains are not permitted to exceed 24 miles per hour, and acid rain dissolved so much of the gold roof of Poland's Sigismund Chapel of Walwel Cathedral that the roof had to be replaced. Industrial effluents and municipal sewage commonly flow untreated into all major rivers in the Soviet Union, resulting in mammoth fish kills, and the Soviet Union has less land set aside for game preserves and parks than any other developed country in the world. Fish has almost vanished from the Chinese diet because of industrial pollution and landfill projects; the Chinese government has literally turned state-owned forests into deserts; and over 8 million acres of land in northern China were made alkaline, and therefore unproductive, during the Great Leap Forward.[70] Establishing private property rights in natural resources, along with well-enforced rights of individuals to be free from pollution, are essential to finding solutions to environmental problems. Socialism or state ownership is incompatible with such a system of rights.

The Future of Fossil Fuels

One of the biggest successes of tax-funded environmental intervention has been to secure, through the political process, an extraordinary halt to the development of coal, oil, and natural gas. Legislation has sharply reduced domestic energy production in the United

States, reducing economic growth and making the country more dependent on foreign sources of fuel, such as petroleum from the Middle East. The federal government has nationalized (or confiscated) millions of acres of coal reserves in the West and has declared federal ownership of seabeds where larger reserves of oil are found.

Government ownership of coal reserves has always created controversy over what the right volume of leasing should be and what constitutes an appropriate lease price, and certain environmental groups used this confusion to obtain a moratorium on coal leasing in 1971. The federal moratorium on coal leasing lasted ten years. The moratorium was lifted in 1981, but the groups continued to strangle the coal industry with the regulations they had helped set in place in the meantime. To proceed with coal production, a company must comply with all the directives and red tape required by the National Environmental Policy Act of 1970, the Clean Air Act of 1970 and its 1977 amendments, the Clean Water Act of 1972 and its amendments, the Coal Leasing Act amendments of 1976, the Surface Mining Control and Reclamation Act of 1977, the Endangered Species Act of 1973, the Safe Water Drinking Act of 1974, the Solid Waste Disposal Act of 1971, the Federal Water Polution Control Act amendments of 1972, the Mine Safety and Health Act as amended, the Resource Conservation and Recovery Act of 1976, the Coastal Zone Management Act of 1972, the Fuel Use Act of 1978, and the Public Utilities Regulatory Policy Act of 1978, in addition to myriad other federal, state, and local government regulations. Even if a company complies with this mountain of regulation, the tax-financed environmentalist attorneys are likely to claim that the lease price is too low and not in the national interest.

These special-interest groups even criticize private companies in the coal industry for not mining coal on land that is already leased. A so-called resource specialist for the National Wildlife Federation recently testified before the Senate Subcommittee on Energy and Mineral Resources that

> there are 249 federal leases covering 338,000 acres and containing 6.6 billion tons of coal for which no mine plans have been submitted [by coal companies]. Another way of viewing this is that 44% of all leases, 42% of all leased acreage, and 40% of all leased reserves in 1981 were held by lessees who had not submitted mine plans [to the government]. . . . The question the coal industry has not answered here is, if a company has old federal coal leases . . . and has been holding them without producing any coal on them,

why should that company be able to obtain additional federal coal leases?[71]

The National Wildlife Federation has failed to recognize that what these coal producers are doing is conserving resources. These companies believe that the value of coal is going to increase in the future, so they are holding off production to maximize their profits—just the opposite of the rapacious, short-sighted behavior of which they are being accused. The present value of conserving these resources is greater than the value of extracting them now, and the higher the expected future land value, the more land that will be purchased or leased by speculators to be held for future use. Through foresight and risk taking, the speculator benefits society by both producing and conserving the resource. But this has been completely ignored by such resource specialists, who specialize in stopping the use of resources. It is not true that future generations have no voice in today's decision making, as some have claimed, for firms take into account the opportunity costs of present consumption. The image of business firms as having exceedingly short time horizons is a myth. If anything, it is government decision making that is shortsighted, for the politician's time horizon rarely extends beyond the next election.

Coal production (and employment in the coal and related industries) has been reduced by regulation intended to purify the air, but there is evidence that regulation has been counterproductive. In 1971 EPA mandated the scrubbing of coal to rid it of most of its sulfur content. Despite billions of dollars spent on scrubbers, however, the end result is possibly more pollution. For one thing, not all coal has the same sulfur content, and scrubbers do not work well on low-sulfur coal, so that the sulfur the technology is supposed to eliminate has to be added artificially to make the scrubbers work. Furthermore, scrubbers produce huge quantities of sludge, the disposal of which requires the permanent removal of thousands of acres of land, often farmland, from productive use. Scrubbing also requires massive volumes of water, which creates serious problems in the western states. Perhaps the most ironic thing about the coal-scrubbing saga is that despite the enormous costs that consumers (ultimately) have been forced to pay to rid the air of sulfur dioxide, scientists still do not know with certainty whether sulfur dioxide is harmful to health. Many scientists believe that it is not sulfur dioxide but the sulfate compounds into which sulfur dioxide

165

can be transformed over time that are damaging.[72] Until we understand this process, it is possible that all the money spent on scrubbing may have been wasted.

During the 1970s, the federal government's petroleum price control and entitlements programs created an energy crisis, made the United States more dependent on unstable sources of foreign oil, and kept oil prices higher than they would have been with deregulation. Now that the war between Iran and Iraq has been raging for several years and serious concerns are being voiced about our nation's ability to conduct trade with oil producers in the Middle East, there has been much talk about easing up on the irrational, self-defeating restrictions that have been placed on the development of domestic energy sources, especially offshore oil fields. This is especially important because no nuclear power plants have been ordered since 1978, coal production has been hampered, and several electric utilities are predicting bankruptcy.

Congress has adopted another policy advocated by the above-mentioned special-interest groups—a moratorium on offshore leasing of federally owned lands under the seas. There are tremendous reserves of oil under the Outer Continental Shelf, but Congress withdrew 736,000 acres in 1982 and increased this to more than 52 million acres in 1984 by attaching an amendment to an appropriations bill.[73] In 1984 only about 2 percent of the nation's federally controlled offshore acreage was under lease for oil and gas operations, while net imports of crude oil and refined oil products were rising.[74] The most direct impact of the moratorium has been to increase the price of energy by restricting its supply, but there have been secondary effects that are less noticeable but just as important. One of these effects is the loss of thousands of employment opportunities that the additional economic activity would generate. As one energy analyst has stated:

> [C]ompanies in Connecticut, Massachusetts and Rhode Island make sophisticated computer equipment that is used in seismic surveys. Specialized maps are produced in California and Florida. Steel made in Alabama, Ohio and Pennsylvania is used to fabricate offshore rigs and platforms at shipyards in Alabama, California, Louisiana, Maryland, Mississippi and Texas. After the rigs are assembled, they are painted and treated with protective coatings made in Missouri and New Jersey. Engines to power the rigs come from Illinois and Michigan. Cranes that hoist equipment and supplies are made in Nebraska, Pennsylvania, Texas, Washington

and Wisconsin. Specialized drilling tools, drilling fluids and cement are provided by plants in Arkansas, California, Nevada, Oklahoma, Utah and Wyoming. Heaters to warm offshore work areas and living quarters are made in North Dakota. Crews and supplies are transported to and from offshore rigs by helicopters and workboats from Alaska, Connecticut, Louisiana, New York, Oregon, Texas, and Washington. Special shoes, hard hats and work clothes are manufactured in Kentucky, Minnesota, Pennsylvania, Tennessee, Texas and Wisconsin.[75]

In giving in to political pressures, the federal government has eliminated thousands of employment and business opportunities. Perhaps this explains why the moratoriums have been implemented rather surreptitiously. The leasing moratoriums have moved through Congress very quietly, without formal hearings and the media attention that is usually given to such hearings. Recorded votes were never taken, either in committees or on the floor of the House or Senate; the moratoriums were simply pushed through as amendments to various appropriations bills. This type of underhanded behavior is inevitable and is the price we must pay for government ownership of offshore resources. Politicians are using their positions to win votes and campaign contributions from some environmentalist groups and a handful of citizens who oppose offshore oil exploration—but at great expense to the rest of the nation. Privatization of all offshore areas would be more conducive to both energy development and higher employment and would also be ecologically sound as long as liability laws are appropriately designed. Undersea oil has been produced since the 1890s, and although there have been a few oil spills, they have had no permanent effects on beaches, bird populations, or aquatic life. In fact, natural oil seeps have been responsible for putting more oil into coastal waters than has drilling.[76]

Does Capitalism Cause Cancer?

Another manifestation of the tax-funded environmental intervention is the vast array of regulations that ban or severely limit the use of many chemicals, foods, and other products because they are alleged to be carcinogens. Since at least the mid-1970s, the U.S. public has been bombarded with threats that possible carcinogens include scotch whisky, the caffeine in coffee, diet soda, most food additives, children's pajamas, and thousands of other products. This has led to what is known as the environment-causes-cancer hypothesis, which holds that cancer is mainly caused by things, especially chemicals, added to the environment by modern industrial societies. Proponents of this view are fond of proclaiming that 80 to 90 percent of all cancer is environmentally caused. These claims, however, should be viewed skeptically in light of the record of truthfulness (or lack of it) that the claimants have accumulated, and the fact that there could not possibly be a stronger case made for government regulation and control of industry than the claim that unless this is done we will probably die of cancer. The case for disregarding the costs of pollution control is stronger if it is believed that pollution produces a higher incidence of cancer. Recent research, however, shows that the environment-causes-cancer hypothesis may be one of the all-time great scientific flimflams. This is how an extremely thorough investigation of the causes of cancer by Edith Efron has been described:

> *The Apocalyptics* [Efron's book] is the fully documented revelation of one of the most astonishing scientific scandals of our time: the ideological corruption of cancer research in the United States. After years of diligent investigation, it is Edith Efron's contention that an extreme environmental movement . . . has politically distorted research in environmental cancer, saturating the United States with theories of cancer that are pure myth. . . . The . . . chief misrepresentation . . . is the "Garden of Eden" theory of cancer, namely that cancer is a man-made by-product of rampant industrialism and that nature is pristine and pure. This theory is false, and scientists have known it for years. Yet despite abundant scientific evidence of natural carcinogens, governmental agencies fail to report on most of them and instead issue warnings only about industrial carcinogens.[77]

Efron's book is a painstaking, encyclopedic examination of cancer research in the United States and much of the rest of the world. She demonstrates that what legitimate cancer researchers know about the causes of cancer and what the public has been led to believe are very different. In 1975, for example, Irving Selikoff, a nationally known authority on cancer and its causes, addressed the Scientific Committee on Occupational Medicine in Milan, Italy, and described what he called the Paradox of Rehn, which holds that since the early 1900s it had been suspected that industrial chemicals may cause cancer but as of 1975 there was no evidence in support of that notion. In summarizing the state of environmental cancer research as of 1975, Selikoff stated:

In 1895, Rhen reported the first three cases of cancer of the bladder among aniline workers. When additional cases of this association were identified in the next 15 years . . . it was projected that the developing chemical industry . . . would bring with it a host of problems and an unhappy harvest of cancer. This prediction, in the next decades, seemed far from unreasonable when our laboratory colleagues demonstrated carcinogenicity of literally hundreds of chemicals in animal test programs. Yet, by and large, the prophecy was not seen to be fulfilled in the first half of the 20th century. Even until recently, human chemical cancers have been relatively few and seemingly restricted in type and number, almost as exceptions to the broad spectrum of human cancer.[78]

Nevertheless, 1975 was the year in which a flood of regulation began banning hundreds of suspected carcinogens, even though there were no scientific breakthroughs immediately after Selikoff offered his remarks. Regulation gained significant momentum with the passage of the Toxic Substances Control Act of 1976, which greatly expanded the federal government's authority to protect us from unproven carcinogens.

Efron also demonstrates how a number of axioms of many involved in cancer research are simply untrue. The first is the Garden of Eden axiom that states that there are no (or few) natural carcinogens. Efron surveyed the scientific literature and found volumes of natural carcinogens that have been all but ignored by the government, the media, and especially the environmentalist interest groups. Efron also compiled a long list of research results showing that there are much higher incidences of different types of cancer in less industrialized societies than in more industrialized societies, which contradicts the environment-causes-cancer hypothesis. She further examined predictions of a coming "age of cancer," to use Ralph Nader's phrase. For example, Umberto Saffiotti of the National Cancer Institute warned *Time* magazine in 1975 that cancer in "the last quarter of the 20th century would emerge from the industrial system."[79] These views were quickly embraced by the press with Dan Rather of CBS claiming that "we are suffering a cancer epidemic in slow motion" and the *New York Times* writing of "a monstrous epidemic of occupational cancer."[80] Fortunately, the evidence pointed in the opposite direction. In 1977 the World Health Organization reported that in many countries, including the United States, "death rates were either stationary or declining"; in 1978, the National Center for Health Statistics reported that "death rates from all causes [of cancer] had decreased during the years 1940 to 1976"; in 1979 the American Cancer Society reported that the "overall incidence of cancer has decreased slightly in the past 25 years"; and in 1982 a National Research Council committee said that "the overall age-adjusted cancer rates have remained fairly stable over the past 30 to 40 years."[81] Philip Handler, former president of the National Academy of Sciences, concluded:

> Indeed, the United States is not suffering an "epidemic of cancer," it is experiencing an "epidemic of life"—in that an ever greater fraction of the population survives to the advanced ages at which cancer has always been prevalent. The overall, age-corrected incidence of cancer has not been increasing; it has been declining slowly for some years.[82]

With the help of taxpayers' funds, government and its special-interest allies seem to have used the public's concern over pollution to perpetrate a colossal hoax on the public. As Edith Efron concluded:

> [M]ost [news] reporters—thus, presumably, most Americans—appear to . . . "know" the apocalyptics' "axioms" or variants of them. They "know" the latest carcinogen in the headlines, whether the data are valid or not—until they forget it. They "know" that they are being massacred by "pollution." *They "know" primarily what is false or unknown—and they rarely know how to identify the actual threats to their lives.* That, too, is the result of the "dumping," of the ventilation of "gratuitous nightmares," of the cries of wolf by the "moralists" who are breaching the "ethics and norms of science." They have rendered most citizens incapable of differentiating between known and unknown hazards. And that, too, is the meaning of the fable of the boy who cried wolf: The ostensible protector of the community actually *disarmed* the community. . . . *Were a physician to treat a patient for ten years by terrorizing him incessantly with hypothetical or false warnings of threats to his life, while failing to inform him of, and to treat, the known diseases from which the patient actually suffers, that physician would be recognized as a sadistic incompetent.* That is actually how the cancer prevention establishment has been "treating" this whole nation.[83]

Many environmentalist interest groups are an important part of this "cancer prevention establishment." They have shunned the scientific method and have avoided the truth if it does not fit their anticorporate biases. Even worse, some have gloated over their corruption of science in one of the most important fields of research, cancer prevention. They are clearly pleased that the public now seems to believe that there is no truth that can be gleaned from scientific research and that one scientist's opinion is just as good as another's. One of the latest media campaigns illustrates this mentality.

The July-August 1984 issue of *Environmental Action* magazine includes an article on fluoride that contains the following remarks:

> For further information on fluoride, a few addresses are given below. But you've been forewarned—expect two very different stories. There is in New York City a resource center where journalists with scientific questions may call to be put in contact with one of the many scientists the center has on file. "Fluoride?" asked the receptionist. "Do you want to speak to a pro-fluoridation scientist, or an anti-fluoridation scientist?" "But I thought scientists are supposed to be neutral?" I asked. "Not where fluoride is concerned."[84]

The message of the article is that there is "an incestuous relationship between government [regulatory] agencies and the industries they're supposed to regulate," so that fluoride, since it was invented and developed by industry, should be added to the ever-expanding list of dangerous chemicals.

Polluting the Public Policy Environment

One point we wish to stress in this chapter is that the environmentalist movement often alluded to in public policy circles is not quite a homogeneous group. Environmentalists do not all think alike. However, there is a large and (politically) influential element of environmentalism that shares a strongly interventionist philosophy. And as discussed here, it is this element that with the aid of taxpayer funding, has helped create a great many environmental problems by promoting massive federal programs that coerce taxpayers into subsidizing the destruction of their own environment.

It is important to note that the views of the leaders of many of the interventionist environmentalist interest groups diverge sharply from the views of millions of U.S. citizens, including many of the groups' own members. As the presidential election results of 1980 and 1984 reveal, most voters believe in Ronald Reagan's private-property, free-enterprise philosophy (whether he practices what he preaches is another matter). This philosophy, however, is at odds

171

with such destructive environmental policies as government ownership of millions of acres of land, which is a predominant objective of many environmentalist interest groups and the government bureaucracy that supports them at the taxpayers' expense.[85]

Some of the above-mentioned special-interest groups are undoubtedly well intentioned, but their good intentions have proven very costly to society. And some people, such as many involved in the various *Limits to Growth* studies, openly admit their intellectual dishonesty because of their strong feelings about the goals they hope to achieve.

VIII. Poverty, Politics, and Social Programs

Initially the scene of such [political] activism will have to be local, but community organizations should also devote some energies toward the long-range goal of stemming the present national political move in the direction of federal government abdication of responsibility for meeting the needs of the poor. It will be at the federal level, via congressional action, that critical decisions will be made in the years ahead concerning the government's role in responding to particular social needs. Community organizations across the country should be about the business of producing local victories that provide the base from which a national movement can be built.

—National Citizen's Monitoring Project of
the Working Group for Community
Development Reform
Citizen Monitoring—A How-To Manual

What is in fact being sought and achieved under the banner of "social justice" is the redistribution of decision-making authority. Decision makers acting as surrogates for others in exchange for money or votes are being either replaced or superceded by decision makers responsible largely or solely to the pervasive social vision of their clique. . . . It is [this] . . . more moral or ideological set of decision makers who originate and impose standards, i.e., who reduce freedom.

—Thomas Sowell
Knowledge and Decisions

Few issues generate more heat and less light than how much public money should be spent on social programs. While some people argue that too much is being spent on the nation's needy, others are convinced that the poor are suffering because poverty programs have been cut to the bone and far too little of the nation's resources is allocated for the poor, the sick, and the elderly. For example, a 1984 article in *Business Week*, "Why There's No Welfare

173

Fat Left to Trim," concluded that "Current programs are very close to the minimum level of support that a wealthy society has decided to provide to its poorest citizens."[1] According to the article, the Reagan administration apparently had decimated social programs because

> Congress readily agreed to Reagan's proposals for deep slashes in a broad array of welfare programs—reductions that greatly toughened eligibility standards for food stamps, Medicaid, and other major benefit programs. . . .
>
> As a result of this clean sweep, politicians and welfare experts generally agree that there is little room left for additional cuts. Says Henry Aaron, former assistant secretary of the Health, Education and Welfare Dept.: "This closet has been cleaned."[2]

The article noted that after adjusting for inflation, spending on welfare programs was about the same in 1984 as it was in 1980.

A similar assessment was published at the same time in *U.S. News and World Report:*

> By many accounts, life for the urban underclass became bleaker in recent years. Since 1980, a harsh economy and cuts in federal social-welfare programs have combined to reduce by 9.4 percent the average income for the poorest one-fifth of American households, according to the Urban Institute, a Washington research group.[3]

This analysis described the plight of "America's underclass" as desperate, and it contended that the share of the nation's population with poverty-level income had risen to 15 percent in 1982 from a low of 11.4 percent in 1978. In 1960, prior to the initiation of the Great Society programs, the poverty rate was 22.2 percent.[4] On the basis of these two articles, the situation in the 1980s seems bleak.

Other sources, however, have reached remarkably different conclusions. For example, J. Peter Grace, director of the President's Private Sector Survey on Cost Control, surveyed only means-tested programs for the poor, such as Aid to Families with Dependent Children, food stamps, and Medicaid—which accounted for $124 billion in expenditures in 1982—and found that "In theory, the $124 billion should have not only brought all households out of poverty, but been sufficient to bring all households to 125% of the poverty level with $47.5 billion left over for other purposes such as reducing the federal deficit."[5] The Grace Commission report was written after many of the purportedly devastating cuts in social programs had already been made. Yet, as a little arithmetic readily reveals, spending only $61.2 billion on means-tested programs alone could have brought every household in the nation out of poverty. In short, the means-tested programs, even if cut by half, would still be adequate to eliminate poverty. The means-tested programs are not the only ones in existence, for additional billions of dollars are spent on such programs as the Jobs Corps, the Legal Services Corporation, Head Start, and Volunteers in Service to America (VISTA).

Other commentators have also observed the massive amounts of spending on social programs relative to the number of poor, but few of them have stated the facts as forcefully as William E. Simon, a former secretary of the treasury:

> From 1965 to 1976 the amount of government money spent for "social welfare" functions broadly defined exploded from $77 billion a year to more than $331 billion—an increase of better than $250 billion in the amount of money being spent each year allegedly to help the needy. Interestingly, the number of poor people in America hardly changed at all during this period—continuing to hover at about the 25 million mark, according to the official figures (which overstate the problem by leaving out in-kind benefits).
>
> A little arithmetic is sufficient to show that if we had taken this $250 billion increase in social welfare spending and simply given it to those 25 million poor people, we could have given each and every one of them an annual grant of $10,000—which is an income, for a family of four, of $40,000 a year. We could have made all those poor people relatively rich. But we didn't.[6]

For his analysis, Simon included the substantial state and local expenditures on social programs with the federal allocations. He then rhetorically asked: "So where is the money?"[7] This question deserves an answer.

An Overview of Welfare Expenditures

In every society there are individuals who for a variety of reasons and through no fault of their own cannot take care of themselves. Many people believe that there is some role of government in providing assistance—at least temporarily—to alleviate hunger and malnutrition and to mitigate the consequences of misfortune for

175

such individuals. Although there is broad political support for some government expenditure to assist those who are less fortunate, there is evidently widespread disagreement about the amount that should be spent. A commonsense approach would dictate that the appropriate level of expenditures should be directly related to the extent of need, that is, the number of individuals who are needy and the amount of money required to enable these people to meet some minimum standard of living. In 1964 the Social Security Administration developed an official standard of need for the United States—the poverty threshold—using a U.S. Department of Agriculture (USDA) survey conducted in 1955. This survey showed that families of three or more people spent about one-third of their income on food, so the Social Security Administration initially set the poverty threshold at three times the estimated cost of USDA's so-called economy food plan for 1961. Each year, the Bureau of the Census adjusts the poverty threshold in response to changes in the Consumer Price Index to account for the effects of inflation. Given this information, it is possible to determine the amount of expenditure required to bring every needy individual in the nation up to the poverty threshold.

Jonathan R. Hobbs has made this calculation for the years 1979 through 1983, and his estimates are shown in Table 8.1, column 2. (Note that the estimates of need include an annual increase of 1.5 percent to allow for administrative overhead, this rate being based on the actual overhead rate for the Social Security Administration.) The data indicate that curing poverty is an expensive undertaking,

Table 8.1
WELFARE NEED AND WELFARE SPENDING, 1979–83

Year	Need Based on Poverty Threshold ($)	Welfare Expenditures ($)	Ratio of Need to Actual Expenditures
1979	70,189,740	278,386,195	25.2
1980	85,953,062	324,941,211	26.5
1981	95,235,993	369,244,788	25.8
1982	103,331,052	403,519,754	25.6
1983	109,871,908	413,244,030	26.6

SOURCE: Jonathan R. Hobbs, "Welfare Needs and Welfare Spending," Heritage Foundation Backgrounder no. 219 (Washington, 1982), p. 3.

requiring about $110 billion in 1983. However, actual expenditures on welfare programs by federal, state, and local governments, shown in column 3 of Table 8.1, far exceed the amount required to alleviate all poverty in the United States. Nearly $4 are expended for each dollar of need based on the poverty threshold. It is clear that the taxpayers are not getting a good return on their money.

The statistics on the number of individuals below the poverty threshold include only reported cash income; they do not include in-kind transfers to the poor, such as food, housing, medical care, and other services. Nor are the billions of dollars of goods and services provided by private charitable organizations included as income for the needy. Thus, many more people are counted as being below the poverty line than would be the case if in-kind and private transfers were taken into account. Nevertheless, little progress was made between 1979 and 1983 in curing poverty (see Table 8.1), even though there was a steady increase in both the amount required to raise all individuals to the poverty threshold and the amount of welfare expenditures.

The federal government is the source of the vast majority of social program expenditures, and both this outlay and the number of programs have risen dramatically over time. By 1982 there were 49 major national welfare programs encompassing a wide range of income-transfer schemes, from Social Security, Aid to Families with Dependent Children, and unemployment compensation to such in-kind services as Medicaid and Medicare, Comprehensive Employment and Training Act (CETA) assistance, and food stamps. Federal outlays for welfare programs between 1950 and 1980 are shown in Table 8.2 and have been combined in four categories: cash transfers, noncash transfers, social services, and training and employment. To eliminate the effects of inflation, all expenditures are reported in 1980 dollars. After adjustment for inflation, total outlays for welfare programs were 30.8 times as great in 1980 as they were in 1950. Much of this increase can be attributed to the relative growth of noncash transfers, which rose 14,622 percent between 1950 and 1980; in contrast, cash transfers were only 21.4 times greater in 1980 than in 1950. Social services in 1980 cost 59 times as much as similar services in 1950, and spending for vocational programs rose more than 147 times during these three decades. During the same period, total population increased by only 48 percent, so the rise in total spending on welfare programs of nearly 3,000 percent in constant dollars is far out of proportion.

Table 8.2
FEDERAL OUTLAYS FOR SOCIAL WELFARE PROGRAMS SINCE 1950 ($ Millions)*

	1950	1955	1960	1965	1970	1975	1980
Cash transfers							
Old-age, survivors, disability (Social Security)	2,666	13,556	30,470	44,073	62,578	96,874	120,262
Unemployment and compensation programs	785	1,238	1,467	1,950	2,496	7,336	18,023
General welfare programs**	3,726	4,404	5,132	6,433	9,412	15,723	15,166
Total	7,177	19,198	37,069	52,456	74,486	119,933	153,451
Noncash transfers							
Medical care***	150	217	853	2,176	21,169	35,055	53,020
Infants and children's programs	361	614	975	1,579	2,007	3,639	5,752
Housing	—	—	398	607	1,227	3,554	5,514
Food stamps	—	—	—	—	1,216	7,144	9,117
Other	—	—	163	788	3,453	3,566	1,827
Total	511	831	2,389	5,150	29,072	52,958	75,230
Social services							
Institutional care	82	150	72	93	46	30	—
Other social service programs	—	—	—	405	2,687	3,959	4,835
Total	82	150	72	498	2,733	3,989	4,835

Training and Employment

Vocational and adult education	92	89	119	1,105	1,271	1,431	863
Vocational rehabilitation	61	79	177	379	1,195	1,239	427
Jobs programs (CETA)	—	—	—	—	—	2,283	9,589
Total	153	168	296	1,484	2,466	4,953	10,879
Grand Total	7,923	20,347	39,826	59,588	108,757	181,833	244,395

SOURCES: *Statistical Abstract of the United States* (Washington: Bureau of the Census, selected years); *Budget of the United States Government, Fiscal Year 1982* (Washington: Office of Management and Budget, 1981); *Social Security Bulletin 44*, no. 11 (November 1981).

*Figures are in constant 1980 dollars.

**Primarily AFDC and Supplemental Security Income.

***Medicare, Medicaid, and civilian hospital and medical care.

The origins of this dramatic growth in spending can be traced to the early 1960s, when the Kennedy administration proposed a new approach to government assistance to the poor. In his welfare message to Congress in 1962, Kennedy emphasized the importance of ending the dole and helping individuals to help themselves. As the *New York Times* editorialized,

> President Kennedy's welfare message to Congress yesterday stems from a recognition that no lasting solution to the problem can be bought with a welfare check. The initial cost will actually be higher than the mere continuation of handouts. The dividends will come in the restoration of individual dignity and in the long-term reduction of the need for government help.[8]

The new approach was to provide a "hand," not a "handout." After more than two decades of experimenting with the new approach, the results appear to be vastly different from those suggested by the *Times*. The prediction that the initial costs would be higher was realized with a vengeance, but taxpayers in the 1980s are still waiting for the "long-term reduction" in the need for government assistance. The prospects do not seem to be improving. If anything, it seems that poverty is expanding rather than contracting, despite the hundreds of billions of dollars that have been expended each year.

Before the Johnson administration began waging the War on Poverty, the percentage of the United States population with reported cash incomes below the poverty threshold had steadily declined. In 1949 32.7 percent of the population was beneath the poverty threshold; by 1954 the percentage had declined to 27.9 percent; by 1959 the rate had fallen to 22.4 percent. In other words, progress in reducing poverty was being made at the rate of about 1 percentage point per year prior to the explosion in social problems that began during the early 1960s. Progress continued throughout the 1960s, largely because of the economic growth during that decade, but there was little improvement thereafter. By 1973 the number of people with incomes below the poverty threshold had reached a low of 11.1 percent. By 1982, however, the number had climbed to 15 percent. Given the amounts of money being spent by the federal government to alleviate poverty during the 1970s, it seems incredible that the problem could become more severe. As Charles Murray has observed:

All we are measuring with the official definition of poverty is cash income after taking government transfers into account. The recipient of the benefits does not have to "do" anything. To reach zero percentage of people beneath the poverty line, all that needs to be done is send out enough checks with enough money to enough people. Starting in the late 1960s, these numbers all started to increase—number of checks, size of the checks, number of beneficiaries. . . .

[T]he budgets of the 1970s were being focused on a much smaller number of people than earlier, smaller budgets. In 1950, there were an estimated 45.5 million people living beneath the poverty level; in 1960, 39.9 million; by 1970, only 25.4 million. Given these conditions—more money, fewer poor, just a matter of distributing money, logic suggests that . . . [the rate of decline in the percentage of the population with incomes below the poverty threshold] should have gotten much steeper in the 1970s. It seems impossible that it could have flattened out.[9]

While the proportion of the population in poverty had flattened out during the 1970s, total population had increased, so that the number of people in poverty has been rising rapidly since 1978. By 1982 more than 34 million Americans were officially living in poverty, an increase of almost 10 million since 1978. The War on Poverty is not only costly, it is also a losing proposition. There are more Americans officially living in poverty today than there were in 1965, when the rapid expansion in the number of programs and benefits was just getting under way.

It is clear that our failure to solve the problems of the poor cannot be attributed to stinginess on the part of U.S. taxpayers, for the resources committed to the problem by federal, state, and local goverments—combined with those of the private sector—should be more than adequate to address the problems of the poor. Alternative reasons must be found to explain why the welfare system expands rather than reduces poverty. Changes in the system are inevitable because recent trends in welfare spending and the number of people in poverty simply cannot continue for long without bankrupting the nation. Because all social programs involve transferring income or resources from one segment of society to another by political means, the shortcomings of the welfare system must be viewed as a political problem.

One reason that welfare expenditures do not assist the poor is that some of the funds are directed to individuals in higher-income

181

groups (see Table 8.3). For example, 48.5 percent of the households receiving housing subsidies or living in public housing have incomes about the poverty threshold; and almost one-third of these families have incomes greater than 125 percent of the poverty level. Members of Congress are anxious to subsidize their constituents with tax money, regardless of income, so they convince the voters that the benefits received from government programs exceed the taxes that they must pay for them. Therefore, politicians make every effort to shift the tax burden to other groups or to disguise the real costs of the programs. The poor provide an excellent excuse for initiating social welfare programs that can then be extended to higher-income groups. By 1980 more than half of the federally provided school lunches were feeding children from households with incomes above the poverty threshold (see Table 8.3). It would be politically difficult to justify direct cash transfers to these households because the recipients and the cost to taxpayers would be far too easy to identify. It is much more difficult to determine the value of in-kind benefits and to ascertain who actually receives them. This is one reason why politicians prefer in-kind benefits rather than cash transfers.

A second reason why the welfare system is not reformed is that producers of welfare services in both the public and the private sectors have a vested interest in maintaining and expanding the current system:

> The welfare system sustains a nationwide welfare industry of more than 5 million public and private workers to service 50 to 60 million recipients. The industry has demonstrated that its goal is not to eliminate poverty, but to expand welfare through increased spending, more benefits and programs, centralization of control in the federal government, and expanded employment in welfare-related services.[10]

If poverty were eliminated or even substantially reduced, the employment of millions who have made a comfortable living in the poverty industry would be threatened. It is in their best interests to increase the number of poor people and, once those people are enrolled in poverty programs, to have them remain on the dole.

The much greater growth in in-kind special programs relative to cash grants is part of the strategy employed to maximize the incidence of poverty in the United States:

Table 8.3

Distribution of Noncash Public Transfers, by Income Category

Type of Transfer	Total Recipient Households	Households at or below Poverty Level		Households at 101–125% of Poverty Level		Households at more than 125% of Poverty Level	
		No.	%	No.	%	No.	%
Food stamps	6,769	4,433	65.5	794	11.7	1,542	22.8
School lunches	5,532	2,511	45.4	676	12.2	2,345	42.4
Subsidized or public housing	2,777	1,430	51.5	436	15.7	911	32.8
Medicaid coverage for at least one person	8,287	4,421	53.3	957	11.5	2,909	35.1
At least one of the above	14,266	6,360	44.6	1,860	13.0	6,046	42.4

SOURCE: *Characteristics of Households Receiving Noncash Benefits, 1980* (Washington: Bureau of the Census, 1981), pp. 60, 128.

Most scholarly studies show that the inclusion of in-kind benefits reduces the poverty rate by one-half to two-thirds of the level reported by the Census Bureau. These figures could be further modified to take into account the large amount of unreported income among low-income families. Some estimates of the underground economy place it between 10 and 25 percent of GNP. And one study concluded that individuals with reported incomes under $1,000 were spending $224 for every $100 of reported income. Add to this consideration the fact that among low-income individuals there were would be writers, artists and actors—people whose earning ability is actually quite high.[11]

Thus, the methods used to provide benefits and to count the number of individuals below the poverty threshold guarantee that the incidence of poverty will remain high.

Although the stated goal of the welfare system is to offer a "hand" to those in need so that they can get off the welfare rolls as quickly as possible, which is certainly a desirable objective, the system actually operates to achieve the opposite effect. The welfare system reduces incentives for participants to work and become self-supporting.[12] Even if welfare recipients want to work, the system discourages them from doing so by imposing penalties for their earning additional income. When welfare recipients do go to work, income and payroll taxes are deducted from their paychecks and their welfare benefits are reduced. Further, they have to bear the costs associated with taking jobs, for example, transportation to and from work. The net benefits from working are substantially reduced by these direct and indirect taxes on earned income; for each additional dollar earned, the average low-income family faces an effective tax rate of 62 percent, the highest rate of taxation of any income group.[13] Henry Aaron of The Brookings Institution has shown that the effective rate of taxation for welfare recipients can actually exceed more than 1,000 percent when family income rises to the point where certain welfare benefits are totally lost.[14] The message is clear: Do not earn cash income; or, if income is earned, do not report it.

Moreover, eligibility requirements for social programs encourage the dissolution of the family and perpetuate the family's dependence on welfare. As George Gilder has observed,

> The combination of welfare and other social services enhance the mother's role and obviate the man's. As a result, men tend to leave their children, whether before or after marriage. Crises that would be resolved in a normal family way break up a ghetto

184

family. Perhaps not the first time or the fifth, but sooner or later the pressures of the subsidy state dissolve the roles of fatherhood, the disciplines of work, and the rules of marriage.[15]

Permanent dependence on welfare is increasing, and a substantial and rapidly growing percentage of those on welfare are adopting the public dole as a life-style.[16] The current system rewards individuals for having low incomes and punishes them for increasing their income; it encourages dependency and discourages economic independence; it creates attitudes that undermine the structure of the family and of society and guarantees the perpetuation of an impoverished class. These effects serve the self-interests of those employed in the welfare industry, but they have devastating consequences for their clients.

A third reason why welfare spending has grown so rapidly but has not produced the expected results is that those in need do not receive all the funds or benefits from the programs. There is evidence that the so-called plight of the poor has been used as a justification for politicians and public employees to allocate millions of taxpayers' dollars for explicit or implicit political purposes. Large sums are provided to organizations that purport to study the needs of the poor, to evaluate the effects of existing programs, and to propose new approaches to solve the problems. Although the researchers are supposedly objective and unbiased, their findings inevitably call for additional government spending and rarely criticize past failures. The recipients of government grants know that if the conclusions developed under the auspices of a given grant or contract are critical of the agency providing the funds, the likelihood of obtaining additional resources from that agency is markedly reduced. The bureaucracy is not known for open-mindedness or for being generous to its critics.

Among the organizations that receive large amounts of their funding from poverty programs are the Urban Institute and Welfare Research. The *Washington Post* reported that in 1980 the Urban Institute received $10.5 million of its $14 million budget (75 percent) from the federal government. In that same year, Welfare Research received $1.7 million, or 68 percent of its $2.5 million budget, from the federal government.[17] Such groups provide the intellectual content for arguments that aid to the poor should be increased and that the major problem with poverty programs is that the level of funding is insufficient. Poverty think tanks provide a critical service, but they are rarely involved directly in the politics of poverty.

Given the dismal performance of past efforts at reducing poverty by the government, members of Congress need far more than scholarly studies to justify their ever-increasing appropriation of tax revenues for welfare programs. There are votes to be garnered by appearing to be caring, concerned, and socially aware; however, because many taxpayers are already concerned about the level of welfare spending and the lack of results, there are also political risks associated with alienating some voters who oppose additional welfare expenditures. Although there are many lower-income individuals, they are much less likely to vote than are individuals with higher incomes who bear the burden of the tax system and the costs of welfare. Without demeaning the motives of the poor in any way, Gordon Tullock has stated the matter succinctly:

> The fact is . . . that the poor are generally not highly competent people. That, indeed, is why they are poor. The man who is not capable of holding down a good job is probably equally incapable of efficiently selling his vote in the best market. In other words, he is likely to do badly in the political marketplace as well as the economic. The fact that they are rather inadequate may reflect their heredity, the environment in which they are brought up, or some disabling disease, but the point is that one of the reasons the poor do not seem to do very well in modern welfare states is that they are bad at manipulating the welfare state. The fact that they are, in general, bad at manipulating may also account for the fact that they are not very well off.[18]

Many organizations receive grants and contracts from bureaucracies that are seeking support for the expansion of their programs, and the organizations compensate for the handicap that the poor have in the political marketplace. That is, professionals in the poverty industry organize the poor at the grass-roots level, register them to vote, provide political indoctrination, and make them a political force that the politicians heed. The poverty industry (organizations and individuals who purportedly work to alleviate poverty) constantly lobbies Congress to expand existing welfare programs and to initiate new programs, and the record of appropriations shows that these efforts have been highly successful. But even though additional funds may be obtained, the poor have gained very little because the poverty industry is able to divert much of the increase to its own purposes.

This chapter illustrates these concepts by exploring the history and development through tax-funded political advocacy of the food stamp program.

The Food Fiasco: Hungering for Hunger

The federal government's involvement in providing food stamps began during the Great Depression. According to the Congressional Budget Office, the motivation for this activity was not based on humanitarian motives or concern for the poor, but on "the specific need to increase the consumption of surplus agricultural commodities."[19] The first food stamp program lasted for 46 months, from May 1939 to early 1943 and served about 4 million persons in selected areas. The program ended, not because there were major changes in the needs of the poor, but because the agricultural surpluses were eliminated by World War II and many commodities were in short supply and were rationed.[20] When the program was withdrawn, there was no rash of deaths from starvation or malnutrition. The poor somehow managed to nourish themselves for almost two decades, until President Kennedy began a pilot food stamp program in 1961 that became the precedent for current food stamp programs. In this pilot program, as before, the objective was to remove "price-depressing surplus goods from the market, but it also emphasized the objective of improved nutrition."[21]

Much of the cause of hunger and malnutrition in the United States can be traced directly to the federal government. For decades public policy has systematically discriminated against the poor by making it difficult for them to enter the job market and to earn enough to purchase food.[22] More importantly, the federal government, through the USDA, has made every effort to raise the price of food through its subsidy (welfare) programs for the nation's farmers. American farmers are paid not to produce, acreage allotments take farmland out of production, price supports put floors under the prices that farmers receive for their output, monopoly pricing schemes executed through so-called marketing orders are promoted and encouraged, and the government buys and stores farm commodities to keep prices from falling. The taxpayers pay the farmers, the storage costs for the excess production, and then the supermarket prices that are well above those that would prevail if government were not involved in agriculture.

Huge quantities of food are destroyed each year for the sole purpose of maintaining high prices for farmers, and mountains of dairy and other agricultural products are stored by the government to prevent them from reaching the market and putting downward pressure on prices. For example, at the same time that advocates of food programs were expressing distress about the deficiency of Vitamin C in the diets of the poor, federal policies raised the prices of citrus. About 40 percent of oranges and 75 percent of lemons grown in California were wasted or destroyed under federal programs in 1983: "more lemons were dumped . . . than sold fresh to American consumers."[23] In addition, imports of some foodstuffs—sugar, for example—are restricted because they can be produced abroad for far less than they can be produced domestically, and cheap imported foods would force down domestic prices. During the last year of the Carter administration, price supports cost $3.5 billion; only four years later the cost had skyrocketed to an estimated $21 billion.[24] Given that the federal government routinely spends billions of dollars each year making food expensive, it is hardly surprising that some Americans find it difficult to purchase adequate food on a limited income.

Common sense dictates that the first step to reducing hunger and malnutrition in the United States would be to make food more affordable by ending the costly public policies that have increased food prices for decades. This step has not been taken. Indeed, the ostensibly conservative and free-market Reagan administration has increased rather than reduced farm subsidies, and Congress must share some of the blame because agricultural policy is a thinly disguised welfare program for farmers and dairymen that has rapidly grown to scandalous proportions. H. L. Mencken took the measure of the American farmer more than half a century ago and fulminated:

> Let the farmer, so far as I am concerned, be damned forevermore. To Hell with him, and bad luck to him. He is a tedious fraud and ignoramus, a cheap rogue and hypocrite, the eternal Jack of the human pack. He deserves all that he ever suffers under our economic system, and more. Any city man, not insane, who sheds tears for him is shedding tears of the crocodile.

> No more grasping, selfish and dishonest mammal, indeed, is known to students of the *Anthropoidea*. When the going is good for him he robs the rest of us to the extreme limit of our endurance; when the going is bad he comes bawling for help out of the public

till. Has anyone ever heard of a farmer making any sacrifice of his own interests, however slight, to the common good? Has anyone ever heard of a farmer practicing or advocating any political idea that was not absolutely self-seeking—that was not, in fact, deliberately designed to loot the rest of us to his gain?[25]

Farmers have always been a politically powerful group. Historically, most Americans lived on farms, and the political clout of the agricultural lobby was derived from sheer numbers. Over the past century, however, technology has greatly altered agriculture, and output has increased dramatically, even though only a small percentage of Americans now live on farms or derive their incomes from agriculture. But the political power of the farm lobby did not wane as the number employed in agriculture declined. Farmers and dairymen are still among the best organized special-interest groups. They contribute heavily to election campaigns at all levels of government, exist in every state and congressional district, and have a cabinet-level federal department to represent their interests.[26] Eliminating the farm programs that keep prices above free market levels would threaten farmers' subsidies and the jobs and employment security of tens of thousands of bureaucrats who work in USDA. The food stamp program was initiated to dispose of embarrassing levels of agricultural surpluses and to disguise the fact that the powerful farm lobby was receiving massive amounts of welfare from taxpayers. Farm subsidies and price supports encourage agricultural output and at the same time discourage consumption. Food stamps were adopted to increase the consumption of food and to reduce surpluses without lowering prices, that is, without altering federal agricultural programs, a move that would have alienated both the farm lobby and the Department of Agriculture bureaucracy. A case may even be made that our concern about hunger in other countries has been motivated, at least in part, by a desire to dump surplus U.S. agricultural commodities.

The food distribution programs begun by the federal government prior to 1964 failed to significantly reduce agricultural surpluses. Thus, an intensified effort was needed that would increase the subsidized consumption of food by lowering eligibility requirements, broadening the scope of existing programs, increasing the number of programs, and raising the level of the subsidy. By 1983 a total of 13 food assistance programs were in operation, 10 of which were directed at children. In addition to the food stamp program, there was the Summer Feeding Program; the Child Care Food Program; the Supplemental Feeding Program for Women, Infants, and Children (WIC Program); the Congregate Feeding Program for the Elderly; the School Breakfast Program; the National School Lunch Program; and others. Programs proliferated, and so did the costs.

For some programs there is no pretense that assistance is only for those in need. To encourage the consumption of food, all individuals over 60 are eligible for taxpayer-provided meals fives times per week regardless of their income; their spouses are also eligible for the Congregate Feeding Program for the Elderly regardless of age. If the elderly cannot get to the feeding center because of infirmity or inconvenience, the taxpayers provide delivery service through Meals on Wheels. The elderly are also eligible for food stamps, but even the elderly poor have been cantankerous about enrolling:

> In March 1972 President Nixon announced Project FIND to locate and recruit 3 million elderly poor for food assistance. Despite mass mailing of information to almost 30 million retirees, and despite home visits and telephone campaigns by 36,000 Red Cross volunteers, only 190,000 elderly signed up. The GAO [U.S. General Accounting Office] found that in most counties surveyed, recruiting efforts enticed fewer than 3 percent of the elderly poor onto the food dole. Apparently, many felt that despite having been labeled poor by some bureaucrat, they could feed themselves.[27]

The elderly are not cooperating fully with USDA's plans for reducing food surpluses. One nutrition survey ominously reported that "regardless of income, persons 60 years of age and older *consumed far less food than required.*"[28] The nation's senior citizens, however, do not appear to be in any danger of wasting away from lack of nourishment. The life expectancy for both men and women at age 60 has risen steadily for decades: By 1983, on the average, 60-year-old females could expect to live another 23.9 years and 60-year-old males could expect to live another 19.5 years. In any event, the food problems of the elderly can hardly be viewed as acute.

Eligibility standards for the food stamp program have been lowered so that even middle-income families have little difficulty in qualifying. One food advocacy group, whose major purpose is to increase the number of people enrolled in the program, provided an example in which a family of six with four cars (including a

190

camper and a dune buggy) could still manage to meet the food stamp limitations on assets.[29] Income limitations to qualify for food stamps have also been reduced. In Alaska, for example, a family of four with a net monthly income of $970 is entitled to food stamps. Net income is what remains after certain deductions have been made. For example, there is a work deduction under which 18 percent of pay from a job or training program is not included; there is a standard deduction of $85 per household; there is a dependent care deduction; and there is a shelter deduction. (A medical deduction also applies if a member of the household is elderly.) The regulations are complex and vary from state to state, but a rough approximation reveals that four-person households with total incomes above $15,000 per year may legally receive food stamps.

Many of the programs overlap. For example, we can assume that children who receive taxpayer-provided breakfasts and lunches at school also eat three meals a day at home from the food stamp program. Food stamp recipients are also eligible for the WIC program and for commodity distribution programs. According to the Congressional Budget Office, federal food programs do much more than prevent hunger or malnutrition: "Today, the food stamp program goes beyond providing recipients the wherewithal to increase food consumption and, on the average, for every one dollar of bonus food stamps transferred, approximately 43 cents is freed for nonfood purchases."[30] In effect, the food stamp program is so generous that it goes far beyond meeting the food needs of families that cannot provide for themselves; it permits recipients to take money that would have gone for food and spend it on other items.

Given USDA's objective to increase the consumption of commodities, it is not surprising that there has been a great deal of fraud in federal programs and that little effort has been made to reduce the level of fraud or to punish those involved. In 1977 the General Accounting Office reported:

> The Government is losing over half a billion dollars annually because of overissued food stamp benefits caused by errors, misrepresentations, and suspected fraud by recipients, and by errors by local food stamp offices. For every $100 of the more than $5 billion in annual benefits issued nationally, overissuances account for about $12. Only about 12 cents of that $12 dollars has been recovered. The . . . projects GAO reviewed were doing little to identify and recover the value of these overissuances.

191

. . . [A]bout half of the dollar value of claims established for stamp overissuances were classified as involving suspected fraud by recipients, but very few recipients were prosecuted or otherwise penalized. . . . If some semblance of integrity is to be maintained in this program, food stamp recipient fraud cannot be allowed to continue unchecked. Administrative adjudication and penalty assessment could be an effective deterrent.[31]

The report apparently had no effect, for six years later GAO again reported:

In fiscal years 1980 and 1981, about $2 billion in food stamps benefits was overissued and about $500 million was underissued because of food stamp agency errors and fraud. The net drain on program resources could have provided benefits to about 1.7 million needy people for 2 years.

Without specific direction and emphasis from the Department of Agriculture, States collected only about $20 million, or 1 cent of each overissued dollar, during the 2 fiscal years.[32]

Public outrage about fraud and abuse of the program led to congressional pressure for so-called workfare. Under this program, every unemployed recipient who is able to work would be required to do so to obtain food stamps. Although there was much fanfare about cracking down on malingerers, nothing of substance was done.[33] In an evaluation of the workfare requirements in 1978, GAO found that of 620 able-bodied food stamp recipients required to register for work, only 3 actually got jobs and 384 were not even registered for work at the local employment service offices responsible for helping them find jobs.[34] The penalties for failure to participate, although rarely imposed, were hardly burdensome: An individual who refused to work would not receive benefits for 30 days; other family members would not be affected and would continue to receive their benefits. Complying with the work requirement was also simple. According to GAO, "Merely showing up at the worksite constituted compliance with the workfare obligation."[35] USDA sought to mollify congressional critics and soothe the irate public, but if stringent restrictions about working had been applied to recipients, the number participating in the program might have been reduced.

Are federal and food programs effective? After billions of dollars have been spent, the answer to this question is still unknown. In late 1975 a report published by the National Academy of Sciences concluded:

> Little or no effective evaluation of the impact of these programs [for example, food fortification, nutritional labeling, nutrition education, and supplemental feeding programs, such as food stamps, surplus food distribution, school lunches, and women and infant children feeding] on the nutritional well-being of the target groups has been carried out. The cost-effectiveness of these programs versus other means of expanding purchasing power has not been evaluated for their relative impact on nutritional goals. As a consequence there is little information with which to assess the continuing value of these programs.[36]

USDA, however, was not anxious to provide thorough studies of the impact of the programs. Five years later the Congressional Budget Office indicated that "ad hoc assessments have served as the major evaluations supporting the continued growth and expansion of the programs."[37] Consistent and reliable data "have not existed," and the evidence is still "fragmented."[38]

Studies on diet conducted at Pennsylvania State University reported that households participating in the food distribution program had no better diets than similar households that did not participate. Further, the study concluded that food stamps provided some improvement in the diets of families experiencing temporary shortages of funds; that is, when more than two weeks had elapsed since the family received income from its last major source of pay. But when households had received income within two weeks preceding their interviews, the impact of food stamps on their nutrient intake was insignificant.[39] A more recent assessment of federal food programs takes a dim view:

> If federal food assistance was intended to fight hunger, then it was an abject failure, since the poor consume fewer calories now than in 1955. The decline in calorie consumption among the poor stems largely from decreased fat intake and is mainly a result of personal choice. If hunger were widespread among the poor today, they would buy more calorie-dense, fatty foods, and fewer fruits and vegetables. Scattered cases of individual hunger may exist, but it makes no sense to make 40 million people eligible for food stamps because of half a dozen families shown on the evening news.[40]

193

If the objective of federal food programs is to prevent malnutrition, then much more could be achieved much less expensively by simply fortifying foods with vitamins. The Congressional Budget Office indicated in May 1980 that "vitamin fortification could provide for 100 percent of a child's recommended dietary allowance for less than $3.00 a year in ingredient costs."[41] There is no doubt that a major problem with American eating habits is a lack of understanding about what is required for good nutrition. The federal government is engaged in major research and information dissemination, with more than 125 federal programs conducted by an alphabet soup of 42 agencies dealing with nutrition.[42] The involvement of the federal government in nutrition is part of the problem. According to GAO, information is given piecemeal and sometimes is duplicative, conflicting, and confusing."[43] Consider the recommendations made in federal government reports dealing with polyunsaturated fat. Five federal reports indicate that good nutrition requires an increase in polyunsaturated fats; five others indicate that polyunsaturated fats should not be increased. To add to the confusion, one report specifies that polyunsaturated fat should be increased "for high risk groups."[44] Is it any wonder that the average consumer is not knowledgeable about nutrition?

Federal food programs have clearly gotten out of hand. Tens of billions of taxpayers' dollars are being spent annually on programs, even though there is virtually no evidence that the expenditures are producing substantive benefits. Fraud and abuse are rampant, and no real effort has been made to correct these problems. Federal food programs do not even meet federal standards: In 1978 GAO reported that 40 percent of the lunches served under the school lunch program did not meet the USDA's own requirements and were significantly lacking in as many as 8 of the 13 nutrients for which standards had been set.[45] In 1979 GAO found that 20 percent of the child care food centers had unhealthy conditions, including vermin, and that 62 percent of the centers failed to meet nutritional standards.[46] In another study conducted in 1981, GAO still found lunches in federal programs lacking in 7 of 14 required nutrients and evidencing a substantial waste of food.[47] There are alternatives that offer results at much lower costs, but they have been given short shrift or have been totally ignored.

In May 1980 the Congressional Budget Office questioned whether hunger and severe malnutrition in the United States were ever serious problems, even before the War on Poverty was initiated:

What are the nutritional problems that are to be addressed by government intervention? Hunger and severe malnutrition are *not serious public health problems* in the United States today although some subgroups of the population may be affected. Despite some limited cases of severe malnutrition found by the Senate Subcommittee on Employment, Manpower and Poverty in the Mississippi Delta in 1967, statements that severe malnutrition exists on a national scale have never been documented, even during the early years of the "War on Poverty" programs [emphasis added].[48]

Hunger in the Mississippi Delta in 1967 is hardly surprising. Federal government agricultural policy wrecked the local economy by making agricultural labor subject to the minimum wage in 1966 and by increasing cotton set-aside payments, which resulted in less cotton being planted. To save on labor costs, planters turned to mechanical cotton-pickers, throwing tens of thousands of farm laborers out of work, according to USDA. Because cotton acreage was reduced at the same time, the demand for labor was lowered even further. Unemployment was severe in the area, and without income, people found it difficult to buy food.[49]

From this episode, however, a team of physicians sponsored by the Field Foundation extrapolated wildly to the entire United States and reported findings that were used as the basis for the hysteria about hunger that prevailed throughout the 1970s and continues today:

> Wherever we went and wherever we looked we saw children in significant numbers who were hungry and sick, children for whom hunger is a daily fact of life, and sickness in many forms, an inevitability. The children we saw were more than just malnourished. They were hungry, weak, apathetic. Their lives are being shortened. They are visibly and predictably losing their health, their energy, their spirits. They are suffering from hunger and disease, and directly or indirectly, they are dying from them—which is exactly what "starvation" means.[50]

Hunger Hysteria: Federal Funding of Political Advocacy for Food

The report of the Field Foundation physicians was given wide circulation through congressional hearings and the media. The issue of hunger had intrinsic appeal because of its human interest content, and liberal politicians quickly seized the issue as a means of demonstrating their caring and concern for the less fortunate. USDA bureaucrats, always in search of ways to increase their budgets and the number of programs under their control, quickly recognized that the hunger issue was a potential bonanza. The output of the nation's farms could be mobilized in the War on Poverty, and it would be possible to attempt once again to reduce the costly food surpluses that were accumulating by providing large-scale federal subsidies for the purchase of domestic food.[51] To accomplish these USDA goals, Congress would have to appropriate funds for food programs, and so members of Congress would have to be persuaded that votes could be won by providing food subsidies for people who, on the whole, could feed themselves. In short, a politically active grass-roots lobby was needed to pressure Congress and to develop constituents for the programs. By law, however, federal employees are not permitted to lobby for programs, even though they routinely do so under the guise of providing "public information,"[52] and the organization and development of a vocal grass-roots constituency for food programs is a task for which the federal bureaucracy is not well suited. The activity is too visible (the whole idea of such a campaign is to arouse certain segments of the public), and it is time consuming.

Given that federal employees in USDA cannot easily lobby Congress, another approach to generate political support for government programs involves lobbying activities conducted by private organizations that are financed by government grants and contracts. Although it is also illegal for federal funds to be used by any organization for political activity, the law had never been strictly enforced. Further, even if an organization were challenged on the use of tax money for political advocacy, the repercussions would be felt by the grantee rather than by the grantor. Especially during the Carter administration, liberal political activists had become entrenched in the federal bureaucracy and largely controlled the allocation of funds from the Community Services Administration (see chapter 9) and the Legal Services Corporation (see chapter 12). Other agencies were also providing funding and other support for political advocacy groups dealing with government involvement in a host of issues, including housing, welfare rights, civil rights, senior citizen concerns, and health care. The food programs were just another form of income transfer, and funds were made available to finance political advocacy groups that specialized in this issue: "The Community Services Administration funded scores of local and national food stamp advocate organizations to increase enrollment in food stamp programs. . . . Total funding for food advocacy organizations probably exceeded $100 million in the 1970s."[53]

In addition to the organizations concentrating on food programs, many others joined coalitions that were concerned with a variety of related issues. Table A8.1 (in appendix) provides information on selected grants to a sample of the advocacy organizations involved in welfare rights, showing that vast amounts of federal tax funds and other resources have been allocated to these groups. A review of the activities of the Food Research and Action Center (FRAC) and some of the other organizations in the food and welfare rights movement reveals their political orientation.

The Food Research and Action Center

A brief summary of FRAC's history, objectives, methods, and funding appears on the inside front cover of its 1981 publication entitled *Food and Nutrition Issues in the Food Stamp Program:*

> The Food Research and Action Center (FRAC) was organized in 1970 as a nonprofit law firm and *advocacy center* working with the poor and near poor to end hunger and malnutrition in the United States. FRAC works primarily with the Federal food programs— the food stamp, school lunch and breakfast, elderly nutrition, child care food, summer food, and women, infants and children (WIC) programs as vehicles for addressing this nation's hunger problems. However FRAC's premise in its work is that the Federal food programs cannot solve the problems of this nation's poor; hunger and malnutrition are caused primarily by a lack of income, and *are tragic symptoms of the maldistribution of economic resources in this country.*
>
> Therefore, in the 1980s FRAC will be engaged in efforts to help groups around the country work with the food programs, not only to meet the immediate needs of America's hungry, but also as an *organizing tool for poor people and their allies in the larger effort at creating meaningful social change.* This work will focus on three areas:
>
> —to represent the interests of the poor and the near poor in the development and implementation of the federal food programs, and to protect their rights with litigation and legal support to local Legal Services offices and other legal advocacy groups;
>
> —to help community groups and coalitions work to improve the food programs through *local organizing and advocacy efforts,* and to promote the development of organization among recipients

and their friends to tackle food and other poverty-related issues; and

—to develop written materials to help people understand the food programs, *to undertake the training of community advocates working with the programs, and to understand national and state legislative issues around the food programs and welfare reform so they can express their views and have some impact on the legislation.*

FRAC is funded jointly through the Community Food and Nutrition Program of the *U.S. Community Services Administration,* the United Methodist Church, the *Legal Services Corporation* and by other church and foundation sources [emphasis added].[54]

FRAC readily admits that food programs are an "organizing tool" in the "larger effort at creating meaningful social change." The direction of social change is not difficult to discern: Clearly, the objective is to remedy the "tragic symptoms of the maldistribution of economic resources in this country." Food program funds are being used to promote the ideas of political activists, and some of the taxpayer support has been provided by the Reagan administration: "The *New York Times* reports that *two-thirds* of FRAC's 1981 budget was tax-subsidized, some $600,000; in 1982, FRAC received $120,000 in federal subsidies."[55] The Legal Services Corporation "gave $50,000 to the Food Research and Action Center (FRAC) in Fiscal Year 1983."[56] Given this heavy reliance on taxpayers' funds, FRAC's vocal resistance to budget cuts by the Reagan administration and particularly to the disbanding of the Community Services Administration is understandable.

FRAC has vociferously opposed the Reagan administration's tax and economic policies. In its monthly newspaper, *Foodlines,* there is a recurring theme that these policies are unfair and they must be changed. For example, the June 1983 issue stated that "new taxes should be raised from those who are not now paying their fair share of the tax burden, i.e. corporations and the wealthy."[57] The sample issue urged readers to contact their congressional representatives: "After two years of budget cuts, we have a chance to get a budget adopted that would ADD money to the federal food programs. Members of Congress, particularly those on the Budget Resolution Conference, must hear from you."[58]

FRAC encouraged participation in the "National Let Them Eat Cake Sale," which was held October 3, 1983, in various cities as a media event. Pastries were baked and given unlikely names (Guns-

or-Butter Cookies, Banana Republic Cream Pie, and Upside Down Budget Cake) and games were played (Wheel of Reaganomic Misfortune, the Social Safety Net Jump, and Test Your Political Strength) to "educate participants about the effects of Administration policies."[59] As announced, "The First National Let Them Eat Cake Sale will also provide a unique opportunity to organize a vital new constituency through coalition-building at the local and national levels. This highly visible forum is sure to garner media attention and attract new members for citizen action groups."[60]

FRAC's propaganda goes far beyond food issues. An article in the June 1983 issue of Foodlines, "Soviet Attack: The Exaggerated Threat," dealt with foreign affairs and defense issues.[61] More than a casual interest is involved in FRAC's discussion of U.S.-Soviet strategic capabilities, in that the organization advocates a reduction in the U.S. defense budget. FRAC joined with the National Anti-Hunger Coalition (NAHC) to form FACT (Feed America's Communities Today), a campaign "to Fight Domestic Hunger and Guarantee People the Right to Eat."[62] To finance FACT's goals, an additional $7.5 billion dollars is needed, and "simple, common sense, formulas" are proposed to raise the funds, such as "a 2% general efficiency reduction in Pentagon spending."[63]

FRAC evidently enjoys a close working relationship with the USDA officials involved in food programs. A FRAC brochure describing its activities and goals reports that "FRAC's attorneys worked *with* Department of Agriculture officials to restore critical food benefits to retarded and handicapped children in day care settings" (emphasis added).[64] Although the brochure indicates that "providing information to the Congress" is the principal technique used by the organization to influence legislation, it also states that "at the request of congressional offices and veterans' groups FRAC staff drafted legal language to protect the right of disabled veterans to food benefits."[65] Drafting legislation goes far beyond providing information, but FRAC has often liberally interpreted both its mandate and its methods. For example, GAO has claimed that "a March 1979 booklet about the Food Stamp Program, published by a research and action group in Washington, D.C., advised food stamp recipients that they did not have to make restitution for receiving too many benefits."[66]

Since President Reagan took office, FRAC has devoted most of its efforts to opposing administration policies. The organization is using federal grants "to help people sue the [Department of Agriculture] and bring class-action suits to block proposed cutbacks in nutrition spending."[67] FRAC's opposition to Reagan administration policies goes far beyond the food issue, however, in that proposed budget cuts to the agencies that help fund FRAC and similar groups present a major threat to their continued existence. To counter the Reagan administration's efforts to reduce spending on domestic programs, FRAC played a major role in forming a powerful coalition of tax-funded advocacy groups, labor unions, and religious organizations called the Fair Budget Action Campaign (FBAC) (see Table A2.3). The "Statement of Purpose" of FBAC contended that

> the budget policies of the Administration and the Congress—deep cuts in human needs programs, the largest peacetime military buildup in the nation's history and massive shifts in the tax burden from corporations and the wealthy to middle and low income taxpayers—are leading the country to disaster and economic hardship. We believe that the crises caused by these misguided policies require a unified response on the part of organizations which have traditionally worked on a more narrow range of issues (i.e., human services, taxes, peace). We are therefore initiating a Fair Budget Action Campaign to work for the maintenance of vital human services, equitable taxation and sensible military spending. We will attempt to achieve these ends through cooperative grass-roots action among our constituencies and intensive public education on the devastating effects of the Reagan budget policies.[68]

Although the voters elected Reagan and thereby endorsed his policy changes, advocacy groups involved in FBAC used tax funds to oppose these policy shifts: "Together we can stop or at least greatly impede the Reagan Budget."[69]

For each Reagan budget, FBAC produces *An Organizer's Manual* that reviews the budget, offers alternatives, and contains a primer for "Local Organizing for a Fair Budget."[70] The second issue of the manual, *Information on President Reagan's 1983 Budget Cuts*, contained scathing criticism of almost every element of the proposed budget. Consider the description of "Reaganomics":

> The Reagan Administration's economic plan amounts to an attack on the entire relationship between the American people and their government. Beginning with the New Deal in the 1930s this country made a commitment to help those in need—the unemployed, the disabled, the elderly, the poor. Individual charity wasn't enough. Government assistance was needed to help the people left out by the raw operations of the market system.

200

Return to the 1920s. Under the guise of a new approach to solving economic problems, conservatives are proposing what they have always proposed: Favors for the wealthy, big business and special interests; a cold shoulder for the unemployed, the poor and the disadvantaged.[71]

After much rhetoric on the budget, careful attention was directed toward the political activities necessary to defeat the Reagan economic program and the budget cuts. The third part of the manual, devoted to local organizing, covered such topics as building coalitions, developing community impact data, fundraising at the grass roots, holding an accountability hearing, holding a public forum, lobbying, working with the media, holding public demonstrations, and registering and educating voters. FBAC expressed concern about using government funds in voter registration campaigns, but it also suggested an expedient that would minimize the difficulties:

> The use of government funds for registration may raise problems. Even if the use of particular government funds for registration is not barred, groups using such funds should be aware that this may result in government audits or other governmental scrutiny aimed at challenging the appropriateness or legality of the activity or, perhaps, the tax-exemption of the group. . . .

> To minimize restrictions and legal hassles, many groups have found it wise to establish coalitions for voter registration. This allows one group to share responsibility, costs, and risks. It also broadens the base for effort, making it much more effective. Groups under tough legal restrictions then limit their aid to the coalitions to volunteer and after-hours work by staff and to similar nonorganizational support.[72]

Further, the FBAC manual noted that "all registration activities by tax-exempt groups *must be non-partisan—they must not favor a particular candidate or party.*"[73] (Of course, given that all of the groups in the coalition are adamantly opposed to the Reagan administration's policies, it is unlikely that FBAC was nonpartisan during the 1984 campaign.) Other advice in the manual intended for political organizers ranged from the mundane to the sublime; for example, "[Y]ou may wish to establish legal counsel for your demonstration in advance, particularly if you are planning a sit-in, boycott, or any other non-violent activity that does not remain within the bounds of local, state, or federal law."[74]

Without question, these advocacy groups are thinly disguised political organizations whose leaders are well aware of the illegality of their activities as tax-supported entities. The fiction that such groups operate in the public interest and are apolitical has been preserved primarily because the federal government has not enforced the law and exposed the political nature of these groups. Politicians have found that the costs of exposing such abuses are too high, for any attempt to question or restrain the entrenched privileges that these organizations have enjoyed would produce a firestorm of protest and righteous indignation from the media. Moreover, there is little criticism from advocacy groups on the political right because some receive government funds as well and others are ever hopeful of getting their hands into the public till (see chapter 14). Although most of the advocacy efforts are directed at the federal government, considerable work has been done at the local and state levels of government as well.

FRAC makes every effort to implement its political goals by organizing at the grass-roots level. To obtain the participation of citizens who may not ordinarily be politically active, FRAC focuses on specific issues, such as campaigns for school lunch and breakfast programs. FRAC-produced how-to manuals, written in an easily understood style, outline in detail every aspect of an organizing campaign by a pressure group. One such manual, FRAC's *Guide to Quality School Lunch and Breakfast Programs,* illustrates this concept at the local level, and gives "special acknowledgement to Paula Roberts of Legal Services Corporation for her valuable assistance in the earlier development and publication of this guide."[75] Clearly, the relationship between FRAC and the government agencies that provide its funding can hardly be described as being at arm's length. It is also interesting that FRAC refers in the manual to the meals provided through school lunch and breakfast programs as "free"—there is no indication that taxpayers fund the programs.

After providing a brief review of the meal programs, the FRAC manual is devoted to organizing a political campaign for federally subsidized school meals. The campaign begins with the formation of a committee that recruits allies from such sources as welfare rights activists, unions, and community service agencies. The committee's organizers are also encouraged to broaden the coalition:

> Other groups to consider are dairy associations, local and state food co-ops, farmers and grocers since they would benefit eco-

nomically if the program were implemented. You may find that a breakfast campaign has the potential for uniting people who would ordinarily be on opposite sides of the fence. At any rate, the broader based the group, the better![76]

The message is clear, though subtly stated: In ordinary circumstances the business community is on the opposite side from that of welfare advocates, but when profit is involved, businessmen have flexible attitudes. FRAC has little patience with opponents, especially elected officials:

> If the school board is unwilling to commit itself, or if they are simply opposed to a breakfast program, you must double your efforts. Find more advocates, enlist editorial support and additional press coverage, and work on individual board members or school officials. Over the long run, you might have to work to defeat the hostile board members at election time and replace them with supporters.[77]

According to welfare advocates, real progress can only be made if sympathetic officials hold elected office.

Appendixes to this manual contain a complete sample set of materials for mobilizing community opinion and political support, including by-laws for the committee, a community flyer, an agenda for a community conference or public meeting on school food programs, a statement to be presented to the school board, and a press release to gain access to the media. All that is required is that the appropriate blanks be filled in. For additional assistance, the names and addresses of "advocate groups and FRAC fieldworkers" are provided.[78]

FRAC's political agenda at the state level of government, as set out in another manual, *Guide to State Legislation,* is much more sophisticated than that pursued at the local level.[79] The first chapter of this FRAC manual deals with "lobbying the state legislature" and contains a wealth of information about dealing with state legislators and interest groups and forming networks or coalitions. The remainder of the text deals with political objectives at the state level with regard to food stamps, school lunch and breakfast legislation, and the food sales tax. If elected representatives are perceived as unsympathetic to the welfare cause, the manual suggests that this obstacle could be evaded by dealing with the state's unelected bureaucrats:

If your state legislature generally reacts favorably on poor people's issues, you should probably pursue food stamp issues with them. But if the legislature is reactionary, stay away from them and concentrate on administration advocacy with the state public welfare department. A reactionary legislature could very well take a bill designed to limit verification [of recipients' incomes and allowable expenses] and turn it into a law requiring verification in all areas permitted by federal regulation.[80]

Tactics represent a relatively minor part of this manual. Instead, much attention is given to specific proposals for legislative changes to food programs that FRAC advocates, including requiring bilingual materials in the food stamp program, making it easier to obtain food stamps quickly, requiring more formal (and more costly to the taxpayer) hearings when actions adverse to food stamp recipients are taken, making workfare more difficult to implement and enforce, mandating that schools offer food programs for students, regulating food served in school programs, and increasing state expenditures for a variety of purposes relating to food programs (for example, the purchasing of kitchen equipment for school cafeterias). In some cases the manual offers model legislation, often based on laws enacted in other states where the welfare lobby has been successful.

The campaign against sales taxes on food is based on the regressivity of this tax, that is, lower-income households pay a greater proportion of their income for such a tax than do higher-income households.[81] A sales tax on food also raises the effective price of food and therefore reduces consumption. It is interesting that FRAC is concerned when sales taxes increase the price of food, but not when federal agricultural policies produce the same result. The reason for this asymmetry is that FRAC can use the sales tax issue as a vehicle for attacking the rich. At every opportunity, FRAC denounces and condemns corporations and higher-income taxpayers:

> [T]hose with the most political power (corporations and wealthier individuals) have disproportionately light tax burdens.[82]

> There are innumerable ways to replace lost food tax revenues and shift the burden because there are innumerable features in states' tax systems which enable corporations and wealthy individuals to legally evade paying their fair share of the tax burden.[83]

> When identifying new revenue sources, we must focus on those taxpayers who benefited the most from the Reagan tax bill—since

that's where the new "tax base" was created. And since the biggest beneficiaries were corporations and wealthy individuals that's where our attention should be focused.[84]

FRAC's political goals are directed as much against wealthy individuals and corporations as they are toward advocating food programs. FRAC's allies, regardless of the stated purpose of their organizations, also attempt to redistribute income and limit the rights to private property. Social change is the ultimate goal. The policies and objectives pursued by the Association of Community Organizations for Reform Now (ACORN), one of the members of the FBAC coalition, clearly illustrate this political orientation.

The Association of Community Organizations for Reform Now

ACORN was founded in 1970 as the Arkansas Community Organizations for Reform Now, a project of 1960s welfare rights organizers who were attempting to build a new neighborhood-based activism among low- and moderate-income families. ACORN's founder, Wade Rathke, had been the chief organizer for the Massachusetts branch of the National Welfare Rights Organization. For nearly five years, ACORN operated exclusively in Arkansas, primarily in Little Rock neighborhoods. Affiliated state branches were then established in South Dakota and Texas.[85] By 1983 ACORN had established groups in 27 states and claimed over 60,000 families as members.[86] As the geographical scope and size of the organization grew, the "Arkansas" in its name was replaced with "Association."

ACORN's success can be traced directly to taxpayer financial support. Nevertheless, ACORN has always stressed its financial independence as a member-supported organization: "ACORN has always been committed to the principle of financial self-sufficiency and we've made great strides toward that goal. The principle is important because only an organization that raises and controls its own funds can be truly independent. Because ACORN members pay the organization's way, we call the shots."[87] There is considerable doubt, however, whether ACORN would have even survived had not federal support been given through VISTA (the domestic version of the Peace Corps). At ACORN's urging, VISTA initiated the Community Organizations Research and Action Project (CORAP), which assigned its volunteers to work with neighborhood groups. The CORAP grant was awarded in September 1977 and provided $470,475 for training 100 VISTA volunteers, 80 of whom were delegated to ACORN activities in Arkansas, Texas, Missouri, Tennessee, Louisiana, Florida, and South Dakota. The link between ACORN and CORAP was so close that it was

> difficult to distinguish between the makeup and operation of the organizations. The officers of both the CORAP board and the ACORN board are the same individuals. The project supervisor and the project coordinator are paid under the grant for full-time employment, but both are also on the ACORN payroll. Training under the grant is provided by the Arkansas Institute for Social Justice . . . another spinoff organization run by two former ACORN organizers.[88]

ACORN's account of the meeting of its executive board on October 15, 1977, indicated that "our financial situation is such that we can no longer afford to be as distant [from federal funding]—unless we are willing to see the organization risk death."[89] ACORN organizers were placed on the VISTA payroll to conserve resources.

ACORN has actively tapped a variety of federal agencies for financial support, including a $60,000 grant from the National Endowment for the Humanities for Louisiana ACORN to "plan for a two-year educational program in the humanities for low and moderate income members." This project was to be undertaken in cooperation with the Institute for Social Justice. In 1981 the endowment's award was renewed and increased to $201,558; the purpose of the grant, however, was more explicitly stated. The rather ambiguous "humanities program" translated into "explaining the history of social movements." The Community Services Administration awarded Texas ACORN $25,000 in 1981, and ACTION gave $2,000 to Oklahoma ACORN in 1980. This list of federal grants is indicative—and by no means exhaustive.

ACORN is a political organization with its own "People's Platform." The platform's preamble, in part, states:

> We come before our nation, not to petition with hat in hand, but to rise as one people and demand.
>
> We have waited and watched. We have hoped and helped. We have sweated and suffered.
>
> We have often believed. We have frequently followed.
>
> But we have nothing to show for the work of our hands, the tax of our labor. Our patience has been abused; our experience misused. Our silence has been seen as support. Our struggle has been ignored.

Enough is enough. We will wait no longer for the crumbs at America's door. We will not be meek, but mighty. We will not starve on past promises, but feast on future dreams.

. . . We will continue our fight until the American way is just one way, until we have shared the wealth, until we have won our freedom. . . .

Our freedom shall be based on the equality of the many, not the income of the few. Our freedom is the force of democracy, not the farce of federal fat and personal profit. In our freedom, only the people shall rule.[90]

The planks of the People's Platform contain wide-ranging proposals for overhauling the nation's economic system. The energy plank ("put people before profits at the utilities") indicates that publicly owned (that is, government-owned) utilities are preferable to privately operated firms; rates should not be based on the cost of providing service or consumption, but on "social considerations"; discontinued service for nonpayment of bills should be prohibited or severely restricted; and consumers should control state regulatory commissions. The platform also calls for price controls on gasoline, heating oil, and propane. The health-care plank calls for a national health care system "controlled by democratically elected community-based committees," with fixed salaries for doctors and around-the-clock free neighborhood clinics. The housing plank demands at least 1 million new units of federally subsidized housing each year, rent controls, limitations on eviction of tenants, and every type of housing subsidy imaginable. The jobs and income plank proposes to guarantee a minimum annual family income at the Bureau of Labor Statistics "median living standard," public jobs programs, every conceivable form of welfare and disability payments (pegged to the cost of living), and the "rights of workers." Other planks deal with rural issues, community development, and banking. The tax plank advocates "reform" that translates into eliminating taxes for low- and middle-income wage earners and establishing much heavier taxes for upper-income households and big corporations. The representation plank would require all corporations to have worker representatives and low-income members on their corporate boards. Throughout the platform, the corporation is singled out as the major cause of all social and economic problems, and such groups as workers, farmers, tenants, consumers, and communities are to be given "rights" to organize and be

207

collectively represented in their "confrontations" with business corporations.[91]

ACORN attempts to implement its program through political action. In an effort to put some distance between the organization and its political activities, a political action committee has been formed:

> APAC is the political arm of ACORN, exercising our strength in electoral campaigns. APAC is a committee of the ACORN citywide or statewide board. . . . It takes the lead in screening and endorsing candidates for political office, planning and carrying out voter education and get-out-the-vote efforts.

> Unlike other Political Action Committees (PACs) which exist to make financial contributions to candidates, APAC exists to move the organized power of low and moderate income people at the ballot box. Its strength is not in the size of its budget but in its house-to-house and precinct-by-precinct work.[92]

The distinction between ACORN and APAC is one of style rather than substance. Since its founding, ACORN has always been actively involved in politics, beginning with local issues and local elections and soon expanding to statewide political issues and campaigns. An article in the *New Republic* in 1974 described ACORN's political goals: "By 1976 ACORN hopes to have . . . enough political clout to start influencing legislative races . . . [and to pass] legislation to benefit its constituency."[93] Evidently, ACORN met its timetable; in the 1978 Arkansas primary election, at least one of the taxpayer-provided VISTA volunteers from the CORAP grant was "instructed by his ACORN supervisor to participate in a mailing of a slate of endorsements to ACORN members, develop and reproduce a flyer endorsing candidates to State and local office for distribution at neighborhood meetings, cover the polls and pass out a slate of ACORN endorsements, and distribute endorsed candidates' literature to members."[94]

ACORN not only endorses candidates but also has its members run for elected office. In 1974 ACORN members filed and ran for every seat on the governing body of Pulaski County, Arkansas, the location of the city of Little Rock, and effectively gained control of the budget.[95] ACORN has advocated change-of-government initiatives in several cities to replace at-large election systems with ward-by-ward or neighborhood systems. In the 1982 elections in Arkansas, Colorado, and Michigan, ACORN initiated proposals for the statewide election of utility commissioners.[96] The organization has had considerable success in its political campaigns at the state and local levels: Homesteading programs have been adopted in at least six cities; the sales tax on medicine has been repealed in Arkansas and Missouri; so-called lifeline telephone rates have been started in six states; and increased payments and expanded eligibility for federal energy assistance have been obtained in seven states.[97]

During the late 1970s, ACORN became more actively involved in national politics and began to use its local organizations to elect delegates to the Democratic National Convention; further, 42 ACORN members were delegates or alternates at the 1980 convention.[98] At state caucuses and conventions, ACORN has also become an important political force.[99] After the 1980 election, much of ACORN's energy was devoted to opposing the Reagan administration, and, according to its membership newsletter, *ACORN USA*, the organization was going to make every effort to defeat Reagan in 1984:

> [O]n June 18, ACORN Founders Day, every ACORN city will hold a caucus to kick off our involvement in the 84 presidential campaign. Candidates or their representatives will be invited to state their case. Then, ACORN members will vote for their favorite candidate and designate which ones are "unacceptable."
>
> The caucuses will be a signal to the candidates that ACORN members are ready to work hard to beat Reagan next year.[100]

Other articles in the newsletter have dealt with political campaigns and issues at the national level. Even though ACORN's political activities are supposedly conducted through APAC, no mention has been made of this organization in these articles.

Like FRAC, ACORN is essentially a political organization operating with taxpayer support under the guise of a public interest group working for the poor. Other organizations receiving taxpayer funding (see Table A8.1) operate in a similar vein. Although the specific areas of interest may differ from organization to organization, the groups are all members of the same family. One of the major reasons that these groups are so similar is that the cadre of personnel who organize and direct them usually come from the same source and receive similar training (see chapter 2). The constituent groups that comprise the welfare rights coalition do not arise spontaneously at the local level, but are the result of a carefully planned strategy to initiate and nurture their formation and development. ACORN has played a major role in this strategy by spawning the Institute for Social Justice (ISJ).

The Institute for Social Justice: An Organization for Organizing

According to the *Acorn Members Handbook, 1983*, ACORN has helped establish at least four organizations, including ISJ, which is

> a national training and research center, now headquartered in Dallas, Texas. Since 1972, the Institute has shared ACORN's experience and skills with community groups, legal services programs, church groups, community action agencies, and other local and national organizations. The Institute conducts special research and educational projects in conjunction with ACORN, and carries out local, regional, and national training programs for ACORN leaders.[101]

ISJ's training of organizers goes far beyond ACORN's needs. As early as 1975, ISJ was actively involved in training large numbers of activists. As Wade Rathke explained to the *New York Times*, "In 1975, . . . it trained 450 persons for 55 other organizations."[102]

ISJ publishes a quarterly journal, *The Organizer*, which contains practical suggestions for successful organizing, as well as more esoteric articles that provide the intellectual foundations of the movement. In the Spring 1982 issue, an article entitled "Going to Court: A Research Guide" suggested that court records can be used as a source of "personal information on target figures that can be deeply private and perhaps intensely embarrassing."[103] Other "tactical" suggestions appeared in "The Seven D's of Defense," an article in the Winter 1983 issue that proposed:

> A strong offense in an organizing campaign requires begin [sic] ready to counter any defense your adversary might employ. . . .
>
> I've grouped the most familiar counter tactics into several categories that I call "The Seven D's of Defense": Deflecting, Delaying, Denying, Deceiving, Dividing, Discrediting, and Destroying.[104]

The same issue contained an article entitled "Realigning the Democrats," in which Richard A. Cloward and Frances Fox Piven contended that "What the Left needs is a national strategy that can translate these convictions [about economic rights] into the power to block the corporate agenda."[105] Cloward and Piven proposed a strategy that includes protest and conflict:

210

[T]hrough collective protest, millions of politicized poor and minority voters will enter the Democratic Party. A class-based party, including women, minorities, industrial workers, and the tens of millions of beneficiaries of the welfare state, will be in the making. And with the realignment, perhaps the increasing politicization of the American electorate will be matched by an ideologically oriented party politics.[106]

Given that the activists who promote the liberal causes espoused by the organizations that receive taxpayers' dollars receive similar training and read the same ideological materials, it is not surprising that the goals and methods are so similar throughout the welfare rights movement. Without exception, it can be demonstrated that in this movement, the basic agenda is the same: the redistribution of income through the auspices of the state, and greater government control over every aspect of the private sector.

Rural America: ACORN in the Countryside

Rural America is the countryside's counterpart of ACORN—a group that organizes low- and middle-income families for political activities in rural areas. There are, of course, differences in emphasis between the two organizations. For example, while ACORN is concerned with urban pollution, Rural America approaches environmental issues from a pesticide perspective. According to Rural America:

> The poverty and powerlessness of rural Americans is no accident. . . . It is the result of social and economic policies. For much of this country's history, and especially the last 100 years, rural America has been viewed as one huge factory—a food factory, an energy factory, a timber factory—and its people have been seen as a source of cheap labor to keep these factories operating. For the most part, public policies have been designed to support narrow economic interests engaged in the exploitation of rural resources and people. Tax laws, government subsidies, research and so-called development programs have been aimed at removing the wealth of rural America as fast and as profitably as possible for the benefit of corporate interests.[107]

Rural America has proposed a political platform that is remarkably similar to ACORN's. Its platform proposals include the rights of citizens to welfare, the extension of the food stamp program, access of Rural America representatives to the policy-making body

211

of the Department of Health and Human Services and representation on the National Health Planning Council, "alternative forms" of land ownership, farmers' strikes, expanded union rights, increased federal funding for employment training centers, federal funding for rural health centers, free school meals for all students, elimination of corporate control of energy production, and an increase in federal funds for legal aid.[108]

This ambitious agenda is to be implemented through political action financed with taxpayers' funds. Organizing Rural America chapters throughout the nation and finding grass-roots support for its political goals have been underwritten by the federal government. Even the manuals for the political activists have been produced with tax funds. Rural America uses two "guides for organizers": (1) *Getting People Together in Rural America—A Beginner's Guide to Consumer Organizing*, and (2) *Making Democracy Real in Rural America—A Guide to Organizing and Advocacy in Rural Areas*. A statement on the front cover of *Getting People Together* recognized that "the research and preparation of this report were supported by the Office of Consumers' Education, U.S. Department of Health, Education and Welfare."[109] *Making Democracy Real* acknowledges that "this handbook was prepared under a grant from the Community Services Administration to explore non-service delivery organizing in rural areas."[110] In addition to providing the resources to produce training manuals, the federal government has arranged for VISTA volunteers to staff Rural America organizing drives and has given grants and contracts for hundreds of thousands of dollars (see Table A8.1) to further the organization's goals. According to *Making Democracy Real*, organizing is done for only one purpose:

> Simply put, the purpose of organizing . . . is to influence private and public institutions to make them more responsive to the needs of low and moderate income people. This may involve the creation of new institutions and the launching of new services or it may simply mean making already existing services more accessible and equitable for particular constituencies. . . .
>
> Advocacy and reform movements are firmly rooted in the American tradition. The underlying objective is to make real the American ideal that every person or group *has a right to an equitable share of society's goods and services and a right to participate in basic societal decisions* [emphasis added].[111]

212

The phrase "equitable share of society's goods and services" conveniently ignores that society does not own goods and services—individuals do. To redistribute the wealth implies that it must be taken from some and given to others through the auspices of the state. For this reason, residents of rural areas must "participate in basic societal decisions." The problem, according to the leaders of Rural America, is that those in rural areas have not been participating in the way that the activists would like and have not previously adopted the activists' definition of "equitable share." Through the organizing process, activists can indoctrinate their clientele about the "correct" interpretation of "equitable share" and can direct their "participation" in decision making.

From Streetlights to Social Change: Potholes to Politics

All advocacy groups that engage in grass-roots organizing are essentially seeking to change society by using the interests of low- and middle-income individuals in welfare issues as a vehicle for their own political objectives. When organizing is done at the grass-roots level, however, the socialistic objectives of the organizers is never revealed. Rather, the group is formed around local issues, such as street repairs, installation of a stoplight, or some other issue of local concern. A major difficulty in mobilizing the rural poor, as Rural America's training manuals clearly reveal, is that attitudes about self-reliance must be "overcome."[112] In other words, it is essential that as many people as possible become dependent on the state rather than self-supporting, in that political activists are only useful to a constituency whose members depend on the state. The welfare rights activists do not intend to assist their clients in achieving independence, for it would not serve their ultimate purpose of using their members' political power to achieve change in society—change that produces a redistribution of income from the most productive members of society to others who are less productive. The constant clamor for greater welfare spending and for the development of new programs is part of the relentless drive to have the government control the allocation of resources and the distribution of wealth.

Moreover, it is important to acknowledge Charles Murray's evidence presented in his book, *Losing Ground*, that as welfare spending by government has increased dramatically, the problem of poverty has gotten worse.[113] In fact, progress in reducing the incidence of poverty in America was being made throughout the 1950s and early 1960s, thanks to economic growth. But it was about the same time—the late 1960s—that the welfare state programs ballooned with President Johnson's Great Society programs that this progress was halted and even reversed. This, of course, was predictable (and was predicted by many), for the U.S. welfare state makes it financially unattractive for the poor to become economically independent. Tax-funded politics has helped construct this calamitous system, and now that the system has failed, the tax-funded antipoverty industry does all it can to maintain the system and stand in the way of true reform.

Research has consistently shown that the level of welfare spending far exceeds the amount required to place every individual above the poverty threshold. From the viewpoint of the welfare rights activists, however, the disappearance of poverty would portend disaster. The welfare industry depends on the poverty issue to justify a flood of federal dollars that is a source of income and employment and, most important, serves as a tool to be used to reorient the U.S. economic system in a way that conforms to its own definition of "fair." It is important to recognize that successful grass-roots organizing can build a large and powerful lobby that the organizers can control and manipulate to their own advantage. The motto may be "power to the people" and may be based on a people's platform, but the leaders of the welfare rights movement will ensure that their own agenda is implemented. The sad, and often unrecognized, truth is that the programs that purport to aid the poor often primarily benefit those in the poverty industry.

IX. The Antipoverty Industry: Personal Gain from Compassion

Few, save the poor, feel for the poor.

—Letitia Landon
The Poor

The poor shall never cease out of the land.

—*Deuteronomy* XV:11

The antipoverty industry consists of hundreds of independent organizations, both public and private, that receive funding from a wide variety of agencies through a bewildering array of programs to purportedly alleviate the problems of poverty. When confronted with such a complex, researchers generally focus on broad aggregates so that the system can be more simply understood and analyzed. Such an approach, however, has a serious shortcoming: When emphasis is given only to the number of grants received, the dollar amount of those grants, or the sources of funding, one loses sight of the problems of the individuals whom these organizations purport to serve. In effect, the forest obscures the trees. It is obviously impossible to examine in depth every grant or organization, but a close examination of individual elements of the antipoverty industry can be most revealing. A more detailed analysis can illustrate the ways in which tax-funded poverty programs are used both for political purposes and to enhance the income and well-being of the officials who direct the programs. Reviewing one such organization, The East Los Angeles Community Union (TELACU), which was formed to aid needy Hispanics in the Los Angeles area, can provide useful insights into the antipoverty industry.

The East Los Angeles Community Union

East Los Angeles is one of the many jurisdictions that make up the Los Angeles metropolitan area. The vast majority of its inhabitants—87 percent, according to the 1970 census—are Hispanic. Demographic data for East Los Angeles indicate that relative to the

215

United States as a whole during the 1960s and 1970s, the area was economically depressed, with below-average per capita and median incomes, a lower level of educational attainment, and higher rates of unemployment. At 16.7 percent, the proportion of individuals in East Los Angeles living below the poverty level in 1970 was considerably higher than the proportion for the nation, 10.1 percent. The economic statistics reveal that East Los Angeles may also be considered an economically depressed area. To alleviate these problems, large amounts of federal, state, and local tax dollars have been provided.

At the front lines in the War on Poverty in East Los Angeles was TELACU, incorporated on May 28, 1968, as a special type of nonprofit organization called a community development corporation (CDC). Under Title VII of the Community Services Act of 1964, CDCs may receive federal funding from the Special Impact Program of the Community Services Administration (CSA). This program takes the community economic development approach to eliminating poverty and permits the organizations it funds to undertake an almost unlimited range of antipoverty projects, as determined by local needs. TELACU's operations were under the direction of a board of directors composed of members of the community and representatives of local organizations.

Based on the critical economic and social problems facing the community, the board initially stated that TELACU's efforts would be directed toward four major objectives: (1) increasing the income of the residents of the special impact area, with emphasis on the economically deprived; (2) expanding employment opportunities for these residents; (3) achieving partial financial self-sufficiency in the organization's operations; and (4) helping represent the needs of the community by working with city, county, state, and federal governments.[1] The articles of incorporation explicitly stated that TELACU was not to be actively involved in political activities: "No substantial part of the activities of this corporation shall consist . . . of attempting to influence legislation and the corporation shall not participate in . . . any political campaign on behalf of any candidate for political office."[2]

Given the economic conditions in East Los Angeles, most would agree that these objectives seemed worthy and well-intentioned. On the surface, TELACU responded to the problems by seeking seed money to establish local business enterprises that would become self-sustaining and provide an economic stimulus for further growth

216

and development in the community. When Congress passed the Economic Opportunity Act in 1964, it stipulated that funds would not go directly to those in need; instead, the funds would be used by local organizations to assist in meeting local needs by creating job opportunities and training the poor.

CSA began funding TELACU in 1972. From modest beginnings, the organization prospered, becoming the largest private, nonprofit antipoverty organization in the Los Angeles area and the fifth largest in the nation.[3] The officers of TELACU were extremely adept at raising funds from private foundations and from city, county, state, and federal governments. At TELACU's zenith, about $10 million per year was added to the corporation's coffers from government sources. Between 1972 and 1982, TELACU obtained at least $25 million in grants from CSA. By 1982, TELACU had become a $50 million conglomerate.[4]

Department of Labor Audit

A wealth of information is available about TELACU from a U.S. Department of Labor (DOL) audit of the organization for the years 1976 through 1979.[5] Unfortunately, the audit does not provide a comprehensive analysis of TELACU's activities, because officials refused to cooperate with the audit task force:

> Many areas of testing remain unaccomplished because of TELA-CU's lack of cooperation, which resulted in a significant curtailment of our audit. . . . From the start of the audit TELACU did not cooperate and refused to provide necessary requested information. Verbal requests were ignored and phone messages were left unanswered. It appears that the primary reason for their lack of cooperation resulted from our request to review profit making venture records.[6]

DOL tried to get TELACU's officers to cooperate from April 23, 1980, through June 30, 1981, in a series of 36 meetings to elicit information about the organization's financial affairs. DOL met with little success. TELACU's attitude ran directly counter to the *Code of Federal Regulations* (45 CFR Subpart 1068.42-9[a]), which provides that

> audits and examinations of grantee's operations may be conducted by CSA auditors, auditors from staff of other Federal Agencies, State and local auditors and U.S. General Accounting Office. Grantees and delegate agencies must cooperate fully with General

217

Accounting Office (GAO) and CSA auditors when they conduct audits and examinations of grant programs.

In response to claims that the organization had failed to cooperate, TELACU first asserted that "the statement is false and calculated to distract attention from the auditors' own inability or unwillingness to comprehend the materials or programs audited . . . [and] to camouflage their inability to conduct an audit of this scope."[7] In effect, according to TELACU, the auditors were lazy, if not incompetent. Second, in a letter dated July 9, 1980, TELACU claimed that the federal government had "no right to examine the books and records of the profit making venture." The reason offered for this assertion was that once federal funds are deposited into a profit-making company, "those grants monies lose their separate identity" and, therefore, the federal government loses all "power to examine the operation of the business enterprise."[8] TELACU asserted that representatives of the taxpayers who had provided the funds had no right either to investigate how the funds had been spent or to assess the results that had been achieved.

There may be a less-charitable rationale for TELACU's reluctance to cooperate. A comprehensive audit would have shown that TELACU did little to aid the poor in East Los Angeles and that much of the funding the organization received was used primarily to benefit its officers and directors. TELACU is not an isolated example of the misuse of funds that taxpayers have provided to ease the plight of the poor. As discussed later in this chapter, there are several other organizations that have received tax dollars to provide for the needs of less-fortunate Americans. Political activity pervades these organizations, which use the poor as pawns to obtain funding for political purposes.

Taxpayer Financing of the Antipoverty Industry

All antipoverty organizations excel in obtaining taxpayers' funds from all levels of governments (see Table A9.1, in appendix, for a sample of TELACU projects for fiscal years 1976 through 1979). A partial list of TELACU's programs, for example, includes economic planning, development of a handbook for similar organizations, revitalization of commercial areas, establishment of an industrial park, historic preservation, employment and training opportunities, energy assistance, health services, handicapped assistance, senior citizens' cooperatives, transportation and assistance, transportation-assessment studies, and regional economic development. No stone was left unturned in the quest for tax-funded support. TELACU received at least 76 grants and contracts totalling more than $32.4 million (see Table A9.2). The budgets for some of the grants are not known, but it is clear that the vast majority of the funds—at least $30.5 million—were obtained directly or indirectly from federal sources. The DOL audit questioned about $4.2 million of the expenditures, and $371,000 had been questioned in an earlier audit. Thus, even the limited DOL audit questioned about 15 percent of the organization's expenditures.

Had a comprehensive audit been completed, more evidence of questionable spending might have been brought to light. Even though the auditors may have accepted as legal many of TELACU's expenditures, such as TELACU officers having a preference for Mercedes-Benz automobiles leased with taxpayers' funds, many taxpayers would undoubtedly question the propriety of agents of antipoverty organizations using tax funds for such purposes.

TELACU's Adventures with Venture Capital[9]

A major activity for CDCs is to use grant and contract funds for venture capital to establish new business enterprises to breathe economic life into a depressed area. In theory, new firms create employment and training opportunities for disadvantaged and unemployed workers. These businesses should meet the needs of local residents and, by offering goods and services for sale, become self-sustaining. There was an acute need for economic opportunities for Hispanics in the East Los Angeles area, and TELACU's name would seem to indicate that the needs of the poor there were its primary concern. The *Code of Federal Regulations* (45 CFR Subpart 1076.40.3[a]) specifies that

> by funding a CDC under Title VII, OEO [the Office of Economic Opportunity] had determined based on recommendations and statistics submitted by the CDC, that the CDC's special impact area has a potential for economic viability and *has sufficient targets for investment of venture capital.* Given the tremendous needs of the special impact area and the limited resources available under Title VII, it is therefore expected that *all CSA investment capital funds will be used for ventures located within the special impact area* [emphasis added].

Economic distress, if not federal regulations, would indicate that all of TELACU's grant and contract funds should have been used to assist local citizens. Nothing could be further from the truth. The auditors found that TELACU routinely invested not only outside East Los Angeles but also outside the state of California. Funds intended for poor Hispanics in southern California were invested in Montana, Wisconsin, Illinois, Georgia, and New York. One may be able to justify investing outside the special impact area if such investments were so extraordinarily profitable that they could provide a large flow of income to support activities that were undertaken within the area. But there was little likelihood that the residents of East Los Angeles would benefit from some of TELACU's out-of-state ventures. Five of these ventures are briefly described below (see Table 9.1 for a more complete listing).

New York City: Nuestro Publications. As of December 31, 1978, TELACU had invested and loaned $443,023 to Nuestro Publications. TELACU Venture Capital had also pledged a $200,000 time certificate of deposit as collateral in guaranteeing certain debts of the New York company. Moreover, in July 1979, TELACU paid Donnelley and Sons Company $250,900 for guarantees made on behalf of Nuestro, without CSA's knowledge or approval. During the same time period, Nuestro's accounting records revealed a stockholders' deficit of $1,562,600. In addition to the loans and guarantees, TELACU also provided more than $22,000 in direct loans to officers of Nuestro Publications. The DOL audit concluded that "Nuestro Publications' financial position is poor, and TELACU's investment and loans to this organization appear to have little value."[10]

Browning, Montana: Blackfeet Indian Writing Company. In 1976 and 1977, TELACU loaned $200,000 to the Blackfeet Indian Writing Company, and the loans were still outstanding in November 1982. Prospects for repayment are less than sanguine, given that the ballpoint pen firm has not earned a profit since its inception and its liabilities are substantially larger than its assets.

Michigan: Michigan Peninsula Airways. When asked to explain the investments outside the barrio, Gustavo Paladines, who served as director of economic development for TELACU, told the *Los Angeles Times* that "I went to a very good business school and I never heard that a decision for a business investment had to be predicated on a geographical location. What does 5 miles, 500 miles or 5,000 miles

Table 9.1

TELACU SUBSIDIARIES, REVENUES, AND NET PROFITS
OCTOBER 1, 1976–SEPTEMBER 30, 1979

TELACU Venture Company and Year of Incorporation	Gross Revenues ($)	Outside Income (%)	Total Expenses ($)	Net Profit ($)
TELACU Industries (1975)	511,359.14	3.4	750,342.30	(238,983.16)
TELACU Investment Company (1975)	304,306.73	98.6	866,331.60	(562,024.87)
Interamerican Entertainment (1978)	366,586.00	100.0	1,168,066.84	(801,480.84)
TELACU Travel (1978)	143,608.44	79.1	248,535.00	(104,926.56)
Eastland Leasing (1976)	752,177.37	13.9	601,846.31	150,331.06
First Southwest Capital (1976)	55,316.59	100.0	56,268.75	(952.16)
Ventures Inc. (1978)	52,019.99	84.1	192,900.99	(140,881.00)
Community Research Group (1978)	359,008.93	3.1	269,955.73	89,053.20
Community Mortgage Corporation (1978)	36,300.00	0.0	1,519.22	34,780.78
TELACU Financial Services (1976)	75,132.00	100.0	72,192.00	2,940.00
TELACU Currency and Exchange Company (1972)	979,590.97	100.0	940,083.32	39,507.65

Table 9.1 (continued)

TELACU Venture Company and Year of Incorporation	Gross Revenues ($)	Outside Income (%)	Total Expenses ($)	Net Profit ($)
TELACU Venture Capital (1976)	153,789.84	71.0	401,381.67	(247,591.83)
Community Planning and Development Corporation (1973)	317,812.78	16.3	541,311.85	(223,499.07)
TELACU Management Services (1975)	244,244.61	7.3	119,833.40	24,411.21
Intercity Energy Systems (1979)	62,434.80	0.0	50,967.96	11,466.84
TELACU Community Credit Corporation (1978)	57,928.00	100.0	49,362.00	8,566.00
Community Thrift and Loan (1976)	2,670,173.00	96.4	2,884,330.00	(214,157.00)
Aqua Pets Industries (1979)	3,078,466.00	100.0	3,633,571.00	(555,105.00)
TELACU Development Corporation (1977)	57,177.00	28.1	151,191.00	(94,014.00)
TELACU Industrial Park (1977)	427,319.00	100.0	1,583,416.00	(1,156,097.00)
Total	10,704,751.19		14,583,406.94	(3,978,655.75)

SOURCE: *Report of Audit: The East Los Angeles Community Union (TELACU) Los Angeles, California, January 1, 1976–December 31, 1979,* vol. 2 (Washington: Department of Labor, 1982), p. 12.

[away from Los Angeles] have to do with an investment?"[11] Paladines's financial acumen, however, leaves something to be desired. He directed that more than $100,000 of Small Business Administration funds obtained by TELACU be invested in Michigan Peninsula Airways, "a fledgling, minority-owned company now beset by creditors." In addition, a TELACU subsidiary bought a modified DC-8 jet (one of Michigan Peninsula's two planes, both of which lacked navigational equipment) to lease to the company. TELACU's stock in the company, purchased with taxpayers' dollars, is now worthless.[12]

Hartford, Connecticut: WHCT-TV.[13] One of TELACU's most lucrative ventures outside of California was the purchase of a UHF television station in Hartford, Connecticut. CSA provided TELACU with $250,000 to pay for consultants, lawyers, and the appraisal costs of the Hartford station and of two stations in California. The purchase of the California station was not permitted by the Federal Communications Commission (FCC), but TELACU sought the assistance of a group of Virginia businessmen (including Lieutenant Governor Richard Davis and a former congressman) to finance the $4-million acquisition of the Hartford station. The Virginia syndicate would get 51 percent of the stock; TELACU Industries, a wholly owned subsidiary of TELACU, would get 39 percent; TELACU's president, David Lizarraga, would receive 6 percent; and Gustavo Paladines, the Michigan Peninsula Airways promoter, would receive 4 percent. The Virginians needed TELACU's participation to qualify for the 25 percent price discount on the station under FCC policy on distress sales. Without having risked a cent of their own funds, TELACU officials will be able to personally profit when the stock can be sold three years after the close of the transaction. If the station were to be sold at its purchase price, Lizarraga would receive close to $250,000. Lizarraga refused to comment on the Hartford deal, but Paladines said that "he [Paladines] deserves the stock because he worked hard to put the deal together and was not sufficiently compensated by his $55,000 annual salary."

Washington, D.C.: Townhouse. TELACU spent $320,000[14] to purchase a three-story townhouse in Washington, D.C., at 1812 19th Street, NW (near fashionable Dupont Circle). It is unclear how buying a building in the nation's capital may be necessary to alleviate poverty in southern California. TELACU officials often travel to Washington on business, and perhaps they need a home away from home.

Traveling with TELACU

TELACU officials apparently viewed travel as an important part of their mission to help the poor in East Los Angeles:

> TELACU's overseas travel expenditures have ranged from a trip to Mexico City for the board of directors and their guests to a $25,000 bill for travel and other expenses connected with a trip to Switzerland and Lebanon. The purpose of the latter trip, described by one of the travelers as "a wild goose chase," was to find financing for a hotel and convention center that was never built.[15]

Not all travel was international. TELACU officials found South Lake Tahoe to be the ideal location for a training seminar, and the expenses of 20 spouses were also paid so that they could attend.[16] Nor was all travel for seminars. One official was permitted to drive a TELACU van about 4,000 miles to take a vacation in Racine, Wisconsin. The practice was not uncommon, for "certain TELACU officials were provided company cars 'which they were then free to use on their own time. . . . There were no restrictions on how far you could travel in those cars.' "[17]

Poverty and Pleasure: InterAmerican Entertainment

One of TELACU's most flamboyant ventures was InterAmerican Entertainment Company, established in 1978.[18] TELACU received at least $900,000 in federal grants and contracts to pursue such projects as acquiring television stations and buying the rights to television programs produced in Britain and elsewhere for distribution in Latin America. "Love for Lydia" and "The Professionals" were two of the offerings selected for distribution. A leading Mexican television financier, Julio Gonzales-Reyes, was recruited to head the company, and he was promised 10 percent of the profits— he expected to make $1 million within five years:

> He was given a new TELACU Mercedes-Benz and a generous travel allowance to visit Europe "at least four times a year."

> He went to London, Cannes and Milan to buy films and then traveled to "every country in South America at least twice a year to sell the films after they had been dubbed into Spanish. . . ."

> "My style turned some people off," he acknowledged. "I'm from a rich family and I'm used to a good life."

224

Gonzales-Reyes said that he worked out of a "lavish office" and spent funds supporting a life style that would make him appear successful in the fast-paced entertainment world.

Even with help from government grants, Gonzales-Reyes said, the company could not make it.

"My life at TELACU was one of excuses to my friends and clients—why I couldn't pay, why the films weren't ready," he recalled.[19]

InterAmerican Entertainment Company failed in 1981.

Despite the pronounced goal of self-sufficiency for the enterprises formed by TELACU, failure was all too common. Table 9.1 lists the 20 companies that TELACU established, the year of their incorporation, and, for fiscal years 1976–79, their gross revenues, the percentage of revenues from outside (that is, nongovernmental) sources, their expenses, and their net profits. InterAmerican Entertainment operated at a loss of more than $800,000 in fiscal years 1976–79. Only 8 of the 20 firms managed to operate in the black, and the total losses were about $3.9 million. Almost three-fourths of all revenues were obtained from federal, state, and local government grants and contracts for social programs. It is interesting that those companies that generated 96 percent or more of their revenues from outside of TELACU incurred either substantial losses or generated only small business gains. When the companies relied heavily on social programs for revenue, they generated profits.[20] There is little evidence that the companies were becoming self-sustaining as ongoing business enterprises.

An examination of two of TELECU's venture companies, Aqua-Pet Industries and TELACU Industrial Park, illustrates how the organization operated and how its investments failed.

Going Under: Aqua-Pet Industries[21]

Between 1976 and 1979, TELECU invested more than $700,000 of taxpayers' money in Aqua-Pet Industries, a small manufacturer of aquariums located in the San Fernando Valley. The plan was to move the company to TELACU's new industrial park (see below). When application was made for the grants to acquire the company, TELACU officials projected that sales would be $16 million by 1982. The projections were far too optimistic:

"The money they invested basically went down the tubes," said David Cohen, a former official with the Community Services

225

Administration which gave TELACU money for Aqua-Pet and other investments.

"The investment is an example of a failure," he said.

The story of the company's failure is wrapped up in a tangle of lawsuits, with charges and countercharges of incompetence, mismanagement and fraud.

Larry Kelmanson, one of Aqua-Pet's founders, charged in one suit that TELACU officials "took part in a fraudulent plan—whereby the income, revenue and profits of Aqua-Pet were . . . diverted to themselves."

He reportedly settled the suit for $70,000.

In another lawsuit, [Tony] Lewis [a former owner of the company] accused TELACU of squeezing him out of the company without paying him the $50,000 he was due. TELACU spent thousands of dollars defending the lawsuit and ultimately settled with Lewis for $80,000, he said. . . .

"One hundred and twenty people are out of work now because of them," Lewis said. "I don't understand how they continue to get financing and continue to lose money."[22]

Aqua-Pet was a profitable company when it was acquired, but under TELACU management, the concern had managed to lose more than $555,000 in one year and declared bankruptcy in 1981.

Wheeling and Dealing in Real Estate: TELACU Industrial Park

TELACU officials sought investments in real estate as well. Although most of their venture companies were foundering, TELACU officials decided to establish TELACU Industrial Park on a 46-acre site that until 1975 had been a B.F. Goodrich tire factory.[23] When the tire factory closed, nearly 900 employees lost their jobs, and it was thought that a thriving industrial complex would help revitalize the area. TELACU purchased the property in 1977 for $5 million. (Three private bidders had offered between $3 million and $3.5 million for the property, but then the private purchasers were not financed with taxpayers' funds.) In theory, firms operating in the park would hire residents of the East Los Angeles barrio, but in fact very little additional employment resulted. The two major tenants, Stationers Corporation and The Federated Group, brought their work forces with them.

TELACU had planned to start labor-intensive businesses in the industrial park to provide employment—a wallpaper company, a furniture-manufacturing concern, and a bank in which TELACU had invested more than $1 million of taxpayers' money. However, only the ill-fated Aqua-Pet Industries actually located in the park. The industrial park scheme lost $1.1 million between 1977 and 1979 (see Table 9.1). In June 1983, the Los Angeles County Board of Supervisors placed a lien against portions of the industrial park after DOL warned that the county could be held liable for $320,000 in disallowed TELACU expenditures.[24]

TELACU Development Corporation (TDC), a subsidiary of TELACU, was also involved in real estate activities, but in a less decisive way, as the auditors' report reveals:

> In February 1979 TDC entered into an agreement with Erling and Ethel Christensen to acquire land valued at $285,000. TDC was required to pay the Christensen's [sic] a $20,000 advance to be applied against the purchase or default if the deal was not consummated at the close of escrow, May 1979. However, a further stipulation in the agreement allowed TDC to pay an additional $5,000 per month not to exceed three months after the original escrow closing date. This would allow extensions on the escrow closing date up to three months beyond the original May 1979 closing date. However, the $5,000 monthly payments would not be applied against the original purchase price.
>
> We found that TDC did not pay the $265,000 ($285,000 less the $20,000 down payment) balance on the purchase of the land by the May 1979 escrow closing date. They exercised their option to extend the escrow for two additional months by paying the required $5,000 per month. Finally, TDC decided not to purchase the property and forfeited $30,000, the $20,000 down payment and the $10,000 privilege for extending the original closing date an additional two months.[25]

TDC incurred a net loss of $94,000 between its founding in 1977 and 1979.

TELACU's Successes

The failures and financial disasters uncovered by the DOL audit and the media did not faze TELACU officials, who asserted that "financial soundness is not always measured in the simple terms of profit and loss."[26] Moreover, TELACU officials claimed that "one does not have to look far for evidence of TELACU's success— TELACU's annual financial statements provide ample support."[27] As evidence of "an established record indicating accomplishment,"

227

TELACU offered its "establishment of a $1 million rural loan fund."[28] If the rural loan fund is an example of accomplishment, antipoverty activities are in far worse shape than most Americans could possibly imagine. In 1979, TELACU managed to have its special impact area formally expanded to include all of California, including rural areas. Evidently, TELACU's officials did not find the needs of the poor in the urban barrio to be sufficiently challenging:

> TELACU's rural loan program, set up in January, 1981, was supposed to serve needy people in rural areas throughout California and Nevada. During the program's 19 months of operation, it was supposed to have made at least six loans. It in fact made only one, to the Bravo Manufacturing Co., which . . . was ineligible because it is in the non-rural city of Fremont, which has a population of 100,000.[29]

The loan program for needy people in rural areas did not help a single individual, even though CSA had given TELACU $1 million for this purpose. The loan that was made was for $30,000, $10,000 less than the administrative costs that were charged to the program. Rather than aiding the rural poor, TELACU invested the funds in high-yielding certificates of deposit and earned more than $230,000 in interest. Federal regulations (45 *Code of Federal Regulations* 1050.43[b][1]) clearly state that interest earned on program funds must be returned to the Treasury: "Interest earned on the investment of CSA funds will be reported on SF 272 item 13.a [Federal Cash Transactions Report] . . . and a check payable to the Treasury of the United States for the earned interest should be attached to the report and sent to the CSA office responsible for administering the grant."

TELACU was not pleased when the government demanded repayment of the unused loan and the interest. TELACU argued that at least some of the interest had been used to provide programs (even though no eligible loans were made) and that the interest would be needed to pay an estimated $175,000 in legal fees for fighting the ruling in court. In addition, the rural loan grant was given under conditions that had never prevailed. Therefore, TELACU asserted that it should not be bound by the terms of the grant. TELACU's president, David Lizarraga, testified that he did not even read the grant documents when he signed them because "I've received grants in the millions and they've never had any conditions."[30]

One must have some sympathy for Lizarraga's plight:

> Lizarraga was one of several grant-seekers who lined up at CSA on the last day of Carter's Administration to sign documents "bang, bang, bang," accepting millions of last-minute grant dollars, according to a disposition by Gerrold Mukai. He headed the CSA office that gave TELACU about $25 million in venture capital and operation expenses over the years.

> Mukai, who became a TELACU consultant, said that just a few days earlier CSA had received authorization to award about $20 million and was rushing to make the awards before Ronald Reagan's Administration took over. . . .

> "We who were politically appointed were engaged in clearing the agency," Mukai recounted in a deposition. "The staff was engaged in providing a pizza . . . party for all of us out in the hall. . . . Various people would come in, we would wave them in, they would sign, we would sign, and they would leave."[31]

Under the circumstances, it is difficult to imagine how Lizarraga could be expected to read and study the terms of TELACU's million-dollar rural loan grant.

Evidently, the auditors were impressed by TELACU's successes, for page 42 of the audit report states that "We have deleted our finding concerning TELACU not achieving self sufficiency." Some could argue that the taxpayers' watchdogs were too easily thrown off the scent.

TELACU's Financial Affairs

The auditors found that TELACU's managers consistently took a cavalier attitude about the taxpayers' funds entrusted to the organization to assist the poor. Keeping track of money was simply not a major concern:

> TELACU established at least 380 bank accounts during our audit period (195 checking accounts and 185 savings and time certificate of deposit accounts). The number of bank accounts were established to assure individual transactions were controlled. However, the large number of interfund and intercompany transactions made it impossible to trace funds. TELACU was unable to provide an inventory of bank accounts, and many of the bank accounts were accidentally discovered during the course of our audit. Many of the savings accounts and TCD accounts were not entered in the books. At this time we do not know if all bank accounts were discovered.

In addition, our review noted that TELACU used bank debit memo and wire transfers extensively to transfer funds across the country and into other parts of the world. (Transfers to other parts of the world included the countries of Switzerland and France).[32]

Controls were all but nonexistent. For example, "about $240,000 in cashable certificates of deposit were once discovered lying loose in an employee's desk drawer. . . ."[33] Given the critical need that TELACU stressed in applying for grants, it is surprising that the organization was not aware of how much money it had or where it was deposited. One would think that the funds would have been carefully managed and that every effort would have been made to use the funds to alleviate the plight of the poor.

Attitudes toward expenditures were also casual. The auditors "were unable to locate documentation to support $15,847,559 in bank debit entries."[34] Some of the financial transactions that were documented raise serious questions about TELACU's operations, as discussed below.

Loans to Officers. During the course of the DOL audit, four separate loans to David Lizarraga were discovered: (1) $5,000 loan from TELACU Currency Exchange Company (TCEC), (2) $10,000 loan from TCEC, (3) $5,000 loan from Community Mortgage Corporation (CMC), and (4) $25,000 notes payable. Not only is the practice of making loans to officers from taxpayers' funds of dubious propriety, but often the method of repayment in this instance was highly questionable.

The TCEC loan was recorded as "TELACU loan fund to David Lizarraga, President-TELACU. . . . The money was borrowed by D. Lizarraga for private investment purposes,"[35] and some of the journal entries relating to the loan had been obliterated. The loan allegedly was partially repaid with a bonus check from another TELACU corporation, TELACU Industries (TI), made payable to Lizarraga. The auditors reported:

> A bonus check from TI was written on January 24, 1978 for $4,400 to David C. Lizarraga. Within one week D. Lizarraga endorsed the check over to the General 451 account which applied the $4,400 payment to the $5,000 receivable due from TCEC. Thus the balance due from TCEC was reduced to $600. (Our review of D. Lizarraga's personnel file and minutes of the meetings from TELACU board of directors meetings disclosed no authorization for a bonus of $4,400.)[36]

230

The remaining $600 was supposedly paid by Lizarraga with a check from another TELACU corporation, Community Thrift and Loan Company (CT&L). The check number recorded in the TELACU books, however, did not exist. Similar conditions prevailed with the $10,000 loan from TCEC, in that some of the journal references were obliterated and Lizarraga allegedly repaid the loan with a check that had a nonexistent number. The auditors noted that "we are unable to conclude when the cash was first withdrawn, whether the $10,000 represents all or only a part of what was first withdrawn, and whether David Lizarraga was in fact repaying funds previously borrowed."[37] The loan from Community Mortgage Corporation was equally obscure in terms of its repayment.

The details surrounding the $25,000 notes payable to Lizarraga from InterAmerican Entertainment are somewhat more imaginative. The auditors found that the note payable appeared in InterAmerican's books without explanation, and they essentially concluded that there was no logic to paying $25,000 to Lizarraga.[38] TELACU's response to the auditors' questions regarding this matter further clouded the issue. It claimed that Maravilla Development Inc., a private corporation controlled by Lizarraga's wife, had made interest-free loans to various TELACU subsidiaries totaling $62,000, including $25,000 to InterAmerican. The $25,000 payment to Lizarraga was a payment on this loan. The auditors could find no record of the transactions with Maravilla, and articles of incorporation for Maravilla revealed that David Lizarraga, not his wife, was president of the company.

The whole episode raises far more questions than it answers. For example, why was Maravilla willing to lend money interest free? Why did TELACU borrow at all in view of the millions that it had in bank accounts and certificates of deposit around the world? The auditors gave up: "TELACU did not response [sic] to many of the issues raised in the finding."[39] Other officers also received dubious or, in some cases, blatantly illegal payments from TELACU.

TELACU Officials Enrolled in CETA Programs. The Comprehensive Employment and Training Act (CETA) provides job training for the unemployed. The *Code of Federal Regulations* expressly forbids the hiring of anyone under the program who works for a CETA subgrantee or members of their family (29 *CFR* Part 98.22[a]). TELACU openly ignored this restriction. Joe L. Gonzales, chairman of the TELACU board of directors and a prominent businessman, owned two art galleries and an export-import company and was a noted restorer of historic art. Both he and his wife were enrolled in the CETA programs administered by TELACU, but found the prospect of public disclosure of this fact distasteful:

> "You come into this gallery and it looks really beautiful and peachy-keen," Gonzales said. "But you don't realize the hardships."

> Gonzales thought it would be "demeaning" and "very embarrassing" if word got out that he . . . was receiving money earmarked for the unemployed.

> "So I told them [TELACU officials], 'Hey, please, I don't want anyone to know.' "[40]

The auditors reported that Joe L. Gonzales and Blanca Gonzales "received in excess of $36,000 over an 18 month period, during which they worked at their art studios rather than as CETA participants." In addition, while Gonzales had formerly served as executive director of TELACU, TELACU paid the art studios in excess of $130,000.[41] One can only speculate how these payments benefited the poor.

Gonzales and his wife each pleaded guilty to two counts of making false statements in the U.S. District Court for the Central District of California. They were "each sentenced . . . [in November 1982] to five years' probation and 1,500 hours of community service" for enrolling in the CETA program and doing no work.[42]

The auditors also questioned the participation of Ruth Berkemeyer in the CETA program and (mistakenly) identified her as the wife of Carlos J. Garcia, the secretary and general counsel of TELACU. Berkemeyer was, in fact, Garcia's mother-in-law, a "low-income senior citizen" who, TELACU contended, was eligible for the program.[43] But "the woman's daughter said her mother had been in a convalescent home for several years."[44] Aside from the nepotism issue, it is difficult to comprehend how an aged individual confined to a convalescent home for years could have participated in job training or benefited from it.

TELACU officials also gained from the programs in more indirect ways. Grants were given to the organization to repair homes of the elderly and the needy and to provide insulation and other forms of weatherization. Workers were used to improve the homes of TELACU officials as well.[45]

Excessive Payments to Employees. TELACU officials were compensated by salaries, fringe benefits, and expense accounts, but they often believed that they were entitled to much more. Consider the case of Leonard Rutkin, a former stockbroker in New York City who served as TELACU's director of economic development between 1975 and 1979. While Rutkin was paid a full-time salary by TELACU, he was also being paid as a consultant. The auditors reported that "our review disclosed Leonard Rutkin, former Vice-President for TELACU Industries (TI), left TELACU owing the organization $66,974.24 in outstanding loans, advances and personal expenses. In addition, we found that, as a consultant and salaried employee, Leonard Rutkin was paid $79,330.34 in excess compensation."[46] Rutkin's salary was not terminated even after he left TELACU in May 1979; instead, he was carried on the payroll through December of that year.[47] Rutkin left TELACU in style: He drove off in a silver Mercedes-Benz owned by TELACU's leasing company and was still driving it in March 1982: " 'He got the car and nothing was ever signed,' recalled Gil Crews, a former TELACU official in charge of company cars. 'When he left, he just kept driving it.' "[48]

The DOL audit report indicates that no effort was made to recover the Mercedes-Benz or the funds that Rutkin owed to TELACU. Rutkin's financial legerdemain with taxpayers' funds went far beyond running up thousands of dollars in credit card charges, collecting consulting fees, and expropriating an expensive automobile. The *Los Angeles Times* revealed that Lizarraga used poverty funds to purchase a condominium, which he then rented to Rutkin. When Rutkin left TELACU, according to the *Times,* he "traveled around the country helping other anti-poverty agencies set up profit-making networks."[49]

Gustavo Paladines also remained on the payroll for at least six months after he resigned from TELACU, and he even managed to get a $10,000 raise after he left the organization. His physical association with the antipoverty agency did not end with his resignation, however, for he was also provided free office space to set up his own export business. His attempt to get a $200,000 Small Business Administration loan through TELACU, however, was not successful.[50]

Other TELACU officials also profited from their affiliation with the organization, but in a much more indirect fashion. Conflicts of interest were of little concern to TELACU officials. Joe Gonzales,

TELACU's board chairman who enrolled himself and his wife in the CETA programs, had substantial dealings with TELACU:

> [B]etween the period October 1976 and March 1980, TELACU disbursed over $129,000 in venture capital and social program funds to Joe L. Gonzales and related for profit companies. . . .

> [I]n calendar year 1980 business dealings between TELACU and Joe L. Gonzales had grown substantially. For example, during calendar year 1980, the Joe L. Gonzales General Contractor Company was involved in a $338,000 contract with TELACU Industrial Park, Inc., a TELACU subsidiary company.[51]

At the same time, Gonzales arranged to have at least two of his employees placed on TELACU's payroll so that they could work at taxpayers' expense. An employee at one of Gonzales's art studios was hired as a CETA participant, and an employee of his construction company was enrolled by TELACU as a "weatherization coordinator" and paid from a U.S. Department of Energy grant that had been awarded to the California State Office of Economic Opportunity.[52]

DOL auditors indicated that Roy Escarcega, vice president for TELACU's Urban Development Division, had also been involved in transactions that generated conflicts of interest. Escarcega headed the social services activities "for more than five years, except for a suspension in 1980 after he was accused by six women employees of sexual harassment."[53] Escarcega also wheeled and dealed with TELACU's social service grants:

> Three Los Angeles County agencies: Agency on Aging, Community Development Department, and the Road Department, contracted with TELACU to administer and operate five social service type programs. Those programs, which operated between July 1978 and July 1980, were administered by TELACU at 4748 Brooklyn Avenue in East Los Angeles.

> Our review disclosed the building was owned by DCR Development, Inc., a for-profit company. Our review also disclosed this company was owned by three brothers, David, Cris, and Roy Escarcega.[54]

The auditors also indicated that CETA funds had been used to hire workers and to purchase materials to repair the DCR building, as well as the residences and business real estate of TELACU officials.[55]

234

The foregoing discussion of TELACU's activities documents graft, corruption, conflicts of interest, illegal and imprudent expenditures, and double dealing. The DOL audit was much more extensive than chronicled here, but enough detail has been given to indicate that the poor never receive or benefit from much of the money allocated to TELACU for antipoverty programs. As the discussion below reveals, TELACU, unfortunately, is not atypical of the antipoverty industry: A great deal of the money never reaches the poor but is used to benefit those who profit from poverty—by working in the antipoverty industry. It is hardly surprising that the war on poverty is not being won.

In TELACU's case, the funds were often wasted even when they were used for their stated purposes. The *Los Angeles Times* investigated TELACU's claims about training and creating employment opportunities for minorities and reported that "through a variety of government programs, TELACU claims that it trained and found work for 2,144 people between 1969 and 1981."[56] In an average year TELACU produced only about 165 jobs, despite millions of dollars received from the government each year for this purpose. There is evidence that even the very modest success that TELACU claimed may be overstated.[57]

Critics of the Reagan administration claim that social programs that aid the poor, the elderly, and the sick have been drastically curtailed and that much suffering has been caused by reductions in spending programs for such purposes. Despite TELACU's dismal performance for more than a decade, however, the Reagan administration provided $6 million in grants for TELACU to construct a modern, three-story headquarters building. Former board chairman Joe Gonzales was the project designer of the 40-foot mural depicting Latino heritage in brilliant colors above the building's entrance. Moreover, "the office of executive director David Lizarraga is no cubbyhole. He's got his own bathroom, shower, and kitchenette—besides an office with plush carpeting and designer furnishings that include a gleaming round walnut desk with matching coffee table and a $400 wastebasket."[58]

Those decrying the cuts in social programs are the leaders of the antipoverty industry who have spent years doing well by purporting to do good.

One would like to believe that TELACU is an isolated and extreme example of abuse of taxpayers' money intended to aid the poor, but such is not the case. Fifty-two CDCs have been formed across the nation. In August 1982, the *Washington Post* reported that "in one recent six-month period 37 officials of such CSA-funded groups were indicted, 34 convicted, and prison sentences of 45 years and fines of $91,000 were ordered."[59] Despite the sordid record, no criminal charges have ever been filed against TELACU officials.

Other Cases of Profiting from Poverty

It is instructive to examine briefly some other cases illustrating the way in which the antipoverty industry thrives on the plight of the poor and employs human suffering as the *entreé* to taxpayers' funds.

Pride or Prejudice?

Housing is a major concern of the nation's poor and elderly, especially for those who live in high-cost urban areas, such as the nation's capital. In 1974, P.I. Properties was established as a non-profit real estate arm of Pride, Inc., a black self-help organization that was established in 1967 by the future mayor of the District of Columbia, Marion Barry, and his then-wife, Mary Treadwell. P.I. Properties was formed to take over the 285-unit Clifton Terrace apartment complex on 14th Street, NW, from the U.S. Department of Housing and Urban Development (HUD). In its heyday, Clifton Terrace had been a fashionable address, but it had fallen on hard times and was home to hundreds of low-income and elderly families and individuals. HUD had acquired the property through a mortgage default and wished to transfer the management and operation of the property to a private organization. HUD decided to sell the building to P.I. Properties for $820,400, even though the complex had been appraised at $1.2 million. The sale was also remarkable in that no down payment was required. As events developed, however, the sale price was immaterial, for P.I. Properties made only four monthly mortgage payments during the first three years of ownership.[60] Other bills went unpaid as well. For example, Treadwell did not pay the utility bills, and the taxpayers, through HUD, paid $93,566 to "protect the department's [HUD's] credibility, as well as to save the department from further embarrassment."[61]

The taxpayers were not the only ones to suffer from P.I. Properties' management of Clifton Terrace:

236

[D]uring the years of P.I. management, tenants at Clifton lived in some of the most degrading ghetto-like conditions in the city. . . . During the winter of 1976–77 the heat was shut off several days at a time, because of unpaid bills. Electric power was shut off several times, again because of unpaid bills.

Maintenance was minimal. Rats roamed freely through apartments and hallways. Garbage accumulated for weeks at a time. The stench of trash and urine regularly filled the halls and other public areas.[62]

Rent was collected from the tenants to pay the mortgage, utilities, and other expenses, but virtually nothing was done to provide services for the residents or to repay the loan from HUD. Again, the question arises: What happened to the money? Treadwell and other officials of P.I. Properties benefited by taking $600,000 from the corporation for their personal use. The antipoverty officials had very expensive tastes: "While the tenants of Clifton Terrace had to plead for such basic services as heat, hot water and electricity, Treadwell lived in a $900-a-month apartment at the Watergate and drove Mercedes and Jaguar sports cars."[63] Treadwell also had expensive travel tastes and would frequently visit Montego Bay in Jamaica to stay at a villa, with the services of a cook, laundress, maid, and gardener.[64] The other two principal officers of P.I. Properties, General Manager Robert E. Lee and Joan M. Booth, Treadwell's sister who managed Clifton Terrace, had similar tastes and had little sympathy for those who lived in the apartments:

Treadwell, Lee and Booth customarily referred to the tenants of Clifton Terrace as "niggers" and "animals."

"I don't give a damn about them in terms of their problems," Lee declared in an interview. "My intention was never to help anyone but me."

As for Booth, said Lee, "Joan was in Clifton for the same reason Mary was in it and I was in it—for the money."

P.I.'s long-term goal was to force all the tenants out of Clifton Terrace and to convert the apartments into luxury condominiums.

Profits were the only goal.[65]

In a series of articles in October 1979, the *Washington Post* described the elaborate means P.I. officials used to bilk hundreds of thousands of dollars from the tenants and the taxpayers, and the interested reader may consult this source for further details. It is sufficient to note here that many of the ruses employed were remarkably similar to those used in the TELACU case. Treadwell, Lee, and Booth were all convicted in criminal proceedings against them for their role in the Clifton Terrace fiasco.

Bates Street and Beyond

One of the worst slums in Washington, D.C., is Bates Street, a collection of 163 abandoned or dilapidated houses in the northwest section of the city. The D.C. government sought to turn the slum into a model community by using $15 million to hire a private developer to rehabilitate the houses. As is typical, most of the funds were provided by taxpayers through federal grants, and performance failed to live up to the promises:

> [S]ix years after construction began, it is still unfinished and $4 million in interest-free loans of public funds to the project have never been fully accounted for, according to the D.C. auditor.

> The development firm chosen for the project and its related entities finished 105 units—many with inadequate heating systems and other deficiencies—before running out of money. In effect, about $90,000 per unit was ultimately spent by the city on the housing and ancillary improvements. Originally, the anticipated cost had been $45,000 to $60,000 per unit.[66]

The higher costs should not be surprising, given that officials of the development firm, Bates Street Associates, had a taste for Mercedes-Benz and Lincoln automobiles.[67] Other funds designated to help improve housing were used to refurbish the homes of the director of housing for the District of Columbia, Robert L. Moore, and the developers.

> Work done in late 1979 or early 1980 on Moore's house . . . included enlarging a second-floor bedroom, installing two closets and a dressing table; repairing a ceiling in anther [sic] part of the house; putting in new storm windows and an electric garage door; installing a metal fireplace in his downstairs den, sanding and refinishing the downstairs floors, installing carpeting and repairing steps on the back porch.[68]

The problems with the Bates Street project are not unique. HUD funds provided by taxpayers have been abused throughout the nation. In Memphis, for example, $5.7 million intended to subsidize housing for the poor was parlayed into a $24.5 million portfolio of

238

bonds that were speculatively traded in search of profits for the Memphis Housing Authority.[69] The pattern of diverting employees and materials designated for improving the housing of those in poverty to the well-paid executives of the housing agency was also observed:

> Authority workers were pulled off their jobs in 1981 to repair the home of executive director Lawrence Wade. . . . The workmen reportedly installed paneling, ceramic tile, a bar and half-bath in Wade's attic and two air-conditioners purchased by the agency at a discount. They also fixed the personnel director's roof and worked on an office building partially owned by Wade.[70]

Auditors had also uncovered many other violations of federal regulations that served the interests of those who ran the housing agency and their business associates, including the subsidization of ineligible landlords, failure to solicit competitive bids, understating of income to increase federal funding, conflicts of interest, payment for goods never installed and services never provided, and missing records.[71] These problems are far from unusual. Other instances of flagrant abuse of taxpayers' money allocated for housing programs for the poor were also cited in Camden, New Jersey, and in Boston.[72]

Where Does the Money Go?

One reason that the social programs passed by Congress to aid the poor have had so little impact in curing poverty is that substantial sums have been diverted from helping the needy to feathering the nests of individuals in the antipoverty industry. There are many who are literally getting rich by claiming to aid the poor. There is overwhelming evidence, supported in many cases by criminal convictions, that social programs are being manipulated for personal gain and that the poor are merely being used as an excuse to obtain vast sums of taxpayers' money from all levels of government. These revelations are hardly new. For years, federal auditors have documented wrongdoing in all kinds of social programs, and academicians and others have repeatedly exposed such antics.[73] The question, then, is not so much "Where does the money go?" but "Why has the money been going down the same ratholes for so long?"

Congress and the executive branch have long been aware of the gross misuse of social program funds, as have officials at the state and local levels of government, but nothing has been done to curb these patently illegal acts. One would think that members of Congress, who on every possible occasion openly profess their concern for the poor, would take corrective action. Neither members of Congress nor other elected officials have made an effort to aid the poor by simply ensuring that the funds allocated for their benefit actually reach them. The only conclusion that can be drawn is that some politicians benefit from the system as it now operates.

Politics and Poverty

There must be a direct link between politics and poverty, so that even though antipoverty organizations fail to alleviate poverty, they advance the political goals of elected officials who provide them with funds. The record shows that the organizations that purport to alleviate poverty are heavily involved in political activity.

TELACU's Political Activity

Although TELACU's articles of incorporation specifically stated that the organization was not to be engaged in politics, the provision was largely redundant, given the limitation imposed on such activity by the Community Services Act (Section 603[b]):

> Programs assisted under this Act shall not be carried on in a manner involving the use of program funds, the provision of services, or the employment or assignment of personnel in a manner supporting or resulting in the identification of such programs with . . . any partisan or non-partisan political activity associated with a candidate or contending faction or group in an election for public or party office.

The legislation governing the agency that provided much of TELACU's funds dictates that grantee agencies must not be involved in either partisan or nonpartisan political activities. The evidence indicates, however, that TELACU was a highly political organization. The DOL auditors found that

> David Lizarraga is the founder and president of an unincorporated non-profit political organization called Hispanic American Democrats (HAD). Though we were unable to determine when the organization was created, we do know that HAD was headquartered at 6055 E. Washington Blvd., Suite 208 in the City of Commerce. The HAD headquarters is also the business address for TELACU Industries, Inc. (TI). It appears that David Lizarraga used TI facilities and resources to assist in the operation of the HAD

240

activities. It also appears that CSA funded TELACU personnel were used in the operation of the HAD activities.[74]

In response to the auditors' claims that TELACU's officers were involved in politics, the organization also pointed out that Lizarraga "was also active in Democratic Party politics, running for and serving as Southern California Chair of the California Democratic Party."[75] The auditors reported that TELACU Industries had guaranteed payment of two $10,000 loans to the Friends of David Lizarraga Committee to support Lizarraga's political ambitions.

As a CDC, TELACU was organized under an act of Congress, and federal law explicitly prohibits contributions for political purposes. The law (2 USC Section 441 b[a]) states in part:

> It is unlawful for any corporation organized by authority of any law of Congress to make a contribution . . . in connection with any election to any political office, or in connection with any primary election . . . or for any corporation whatever . . . to make a contribution . . . in connection with any election at which . . . a Senator . . . in Congress is to be voted for.

Nevertheless, two of TELACU's officers, Lizarraga and Carlos J. Garcia, attended a dinner for Alan Cranston at which tables were purchased for $2,000. TELACU Industries reimbursed Lizarraga and Garcia $1,000 for their expenses in connection with the dinner.[76] In their response to the auditors, TELACU officials admitted making the contributions and indicated that "TELACU created a Political Action Committee on March 21, 1981 for the purpose of reporting political contributions separately."[77] The audit report then states that "TELACU's response indicates that a positive corrective action plan has been taken that would essentially fulfill the thrust of our recommendation."[78] It was not explained how the auditors could conclude that creating a political action committee to report illegal political contributions is a positive corrective action plan.

TELACU's political activity goes far beyond purchasing tables at fundraising dinners. In March 1982, the *Los Angeles Times* reported that

> during the last three years, TELACU has made about $65,000 in political contributions through its subsidiaries, often to politicians who vote on TELACU's funding. . . .
>
> The donations were made to state and local campaigns, governed by less-restrictive laws which permit corporate contributions.[79]

241

Conflicts of interests are abundant in TELACU's political dealings. Los Angeles City Councilman Arthur K. Snyder was involved in a lease with one of TELACU's subsidiaries at the same time that the council was making grants to TELACU. For this and other political irregularities, Snyder was fined $14,000.[80] Other Los Angeles councilmen and officials have received more direct aid. In 1982, for example,

> donations of $3,000 each were given, for example, to Los Angeles City Councilman David Cunningham and Los Angeles County Supervisor Ed Edelman, who, by virtue of their votes and key government posts, have helped steer millions of dollars in federal grants to TELACU.
>
> The city and county of Los Angeles have awarded TELACU about $7 million in grants since a federal criminal investigation of TELACU was launched in 1980.
>
> Cunningham received the contribution when he was chairman of the City Council's grants committee voting on TELACU's grant applications. He said: "I don't see any conflict of interest."[81]

In December 1980, Andy Camacho, a politically prominent attorney from Encino, was given a loan of $30,000 by TELACU—almost at the same time that President Carter appointed him to a national board that had oversight powers on antipoverty organizations, including TELACU.[82] TELACU Investment Company directed a $150,000 loan that had been obtained from the Small Business Administration to Estaban Torres, a union activist who had been instrumental in founding TELACU:

> As an assembly-line welder at a Chrysler plant during the 1950s, he became active in the United Auto Workers (UAW), and he gradually worked his way up the union hierarchy. He was sent to Central and South America as an organizer, and after working with Latin American unions in the 1960s he was tapped by UAW President Walter Reuther to start a community action project in the heavily Hispanic East Los Angeles. Asked to develop a prototype for a "community union," Torres in 1968 founded The East Los Angeles Community Union (TELACU), which eventually grew into one of the five largest anti-poverty agencies in the country.[83]

In 1974 Torres unsuccessfully sought the Democratic nomination to a seat in the House of Representatives; later, he was appointed ambassador to UNESCO and served as a White House adviser to

242

President Carter. Torres had close ties to TELACU officials and, while he was a White House adviser he "recalled giving TELACU pointers on sources for government grants." The pointers led to a "State Department grant TELACU got in 1980 to work in Ecuador and proposals for projects in Panama and Bolivia." Torres again ran for Congress in 1982 and hired George Pla, a former TELACU executive vice president, as his campaign manager.[84] His 1982 bid for Congress was successful—the area had been redistricted and Torres "had the backing not only of East Los Angeles Hispanic leaders but of United Farm Workers leader Cesar Chavez and other national figures."[85]

TELACU also directly helped its officers and political allies by using CETA workers in campaigns. In 1978, CETA workers gathered signatures for Lizarraga to aid his efforts to be a delegate at a political convention, and they were used to get out the vote for Jimmy Carter in 1976:

> Former CETA secretary Anna Hernandez recalled "They gave us a (precinct) packet and told us what routes to go."
>
> On the front of the packet was a photograph of Carter and his running mate, Walter Mondale.
>
> The packet contained a computer printout of addresses to be contacted. It instructed walkers to tell voters: "I am from the Carter-Mondale headquarters. I would like to remind you to vote today if you have not and keep in mind the Democratic slate."[86]

In 1978, CETA workers were taken in TELACU vans to political rallies during working hours. The rallies supported beleaguered Rep. Edward R. Roybal (D-Calif.), then facing disciplinary action from the House Ethics Committee for lying under oath about a cash political contribution that had not been reported. " 'Over the years', Roybal said, 'he has supported TELACU and vice versa.' "[87] TELACU developed close relationships with political officials who could support the organization in its quest for funding. Taxpayer funds were used for political contributions and to provide resources for election campaigns, and elected officials steered grants and contracts to TELACU. Favors were also provided to bureaucrats. Gerrold Mukai was instrumental in directing CSA grants to TELACU, and he was then given a check for $50,000 from a TELACU subsidiary when he left government service. In 1982, David Lizarraga neatly summed up the political goals of TELACU: "We are an organization that is very political and very successful. . . . Ten years ago, we were on the streets and frustrated. We found that the only way to have an impact on government is to infiltrate government. . . . In 10 years, we have learned to make the system work for us."[88]

Politics in Other Antipoverty Agencies

In other examples of the abuse of antipoverty funds, politics have also played a key role. In Boston, the Neighborhood Development Agency (NDA) received about $25 million annually in community development grants. HUD auditors found that NDA was paying the salaries of employees who had nothing to do with housing problems; instead, they were conducting political polls for Mayor Kevin White and others. NDA employees circulated petitions, handed out absentee ballots, and raised campaign funds. Grants for renovations of homes and businesses were influenced by whether or not the applicant had contributed to political campaigns. Some NDA officials were given large pay raises (92 percent in one case), but the recipients were required to kick back some of the increase to the mayor's campaign fund. Little in the way of housing improvement was undertaken. One contractor was paid $90,000 to renovate 256 homes, but none was renovated; weatherization grants for 3,142 homes reached only 507 homes. In 1982 HUD auditors determined that $4 million was misspent or unaccounted for.[89] Thus, housing funds provided by the taxpayers were expropriated for political purposes. The poor suffered and the politicians flourished.

In the case of P.I. Properties in Washington, D.C., the mastermind of the Clifton Terrace housing scheme has been described as a "street activist," that is, a political organizer with power connections within government.[90] Mary Treadwell was able to continue to divert funds intended for the poor to her own uses because she "frequently invoked her friendship with then HUD secretary Patricia R. Harris, who later became secretary of Health, Education and Welfare."[91] In addition, Treadwell had been married to the city's mayor, although the mayor himself has never been accused of wrongdoing in this matter.

Antipoverty Programs and Political Spending

A clear and familiar pattern emerges from these case studies. Private, nonprofit antipoverty organizations are essentially thinly disguised political entities that channel campaign contributions to and get out the vote for favored politicians. Most of the private,

244

nonprofit antipoverty organizations that receive tax funding have a common characteristic: They deal with the grass roots, that is, with individuals who vote in specific districts, such as wards, precincts, and congressional districts. As every politician knows, it is costly and time consuming to reach individual voters and to organize grass-roots support for campaigns. Antipoverty organizations are especially important in organizing political support because they bring into the political process individuals who typically do not participate in large numbers. Not only do the officials of antipoverty agencies ensure that the poor vote, but they encourage and instruct the poor in voting for the "right" candidates.

Politicians are anxious to secure as many resources as possible to use in their campaigns. If the costs of organizing the poor can be shifted to the taxpayers, campaign contributions from other sources can be used for other purposes, for example, expensive media advertising. The bottom line is that tax dollars are converted into political contributions by laundering grants and contracts through groups that purport to aid the nation's poor. In return for political loyalty and assistance, politicians appropriate funds for antipoverty programs and use their influence to direct the money to those groups that will provide assistance and resources in the next campaign.

Little changes when incumbents are voted out of office, for the newly elected officials recognize the importance of the political power that many of the antipoverty organizations have been able to develop, and they are unwilling to alienate such constituencies. In effect, poverty programs have evolved into a large-scale spoils system for incumbent politicians at all levels of government, and helping the poor by providing better housing and job opportunities has become subordinate to using the funds for political gain. In addition, a cozy relationship has developed between the antipoverty industry and the bureaucracy. Politicians are eager to have public programs headed by individuals who will serve their interests and who are sympathetic to the subtleties of the political process. Public agencies that purport to aid the poor are staffed by political appointees who fully understand that their positions, salaries, and prestige are directly dependent on their elected patron remaining in office. Because of this simple fact, it is not surprising that so much tax money intended for the poor is diverted to political purposes. We do not wish to imply that all funds appropriated for poverty programs are skimmed and that the poor receive nothing.

It is certainly true, however, that the poor receive far less than what Congress formally allocates to them because the officials of anti-poverty programs enrich themselves at the expense of the poor and funnel large amounts of money to their political allies. Consequently, the poor and the taxpayers suffer while the politicians, bureaucrats, and their allies in the antipoverty industry prosper.

We also do not wish to leave the reader with the impression that the elimination of waste, fraud, and abuse would cure the nation's poverty problems. Even if tax-funded political advocacy were halted, the perverse incentive effects (see chapter 8) that discourage individuals from getting out of poverty would still remain. A fundamental overhaul of social programs is badly needed, and opposition to the changes required would be reduced if the groups that prosper from the plight of the poor did not receive tax funds to promote the agenda of the antipoverty industry.

X. Politics and the Redefinition of "Civil Rights"

[The Civil Rights Act of 1964] does not require an employer to achieve any kind of racial balance in his work force by giving preferential treatment to any individual or group. . . . [Subsection 703(j) under Title VII of the Civil Rights Act] is added to state this point expressly.

—Sen. Hubert Humphrey

The very meaning of the phrase "civil rights" has changed greatly . . . since the Civil Rights Act of 1964. Initially, civil rights meant, quite simply, that all individuals should be treated the same under the law, regardless of their race, religion, sex or other such social categories. . . . Many Americans who supported the initial thrust of civil rights . . . later felt betrayed as the original concept of equal individual *opportunity* evolved toward the concept of equal group *results*.

—Thomas Sowell
Civil Rights: Rhetoric or Reality?

Prior to the Civil Rights Act of 1964, there were many more examples of government-sanctioned discrimination against various minorities, especially blacks, than there are today. The early advances made by the civil rights movement[1] embodied additional guarantees of equality of opportunity, supported in large part by equal opportunity legislation and regulation that, in theory, protects individual rights to life, liberty, and property. The courts also enforced the equal protection clause of the Constitution more vigorously. The new laws and regulations were accompanied by the creation of new government bureaucracies with new empowerments to enforce them. But there is always the risk that governmental empowerments, however well intentioned, may be abused for political gain. The predominant activity of modern government is not to protect private property rights, as is suggested by the Civil Rights Act of 1964, but rather to rearrange rights in ways that dispense special privileges to politically active groups and spread the costs among less politically aware citizens.

A number of scholars have concluded that many of our economic and social problems have been created when government has abandoned its proper role of protecting individual liberties in favor of destroying them for political gain.[2] Civil rights legislation and regulation, unfortunately, are a case in point. Along with the rapid growth of the size and scope of government over the past two decades has come a perversion of the term "civil rights." Much of what many civil rights special-interest groups seek to achieve through the political process is not exclusively the guarantee of equal rights of all citizens. Rather, they seek preferential treatment for certain groups of people whom they refer to as their "clients," for example, blacks, the poor, and some women. These special-interest groups often seek these preferences even if they violate the civil and economic rights of others in society. In short, civil rights has been turned on its head: It now has less to do with equal opportunity than with special privileges provided by the state.

Tax-funded politics has played an important role in this process. The special-interest groups that purportedly represent minority groups in society have received millions of taxpayers' dollars to support their activities. It should come as no surprise, therefore, that their objectives have changed from protecting civil rights—the principal interest of minorities that are discriminated against—to participating in interest-group politics, which is the principal interest of the Washington establishment.

In this chapter we contend that before the civil rights movement became so heavily reliant on government funding, it had greater incentives to focus on the true interests of minorities. Now, however, it often ignores these interests in favor of satisfying the interests of a major funding source, the federal government.[3] This change benefits the Washington establishment and the unelected spokesmen for minority groups who have assumed positions of prominence and wealth; but it is doubtful that much of what is being done in the name of oppressed minorities actually helps minorities. Many black citizens, in particular, are beginning to realize the disparity. For example, Glenn Loury of Harvard University wrote in an article for the U.S. Civil Rights Commission in 1984: "The evidence of which I am aware suggests that, for many of the most hotly contested public policies advocated by black spokesmen, not much benefit 'trickles down' to the black poor."[4]

248

Tax-Funded Politics and Civil Rights Organizations

There are dozens of civil rights lobbying organizations, but we will discuss only a few of them here to illustrate the part they play in the government process. Table A10.1 (in appendix) lists selected federal government grants given to various civil rights organizations, including such groups as the National Urban League, Jesse Jackson's People United to Save Humanity (PUSH), and the National Organization for Women (NOW). The last group may seem out of place here, in that women constitute a majority of the U.S. population, but such groups as NOW claim to represent a minority just as do the National Urban League and the National Association for the Advancement of Colored People (NAACP). Although these federal grants have been distributed in the name of promoting the interests of various minorities, there is much evidence that civil rights organizations consistently promote liberal and even radical political programs that are at odds with what the minorities have voiced as their own preferences. In a *Wall Street Journal* article ("Are Black Leaders Listening to Black America?"), journalist Joseph Perkins has written:

> Black leaders react in traditionally knee-jerk liberal fashion to issues across the board, even though, in general, black Americans are decidedly conservative on a number of issues. The [Congressional] Black Caucus, for example, advocates a "right" to abortion, forced busing and bans on organized school prayer, whereas 62% of blacks oppose abortion (National Opinion Research Center, 1984), 52% oppose busing (Associated Press, 1983) and 71% support school prayer (Gallup, 1984). . . . Black leaders have demonstrated not only a propensity to ignore the feelings of their constituency on numerous issues, but a predilection to promote liberal—oftentimes radical—policies.[5]

There is further evidence that civil rights leaders ignore the preferences of those they claim to be leading. By enacting the Civil Rights Act of 1964, Congress declared itself in favor of equal opportunity but opposed to affirmative action quotas based on race or sex. This position is also held by the majority of U.S. citizens, including most blacks and an even larger majority of women.[6] Blacks have rejected preferential treatment by 64 percent to 27 percent, and 80 percent of women have also rejected it. Yet the emphasis of the civil rights organizations has been precisely in favor of special treatment in the form of quotas and other set-asides for

249

women and minorities. On the issue of income redistribution, or distributive justice, there are four times as many blacks who believe that people with more ability should earn more as there are those who believe that government should forceably equalize earnings.[7] This, too, is greatly at odds with the views of the civil rights establishment, which often assumes a radical redistributionist philosophy.

On the issue of criminal justice, public opinion polls have consistently shown blacks to be among the strongest supporters of giving criminals stiffer sentences, but most civil rights organizations have led lobbying efforts to reduce criminal punishment. With respect to so-called women's rights, it is interesting that even though NOW claims to represent women, public opinion polls show that a majority of women in the country disagree with its policy prescriptions, as evidenced by the 57 percent of the women's vote that Ronald Reagan received in the 1984 presidential election, despite NOW's strong support of Walter Mondale and all of the stories in the media of a gender gap. Thus, it appears that many civil rights organizations are using taxpayers' funds to promote a political agenda that is not necessarily helpful to or desired by the majority of people in minority groups.

The civil rights organizations themselves, however, do very well financially, regardless of whether they are helping their constituents. For example, during the 1970s the National Urban League and its affiliates received more than $100 million each year in federal grants. In federal jobs training legislation, Congress actually suggested that the National Urban League be favored for funds set aside by the secretary of labor.[8] Even though there is undeniable evidence that federal jobs training programs have been abysmal failures (even liberal Democrats did not defend CETA in 1982), the National Urban League is a steadfast defender of such programs, many of which are administered by its affiliates.[9]

Consider a 1981 U.S. Department of Labor grant for $4,696,170 that the National Urban League received for a project entitled Seniors in Community Service.[10] The funding included more than $160,000 for the league's personnel salaries and an additional $28,000 in fringe benefits. The budget also included $33,499 for travel to visit sub-grantees, the majority of which were local National Urban League chapters. Another $342,876 was budgeted for general administrative costs, along with $12,000 for telephone expenses, $19,000 in additional travel expenses, and $18,000 in per diems for

250

two National Urban League conferences. The National Urban League also benefited from the grant by being allowed to channel some of the funds to its affiliates to "administer" the Seniors in Community Service program. According to the league's grant proposal:

> [E]mploying agencies for participants under the projects will be public or private non-profit, non-partisan organizations which will provide: job supervision, orientation, job training, support services and transition opportunities to program participants. Such agencies may include, but are not limited to: schools, child care facilities, hospitals, neighborhood centers, environmental agencies, *Urban League affiliates*, Red Cross, United Way, public libraries, neighborhood associations, public agencies providing a direct community service, etc. [emphasis added].[11]

The National Urban League, like other civil rights organizations, benefits directly from various welfare state programs regardless of whether the programs are successful. As long as the programs persist and grow, National Urban League employees and administrators will enjoy income-earning opportunities.

There is little doubt that the league is heavily involved in tax-funded politics. It is part of the network of tax-funded lobbying organizations. For example, among the activities listed for the Atlanta subgrantee of the grant mentioned above is participation in the July 1982 Conference of the National Council of Senior Citizens (see chapter 11). One of the activities at the conference was "a . . . group meeting [where] participants were given information on public benefits and voter registration. All seniors not registered to vote were registered during the meeting."[12] The league, then, apparently used taxpayer funds to register voters who would provide political support for the government programs that the league itself administers.

The National Urban League has been sharply critical of the Reagan administration's attempts to alter welfare state programs, even while receiving millions of dollars in federal grants.[13] Some insight into the league's political views can be found in its journal, *The Urban League Review*. Each article in the winter 1982–83 issue is basically a condemnation of the Reagan administration's policy proposals. None of the authors found any merit whatsoever in any of the administration's proposals for changing existing welfare state programs. Surely there must be *some* merit in the proposed changes. In "Gutting the Great Society," Tom Joe concluded: "There is little

251

doubt that the much discussed economic gains blacks have made in relation to whites over the last two decades will diminish as these [welfare spending] cutbacks take place."[14] This contradicts a great deal of scholarly research that has shown that increased welfare spending has coincided with an increase in poverty, especially among blacks,[15] and that economic progress among blacks appears to have been stalled precisely when the Great Society welfare programs began to grow. Such evidence is studiously ignored by the National Urban League. In "A Dream Denied: The Black Family in the Eighties," James McGhee, director of research at the National Urban League, warned of the impending destruction of the present black middle class if the welfare state is tinkered with. Robert C. Smith, in "Black Leadership in a Neoconservative Era," offered the following advice to the leaders of civil rights organizations:

> The attacks on liberalism today are understandable. . . . However, it is an error (maybe of historic proportions) for progressives, especially blacks, to join in the chorus of criticism because liberalism has not failed; rather, it has not been . . . adequately funded. This is not to say that it may not be necessary to move in the United States toward an explicit social democratic agenda (in the form of systematic national planning; nationalization of some industries, especially energy and armaments; a permanent system of restraint . . . on wages and prices [i.e., price controls], credit controls and a more progressive and effectively administered inheritance tax) but rather it is to say that the task today is more modest—the maintenance of the liberal hour in a time of conservative reaction.[16]

In sum, the National Urban League, and many other tax-funded civil rights organizations, depend on and therefore support the welfare state. The leaders of these organizations are able to gain power, prestige, and wealth by organizing political support for the welfare state and by ensuring that large numbers of minorities participate in welfare state programs. They even organize voter registration drives to ensure voter support for programs that their organizations often administer. Sadly, many of the policies strongly advocated by these groups have been shown to harm the very people they claim to protect, the victims of discrimination.

Affirmative Discrimination

There has been a major shift in emphasis among the so-called civil rights organizations on the subject of affirmative action and

252

equal opportunity laws. In the spirit of the Civil Rights Act of 1964, equal opportunity laws require that individuals be judged on their qualifications as individuals without regard to race, sex, national origin, and so forth. What are now being called affirmative action laws, however, insist that people be judged with regard to such group membership; such laws constitute a mandate that some citizens receive preferential treatment over others, regardless of the civil rights of those who may be the victims of such treatment.

The term "affirmative action" has been completely distorted. The phrase was first used in the context of discrimination by President Kennedy in 1961 when he issued Executive Order No. 10,925, which read that federal construction contractors "should take affirmative action to ensure that . . . employees are treated . . . without regard to their race, creed, color, or national origin."[17] Today, for contractors to comply with federal regulations, they are required to pay specific attention to race, creed, color, or national origin in making their employment decisions. It is not coincidental that during the 1950s and early 1960s, early civil rights leaders such as Martin Luther King, Jr., and organizations such as the NAACP and the Southern Christian Leadership Conference were not heavily dependent on federal funding and did not advocate special preferences for minorities. They fought for *equal opportunity*. However, as affirmative action laws are now enforced, they try to remedy past discrimination, which was pervasive and repulsive, by even more discrimination against the 15 percent of the U.S. population that the federal government has not defined as being part of a minority group. It is not even clear that such reverse discrimination policies help those individuals who may have suffered from discrimination in the past.

There are a great many reasons for differences in income among whites and nonwhites, men and women, and so forth. Simply finding that a difference exists and remedying that difference by governmentally sanctioned preferential treatment ignores factors that may be far more important than discrimination. For example, age differences among different groups are significant: Blacks are a decade younger, on average, than the Japanese; Jews are 25 years older, on average, than Puerto Ricans; Polish Americans are twice as old, on average, as American Indians.[18] Furthermore, there is a much larger wage gap between age brackets than between blacks and whites or between men and women because of differences in experience, training, and learning.

Cultural differences among population groups are also important. For example, people who marry earlier are more restricted in their employment opportunities than those who marry later. Educational emphasis is also important, as different fields of study lead to different career paths. Mathematics provides preparation for relatively high-paying work in business, economics, engineering, computer programming, and statistics; preparation in history and English is not as lucrative. Although such a finding is often dismissed as bigotry, there are also differences among groups in work habits, discipline, attitudes, and so on that affect job performance and earning capacity.

In short, there are several reasons for wage differences among different groups in society, and discrimination is only one of them. By focusing on discrimination, government authorities and professional civil rights lobbying organizations have ignored many alternative and possibly superior means of improving the lot of minorities in U.S. society. Furthermore, there is evidence that this approach has actually harmed minorities. As Thomas Sowell has written:

> Much has been made of the number of blacks in high-level occupations before and after the Civil Rights Act of 1964. What has been almost totally ignored is the historical *trend* of black representation in such occupations before the Act was passed. In the period from 1954 to 1964, for example, the number of blacks in professional, technical, and similar high-level positions more than doubled. In other kinds of occupations, the advance of blacks was even greater during the 1940s—when there was little or no civil rights policy—than during the 1950s when the civil rights revolution was in its heyday. The rise in the number of blacks in professional and technical occupations in the two years from 1964 to 1966 (after the Civil Rights Act) was in fact *less* than in the one year from 1961 to 1962 (before the Civil Rights Act). . . . The Civil Rights Act of 1964 represented no acceleration in trends that had been going on for many years.[19]

Sowell also has found that the history of Asians and Hispanics shows long-term upward trends that began years before the civil rights act was passed in 1964. Those trends were not noticeably accelerated by the act or by later affirmative action policies. From such evidence Sowell has concluded that ignoring these trends makes before and after comparisons misleading—but this is exactly what civil rights organizations have done. There is also some evidence that affirmative action policies have harmed the relatively disadvantaged within the groups singled out for special preference. Sowell has found that the relative positions of these groups declined under affirmative action:

> In 1969, *before* the federal imposition of numerical "goals and timetables," Puerto Rican family income was 63 percent of the national average. By 1977, it was down to 50 percent. In 1969, Mexican American family income was 76 percent of the national average. By 1977 it was down to 73 percent. Black family income fell from 62 percent of the national average to 60 percent over the same time span. There are many complex factors behind these numbers. The point here is simply that they do not support the civil rights vision.[20]

Data about individuals tell the same story. Those blacks with less education and job experience—the truly disadvantaged—have fallen further and further behind during the era of affirmative action. By contrast, blacks with more education and experience have been advancing economically, both absolutely and relative to their white counterparts. Black male high school dropouts with less than six years of work experience earned 79 percent of the income of their white counterparts in 1967, but this figure fell to 69 percent by 1978—after affirmative action programs were in place. Over the same years the income of black males who had completed college and had more than six years of work experience rose from 75 percent of the income of their white counterparts to 98 percent.[21] None of these statistics support the claims made by those who promote quotas and set-asides (that is, affirmative action), but Sowell has offered a straightforward, elementary economic explanation of them:

> To explain such diametrically opposite trends within the black community on the basis of whites' behavior would require us to believe that racism and discrimination were growing and declining at the same time. It is much more reconcilable with ordinary economic analysis. Affirmative action hiring pressures make it costly to have no minority employees, but continuing affirmative action pressures at the promotion and discharge phases also make it costly to have minority employees who do not work out well. The net effect is to increase the demand for highly qualified minority employees while decreasing the demand for less qualified minority employees or for those without a sufficient track record to reassure employers. Those who are most vocal about the need for affirmative action are of course the more articulate minority members—the advantaged who speak in the name of the disad-

vantaged. Their position on the issue may accord with their own personal experience, as well as their own self-interest.[22]

The Minimum Wage Law

Based on decades of research, it is the nearly unanimous opinion of economists that the minimum wage law prices out of the market precisely the people that the law is supposed to help—those with relatively little education and work experience.[23] Especially hard hit by this law are black teenagers who are deprived of opportunities to participate in their first work experience at an early age.[24] Most civil rights organizations, however, advocate increasing the minimum wage, which would surely result in more unemployment among black teenagers, which is already several times higher than the overall unemployment rate and as high as 60 percent in some cities. The major political allies of these organizations are labor unions, whose members include almost no black teenagers.

Why would groups that supposedly represent the interests of blacks support such a destructive law, and why would labor unions lobby for a law that they say benefits black teenagers who do not generally belong to labor unions? The answer lies in the need for civil rights organizations, which claim to represent only a minority of the population, to form coalitions with other special-interest groups to get what they want. The AFL-CIO benefits from increases in the minimum wage because its members compete with relatively unskilled, nonunionized black teenagers. Pricing black teenagers out of the market, therefore, improves the job security of union members. In return for supporting increases in the minimum wage, labor unions help civil rights organizations lobby for increased welfare spending. These political strategies persist because the benefits received are earmarked for specific groups (for example, food stamp recipients), and the costs are well hidden. Few black teenagers (or any teenagers), for example, are likely to fully understand that one reason why it is so difficult for them to find work is that few employers can afford to hire them, owing to the minimum wage law and other regulations. The costs are even more disguised as labor unions and some civil rights organizations constantly put out misinformation about the effects of the minimum wage law. They apparently provide this misinformation so that union organizers can protect their members from competition and civil rights

256

leaders can claim credit for providing government benefits to their clients.

There are some encouraging developments, however. The National Council of Black Mayors has endorsed the idea of a two-tier minimum wage whereby teenagers could receive a lower wage and not be priced out of the market. For this plan to prevail, however, the leaders of the tax-funded civil rights organizations must be convinced that logrolling with labor unions on this issue is not profitable—a formidable task, to say the least. As long as the leaders of civil rights organizations believe that minorities must seek special treatment by government rather than individual initiative through equality of opportunity, they must continue to play the game of interest-group politics.

Occupational Licensing

Another unfortunate result of the close political link between the tax-funded civil rights organizations and labor unions is that the civil rights organizations have helped the unions maintain a system of occupational licensing laws. Literally thousands of occupations, from fortune telling to the practice of medicine, require special governmentally sanctioned licenses, and one effect of these laws has been to reduce the employment opportunities available to minorities.[25] Licensing laws are routinely used by incumbent practitioners to establish monopoly rights in various trades, many of which are unionized. Trucking licenses are allocated by the Interstate Commerce Commission, which restricts the supply of trucking services and allows trucking firms and the teamsters union to earn monopoly profits. State and local governments restrict entry into the taxi business, charging as much as $60,000 for the so-called right to drive a cab. Hairdressers must often pass written as well as practical tests, a practice that denies licenses to many people who are excellent hairdressers (and who pass the practical portions of the exams) but who are not adept at written examinations. For decades, plumbers and electricians have excluded blacks from entering their occupations because of racist licensing restrictions enforced by state and local governments.[26] These are just a few examples taken from a long list compiled by Walter Williams in his book *The State Against Blacks*.

By becoming so heavily involved in politics and by receiving millions of taxpayer dollars, some civil rights organizations have painted themselves into a corner on the issue of occupational licensing. We now observe such perversities as Rep. Charles B. Rangel (D-N.Y.), a member of the Congressional Black Caucus, defending beautician licensing laws on national television, even though these laws have caused a black failure rate (to enter the occupation) that is three times the rate of whites.[27] However well intentioned they may be, Rangel and other like-minded politicians know the value of the political campaign support that labor unions can provide, and they hesitate to take action that would jeopardize that support. Rather than working to open up job opportunities for minorities, some civil rights organizations defend the laws that effectively deny minorities those opportunities. Taking this position helps labor unions protect their members from labor market competition from minorities, and in return the unions help civil rights organizers lobby for increased welfare spending, which will relegate minorities to a safer place in society where they cannot compete with unionized labor. All of this is done in the name of helping minorities.

Women and Civil Rights

Even though women make up a majority of the U.S. population, several tax-funded women's groups, such as NOW, have declared women to be a minority. Accordingly, these groups routinely complain that women, too, deserve special privileges from the state because of past discrimination. In short, much of the women's movement, like the rest of the civil rights movement, is not concerned so much with guaranteeing equal opportunity as with dispensing special privileges to some people at the expense of others.

Wage discrimination on the basis of sex has been legally banned since the mid-1960s, and the Fourteenth Amendment protects the equal rights of all citizens, including women. It is likely, therefore, that what women's groups mean when they speak of equal rights legislation is not the further guarantee of equal opportunity, but rather equality of results, that is, a redistribution of income. Tax-funded women's groups are often heard to say that women earn on average about 60 percent of what men earn. This figure is repeated endlessly, usually in a tone of moral outrage, to support the belief that the reason for the difference is sex discrimination. Their solution to this so-called problem is usually a government program to redistribute income.

In fact, there are many reasons that men and women receive different wages. Therefore, equalizing wages through government action would not achieve true equality but would create special privileges for one group (some women) at the expense of other groups. For example, women work substantially fewer hours than men because a larger proportion of women work part-time.[28] Women also average fewer continuous years of employment on a given job, usually because of marriage and motherhood.[29] In these cases, women choose to earn less in return for other benefits, such as staying home with small children. An examination of the income status of single women compared to that of single men shows that the wage differences largely disappear in this case. In the 25–64 age bracket, women who remain single earn 91 percent of the income of men who remain single.[30] Moreover, the remaining 9 percent cannot necessarily be attributed to discrimination, for women generally choose occupations that are not as lucrative as those chosen by men. For example, women do not choose to enter such fields as mathematics, economics, science, and engineering as frequently as men do. Nor are they as attracted to physically taxing occupations, such as carpentry, ironworking, lumbering, and coal mining. These are all occupations that pay relatively higher wages than do many safer occupations that women often choose.

The ramifications of marriage and parenthood are profound, but they are often overlooked by those who see discrimination as the predominant cause of male-female wage differences. According to Sowell:

> Marriage increases a man's rate of participation in the labor force compared to single men and reduces a woman's labor force participation rate compared to single women. A married man's hours worked annually increase with the number of children. A married woman's hours decrease as the number of children increases. Married men work more and earn more than single men, while it is just the reverse with women. Married men with children work the most and earn the most, while married women with children work the least and earn the least. Altogether, married women living with their husbands average only 25 percent of the annual income of married men living with their wives. The big difference is not between men and women, but between married women and everyone else.[31]

Women's rights activists may disapprove of the choices women make—that is, entering occupations, such as secretarial work, that are easy to move into or out of—but this situation is completely different from saying that differences in wages are caused by employer discrimination. Moreover, if male-female wage differences were caused primarily by employer discrimination, it would be hard to explain why the difference is 9 percent in the case of women who never marry but 75 percent in the case of married women living with their husbands. As Sowell has further stated:

> The central "59 percent" cliche would require us to believe that employers could survive in a competitive market, paying nearly 70 percent more for given labor than they have to, whenever that labor is male. Even if employers were that needlessly generous to men, or so consumed by ideology, waste of this magnitude would be economically fatal to those businessmen who happened to have more men on the payroll than their competitors. Far smaller differences in cost have sent innumerable businesses into bankruptcies. As in so many other areas, the civil rights vision is so preoccupied with individual *intentions* that it ignores *systemic* effects. . . . Researchers who take literally statistics based on the fact that the man's name alone appears on his paycheck set the stage for much misunderstanding of social reality.[32]

Although sex discrimination certainly exists, normal labor market analysis can explain almost all of the differences that occur between the wages of men and women. Much of this analysis is just plain common sense, but it has been routinely ignored by the civil rights and women's rights activists. Their narrow perception has led them to advocate such ideas as equal pay for work of comparable value, which is not the same as equal pay for equal work. Instead, this scheme would have groups of government bureaucrats decide the comparable worth of different types of jobs and set wages accordingly. For example, a librarian could be considered to be of comparable worth to a chemist or an engineer if the small handful of bureaucrats deemed it so. In short, wages would not be set by supply and demand and by how markets evaluate job performance, but by the personal preferences and prejudices of a small group of bureaucrats. The determination would be totally arbitrary and subjective, regardless of the attempts made to make the process sound scientific by having bureaucrats assign points to various job categories. Bureaucrats applying comparable worth would ignore such factors as the relative scarcity and productivity of different types of labor, which vary considerably from job to job and from individual to individual. They are also likely to ignore what workers themselves want. A carpenter and a secretary may be given the same number of points, but that does not compensate the carpenter for working outdoors in cold winter weather while the secretary works inside a comfortably heated building. Carpentry may pay more to compensate for these differences, but such compensation could be outlawed by comparable-worth legislation.

If women choose to enter occupations that are dangerous, more strenuous, require more education and training, or that are permanently full time, they are usually free to do so. In so doing, they can increase their wage income without participating in all of the injustices that a bureaucratic system of comparable-worth regulation would entail. Ironically, many occupations that are predominantly male are so because of occupational licensing restrictions, but women's rights organizations rarely attack these regulations. Sowell has offered a reasonable explanation for this phenomenon:

> In a sense, such claims [in favor of comparable worth] are a reassuring social sign that civil rights activists, whose own employment and visibility depend upon maintaining an adequate flow of injustices, are forced to resort to things like "comparable worth" in order to keep busy. It is also virtually a lawyers' full-employment act, since it will be possible to argue interminably on both sides as to the items that go into the job point totals. . . . Moreover, labor unions have every incentive to embrace this doctrine, since achieving "comparability" can only be done by raising some salaries, not by lowering others. This is especially so in government employment, since no politician wants to be on record against equality, comparability, or equity. The net result is likely to be that taxpayers will end up paying far more than necessary to get the public's work done.[33]

Tax-funded civil rights and women's rights organizations have co-opted the term "civil rights" to describe their own personal political agendas, agendas that do not necessarily have anything to do with civil rights. Their goals include income-redistribution schemes that the public may not find as palatable if they were not shrouded in civil rights rhetoric. It is no surprise that civil rights organizations have ignored the fact that many of these schemes actually harm minorities and women. Admitting that government programs to help minorities have failed or have made things worse would jeopardize additional government funding, not only of the programs but also of the civil rights organizations themselves. Further examples of tax-funded politics will illustrate what a lucrative business this can be.

When PUSH Comes to Shove

Jesse Jackson's People United to Save Humanity (PUSH) has received millions of taxpayers' dollars. Jackson is undeniably one of the best known of the civil rights leaders, most recently because of his spirited attempt to secure the Democratic party's presidential nomination in 1984 and for his voter registration drives that organize mostly black voters to support various causes. Jackson is a professional politician, although his role is more that of a political middleman between elected officials and black citizens. His views are consistent with the modern civil rights vision: supporting forced busing, quotas, and increased welfare expenditures and opposing such policies as tuition tax credits, tax reduction, and expenditure restraint. He also supports many of the other policies advocated by the far left in U.S. politics. He is among the harshest critics of President Reagan, he has been widely quoted as saying "Long live Fidel Castro" while on his visit to Cuba in 1984, and he is still remembered for his embrace of Palestine Liberation Organization leader Yasser Arafat in 1978.

Jackson's PUSH organization is divided into several nonprofit corporations, including the PUSH Foundation, an Ohio trust based in Chicago; Operation PUSH, an Illinois nonprofit corporation with many affiliates across the country; PUSH International Trade Bureau, Inc., another Illinois nonprofit corporation that works with corporations; and PUSH for Excellence, Inc., an Ohio nonprofit organization with offices in Chicago.[34] A major focus of Jackson's operation is to "run programs in schools designed to improve the motivation and achievement of minority school children."[35] In claiming to pursue these goals, PUSH received more than $5 million in federal grants from 1977 to 1981 from the departments of Education, Labor, Health and Human Services, and Commerce, as well as millions of dollars in state and local government grants. The city government of Los Angeles, for example, gave PUSH $667,000 for the 1978–79 school year.[36] There is reason to believe, however, that some of these funds have been used for purposes other than "vitalizing" black students with slogans about Jackson's "5 A's"—attention, attendance, attitude, atmosphere, and achievement.

In 1983, the U.S. Department of Education's Office of Inspector General completed nine audits of federal grants awarded to PUSH. The auditors concluded that of the $4.9 million given to PUSH from 1977 to 1981, nearly $2 million was spent in ways that may have violated regulations prohibiting the funding of organizations engaged in political activity.[37] Even though the grants were awarded to PUSH-EXCEL, Jackson's youth education organization, the auditors found a disturbing pattern: "PUSH-EXCEL and PUSH share office space in a Chicago building owned by PUSH. They also share certain programs and supportive service personnel. Common expenses were also shared by both organizations."[38] The auditors found that the taxpayers had paid travel expenses and registration fees for employees of Operation PUSH to attend at least three of their national conventions in 1979, 1980, and 1981. Other examples of questionable spending include the following:

- A $1 million contract awarded to provide aid to "inner city school students to promote excellence and improve motivation" was used to buy basketball uniforms for a fund-raising celebrity game, a contribution to a Los Angeles high school for a dinner dance, costs relating to a girls' basketball tournament, and band activities. PUSH also charged the government for entry fees for a parade float sponsored by the Los Angeles Chamber of Commerce.[39]

- A grant made by the Department of Education's research arm, the National Institute of Education, was used to print 10,000 Christmas cards bearing an autographed photograph of Jesse Jackson.

- A $656,644 grant awarded by the Department of Education in March 1981 was used for insurance for a dance group, donations to a Chicago track club, and airfare to coordinate the Black Leadership Conference in Holly Springs, Mississippi.

- A grant was used to help mail out 2,000 fund-raising letters to area businesses and regular contributors, to write letters to foundations seeking donations, to sell tickets for a dinner playhouse that would raise funds for PUSH, and for holding business luncheons to obtain donations.

After evaluating these and other grants, the Department of Education declared that Jackson had "misused" more than $1.7 million in grants and recommended that the money be returned. In general the auditors believed that the money had been mishandled "because of a lack of documentation for some expenses, claims for salary or expenses performed by project employees who were doing nongrant related work and claims for expenses not connected with the projects."[40] In several cases, money had been withdrawn from program accounts, "but no justification for expenditures was offered."[41] Although the Department of Education insists that nothing done was of a "criminal nature," these uses of taxpayers' funds leave open the possibility that some funds may have been used to finance Jackson's political organization, including his voter registration drives and his bid for the Democratic presidential nomination. In any case, it is clear that much of the grant money has been used in ways that are not directly related to educating minority youth. PUSH's own records, for example, show that PUSH-EXCEL has paid out more money in recent years for salaries than for program services.[42]

Women and "Educational Equity"

In 1974, Congress passed the Women's Educational Equity Act (WEEA) because "Educational programs in the U.S. . . . are frequently inequitable in as much as programs relate to women. . . . It is the purpose of this [act] . . . to provide educational equity to women." As is usually the case with government expenditure programs, however, rhetoric and reality are divorced in this act. This legislation has been used as a conduit through which numerous radical women's groups can finance their political activities. A survey of some of the grant recipients will demonstrate how the U.S. taxpayers are unknowingly financing a radical political agenda advocated by various so-called feminist special-interest groups.

The Council on Interracial Books for Children

A federal government grant to the Council on Interracial Books for Children apparently violates the U.S. Department of Education's congressional mandate not to get involved in curriculum programs.[43] In July 1981, the Department of Education gave the council the second installment of a two-year, $244,000 grant. In the name of promoting educational equity for women and minorities, the council said that its objective was to "reeducate" American children by producing new textbooks that reflected its views. Consider the following passage from a 1980 council publication, *Guidelines for Selecting Bias-Free Textbooks and Storybooks:*

> Implicit in all of the textbooks surveyed is the assumption that the U.S. society is a true democracy. . . . The distortion which results is serious, for by calling our government and economic systems "democratic," the textbooks deny the realities of capitalism and all that goes with it—classes, conflicting class interests, and the ongoing struggle between those few who control wealth and those many who are trying to share wealth.

Through the council's efforts, "Textbooks can mold human beings with counter-values that may help to restructure the society."[44]

The council and similar groups receive government funding through WEEA and at the discretion of Leslie Wolfe, a career bureaucrat who makes all funding decisions regarding WEEA projects. Although Congress intended that WEEA grants be dispersed among a wide variety of groups, Wolfe has directed most of the grants to a handful of organizations that are ideologically compatible with the Council on Interracial Books for Children. For example, of the 55 grants awarded in 1981, only 3 went to state and local educational agencies. More than half of the remaining grants went to political interest groups, such as the council, NOW, and Women's Action Alliance.[45]

The council's 1980 WEEA grant was for a project entitled Equity Models for Basal Readers, whose goal was to produce bias-free elementary school textbooks. To accomplish this task, a list of guidelines was established, including the following:

> Let's make it clear that we have no desire to see children's books that would solely help the dominated get a bigger piece of the pie. We don't like the pie, period. . . . We are not interested in seeing different people win a place in the status quo, the present social structure. We are challenging the structure itself because it promotes anti-human values.[46]

The stated goal of "bias-free texts" can hardly be accomplished by such ideologically biased attacks on the free enterprise system. The council clearly holds the present "economic system" accountable for racist and sexist attitudes and proposes to propagandize against it:

> Texts may imply that individual bigots, or groups of ignorant and prejudiced people, are to blame for some unfortunate situation, while ignoring a society that manipulates and encourages working-class divisions. . . . *Because the economic system is not held accountable,* students are led to believe that education and greater tolerance will eliminate societal flaws. . . . Racism, sexism, and economic exploitation are not occasional aberrations of the U.S. system, but deeply ingrained mechanisms of the national social and economic structure [emphasis added].[47]

The council concluded that "one of the great myths of U.S. society is that we have no class problem or class conflict. . . . Stemming

265

from this refusal to recognize the conflict of class interests is the refusal to link sexism and racism to economic exploitation. . . . Individualism is a philosophy of life; it has not always existed in every human society and should be discouraged as a highly negative force."[48]

With these themes in mind, the council proceeded to develop, at taxpayers' expense, a series of textbooks. It also retained several outside consultants, many of whom were also recipients of grants from the Department of Education.[49] Armed with federal grants and a team of tax-funded supporters, the council produced readers and teachers' manuals for the third and fifth grades, and field test sites were chosen in Arizona, Massachusetts, Florida, and California. A small sample of these materials reveals their propagandistic nature. The following "background material" is found in a teacher's manual:

> Hispanics are among the poorest people in the U.S. . . . Housing and health facilities are grossly inadequate and political power is limited. These problems are aggravated by cases of police brutality, and inequitable treatment by the courts. Discrimination and institutional exclusion limit possibilities for rapid change in their social, economic, and political conditions.[50]

In contrast to this description of life in the United States under "capitalism" is a description of life in communist Cuba. The Cuban government is portrayed not as oppressive but as compassionate and just, as in this story:

> The woman is a ballerina who is going blind. Her country is Castro's Cuba. A section [of one of the Council's texts] entitled "Newcomers" tells the story of "Alicia Alonso," a world-famous ballerina who elects to stay in Cuba after the Castro-led revolution. She is going blind, but the Cuban government gives her all the assistance she needs to set up schools throughout the Cuban countryside. Her courage in continuing to dance, despite her growing handicap, is matched only by the brotherly nature of the Cuban government, which is depicted as the provider of all worldly needs.[51]

On the subject of women in the workplace, the books provide stories of U.S. "sweatshops" where

> [w]omen factory workers faced many problems: long hours, low pay, inhumane work conditions, constant exposure to the risk of

serious personal injury, and unequal pay as compared to men. These conditions were the result of exploitation of women by their employers. Their wages were purposely kept low so as to save employers money and increase their profits.[52]

In a section entitled "Taking Action," a warning is issued: "Sweatshops have reappeared in large numbers." Teachers are advised to have students "Write and deliver a speech to co-workers telling them the advantages of joining a union."

The council hopes to sell these texts commercially. This could be a very profitable enterprise because the taxpayers have underwritten a large part of the expense.

The National Student Educational Fund

Another recipient of WEEA funding is the National Student Educational Fund (NSEF), which received $232,000 from the U.S. Department of Education in 1981. The main product of the grant was a national "feminist conference" held in Washington, D.C., and an accompanying manual entitled *Empowering Women*.[53] The manual is largely a collection of articles written by other WEEA-funded women's groups, such as the Women's Equity Action League. These articles are available elsewhere, often free of charge. Although NSEF is required to focus its tax-funded activities on educational issues, the organization uses WEEA's broad definition of "educational" as a rationalization to engage in tax-funded political activity. *Empowering Women*, for example, discusses the distressing state of the national economy and advocates laws to strengthen unions, to allow more welfare spending, to require more stringent product safety regulation, to set affirmative action quotas, and to encourage other "progressive" policies that may motivate "socialist feminists" to "directly challenge the right of the ruling class to divide up the economic pie."[54]

NSEF also uses taxpayers' funds to indirectly support its lobbying counterpart, the U.S. Student Association (USSA). Both groups have participated in Solidarity Day protests in Washington, D.C., and the director of the USSA has traveled to Moscow to discuss "struggles for peace." USSA's vice chairman served as national secretary to the Young Workers Liberation League, reportedly an affiliate of the Communist Party U.S.A.[55] Because of these activities, several USSA chapters across the country have withdrawn from the organization.

267

The final 44 pages of *Empowering Women* contain technical advice on political organizing, including advice on leadership, coalition building, fund raising, and media relations. There is even an article on how to procure federal grants to finance these activities. But a large portion of the manual and of other NSEF publications is devoted to arguments against proposed budgetary cutbacks in the area of "women's programs." It is not apparent that any of these actions have anything whatsoever to do with women's equity on college campuses, the stated objective of the grant; nor is there any evidence that the actions have had any impact on college campuses.

The Bay Area Bilingual Education League

Another WEEA grant recipient is the (San Francisco) Bay Area Bilingual Education League (BABEL). In 1981, BABEL received $87,067 from the U.S. Department of Education for its Campesina Project, which would provide a very ambitious program of "training sessions and citizen advocacy leadership, immigration procedures, internal revenue training skills, physical and mental health awareness and prevention, career awareness, educational alternatives and parenting."[56] BABEL's evaluation of its first year of activity under the grant includes its plans: "In each community . . . an organization of Campesina women will be established. The main purpose of this organization is to serve as a platform for community needs and concerns. The formulation of such a group also serves to institutionalize the organization and ensure its continuation." In other words, taxpayers' funds were to be used to garner political support for BABEL so that it could continue to appeal for taxpayers' funding. Other "plans for the future" included a "Chicano Leadership Conference" to "develop a plan of action for the 1980s." A political training manual was also produced, which dealt with such issues as self-awareness, the role of women in society, assertiveness training, identifying needs in one's community, and community organizing and advocacy at the local level of government.

In its second-year progress report to the Department of Education, BABEL made the following statement: "It is necessary to inform and influence legislators at every level if we are to continue to provide opportunities for women to advocate, organize, and ensure that women are seen and treated as equals."[57] Thus, BABEL clearly and blatantly was involved in tax-funded political activity in violation of WEEA.

The types of issues that BABEL lobbies for are bound to be wide-ranging; they are also likely to be consistent with the objectives of the United Farmworkers of America, a union in California. In a summary of its grant proposal, BABEL wrote that it "has the great fortune of being able to utilize the services and resources of the United Farm Workers of America, headed by Cesar Chavez. The Vice-President of United Farm Workers, Delores Huerta, and foremost leader of Campesina, will be a key resource leadership trainer."

BABEL also received $975,000 in 1981 for "Bilingual Education Centers," $82,000 for "Bilingual Educational Training," $36,000 for "Metric Education" (surely a low priority for the U.S. taxpayers), $290,650 for "Civil Rights Technical Assistance Desegregation Assistance Centers," and $52,354 for "the Improvement of Post-Secondary Education."[58]

The Women's Equity Action League

The Women's Equity Action League (WEAL) received at least $1,067,591 in federal grants from 1978 to 1980 from the U.S. Department of Education.[59] A form letter sent to us at our request describing the activities of WEAL states that "WEAL has a small yet influential membership, dedicated to securing the legal and economic rights of women through a program of research, public education and legislative advocacy."[60] Calling these activities "education" may qualify WEAL for Department of Education grants, but the activities are nevertheless pure politics. The June 1983 issue of *WEAL Washington Report*, the organization's newsletter, claimed that "womens' economic equity" was WEAL's main objective.[61] It bemoaned the fact that "women . . . earn about 60 percent of what men earn" and demanded quotas and timetables, among other things, to "remedy" this disparity.

WEAL's legislative agenda is heavily interventionist. The *WEAL Washington Report* (June 1983) listed a number of "primary advocacy" areas, most of which call for abolishing or severely hampering the free-market allocation of resources. "The enforcement of the civil rights laws" is WEAL's primary legislative objective. What the organization means by this is not enforcement of the Civil Rights Act of 1964, but rather its continued distortion in a way that requires employment decisions to be based on race and sex. WEAL supports "the use of written affirmative action programs, with goals and timetables for the hiring and promotion of women and minorities" and "the elimination of job and occupational segregation and the establishment of the principle of equal pay for work of comparable

269

value."[62] Among WEAL's preferred remedies is "class-wide relief," that is, government programs that give special preferences to women and minorities regardless of qualifications or merit.

WEAL also lobbies for expanded welfare spending, especially for "women and children" (the latest version of the "widows and orphans" rationale for the welfare state), government jobs programs, continued funding of the Legal Services Corporation, and "a national policy on child care," in which taxpayers would fund child care centers. In sum, in the name of "educational equity," WEAL is just another special-interest group groping for a redistribution of income. To WEAL, equity means benefiting itself at the expense of others.

The National Organization for Women

One of the best-known women's groups is the National Organization for Women (NOW), which is considered to be an arm of the Democratic party and to have been a major source of campaign support for presidential candidate Walter F. Mondale in 1984. NOW's political objectives are almost identical to those of WEAL and similar groups and, like them, has received taxpayer financing. NOW has set up several affiliates that can receive federal funding, such as the NOW Legal Defense and Education Fund, which received $595,961 from the U.S. Department of Education during the 1980–81 period. There is evidence that these funds were used to promote NOW's political agenda.

One grant for $105,000 from the Department of Education in 1981 was used to finance a media campaign publicizing NOW's positions. The grant proposal included plans for "television news spots," newspaper and magazine ads, radio news features and "public service announcements," talk show presentations, and five brochures to be used as follow-up direct mail pieces to those who responded to the broadcasts and ads. In short, the grant of taxpayers' funds was used to manipulate the news media. Because NOW's views are not widely supported by the general public, it used taxpayers' funds to try to legitimize those views. As the grant proposal stated, "Public service ads can reach millions of people and at an extremely low cost. These are ways of legitimizing the issues—by appearing in mainstream magazines, the message conveyed is that they are mainstream issues."

Another WEEA grant for more than $330,000 went to NOW's Legal Defense and Education Fund to finance a political training

270

manual. The March 14, 1983, issue of the fund's newsletter, *PEER Perspective* (PEER stands for Project on Equal Educational Rights), boasted of a new publication, *Organizing for Change: PEER's Guide to Campaigning for Equal Education:* "Hot off the presses, this is PEER's how-to kit for organizing community groups to campaign."[63] The newsletter quoted a Michigan woman as saying, "With PEER's help, we organized more than 250 community activists, parents and educators in 12 school districts."

These examples of government funding of special-interest groups through WEEA have at least one thing in common: The funding was used to promote the left-wing political agendas of professional women's groups and often had more to do with political indoctrination than education. Moreover, "equity" is not meant by these groups to imply equality of opportunity, but rather special preference at the hands of the state. It appears that taxpayers' support of these objectives is continuing. In the March 15, 1983, issue of the Department of Education's *Education Funding News,* it was announced that the U.S. Department of Education was inviting applications for $5.67 million in new WEEA grants "to develop educational materials and model programs designed to promote womens' educational equity that can be replicated throughout the country."[64] Applicants were instructed to contact Leslie Wolfe, WEEA's program director and the person responsible for the grants that have been given to the National Student Educational Fund, the Council on Interracial Books for Children, and other radical groups.

The League of Women Voters

The League of Women Voters received at least $1,396,842 in federal grants from 1977 to 1982 from such agencies as the Department of State, the National Endowment for the Humanities, the Environmental Protection Agency, and the Department of Energy. The league has specifically stated that one of its primary objectives is "to influence public policy," and it hopes to achieve its political ends through direct lobbying:

> The League does its lobbying on all fronts. In each state and community, members meet with their elected officials at all levels to press for the League's point of view on pending legislation. They also wage letter-writing campaigns in support of program goals. . . . Once laws are passed, the Leagues monitor their administration and go to court in the public interest, if a law needs to be clarified or if enforcement is less than it should be.[65]

The league's lobbying activities almost exclusively focus on ways to increase the degree of government intervention in the economy and on ways that government, not individuals, can "solve national problems." The league is active on dozens of different fronts, including welfare policies, civil rights legislation, housing programs, environmental policy, international relations, campaign finance laws, energy policy, and land use policy. For example, the league has "consistently supported federal [welfare] programs aimed at combating poverty";[66] has advocated school busing; has "endorsed various public service employment programs and public works legislation"; is "in favor of a full employment policy, that is, the concept of [government] assuring a job for all those able and seeking to work"; has supported the Humphrey-Hawkins "full employment" bill; is in favor of goals and timetables governing the use of quotas in hiring women; lobbies for more government-run mass transit systems; lobbies for more government control of land use, including federal comprehensive land use controls; has supported the "windfall profits tax" on the oil industry; is in favor of "forced energy conservation"; and has filed a lawsuit to "force the implementation of the Solar and Conservation Bank," which subsidizes the development of solar energy. In addition to advocating these thoroughly interventionist policies, the league urges continued taxpayer financing of its activities by announcing that government authorities should "ensure more effective citizen participation through such measures as adequate funding for citizen information and review."[67]

The league claims to speak for all citizens, but the phrase "citizen information and review" is merely a euphemism for its own political lobbying activities. The league also supports additional use of intervenor funding to finance its own litigation as it tries to influence government policy through the courts. Its legal activities are similar to the Ralph Nader–style of liberal public-interest law firms (discussed in chapter 5), and the league claims that these activities are a response to "regressive legislation" and "the growth of business-oriented 'public interest' [that is, conservative] law firms."[68] To combat these trends, the league forms political coalitions with such interest groups as WEAL, NOW, Common Cause, the American Civil Liberties Union, Ralph Nader's Public Citizen Litigation Group, the Environmental Defense Fund, the Natural Resources Defense Council, and the Sierra Club Legal Defense Fund.[69]

The Planned Parenthood Federation of America

Planned Parenthood and its many affiliates receive millions of dollars each year from federal and state governments (see Table A10.1). Although these funds are earmarked for family planning services, there is much evidence that they are used to support political activity as well. For example, Planned Parenthood is often a coalition partner with other women's groups. In 1982, the U.S. General Accounting Office (GAO) investigated possible lobbying activities by Planned Parenthood affiliates and found that "Most of the [grant] recipients reviewed for lobbying were involved in some types of lobbying activities. . . . [S]ome . . . used program funds to pay dues to organizations that lobby. . . . In addition, some recipients spent . . . Title X program funds for lobbying."[70] Among the examples of tax-funded lobbying discovered by GAO are the following:

- Two recipients spent grant monies for transportation, lodging, and other expenses associated with attending conferences in Washington, D.C., during which officials visited members of Congress and lobbied against pending legislation to incorporate Title X into a block grant.
- One grant recipient incurred costs writing to Congress to lobby against pending legislation.
- One recipient incurred costs attending a conference that involved lobbying at the state level of government.
- One recipient provided space for about six weeks for a lobbying organization, thereby indirectly involving taxpayers' funds.

These examples indicate that the hundreds of Planned Parenthood affiliates around the country are using taxpayers' funds for partisan political purposes.

Conclusions

The civil rights movement of the 1950s and 1960s grew out of the increasing recognition that government had failed in its basic role of protecting the equal rights of all citizens. It was a response to the numerous examples of government-sanctioned discrimination and violence against blacks and other minorities and the violation of the rights of those citizens to the protection of life, liberty, and private property. Early civil rights legislation sought to remedy some of these injustices. As the civil rights movement grew, however, so

273

did the number of special-interest groups claiming to represent minorities, women, and other groups of citizens who were supposedly victims of discrimination. As these issues became politicized, the meaning of the term "civil rights" was transformed. Today's civil rights movement does not focus on the individual's right to peacefully acquire property and wealth, to enter any occupation, or to compete on a fair basis in the open market. Many, though not all, civil rights interest groups and their government supporters pursue *inequality* of opportunity in the form of job quotas, minority set-asides, and other special, government-sanctioned privileges based on race, sex, or national origin. They have turned the Civil Rights Act of 1964 on its head. Many civil rights lobbyists see civil rights as rights to forcibly take someone else's property through government action. Employment quotas, for example, are simply a form of reverse discrimination, granting special preferences to certain groups at the expense of others. By lobbying for additional welfare spending as a civil right, these lobbyists now claim that their clients have certain rights to the income of other people (that is, taxpayers). In sum, civil rights lobbyists have defined the proliferation of welfare state programs as being a matter of civil rights. It is not unusual to hear protests over proposed cuts in government spending on the grounds that such cuts would violate someone's civil rights, implying that opposition to welfare state programs is the same as opposition to civil rights.

The role of tax-funded politics has been instrumental in this perversion. As the civil rights movement became more heavily funded by the federal government, it began to represent more and more the preferences of the welfare state bureaucracy and the Washington establishment, even when there was overwhelming evidence that many of these programs often harmed minorities. This evolution was almost guaranteed by the large financial stake that many of civil rights organizations came to have in perpetuating welfare state programs. Rather than critically assessing whether the welfare state improves the welfare of minorities, civil rights and women's organizations have spent their time rationalizing, defending, and promoting the programs that they often administer themselves. These groups have formed coalitions with many other special-interest groups, particularly labor unions, to increase their political clout and their ability to convince federal politicians to give them government grants. As a result, the interests of their coalition partners have often taken precedence over the interests of minorities.

One unfortunate example of this development is the strong support given by civil rights and women's organizations to union-backed occupational licensing laws that have been specifically constructed, in many instances, to exclude women and minorities from the labor market. Black teenagers have been "protected" from so-called greedy capitalists by the minimum wage law that denies them the opportunity to work for those capitalists. Women who prefer to work at home have been "protected" from being "exploited" by retailers by federal regulations that ban "homework." Female motorists have been "protected" from discriminating insurance companies by laws that force up the insurance premiums that women pay for automobile insurance to the higher levels paid by men who, on average, are more accident prone. Parents of black children trapped in many of our cities' dangerous and unproductive public schools have been "protected" from tuition tax credits or educational vouchers that would enhance the parents' financial ability to send their children to private schools. In this case, the interests of teachers' unions have been placed above those of minority parents. Even though polls have shown that the majority of blacks are opposed to forced busing, the civil rights lobbyists have continued to push for more busing. Welfare programs that make it financially unattractive for recipients to leave such programs have been stridently defended and even increased. It appears that disadvantaged minorities are being used as pawns in attempts to expand the welfare state and to justify an array of government interventions, many of which harm the minorities in whose name they were established. And the U.S. taxpayers are financing this travesty.

XI. The Senior Citizen Lobby

> The AFL-CIO is continuing its strong efforts to encourage affiliated trade unions to develop active retiree groups and urge them to affiliate with the National Council of Senior Citizens. . . . UAW President Douglas Fraser was the first chairman of the AFL-CIO's Committee on Union Retirees. Fraser has since retired, but AFL-CIO President Lane Kirkland has chosen . . . William Winpisinger, President of the International Association of Machinists, to head the committee. The Machinists union and the UAW have both been key supporters of NCSC for many years.
>
> —National Council of Senior Citizens
> *Progress Report*

> One of the most exciting developments this year has been the establishment of . . . senior organizing and NCSC membership strategies in a number of citizen organizations [including] the Illinois Public Interest Campaign, the Ohio Public Interest Campaign, the Iowa Citizen/Labor Energy Coalition, the Missouri Citizen/Labor Energy Coalition, the Florida Consumer Federation, and the North Carolina Community Project.
>
> —National Council of Senior Citizens
> *Progress Report*

As shown in earlier chapters, the public's compassion for the poor has helped enable government to spend hundreds of billions of dollars on programs designed to alleviate poverty. As has also been shown, however, the professional political activists of the antipoverty industry have captured a large portion of these funds to finance their own personal political agendas and careers. These agendas are often at odds with the interests of the poor. In fact, there is much evidence that many poverty programs have actually perpetuated or increased poverty. Unfortunately, government efforts to help another segment of the population, the elderly, have had similar effects. There is a well-organized and well-financed senior citizen lobby, organized mostly by labor unions and consumer activist groups, that pursues a political agenda that is often at odds with the interests of many elderly citizens. This movement is also heavily financed by taxpayer subsidies amounting to more than $200 million during the 1977–81 period (see Table A11.1, in appendix). In short, the public's compassion for the elderly is being used as a lever to secure taxpayer funding of a political agenda that sometimes seems far removed from the interests of both the elderly and the taxpayers who pay the bill.

Whenever the interests of some segments of the elderly population are served by the senior citizen lobby, it is generally through government action that serves the interests of some people at great expense to other taxpaying citizens. The most notable example is the social security system, which engenders mammoth wealth transfers from the young to the elderly.

A closer look at some of the most heavily tax-financed senior citizen lobbying groups reveals that their actions often have very little to do with improving the welfare of senior citizens. In the name of helping the elderly, many of their actions are aimed at implementing the political agendas of consumer activist groups and of some union leaders, such as William Winpisinger, president of the International Association of Machinists. The Gray Panthers, for example, is an offshoot of Ralph Nader's organizations, and 11 of the 13 members of the National Council of Senior Citizens' board of directors are union presidents.

The National Council of Senior Citizens

The National Council of Senior Citizens (NCSC) is among the most politically active and most heavily tax-financed of the senior citizen special-interest groups. NCSC received at least $154 million during 1978–81 from various federal agencies, including the Department of Labor (one grant was for more than $44 million in 1980), the Department of Health and Human Services, the Community Services Administration, the Administration on Aging, the Department of Justice, and the Federal Trade Commission (see Table A11.1).

Apparently, NCSC receives taxpayer subsidies regardless of which political party controls the White House, for it claimed in its annual report for the fiscal year ending June 30, 1984, that it received $1.15 million from the federal government during that year.[1] If this figure is reliable, it would represent a sharp drop in government funding of NCSC's activities. Nevertheless, this is still a very substantial sum amounting to more than one-third of what NCSC claimed as its total revenue in 1984 and more than three times the contribution of its next largest supporter, the AFL-CIO.

Although much of what NCSC does with its taxpayers' funds is related to such senior citizen issues as social security and Medicare, a major role is to aid in promoting the social policy agenda of organized labor and other members of the anti-industry coalition, such as the consumer activist groups. NCSC is largely under the direction of union leaders (see its board of directors in Table A11.2), and it organizes senior citizens to support the political objectives of labor unions and their allies in return for union support for increased government subsidies to senior citizens. The president of NCSC is Jacob Clayman, past president of the AFL-CIO's Industrial Union Department.

An example of NCSC's tax-funded political organizing activity is its July 1983 Legislative Conference, which was held in Washington, D.C.[2] *Senior Citizen News,* NCSC's newsletter, reported in July 1983 that the conference's "attractions . . . include a massive rally in front of the White House to protest cuts in Medicare and promote health-care cost controls [that is, price controls]; an exciting 'Evening with the Presidential Candidates' [only the Democratic candidates] . . . ; and a series of nine informative workshops to assist NCSC's local leaders."[3] Five of the workshops examined matters such as how to increase government intervention in the areas of food stamps, health policy, energy policy, social services, women's issues, and government-subsidized housing. After instructing the participants on the "necessity" of greater government involvement in these areas, the "skills" workshops focused on how the participants could push their agenda through the political process. These workshops included "How to Make the Best Use of the Media in Your Community, How to Use the Legislative Process Effectively, How to Run a Successful Club, and How to Raise Money."[4] Conference organizers also invited "informative, nationally-known figures" to address the convention, including Sen. Edward Kennedy, AFL-CIO President Lane Kirkland, and Benjamin Hooks, executive director of the NAACP. NCSC also claims to be the biggest "support group" for the AFL-CIO's Solidarity Day marches in the nation's capital and elsewhere that have been organized "to demonstrate . . . opposition to the Reagan Administration's policies."[5]

Union organizers often claim that they participate in NCSC for altruistic reasons, but it is also likely they are interested because the elderly are a source of additional financial support from the dues paid by retired members who would otherwise not pay them. In 1984 NCSC claimed that its membership included 209,443 union retirees.[6] One way in which these retirees are a source of dues revenues for the AFL-CIO, the United Auto Workers, the International Association of Machinists, and other union affiliates is clearly stated in NCSC's *Progress Report:* "In 1983 the National Council of Senior Citizens . . . completed its 15th year as an administrator of the Senior Community Service Employment Program . . . on behalf of the U.S. Department of Labor. . . . The amount provided [by the Department of Labor] between July 1, 1983 and June 30, 1984 is $52,131,913." NCSC reported that this program gives employment to over 10,000 senior citizens and operates 127 projects in 27 states and the District of Columbia. In all likelihood, union membership is a prerequisite for employment in this program, so that the economic self-interest of the union organizers is certainly being served. Moreover, it is important that like all other government "jobs programs," this one could not actually "create jobs," as its supporters claim, because the $52 million taken out of the taxpayers' pockets each year to finance the program reduces private spending in the economy, which leads to lower production and employment there. The composition of employment is changed in a subtle way in favor of more union retirees at the expense of those who are crowded out of the labor market, including some senior citizens. By law, employees in this program must work either for a government agency or a nonprofit organization other than a political party. NCSC fits into the latter category, so it is possible that its own staff members may be paid out of funds appropriated for this program.

Lobbying Activities of the NCSC

"Legislative liaison and research"—or, simply, lobbying—is listed as a major item on NCSC's agenda. As stated in NCSC's 1984 *Progress Report:* "This year, the Legislative Liaison and Research Department cooperated closely with Congressional committee staff, NCSC General Board members, a variety of national coalitions and key grass-roots leaders around the country to improve NCSC's visibility both in Washington, D.C. and in the field."[7] As an indication of the types of issues NCSC has joined "national coalitions" to support, consider some of its coalition partners (many of which have been discussed in other chapters): the Citizen/Labor Energy Coalition, the Consumer Federation of America, the Center for Science in the Public Interest, Consumers Union, the Ohio Public

Interest Campaign, the Illinois Public Action Council, Congress Watch, the Community Nutrition Institute, the Infant Formula Action Coalition, and the AFL-CIO. NCSC, as a recipient of hundreds of millions of taxpayers' dollars and as part of a national coalition, claims to have spent much of its time loudly opposing what it has described as the Reagan administration's "new and dramatic cuts in dozens of the most important social, economic and welfare programs" in 1984.[8] As NCSC has stated, "Immediately after the President's [1984] budget was released, the Legislative Liaison and Research staff began lobbying independently and in coalition with other national organizations against new program cuts."[9] Furthermore:

> These efforts were rewarded. . . . [T]he House of Representatives passed a Democratic-sponsored budget resolution for FY 1984 that rejected most of the President's proposed cuts in social programs. . . . The House restored funding to programs . . . including: $900 million . . . for the Food Stamp Program, $192 million for housing . . . , $950 million for Low Income Energy Assistance, $105 million for Older Americans Act programs, $650 million for Social Services . . . , and restoration of funding for the Legal Services Corporation."[10]

Promoting Tax-Funded Politics. Another of NCSC's major legislative efforts has been its lobbying against restrictions on tax-funded politics. As written in the organization's *Progress Report:*

> Last January [1983], the Office of Management and Budget attempted to restrict the ability of non-profit organizations to lobby and to participate in the legislative and governmental decision-making processes by proposing changes in the rules governing cost accounting by non-profits. . . . The OMB proposals would have prohibited non-profits from using Federal funds to engage in any type of "political advocacy". . . . NCSC joined a broad coalition composed of non-profit organizations to oppose the proposals and, within a very short period of time, there was considerable pressure on OMB to withdraw the regulations. In early March, OMB did withdraw the proposals.[11]

NCSC also involves itself in such issues as natural gas regulation, telephone rate-making policy, the social security system, the health care system, housing policy, government support of the Legal Services Corporation, the railroad workers retirement system, and military policy.

Opposing Natural Gas Deregulation. NCSC clearly acts against the interests of senior citizens in lobbying for continued regulation of the price of natural gas. The regulation of natural gas prices causes shortages and has caused prices to be higher than would otherwise occur (see chapter 6). Nevertheless, in joining in the zealous attack on the "profits of the big oil companies" NCSC has boasted that it

> participated in the Citizen/Labor Energy Coalition (C/LEC) efforts to have consumer legislation on gas pricing and producer/pipeline contracts introduced in Congress and joined the drive to sign co-sponsors onto bills that would roll back prices, extend price controls, [and] revise current anti-consumer gas contracts. . . . In addition, NCSC groups throughout the country participated in "Gas Protest Days" in September. . . . C/LEC is presently working with Senate allies to fashion a pro-consumer bill.[12]

Distorting the Market for Telephone Services. NCSC is also opposed to pricing telephone services based on the cost of providing service. For years, because of regulation, long-distance telephone calls have been priced above marginal cost, resulting in cross-subsidization from long-distance callers to local users. In 1982 the Federal Communications Commission proposed ending this arbitrary and unfair subsidization scheme by charging customers according to the true cost of providing the service. Being a net beneficiary of the subsidy, "NCSC joined with representatives of labor, rural areas, consumers and seniors to fight for legislation which would repeal access charges. Consumers won a great victory in November 1983 when the House of Representatives passed a bill to repeal the charges."[13] Although NCSC claims to represent consumers, those long-distance callers who are being charged supracompetitive rates are clearly worse off because of the existing regulation. NCSC obviously excludes long-distance callers from their definition of "consumers" and instead dwells on the "massive lobbying efforts waged by AT&T" and the evils of big business.

Government-Subsidized Housing. Government-subsidized housing is another major focus of NCSC's lobbying activities, especially "Section 202 Senior Housing" and "Section 8 rental assistance programs," which are administered by the Department of Housing and Urban Development (HUD). Section 8 housing includes rent subsidies for the poor and the elderly. With Section 202 housing, HUD loans money to a developer, who builds public housing projects;

the developer then pays off the loan with the help of federal operating subsidies approved by Congress and given to the tenants. Thus, government revenues are used to pay back money the government lent in the first place. NCSC claims that one of its top priorities is both expansion of Section 202 public housing projects and opposition to voucher plans that have been proposed by the Reagan administration to give poor and elderly families housing vouchers to be used for whatever type of housing they prefer.

Despite NCSC's preferences for subsidized public housing, there is much evidence that it has failed to meet the housing needs of the poor and elderly and that vouchers would serve their interests much better. For example, despite HUD's having spent more than $76 billion pursuing the goal of "decent housing for every American" by 1976, millions of Americans still live in housing that is substandard. This is a puzzling statistic, for if the $76 billion had been spent on housing, HUD could have purchased more than 1.5 million new $50,000 single-family homes.[14] The answer to this puzzle can be found in an examination of the way in which this money was actually spent. For example, the *Washington Post* reported that HUD has made rehabilitation loans to homeowners who make over $50,000 a year to install home greenhouses and skylights. HUD spent about $5 million on a program funding projects for "arts, urban design, user needs design . . . , preservation of historic or other structures," and so on. HUD spends nearly $1 million a year on its fair housing and equal opportunity research program, even though other agencies, such as the Legal Services Corporation and private law firms, fund similar programs; HUD spends nearly $4 million a year on its state and local policy analysis research program, including a $50,000 grant to the National Association of Schools of Public Affairs and Administration to evaluate master's degree programs at 175 schools. HUD's Cincinnati Office paid $1,000 and more to mow a 2.2-acre tract of lawn. HUD spent more than $50 million each year on research projects that have been done elsewhere. HUD spent about $22 million a year on travel, often first class, for its own employees. Despite all the television horror stories about substandard housing, HUD spends millions of dollars renovating college dormitories at such places as Cornell University, projects that can hardly help "the poor and the elderly." The list is almost endless.[15] Whenever HUD does spend money on housing projects for the poor and the elderly, the results are usually disappointing and are frequently disgraceful. Hundreds of housing policy failures have been reported by the news media, including the following story by *Washington Post* reporter Jackson Diehl:

> Billions of tax dollars were spent nationally—and millions were poured into the Pumpkin Hill Apartments [in South Laurel, Maryland]—in pursuit of this Kennedy-Johnson dream of decent, affordable housing for every American. What millions of tax dollars bought in the case of Pumpkin Hill are apartments that Prince Georges County Executive Lawrence J. Hogan recently called "threats to human life." Pumpkin Hill, moreover, is one of six federally subsidized housing fiascoes in Prince George's County. Almost $35 million—five times the amount the government set out to spend—has been poured into the Pumpkin Hill, Central Gardens, Washington Heights, Baber Village, Nalley, and Glenarden apartment projects. What HUD has to show for that $35 million today are six ugly and dangerous suburban slums. The big losers—besides the taxpayers—are the very people that the 2,140 apartment units were built to help. Low and moderate-income families in Prince Georges—who in some cases could only watch helplessly as their homes were deliberately condemned as a way of herding them into the projects—have suffered through their swift decline. Some of these families are worse off than they were before. In all too many cases, the winners have turned out to be the private developers who snapped up federal loans and subsidies designed to encourage construction of these apartments. Some of them, with little or no investment, have walked away from these projects millions of dollars richer.[16]

One reason why government-subsidized housing has not always helped the poor and the elderly and has sometimes even hurt them is that those who are more adept at manipulating the political process—such as bureaucrats, contractors, developers, unions, academic researchers, and lawyers—are able to transfer large portions of the government largesse to themselves, all the while claiming to be acting on behalf of the elderly or some other group that draws public sympathy.

The Reagan administration has responded by proposing to use the same government funds for vouchers for the poor and elderly to ensure that these people, not the developers, researchers, and career bureaucrats at HUD, benefit from the programs. Under this proposal, millions of dollars could be saved and those in need could receive more and better housing. But NCSC continues to oppose the voucher program, primarily because those who really benefit from government-subsidized housing stand to lose their benefits. If the poor and the elderly could simply choose where to live, how could developers make millions by constructing more slum housing? How could academic researchers study how to improve housing conditions for the poor if a way were found to satisfy the poor? What would the bureaucrats at local public housing authorities do if there were limits on how much more housing they could build and administer? What would HUD bureaucrats do if there were no housing crisis? And it is clearly not in the economic self-interest of labor unions—which direct the activities of NCSC—to reduce the amount of government-subsidized housing projects, regardless of whether or not such projects help the elderly. Constructing public housing is a major source of employment for unionized labor and of dues for the unions whose presidents sit on the NCSC board of directors. It appears that the desire for increased union dues has relegated the welfare of the elderly to secondary importance at NCSC.

NCSC-PAC, Union Organizing, and Networking. Perhaps the major focus of NCSC's tax-funded political activities is on three issues—social security, Medicare, and Medicaid. These issues are dealt with separately later in this chapter. For now, it is useful to first consider how NCSC and its allies use taxpayers' funds to influence these and other policies—information that can be gleaned from NCSC's own description of its political activities.[17]

In 1983 NCSC formed the NCSC Political Action Committee (NCSC-PAC) "to influence the nomination and election of candidates to office . . . who are committed to promote the interest of senior citizens of the United States [that is, NCSC's version of those interests] in harmony with the national interest."[18] Thus, NCSC-PAC claimed it would pursue only those issues in which its own self-interest overlaps with "the national interest." This, of course, is impossible, but it is typical of special-interest groups to claim that they represent only "the people" or the "public interest." After raising more than $220,000 in 1983, NCSC-PAC proceeded to make campaign contributions, to mobilize senior citizens to support the election of certain candidates, to train "volunteers" to work on phone banks to solicit votes, to help register voters, and to engage in other political activities. NCSC felt that it was necessary to politically mobilize in this way because "time and time again, NCSC and its local affiliates have had to respond quickly and effectively to attacks from the conservatives in Congress and the Administration."[19]

To respond to these threats, NCSC claims to have built "stronger ties with a larger number of unions" and is "building stronger relationships with citizen networks throughout the country." NCSC also claims to have "offered extensive aid to a number of unions to design and maintain retiree programs that involve retirees in political activities, community education programs, voter registration, fund raising for political campaigns, legislative actions and helping to organize new union members."[20] Thus, tax revenues not only are helping promote NCSC's political agenda but also are being used for union organizing. The "citizen networks" are mostly radical left-wing groups, such as the Illinois Public Action Council, the Citizen/Labor Energy Coalition, the Ohio Public Interest Campaign, the Consumer Federation of America, and Congress Watch. NCSC has joined with these groups on a wide variety of issues, ranging from opposing decontrol of oil prices to favoring the ban on Nestlé infant formula. One coalition partner that has gained much media attention and that has also received taxpayer subsidies is the Gray Panthers, an offshoot of Ralph Nader's organization.

The Gray Panthers

The Gray Panthers has received hundreds of thousands of dollars in cash subsidies from the federal government (see Table A11.1). It has also received the services of VISTA volunteers to help "organize," run "training conferences," develop "the Gray Panthers network," and run a "media conference," among other things. The Gray Panthers was founded in 1970 by its current "national convener," Maggie Kuhn, and five others.[21] In 1973 the group merged with Ralph Nader's Retired Professional Action Group. Although the Gray Panthers claims that senior citizens are its main concern, it also stresses that "nearly half of [the Gray Panthers'] members are under 65, and the issues addressed by the group are not confined to those dealing with older people."[22] An examination of the issues in which the group is involved and of the stands it takes reveals that it is often more concerned with harsh, anticorporate political posturing than with helping the elderly. A statement in *Public Interest Profiles* reads:

> The goals of the Gray Panthers are . . . to advocate for fundamental social change that would eliminate injustice, discrimination

286

and oppression in our present society . . . and heighten opportunities for people to realize their full potential. . . . to act independently and in coalition with other movements to build a new power base to achieve short-term social change and ultimately a society which will put the needs of people above profits, eliminate the concentration of corporate power, and serve human needs through democratic means.[23]

The Gray Panthers claims 110 affiliates in more than 30 states and insists that "Whether on a national or local level, the methods of the Panthers are the same—advocacy, education, and model projects which will demonstrate concrete steps toward social change."[24] According to *Public Interest Profiles*, "The flamboyant, media-drawing tactics for which the group is most notorious—the demonstrations, rallies, and picketing—constitute but a few of the many tactics in the arsenal."[25] As an example, a Long Beach, California, chapter was the major force in 1981 behind the Long Beach Coalition for a Fair Budget, which "has banded together to fight inhuman budget cuts, the increased military budget, and fraudulent tax reforms" proposed by the Reagan administration.[26] In New York, Gray Panther members announced a "Jelly Bean Award" aimed at castigating congressional supporters of President Reagan who were said to demonstrate "opportunism and mean spirit" by voting for the president's economic programs; the first "winner" was Sen. Daniel P. Moynihan (D-N.Y.). The Gray Panthers has also participated in several national coalitions and has supported Big Oil Day (October 17, 1979), Big Business Day (April 17, 1980), and Solidarity Day (September 19, 1981). In short, the Gray Panthers is part of the radical left in American politics, and, in the name of protecting the elderly, it has used taxpayer subsidies to pursue its objective of greater government control over resource allocation.

The Policy Goals of the Gray Panthers

Price controls on medical services and increased government spending on Medicare, Medicaid, and social security are top priorities for the Gray Panthers.[27] Nationalized health care is another priority: "We would like to see the U.S. join other industrialized countries in the world and develop a National Health Service."[28] The Gray Panthers completely ignores the bureaucratic ineptitude that plagues government provision of health care. The group misinforms the public by claiming: "And don't let your doctors tell you that care there [in Great Britain, where health care is nationalized] is bad. British people get good medical care and pay a lot less for it."[29] How would this new, mammoth bureaucracy be financed? Raising taxes is the appropriate solution, for in another case of unsubstantiated doubletalk, "Today the poor pay the highest proportion of their earnings in taxes—the rich pay the least."[30] According to Internal Revenue Service data, however, in 1980 the highest 50 percent of income earners paid 93.5 percent of federal taxes; the highest 25 percent paid 73.8 percent; and the highest 10 percent paid 49.7 percent. Moreover, preliminary IRS data for 1984 reveal that because of the tax-rate reductions set in motion by the Reagan administration and Congress in 1981, higher-income individuals increased their share of tax payments from 1980 to 1983.[31] Nevertheless, the Gray Panthers proposes tax increases of $1,780 annually for families with incomes of $20,000 per year, gradually increasing to additional taxes of $7,380 for families with annual incomes of $60,000. According to this scheme, a middle-class family consisting of, say, two working high school teachers would pay $4,000 to $5,000 more per year in taxes. According to the Gray Panthers, "society as a whole is willing and able to finance this."

Opposing Privatization. The Gray Panthers also organizes opposition to efforts to privatize hospitals and nursing homes. Like every other enterprise, there is every reason to believe that the provision of health care by private, competitive firms would be more cost effective and of higher quality than bureaucratic, government provision. The Gray Panthers, however, has opposed privatization because the profits of some private providers "are enormous."[32] The Gray Panthers also "doubt very much that corporations can be trusted." The group warns its allies that "the AFL-CIO has alerted the Gray Panthers to the possible dangers of the possible sale or lease of [George Washington University] hospital [in Washington, D.C.] to American Medical International, a private firm."[33] The AFL-CIO does not seem particularly disturbed over the quality of health care when affiliated nurses unions go out on strike, and it seems peculiar that it becomes concerned about patient care only when that care is provided by certain private (especially nonunion) companies.

Housing Policy. Like NCSC, the Gray Panthers devotes considerable effort to housing policy, especially by promoting greater subsidization of public housing and the adoption of rent-control

288

laws. The group is a member of the National Low-Income Housing Coalition (which has also received taxpayer subsidies). The coalition lobbies for such legislation, and it is also involved in the National Tenants Union, which is mostly concerned with rent-control laws. As stated in *Shelterforce*, a magazine published by the "national housing movement," the Gray Panthers is "the most militant and active group of senior activists. . . . In the coming year the two priority issues of the Gray Panthers will be housing and disarmament."[34] This magazine also has described how the National Tenants Union and its Gray Panthers affiliates are aided by taxpayer subsidies: "Many tenants associations employ organizers, counselors, and other people through . . . federal programs. . . . These funds will become more and more tied to local politicians [because of the Reagan administration's federalism proposals], often the very people that tenant groups consider their adversaries." These federal programs include the Solar Energy and Conservation Bank, Urban Development Action Grants, CETA grants, VISTA and ACTION grants, the Legal Services Corporation, the Community Services Administration, and the National Consumer Co-op Bank.

In lobbying for rent controls, the Gray Panthers and its affiliates contribute to the housing shortages and slum conditions that plague many cities and that often harm senior citizens, at least those who cannot find adequate housing because of rent-control–induced shortages. The rhetoric of rent control is sometimes appealing, but the effects are disastrous (see chapter 4). In New York City, where rent controls have existed since World War II, only 2,000 rental units are built annually, although approximately 30,000 units are simply abandoned each year by their owners because they are not profitable.[35] Washington, D.C., implemented rent-control laws recently and watched its rental housing stock slip from 199,000 to 175,000 units in eight years.[36] The rental housing construction crisis seems to be spreading nationally. The percentage of new housing starts devoted to rental apartments fell from 57 percent during the 1970–77 period to 9 percent during the 1980s.[37] Consequently, government-owned rental housing has replaced that which is privately owned. The proportion of federally subsidized multifamily rental units increased steadily from 22 percent in 1972 to about 75 percent in 1979.[38]

By lobbying for rent-control laws and other land-use regulations, the Gray Panthers and other senior citizen advocates are contributing to a housing crisis for the poor and many of the elderly in the nation's cities. Every professional economist who is familiar with housing market issues knows this, as do scores of journalists, policymakers, and other government officials. Perhaps this is why the federal government went to court to gain exemption from any local rent-control ordinance attempting to regulate apartments owned or subsidized by HUD. Federal politicians do not want local politicians destroying their neighborhoods. Nevertheless, the laws persist in many cities and are even being extended to new areas, thanks to the successful use of rhetoric and disinformation by the rent-control advocates.

In one perverse sense, rent control has been a success. By causing the deterioration and abandonment of rental housing, rent controls and other land-use regulations (building codes, environmental restrictions, zoning restrictions) have stimulated a demand for billions of dollars in government-owned and -built rental housing units. This construction has been a boon for the construction business and the labor unions whose members work on such projects at wage rates that are artificially inflated by the Davis-Bacon Act.[39] Ironically, many of the citizens who are being forced into substandard housing by these policies are paying taxes that indirectly subsidize the political activities of the groups that support the policies.

Social Security. Social Security is by far the most important issue for the Gray Panthers and other tax-funded senior citizen groups, such as NCSC, the National Retired Teachers Association (which received more than $115 million in taxpayer subsidies between 1980 and 1982), and the National Council on Aging. In recent years the news has been filled with stories of a Social Security crisis, with expenditures on social security payments constantly threatening to exceed social security tax revenues. Huge tax increases were implemented in 1977, when President Carter claimed they would make the system solvent for another 75 years; additional increases occurred when the next crisis hit—in 1983. Once again, we were told the 1983 tax increases would save the system for another 75 years (assuming no inflation or recessions). One reason why the Social Security system seems to be constantly on the edge of collapse is the inherent problems within the system that are simply ignored by last-minute tax increases designed primarily to save the system, at least until the next election cycle is over. Real reform of the system is so difficult to achieve partly because the tax-funded senior citizen lobby is so well organized in its opposition to such reform. Whenever any reform other than increased taxes is mentioned in the halls of Congress, the Social Security lobby stages media-grabbing protests, petition drives, letter-writing campaigns, grass-roots education seminars, face-to-face lobbying, television ads depicting ill or starving senior citizens, and many other imaginative political maneuvers. In short, taxpayer's funds are being used to subsidize a process that guarantees a perpetual Social Security crisis and solidifies government control of the old-age insurance business.

Tax-Funded Politics and the Social Security Crisis

The political role of the senior citizen lobby is to help the Washington establishment—the incumbents in Congress, the Social Security bureaucracy, and sometimes the president—perpetuate what has been called the showpiece of America's welfare state. The Social Security system is by far the federal government's largest program, taking up about one-quarter of the entire budget, or well over $200 billion in fiscal year 1984. The Washington establishment has offered the Social Security system as its best example of how government can serve the common good. Because of this, admitting that the system is in a state of collapse is to admit that government's "most successful program ever" has been a failure.[40] So the Washington establishment must defend itself against any criticism of the Social Security system, however well intentioned and well founded, to maintain its grip on the nation's elderly and on a large portion of the income of every working American. Perhaps this is why the federal government funnels hundreds of millions of dollars to political advocacy groups such as NCSC—to ensure that there is no significant change in the status quo.

Despite the government's efforts to ignore and downplay the system's problems, many prominent economists and other analysts have made valid and powerful critiques of the program. Because the system reduces (but does not eliminate) incentives to save for one's own retirement, the economy suffers from lower savings and consequently from lower levels of capital accumulation and economic growth.[41] Young people entering the system will never receive a fair return on their Social Security investment; in fact, it is very likely be a negative return. Furthermore, the program is coercive; it forces all Americans, regardless of income, preferences, or lifestyle, to participate, and it imposes one insurance plan on all Americans, ignoring the specific needs of various families. And the sys-

291

tem has many inequities, which fall most heavily on some of the most politically vulnerable groups in society—blacks, the poor, women, some elderly, and the young. The cause of these problems is what Peter Ferrara has found to be an inherent contradiction in the system. The contradiction is based on the two basic functions of the Social Security system: insurance and welfare payments. According to Ferrara:

> These two functions are fundamentally incompatible, and the result is very bad welfare and very bad insurance. Insurance pays benefits to individuals on the basis of what they have paid into the program in the past, regardless of their need. Welfare pays benefits to individuals based on their need, regardless of what they have paid into the program in the past. The schizophrenic nature of the program has resulted in its fatal flaw—the social security taxes paid into the system now are not saved and invested through a trust fund as in private insurance, savings, or pension plans, but instead are paid out immediately to current recipients on a pay-as-you-go basis, like a welfare program. This method of operation began when the original funds paid into the system were immediately paid out as benefits to recipients who had paid little or nothing themselves. This was done in pursuit of the welfare objectives of the program. . . . This fatal flaw causes social security to be a bad insurance program that has several negative effects on the economy and the program's participants. For the economy as a whole, [the system] . . . results in a serious decline in savings, which results, in turn, in a loss of capital investment. This . . . results in a decline in economic growth. . . . For the individual taxpayer, the fatal flaw means he loses the interest return he would get on his tax money if it were invested.[42]

This contradiction creates many other problems as well. For example, because there is no trust fund to guarantee future benefit payments, the only guarantee of future benefits is the willingness of future taxpayers to foot the bill. This leaves the program vulnerable to threats of bankruptcy. One thing Ferrara meant by "bad insurance" was that some beneficiaries get more than they pay for and others get less. The get-less group is compelled to take a loss, in that the system is operated by the government, an arrangement that violates basic principles of fairness and justice. Further, because everyone must have the exact same coverage, the system is extremely inefficient in meeting the wide range of individual demands. Who would prefer automobile insurance or life insurance companies to operate in this way?

Perhaps the most important problem with the Social Security system is that it faces a constant threat of bankruptcy whenever there is inflation, which increases benefits automatically and sharply, or when the economy enters a recession, which curtails Social Security tax revenues. Basic reform is needed, provided that the benefits are maintained as promised for all those who have invested in the system, including current retirees. This is a point agreed upon by more and more citizens, including A. Haeworth Robertson, former chief actuary of the Social Security Administration. Robertson believes that given the current system, in 50 years the tax rate necessary to sustain the system will need to be at least 40 percent of taxable income. Fearing a loss of public confidence in the system in particular and in government in general, Robertson has written that "fundamental change in Social Security is both desirable and inevitable."[43] Moreover, he notes, "There is no reason for this country to continue with a social insurance system that is controversial, constantly on the verge of financial collapse, out of phase with the times, and—in my opinion—doomed to ultimate failure."[44]

The only type of reform the Washington establishment has attempted is increasingly frequent tax increases that have only postponed the day of reckoning. The real reforms that have been proposed have been shunned by the Washington establishment. One proposal seems especially appealing, for it, or something similar, has enabled Great Britain to resolve some of its social security problems. The proposal, put forth by Peter Ferrara, is to turn the insurance component of Social Security over to the private sector. Individuals would be allowed to provide for their old age and other contingencies by investing in private insurance, savings, and pension plans through, for example, the expanded use of individual retirement accounts (IRAs). Privatization or denationalization of the insurance function would eliminate much of the political instability associated with all government-operated programs. It would also allow greater freedom of choice, and competition would lead to the invention of new and better plans to meet consumer demands.

Privatization has occurred in at least two countries, Great Britain and Chile, but it has been completely ignored by Congress, by presidents, and by various national commissions organized to study the problems of Social Security in the United States.[45] It is likely that the Washington establishment does not want to give up any of its turf, that is, its control over the retirement investment decisions made by millions of Americans. It would rather continue to use the elderly as political pawns with which to win elections. What congressman has not promised to work to save Social Security from some unnamed but potentially destructive force? This is where tax-funded politics becomes important.

The Washington establishment has successfully squelched attempts at real reform of the Social Security system, but to do so it has needed a great deal of grass-roots and media support. Because the establishment faces budgetary and staff constraints, it uses tax-financed grass-roots lobbying groups, such as the Gray Panthers and NCSC, as well as their labor union allies, to guarantee that no important changes are made in the system. The newsletters published by senior citizen lobbying groups are filled with pictures of their affiliates demonstrating, manning phone banks, and registering voters. The extent to which the Social Security coalition is organized has become well known, and economists usually ascribe this success to the fact that the opportunity cost of a retiree's time is lower than that of someone who is employed. This is probably true, but it takes more than free time to become an effective political coalition; it also takes large amounts of cash, which are often provided by the Washington establishment (see Table A11.1).

The most recent purported reform of the Social Security system occurred in 1983, when the federal government made several changes, such as increasing taxes, delaying cost-of-living adjustments, delaying the retirement age, infusing general revenues into the program for the first time, and forcing employees of nonprofit institutions into the system. The senior citizen lobbying groups were very active during the period preceding these changes, and they appear to be quite satisfied with the results. NCSC, for example, after boasting of its important contribution to the 1983 compromise, stated: "The Social Security compromise signed into law on April 20 is expected to restore the solvency of Social Security over the next 75 years. . . . We can now say that Social Security has been put on a solid financial footing."[46] A more accurate description presents a much more pessimistic view. As Peter Ferrara has reminded us, the same claims were made after the largest peace-time tax increase in history (until that time) was passed in 1977. At that time, the Social Security board of trustees claimed that the tax increase would "restore the fiscal soundness of the . . . program throughout the remainder of this century and into the early years of the next one."[47] Just two

294

years later, the same trustees admitted in their 1980 Annual Report that "the assets of the . . . trust fund would soon become insufficient to pay benefits when due. . . . Accordingly, changes in the law are needed."[48] Now we are expected to believe that the 1983 tax increase will be sufficient for another 75 years.

The only way the government can get away with such gross distortions and wild promises is by repeating these statements and by manipulating the media, which the senior citizen lobby helps to accomplish. Ferrara has told us how the game is played: Rather than being embarrassed by the collapse of the system twice in six years (especially after promising that such a thing could not occur), the Washington bureaucracy and the senior citizen lobby

> took to the countryside to terrorize the elderly they profess to champion. In one of the most shameful chapters in American political history, they sought during the 1982 campaign literally to scare the elderly into providing money and votes for them, telling of plans to slash dramatically, or even completely cut off, their Social Security benefits. These scare tactics were used when no one was even contemplating such cuts—not President Reagan, not his staff, not congressional Republicans, not even "conservative ideologues." . . . Nevertheless, establishment campaigners, with cynical and callous opportunism, used and abused the elderly for maximum short-term political advantage. In the end, these same people were the ones who successfully advanced the one item in the bailout plan that substantially cuts benefits for today's elderly—the taxation of benefits.[49]

The tax-funded senior citizen lobby was especially helpful as it mobilized a coalition called Save Our Security (SOS). The coalition is headed by two former secretaries of the Department of Health, Education, and Welfare, Wilbur J. Cohen and Arthur S. Flemming (who also lectures at the Institute for Policy Studies). The coalition claims that its main objective is "to protect the nearly half-century-old Social Security System against efforts to weaken the protections it offers."[50] Its activities include providing an "extensive research and education program"; increasing awareness of the need for "protecting" the system, that is, avoiding any changes; "strengthening" the system, that is, raising payroll taxes and general fund subsidies; and coordinating grass-roots lobbying efforts and contact with local congressmen. Among the tax-funded groups that are members of SOS are dozens of labor unions, as well as the Center for Community Change, the NAACP, the National Consumers

295

League, the National Council of Churches, the National Council of La Raza, NCSC, the Gray Panthers, National Council on Aging, the National Education Association, the National Senior Citizens Law Center, the National Urban League, and the Women's Equity Action League.

Although this coalition claims to have mobilized to "protect the system," it is not clear who benefits from the system that is being protected. As Peter Ferrara has pointed out, the "rescue plan" finally enacted by Congress and supported by the SOS coalition in 1983 seems to hurt everyone: The elderly will see their benefits cut because of a delay in cost-of-living adjustments and the taxation of benefits; workers will have their Social Security taxes increased, with the burden falling particularly on low- and middle-income workers who pay most of the tax; young people will have their future expected rate of return under the system sharply cut, particularly because of the delay in the retirement age; virtually every worker is being forced into the system, including employees of nonprofit institutions and some federal government employees; and for the first time, massive general-revenue subsidies will be infused into the program, thereby repudiating the principle of self-financing.[51]

Contrary to statements made by NCSC and its allies, there is no reason to believe that these changes will make the system safe for another 75 years—or even for another 5 years. The system remains vulnerable to the inevitability of inflation, which will increase inflation-indexed benefits, and to the equally inevitable recession, which will cut into revenues. This vulnerability is no secret. In April 1983 the Social Security Administration's deputy chief actuary in charge of the program's short-term projections stated, "If [economic] growth is more rapid in 1983, but then restricted by another recession within the next few years, the trust funds could be in a worse financial position than indicated. . . . Depletion of the trust funds would be very likely . . . and could conceivably occur within a few years from now."[52]

The only clear beneficiaries of the Social Security compromise appear to be the Washington establishment and the senior citizen lobby, which continue to accumulate power and income by claiming to be the champions of the elderly. The elderly constitute a captive interest group that has been made even more dependent on the government by the 1983 revisions of the Social Security system. As Paul Craig Roberts of Georgetown University has explained,

The House phased in the taxation of half of Social Security benefits as other income [that is, besides social security income] exceeds certain thresholds. . . . [T]his has the effect of raising the marginal tax rate on other income. . . . The marginal tax rate on income of Social Security recipients increased 50 to 75 percent. . . . The result of the 1983 Social Security legislation was to move a retired individual with $26,000 in private retirement income from a 30 percent marginal tax rate to a 45 percent rate. A retired couple with a private retirement income of $38,000 was moved from a 28 percent to a 50 percent marginal tax rate. Social Security recipients with private retirement income who are still working and have "earned income" in excess of the Social Security earnings limitation can face marginal tax rates in excess of 100 percent until 1990. . . . [C]onsider the case of the single retiree currently in the 30 percent bracket. Since his private income is above the allowable threshold, his Social Security income is subject to tax. For every dollar in private income above the threshold, he has to pay tax on 50 cents of Social Security income until he is paying tax on one-half his Social Security benefits. In other words, above the threshold, every dollar of private income results in $1.50 of additional taxable income. That raises the tax rate on his additional dollar of private income by half, from 30 cents to 45 cents. . . . The increase in the tax rate may be even higher if the added income pushes him up a bracket.[53]

Once people planning for their retirement realize that the penalty for providing a retirement income for themselves in excess of the government-sanctioned threshold is to be hit with a 50–77 percent increase in marginal tax rates, they are likely to save less. Thus, people are likely to become more dependent on (or a captive of) the federal government. As Roberts has concluded, "What we have here is a form of age discrimination. . . . The entire thrust of the Social Security package [of 1983] is to deny the aged any incentive for being independent of the government."[54] This appears to be true not only for retirement insurance but also for health insurance.

Health Care and the Senior Citizen Lobby

Another major concern of the senior citizen lobby is health care, particularly as it relates to Medicare and Medicaid, which are parts of the Social Security program. NCSC and the Gray Panthers, in particular, complain about the rising cost of health care in the United States, but they stand in the way of any attempts to alter the health care industry in ways that would not grant more power over that industry to the federal government. For instance, after citing the rapid increases in the cost of health care over recent years, the Gray Panthers has proposed a program that allegedly will reduce the cost and improve the quality of health care. First, the group urges an expansion of federal Medicare and Medicaid payments. Second, it urges "programs for cost control of the medical industry," that is, price controls that will "put a ceiling on hospital charges and doctors' fees."[55] Third, it promotes government rather than private ownership of health care facilities: "We want to see that hospitals remain non-profit institutions. More and more hospitals are being taken over by private corporations and individuals as profit-making businesses." Fourth, "We would like to see the U.S. join other industrialized countries in the world and develop a National Health Service." These proposals would significantly increase the cost of health care in the United States and would probably reduce its quality. They would satisfy, however, the senior citizen lobby's objective of greater government control of the health care industry.

Expanding Third-Party Payments for Health Care

According to a recent fund-raising letter distributed by NCSC, "The elderly now spend more for health care (out of pocket and as a proportion of income) than they did before Medicare and Medicaid began." It is true that health care costs have increased rapidly. The average cost per patient-day of hospital care increased from $16 in 1950 to $250 in 1980, a 1,463 percent increase—much greater than the increase in the general price level during the period.[56]

One of the principal reasons for these increases is the growth of Medicare and Medicaid themselves. The general effect of such third-party payments is to make the demand for health care (for example, length of hospital stay or number of tests to be run) unresponsive to the price of health care. Consumers will demand a certain amount of care regardless of the price, because the government pays it. Thus, the laws of supply and demand dictate that an increased demand for health care, all other things equal, will drive up the price. And third-party payments, especially since Medicare and Medicaid were enacted in 1965, have increased with a vengeance. Between 1950 and 1970, third-party payments as a proportion of personal health care expenditures rose from 28.7 to 58.2 percent, and medical care prices rose by 125 percent—more than double the 61 percent increase in the general price level. From 1970 to 1980, however, the growth in third-party payments slowed appreciably, increasing only from 58.2 to 66.3 percent. Over this period, medical care prices rose only slightly more than the general price level, 120 percent compared with 112 percent.[57]

There is additional evidence that greater reliance on third-party payments only increases the price of medical care. Consider price increases for different types of medical care. Since 1950 the cost of physician services has increased only slightly more than the consumer price index, and drug prices have actually increased less than the general price level.[58] By contrast, the cost of hospital care has increased by 1,463 percent, and it is hospital costs that are almost entirely supported by third-party payments, with patients bearing only about 10 percent of the costs directly.

Whatever the merits of Medicare and Medicaid, these programs have contributed to the inflation of health care costs, especially hospital treatment. The concern of the senior citizen lobby for rising health care costs and the lobby's push for more extensive third-party (that is, government) payments are essentially contradictory.

Price Controls in the Health Care Market

Imposing price controls to curtail the rising cost of health care is also not likely to have beneficial effects. Nevertheless, the senior citizen lobby perennially aids its congressional allies (such as Sen. Edward Kennedy [D-Mass.]) in trying to generate support for this type of legislation. Price controls on medical services, like price controls on anything else, would lead to shortages and a deterioration of product quality. At the controlled price, the quantity demanded of various health care services would outstrip the available supply, thereby causing long waiting lines. For example, in Great Britain, where the National Health Service provides "free" health care, there were over 750,000 people waiting to enter hospitals in 1979, with waiting time sometimes exceeding three years.[59] Furthermore, the shortages would create a need for someone to allocate the short supply of hospital care, and the senior citizen lobby wants that someone to be a federal bureaucrat. It is unlikely that the poor will fare very well under such a system, in that they would have to curry favor with the political authorities to receive services. And because wealthier people are usually better at manipulating politics than are the poor, the poor will inevitably lose out.

The quality of health care will also be affected. Consider, for example, a physical checkup, which may range in price from $50 to $150, depending on the physician's skill, experience, and thoroughness. There are clearly quality differences in health care, for there are good physicians, bad physicians, and mediocre physicians. With price controls, one could expect a limit to be placed on the quality of care that the poor will receive. Highly skilled physicians will be unwilling to provide the service for only $50 when they could command $100 in the open market. At the same time, less-skilled doctors who charge only $25 will be able to increase their charges for the same service to the higher controlled price.

In sum, price controls do not address the reasons for the increased costs of health care; they only distort the market even further. Although the idea of cost controls may sound appealing, it has been a dismal failure whenever it has been attempted. For instance, the attempts to control health care costs during the 1970s through government regulation turned out to be bureaucratic disasters. As Richard Zeckhauser and Christopher Zook of Harvard University concluded after studying these programs: "Recent government efforts to control health care costs through direct regulation have met with little success. Medical costs remain high and are increasing, despite the institution of a complicated, economically inefficient, and hard-to-manage collection of regulatory programs."[60]

Nationalized Health Care

Nationalized health care is another idea that sounds appealing to many but would surely increase the cost and reduce the quality of health care. A predominant effect of nationalized, allegedly free health care would be a large increase in the demand for health care at the zero explicit price, which would drive up costs and prices. Despite the rhetoric, health care would not be free; the higher prices would be paid in the form of taxes rather than market prices. Thus, nationalization disguises the true cost to health care consumers. If price controls were then imposed to deal with the inflated prices, the problems of shortages and deteriorating quality would soon pervade the industry.

Nationalized health care would create several other problems as well. For instance, how would patients be allocated among hospitals and doctors, given the short supply that would be induced by the zero price? Would they be assigned to hospitals and doctors much like children are assigned to schools? How would "reasonable fees" be decided upon without markets, which reveal information about consumer preferences and costs of resource use? When prices are set by bureaucratic fiat, this valuable information is unavailable.

Such information can be revealed only through the market system, not through the imagination of some bureaucratic planner at the Department of Health and Human Services.

Another problem with nationalization would be the fewer incentives doctors and hospitals would have to provide high-quality care if they were paid the same rate regardless of quality. If doctors are paid according to how many patients they treat, as with Medicaid, would they not have incentives to treat large numbers of patients and perhaps be less concerned with quality?

These are only a few of the problems that would arise under nationalized health care; they are problems that already exist in countries where such systems are in place. It is important to realize that the choice between nationalized health care and private provision is not a choice between free and costly health care, as the senior citizen lobby seems to imply. The choice is between a bureaucratic system of allocation in which the prices paid are in the form of general taxes and a market system in which the prices are more explicit and conform more closely to the benefit principle. In the former case, the type of health care provided would reflect the personal preferences of the health care bureaucracy, whereas in the latter case, consumer preferences would guide the provision of health care as provided by private, profit-seeking individuals and corporations. Thus, the issue evolves around who is to control the health care industry. Will it be the private suppliers, who must be aware of the diverse preferences of consumers, or a paternalistic health care bureaucracy, whose basic premise is that the bureaucracy, not the individual, knows what type of health care should be provided?

Summary and Conclusions

The senior citizen lobby is a collection of nonelected, self-appointed protectors of senior citizens. In the name of representing senior citizens, these special-interest groups pursue objectives that are identical to the political objectives of both the anti-industry coalition and of many labor unions. Without exception, senior citizen groups claim that the market allocation of goods and services, such as natural gas, telephone services, housing, and health care, is detrimental to the interests of the elderly. Government control and regulation of industry are needed, we are told, if the elderly are to be protected. Moreover, these special-interest groups recommend no fundamental changes for the Social Security system, even though the system has for decades been used by politicians as a means of buying votes—a practice that has rendered the system highly unstable and has brought it to the verge of bankruptcy.

Many of the policies that the senior citizen lobby helps to initiate or perpetuate unequivocally make the elderly (and many others in society) worse off by substituting political for market allocation of resources. Price controls do not help the elderly with their health care bills or their ability to find rental housing; government housing programs have displaced thousands of elderly families and have forced them into government-subsidized slum housing; rent controls have ravaged parts of many inner cities, creating serious housing shortages; and natural gas regulation has increased heating bills.

The senior citizen lobby favors government control and centralization, which are not likely to benefit the elderly. Even so, it will help grant the federal government greater power over resource allocation and provide comfortable careers for professional senior citizen lobbyists. Senior citizens have been used as pawns to help incumbent politicians maintain their tenure in office and to consolidate the power of the federal government. The tax-funded senior citizen groups aid in this process by providing misinformation and by trying to convince senior citizens and the public that it is in their interest to turn over larger shares of their incomes to the federal bureaucracy.

XII. Poverty, Politics, and Jurisprudence: Illegalities at the Legal Services Corporation

> We are using taxpayer funds to sue taxpayers themselves, taxpayer funds to have class actions against governments, people, corporations, individuals, and so on, on behalf of special interest concerns that may or may not have been representative of the poor.
>
> —Sen. Orrin G. Hatch
> *Oversight of the Legal*
> *Services Corporation*

In 1965, for the first time, the federal government allocated taxpayers' funds to provide civil legal services to the poor. In that year the Office of Economic Opportunity (OEO) began awarding these funds to local nonprofit corporations, which consisted of primarily legal aid societies that had formerly been supported by charitable contributions, some local and state government grants, and the United Way. By 1970 federal funding for legal services through OEO amounted to about $71.5 million per year. In response to President Nixon's decision to reorganize the executive branch, based on recommendations made by the Ash Commission, Congress enacted legislation in 1974 to establish the Legal Services Corporation (LSC), an "independent, private corporation" funded by taxpayers. The Legal Services Corporation Act of 1974 contained the justification for forming LSC as a corporation: "The legal services program must be kept free from the influence of or use by it of political pressure."

The goals established by Congress in the act were reasonable and well intentioned: "[T]here is a need to provide equal access to the system of justice in our Nation for individuals who seek redress of grievances; there is a need to provide high quality legal assistance to those who would be otherwise unable to afford adequate legal counsel." The Constitution guarantees the poor legal representation in criminal proceedings, and LSC appeared to extend the availability of this legal representation to civil cases, including income-maintenance problems, health matters, and landlord-tenant disputes. Limitations were placed on client eligibility: Only households with incomes of less than 125 percent of the poverty threshold were to be represented. Thus, the establishment of LSC did not appear to be a radical departure from past practices, but merely a natural extension of services that had long been provided by government.[1]

From relatively modest beginnings, LSC grew rapidly. In 1976, the last year of the Ford administration, the annual budget was $92.3 million; four years later, at the end of the Carter administration, the annual budget had more than tripled, to $300 million. Much of the budget growth was stimulated by the "minimum access plan," which provided civil legal services to the needy in every county in the United States.

LSC itself was organized principally as a grant-making agency, a conduit for taxpayers' money to the local organizations that actually provide legal aid. The corporation makes grants to more than 300 legal aid groups in the 50 states, the District of Columbia, Puerto Rico, Guam, and the Virgin Islands (see Table A12.1, in appendix). These groups are private, nonprofit corporations that theoretically provide legal services to the poor.

From a financial perspective, making LSC an independent corporation instead of a program administered by OEO caused a major change in its operations. Under OEO, any funds not spent by the end of each fiscal year had to revert to the U.S. Treasury; however, LSC as a private corporation could accumulate unspent funds. When efforts were being made to increase LSC's appropriations to meet the critical legal needs of the poor, LSC had accumulated millions of dollars that were earning interest. According to a General Accounting Office study conducted in 1980,

> The Corporation's grantees are not required to return funds not expended by the end of the fiscal year. As a result, millions of dollars of unused grant funds have been accumulated by grantees and deposited in checking and interest-bearing savings accounts and, in some cases, invested in interest-bearing Treasury bills.
>
> According to the Corporation, yearend fund carryovers by grantees have been small. However, in three of the four regional offices we visited, some grantees had relatively large carryovers when compared to their total grants. For example, one grantee had a

carryover of $562,000, or 27 percent of its 1978 grant. For 37 grantees, reports by independent auditing firms showed that each had yearend fund carryovers which exceeded $100,000 and averaged 20 percent of grant funding. These 37 grantees accounted for about $8.7 million of 1978 carryovers.[2]

In fiscal year 1980 LSC's total accumulated surpluses exceeded $45.9 million (more than 15 percent of LSC's federal appropriation); in fiscal year 1981 they were more than $60 million (see Table A12.2). In FY 1982 the fund balances held by grantees had declined to $34 million, but interest received during that year on these invested funds was $9.4 million. During the three-year period 1980–82, grantees collected interest in excess of $23.8 million on accumulated surpluses.[3] Some of the grantees had used large percentages of their grants to purchase real estate; "for example, the Birmingham [Alabama] Area Legal Services Corporation purchased a building for $500,000, a figure that represents half of its annual grant."[4] The executive director of the New Orleans Legal Assistance Corporation, an LSC grantee, wrote:

> Through various methods, with the (tacit) agreement and sometimes encouragement of regional and national staff, field programs have been able to accumulate sizable sums of carryover monies. Over the years, NOLA (that is New Orleans) has accumulated a significant fund balance of approximately $469,000. The program had been planning to purchase real property since 1981. In order to do so, many projects were postponed until enough money was accumulated to make a substantial downpayment or outright purchase of property. . . .
>
> While it is true that our clients need our services more than ever, it does not necessarily follow that devoting carryover funds to direct client services is in the clients' best interest in the long term.[5]

It is difficult to discern how the legal problems of the poor are resolved by investments in real estate and interest-earning accounts. There are also questions about the need for the large increases in taxpayer funding that LSC officials were seeking. Moreover, it is evident that those in legal services believed that they knew what was best for the poor—the dictates of Congress notwithstanding.

Courting the Poor?
LSC has always been surrounded by controversy, partly because of the legal activities that its grantees pursued purportedly on behalf

305

of the poor. By any standard, some of the cases taken by LSC grantees seem dubious at best in serving the poor or in ensuring that the federal taxpayers' funds are well spent. Consider the following examples:

- In 1979–81 local legal service grantees in Montana, Iowa, and Connecticut each sued to force the state government to use tax funds for sex-change operations. In the Connecticut case, the attorney for Hartford's Neighborhood Legal Services said that the city has a "legal responsibility to provide medical care." The suit sought between $7,000 and $10,000 to relieve the "frustration, depression, and anxiety" caused by a "gender identity condition."[6]
- California Rural Legal Assistance sued the University of California to stop research that would have improved agricultural productivity. According to the complaint, the development of labor-saving (and cost-reducing) farm machinery would "benefit a narrow group of agribusiness interests with no valid public purpose, contributes to agricultural unemployment or the displacement of farm workers, or the demise of the small family farm, or the deterioration of the rural home and rural life."[7] Taken to the extreme, this logic dictates that all agricultural machinery should be banned. It is well known that capital-intensive agriculture has greatly enhanced productivity and output and has reduced prices, to the benefit of all consumers rather than "a narrow group of agribusiness interests."
- A Texas lawsuit filed by an LSC grantee established the constitutional right to free public education for illegal aliens, and another LSC-funded lawsuit in New York state required payment of welfare benefits to a parent who was an illegal alien.
- In Tampa, Florida, the Bay Area Legal Services persuaded the federal district court to prevent the implementation of statewide functional literacy tests as a prerequisite for high school graduation because the high failure rate among black students was partly attributable to past discrimination.
- The LSC grantee in Ann Arbor, Michigan, brought a suit that required the school board to adopt a plan to make teachers responsive to problems of students who speak so-called Black English and to require teachers to use their knowledge of dialect in teaching students to read.[8]
- In Youngstown, Ohio, the East Ohio Legal Services sued U.S.

Steel Corporation to require the company to sell its mill to a community organization that received tax subsidies.

- LSC grantees in Maine, Massachusetts, Colorado, and South Carolina have entered litigation to reclaim hundreds of thousands of acres for Indian tribes. According to LSC's grantees, fully two-thirds of the state of Maine should revert to the Passamaquoddy and Penobscot Indians; approximately 350,000 people would have been displaced had the suit been successful. Another suit on behalf of the Wampanoag tribe claims ownership of the town of Mashpee, Massachusetts, which covers about 17,000 acres.[9]
- LSC grantees argued that alcoholics should receive supplemental Social Security benefits.[10]

Other examples include suits seeking disability payments for homosexuals;[11] requiring a new school board election in Hereford, Texas; challenging the way federal agents search for illegal aliens; making expulsions from a junior high school in Newburg, New York, subject to racial quotas; supporting antinuclear groups in their attempts to stop power plant construction; blocking increases in transit fares; representing a Ku Klux Klan member in a $1.5 million civil suit in Chattanooga; overturning regulations that suspend welfare payments to participants who refused jobs offered in a Connecticut workfare program; mandating the payment of compensation to inmates in a Louisiana prison that had no income-producing programs; and seeking the release of prisoners in an Indiana facility because of overcrowding.

One case deserves careful scrutiny: *Simer* v. *Olivarez*, a class action suit brought by LSC grantees against the Community Services Administration (CSA) in federal district court in Chicago in September 1979.[12] The continuing resolution that Congress passed to keep CSA operating in FY 1979 contained a $200 million appropriation for emergency energy assistance to help the poor cope with rising energy costs. To ensure that the funds were used to pay heating bills, the Office of Management and Budget had stipulated that funds for this purpose could not be spent after June 30, 1980; after that date, all unspent funds would be returned to the Treasury. Even though CSA had claimed that the poor were in a crisis situation and could not pay their heating bills, $18 million was not spent by the deadline. Several LSC grantees—each having received between $285,000 and $850,000 annually from LSC plus other support from

307

the Department of Health and Human Services—"discovered" these unspent funds and rounded up eight plaintiffs to bring a class action suit contending that returning the unspent funds to the Treasury would violate the Administrative Procedures Act and due process laws. Three of the plaintiffs later said that they had no knowledge of the suit and others claimed that they had been "steered" into the action by the "public interest" law firms.[13]

After preliminary hearings, the suit was settled before trial by arms-length bargaining between CSA and the LSC grantees. Under terms of the settlement, each poor family in whose name the suit was brought would receive $250, the maximum benefit allowed by the energy assistance program. This left $17,998,000 to be distributed. Congress had allocated the money to aid the poor; in their agreement order, the litigants appeared to follow both the letter and the spirit of the law: "So, what we did, your Honor, with the money left over, was to try to provide a program whereby people who would meet all the requirements of the 1979 program would gain the benefits of this money. . . . [T]his is . . . a fair and just way of resolving the matter."[14] There was no intention of giving any money to poor families or individuals, however, and no effort was made to identify "people who would meet all the requirements of the 1979 program." Instead, according to Heather S. Richardson in the *Wall Street Journal*,

> CSA sought a settlement which would allow it to use the funds to finance pet projects which otherwise might have been terminated because of opposition or lack of interest in Congress.
>
> How will the $18 million (less $2,000) be spent? As outlined in the legal settlement, $4 million will go to a hypothermia program run by former CSA grantees to alert people to the dangers of freezing to death; over $2 million will be spent to subsidize solar power programs; and roughly $3 million will go to public advocacy and legal services. The remaining $4 million, originally intended for emergency energy conservation kits, will probably end up in the advocacy kits as well.[15]

CSA was also to receive $350,000 to fund four positions in its own offices, positions that Congress had not approved.

"Thus, CSA and the public advocacy and legal services groups may have hit upon a marvelous recipe to render Congress's intentions moot and feather their own nests: Leave money unspent, be sued and settle as thou and they can best profit."[16] The *Washington*

Post's story on the *Simer* case was headlined "How to Beat Congress by Losing a Lawsuit."[17] Interestingly, the tactics used in the *Simer* case had been successfully applied the previous year in the same court and with some of the same individuals appearing as litigants in *Grieg* v. *Olivarez*.[18]

It seems, then, that LSC and its affiliated grantees do not see the civil legal problems of the poor as their principal concern; rather, their emphasis is on achieving social and political change through the judicial process and on redistributing income and wealth by expanding the welfare system through use of the courts. They are also attempting to undermine the rights of the owners of private property and to expand the role of government in the private sector. Earned rewards, such as high school diplomas based on performance, are to be replaced by so-called rights to which everyone is entitled. These organizations encourage alternative life-styles and try to obtain judicial approval for social programs, such as taxpayer-financed abortions. Under these organizations' ruse of providing access for the poor to the justice system, the taxpayers are being forced to finance social and economic policy changes that many of them would oppose.

Those who are connected with LSC are pursuing their own interests with taxpayers' money. Marshall Breger has argued that "many Legal Services lawyers perceived themselves as strategists in the War on Poverty and . . . focus[ed] their energies on cases of social significance."[19]

Cases with "social significance" are identified solely by the attorneys employed by LSC affiliates; they have enormous discretion in selecting the cases that are pursued, and can even initiate suits for which no client has asked for assistance. There is ample evidence that attorneys funded by LSC are politically liberal: "The radicalization of Legal Services has proceeded apace since the late sixties and early seventies. . . . The National Lawyers Guild, the major organization of radical lawyers in the United States, according to its own report had 1,000 members in 1979 working in Legal Services programs."[20] LSC is a political movement, and tax-financed politics has permeated the agency since its inception.

Politics at the Legal Services Corporation

LSC was established as an independent corporation so that political pressures could not influence its activities. The act establishing the corporation also banned political activities by the corporation and by its grant-receiving affiliates, but loopholes were added to the law that have permitted LSC to broadly interpret its mandate in the political arena. Section 1007(a)(5) of the Legal Services Corporation Act of 1974 [42 U.S.C. Section 2996f(a)(5)] reads:

> [The Corporation shall] insure that no funds made available to recipients by the Corporation shall be used at any time, directly or indirectly, to influence the issuance, amendment, or revocation of any executive order or similar promulgation by any Federal, State, or local agency, or to undertake to influence the passage or defeat of any legislation by the Congress of the United States, or by any State or local legislative bodies, or State proposals by initiative petition, except where—
>
> (A) representation by an employee of a recipient for any eligible client is necessary to the provision of legal advice and representation with respect to such client's legal rights and responsibilities (which shall not be construed to permit an attorney or a recipient employee to solicit a client, in violation of professional responsibilities, for the purpose of making such representation possible); or
>
> (B) a governmental agency, legislative body, a committee, or a member thereof—
>
> (i) requests personnel of the recipient to testify, draft, or review measures or to make representations to such agency, body, committee, or member, or
>
> (ii) is considering a measure directly affecting the activities under this title of the recipient or the Corporation.

Congress also wished to ensure that LSC used no funds for "politically motivated" training by including in Section 1007(b)(6) of the act the proviso that

> [No Corporation funds may be used] to support or conduct training programs for the purpose of advocating particular public policies or encouraging political activities, labor or antilabor activities, boycotts, picketing, strikes, and demonstrations, as distinguished from the dissemination of information about such policies or activities, except that this provision shall not be construed to prohibit the training of attorneys or paralegal personnel necessary to prepare them to provide adequate legal assistance to eligible clients.

Congress further banned organizing by LSC and its affiliates in Section 1007(b)(7) of the act, mandating that "no LSC funds be used" to initiate the formation, or act as an organizer, of any asso-

310

ciation, federation, or similar entity, except that this paragraph shall not be construed to prohibit the provision of legal assistance to eligible clients." In short, Congress took extraordinary measures to prevent LSC from being influenced by or engaging in political activities. Nevertheless, LSC and its affiliates have been determined to use blatant political activism to achieve goals that could not be accomplished through judicial activism.

Ferreting out political activity by LSC grantees is difficult because the Freedom of Information Act does not apply to organizations that receive LSC funding. Nevertheless, there is abundant evidence available from other sources.

LINCs Grants

Among the grants made by LSC were those for the "law in neighborhood and community services grants" (LINCs grants). A survey was sent to recipients by Reagan appointees at LSC to determine how the funds from this program had been used. One of the categories on the survey was "legislative advocacy," and responses indicated that political activity was common. For example:

- The Office of Kentucky Legal Services reported that its client advocacy included "legislative advocacy with clients and client groups around a broad range of issues including Medicaid cuts, child care, etc." The organization also produced a "monthly newsletter on legislative issues (weekly during legislative session)."[21]
- The New Mexico Legal Support Project, in Albuquerque, responded that it had engaged in "Legislative and Administrative Advocacy Training" and the "Development of [a] State Advocacy Network."[22]
- The Texas Legal Services Center, in Austin, reported that it had conducted a "Texas People's Leadership Development Conference"; [begun] Multi-Forum Advocacy Training . . . [and] Set up [a] statewide Advocacy Task Force." The organization was also engaged in "(1) Assisting with a conference to 'Build a Network in Defense of the Undocumented' (2) Block grant/leg. Advocacy Client Training (3) Setting up a (Client)-organizational newsletter which will network all active groups and organizations in Texas."[23]
- The Friends Committee on National Legislation, in Washington, D.C., indicated that it had engaged in "legislative advocacy

against budget cuts in human services program" and had begun a newsletter.[24]

- The Raleigh Tenants Association of North Carolina had "lobbied to pass state laws improving tenant rights."[25]
- The Client's Council of Legal Services of Southeast Nebraska had developed a "welfare-rights oriented client group" and had instigated "legislative advocacy by clients."[26]
- Women Aware, Inc., of Sioux City, Iowa, had sponsored "workshops on legislative advocacy," was an "intervenor in [a] . . . utility rate increase," and co-sponsored a Welfare Rights handbook.[27] The respondent added that "the hand of God [was needed] to place the Moral Majority back into their cages."[28]

One of the most explicit incidents of using taxpayers' funds for political action was described on a LINCs grant report submitted by the Wadley-Bartow Citizens League, of Wadley, Georgia. According to the league's "brief overview of the program":

> We have conducted bi-weekly seminars/workshops, and disseminated information on voter education, citizenship, and the legislative process. Films have also been shown and posters/leaflets distributed throughout the community.
>
> Door-to-door canvassing [was done] in order to stimulate interest and participation. This was done in addition to newspaper articles, leaflets, and radio announcements, plus free transportation.[29]

The objectives of the program were measured "by response and participation in seminars/workshops, increased voter interest in the community, [and] increased voter registration, according to city records." The league also produced "leaflets handed out at seminars/workshops, films on voter education and the political process, posters throughout the community on voter education and citizenship."[30]

When B. A. Johnson filed the report for the Wadley-Bartow Citizens League, he was a candidate for mayor of the city of Wadley. One of the leaflets prepared and distributed depicted a voting machine with careful instruction to "Push Lever 1" for mayor; Johnson's name appeared next to lever 1. Willie R. Strowbridge's candidacy for councilman was aided by similar instructions. At the bottom of the leaflet was the statement "Vote yourself a Xmas present in B. A. Johnson and Willie R. Strowbridge."[31] In effect, taxpayers' money was being used to further Johnson and Strowbridge's campaign. Both Johnson and Strowbridge were elected.

312

The Wadley-Bartow Citizens League received $2,500 from an LSC grant, and the interim report cited above was filed to obtain the 15 percent of the grant that had not been paid earlier. When Johnson's report reached LSC headquarters in Washington, D.C., the political nature of the expenditures was so excessively out of line that J. Kenneth Smith, director of Regional Operations and Support Services in the Office of Program Support at LSC, wrote:

> We have reviewed the Phase II documentation you provided us on your LINCs . . . grant. It would be extremely helpful to us if you would rework your grantee reporting form and delete the references to voter-education, legislative and political process. Perhaps you could rephrase the language to say something to the effect that the project focused on citizenship and advocacy.
>
> I have enclosed the original form that you completed, along with a new form. If you have any questions or need any additional information, please contact . . . me.
>
> Thank you in advance for your cooperation in this matter. I wish you continued success on your project.[32]

Evidently, LSC officials did not want their files to contain evidence that the congressional strictures on political activity had been so wantonly violated.

This was by no means the only LINCs grant that had been used for such purposes. On June 8, 1981, Bea Moulton, director of the Office of Program Services at LSC, wrote a memorandum revealing concern about the LINCs program to her colleagues:

> These grants are in a very sensitive area. They will be subject at some point, I believe, to considerable scrutiny. We need to discuss the other grants you propose to make. They all call for worthwhile, very important, activity. But as described in your forms, it may be the very kind of activity Congress has specifically prohibited from funding. Maybe they can be turned into training proposals. . . . Funding even arguably illegal activity at this time could greatly jeopardize Federal funding for legal services this year and in succeeding years. We just can't risk it.[33]

LSC officials were fully aware of how LINCs grants were being used and that the grants were supporting illegal activities.

The LINCs program has been directed to political advocacy at the local level of government, but LSC funding also has influenced initiatives at the state level.

The LSC-Funded Task Force on California's Proposition 9

In 1980, LSC grantees attempted to defeat California's Proposition 9, which sought to reduce the state's personal income tax rate. LSC affiliates in California had long been politically active at the state level of government. A staff investigation for the Committee on Appropriations of the U.S. House of Representatives, for example, reported that the San Francisco-based California Rural Legal Assistance maintained a permanent office in the state capital, Sacramento, with five attorneys who were all registered lobbyists. Two were active in the legislature, two dealt with administrative advocacy, and one worked exclusively on migrant worker issues. The Western Center on Law and Poverty, based in Los Angeles, shared office space in Sacramento with the lobbyists for California Rural Legal Assistance and had four registered lobbyists engaged in legislative and administrative advocacy.[34]

Alan Rader, an attorney at the Western Center on Law and Poverty and a coordinator for the Proposition 9 Task Force organized by LSC affiliates in California, requested and received $61,655 from LSC to finance the activities of the task force.[35] Thirty local legal service programs throughout California also participated by supplying staff to work with the media and to register voters in welfare offices. In these ways, federal taxpayers were forced to contribute to the cause, directly through an LSC grant and indirectly through the LSC-funded salaries of the attorneys who participated in the campaign. This grant and the activities of the participants violated the law establishing LSC.

LSC's Survival Campaign

Ronald Reagan's election as president in 1980 and the prospect of major changes in LSC resulted in a near panic at the organization's headquarters. LSC President Dan J. Bradley appointed Alan Houseman, then director of the Research Institute on Legal Assistance of LSC, to head a "survival task force," to respond to this new threat. LSC's political nature and activities were revealed in a series of memoranda that Houseman wrote in an effort to develop a campaign that would nullify the effects of any changes in LSC operations that the Reagan administration might attempt to implement. Even though the voters had elected a president who had campaigned on a platform of a different direction for government, LSC was determined that its own political direction was not going to change. Among the changes that Houseman and others at LSC

314

feared the most were "controls on social activism of legal services staff who are engaged in aggressive advocacy, including restrictions on case types and restrictions and limitations on the scope of representation."[36]

On December 1, 1980, Houseman wrote a memorandum entitled "Coalition Building and Strengthening Presence in Community" in which he stated the following:

> It is essential to broaden the political base of local programs for short term and long term survival. In the short term, a strong local political base will be critical if we are to successfully obtain support from Congress for the continuation of an aggressive legal services program. Lobbying in Washington will only be successful if local programs have established credibility and a base in their communities and developed allies who can and will assist them in persuading their Congressman and Senators to support legal services.
>
> A critical means of strengthening the local political base is to develop coalitions and working relationships with local organizations and individuals who would see it in their interest to assure the continuation of an aggressive legal services program.[37]

In Houseman's view, an "aggressive" legal services program meant the "survival of committed . . . political staff" and the "survival of aggressive advocacy (i.e., advocacy which utilizes the full scope of representation including legislative and administrative representation, litigation and community education; advocacy which seeks all possible remedies; and advocacy which is not restricted in what defendants can be sued, e.g., government entities)."[38]

Houseman conceived a survival strategy consisting of three elements: an outside entity to lobby on behalf of LSC, a grass-roots lobbying campaign directed primarily at members of Congress, and a "corporation in exile" to wage the ideological battle against the Reagan presidency. This strategy was implemented, as discussed below.

The Coalition for Legal Services. Even though Congress had prohibited LSC from forming associations and organizations, LSC officials actively participated in establishing the Coalition for Legal Services. As Houseman described the coalition in a memorandum,

> [W]e are attempting to unite and join together in this struggle. We have formed a coalition with PAG [the Project Advisory Group],

315

the National Clients Counsel [*sic*] (NCC), NLADA [National Legal Aid and Defenders Association], the National Organization of Legal Services Workers (NOLSW) and the Minority Caucus. It will be expanding to include others from within the legal services community, such as National Association of Indian Legal Services (NAILS), migrant farm workers group, women's caucus, Organization for Legal Services Backup Centers (OLSBUC), state support and others. It will also expand to include organizations who are allies and supporters of legal services.

The coalition members will be forming an outside entity to lobby and coordinate survival activities on behalf of the legal services community. This entity will be established soon and will begin to function in early 1981.[39]

The coalition's first formal activity was to mail a fundraising letter on February 20, 1981, in which it outlined its purpose: "to provide accurate information about LSC, to develop a network of support for legal services, to advocate in Congress and the media for legal services to the poor, and generally to coordinate the activities designed to preserve the Corporation and legal services."[40]

Several individuals associated with the coalition had close financial ties to LSC. Melville D. Miller and Bernard A. Veney, for example, were both members of the coalition's first board of directors. Miller was also the chair of the Project Advisory Group (PAG), a coalition member organization that had received about $180,000 per year of taxpayers' funds through voluntary contributions from LSC's program affiliates. Veney was the secretary of the coalition and was also the executive director of the National Clients Council, which had received almost $750,000 from LSC in 1981.

Another member group of the coalition, NLADA, was also receiving large amounts of tax dollars and in 1981 received $2,195,000 from LSC.[41] Some of the NLADA funds were used to hire a "full-time experienced lobbyist to work on legal services."[42] Thus, this coalition, which was specifically designed to lobby Congress on behalf of LSC, was being supported by tax dollars.

The Coalition for Legal Services was the brainchild of officials at LSC headquarters in Washington, but apparently, LSC affiliates elsewhere in the country believed that additional coalitions were needed to oppose the Reagan administration, especially if the effort could be funded with tax dollars.

The Coalition for Sensible and Humane Solutions (CSHS). On April 29, 1981, Joseph Lipofsky of Legal Services of Eastern Missouri wrote to Rhonda Roberson at LSC requesting a LINCs grant:

> On behalf of the Coalition for Sensible and Humane Solutions, I would like to make application for funding under the Law in Neighborhoods and Communities Study (LINC's). The enclosed packet gives you some information on this Coalition.
>
> It is our intention to use our LINC's funding for four activities:
>
> 1. To publish a handbook for the "Peoples Lobbyists."
>
> 2. To conduct . . . a "People College of Law" to continue training of community activists in both substantive issues and the process of community education and action, legislative and administrative advocacy as well as their relations to litigation.
>
> 3. To research and to publish a "Peoples Alternative" to budget cuts and tax issues on a state and local level.
>
> 4. To develop an ongoing bimonthly communication on a State-wide basis to focus on budget and tax questions and ways to impact them.[43]

The materials Lipofsky enclosed left little doubt about the organization's aims. According to one enclosure, CSHS was "formed in February 1981 in direct response to President Reagan's budget message to the country."[44] CSHS adopted two basic positions:

> 1) We will oppose *all* federal, state and local budget cuts in programs that meet human needs.
>
> 2) We will oppose the transfer of funds to the states; the so-called "block grants" which endanger the rights and resources of women, minorities, and the poor.[45]

CSHS had wasted no time. Lipofsky's material included a list of activities CSHS had engaged in during its short life, including the attendance of 500 coalition members at budget hearings held in St. Louis by Rep. Richard A. Gephardt (D-Mo.); the attendance of 150 low-income people at a "People's Forum" to give testimony to representatives of Sen. John C. Danforth (R-Mo.) and Sen. Thomas F. Eagleton (D-Mo.); the sponsorship of "massive" letter-writing campaigns to congressmen and senators; and the attendance of a meeting with Senator Danforth on budget cuts.[46]

Despite the blatantly political nature of these activities and of CSHS's objectives, LSC approved Lipofsky's request for funding.

On July 17, 1981, LSC paid Legal Services of Eastern Missouri $17,475 for "community based training" programs that it had "co-sponsored" with CSHS.[47] Two one-day programs were held, one on June 19 in Caruthersville and the other on July 2 in St. Louis. At these training programs, sessions were held on "basic community education," legislative lobbying, referendums and initiatives, "community action," and community/media "outreach."[48] The narrative summary that Lipofsky had submitted to support his grant request indicated that the training program in St. Louis would

> Educate and inform community activists about current federal, state and local budget cutting activities.
>
> Share and develop strategies for fighting back.
>
> Plan for a follow-up statewide conference in August.[49]

Legal Services of Eastern Missouri would remain a favored recipient of federal funds, receiving more than $1.2 million in FY 1983 (see Table A12.1).

Grass-Roots Lobbying. The second strategy in LSC's survival campaign was a carefully orchestrated organizing effort at the grass-roots level. Each LSC regional office designated an individual to coordinate survival activities within its region; each local affiliate was to have its own survival coordinator; and state coordinators were appointed.[50] The coordinators had four objectives: (1) generate a flood of letters to members of Congress urging reauthorization of LSC; (2) generate newspaper editorials praising the legal services program; (3) urge local bar associations to pass resolutions in support of LSC; and (4) arrange meetings with federal legislators to lobby for the reauthorizing legislation.[51]

LSC's Chicago region meeting was held in St. Louis on December 11–12, 1981. During the opening session, Dan Bradley, then president of LSC, gave the "Call to Battle," citing the Proposition 9 task force in California as an excellent example of what a concerted political effort could achieve. The long-term goal of the task force was to "insure the continuation of effective, locally controlled legal assistance effort which are [*sic*] free from political interference." Strategies were to be developed for the media and for the political community, covering local officials, congressmen, state officials and other individuals who make or influence decisions.[52]

LSC had ample previous experience in lobbying Congress and

proselytizing and Rep. James Sensenbrenner (R-Wis.) asked the General Accounting Office to investigate LSC's earlier grass-roots organizing efforts. GAO reported that on April 30, 1980, LSC had

> sent out a packet of materials addressed to: "Persons Coordinating Congressional Relations" that included instructions on effective lobbying of members of Congress at the local level for LSC legislation. The materials provided were as follows:
>
> 1. A statement of "what needs to be done" and "what to send us."
>
> 2. A Legislative update on April 3, 1980. . . .
>
> 3. Fact sheets and background information on the LSC reauthorization and appropriation, including membership lists of the appropriate House and Senate Committees.
>
> 4. One page fact sheet/handouts on possible restrictive amendments.
>
> 5. Examples of supportive Bar letters and resolutions.
>
> 6. Examples of favorable editorials.
>
> 7. Examples of supportive letters from public officials.
>
> 8. A list of state coordinators for the legislative effort. (State coordinators will also receive materials excerpted from the *Congressional Staff Directory*, indicating the Washington and local office addresses and phone numbers and the key staff of each member of their state's Congressional delegation.)[53]

The brochure, entitled "What Needs to Be Done," gave instructions for visiting members of Congress; for securing support from local and state bar associations; for obtaining editorial support in newspapers; for alerting constituents and other concerned groups, including local and state labor organizations, church groups, the League of Women Voters, Common Cause, civil rights organizations, social service organizations, and antihunger coalitions; and, finally, for informing LSC headquarters about "problems."[54] Lobbyists in the LSC cause were directed to report every contact they made with members of Congress and their staffs and to assess the attitude of those people toward legal services and toward any provisions of the legislation or amendments.[55] Detailed information was provided on all aspects of the reauthorization of LSC funding, and lobbyists were urged to oppose any amendment that would restrict legislative representation, the ability of LSC affiliates to represent aliens, the right of a legal services program to receive

319

court-awarded fees, the right of employees to join labor unions, representation in abortion cases, and that would require attorneys to negotiate prior to the initiation of litigation.[56]

The comptroller general concluded: "There is little question that [these activities] . . . constitute 'lobbying,' as the term is used in the applicable restrictive legislation."[57] In a report issued a year earlier, GAO had charged LSC affiliates with lobbying and recommended that the corporation take steps to "more specifically define the legislative restrictions on grantees' lobbying activities and the types of lobbying activities that are not permissible."[58] Although tax funds were being used illegally for political activity, GAO did not believe that there was any way to recover those funds: "Because LSC's regulations and current policies appear to authorize recipients to expend appropriated funds for prohibited lobbying activities in derogation of the . . . restrictions, we do not think, as a practical matter, that the Government would be successful in attempting to recover the illegally expended sums from the recipients."[59] The taxpayers, it seems, are out of luck.

Congress has often attempted to limit LSC's activities, but LSC officials are experts at dodging such restrictions. The Legal Services Act of 1974 placed restrictions on lobbying activities and placed additional limitations on LSC political activities in 1976, 1979, and 1980 to restrict the use of appropriated funds for publicity or propaganda relating to legislation.[60] Congress also tried, without much success, to limit the types of cases that LSC can undertake by forbidding criminal representation; representation for juveniles (until 1977 when the limitation was dropped); school desegregation, Selective Service System, nontherapeutic abortion, homosexual, and gay rights cases; and representation of illegal aliens.[61]

In each instance, LSC officials publicly stated that the corporation and its affiliates would abide by these congressional limitations, and then they continued to flout the law. After GAO issued its report on LSC political activities in May 1981 that had been requested by Rep. Sensenbrenner, Dan Bradley, president of LSC, sent a letter to the comptroller general:

> Your opinion indicates that the Legal Services Corporation and its [grant] recipients have engaged in prohibited grass roots and lobbying activities. You concluded that these activities were carried out pursuant to Corporation regulations and legal opinions that erroneously interpreted the Legal Services Corporation Act and its relationship to riders that have been attached to various

appropriations bills. You have further requested that I take immediate action to halt such grass roots legislative activities.

. . . [W]hile we disagreed with GAO's view of the interpretation
of the various related provisions of existing law, and thus draw
different conclusions about possible violations, we are making
certain changes in our present activities. Prior to receipt of your
opinion, I directed all personnel of the Legal Services Corporation
to stop any and all activities coming within the GAO definition of
grass roots lobbying activities.[62]

The "changes" were being made, but they were not the sort that
may have been expected. Rather than ceasing political activity, LSC
officials decided that alternative organizational structures had to be
developed to carry out both the activities that Congress had expressly
prohibited and those that it was likely to prohibit.

Mirror Corporations. Prior to Ronald Reagan becoming president,
LSC had been able to maneuver around various congressional mandates by using a variety of subterfuges. If a new board of directors
were appointed that was hostile to LSC's political machinations,
then the old stratagems would no longer work. LSC officials thus
conceived the third element of the survival campaign—so-called
mirror corporations as part of the "Corporation in Exile" strategy.

The Boston regional office of LSC was actively involved in the
search for alternative organizations through which it could direct
political advocacy operations. This is evident in a memorandum
written by Friends of Advocacy, a nonprofit corporation formed to
provide legal assistance to the poor, and sent to the board of directors of Connecticut Legal Services (CLS):

As early as January 1981, persons with LSC began to discuss the
notion of programs creating alternative entities calculated to circumvent the anticipated limitations. Within LSC's New England
Region, project directors held meetings for the purpose of dis-
cussing potential responses to anticipated federal restrictions,
including the creation of alternative corporations. In fact, these
regional meetings have continued since then, the next one to take
place October 22nd and 23rd.

On June 18, 1981, our fears unfortunately became reality when
the U.S. House of Representatives passed H.R. 3480, a reauthorization of the Legal Services Corporation which included numerous amendments severely restricting the activities of legal services
programs and their employees. The CLS Board of Directors was

informed of the House's action at a meeting held that very same evening.[63]

LSC headquarters, which was deeply involved in the search for "alternative mechanisms," contracted with the Institute for Non-Profit Management Training to study various options. The proposal was written as a "management training curriculum," so that funding could be provided under the LINCs program. The training program

> will address two specific areas . . . 1) locating and obtaining funding for community based organizations; and 2) training programs for client/community advocates. The goal of the proposed management training program is to improve the capacity of clients (and thus their communities) to productively advocate for themselves and use sound managment [sic] principles and practices to structure and solidify that advocacy and the informed involvement that it gives rise to.[64]

The core of the program was a session on "establishing feeder organizations" to examine "specific strategies for stabilizing the NPO's [nonprofit organization's] funding base through the development of a for-profit arm or 'feeder' organization." The NPO's objective was "to maintain compliance with federal regulations while engaging in certain types of advocacy activities such as lobbying."[65]

LSC also hired a consultant, Gregg Krech, to do a study entitled *Alternatives to Retrenchment.* Among other things, Krech recommended the

> establishment of an independent "sister" corporation which provides services on a fee-for-service basis to ineligible clients [for tax-funded legal services] and donates all the profits back to the legal services program; or the establishment of public interest law firms and social welfare organizations which can provide a wide range of services to poor people with less restrictions.[66]

In effect, the fees generated from providing legal services to clients who were not poor would not be subject to congressional restrictions on federal funds and could be used for lobbying and for financing those cases and representing those clients that Congress had disallowed.

Krech proposed five alternative organizational structures, all of which could launder funds so that congressional restrictions on political advocacy and representation could be subverted.[67] Section 1010(c) of the Legal Services Corporation Act of 1974 had made alternative structures necessary, as Krech noted in his report:

> Interpreted strictly, this provision [1010(c)] attaches all LSC restrictions and prohibitions to any non-public monies of a legal services grantee. Given redirections in LSC funding and expected efforts of programs to develop private sources through fund raising and/ or fee for service, it might not be unusual to find a legal services program receiving only 10 percent of their funding from LSC but having *all* funding subject to the LSC restrictions. . . . As stated earlier, private funds will almost certainly be subject to the same restrictions as LSC funds according to section 1010(c) of the Act. If you contemplate the *potential* use of new funds for activities which are not a permissible use of LSC funds, these new funds still have to be raised and used outside of the LSC corporate entity. Raising money through the LSC entity will provide additional money, but that money will become subject to the same restrictions as the LSC money. Raising money through a separate entity allows the money to be raised while discretion is maintained as to its use.
>
> . . . There are inherent limitations on 501(c)(3) corporations [i.e., nonprofit, tax-exempt organizations] with respect to the conduct of unrelated business activities and legislative influence. Other corporate forms provide greater flexibility to charge fees and lobby.[68]

There are indications that the mirror corporation strategy has been implemented. In 1982 the New Haven Legal Assistance Association (LAA) transferred its annual grant of $543,000 to the South Central Connecticut Legal Services Corporation. New Haven LAA continues to operate as a separate structure, funded through "alternative funding sources" and free of any restrictions Congress may impose on recipients of federal funds. But South Central handles no cases; it simply acts as a screening and referral entity, primarily for New Haven LAA. South Central pays New Haven LAA a set rate for every case it handles. Although the two programs are legally separate, they are "operationally integrated," sharing the same office, the same phones, and the same attorneys, and being managed by the same executive director. The legal separation, however, has made it possible for New Haven LAA to ignore congressional restrictions on use of taxpayers' funds.[69]

Using similar tactics, on January 4, 1982, Texas Rural Legal Aid transferred $760,000 to a separate entity, the Texas Rural Legal Foundation, to provide legal services to eligible clients.[70] Texas Rural Legal Aid was very active politically and had brought suit to prevent the special senatorial election in Texas won by a conservative congressman, Rep. Phil Gramm.[71] It is anyone's guess how stopping a senatorial election would have served the legal needs of the poor.

LSC affiliates were also concerned about the fund balances that had been accumulated. At a meeting on August 27, 1981, there was a panel discussion on "creative ways of using fund balances," including "hiding fund balances."[72] Evidently, there was some fear that Congress might use the balances to justify cutting LSC's appropriation or that members of a new LSC board of directors would recall the balances to headquarters. Mirror corporations had been viewed by LSC officials as a repository for fund balances that would not be open to public scrutiny.

Training and Organizing for Political Advocacy

LSC headquarters was also concerned about the allocation of the corporation's funds under the Reagan administration and in 1981 decided to spend considerable sums on "training manuals." LSC's Office of Program Support awarded contracts to produce "between 35 ad 50" training manuals to be made available to grantees, regional training centers, and client groups "in connection with education and training programs."[73]

Given the mandate of LSC, one would expect LSC training manuals to focus on helping attorneys represent the poor in the courts. Most of the manuals, however, emphasize organizing for political activism, and references to the judicial process are typically made only in the context of how the courts may be used to further such organization. For example, consider *The Law and Direct Citizen Action*, a training manual developed by the Institute for Social Justice (see chapter 8) using taxpayers' funds provided by LSC's Advocacy Training and Development Unit. The preface to the manual states:

> This handbook is written for community organizations and the legal workers who advise them. It is a guide to the areas of the law that affect direct citizen action. The law both creates rights and restricts them. Some laws—for example, the First Amendment, the Freedom of Information Acts—can be very useful to organizations seeking to bring about social change. But often the law can stymie action—whether by permit requirements or by

mass arrests. This handbook is a guide to how to use the law and not let the law be used against you.[74]

"Social change" is a recurring theme throughout these manuals and is a code word for the left-wing political activity that characterizes LSC, its affiliated groups, and the network of organizations that LSC helps to fund. According to this particular manual, social change can be achieved only by power, and power is obtained by organizing:

> It takes power to achieve significant social change. People get power by organizing. Social change organizations provide a power base from which people can take systematic collective action on their own behalf. The strategies and tactics of such organizations may vary, but whether they engage in electoral politics or direct action, community education or militant disruption, consumer boycotts or picket lines, their ultimate strength lies in their ability to mobilize and empower large numbers of people.[75]

Organizing is viewed as the only way that problems may be effectively addressed. In fact, the role of the individual attorney in helping an individual client is derogated: "A victory won through direct action by fifty members is more meaningful in the long run than a triumph achieved by a single leader (or lawyer).[76] Moreover:

> Organizers—good organizers—are trained to empower people to take collective action on their own behalf. Lawyers, on the other hand, are trained to be advocates who act on behalf of their clients. As a result, many lawyers are oriented toward solving specific problems by using the legal system to win individual cases— instead of helping people solve their own problems by direct action.
>
> But there are other lawyers who believe in the basic principles of organizing to achieve social change. They want to know what kinds of assistance they can provide and how best to provide it. This handbook is intended to help them and to help community organization leaders and members as well, by helping them understand the limitations the law imposes, the opportunities it provides, and the reasons behind the advice their lawyer is giving them.[77]

A lawyer's role, then, is to "protect the members of the organization" and to "fight back," not to represent individuals. An attorney can force opponents of the organization to "cave in" by "imposing liability and money costs on others."[78] Evidently, the ends justify the means, for the manual indicates that "exposure" is a useful tool and "the threat of scandal and ridicule is a powerful one."[79] If lawyers follow the appropriate prescriptions, they "have a unique opportunity to help give *real* 'power to the people.' "[80]

In addition to a philosophical discourse about the importance of organizing for advocacy and an attorney's role in that process, this particular manual offers practical suggestions, such as how to file a series of small suits so that "the opposition's costs may be significantly higher if it has to defend itself against a lot of small suits which are factually distinct that [*sic*] if it has one massive class action to defend, and this can enlarge the organization's bargaining power."[81] Of course, it is expensive for the plaintiff to file a large number of small suits, but as long as the costs are paid by the taxpayers the organization seeking social change does not bear the burden.

Moreover, organizations and their attorneys should not let the law stand in the way of their objectives; the manual argues that it may be more effective to flout the legal system than to abide by it. In answering the question "Should a group apply for a permit [for a demonstration]?" the manual offers the following advice:

> This is a question that cannot be answered in the abstract. This is a decision that should be made be the group, not the attorney. The attorney should not get too involved in tactical discussions. One experienced organizer argues that the organization should select the best tactic for the situation, then look at the law. If the group starts its selection of tactics by looking at the law, the result can be narrow, unimaginative, or restrictive tactics. Lawyers often tell groups what they can't do instead of what they can. Choose the tactic, then decide how much to modify it (if at all) to comply with applicable regulations or ordinances. For example, a tenants' group may wish to picket a landlord at his house or confront a public official at her office. The group may feel that surprise or catching the target off-guard is a major part of its strategy, so it does not want to apply for the necessary permits.[82]

In essence, LSC, chartered by Congress and charged with using the law to help the poor, has spent tax dollars to finance a manual that advocates illegal activities. The sentiments expressed in *The Law and Direct Citizen Action* are characteristic of those found in other "training manuals" funded by LSC, including *Communication Skills, Community Advocacy and Leadership/Community Development*, which was produced for LSC's Office of Program Support. The familiar themes of advocacy and organizing for social change appear throughout this document:

> There is a tremendous amount of discussion in this country today about the difficulty in addressing many issues confronting poor people. There are probably just as many complaining about a lack of knowledge about where and how to get involved in social change. Although many people are very interested in social change, they do not understand where and how to begin work on issues that affect it.
>
> . . . Many helping professionals are concerned with their clients and are interested in social change.
>
> For many years, . . . lawyers . . . and other helping professionals have tried with limited success to bring about change. Their approach has been to work hard on individual cases and take on as many clients as possible. However, this effort to meet the needs of the community/client has not had the impact that is needed or desired to create real social change. As resources continue to diminish, it is encumbant [sic] upon all concerned to find new ways to complement the programs of present social/legal services.[83]

This manual also stresses the need for "organizing" for social change, in that dealing with individual clients has not produced what the activists consider to be desirable results. The material in the manual illustrates the concept that legal services advocates should not respond to individual requests for legal assistance but that they should proselytize for change. Consider three cases suggested for "advocate role play situations." One case poses the problem of a "Black lawyer who is attempting to convince residents of a poor white apartment building to organize a rent strike." In another, "A white paralegal is attempting to convence [sic] a number of mainly Black and Hispanic prisoners to file a class action suite [sic] becuase [sic] of overcrowding in the county jail." In yet another, "A lawyer, living in a very economically depressed area of a city, is trying to get the poorest people to organize a food co-op."[84]

When congressional oversight hearings were held on LSC, there were numerous protests about the involvement of legal services activists in all sorts of organizing activities, including union organizing.[85] Apparently, the training and education program was effective, for LSC affiliates instigated or were involved in many activities

327

that had little or no connection with LSC's basic mission. Furthermore, this advocacy and organizing activity was undertaken in spite of the federal law prohibiting organizing activity.

The Verdict on the Legal Services Corporation

LSC has been clearly riddled with illegal political activity. Hundreds of millions of taxpayers' dollars have been used to fund the political goals of a determined group that has used the needs of the poor as an excuse to obtain vast sums of money from the government. Tax monies have been diverted to elect candidates to office, to defeat or support legislation at all levels of government, to finance administrative and congressional lobbying, to organize at the grass-roots level for political purposes, and to fund a host of allied organizations. Many of the cases pursued by LSC and its affiliates are bizarre and have nothing to do with alleviating the legal problems of the poor. Attorneys associated with LSC affiliates have sought to advance their version of political utopia, and these proselytizers may have been convinced that their expertise would place them in leadership positions if the political changes being advocated with tax funds were put in place.

For years, LSC has been criticized for its blatant and illegal political activity. While LSC officials were publicly denying any wrongdoing or any untoward political actions,[86] internal memorandums and other documents show that they were fully aware of and concerned about the propriety and legality of their activities. LSC's president, Dan Bradley, was seeking increased funding from Congress, but LSC was diverting, for its own uses, tens of millions of dollars originally intended to help the poor. When testifying about LSC's FY 1982 budget, Bradley stated that "the painful reality is, however, that legal services programs already operate at the margin. There is little that can be done to meet rising costs, short of reducing available service."[87] In contrast to Bradley's grim assessment of LSC's fiscal status, LSC affiliates had amassed tens of millions of taxpayers' dollars in unspent balances in the period from FY 1980 to FY 1982 and had purchased $15.5 million in real property and $17.8 million in equipment during the same period. LSC headquarters openly encouraged the diverting of program resources away from services for the poor by hiring consultants to develop "alternative corporate forms" and to find "creative ways" to use fund balances; LSC even drafted sample documents to be used in acquiring real estate.[88] During the same period, $2,257,000 was

328

spent for dues to various organizations, including labor unions, and payments were made to the Committee on Political Education (C.O.P.E.), the AFL-CIO political action group, and similar organizations.[89] Bradley also failed to mention the interest income from unspent fund balances that had been invested or the millions of dollars in legal fee awards that LSC grantees were collecting from their lawsuits (see Table A12.2)—awards that taxpayers also paid when the suit was brought against local, state, or federal government agencies.

There might not have been much money to provide legal services, but that did not stop officials associated with LSC affiliates—officials such as Bernard A. Veney, executive director of the National Clients Council—from living well at taxpayer expense. During the first nine months of 1983, for example, Veney's expense account tabs included the following:

> $177.90 for a stay with his wife at an inn a few blocks from his Washington office;
>
> $180-a-day suite at the Burbank Airport Hilton during a California training seminar;
>
> $171.60 for lodging at a Jackson, Wyoming, resort;
>
> a $419.47 tab at the posh Georgetown Hotel in Washington during another training seminar;
>
> $10,069.51 in car and limousine rentals when Veney commuted between Washington and his home in Columbia, Md. [an outlying suburb of Washington];
>
> a $6,456 salary advance which was still outstanding from August, 1982; and,
>
> a $738 plane ticket for his son who was not employed by the Clients Council.[90]

So much LSC money was diverted to political activity, frivolous lawsuits, organizing campaigns and training, slush funds, real estate, and other purposes that it is reasonable to question whether LSC and its affiliates were concerned at all about the legal problems of the poor. Apparently, their greatest concern was to use the poor to obtain resources that would support the agenda of LSC activists and spread their propaganda. At the same time that LSC was furthering its political causes in the courts and legislatures at taxpayer expense, the organization's survival campaign was undertaken to keep the corporation free from political interference, as if such an assertion could justify the subterfuges and stratagems devised under that scheme. LSC's principal problem was that a board of directors appointed by the Reagan administration might have a different view of LSC's purpose and might try to alter the corporation's policies toward legal services for the poor.

In 1982 the worst fears of LSC officials were realized when President Reagan appointed new board members and officers. The response was a campaign of smear and innuendo that was intended to divert attention from LSC and its activities and to focus on the new appointees. Many files from the period 1980–82 in LSC's Washington office were destroyed, and the appointees had to scour regional offices to obtain copies of important correspondence and memoranda.[91] The denial of information to Reagan appointees was only a small skirmish in the major battle over the integrity of the appointees, which focused on the consulting fees and travel expenses the Reagan board members had charged to LSC. LSC bureaucrats and their allies orchestrated a major media campaign to discredit the board members and to preserve the corporation. The media rose to the bait and produced a barrage of articles questioning the propriety of the board members' behavior.[92] A GAO investigation concluded that there was no impropriety committed by the president's LSC appointees:

—payments to Board members complied with the law and LSC's regulations and policies,
—LSC's practices for compensating Board members were comparable to those followed by other Government corporations,
—the new LSC president's contract was properly negotiated and consistent with the contracts of past LSC presidents and presidents of other Government corporations, and
—LSC Board members, appointed by the President while the Senate was in recess, were entitled to compensation.[93]

Although the charges were without substance, the damage had been done. The smear campaign had produced a smoke screen behind which LSC's congressional allies could maneuver. LSC continued to receive funding under continuing resolutions that kept the corporation's activities from being closely examined.[94]

Intimidation was also brought to bear on the Reagan appointees when death threats were made against the LSC board chairman and president.[95] Evidently, the pressure tactics worked, for LSC still exists, which is no small accomplishment after three attempts by Reagan to end its financing. Indeed, the corporation is prospering; in January 1984, the board of directors voted to request a budget of $325 million for FY 1985, an increase of 18 percent over 1983 and the largest budget LSC had ever sought.[96] The budget process was interesting: "Board members had planned to seek a 4.4 percent increase, but agreed to increase it after protests last month that the amount was not enough and after accusations that board members were trying to destroy legal aid programs."[97] One would think that the board's first objective should be to dismantle some of LSC's programs, particularly its illegal political, organizing, and training activities. No budget increase would be necessary if the resources devoted to illegal activities were used instead for their intended purpose: providing legal services to the poor.

Despite abundant evidence of blatant wrongdoing, little has been done to correct LSC's abuses of its mandate. Congress has placed various restrictions on the corporation's operations from time to time, but it has never effectively brought LSC under control, and no attempts have ever been made to enforce the restrictions. Sen. Orrin G. Hatch (R-Utah) has offered an explanation:

> To question the activities of the Corporation and its 326 grantees is, of course, politically disadvantageous. One is led to believe that the nobility of the Corporation's purpose makes any question as to the propriety of some of its activities nothing less than a vicious attack on the poor themselves. This misinformed, oversimplified presumption has scared away much needed review and has provided the Corporation with a congressional carte blanche to operation without oversight, without review, and without criticism.[98]

The apostles of the poor have carefully cultivated the notion that questioning a program that is intended to help the poor is an attack on the poor. This attitude serves their interests and the interests of those in Congress who benefit from the political activities and the organizing that LSC has so generously funded with taxpayers' money.

LSC and its affiliates deal not only with political issues but also with candidates. Those in Congress who support LSC appropriations and do not question how the funds are spent are supported at election time by the grass-roots organizations nurtured by LSC. Thus, a cozy relationship has developed between those in Congress who appropriate funds and those who spend them. The taxpayers are the losers, for they finance the grass-roots political activity that sends to Congress those individuals who benefit from the illegal use of tax monies and who have every incentive to continue this practice. The poor also lose, for funds originally allocated to benefit them are shamelessly diverted for political purposes that primarily benefit the apostles of the poor.

LSC has built a powerful constituency in support of its program and appropriations. One of the most important groups in the coalition is the American Bar Association (ABA), the professional association and lobbying arm of the nation's lawyers. LSC and its affiliates provide direct employment for nearly 5,000 attorneys,[99] and thousands of other attorneys obtain income by participating in LSC lawsuits. If LSC funding were terminated, a depression would hit the legal profession, as thousands of lawyers would be out of work and in competition with other practicing attorneys. There is already a surfeit of lawyers in the United States, and a steady stream of graduates from the nation's law schools continues to swell the ranks of the profession. Thus, there is a powerful economic rationale for the ABA's interest in LSC's funding; and, according to the *Washington Post*, the ABA "engaged in a massive lobbying campaign" to protect its stake in the program.[100]

In addition to lobbying for LSC, the ABA also responded to the 1980 election of Ronald Reagan by establishing special trust accounts in more than 30 states called "interest on lawyers' trust accounts."[101] In six states the bar associations have made this program mandatory for all lawyers. How it works is that participating lawyers deposit their clients' cash for such things as filing fees and real estate escrows in a statewide account. The interest accrued goes not to the clients but to LSC. The total contribution was $16 million in FY 1984 and is expected to be as much as $50 million in FY 1985.

In 30 states, this program was set up by the bar associations without legislative approval, and in no state does a client have a legal right to say whether he wants the interest to go to the LSC or not. This has infuriated some clients, such as Evelyn Glaeser, an elderly widow who filed suit in Florida federal court claiming her due process rights were violated when the interest proceeds of a small trust account her husband left her went to LSC.[102] Glaeser's suit was the first in federal courts as of early 1984, although four state courts had by then ruled the system unconstitutional.

The ABA may also hold this positive view of federal funding for attorneys because the ABA itself has been highly successful in getting taxpayers' funds for its own use. Millions of dollars in grants and contracts from numerous federal sources have been given to the ABA for a variety of "studies" (see Table A12.3). Once one group has its hand in the taxpayers' pockets, it is difficult to be objective about the way in which other groups dispose of their tax dollars.

Every group that receives funding from government is implicitly threatened whenever efforts are made to eliminate or reduce the funding of even one recipient. For this reason, enormous pressures are brought to bear on politicians whenever spending cuts are contemplated. These pressures are all but irresistible, for individual taxpayers rarely offer determined resistance to the special-interest groups that surround every legislative body. At the very least, however, politicians have an obligation to ensure that public funds are spent only for the purpose for which they were appropriated. Alternative methods of delivering public services should be used to avoid the abuses that are so common when bureaucracies pursue their own interests at public expense.

XIII. Tax-Funded Unionism: The Politics of Unemployment

> Every piece of social welfare legislation enacted in the last two decades carries a union label.
>
> —George Meany
> *AFL-CIO News*

> We've got the finest political organization in the country right now in the AFL-CIO.
>
> —George Meany
> *Washington Daily News*

The academic literature in the fields of labor relations and labor economics, as well as the popular press, have given far more attention to the economic goals and effects of U.S. unionism than to its political dimensions. This is partly because U.S. unions are less directly involved in political activity than unions elsewhere, particularly in western Europe. Unions, for example, have never successfully sponsored a political party in the United States. Nevertheless, we cannot escape the fact that all unions are inherently political organizations. If unions are successful in attaining even some of their economic goals, their gains must be protected from market forces that would erode them, and U.S. unions inevitably seek that protection through government intervention. Moreover, unions have found that they can use their political clout to obtain hundreds of millions of taxpayers' dollars each year to foster union activities, primarily organizing workers to offset the precipitous decline in union membership that has occurred since the 1950s. Because many taxpayers and voters would object to making direct grants to labor unions for organizing and political activities, the transfer of these funds is carefully disguised by using grants and contracts under government programs to reduce unemployment and to promote worker safety. Few groups in the private sector have been as successful as labor unions in raiding the public purse.

335

The Political Imperatives of American Unions

Economists have produced a vast amount of research demonstrating that on average, the wage rates of unionized employees are considerably higher than those of nonunion employees. This literature has been reviewed elsewhere, and it is sufficient to note here that estimates of the union-nonunion wage differential are as high as 60 percent, although the differential varies over time and across industries, sexes, races, and occupations.[1] When the union wage is far above the nonunion rate and when labor costs are a significant component of total production costs, the union's success can create a major threat for both the company and the union. When there is an ample supply of nonunion employees who are able and willing to perform the same work for a lower market wage rate, the threat of competition from alternative sources of supply is very real. Entrepreneurs in search of profits would view this set of circumstances as an excellent opportunity to enter the market with nonunion labor at lower cost, which could drive the company out of business by offering lower prices to consumers. The union would disappear, and so would the jobs.

The union and the company have a very real common interest: the survival of the firm. Any threat to the financial health of the company is a direct threat to the union. Both parties are vitally interested in keeping competitors out of the market, a difficult task when nonunion labor is available and when there are few barriers to entry by new firms. The union and the company, therefore, must cooperate to ensure their mutual survival, and the protection of government is sought in the political arena to reduce, and if possible to eliminate, the threat of competition from nonunion firms.

The competitive environment in which a company and its union operate greatly influences the political tactics they adopt to control competition in the market by restricting entry and output. There is a vast difference between the market for goods and products and the market for services. Competition for services is limited almost exclusively to domestic producers. It is usually prohibitively costly for workers in foreign countries to deliver services in the United States (for example, to educate students or to provide health care); however, for tangible goods, such as steel, textiles and apparel, and automobiles, employees abroad can produce goods at wage rates prevailing in those countries and ship them to the United States. Companies producing goods must compete on a worldwide basis, whereas companies providing services must compete only against other domestic producers. The distinction is critical, for it dictates that different political strategies in seeking government protection from lower-cost competitors must be pursued by those companies and unions that produce goods and those that produce services. Protectionism is sought to reduce foreign competition, whereas licensing, franchise arrangements, and other forms of government regulation are sought to limit domestic competition.[2] In both cases, however, the primary objective is the long-term survival of the company and its union.

Labor unions actively participate in politics primarily to extend and to prevent the erosion of the special privileges that government has granted to protect them from competition and to obtain funds from taxpayers that can be used for union purposes. From the perspective of union leaders, candidates who are sympathetic to union goals must be elected to office and resources must be available for lobbying for the special-interest legislation that is so essential to organized labor. The political activities of labor unions are well known and have been documented and need no further elaboration here.[3] What has not been publicized is the extent to which taxpayers are supporting the political and other goals of union leaders.

From 1977 to 1982 taxpayers provided in excess of $161.7 million dollars in support of organized labor through grants and contracts, primarily from the U.S. Department of Labor (see Table A13.1, in appendix). Although some of the funds were awarded during the late 1970s, most were for activities conducted in the early 1980s. There are a number of reasons to believe that our tabulation of taxpayer funding to labor unions grossly understates the actual amounts involved. First, our listing is admittedly incomplete: Time and resources prevented more than a cursory accounting of all federal grants to unions. Second, additional tens of millions of dollars were undoubtedly obtained from state and local governments: A number of federal programs provide funds to state and local government entities, particularly for job creation and training of the unemployed, and unions have been extremely adept at capturing these funds. Third, some grants are difficult to trace because unions have created fronts, such as the Human Resources Development Institute, which they control and use solely for the purpose of obtaining taxpayers' funds. Finally, labor unions have carefully cultivated other groups, such as the National Council of Senior Citizens, and have obtained tens of millions of dollars each year

337

from all levels of government to support these union-dominated groups that may appear to have very little to do with labor unions (see chapter 11). These groups play a critical role for unions by providing a vehicle for obtaining vast amounts of taxpayers' dollars, which may then be used to further union leaders' political and social goals.

It is clear from the data that the Department of Labor is a conduit for transferring millions of taxpayers' dollars each year to organized labor (see Table A13.1). Unions have also successfully approached other agencies for tax dollars, but the bulk of the money comes from the Department of Labor for employment and training purposes. Union leaders have turned the unemployment issue into a gold mine. It is no surprise that unions have made every effort to oppose the Reagan administration's budget cuts through editorials, rallies, and extensive lobbying because a reduction in federal spending could endanger the funds that unions and their affiliated organizations have come to expect.

Promoting Unionism with Tax Dollars: Profiting from Unemployment

Labor unions have always advocated and lobbied for increased government transfers and subsidies, not only for the unemployed but also for welfare recipients, farmers, and a host of other special-interest groups. In part, their interest in expanded programs that transfer resources from employed to unemployed workers is based on the belief that such programs "serve to mollify people who are unemployed or partly employed and keep them from invading the industrial labor market and bidding against employed labor union members."[4] The incentive for union support for farm subsidies that raise the price of food for all consumers, including union members, is the "competitive threat of the rural population pressing in upon the industrial workers who through forcibly elevated wage rates have already priced many of their workers into unemployment."[5] In effect, the taxpayers should subsidize farmers so they will stay on the farms and subsidize the unemployed so they in turn will remain out of work rather than compete for jobs with employed union members who pay dues. Union leaders have also strongly advocated government-funded job training and job creation programs, for such programs offer employment opportunities for potential union members and a source of revenue for the unions.

Federal efforts at job creation can be traced to the Great Depres-

338

sion. In November 1933, President Roosevelt inaugurated the Civil Works Administration to place the unemployed on the federal payroll—a program that has been described as "politicians banging on a tin pan"[6]—but the program was abandoned less than four months later because it was ineffective and expensive. The second federal attempt to reduce unemployment was the Works Progress Administration (WPA), which began in 1935 and continued throughout the rest of the 1930s. More individuals were enrolled in work relief efforts in 1938 than in any preceding year, and the unemployment rate was higher in 1939 than in 1931, two years after the stock market crash. Evidently, federal programs did little to alleviate the problems of the unemployed during the 1930s; it was World War II that finally brought the economy out of the doldrums.

Political efforts to combat unemployment resurfaced when President Kennedy signed the Area Redevelopment Act (ARA) on May 1, 1961. This act established the Area Redevelopment Administration in the Department of Commerce to aid "depressed areas" with grants and loans and with funds for training the unemployed. In that same year the Youth Employment Opportunities Act provided jobs for 21,800 unemployed youth in an effort to combat teenage unemployment, which had reached crisis proportions, largely because of the minimum-wage law that labor unions had long championed.[7] In 1962 Congress passed the Manpower Development and Training Act (MDTA), which was designed to retrain workers displaced by technological advances by giving them classroom instruction, remedial education, on-the-job training, and job placement. Eventually, the scope of the program was broadened to include the economically disadvantaged, minorities, and unemployed youth. Under MDTA, training was offered for such occupations as waiter, waitress, dishwasher, and hot-air balloonist. Concern about the unemployed reached new heights when, in 1964, President Johnson initiated the War on Poverty and established the Job Corps, which was to provide the vehicle for moving poor youth into the middle class through job training. This program was followed in 1965 by enactment of the Neighborhood Youth Corps, a program for urban teenagers that was to reduce the rate of high school dropouts and to provide work experience.

Despite the proliferation of programs and mounting costs, there was no significant decline in unemployment. So, in 1971, the Emergency Employment Act was passed to increase the number of employees in state and local government. Even Congress found the

339

federal efforts at training and job creation confusing, and to remedy the apparent deficiencies—unemployment remained stubbornly high—the Comprehensive Employment and Training Act (CETA) was passed in 1973. Congress appropriated billions of dollars for training, job placement, and job creation, but with little result. In an article in the *Washington Post* in 1979, John Berry and Art Pine examined federal efforts to aid the unemployed:

> Over the past 19 years, the United States has spent $85.8 billion on programs to train the poor and "hardcore" unemployed and fit them into today's job market.
>
> By almost all accounts, that effort has been a bust.
>
> For all the outpouring of federal, state and local money over the years, there are few experts, even among those who support the current round of programs, who claim that they have been effective—other than to provide income for the recipients.
>
> Moreover, despite the massive investment—$15 billion in the current fiscal year alone—experts still don't know such basics as which kind of programs work best, what impact they have over the long run and what changes, if any, to make for the future.[8]

Berry and Pine made this pessimistic prediction: "[I]f the government doubled all its current outlays for employment and training programs, it 'might' lower the jobless rate in five years by 0.2 to 0.3 percentage points—if the expansion were managed efficiently."[9] The implications of this statement are ominous, as can be illustrated by some simple arithmetic. If government spending on all job-related programs were to double, the amount allocated for 1979 for this purpose would be about $30 billion; over a five-year period, the total spent would amount to $150 billion. If the unemployment rate were lowered by 0.3 percent from, say, 8 percent to 7.7 percent, the number of jobs created (assuming the number of individuals in the labor force to be 110 million) would be about 330,000. Thus, it would cost the taxpayers more than $450,000 to create each job, and this figure is optimistic because it is assumed that the programs are managed efficiently—a highly dubious assumption given government experience with jobs programs.

Numerous studies have found federal employment programs to be costly, ineffective, and filled with corruption and patronage. For example, the General Accounting Office has issued many reports citing program abuse and questionable practices.[10] Consider the Job Corps:

Despite a big advertising campaign and kickbacks to recruiters, the Job Corps could not meet its 1968 recruitment goals. And of those who were enrolled, the GAO found that 22 percent were ineligible for one reason or another. Its results were no more impressive. Of 326 Corps members who left the program in 1967 and were reported to be employed immediately thereafter, a GAO survey one year after of reported employers found that 22 percent indicated that the Job Corps terminee had never worked for them. Of the remaining 282, 211, or 75 percent, had left their jobs. Only 71 of the 362 reported employed were still working at their first job. And only 25 percent of employed terminees were working in areas in which they had received training. The GAO found that one Job Corps center listed its terminees as employed solely by confirming that they had an interview scheduled.

In 1979, the GAO reported that the Job Corps was still failing, and still masking its failure with statistical buncombe. For the mid-1970s the Corps claimed a placement rate of 90 percent of terminees; but the GAO found that, for 1975, "only 36% of those youths who had been in Jobs Corps at least 30 days were placed." For 1972 Job Corps participants, those who dropped out after thirty days or less earned more on the average in 1976 ($2,027) than those who stayed in between one and six months ($1,896).[11]

Other federal programs presented similar problems. During one twelve-month period in 1978–79, for instance, a crackdown on misuse of CETA funds produced 67 indictments and 24 convictions.[12] Cities that received funds to create jobs in the public sector simply placed many of their regular employees on the federal payroll, courtesy of CETA. At one time, CETA workers made up more than one-fourth of the city hall work force in Hartford, Connecticut, and one-third of that in Buffalo, New York.[13] Furthermore, when patronage positions were paid from CETA funds, the pay scales could be generous: "56 CETA recipients on the . . . payroll averaged $18,000 a year for jobs that paid only $8,751 in other government agencies."[14]

Studies of federal job-creation programs have shown that one reason for program failure has been that only a fraction of the funds allocated for employment ended up in employment budgets. Edward Gramlich has estimated that only 45 percent of annual federal grant dollars went for employment purposes.[15] Ronald Ehrenberg has demonstrated that for the years 1958–62 and 1965–69, only 22 percent of the additional federal funds appropriated for job-creation programs actually appeared in employment budgets.[16] Other analyses have reported that only between 6 and 9 percent of federal grant dollars end up in the wage bill.[17] These observations are not surprising in light of the findings reported in earlier chapters of this book.

When the federal government initiates a program that provides funds for some purpose, special-interest groups immediately form and attempt to gain control over the money and to use it for their own purposes. These groups include the bureaucracy that distributes the grants, the grant recipients, the trainers and recruiters for the programs, those who "evaluate" the "impact" of the programs, and so forth. There is an entire industry that is dependent on the plight of the unemployed (similar in every respect to that which thrives on the plight of the poor), which is used as the primary rationale for diverting taxpayers' dollars to those who benefit from unemployment. The unemployment industry is politically powerful and also, thanks to politicians who generously distribute the taxpayers' money, well financed. Thus, even though federal jobs programs have and will continue to fail, the appropriations continue to be disbursed.

Federal job-creation programs are really nothing more than a shell game. The federal government cannot create anything; all it can do is take something from one group and give it to another. When jobs programs are enacted, taxpayers must finance them, which often leads to an increase in taxes. An increase in taxes reduces the amount of income that taxpayers have available to spend on goods and services, so the demand for goods and services falls and employment in the private sector is reduced. In this way, tax-supported federal jobs programs must create unemployment in the private sector. Even if the funds are obtained through deficit spending, the same result occurs, albeit in a more subtle and indirect way. Public-sector jobs are created at the expense of jobs in the private sector, and for this reason government jobs programs can never solve the nation's unemployment problem. Politicians prefer jobs programs to other potential solutions because the groups that benefit are more politically active and influential than those who pay for the programs. Viewed in this way, federal tinkering in the job market is a way for politicians to use the unemployed as an excuse for transferring taxpayers' funds to their political allies.

Developing Human (or Union?) Resources[18]

The billions of tax dollars allocated to ease the nation's unemployment ills through CETA and other so called jobs programs have been a major temptation for labor unions as their membership and revenue base continues to erode. To avoid the criticism that could be expected if grants were made to unions directly, the AFL-CIO set up a front organization, the Human Resources Development Institute (HRDI), which was incorporated in Delaware in 1968. Who would criticize an organization devoted to "developing human resources?" But there has been little distinction to be found between HRDI and the AFL-CIO. HRDI officers and members of the HRDI board of trustees have all been prominent union leaders: the late George Meany was board chairman, and other members included Lane Kirkland, Glenn E. Watts (Communications Workers of America), Martin Ward (plumbers union), Lloyd McBride (United Steelworkers of America), John H. Lyons (ironworkers union), and other union presidents. The HRDI president, Alan Kistler, was AFL-CIO director of organization and field services; the secretary-treasurer, William Collins, was comptroller of the AFL-CIO; Michael M. Arnold, who became the executive director in 1979, had been active in the bricklayers union for 22 years and had held other HRDI posts as well.[19] Moreover, HRDI's national headquarters office has been located at 815 16th Street, NW, Washington, D.C., the building that houses AFL-CIO headquarters. HRDI has the AFL-CIO logo on its stationery and publications. HRDI employees have used the same credit union, computer facilities, and accounting systems as AFL-CIO employees. Any questions about HRDI's links to organized labor can be answered by the brochure entitled *Human Resources Development Institute: Manpower Arm of the AFL-CIO*, which states that

> HRDI is an integral part of the American labor movement and works closely with international unions, state and local labor councils, local unions, and with the AFL-CIO's trade and service departments. HRDI's national office is in the AFL-CIO headquarters building in Washington, D.C. Its field staff—men and women drawn from the ranks of experienced unionists—are located in some sixty U.S. cities and work closely with government, business and community groups in developing our human resources. HRDI helps the nation's workers and potential workers in many ways:
>
> HRDI staff assist unions and management in developing and implementing programs to train or upgrade workers for specific job opportunities.
>
> HRDI staff advise both unions and employers on how they can

utilize training programs to meet specific needs of a plant or industry.

HRDI staff serve as a link between organized labor and government in the implementation of the Comprehensive Training and Employment Act (CETA).

HRDI staff advise organized labor's representatives who serve on state and local manpower planning councils how to develop and maintain programs that effectively meet local training and employment needs.

HRDI staff, through their close contacts with local unions and employers, develop information on job openings and provide placement services to persons seeking work.

HRDI operates special programs for veterans, Native Americans, handicapped persons, performing artists, and other groups with exceptional employment problems.[20]

The above listing clearly emphasizes aid to unions rather than aid to individual workers seeking employment opportunities or training.

HRDI has been funded with federal tax dollars, primarily through the Department of Labor, the Department of Health, Education and Welfare, and the Department of Education. Although a complete listing of grants and contracts to HRDI could not be obtained, the following is a partial listing of Department of Labor grants—totaling $31,968,830—that HRDI received between 1979 and 1983:

Contract Number	Amount ($)
99-0-264-33-54	448,285
99-0-264-42-10	15,888,626
99-0-264-42-05	1,745,119
99-9-264-32-03	350,000
99-6-264-42-04	5,138,930
99-9-264-42-12	6,997,870
99-3-264-98-21	1,400,000

Tax dollars have supported the national headquarters of HRDI, 7 regional offices, and as many as 65 field offices. HRDI was so dependent on CETA funding that when the Reagan administration ended the program, the number of HRDI field offices was reduced to 12.[21]

HRDI's primary goal has been to obtain tax dollars for local unions

344

and other union organizations, an objective mandated by the AFL-CIO leadership:

> The 1977 AFL-CIO convention called on the local HRDI staff to provide technical assistance to local unions and other organizations which wish to receive federal funds to operate employment and skill training programs designed to benefit unemployed and disadvantaged groups and individuals.

> In 1978 alone, HRDI local representatives were responsible for the development of 410 funded programs nationwide—totaling $30,037,398 and mostly funded through CETA—on behalf of local unions or labor organizations.[22]

Thus, in addition to getting federal dollars for its own operations and programs, HRDI has played a major role in obtaining additional millions of dollars each year for other union organizations:

> HRDI continues to assist interested local unions and other labor organizations to obtain federal funds to operate employment and training programs. Between January 1980 and April 1981, HRDI helped obtain funding for 396 programs. . . . Altogether, over $27.7 million in federal funds went to unions and other groups as a result of HRDI's program development efforts.[23]

HRDI also has provided technical expertise to local unions and other labor organizations with regard to the CETA program. The CETA program was executed at the state and local levels of government through federal grants to prime sponsors, that is, states, counties, and municipalities with populations of at least 100,000. Each prime sponsor developed an annual plan with the advice of the state or local CETA planning council showing how the funds were to be used, and regulations required that every CETA planning council have union representatives. HRDI emphasized to local units of organized labor that "it is important for organized labor to take full advantage of the CETA planning system. In this way, labor can help channel CETA money into programs that are in the interests of both labor [that is, unions] and the community at large."[24] HRDI noted that CETA permitted unions to "create jobs for laid-off members, retrain members with outdated skills, prepare young people for entry into union jobs or apprenticeship programs, and bring unemployed men and women into good union positions."[25] In effect, tax funds were to be used to provide services specifically to union members or prospective members. To ensure that CETA funds were used to increase union membership, HRDI "provided on-site assistance to labor organizations throughout the country . . . and it assisted state and local labor organizations with the nomination of labor representatives to new planning councils, providing technical services to the labor appointees."[26] Apparently, the issue of conflict of interest was never raised, even though having union representatives on committees that made funding decisions about grants to union organizations was a blatant conflict of interest.

HRDI has taken its role as adviser to unions very seriously:

> Between January 1978 and April 1979, HRDI local representatives provided technical assistance to organized labor on 3,616 occasions. The assistance varied in each instance and ranges from helping local unions understand government regulations covering employment and training programs, to helping unions protect against abuses of CETA rules that might adversely affect the union.
>
> As part of its core contract, HRDI received funds from the Department of Labor to provide technical assistance to organized labor. . . .[27]
>
> HRDI has increased its efforts in technical assistance services to help assure the effective implementation of CETA's labor standards. From January 1980 through April 1981, HRDI rendered technical assistance services to labor organizations on 6,012 occasions to representatives of organized labor who serve on state or local prime sponsor planning councils.[28]

CETA was replaced by the Job Training Partnership Act (JTPA), which was passed in October 1982 and which became fully effective on October 1, 1983. The title of the legislation was different and the level of funding was lower for JTPA than for CETA, but the role of HRDI and the unions remained the same. "Recognizing labor's opportunities to influence state and local training policies under the new act, the AFL-CIO Executive Council in February 1983 gave HRDI a strong mandate to help labor organizations assume an active role in the implementation of JTPA in their communities."[29] HRDI's assistance included the "nomination of labor representatives to new planning councils [and] providing technical services to the labor appointees."[30] The funding of unions carried out under CETA was continued under JTPA; nothing of substance was altered.

The scope of HRDI's activities is very broad, encompassing a bewildering range of programs catering to a wide variety of special-interest groups. But there is a common theme to all HRDI programs:

346

The emphasis is not on assisting individual workers to improve their training and to find jobs, but on promoting unionism and assisting unions to obtain members. Consider the following examples.

Job Development and Placement. Federal programs emphasize the creation of new jobs and the placement of disadvantaged workers in these jobs. No provision in the law requires that the new jobs be created solely at unionized firms. HRDI and the labor groups that it assisted, however, always stressed the importance of work in a union environment. Literature describing HRDI's job development and placement efforts specifically states: "By developing jobs covered by union contracts, HRDI usually assists the disadvantaged worker in obtaining higher wages and better working conditions."[31]

Large amounts of federal money were available for the training and job placement of the handicapped or disabled. HRDI and local unions actively sought these funds as a means of increasing the membership of organized labor, as is indicated by the title of one of HRDI's brochures: *Opening doors for the disabled . . . to good union jobs.*[32] The brochure describes "How Unions Are Helping the Disabled":

> Unions recognize the capabilities of many disabled people to master a trade. Unions work cooperatively with employers to help the disabled make new strides in employment and develop work skill.
>
> With union support, creative training and worksite accommodations are helping bring handicapped workers into union jobs and training programs.
>
> Some unions have helped revise physical requirements so disabled workers can qualify for apprenticeship—without reducing the high training standards that are the hallmark of the apprenticeship system.
>
> Other unions have developed agreements with management to make worksites, tools, and equipment accessible to disabled workers.
>
> These kinds of activities make the most of union expertise on behalf of handicapped workers, including union members.[33]

The brochure gives no indication whatever that the services provided to the disabled by the unions were financed by the taxpayers. An uninformed reader would naturally assume that organized labor has a compassionate concern for the handicapped and is devoting its own resources to address the employment problems of the disabled: "The AFL-CIO Human Resources Development Institute is working to realize labor's goal of good [that is, union] jobs for the disabled."[34]

The proposals that HRDI submitted in search of funding clearly reveal that emphasis was to be given to placing the handicapped in union jobs. In April 1979 HRDI submitted a proposal to the Virginia State Vocational Rehabilitation Department entitled "To Provide the Handicapped With On-The-Job Training," which stated: "A major effort will be to place handicapped persons into union jobs that will pay union wages, provide fringe benefits, union membership and job security after the o-j-t has ended."[35] The proposal also noted that "the majority of HRDI's placements have been in union jobs."[36]

Federal contracts also openly stipulated that placements were to be primarily in unionized firms. Vince Moretti, the coordinator of handicapped programs at HRDI headquarters, sent a memorandum about union placements to all handicapped placement staff on August 21, 1978, stating: "The H.E.W. and D.O.L. contracts both emphasize the importance of our commitment to placing clients in union positions. I fully realize that every effort is being made to direct a great portion of your activities in this area and we are hopeful that the placements in the union column will continue to increase."[37] HRDI headquarters staff instructed the placement specialists that "all contacts are to be 100% union involved. This means only union representatives and union companies be contacted and all phases of development and placement be confined to this area."[38] Other programs that are directed by HRDI and local unions also stress the role of unionism.

Youth Programs. In the brochure *HRDI Helping Youth,* training programs have been described as being operated exclusively by unions:

> HRDI works with labor organizations to develop training programs that give young people marketable skills. Some of these are training programs sponsored and operated by the union itself. HRDI helps labor groups make use of federal funds for many of these programs. The participation of organized labor in these programs contributes to their relevance.[39]

The principal criterion for judging the "relevance" of HRDI's youth efforts has been whether or not they served the goals of the unions involved. A memorandum from HRDI headquarters about the Norfolk, Virginia, youth program emphasized that "this is a trade union program and . . . there have to be close ties to the local unions representing employers where enrollees are placed or efforts are being made to place them."[40]

In April 1979 HRDI received a grant from the Department of Labor for a pilot program to help train about 245 disadvantaged high school students in seven cities. Training was only one aspect of the grant: "Besides serving these young people, a goal of the pilot program is to demonstrate that active union involvement in summer youth programs will lead to better program results than when unions are not involved."[41] Thus, it was a forgone conclusion that "active union involvement" produced "better results" in youth training. There was also time for a little indoctrination: "The program will explain union membership [to the youth]."[42]

HRDI and the local unions participating in CETA and other federal, state, and local government programs always reported to the sponsoring agencies that their efforts at training and job development had been huge successes, even though the billions of taxpayers' dollars spent on these activities did not markedly reduce the unemployment rate. The claims were vastly overstated. A former employee of the HRDI office in Norfolk, for example, has testified that it was standard operating procedure to claim multiple credits for each client served. For example, a handicapped, black female under 18 years of age with a criminal record would be claimed as a placement credit under at least five different programs (disabled, minority, female, youth, offender). The record would appear to indicate that five separate jobs had been created for five different individuals, even though only one person had been placed in one job.[43]

Other Programs. HRDI and other union organizations participated in numerous other programs that received funding from federal, state, and local governments, and each program stressed the placement of workers in firms covered by collective bargaining agreements. For example, in providing aid to ex-offenders, "HRDI assists released prisoners to find jobs in unionized plants."[44] Similar statements apply to HRDI programs for Navajo Indians, veterans, women, building trades training, and artists.[45]

The principal goal of all HRDI and related programs is to provide

349

revenues and employment for unions and increasing the membership rolls of organized labor. Unions have missed no opportunity to obtain funds from the taxpayers to finance their operations and objectives. Consider the use of "cultural activities" for organizing purposes.

Federal Funding of Union Organizing: Cloaking Unionism in Culture

Although it is illegal to use federal funds to promote unionization, District 1199, National Union of Hospital and Health Care Employees, in New York City developed a unique program to disguise the promotion of unionism as culture. In January 1979 District 1199 began its Bread and Roses program, purportedly to bring culture to its members. The title of the project was adopted from a slogan used in 1912 by striking textile workers in Lawrence, Massachusetts, who carried banners proclaiming "We Want Bread and Roses, Too." Rachel Cowan of the *Village Voice* described District 1199 and the Bread and Roses programs as follows:

> District 1199 has become the darling of the endowments and a model for other trade unions. Yet the cultural vision that informs Bread and Roses is linked tightly to the politics that previously set 1199 on the radical fringe of the American labor movement and in frequent opposition to the government. Underlying both is a strong commitment to racial and economic justice.[46]

Having packaged the project as culture, District 1199 initially sought and received $300,000 from the National Endowment for the Humanities (NEH), $80,000 from the National Endowment for the Arts, $28,000 from the New York State Council on the Arts, and $14,000 from the New York Council for the Humanities—all tax-funded organizations—as well as additional funds from private sources.[47] With a total budget of $1.3 million, District 1199 launched a series of cultural events, including drama, music, and poetry readings at some 30 hospitals where union members work, art exhibitions, a Labor Day celebration, posters, concerts, and books. Without exception, these events and materials have encouraged unionization and supported organizing activities; far more than cultural education has been involved. For example, part of the funds was used to entertain and boost the morale of striking nurses. The *AFL-CIO News* for May 8, 1982, printed a picture of a musical revue with the caption "Musical revue brought picket line relief for 2,000 members of District 1199 who had been on strike for 27 days in support of 78 registered nurses before a settlement was reached with Long Island Jewish Medical Center in New Hyde Park, N.Y. The performance was provided by the union's continuing Bread and Roses program."

The publications produced for Bread and Roses also actively advocate unionism. For example, Georgeen Comerford's *1199: A Family Portrait—Photographs of Hospital Workers,* a collection of photographs published as part of the program using NEH grants, includes two photos of union organizers (pp. 20, 26), and a photo of "1199ers and mass rally" (p. 27), but it omits any depiction of nonunion hospital employees, such as the administrative staff, and no mention is made of physicians and surgeons.[48] The introduction to the book reads: "At a time when funds for social services are being constricted, her [Comerford's] images [emphasizing unionization] will insure that we will no longer look upon hospital jobs as expendable budget items."[49]

Another book, *One Strong Voice . . . Or an Out of Tune Chorus?,* is a pictorial history of the development of the nursing profession, with much emphasis on the importance of the "collective struggle."[50] For example, "The private duty experience also left nurses with almost no legacy of collective struggle over working conditions nor any experiences with forming on-going alliances with other health workers."[51] The book concludes with the admonition that

> women health workers can use their strength, their numbers, and the part of their long history of struggling for dignity on the job and for decent patient care, to be ONE STRONG VOICE in the health sector. This history does suggest that if women health workers retreat from struggles over working conditions, staffing, or how care is to be determined, or let administrators use only the dollar yardstick, the search for meaningful work and for decent health care will be endless.[52]

In a similar vein, *Lawrence 1912: The Bread and Roses Strike* is an illustrated history of the textile workers' strike. The opportunity is not lost, however, to relate the past to the current difficulties facing unions. In the preface, Sol Stetin, senior executive vice president of the Amalgamated Clothing and Textile Workers Union (ACTWU), writes that

> when clubs and bullets failed to defeat the workers' determination to join the Textile Workers Union of America in the 1930's and

40's the industry resorted to its ultimate weapon, moving South where unions were weak and wages low.

Since 1933, I have had the privilege of participating in the historic struggle of America's textile workers to organize. At no time in that period has there been a brighter outlook for textile unionism. Thanks to the courage and determination of textile workers throughout America and Canada, we're on the verge of a breakthrough in our campaign to organize the giant J. P. Stevens Company.

The Stevens workers have demonstrated that the spirit of Lawrence lives on. In 1912, textile workers in Lawrence demanded "Bread and Roses Too"—not just better wages, but a return of their human dignity. The 500,000 members of ACTWU have pledged themselves to struggle, until the dream of the Lawrence strikers of 1912 becomes a reality.[53]

In the text it is argued that the South can become a "second Lawrence" because ACTWU has made the "towns to which the mill owners fled" no longer "safe havens." The "battle" for the unionization of J. P. Stevens will be "time consuming—as was Cesar Chavez' fight to organize the Farmworkers," and will involve "a nationwide boycott"; the Stevens campaign and the revival of interest in the Lawrence strike, however, make it "possible for America to believe, once again, that economic justice is a goal that can be achieved."[54]

"Justice" is a matter of great concern to union officials, who are convinced that it can be achieved only through unionization. "The Working American," an art exhibition shown by District 1199 at its headquarters as part of Bread and Roses and taken on tour to six major cities through the auspices of the Smithsonian Institution, was also reproduced as a book. The book's foreword was written by Moe Foner, project director of Bread and Roses and executive secretary of District 1199. He concluded:

Our Union has blazed many trails in the past. We dared to undertake the task of organizing low-paid, minority group hospital workers who, until 1959, were considered unorganizable. We committed ourselves fully in the civil rights movement and the struggle to end the Vietnam war. We see our current effort in the cultural field as a logical extension of our long-standing commitment to help build an America where we can *all* have bread—and roses, too.[55]

Part of the cultural package assembled by District 1199 included conferences on several topics, including health care. At one conclave, Princeton economist Uwe Reinhardt advocated the need for national health insurance and condemned the high incomes earned by physicians.[56] Other Bread and Roses activities included having luminaries visit and present their views of the activities. Jane Fonda, after her tour of the art gallery, commented that "Bread and Roses is an exciting use of culture to further the struggles of working people."[57] Gloria Steinem asserted that the Bread and Roses program "will inspire female and minority workers . . . the organizing wave of the future."[58] Among others participating in Bread and Roses activities were Harry Belafonte, Ossie Davis, Sam Levenson, Andrew Young, Coretta Scott King, and Ricardo Montalban.

Pro-union propaganda was stressed at discussions held after films or lectures. A "discussion guide and fact sheet," prepared by District 1199 for use in conjunction with *Rise Gonna Rise*, a pictorial history of southern textile workers, includes so-called facts about labor unions, such as the geographical concentration of membership, and offers a number of opinions, such as that "in part to avoid unions, corporations often close their northern plants and move their business to the South."[59] There are also some purported facts about J. P. Stevens & Company and ACTWU's organizing difficulties at the company's facilities, followed by a series of discussion questions, including "A. Should workers have unions? Why? B. Would you like to be a textile worker in the South? C. Are workers today proud of the jobs they have? Should they be?"[60]

In none of the materials developed for the Bread and Roses series is the dark side of unionism shown. The strike is glorified in posters and books, but there is no mention made of the strike-related violence that union members often direct at nonunion workers. In their extensive study of union violence, Armand Thieblot and Thomas Haggard have found that, after adjusting for size of membership, the National Union of Hospital and Health Care Employees is the second most violent union, with 5.7 incidents per 10,000 members; the United Mine Workers of America is the worst offender.[61] It is also evident in HRDI materials that are made to educate participants about the potential costs of unionization. Information about union activities, however, is made readily available:

> Up to date information on two labor-initiated boycott campaigns was available at booths staffed by representatives of the United

Farm Workers and the Amalgamated Clothing and Textile Workers Union. The Farm Workers signed up 150 persons who volunteered to help in its boycott campaign against California-grown iceberg lettuce. The Amalgamated publicized its boycott drive against products made by textile giant J. P. Stevens, which continues to violate Federal laws in its effort to prevent unionization of its plants.[62]

The Bread and Roses project was considered to be such a success by District 1199 officials that a book, *Our Own Show: Organizing Cultural Programs for Working People,* was prepared using funding from the Department of Labor and other sources to instruct other unions about forming their own cultural programs. One of the benefits cited for such activities is that "farm workers, J. P. Stevens textile workers, poultry workers, and others involved in difficult union organizing battles had a chance to publicize their struggles."[63] The project director also makes it clear that far more than exposure to culture is at stake: "Cultural programs, we have found, provide our members with both entertainment and education while creating a new enthusiasm for union involvement, and that is enough to make cultural activities worthwhile for any union."[64]

From the perspective of District 1199, cultural programs are especially worthwhile if much of the cost can be passed on to the taxpayers:

> At both the national and state levels, government agencies have been established to provide funds for cultural programs. Labor's ability to influence these agencies to give money to programs for working people varies from state to state and may depend on who is in charge of the agencies at a particular time. But since these public funding sources are financed with workers' tax dollars, workers have every right to expect to be served by them.[65]

The logic in this statement is seriously flawed. While it is true that public funding sources are financed with workers' tax dollars, it is also true that businesses pay substantial sums to all levels of government. Moreover, only a small proportion of U.S. workers are union members or even can be shown to benefit from the existence of unions. Overall, unionists contribute only a small proportion of total tax revenues. Further, it is not clear that even all union members benefit from these so-called cultural activities. Indeed, if the acquisition of culture were essential to the life-style of union mem-

354

bers, it would be logical for unions to finance cultural programs from dues collected from members, rather than seek taxpayer funding. It is interesting that nonunion workers do not seem to have the same craving for or claim to culture that union leaders believe their own members deserve and need.

Union determination to obtain tax funds for cultural programs is shown by the AFL-CIO's establishment of the Labor Institute for Human Enrichment, which is to "assist unions in participating in state arts and humanities councils which give grants to support cultural programs."[66] NEH, to assist the unions, established a "Labor Liaison" to facilitate the processing of grant applications prepared by unions.

Funds received from tax-supported state arts and humanities councils have been used for purposes that would be difficult to describe as cultural. For example, the Virginia AFL-CIO received funds for a series of discussion sessions on such topics as plant closings, job safety and health, and women and minorities in the work force; in Delaware, the AFL-CIO Community Services Department obtained state tax funds to finance a discussion series on retirement; and in Hawaii, Local 142 of the International Longshoremen's Association held tax-funded meetings to discuss programs for developing housing for workers.[67] These activities may be of vital interest to union leaders and their members, but it seems farfetched to package such issues as culture in order to obtain taxpayers' funds to support them. Union dues that supposedly pay for the services that unions purportedly provide their members should be spent for such purposes. To the extent that tax funds can be obtained to provide services for union members, the dues revenue that unions collect are then freed for other uses, including political activity.

Some organizations that obtain federal funds or other resources from taxpayers also engage in union organizing without making any effort to disguise this illegal activity. The Domestic Volunteer Service Act (Section 404) specifically prohibits individuals in the VISTA program from engaging in union organizing, and it prohibits funds appropriated under the act from being used "directly or indirectly" for such purposes. In September 1977, however, ACTION arranged a grant for nearly $500,000 to place 80 VISTA volunteers with the Association of Community Organizations for Reform Now (ACORN).[68] At the October meeting of ACORN's executive board, a motion to organize a union of household workers in New Orleans was unanimously approved; the Household Workers Organizing Committee was established and it subsequently shared space in the building that ACORN occupied in New Orleans. An ostensibly separate organization was created, the United Labor Organizations, that was theoretically independent of ACORN but that was also housed in the same New Orleans building as ACORN. Five VISTA volunteers worked actively with the Household Workers Organizing Committee for several years, until ACTION's Office of Compliance finally directed that the assignments be terminated.[69]

Conclusions

In 1961 the federal government began to appropriate tax dollars for job placement and training for the unemployed. After more than two decades of increasing federal expenditures to reduce unemployment, however, there is no evidence that these efforts have worked. Rather, the programs have destroyed jobs in the private sector and have been riddled with corruption and abuse.[70] Even though the unemployed have not benefited from the taxpayers' dollars allocated for their use, labor unions have been able to manipulate the programs to obtain hundreds of millions of such dollars to finance their own objectives in at least six ways. First, unions have used the funds to employ their own members as placement specialists and trainers so that federal jobs programs have provided employment for unionists. Second, the federal, state, and local government grants for jobs programs have permitted unions to use tax dollars to pay part of the overhead costs of their activities. In the absence of taxpayer funding, the overhead would have to come from revenues collected from members. By having the taxpayers pick up some of the expenses of union operations, at least part of the unions' dues income has been freed for other purposes, including political activity. Third, by directing their job placement efforts to firms with collective bargaining agreements, unions involved in federal jobs programs have been able to recruit members to offset the continuing decline in their membership. Fourth, CETA regulations permitted private, nonprofit contractors to hire unemployed workers at the taxpayers' expense, so that unions could pay some of their staff courtesy of the taxpayers (although there are no data on the extent to which this has occurred). Fifth, union-directed training and placement programs have offered an excellent opportunity for promoting unionism and educating the unemployed about union membership. Finally, taxpayers' funds have been used to

356

assist union members to retrain and find alternative employment, even though there is evidence that union wage rates cause unemployment for some union members.

Although it is against federal law for tax funds to be used to promote unionization, a strong argument can be made that federal funds obtained by unions through jobs and placement programs have been employed primarily for this purpose. Other tax-funded programs, such as cultural enhancement through the two national endowments for the arts and humanities, have also been a generous source of taxpayers' money to support union organizing and promotional activities. Even poverty programs have provided resources to groups that have openly engaged in union organizing activities.

Labor unions are well financed (in no small part owing to the taxpayers) and are very politically active. Politicians who receive campaign contributions and other campaign assistance from organized labor are anxious to court the unions, and the plight of the unemployed offers an excellent rationale for appropriating billions of dollars each year for jobs programs that permit unions and their front organizations to obtain vast sums for their activities. Even though the benefits to the unemployed may be marginal at best, politicians are much more concerned about courting the politically powerful. The bureaucracy is anxious to have jobs, training, and placement programs expand, for they provide public sector employment and promotion opportunities for those who administer and direct the programs. Thus, the bureaucracy and the unions have formed an alliance that profits both at the expense of the taxpayers.

Although the public is not generally aware of it, labor unions use tax funds to help finance strikes. For example, strikers have access to welfare funds and food stamps, and the sums involved are hardly trivial. A Wharton School study by Arnold Thieblot and Ronald Cowin estimated that in 1972 strikers received $329 million in public welfare support, excluding unemployment compensation.[71] The authors concluded that "public welfare support is widely available to strikers, that its use is already substantial, and that its use is rapidly growing."[72] In this way, hundreds of millions of dollars are being given each year directly to union members who support union activities. By subsidizing strikers, the government encourages disruptive job actions, lengthens their duration, and exacerbates the unemployment of other workers who are indirectly affected.

In view of the Reagan administration's opposition to some of the spending that has benefited unions, it is hardly surprising that the

AFL-CIO and its affiliated groups have relentlessly campaigned against virtually every cut in federal spending. The professed concern at Solidarity Day rallies and in union publications has always been the plight of the unemployed, the poor, and the disadvantaged. The truth, however, is much different. Labor unions and their members constitute a special-interest group that is a major beneficiary of government programs, even though union members and officials are among the highest paid workers in the United States. The argument that unions are uniquely qualified to operate programs to cure unemployment does not withstand close inspection: The record shows that when unions operate jobs programs, the primary goal is that of promoting unionism, rather than providing job training and placement for the unemployed. Federal jobs programs may be viewed not so much as a means of helping those in need of jobs but as a guise that politicians employ to give billions of taxpayers' dollars to their politically powerful allies in organized labor.

XIV. Funding the Right

> I consider [the National Endowment for Democracy to be] one of
> the most wasteful and mischievous expenditures of funds . . .
> that we have ever seen. It hands over in large blocks to the
> Chamber of Commerce; the AFL-CIO; and to the political par-
> ties . . . moneys to be used without any accountability whatso-
> ever.
>
> —Rep. Richard L. Ottinger
> *Congressional Record*

> Defense contractors are spending large sums of money to lobby
> for their weapons and are reporting only a fraction of these costs
> under the loophole-ridden 1946 Federal Regulation of Lobbying
> Act. In 1974–75, for example, the [government auditors] ques-
> tioned more than $2 million as possible lobbying expenses.
>
> —*Common Cause*

Any study of tax-funded politics would be incomplete without
an analysis of tax funds that conservative groups obtain to advance
their political agenda. But labels such as "liberal" and "conservative" and "right" and "left" are often misleading and add confusion
to the discussion, for the ideologies neither of the right nor the left
can be regarded as monolithic and accepted without question. Among
groups at each end of the political spectrum, however, there are
broad areas of agreement on issues, although priorities and emphases
may vary. The political agendas of the right and the left may even
coincide on some occasions. For example, free-enterprise economists who had long advocated the deregulation of the airlines were
supported in that instance by liberal consumer advocates. Furthermore, Ralph Nader cooperated with the National Taxpayers Union,
a group widely regarded as conservative, in opposing the increase
in quotas for the World Bank—the so-called big bank bailout bill.
Although Nader opposed the plan because it would subsidize large
banks by propping up their dubious loans to foreign countries, and
the taxpayers' coalition opposed it on the grounds that public funds

should not be used to pay for mistakes made by private banks, the objective of both parties was the same. Unfortunately, such instances of cooperation are the exception rather than the rule.

It is important to recognize that conservatives and liberals generally espouse the same ends, for example, the elimination of poverty and discrimination, higher living standards for all Americans, a cleaner environment, improved health care, and more economic opportunity. However, they are often at odds about the most effective means of achieving these goals. In general, liberals view the government as the prime mover in setting economic and social policy, whereas conservatives believe that the private sector is more effective and efficient. Without a lengthy discourse on ideology (which would likely satisfy no one and in any case is unnecessary for our purposes here), we consider conservatives (those on the right) to be those who believe that government is too large, costly, inefficient, and overly interventionist in the private sector and that the public sector should be reduced in the size and the scope of its activities. We consider liberals (those on the left) to be those who believe that high costs and inefficiency are a necessary price to be paid for the public sector to accomplish social goals: They believe that the principal reason that government has failed to eliminate poverty and achieve the good life for everyone is that taxpayers have been unwilling to fund needed public programs and that the size and scope of government should be increased. These definitions may be grossly oversimplified and perhaps even somewhat inaccurate, but they are useful in this analysis of tax-funded politics.

Tax Funding the Right

Exposés of conservative groups have carefully examined all aspects of their operations, including their sources of funding.[1] In every case, references to taxpayer support are rare, if mentioned at all. For example, investigative reporter Connie Paige claims in the subtitle of her book, *The Right To Lifers*, that she would document "who they are, how they operate, and where they get their money."[2] Appendix A of the book lists the "New Right's Money Tree," which includes such corporate donors as Ford, Mobil, IBM, Castle and Cooke, Pizza Hut, General Motors, Coca-Cola, Firestone, and such foundations as Bechtel, Adolph Coors, Fred C. Koch, Samuel Noble, John M. Olin, J. Howard Pew Freedom Trust, Sarah Mellon Scaife, and Smith-Richardson.[3] Appendix B lists "Fundamentalist Donors" who made contributions to the "principal U.S. evangelical organizations" between 1970 and 1980.[4] Neither appendix lists any government grants or contracts and, given the level of detail in appendix B (which lists donors, recipients, amount, date, and "background on donors"), tax funds would have been included had they been received. Paige mentions only one grant of tax funds to a conservative organization:

> [The] Heritage [Foundation] would also receive adverse publicity. The Scripps-Howard news chain would print a story in March 1978 about how the foundation had received a $46,000 federal contract for a transportation study in New Hampshire via Governor Meldrim Thompson, a Heritage associate. The U.S. Department of Commerce would investigate and would eventually force Heritage to return part of the grant. By that time, however, the foundation was well enough established to withstand the damage of such a disclosure.[5]

Two interesting items stand out: (1) the amount of the grant to Heritage is trivial compared with the hundreds of millions of dollars routinely funneled to liberal groups, and (2) the government required that part of the grant money be returned, an event that rarely occurs with grants to liberal organizations, even though they may have used the funds for dubious, if not illegal, purposes.

In sum, investigative reporters such as Paige have scrutinized every aspect of many conservative organizations and have found almost no taxpayer funding of their activities. Our own research corroborates this: Although there is some taxpayer funding of various conservative groups, the amounts of money involved are trivial compared to the hundreds of millions of dollars received by liberal organizations. Nevertheless, as a matter of principle, we believe that taxpayer funding of any political activity—conservative, liberal, or whatever—has no place in a free society and should be stopped. Although taxpayer funding of the right is a relatively small phenomenon, there has been, not surprisingly, quite a bit of it during the Reagan administration, as the following examples reveal.

In late October 1984, after the conservative Reagan administration had been in power for nearly four years, the *Washington Post* published a story entitled "Conservatives Get Grants."[6] The *Post* story reported concern that the Legal Services Corporation had awarded "large grants to three conservative groups whose political objectives closely mirror those of the Reagan administration."[7] A grant for $337,000 was made to the Constitutional Law Center located in

Cumberland, Virginia, and headed by James McClellan, a conservative constitutional scholar and former aide to conservative senator John P. East (R-N.C.), to "provide direct delivery, technical assistance, training and publications on legal issues concerning the protection of the constitutional rights of the poor." A grant for $337,000 was also given to the National Center for the Medically Handicapped, in Indianapolis, to provide technical assistance, training, and publications on "legal issues concerning treatment of the critically or terminally ill, handicapped and medically dependent poor persons." A grant for $400,000 was made to the Oakland Urban Legal Foundation in California for "developing programs to increase private lawyers' participation to provide no-cost or reduced-cost services for the poor."[8]

Rep. Peter W. Rodino, Jr. (D-N.J.), chairman of the House Judiciary Committee, asked the General Accounting Office to investigate whether the "three groups are eligible for funds under the Legal Services Act."[9] The GAO report did conclude that there were "improprieties" in the funding of these programs.[10] In an interview with the *Post*, Rep. Barney Frank (D-Mass.) stated that the grant to the National Center for the Medically Handicapped might help poor people, but "he described the other two as 'simply ideological' . . . These groups are pretty far out."[11]

Other grants to conservative groups have also generated controversy in the media. The U.S. Information Agency (USIA), through its private-sector initiatives program, has given seed money to foster educational exchange projects. One grant for $428,000 was made to the Claremont Institute, in California, "to bring young conservatives to the U.S." A grant of $192,145 was given to the Washington-based Ethics and Public Policy Center, headed by Ernest Lefever, to hold seminars for European church leaders in the forefront of the antinuclear movement. Jack Anderson described the USIA's actions in making these grants as "doling out bundles of money to conservative organizations with the right ideological tilt."[12]

USIA also made a grant of $162,810 to the Mid-America Committee for International Business and Government Cooperation "to bring 14 official press spokesman from right-wing Latin American regimes to Washington."[13] The committee and its activities were described in the *Washington Post* as

> a rather obscure businessmen's lobby dealing with the southern hemisphere [that] wants to teach these spokesmen how to manipulate the American media—a cause the USIA seems to endorse.

Your tax dollars have already provided hospitality for Carlos Infante, Gen. Pinochet's international press director; Guy Mayer, the Haitian director of information; Pablo Nuila, the chief of Army Information in Guatemala, and 11 others.

The American hosts were selected with equal impartiality, ranging from John McLaughlin of the National Review to M. Stanton Evans and Patrick Buchanan. Thus was vindicated the promise of the $169,810 "grant agreement" which mentions the diversity of the American press and stresses that:

"The understanding of these differences is essential if the attendees are to learn to handle the media to the best advantage, i.e., not defensively, but assertively."[14]

The program was directed by Ian McKenzie, formerly a publicity aide to Nicaraguan dictator Anastasio Somoza. The trainees from Latin America also had meetings on Capitol Hill—with an aide to Sen. Jesse A. Helms (R-N.C.) and with a member of the Republican Policy Committee.[15]

USIA's programs have long been carefully scrutinized by the media because of the friendship between USIA's director, Charles Z. Wick, and President Reagan, and because of Wick's flamboyance, perhaps best described as "full Hollywood." Wick travels extensively and expensively on taxpayers' funds, eschewing the conservative credo of economy in government:

In the last two years, Wick has spent 177 days abroad in such places as London (three times), Paris (five times), Geneva (three times), Rome, Amsterdam, Bonn, Mexico City, Rio de Janeiro, Peking, Tokyo, Vienna, Bangkok, Budapest, Jakarta, Johannesburg and Casablanca.

He travels with three or four bodyguards, flies either first class or on the supersonic Concorde, stays in luxury hotel suites, is met by limousines and hands out $5 tips to bellhops and pool attendants. Wick, a one-time music arranger and show business agent, has brought a box-office approach to the USIA, transforming it from a rather stodgy bureaucracy to a Hollywood-style production in which Wick is unquestionably the star.[16]

These antics provide ample grist for the media's mill and ammunition for liberal activist groups denouncing cuts in federal spending for social programs. From the perspective of the taxpayers, Wick's Cecil B. DeMille mode of operation is extravagant and unnecessary;

such excesses on the part of conservatives in government also generate suspicions about whether grants distributed by USIA under Wick's direction are cost effective—an issue that warrants careful consideration.

Criticism has also been generated by the involvement of federal officials in the process of informing groups with conservative views about how to apply for government funds. Myron E. McKee, special assistant to the executive officer of ACTION, the federal volunteer agency, sent a letter to 46 state offices of Birthright, an anti-abortion agency, urging them to apply for federal funds. The letter, written on plain white stationery but mailed with the agency's postal frank, provided advice on how to apply for "paid Vista volunteer positions. . . . Each state [organization] should apply for at least 10 paid Vista positions."[17] The letter contained application materials and a model application (previously filed successfully by Birthright of Massachusetts, which received $99,000) and promised an answer to the application within 30 days. Subsequently, McKee was informed that he must reimburse the agency $150 for postage.

Although evidence indicates that government grants have been provided only on a sporadic basis to conservative groups, we have found one organization that has consistently received tax-funded support: the American Enterprise Institute for Public Policy Research (AEI). The *Washington Post* reported that AEI received $260,000 in 1982 and $234,000 in 1983 from federal agencies, sums representing about 2 percent of the organization's budget.[18] AEI's own report of federal funding awarded (but perhaps not spent) in 1983 reveals a higher level of taxpayer involvement than reported in the *Post:*

> AEI has received a one-year grant of $250,000 from the U.S. Department of Commerce to undertake a major study on the relationship between technological innovation and economic adjustment. The project will look at public and private research and development policies aimed at maintaining and enhancing America's international competitiveness in both traditional and high-technology areas.[19]

> AEI has received $335,000 from the U.S. Department of Health and Human Services to evaluate innovative approaches to the financing and delivery of health services under the Medicaid program serving low-income households.[20]

> AEI has received a three-year grant of more than $390,000 from the National Endowment for the Humanities to help pay the costs

of several activities of the Institute's constitution project, "A Decade of Study of the Constitution."[21]

AEI also acknowledged support from USIA and the Agency for International Development (AID), which partially funded an AEI international conference on the writing of constitutions.[22] In conservative circles, AEI is much closer to the center of the political spectrum than are many other so-called conservative public policy groups. This may help to explain some of AEI's success in obtaining taxpayers' dollars. At the very least, it may be argued that AEI differs from many conservative groups in that it actively seeks support from government agencies.

The ideological and philosophical prohibitions that many conservatives have against seeking tax dollars to support their activities are sometimes eroded by the requirement that all monies that Congress appropriates for an agency for a given fiscal year must be spent within that year. Research or other program funds appropriated by Congress must go to some individual or organization, and conservatives sometimes argue that it would be better for these monies to be captured by the right rather than to have the tax dollars continue to support the activities of groups on the left.

Taxpayers do not necessarily gain, however, when taxes are used to support ideologues, regardless of their persuasion. Consider the Office of Juvenile Justice and Delinquency Prevention (OJJDP), a part of the U.S. Department of Justice. When the director, Alfred Regnery, was confirmed in November 1982, a high priority was to eliminate the use of about $60 million by left-wing organizations for political advocacy under the guise of finding solutions to youth crime.[23] Regnery was successful in cutting off the funds, but the budget was not reduced by Congress; so other grantees were sought. Projects that have been funded by OJJDP include the following

—A two-year grant for $800,000 was awarded to Judith Reisman, now a research professor at American University and formerly a writer and producer for the "Captain Kangaroo" children's television show. Professor Reisman is studying cartoons from *Playboy, Penthouse,* and *Hustler* magazines to assess erotica and pornography. The first cartoon collection (including samples of "Chester the Molester" from *Hustler*) illustrates "sexualized children in mainstream pornography."
—$4 million was given to the National School Safety Center for George Nicholson, the Republican loser in the 1982 California

365

election campaign for attorney general, to study school violence. The grant indicates that the funds will be used "to restore our schools as temples of learning," a feat to be achieved by sending pamphlets (such as "Truancy Reduction: The Hooky Handbook") and speakers to schools through the nation. Tens of thousands of dollars will be spent to purchase computers, word processors, photo-compositors, and videotapes.

—A $900,000 grant to Washington Consulting Group was cancelled after $400,000 had been spent because a cousin of Vice President Bush was on the payroll. The task statement for the contract revealed that Washington Consulting Group was to provide "support to the OJJDP in issues related to the reauthorization of the JJDP Act," the legislation providing agency funding.[24]

Between November 1982 and April 1984, more than 85 percent of the OJJDP grants and contracts were made without competitive bidding, and $16.4 million of taxpayers' funds were allocated in this way.

The National Endowment for the Humanities (NEH) provides a second example of the redirecting of federal funds from liberal groups to conservatives. During the Carter administration, NEH was headed by Joseph Duffey, who had been "increasing Federal support for women's, minority, labor and ethnic studies, and for avant-garde scholarly fields such as semiotics" [the theory of symbols and symbolism].[25] In 1981 the Reagan administration appointed William J. Bennett as chairman of NEH to succeed Duffey, and changes in the agency's program priorities were made. Previously, Bennett had assisted in the preparation of the chapter on NEH in the Heritage Foundation's study, *Mandate for Leadership*. Under Bennett's direction, funding policies shifted more toward the political right:

> When liberal Democrats dominated the agency, they tended to support projects they agreed with, so it should come as no great surprise that conservative Republicans do the same. Indeed, the endowment has been used by both sides as a weapon in the culture wars. But a study of Bennett's methods and policies, based in part on confidential reports, shows he has politicized the grants process to an unprecedented degree.

> For starters he sharply reduced funding in many areas that had been emphasized by Duffey. For example, grants to projects dealing with women dropped by 37 percent (from 143 to 90) between

fiscal 1981, the last complete year of Duffey's chairmanship, and fiscal 1983, the first complete year of Bennett's, according to endowment statistics. Grants to labor unions dropped by 100 percent (from six to zero) during the same period, and grants for studies in semiotics dropped by 50 percent (from four to two).[26]

The reference to the politicization of the grants process to an "unprecedented degree" is based on the observation that conservatives were beginning to receive funding from NEH, thereby displacing some liberal groups that had been on the public dole for years. Evidently, in the view of the media, grants to liberal groups are totally apolitical, despite overwhelming evidence to the contrary (see, for example, chapter 13, which discusses the use of NEH funds by labor unions). This double standard, which infuriates conservatives, seems to be prevalent in the media.

Among the NEH grants awarded to conservative groups are the following:

—$30,000 to Accuracy in Media (AIM) to assess the Public Broadcasting System's 13-part documentary on the Vietnam War, "Vietnam, a History." NEH had originally financed the PBS film with a $1.5 million grant and AIM had requested $200,000 to prepare a two-hour assessment. The AIM request was reduced because $30,000 is the maximum amount that the chairman can award at his own discretion for an "emergency grant" that does not require a vote of the NEH council. NEH had received 300 letters calling the documentary ". . . biased, unfair, and inaccurate."[27]

—up to $140,000 for the Claremont Institute in California "to support scripting for 60-minute docu-dramas for television as part of a five-part series focusing on Winston Churchill's decisions and actions during the period September 1939 to December 1941.[28]

—$453,076 to Public Research, Syndicated of Claremont, California ". . . to distribute articles on the Constitution to newspapers across the country."[29]

—In 1983, the Claremont Institute was awarded $303,580 ". . . for conferences and lectures on the bicentennial."[30]

—The Hoover Institution at Stanford University was awarded a $900,000 matching grant in December 1983 for its library and archives.[31]

—a grant of $654,540 for summer seminars for high school teachers was made to the Humanities Institute of the University of California at San Diego. This Institute is headed by Ronald Berman, a Nixon appointee who served as chairman of NEH from 1971 to 1977.[32]

—approximately $50,000 to the World News Institute headed by Richard Bishirjian to support a ". . . ninety-minute TV program on the political and philosophical influences on the Founding Fathers, based on *The Roots of American Order* by conservative scholar Russell Kirk. Kirk was a member of the Reagan transition team that studied the endowment; Bishirjian headed that transition team."[33]

Although Alfred Regnery broke up the old-boy network that provided funding for the left through his office (OJJDP) and William Bennett attempted to do the same at NEH, as did Charles Wick at USIA, the real issue is whether the taxpayers are now better off. The activities of organizations involved in public policy matters are, by definition, political in nature. Such organizations inevitably promote their vision of what is best for society by encouraging the widespread adoption of the moral and ethical values that those who manage their budgets endorse. In a free society, all points of view must be heard. But when government decides to fund some groups but not others, an advantage is provided to those who receive support. As Milton Friedman has observed, it is impossible for government to fund all propaganda: "If it [government] gave to all who asked, it would shortly find itself out of funds, for . . . [government] cannot repeal the elementary economic law that a sufficiently high price will call forth a large supply."[34]

It may be argued that Congress has appropriated funds for public policy groups, that the funds must be spent for specified purposes, and that the election of President Reagan implies that the funds should be distributed as his political appointees direct to reflect the desires of a majority of the voters. Those conservatives who advocate defunding the left, however, have never called for funding the right. As discussed in greater detail in chapter 15, the potential for misuse or waste of taxpayers' dollars is great whenever government financially supports groups involved with public policy issues.

Tax-Funded Corporate Politics

Corporations are among the most active participants in U.S. politics. Each year, corporations contribute millions of dollars to political candidates and spend millions more in lobbying at the federal, state, and local levels of government. Those corporations that obtain tax funding for their political activities are generally government contractors, especially defense contractors, who have direct business dealings with government. Most conservative groups do favor a strong national defense and a high level of defense spending, which supports the lobbying efforts of defense contractors for increased expenditures on weapons programs. This commonality of interest is one reason why corporate politics are regarded as conservative. The conservative label has also been attached to businessmen because they often espouse the virtues of competition and free enterprise; however, they frequently seek taxpayer subsidies, protection from foreign competition, and special privileges from government because their particular industry and company face special problems. They tout free enterprise and competition as being desirable for other industries and other companies. Unlike conservatives, government contractors seek an expanded role for government and increased public expenditures because they can potentially profit from such policies.

Unlike public policy activists who obtain tax funds under the guise of helping the poor, the hungry, and the unemployed and then divert the money for political purposes, corporations have no convenient smoke screen for hiding tax-funded contributions for their political activities. Although politicians benefit from the campaign contributions received from corporations and are anxious for them to continue, they are sensitive to the public perception of corporate greed. A simple expedient that is often used to channel tax funds for political purposes to some corporations is to build the funds into the contracts between the government and the corporations. Common Cause, a self-styled public interest group, has criticized this practice:

> The government has footed untold millions of dollars of defense contractors' lobbying expenses because the Defense Department has no definition of "lobbying" and therefore no regulation that specifically prevents lobbying costs from being charged against government contracts.

> Sen. William Proxmire (D-Wis.) is incredulous. "Every citizen has the right to communicate with his elected representatives. However, no citizen has the right to ask the government to reimburse the costs of these communications and, to my knowledge, no segment of society other than government contractors has had the temerity to make such a request."[35]

Defense contractors also have "entertained military and congressional personnel with parties at hunting lodges on the Maryland shore, goose hunts, rides on corporate jets and yachts, and football tickets."[36] Taxpayers also pay for corporate public relations campaigns that polish the image of government contractors, especially those who contract with the military.[37] Politicians benefit from the political expenditures of defense contractors, so it is hardly surprising that there is little furor raised when it is revealed that taxpayers have paid more than $600 for toilet seats in aircraft, and hundreds of dollars for individual items such as bolts, nuts, and simple tools, including coffee makers.

The sums involved in corporate lobbying at taxpayer expense are not known, for the information is proprietary. Common Cause contends, however, that

> Defense contractors are spending large sums of money to lobby for their weapons and are reporting only a fraction of these costs under the loophole-ridden 1946 Federal Regulation of Lobbying Act. In 1974–75, for example, the DCAA [Defense Contract Audit Agency] questioned more than $2 million as possible lobbying expenses.

> This total does not include those amounts which the contractors voluntarily did not charge to the government, so the actual amounts spent on lobbying are not known. In those same years, only three . . . companies had registered lobbyists and they reported spending only $89,251.20.[38]

Corporate executives are concerned about social responsibility, that is, the role of the corporation in solving society's problems, and the National Alliance of Business (NAB) was formed in 1968 to marshal "the resources and expertise of business for the task of preparing jobless Americans for productive work."[39] NAB's goal was to form a partnership between business and government to aid the unemployed:

> The Alliance was born of a partnership forged by President Johnson and the leaders of some of America's largest corporations. These far-sighted citizens recognized the dangers inherent to a free society in allowing citizens to live without productive work or hope for a better life.

> They saw that building a partnership of business and government was the best route for tapping new resources to shape a more efficient, humane and responsible society. And their collective

vision of the urgent need to bring every public and private resource to bear in the search for solutions to joblessness still guides the work of the Alliance.[40]

Despite the claim that NAB would "bring every . . . private resource to bear" on the problem of joblessness, consider the organization's operating budget, with dollar amounts shown in millions:[41]

Year	Operating Expenditures ($)	Federal Sources ($)	Other Sources ($)	Percent Federal
1980	13.0	12.8	0.2	98
1981	11.4	10.7	0.7	94
1982	9.7	8.8	0.9	91
1983	11.2	9.0	2.2	80
1984	10.1	5.4	4.7	53

During these years, corporations were claiming credit for acting in a socially responsible way, and the taxpayers were paying most of the bill. From 1980 through 1982, more than 90 cents of every dollar that NAB expended was provided by tax funds. Most of NAB's 232 corporate sponsors appear on the Fortune 500 list, but in 1980 the corporate community contributed only $200,000 to NAB, an average of less than $1,000 per company.[42] Under budget pressures from growing deficits and the emphasis on private-sector initiatives, grants to NAB from the Department of Labor (the source of most of NAB's federal funds) declined and the business community finally began to contribute more substantially to the "urgent need." Even by 1984, though, the taxpayers still provided more than half of the support for NAB's programs. Social responsibility is easy if taxpayers' funds can be used to subsidize the effort.

The National Endowment for Democracy

Government funds have a peculiar characteristic: Once wrested from the taxpayers, they belong to everyone—and therefore to no one. All that is required to dip into the public till is to form a political coalition to appropriate funds for a given purpose. The National Endowment for Democracy illustrates this up-for-grabs nature of taxpayers' funds.

The seeds for this endowment were sown in a speech given by President Reagan to the British Parliament on June 8, 1982. Reagan indicated that not enough was being done to encourage democratic

371

institutions in other countries and stated that his objective was "to foster the infrastructure of democracy—the system of a free press, unions, political parties, universities—which allows a people to choose their own way, to develop their own culture, to reconcile their own differences through peaceful means."[43]

Reagan's statement led to two legislative proposals. First, in February 1983, legislation was introduced to authorize Project Democracy, a program that would fund projects to export democracy through USIA, AID, and the Department of State. Under Project Democracy, 28 existing educational and cultural exchange and training programs were to be expanded and 20 new initiatives were to be started. USIA was primarily responsible for Project Democracy, and the agency's budget increased to support this project and other programs rapidly: From fiscal year 1983's budget of $545.5 million, USIA requested an additional $166 million in appropriations for FY 1984 and $885.4 million for FY 1985.[44] USIA has long promoted a better understanding of the United States abroad through preparing or arranging academic exchanges, international visitors programs, radio broadcasting, films and television programs, libraries, books, magazines, commercial bulletins, art exhibitions, and tours of artists and orchestras. The second legislative proposal, introduced in April 1983, was to authorize funding for the National Endowment for Democracy (NED), a nongovernmental organization designed to finance and coordinate private-sector programs to encourage democracy abroad through Project Democracy. The evolution of Project Democracy in general and NED in particular is a classic example of coalition politics that fleece the U.S. taxpayers.

In 1979 Democratic and Republican leaders had established the American Political Foundation (APF), a private, nonprofit organization intended to undertake bipartisan political exchanges.[45] APF was inspired by the foundations that had been established by the four major political parties in West Germany, and that were funded by the West German government.[46] Taxpayer funding of foundations established in the United States by the Republican and Democratic parties, however, would have created a firestorm of criticism for politicians who voted to appropriate the funds, for it would have been perceived as a slush fund for the two political parties. APF remained almost inactive until President Reagan's speech in London in 1982. Then APF, now also representing the AFL-CIO and the U.S. Chamber of Commerce, arranged a grant from AID for a feasibility study of the proposed Democracy Program. Inclusion of labor unions and business in the project ensured lobbying support from these groups, and the public would no longer perceive the undertaking solely as a vehicle for funding political parties.

The grant agreement between APF and AID specified that the study was to determine the "feasibility of various programs and institutional arrangements to promote the development and strengthening of democratic forces overseas."[47] AID was to provide half of the $300,000 needed for the six-month study, with the remainder coming from matching private-sector grants. Despite concern about the urgent need for private-sector initiatives in promoting democracy abroad, private support for APF did not materialize:

> Soon after the $150,000 grant was awarded [by AID], it became clear that the expected private matching funds would not materialize despite APF fund-raising efforts. Although the APF solicited contributions from over 50 private sector organizations and foundations, the AFL-CIO was the only organization to contribute. Its $25,000 contribution was made to further the work of the APF and ultimately was not spent for Democracy Program expenses.[48]

The study ultimately cost $400,000 in taxpayers' funds, an expensive proposition given that the study's findings had been decided long before the work was completed. The GAO audit of the APF grant reported:

> The AID grant agreement described the project as a "feasibility" study and stated that, in undertaking the study, no assumption would be made on the desirability or operating conditions of any particular program or structure. Staff members advised us, however, that the Democracy Program was not a feasibility study in the academic sense but instead was a study to work out a mechanism by which labor, business, and the two political parties could conduct programs abroad promoting democratic institutions and processes. They therefore saw their role as one of examining how their respective interest groups might best be involved in the envisioned new program.
>
> The first grant agreement also stated that the Democracy Program would "recommend alternative ways in which democratic forces overseas can be supported through ongoing programs and/or new mechanisms." We found, however, that the staff decided very early in the study that new private sector programs and mechanisms would have to be established and that they focused little

attention on whether existing government and/or private agencies might expand certain activities toward strengthening democratic institutions. . . . The Democracy Program did not recommend alternatives but simply described in its final report the types of programs that business, labor, and the two political parties might conduct from Endowment grants.[49]

At the outset of the feasibility study, a list of questions was sent to all U.S. embassies soliciting views on what activities a new program promoting democratic institution building might include. Over 100 posts responded, but

Although the final report of the Democracy Program states that the cable responses were valuable in designing the new program, it does not discuss the issues they raise. Further, only two of the five regional reports prepared by the research staff discuss the cables' contents. The program director told us that the cable responses were not discussed in the final report because some of the material in them was sensitive and should not be publicly discussed.[50]

The advice of some of the experts hired to produce task force reports was also ignored. For example, the task force on democratic electoral processes

concluded in its report that past private sector consultant efforts related to electoral processes had filled foreign needs reasonably well and that a large-scale, high priority effort by a new U.S. program to aid democracy abroad was not needed. They further concluded that (1) there was no logical reason why the Democratic, Republican, business, and labor foundations envisioned as the operating arms of the Endowment should perform the limited activities the task force proposed and (2) the Endowment itself might more appropriately carry them out. These conclusions were not mentioned in the body of the study.[51]

The study's final report focused exclusively on the roles to be played by business, labor unions, and the two political parties; no reports were prepared to examine how existing organizations (for example, churches, the media, foundations, and universities) might also be involved. This omission is not surprising, given the composition of the APF executive board: Democratic National Committee Chairman Charles T. Manatt, Republican National Committee Chairman Frank J. Fahrenkopf, Jr., Ambassador William E. Brock III,

AFL-CIO President Lane Kirkland, U.S. Chamber of Commerce Vice-President Michael Samuels, and Sen. Christopher J. Dodd (D-Conn.).

The report was ready in October 1983, but it was not released until February 1984. The APF board of directors had approved the proposed NED structure on March 16, 1983—months before the report recommending the appropriate structure was complete. Time pressures prevented the study's results from influencing the recommendation to establish NED: "At the outset of the study, the Democracy Program Board and staff recognized that an off-election year such as 1983 was the best time for the Endowment's legislation to be considered"; and, even though the content of and analysis in the study were incomplete, the staff "appears to have devoted much time and attention to legislative matters."[52] The legislative timetable was discussed at the board's first meeting, and internal memoranda reveal concern about meeting legislative deadlines: "[w]e are racing the congressional clock in completing our work."[53]

As originally proposed, NED would be a private, nonprofit corporation chartered in the District of Columbia and financed by an annual grant from USIA. It was prohibited from carrying out programs on its own and could only serve as a conduit for funds to other organizations that submitted proposals for projects to encourage democracy abroad. NED's private status was important in that the organization's activities were not subject to the Freedom of Information Act. During debate on the measure in Congress, Rep. Richard L. Ottinger (D-N.Y.) asserted: "There are no adequate mechanisms for tracing the use of the public funds and indeed the use of those funds are not even subject to the Freedom of Information Act so that the public can find out how their money is being used."[54] As a private entity, NED could also engage in activities that would be illegal for a government entity to undertake. In short, NED could launder funds so that legal restrictions on tax-funded support for certain activities could be bypassed. Congress was informed by USIA officials of the intent of NED's funding of illegal activities in budget hearings for USIA:

> Some of the activities to be assisted with NED funding, which USIA does not and, *in many cases, cannot legally fund,* include basic union-building abroad, assistance to International Trade Secretariats of various unions, political training for trade union leaders, assistance to trade union exiles and their families, support for the work of international labor organizations, aid to efforts to organize

unions in totalitarian and dictatorial countries, training of Third World political leaders within their own regions, assistance to political parties and affiliated organizations in election activities, assistance in conducting national public opinion polls and voter education programs, assistance in formulating party programs, organizational structure and behavior, work on integrating the local traditional sector into the democratic process, and help in formulating party approaches to issues of governance [emphasis added].[55]

USIA officials, then, readily admitted that one of NED's objectives was to permit the expenditure of federal funds for purposes that Congress had declared illegal. A private corporation, especially one exempt from scrutiny under the Freedom of Information Act, can safely engage in activities funded with tax dollars that would be illegal for government entities. From the outset, NED was established to flout the law. Presumably, Congress had good reason for prohibiting government agencies from undertaking certain projects when the limitations were put in effect. The design of an organizational structure to circumvent these restrictions seems, at best, suspect, as noted by Rep. Jim Leach (R-Iowa): "[W]e will do abroad what we are precluded from allowing here in this country; we are proposing something that does not reflect our own values or our own law."[56]

The proposed appropriation for the NED stipulated how almost all the $31.3 million initial budget was to be allocated: $13.8 million was to be earmarked for the Free Trade Union Institute of the AFL-CIO; $2.5 million was to be set aside for the private enterprise development program of the National Chamber Foundation, the nonprofit arm of the U.S. Chamber of Commerce; $5 million was to be given to each of the two political parties, which had incorporated separate "international relations institutes"; $5 million would cover NED's operating expenses (evidently, there was little hope that private funds would cover operating expenses, given the lack of response from the private sector when APF had appealed for contributions); and what was left would be awarded to other private-sector grantees who submitted proposals for funding. The proposed budget contained something for everyone. Even before Congress voted on the proposed funding, the representative of the U.S. Chamber of Commerce complained that the labor unions were getting more than the business community from the public purse:

I do not believe that the $2.5 million figure for business programs is an adequate level when compared with the amounts of $5 million being allocated to each of the two parties and the $13.8 million to labor. Although the disparity with labor is the largest, it is understandable in the context of labor's long involvement in similar international programs. It would be folly in the first year to fund beginning institutions on a level comparable to those in existence. Business enters this process, however, with the goal of becoming organized and effective so that future funding levels for business will be comparable to those of labor. I would, however, expect greater funding comparability with the political party activities. . . . If the Congress believes the parties' foundations [i.e., their international relations institutes] both deserve and can well spend $5 million each in fiscal year 1984, I would hope that the Congress believes business both deserves and can well spend $4.5 million in fiscal year 1983.[57]

At the same time that business leaders were complaining about perceived inequities in funding, they kept up a steady stream of criticism about the size of the federal deficits.

The AFL-CIO was to receive far more than the other participants because $13.8 million was the level at which the federal government had already been funding the Free Trade Union Institute through AID grants, even though AFL-CIO president Lane Kirkland claimed that this work had been undertaken with "our own funds."[58]

There are serious questions about the need for taxpayer funding of business groups to promote democracy in other countries. There are already widespread U.S. business interests throughout the world. U.S. oil companies, banks, computer companies, and so forth have overseas branches staffed, at least in part, by U.S. nationals. The number of U.S. companies in 52 countries is sufficient for the formation of American chambers of commerce to represent the interests of U.S. firms in those places. U.S. businessmen have connections with foreign nationals in vitually every country in the world. If these businessmen are incapable of transmitting ideas about private enterprise to their foreign counterparts, why should there be any expectation that giving millions of tax dollars to the U.S. Chamber of Commerce will produce any results? If U.S. businessmen working in foreign countries are successful in promoting private enterprise and democracy, why should taxpayers contribute to the effort?

377

Two issues arise in an examination of funding political parties for international programs. First, members of Congress have never had a shortage of funds for foreign travel—junketing is a way of life, and taxpayers have paid dearly for the itinerant tendencies of members of Congress and their staffs and families. NED appears to be another source of funds for congressional travel:

> The endowment dispatched one bipartisan delegation of earnest dogooders to the Caribbean and Europe. Did the apostles of freedom visit countries where some enlightenment on the principles of democracy is sorely needed? Not on your life.

> They went to Jamaica, where the beaches are inviting, the people are free and the government already democratic. They also stopped by such solidly democratic capitals as Stockholm, Brussels and Paris. The delegation even brought the message of democracy to Geneva, capital of the world's oldest democracy.[59]

Second, some of these popular fact-finding missions could have the promotion of democracy and private enterprise as objectives, but Rep. George Miller (D-Calif.) questioned whether political parties could explain our political system to the American public, let alone to foreigners:

> Our political parties have enough trouble explaining the two-party system to the American public. If you want to spend $31 million, give it to the parties to tell them what is going to be going on in San Francisco and Dallas [locations of the 1984 national party conventions].

> I do not think they can explain it for $100 million.[60]

During the congressional debate on NED, the proposal's opponents, led by Rep. Hank Brown (R-Colo.), expressed two major concerns. The first was that the organization would use tax monies to influence foreign elections. Rep. Bill Emerson (R-Mo.) referred to the appropriation measure as the "Taxpayer Funding of Foreign Elections Act"[61] and asked:

> [W]hat is the Republican Party of the United States of America doing with taxpayer money supporting one side or another in a political situation in a foreign country? I would argue that it would be violative of the laws of the United States if a foreign government attempted to influence our politics. The potential of such activities being profoundly counterproductive is overwhelming.[62]

Representative Leach feared that those who would become involved in foreign affairs through NED lacked the expertise needed to be effective: "More and more people become involved in foreign affairs without particular background for that involvement."[63]

The second concern of the NED opponents in Congress was that public rather than private funds were to be used, as Representative Leach stated:

> If this is such a terrifically good idea, why do not the political parties and the labor unions involved simply ask their membership for funds and let them go to their membership and suggest that these activities are to be funded through their membership, in which case the idea can stand on its own merit. But to go to the taxpayers implies that maybe the merit is not so strong and maybe we ought to reassess this process itself.[64]

Rep. Judd Gregg (R-N.H.) reiterated this concern:

> If the private sector is the proper place to do this, then it should be the private sector funds that do it. That is the traditional role I believe that the private sector assumes. It is not appropriate for us to be underwriting this effort, any more than it is appropriate for us to be subsidizing other political activities in the private sector.[65]

Representative Miller asserted that the use of federal funds in such a project would detract from it and would "cloak it in the misgivings, in the cynicism of many of these countries, by having Federal funds involved in it."[66]

Authorizing legislation for NED (Public Law no. 98-164) was passed on November 22, 1983, awarding NED an annual grant from USIA; the FY 1984 appropriation (enacted as part of Public Law no. 98-166) was passed on November 28, 1983. Congress deleted the funds earmarked for the international relations institutes of the two political parties and appropriated a total of $18 million for NED's operations and programs. At the April 1984 meeting of the board of directors, NED's budget was allocated as follows:

—$11 million for the Free Trade Union Institute of the AFL-CIO;
—$1.7 million for the National Chamber Foundation's Center for International Private Enterprise;
—$1.5 million from discretionary funds for each of the international institutes of the Democratic and Republican Parties; and
—$2.3 million for Endowment administration and discretionary grants to other organizations.[67]

The funds were awarded to the international relations institutes of the two political parties "on the same basis as the earmarked institutions." Indeed, these two grants were awarded even though the two political party organizations had not "presented comprehensive program proposals and without being considered with other applicants for discretionary funding."[68] The congressional conference report on NED's funding removed the earmarking of funds for the two political parties, but noted that this was done "without prejudice to their receipt of funds from the Endowment."[69] Table A14.1 (in appendix) lists all NED grants for FY 1984; Table A14.2 lists NED grants awarded through March 31, 1985, for FY 1985.

From the outset, the NED grants were embroiled in controversy. The AFL-CIO Free Trade Union Institute quickly became involved in elections in Panama: "Eugenia Kimble, executive director of the AFL-CIO's institute, said it spent $20,000 organizing a May Day rally to get out the union vote in the election, not to promote the union-endorsed candidate, Ardita Barletta, who won amid charges of fraud."[70] This involvement brought scathing criticism from Ambassador James E. Briggs, who sent a classified cable to the Department of State (subsequently leaked to the media) which, in part, stated, "The embassy requests that this harebrained project be abandoned before it hits the fan."[71] In its study of NED, GAO interviewed representatives of each of the earmarked recipients to assess the "interface" among NED, its grantees, and the Department of State. The AFL-CIO representatives had reported that "since the AFL-CIO has been functioning abroad for years, the institute will not require advice on its operations from the State Department. Further, the labor official believes that the institute's activities might be compromised if it becomes too closely associated with the government."[72]

Apparently, even Briggs began to see the benefits of funding NED and its grantees. In a second cable sent to the Department of State, Briggs reversed his earlier views: "I am a strong and enthusiastic supporter of the NED and its purposes. . . . I look forward to the NED's assisting in the development of democracy in Panama . . . and believe it very important that the NED be funded as originally envisioned." This cable was unclassified and was quickly distributed to the media and to members of Congress.[73]

Similar incidents are likely to occur, but they may be difficult to detect because NED has resisted congressional oversight and standard audits:

Endowment officials have . . . resisted including provisions in the final grant agreement which would allude to USIA control or oversight of the Endowment's finances, programs or administrative operations. . . . [Moreover,] attorneys for the endowment have resisted acknowledging USIA audit rights, asserting that authorizing legislation already included a "comprehensive set of oversight requirements designed to ensure the complete operational integrity of the Endowment."[74]

In sum, NED, as described by Rep. George W. Crockett, Jr. (D-Mich.) is "at best a boondoggle."[75] Lobbyists for the AFL-CIO representing labor, lobbyists for the U.S. Chamber of Commerce representing business, and the two political parties used the NED concept to build a coalition to obtain tax funds that could be used for their own purposes. Although it was claimed that there was an urgent need for private-sector involvement in foreign affairs, neither the chamber nor the political parties had used their own funds for such purposes before NED was created. The AFL-CIO's Free Trade Union Institute had been in existence for a number of years prior to NED's establishment, but it had been receiving taxpayers' funds through AID. There is no evidence that private groups have any special expertise in foreign affairs, and on at least one occasion—the involvement of the AFL-CIO in Panamanian elections—such private action may have been harmful. The programs and goals of NED overlap and duplicate the work being pursued by professionals in the Department of State, USIA, and AID. Further, government agencies are subject to the Freedom of Information Act and are prohibited from engaging in activities that NED seems determined to pursue. Like most other federal programs, NED will be all but impossible to terminate now that it has become established. Taxpayers are now supporting political activity abroad as well as at home; there appears to be almost no limit to the uses that can be found for tax dollars.

Concluding Comments

The conclusion that organizations on the right receive only a trickle of funds from the U.S. Treasury in comparison with the torrent that flows to groups on the left is based on three observations. First, listings of grants and contracts obtained under the Freedom of Information Act from many agencies contain few entries for conservative groups. Second, exposés of conservative organizations and movements that investigate their funding sources rarely if ever reveal the receipt of taxpayers' funds. Third, the media have given considerable attention to the grants and contracts that have been directed to conservative organizations and, without exception, these have proved to be small in number and in dollars relative to the hundreds of millions of dollars that are regularly disbursed—with little media attention—to liberal organizations. This disparity can be explained by the ideology of conservative groups, which discourages seeking government support, and by the resistance of public employees to awarding grants and contracts to organizations that criticize their programs and attempt to shrink the size and scope of government. Those tax dollars that have been awarded to conservative organizations have been used primarily to conduct studies or programs to influence public policymakers rather than for grass-roots organizing and political campaigning. This does not imply that taxpayers are getting more for their money when it is spent by the right rather than by the left. Nor does defunding the left, the conservatives' rallying cry, mean that the tax dollars awarded to the left should be redirected to the right. That would be hypocritical, at best. But unfortunately, such hypocrisy seems to be growing during the Reagan administration, a trend that should be nipped in the bud.

One recent example of funding the political activities of the right by Reagan administration officials is a State Department grant for $45,000 to help sponsor a seminar on "moral equivalence" organized by the Shavano Institute for National Leadership, a Colorado-based conservative organization.[76] The seminar was held in May 1985 at the Madison Hotel in Washington, D.C., where participants were paid honoraria of up to $4,000. Participants included Jeane J. Kirkpatrick, Midge Decter, Norman Podhoretz, Sidney Hook, Irving Kristol, Joseph Sobran, and many other conservative and neoconservative luminaries. The theme of the conference was a critique of the notion of "moral equivalence"—of treating the failures of U.S. society as being no different from those of the Soviet Union. Anyone who asserts that a totalitarian state such as the Soviet Union is the full equivalent of a democracy, however imperfect, surely deserves criticism. However, there is one area in which both the Soviet and U.S. governments do have something in common: They both pay intellectuals to promote the views of the government authorities. Although the Soviets do this on a vastly greater scale, in principle the two governments are in fact morally equivalent in this particular practice. It is ironic that a seminar criticizing the notion of moral equivalence proves a degree of moral equivalence, at least in regard to government support of propaganda, by its very existence.

While the business community has received some federal funds for political purposes, there is little evidence that these grants have been used explicitly for political campaigning and grass-roots organizing, although funds have been used for lobbying. They have been used primarily to improve the public image of the corporate community by demonstrating corporations' social responsibility and concern with social problems. It is easy to be concerned about social issues when the taxpayers are paying most of the bills. Liberal groups have used the plight of various groups in society (for example, the poor, the hungry, the unemployed, the elderly) and causes (for example, "fairness," the environment) as a guise for obtaining funds for political activity. Corporations, on the other hand, would have difficulty obtaining tax dollars for such purposes and thus rely on more subtle approaches, such as loan guarantees, contract over-runs, protection from imports, and other subsidies.

Tax dollars belong to everyone and thus belong to no one. There is an enormous incentive for coalitions to form and lobby for appropriations for new programs that permit organizations to dip into the taxpayers' pockets. This concept has been illustrated by the maneuvering undertaken by the U.S. Chamber of Commerce, the AFL-CIO, and the two political parties to ensure the authorization and funding of NED. Although these groups were unwilling to spend their own resources to encourage democracy in other nations, the lure of tax dollars was irresistible. The temptation to pick the taxpayers' pockets is universal and must be overcome if the tax funding of political activity is to be stopped.

XV. Ideas Have Consequences

[S]pecial interest groups normally have an interest in diminishing the information of the average voter. If they can sell him some false tale which supports their particular effort to rob the treasury, it pays. They have resources and normally make efforts to produce this kind of misinformation.

—Gordon Tullock
Welfare for the Well-to-Do

That's the sort of politician for *my* money!

—W. S. Gilbert
The Gondoliers

As Milton Friedman has pointed out, an important "feature of a free society is surely the freedom of individuals to advocate and propagandize openly for a radical change in the structure of society—so long as the advocacy is restricted to persuasion and does not include force or other forms of coercion."[1] This is unquestionably true in the private sector, but advocacy and propaganda are not proper functions of government. Although government should respond to the desires of the electorate, it should not attempt to influence citizens' views on public policy issues. Government, however, has been making such attempts for decades; by supporting advocacy groups through grants and contracts, it inevitably promotes the propagation of a certain set of ideas that influences the course of public policy. As Richard M. Weaver persuasively argued more than 30 years ago, "ideas have consequences,"[2] and no government is capable of financing the propagation of all points of view; the resources of the public sector are limited, and a willingness to support every advocacy group would quickly exhaust the funds available.[3]

Using tax monies to support advocacy groups violates Friedman's—and Thomas Jefferson's—requirement that in a free society only persuasion is appropriate in promoting changes in public policy. Taxes are not collected through persuasion but under the threat of fines and imprisonment. Whenever tax funds are used for pub-

385

licly or privately produced propaganda, coercion is present. Many individual taxpayers refuse to voluntarily provide financial aid to those groups that have been primary beneficiaries of government funding. Indeed, a major reason why advocacy groups seek taxpayers' funds is that they have been unable to convince private donors that their activities are worthy of support. If propaganda organizations have political clout, however, they can obtain coercively collected funds through the political process. They need only to convince politicians and bureaucrats that the potential benefits of providing tax funds for political propaganda outweigh the potential costs. Thus, any explanation of the political economy of tax-funded politics must provide an understanding of how advocacy groups, public employees who administer grants and contracts, and politicians who appropriate program funds interact in the pursuit of their individual self-interests.

The Political Economy of Tax-Funded Politics

The notion that neither members of Congress nor public employees are aware of the widespread misuse of tax dollars for political purposes can be dismissed out of hand. As reported throughout this book, hundreds of millions of dollars are routinely given to organizations that lobby, make campaign contributions, and engage in grass-roots organizing. For those people who deal frequently with advocacy groups, it is unreasonable to suggest that they do not know how the funds awarded through grants and contracts are actually spent. Neither is the issue of tax-funded politics a new one; the General Accounting Office reported grant violations as long ago as 1948.[4] Moreover, Congress has attached dozens of riders to appropriations bills over the past ten years,[5] and it has repeatedly legislated against the use of tax funds for political purposes, thereby suggesting that Congress is fully cognizant of the scope and magnitude of the abuses. In addition, Congress has not been anxious to enforce those legislative restrictions; otherwise, the imposition of repeated prohibitions for over a decade would have been unnecessary. Congress undoubtedly could halt tax-funded politics, but it has chosen not to do so.

Members of Congress must benefit from passing legislation banning certain activities, for it allows them to assure their constituents that they are unalterably opposed to illegal practices without having to actually enforce the law. As the record shows, Congress has been very adept at ignoring its own laws. For example, even though two

386

laws have been passed requiring a balanced federal budget, deficit spending continues at unprecedented rates.[6] Congress has also frequently exempted itself from laws that apply to the private sector: Its members can legally discriminate in hiring and promotion, are exempt from affirmative action and equal employment opportunity laws, can pay their staffs less than the minimum wage, and can legally ignore health and safety regulations.[7] It is reasonable to conclude that Congress is frequently more concerned about appearances than substance and considers itself above the law.

Tax-funded politics is a serious misuse of taxpayers' funds; it is not only illegal, but it is also immoral because at least some individuals are forced to support ideological causes that they oppose. Tax-funded politics also distorts public policy. Changes in public policy arise from what may be called a clash of ideas. Special-interest groups seek legislation and appropriations from Congress, state legislatures, and municipal governments to advance their view of what is best for society. In many cases, the agenda of advocacy groups on the right of the political spectrum will be diametrically opposed to that advocated by organizations on the left. Planned Parenthood, for example, favors abortion in general and government funding of abortion in particular; Birthright, on the other hand, is totally opposed to abortion. It is no exaggeration to assert that politicians often make public policy decisions on the basis of the old saying that "where there is a lot of smoke, there must be a very big fire." That is, if it appears that a large and powerful constituency supports a particular cause, politicians will respond to its demands by passing laws and regulations or appropriating funds for its programs. The most important measures of the size and power of an interest group are the resources that the group can bring to bear on the political process in terms of campaign contributions, votes, lobbyists, and the attention the media give the group.

Funds are required for advocacy groups to make campaign contributions, hire lobbyists, produce studies that support particular policy initiatives, maintain offices, develop news releases, hold press conferences, and publish newsletters, brochures, and pamphlets. The greater its resources, the more effective an advocacy group should be in presenting its case and in engaging other groups in the clash of ideas. The resources available for a particular cause are a good measure of the intensity of feeling on the issue if support for the group advocating the issue comes from voluntary contributions. A large number of individuals with strong views can express their preferences by contributing funds to a group that promotes that issue. With tax-funded politics, however, a small number of zealots with access to the public purse can obtain resources from government to advance its views even though few individuals in society share the group's philosophy. Whenever government funds any political advocacy group, it effectively penalizes those groups that advocate opposing public policies and provides a distinct advantage to the group or groups that it favors in the clash of ideas.

Should government tip the scales in favor of some advocacy groups at the expense of others? Those who favor tax-funded politics claim that such favoritism is necessary and desirable because otherwise their own particular views would not be heard. As Marshall Breger has noted, this argument is specious:

> Some commentators have claimed that the state must support lobbying by consumer or environmental groups because such groups otherwise would fail to secure a place in the political hurly-burly. This view turns democratic theory upside down.

> The plain fact is that political advocacy groups will not flourish on the basis of government subsidy. Rather they will prosper only insofar as they develop financial roots in the polity. Reliance on the government trough is no sign of the commitment of your adherents to your cause.[8]

An argument frequently advanced by recipients of tax dollars who engage in political activity and who have other sources of income is that tax funds per se are not used for campaigning, lobbying, or organizing. Labor unions, which are among the most politically active groups in the United States, have received hundreds of millions of taxpayers' dollars, in addition to income from membership dues, fines, fees, and assessments. When questions are raised about union involvement in tax-funded politics, there is a strong incentive for union leaders to respond that all political activities are financed from revenues derived from the membership and that taxpayers' funds are used exclusively to support programs conducted by the union. However, it is impossible to distinguish a tax dollar from a membership dollar once it is in the union coffers. The notion that a clear distinction can be made between the use of funds obtained from government and funds from other sources cannot withstand even casual examination.

The evidence presented in this study reveals that virtually all the taxpayers' funds used for political purposes are given to organizations that are on the left of the political spectrum. We make no claim that every dollar these groups receive is used for political purposes. To maintain credibility, each recipient group must provide some services to those people it supposedly represents. Anti-poverty groups must to some extent aid the poor, labor unions must make some effort to relieve unemployment, and so forth. We do assert, however, that vast sums of money are diverted from their intended purposes and are used to support political activities. Hundreds of grants and contracts have been awarded to dozens of politically active organizations, and the sums involved are so substantial that if even a modest proportion of the taxpayers' dollars received were allocated to political activity, the amounts spent would dwarf the reported expenditures of all candidates in most elections (see appendix tables for various chapters). Numerous groups participate in so much illegal political activity that it is hard to believe that large sums of tax money are not diverted for political purposes. Compared to the financing of congressional campaigns, the amounts spent on tax-funded politics must be far greater. In the 1979–80 election cycle, candidates for the House of Representatives and the Senate disbursed a total of $238.9 million; for 1981–82 the comparable figure is $343.8 million.[9] In contrast, labor unions alone received more than $150 million in federal grants during the 1978–81 period (see chapter 13). We also know that the political action committees (PACs) of labor unions dominated all PAC spending for 30 years prior to 1975:

> Labor interests were dominant in PAC activity for more than three decades. Labor PACs supported those who supported the generally liberal social and economic programs of the AFL-CIO. The AFL, the CIO and individual unions had PACs in the 1940s; COPE (Committee on Political Education) began in 1955. By 1968, there were 37 national labor political committees and they spent $7 million. In 1974, 201 of the 608 PACs registered with the Federal Election Commission were labor PACs. They spent $11 million of the $21 million total PAC dollars during the 1974 election cycle. Only 89 corporate PACs existed. This was, however, labor's PAC peak.[10]

There is no question that tax-funded politics has become a big business and that political advocacy groups have had a major impact on the direction of U.S. public policy.

389

The organizations receiving almost all of the funds that are used for political purposes actively promote both the redistribution of income and public-sector control of the private sector. This agenda has been implemented on a large scale, as evidenced by what Terry Anderson and P.J. Hill have called the "transfer society"[11] and by the rapid increase in regulation of the private sector, as documented by Murray L. Weidenbaum.[12] The costs to U.S. consumers of adopting this agenda go far beyond the taxpayers' dollars spent by the advocacy groups; the most important costs arise from the resulting regulations and policy changes. For example, Weidenbaum has estimated that federal government regulations cost the private sector more than $66 billion in 1976; by 1979, this cost had exceeded $102 billion—an increase of more than 55 percent.[13] Despite these enormous costs (more than $400 per capita by 1979), there is little evidence that the regulation of the environment, health, occupational safety, and so on has been cost effective or has even made much impact at all.[14] In some cases, the government regulation of industry has been partially dismantled because it was found to be counterproductive and too costly. For example, the trucking industry has been partially deregulated after nearly 50 years of regulation by the Interstate Commerce Commission, and the Civil Aeronautics Board, which regulated the airlines, no longer exists.[15]

Weidenbaum's estimates of the cost of regulation include only the administrative costs incurred by the government agencies that issue and enforce regulations and the compliance costs borne by those in the private sector. But there are other, less direct costs. Regulations increase the cost of business operations, discouraging new firms from entering an industry and leading to a slowdown in economic growth and lower employment. Regulations adversely affect worker productivity; and if regulatory costs are passed to the consumer in the form of higher prices, inflation is exacerbated and U.S. products are less competitive in world markets. Environmental advocacy groups, for example, have slowed the development of some of the nation's resources and have almost crippled the nuclear power industry so that there is greater reliance on "safe" and "nonpolluting" coal.[16] These long-term effects, though much more difficult to quantify, are nevertheless substantial and could easily outweigh the direct costs of compliance and administration.

With regard to the redistribution of income and wealth, left-wing advocacy groups have been remarkably successful. Huge sums have been spent on programs to ostensibly cure a host of problems, such as poverty, hunger, unemployment, discrimination, and "unfairness." Regardless of the amounts allocated by government for these programs, little seems to ever be accomplished. The public sector annually spends several times the amount estimated as needed to eliminate poverty, but the only result has been an increase in the number of individuals reported as living in poverty (see chapter 8). One outcome common to all these programs, however, is that large sums have been diverted from their stated purposes to support left-wing political activists and their organizations in their efforts to promote what they view as best for society.

These professional political activists claim to champion various causes on behalf of other, less fortunate people. Lobbyists for the poor are typically far from poor themselves (many of them are lawyers), lobbyists for consumer protection are not necessarily the victims of faulty products or dangerous chemicals, antinuclear activists are not the victims of nuclear accidents or may not even be potential victims, social security lobbyists are often young or middle-aged, civil rights lobbyists who oppose tuition tax credits frequently send their children to private schools, and so on. Organizers of many large, left-wing special-interest groups earn a handsome living by lobbying for legislation that provides them with income, prestige, and an opportunity to pursue their own political goals at the taxpayers' expense. They are professionals who establish themselves as middlemen between legislators, the bureaucracy, and the constituents they claim to represent. These activists may be viewed as part of a shadow government that cooperates with politicians and bureaucrats to facilitate the predominant activity of government, which is the redistribution of income and wealth from one group in society to another.

Bureaucrats, Public Policy, and Political Advocacy

The role of public employees in the public policy process is frequently misunderstood. It is widely assumed that bureaucrats are passive agents in the policy process; that is, they merely administer and carry out the programs that Congress designs and funds. The term "civil servant" suggests that bureaucrats merely execute the orders of their masters, the elected members of Congress or, ultimately, the taxpayers. This perception is simplistic and wrong, however, for it ignores the entrepreneurial role played by public employees. The simple truth is that civil servants, like everyone else, are primarily concerned with their own self-interests: salary,

391

rank, perquisites, prestige, and opportunities for promotion. Because prospects for bureaucrats are brightest when their agency's activity and budget are expanding, bureaucrats have strong incentives to promote and stimulate a perceived need for their own activities. The bureaucracy, therefore, is a vigorous lobbyist. As Peter Woll has noted:

> The ability of administrative agencies to marshal support in favor of particular programs is often severely tested, and as a result the agencies have frequently created public relations departments on a permanent basis to engineer consent for their legislative proposals. It has been estimated that the executive branch spends close to half a billion dollars [in 1971] a year on public relations and public information programs. Not all of this expenditure is for political purposes, for there are a number of legitimate public information programs that administrative agencies must undertake. But whatever the percentage may be for non-political purposes, it is obvious that agencies are expending huge amounts of funds, time, and effort on indirect and direct lobbying activities. Administrative personnel engaged in public relations are not so open about their activities as their counterparts in private advertising. . . . The myth that the bureaucracy is "neutral" must be maintained if possible. However, through what might be called undercover devices, the bureaucracy engages in extensive lobbying and propaganda activities. . . . And, regardless of particular congressional outbursts against administrative propaganda and attempts to influence legislation, the bureaucratic strength in the legislative field really stems from congressional dependence upon the information and political support the agencies possess. Congress wants the bureaucracy to play an important role in the legislative process.[17]

There are many examples of bureaucratic lobbying expenditures. In fiscal year 1984, the Department of Agriculture officially employed 144 full-time public affairs persons who had a budget of $6.5 million. The entire department, including sub-agencies, employed 704 people to work in public affairs. The Department of Education had a full-time public affairs staff of 46 persons and a budget of $2.4 million; the Department of Transportation had 21 public affairs professionals with a $1.5 million budget. The Pentagon listed 1,066 full-time public relations employees. Similar programs undoubtedly exist in all other agencies.[18]

Even though large sums of tax revenues are formally appropriated to promote the activities of the federal bureaucracy, these sums are apparently inadequate to ensure the expansion of agency budgets to the extent desired by bureaucrats and politicians. Tax-funded politics is a way of diverting even more tax revenue for the purpose of self-promotion by distributing funds to various special-interest groups that are formally outside the government. The grants and contracts may be given to "help the poor," "protect the consumer," and so forth, but a portion of the money is intended for political advocacy, for support of the government agency that awarded the funds and of the agency's patrons in Congress. The funds flow to groups on the left of the political spectrum because these groups favor an expansion of the role of government in the economy and of government programs and expenditures. By channeling taxpayers' dollars to left-wing organizations, the bureaucracy is merely rewarding its friends and providing support for those who will reciprocate by lobbying and campaigning for increased programs and budgets.

Politicians, Public Policy, and Political Advocacy

Like bureaucrats, politicians pursue their self-interests by increasing their income, prestige, and perquisites of office. Political advocacy funded by the taxpayers plays an important role in this process. Many students of public policy view members of Congress, state legislators, and elected local officials as passively responding to the will of the people, but this view ignores the entrepreneurial role that politicians play in diverting tax dollars to advocacy groups as a means of obtaining resources to win reelection campaigns.

A politician's income, power, prestige, and perquisites depend on winning reelection; money and other resources (such as phone banks and campaign volunteers) are the life blood of electoral politics. Advocacy groups that receive tax dollars repay their political debt by promoting the political careers of incumbents who support them. The groups make campaign contributions, provide campaign workers and volunteers, and register and educate such voters as low-income individuals, who normally do not participate actively in politics. Once reelected, the politician has strong incentives to reward these advocacy groups with tax dollars that will be used to keep the incumbent in power. Grass-roots organizing is a very labor-intensive and expensive activity, but when the taxpayers bear the cost, the incumbent politician has an important edge over his challengers.

393

Even if not facing serious opposition to reelection, the incumbent politician has an incentive to spend time and energy seeking campaign contributions from every possible source, including advocacy groups that receive taxpayers' funds. The incentive is simple: Members of the U.S. House of Representatives can divert leftover campaign funds to their personal use. Under a law passed on January 8, 1980, all members of Congress at the time of enactment could legally use excess campaign funds for personal expenses (other members do the same, even though it is illegal).[19]

Campaigning can be very profitable to the politician under such a law. Consider the case of Rep. Joseph G. Minish (D-N.J.). He had $326,568 in his campaign account when, three weeks before the election, he managed to raise an additional $85,919, apparently to wage a major effort to retain his seat for a twelfth term. According to the Federal Election Commission, however, Minish was able to spend only $142,958, and $269,529 remained when he was defeated. Minish's report to the FEC indicated that more than $13,000 was received "on four days—Nov. 9, 15, 19, and 21—after the election."[20] Minish refused to comment on the planned use of the funds, but he dismissed the possibility of returning it to the contributors because it would have been difficult to decide how much to give to each donor. Other defeated or retiring members of Congress have also pocketed substantial sums; for example, Geraldine Ferraro, the defeated vice-presidential nominee of the Democratic party in 1984, left Congress with more than $105,000 in her congressional campaign account.[21]

The rule with regard to campaign contributions in the Senate forbids any member or former member to convert contributions to personal use. In an investigation of Senate slush funds from campaign contributions, however, the *New Republic* reported as follows:

—Senator Daniel Inouye of Hawaii spent more than $168,322 in campaign funds during 1981 and 1982, a period during which Inouye had no campaign headquarters, no workers, and no telephones. Campaign funds were used for payments to his wife totalling $4,720, two cars ($17,034), and for insurance ($5,582) and gasoline ($1,954). More than $40 thousand were spent on airline tickets; thousands were spent at Washington restaurants and additional hundreds for such items as rented plants and tropical fish and aquarium supplies.

—Senator Matsunaga, also of Hawaii, spent $29,330 in campaign funds in the Senate restaurant in 1981 and 1982.

—Senator D'Amato of New York spent $24,516 in 1981 and 1982 to lease, maintain, insure, and operate two Buicks.

—Senator Alan Cranston of California transferred $66,000 in unused campaign funds to a private checking account.

—Senator Harrison Williams, Jr., of New Jersey took $65,781 in leftover campaign funds with him when he resigned following his Abscam conviction.[22]

The article continued: "In dozens of cases, Senate incumbents have ignored I.R.S. regulations, violated federal election law, and evaded standards for public disclosure and accountability."[23]

Members of Congress seem to be thriving on campaign contributions, some of which come from advocacy groups supported by taxpayers. Our explanation of the process of tax-funded advocacy can be summarized as follows:

1. Politicians allocate taxpayer funds for programs under the guise of alleviating the plight of the poor, the sick, the elderly, the unemployed, . . . and serving the "public interest";

2. The bureaucrats who administer the programs provide taxpayer funds to political advocacy groups through grants and contracts ostensibly intended to carry out program objectives;

3. However, much of the money received by political activists is used to lobby, campaign, and organize support for new programs for the bureaucracy to manage, additional funding for existing programs, and the (re)election of politicians who favor the appropriations which fund the political advocacy.

4. The political advocacy groups proselytize for their programs to persuade the public through the media that greater spending is essential to deal with a pressing social problem; sympathetic politicians receive campaign contributions and assistance in their reelection efforts; these politicians appropriate more funds for existing programs and initiate new programs; the bureaucracy awards more taxpayers' funds to the advocacy groups, and the process recycles from step 1.

The losers are the taxpayers who pay for these shenanigans and the unfortunate members of society who receive only part of the promised benefits of the programs that supposedly are set up to help them. Taxpayers' funds are siphoned off by political activists to promote their views, by public employees who want to finance the expansion of their bureaucratic empires, and by politicians who want funds for reelection contests and for conversion to their personal use. This assessment may seem cynical, for it suggests that political opportunists have used the poor, the unemployed, the hungry, and others in society as pawns to bilk the taxpayers under the guise of compassion. As our research documents, however, this is precisely the role that the poor and those others play in the political process.

There are politicians who oppose tax-funded politics, but criticism of the political advocacy groups on the left is rare and muted. The critics fear that opposition to the programs and organizations that receive funding or that voiced suspicion of the motives of some political activists will cause them to be labeled racist, anti-labor, or anti-poor. They fear attacks by a powerful left-wing network and coalition that has ready access to the media and ample resources at its disposal. The average voter has been misled about these organizations and their goals. As Gordon Tullock has argued:

> [S]pecial interest groups normally have an interest in diminishing the information of the average voter. If they can sell him some false tale which supports their particular effort to rob the treasury, it pays. They have resources and normally make efforts to produce this kind of misinformation. But that would not work if the voter had a strong motive to learn the truth. There is not much point in trying to convince housewives that the canned tomatoes you are selling are much better quality than they are. She may buy one can but as soon as she opens it she finds it is of low quality and doesn't go back. In politics, unfortunately, this rule does not exist, because the voter never has the opportunity to open the can.[24]

Average voters have no real incentives to investigate the activities of government or of organizations that receive government grants and contracts. The costs of doing so are too high, and the benefits of exposing illegalities or shortcomings are negligible. With a great deal of time, effort, and expense, voters may make an opportunity to open the tomato can, but they will receive no rewards for making such sacrifices.

Private organizations that receive taxpayers' funds to support their activities are a feature of many democratic societies.[25] In Great Britain, for instance, private groups that receive tax funds are called *tringos*, an acronym for tax-receiving independent non-government organizations. One incomplete inventory has revealed that in 1982 there were 863 tringos and that the amounts they received in government grants and contracts ranged from £10 for the UNESCO

Participation Programme to £83,843,928 awarded by the Scottish Office to Registered Housing Societies and Associations.[26] Some of the grants awarded were quite curious: The Welsh Office of the Cabinet provided £950 for the National Gypsy Council, and the Department of Employment subsidized the Rare Breeding Birds Panel to the tune of £165.

The problems that the British appear to be having with tringos are similar to those reported in this study:

> Tringos undoubtedly consume huge quantities of public money. Much of this is undoubtedly spent on legitimate objects; some, equally certainly, is not. One can only guess at the exact total.

> Tringos have also grown in numbers, especially since the mid-Sixties. Again, one can only guess at their total numbers. The point is that there is no way of knowing for certain how many there are, how much they receive, or what they spend it on.

> The Civil Service has shown itself extraordinarily reluctant to divulge details about them. They refused even to give them a generic name. Although the term "non-official bodies" was in wide use, the Civil Service refused to admit the existence of such a class until quite recently, despite the fact that the term had been used in official parliamentary responses.[27]

Stopping Tax-Funded Politics

The Office of Management and Budget has been charged with eliminating the tax funding of political activity, and current efforts are rooted in the initiatives begun during the Carter administration. In June 1980, OMB issued Circular A-122, "Cost Principles for Nonprofit Organizations," which established uniform rules for determining the costs of grants, contracts, and other agreements. Like all other OMB cost-principle circulars, Circular A-122 was a management directive to the heads of all federal departments and agencies, and it specified allowable and unallowable costs for federal grants and contracts and how such costs are calculated. The directive specified certain costs that were not to be reimbursed on grounds of public policy, including advertising, fund-raising, and entertainment expenses. Lobbying costs were also not allowed, but the restrictions were vague and, for the most part, ignored.

Under intense pressure to defund the left, the Reagan administration decided to revise Circular A-122 to make it clearer and more effective. On January 24, 1983, OMB published a proposal in the

Federal Register to change A-122's treatment of lobbying activities by defining as unallowable the costs of advocacy activities performed by federal nonprofit grantors and contractors with appropriated funds.[28] The proposed changes would have

> prohibited employees of federal grant or contract recipients from engaging in political advocacy and charging any part of their salary or supporting costs against their federal grant or contract. Employees of companies or of nonprofit organizations receiving government grants or contracts could not accept any salary reimbursement from the government if they engaged in any advocacy at all. If more than 5 percent of the office space of a recipient of government funds were used for advocacy, none of the costs of that space would be reimbursable. No capital equipment, such as photocopiers, could be used for advocacy purposes if partially paid for with federal funds.

> Further, OMB's first draft used an expansive definition of political advocacy which ranged far beyond the traditional definition—influencing campaigns and referenda—to encompass communicating with any member or employee of a legislative body, supporting political action committees and trade associations that have "political advocacy as a substantial political purpose," filing amicus curiae briefs, and efforts to influence governmental decisions by influencing the opinions of the general public. The regulation applied to political advocacy aimed at state and local issues as well.[29]

Broadening the definition from "lobbying" to "advocacy activities," along with the prohibitions and restrictions accompanying advocacy operations, raised a storm of protest. After publication of the proposed revisions, "48,300 comments from the public, from nonprofit and commercial organizations, and from government agencies" were received.[30] No one seemed pleased:

> Those pummeling the administration in the controversy include a number of church-related, environmental, consumer and liberal-left activist organizations, all protesting even the thought of promulgating the regulations, and others such as many conservative groups normally in the president's camp on issues, who have drawn a line in their militancy that the regulations be drafted in the strongest possible language and be vigorously enforced."[31]

At the end of the 45-day period for public comment, the proposed regulations were withdrawn.

The OMB issued a second proposed revision of Circular A-122 on November 3, 1983.[32] This attempt drew no less than 93,600 separate comments (bulk packages of letters and petitions and form letters were counted as single comments), with the vast majority (93.5 percent) favoring the proposed revisions without further changes.[33] This second version significantly eased the restrictions proposed in the earlier draft: Recipients of federal funds could use private funds for lobbying, and the definition of lobbying was more restricted; there were no limitations placed on lobbying at the local level, communicating with government officials on matters other than legislation, litigating on behalf of others, and paying dues to associations that engage in substantial amounts of lobbying.[34] In addition, recipients of federal funds were to facilitate government audit procedures by certifying the accuracy of their cost break-downs. The final version of revised Circular A-122, issued in April 1984, incorporated these alterations.

Despite all the ballyhoo about the effects of revised Circular A-122, it is unlikely that even a minor dent will be made in tax-funded political activity. New regulations that define lobbying and deter-mine what is permissible with taxpayers' funds, who pays for what, accounting practices, and audit procedures are little more than a tempest in a teapot. Lobbying, campaigning, and grass-roots orga-nizing with taxpayers' funds have been illegal for years, but no one has enforced the law.

Our research indicates that prior to 1984 hundreds of millions of dollars were used by advocacy groups for blatantly political activity, often with the full knowledge of the bureaucrats awarding the grants and contracts and of the politicians appropriating the funds. The essential point is that the tax monies given to these groups, at least in part, were intended for political purposes from the outset. The activists were well aware of the role they were to play in the public policy process; they knew (as did the public employees who disbursed the funds) that the political activities they were pursuing were illegal and that little if anything would be done to stop them.

The changes included in revised Circular A-122 suggest that one reason tax funds were used for political activity was that there was no clear definition of lobbying and therefore that the recipients must not have really understood that they were breaking the law. This is manifestly a ludicrous supposition. Moreover, OMB seems to suggest that without proper cost accounting and audit techniques to keep track of expenditures, it was difficult to know how much was spent on illegal activity; thus, it is hardly surprising that federal auditors have not uncovered a widespread abuse of federal funds. This supposition is perhaps even more inane than the no-clear-definition one. Federal auditors from agencies awarding the grants and contracts have no incentives to investigate the abuse of the funds for advocacy, for this advocacy ensures the growth of the auditors' agencies and the expansion of their programs. There are no real incentives to pursue and prosecute activists who misuse taxpayers' money. It should also be noted that tens of thousands of grants and contracts are awarded by the federal government each year—and that even with careful monitoring of contractor and grantee expenditures, a great deal of tax-funded politics would still occur just because of the sheer size of the audit problem. Further, when the General Accounting Office, Congress's audit arm, reported repeated, widespread, and blatant improprieties by certain grantees (see the tale of TELACU in chapter 9), funding was often continued, even under the Reagan administration. Criminal charges are rarely filed, and civil remedies are not often sought. Tax-funded politics benefits too many politicians, bureaucrats, and activists for it to cease just because OMB revised Circular A-122.

There is a simple way to halt tax-funded advocacy: Taxpayers' money that is intended to aid the less fortunate should be given to these individuals directly instead of being funneled through middlemen. If the poor, the hungry, and the unemployed were paid directly through a device such as Friedman's negative income tax proposal,[35] the opportunities for political activists to use tax funds for advocacy purposes would be markedly diminished. Moreover, a scheme such as the negative income tax has advantages that make it intrinsically appealing:

> The advantages of this arrangement are clear. It is directed specifically at the problem of poverty. It gives help in the form most useful to the individual, namely, cash. It is general and could be substituted for the host of special measures now in effect. It makes explicit the cost borne by society. It operates outside the market. Like any other measures to alleviate poverty, it reduces the incentives of those helped to help themselves, but it does not eliminate that incentive entirely, as a system of supplementing incomes up to some fixed minimum would. An extra dollar earned would always mean more money available for expenditure.[36]

400

If the distribution of cash through the income tax system is politically unpalatable, vouchers could be distributed to help the poor obtain education, health care, housing, legal services, and other goods and services.

Political advocacy organizations currently receive most of their funds from government under the guise of helping the less-fortunate individuals in society. But they cannot spend tax dollars that they do not receive. Vouchers or direct payments to the less fortunate would eliminate much of the funding for these groups, thereby resulting in much less tax-funded politics. Undoubtedly, a major reason these groups are so stringently opposed to voucher proposals or any suggestion of direct payments is that their funding disguise would be imperiled. Eliminating the access of advocacy groups to taxpayers' funds will eliminate tax-funded politics. However, passing new laws and regulations, which can be ignored as easily as the ones that have been in existence for years, will accomplish little.

Concluding Comments

We have documented the existence of a well-coordinated network of political activists that has managed to obtain hundreds of millions of taxpayers' dollars each year from the federal government and additional millions from state and local governments for political advocacy. This network is aggressively engaged in a concerted effort to undermine the foundations of private property and private enterprise. If these activists are successful, the market economy that has produced unparalleled prosperity for Americans will be strangled by government planning and public-sector control over the distribution of capital and every major aspect of private-sector activity. In our view, the massive funding that the left has consistently received from the taxpayers has distorted public policy, for the left's ideas have had important consequences in shaping the expansion of government and the growth of the welfare state.

Ideally, we would like to be able to develop an objective measure of the extent to which tax-funded political advocacy has changed public policy over the years. It would be most interesting and informative to know how social programs and regulatory initiatives would have evolved in the absence of tax-funded politics. Unfortunately, this goal is not attainable because, in the terminology of economists, it is not possible to develop a "production function" relating inputs of taxpayer dollars given to advocacy groups to outputs, that is, to changes in public policy.

One indisputable impact of activists on public policy, documented throughout this book, is their ability to divert substantial sums from the public sector year after year to promote their ideology. This phenomenon alone is one indication of the success and impact of these groups on the public policy process. Given the vast sums that have supported liberal activists from the public purse, the clash of ideas through which public policy is formed must have been heavily skewed in favor of the groups on the left of the political spectrum. The evidence clearly indicates that groups that advocate limited government have received miniscule amounts of funding from taxpayers; although these grants are relatively small and few in number, they are illegitimate as well.

Tax-funded political advocacy must be halted by defunding advocacy groups on both the left and the right. We hope that our exposure of tax-funded politics will help bring about this essential change.

Appendix

Table A2.1
Selected "Organizer Training Schools"

Center for Urban Encounter (CUE), Minneapolis	Midwest Academy, Chicago
Highlander Research and Education Center, New Market, Tenn.	National Center for Urban Ethnic Affairs, Washington
	National Training and Information Center, Chicago
Industrial Areas Foundation (IAF), Huntington, N.Y.	New England Training Center for Community Organizers (NETCCO), Providence, R.I.
The Institute, New Orleans	
Laurel Springs Institute, Santa Monica, Calif.	Organize Training Center, San Francisco
Mid-American Institute, Chicago	Pacific Institute for Community Organization, Oakland, Calif.
Mid-Atlantic Center for Community Concern, Brooklyn	

SOURCE: Harry C. Boyte, *The Backyard Revolution* (Philadelphia: Temple University Press, 1980), p. 213.

Table A2.2

MIDWEST ACADEMY "ALUMNI" ORGANIZATIONS, 1983

Carolina Brown Lung Association

National Women's Political Caucus

Nine to Five Working Women's Organization

Massachusetts Fair Share

Wisconsin Council of Churches

Environmental Action Foundation

National Organization for Women

American Federation of State, County, and Municipal Employees

Citizens for a Better Environment

United Auto Workers

Ohio Public Interest Campaign

National Education Association

Community Action Commission

Gray Panthers

Southwest Parish and Neighborhood Federation

Clergy and Laity Concerned

Vermont Alliance

American Nurses Association

Oregon Fair Share

Illinois Public Action Council

Women Employed

Coalition of Labor Union Women

Public Interest Research Groups

Women's Action Alliance

New Jersey Federation of Senior Citizens

American Federation of Teachers

SOURCE: 1983 Midwest Academy brochure.

Table A2.3

NATIONAL GROUP ENDORSERS OF THE FAIR BUDGET ACTION CAMPAIGN

American Coalition of Citizens with Disabilities
American Ethical Union
American Federation of Government Employees (AFGE)
American Federation of State, County, and Municipal Employees (AFSCME)
American Friends Service Committee (AFSC)
American Public Health Association
ASPIRA
Association of Community Organizations for Reform Now (ACORN)
B'NAI B'RITH Women
Center for Community Change (CCC)
Center for Science in the Public Interest (CSPI)
Center on Budget Policy and Priority
Children's Defense Fund (CDF)
Children's Foundation
Clergy and Laity Concerned (CALC)
Coalition for Legal Services
Coalition for a New Foreign and Military Policy
Coalition of Black Trade Unionists (CBTU)
Community Design Center Directors' Association
Community Nutrition Institute (CNI)
Congress Watch
Consumer Coalition for Health (CCH)
Consumer Federation of America (CFA)
Cuban Planning Council

Democratic Socialist Organizing Committee (DSOC)
Disability Rights and Education Defense Fund
Employment Research Associates
Environmental Action Foundation (EAF)
Environmental Action, Inc.
Fellowship of Reconciliation
Food Research and Action Center (FRAC)
Friends Committee on National Legislation (FCNL)
Friends of the Earth
Gray Panthers
Hispanic Housing Coalition
IMAGE
International Longshoremen's and Warehousemen's Union (ILWU)
Interreligious Task Force on U.S. Food Policy
Jobs with Peace Campaign
Latino Institute
League of United Latin American Citizens (LULAC)
Lutheran Council in the U.S.A.— Office for Government Affairs
Mexican-American Legal Defense Fund (MALDEF)
Mennonite Central Committee, U.S. Peace Section
National Anti-Hunger Coalition (NAHC)
National Association of Farmworkers Organizations (NAFO)
National Association of Social Workers (NASW)
National Board of the YWCA of the United States
National Catholic Conference for Interracial Justice

National Child Nutrition Project
(NCNP)
National Committee against
Discrimination in Housing
(NCDH)
National Community Action
Agency Executive Directors
Association (NCAAEDA)
National Consumers League
National Congress for
Community Economic
Development (NCCED)
National Congress of
Neighborhood Women
(NCNW)
National Council of Churches
National Council of La Raza
National Council of Senior
Citizens (NCSC)
National Education Association
(NEA)
National Family Farm Coalition
National Farmers Union
National Low-Income Housing
Coalition
National Rural Housing Coalition
National Tenants Organization
National Urban Coalition

National Urban League
New American Movement
(NAM)
Neighborhood Arts Programs
National Organizing
Committee (NAPNOC)
Puerto Rican Forum
Rural America
Rural America Women
SANE (Citizens for a Sane World)
SER
The Episcopal Church—
Washington Office
Unitarian Universalist
Association—D.C. Office
United Church of Christ—Office
of Church and Society
United Electrical Workers (UE)
United Steelworkers of America
(USWA)
Urban Environment Conference
U.S. Student Association
Wider Opportunities for Women
Women's International League for
Peace and Freedom (WILPF)
Women's Strike for Peace
World Hunger Education Service

SOURCE: *An Organizer's Manual*, 2d ed. (Washington: Fair Budget Action Campaign, n.d.), back cover.

Table A4.1
Indirect Federal Funding of Tom Hayden's Campaign for Economic Democracy

Recipient	Awarding Agency	Grant*	Relation of Recipient to CED	Date
Sierra Club	Environmental Protection Agency (EPA)	$669,253	Sierra Club, FOE, and CED founded Toxics Responsibility Advisory Committee to alert citizens to environmental issues.	1978, 1979, 1980
Citizen/Labor Energy Coalition (C/LEC)	ACTION	$30,000	Hayden is on C/LEC's Board of Directors. C/LEC's policies are largely anticorporate, antinuclear, and "no growth" oriented.	1980–81
C/LEC	Dept. of Energy	$57,640		1979–81
C/LEC	VISTA	8 volunteers		1979–81
C/LEC	Community Services Administration	$200,000		1980
Communitas	Dept. of Justice	$334,761	This "crime control project," established by CED, also uses its funds to promote CED priorities, such as rent	1978

Table A4.1 (continued)

Recipient	Awarding Agency	Grant*	Relation of Recipient to CED	Date
Youth Project	ACTION	$792,157	control. The director is the head of Santa Monicans for Renters' Rights. Youth Project 1978 annual report states that its funds enabled the San Diego chapter of CED to hire its first staff members.	1979–81
Youth Project	Dept. of Labor	$41,990		1980
Youth Project	VISTA	59 volunteers		1979
Center for New Corporate Priorities	Dept. of Labor	$126,000	Anti-industry organization run by Hayden's 1976 Senate campaign manager, Ruth Goldway, ex-mayor of Santa Monica. As mayor, she placed many CETA employees in CED positions.	1978
Laurel Springs Institute	VISTA	$201,238	A training center for CED activists.	1979–81

| Western Sun | Dept. of Energy | $82,000 | Hayden is a director of this federally funded project. He has placed political allies on the payroll to the exclusion of others possibly more qualified in solar energy. | 1979 |

SOURCE: Freedom of Information Act requests.
*Figures represent dollars except where volunteers are indicated.

Table A4.2

Selected Local Anti-Industry Lobbying Organizations

Active Clevelanders Together, Cleveland

Apostles for Justice, Avet, Colo.

Chester Community Improvement Project, Chester, Pa.

Coalition for Social Action, Cedar Rapids, Iowa

Communities Organized for Public Service (COPS), San Antonio, Tex.

Get Action in New Bedford (GAIN), New Bedford, Mass.

Indianapolis Neighborhood Development, Inc. (INDI), Indianapolis

Northwest Community Organization (NCO), Chicago

Oakland Community Organization (OCO), Oakland, Calif.

People Acting for Change Together, Burlington, Vt.

Portland Organizing Project, Portland, Maine

Richmond United Neighborhoods (RUN), Richmond, Va.

Save Our Cumberland Mountains, Jacksboro, Tenn.

Somerville United Neighborhoods (SUN), Somerville, Mass.

Union Sarah Community Organization, St. Louis, Mo.

Southeast Fresno Concerned Citizens, Fresno, Calif.

Syracuse United Neighborhoods (SUN), Syracuse, N.Y.

Adams-Morgan Association, Buffalo

Buckeye Woodland Community Congress, Cleveland

Concerned Citizens Congress of Northeast, Denver

Coalition of Concerned Tenants Union, New Bedford, Mass.

Concerned Seniors of Dade County, Miami

Hartford Areas Rally Together (HART), Hartford, Conn.

Metropolitan Area Housing Alliance, Chicago

North Toledo Area Corporation (NTAC), Toledo, Ohio

Organization of the Northeast, Chicago

People Empowerment Project, Akron, Ohio

Queens Citizen Organization, New York

Roseville Coalition, Newark, N.J.

Sherman Park Community Association, Milwaukee

South East Community Organization (SECO), Baltimore

South End Seattle Community Organization, Seattle

South Side Community Council, Pittsburgh

The Metropolitan Organization (TMO), Houston

410

Treme Community Improvement Association, New Orleans

Twin Cities Organization (TCO), Minneapolis–St. Paul

United Citizen Organization, Buffalo

United Communities Acting Now (UCAN), South Bend, Ind.

United Connecticut Action for Neighborhoods (UCAN), Bridgeport

United Neighbors in Action, Oakland, Calif.

United Neighborhoods Organization (UNO), East Los Angeles

Wilmington United Neighborhoods (WUN), Wilmington, Del.

California Housing Action and Information Network, Los Angeles

California Tax Reform Association, Sacramento

Carolina Action, Raleigh, N.C.

Citizens Action Coalition, Indianapolis

Citizens Action League, San Francisco

Coalition for Consumer Justice, Central Falls, R.I.

Minnesota Communities Acting for Change Together (COACT), Brainerd

Connecticut Citizen Action Group, Hartford

Florida Consumers Federation, West Palm Beach

Georgia Action, Atlanta

Illinois Public Action Council, Chicago

Indiana Housing Coalition, Indianapolis

Massachusetts Fair Share, Boston

Minnesota Citizen Action, Minneapolis

Mississippi Hunger Coalition, Jackson

New Jersey Tenants Organization, Fort Lee

New York Public Interest Research Group/Citizens' Alliance, New York

North Country People's Alliance, Woodsville, N.H.

Ohio Public Interest Campaign, Cleveland

Oregon Fair Share, Portland

United League, Holly Springs, Miss.

Vermont Alliance, Montpelier

SOURCE: Harry C. Boyte, *The Backyard Revolution* (Philadelphia: Temple University Press, 1981), pp. 213–17.

Table A5.1
TAXPAYER FUNDING OF RALPH NADER'S PUBLIC INTEREST RESEARCH GROUPS

Recipient (Branch)	Awarding Agency	Grant*	Stated Purpose	Date
Oregon	VISTA	10,000	Economic development	12/78
California	FTC	44,820	NA	12/76–9/81
California	FTC	3,828	NA	10/79–9/81
California	FTC	10,102	NA	12/76–10/81
New York	FTC	12,169	NA	6/76–9/79
New York	FTC	8,327	NA	6/76–9/79
New York	EPA	3,000	NA	2/79–10/79
Ohio	ACTION	14,478	NA	9/80–9/81
Washington, D.C.	ACTION	48,650	NA	3/80–4/81
Washington, D.C.	ACTION	269,884	NA	3/80–4/81
Pittsburgh	ACTION	10,200	NA	4/81–3/82
Pittsburgh	ACTION	11,664	NA	4/81–3/82
St. Louis	ACTION	9,162	NA	2/81–9/81
St. Louis	ACTION	5,000	NA	9/80–6/81
Trenton	EPA	8,000	NA	10/78–8/79
New York	FTC	24,740	Intervenor funding	1979
California	FTC	46,354	As above	1979
California	FTC	27,521	As above	1979
Massachusetts	VISTA	4 volunteers	Community/consumer outreach	12/77–2/79
New York	VISTA	9 volunteers	NA	4/78
Ohio	VISTA	12 volunteers	Economic-development projects	9/79–9/80

Anchorage	VISTA	4 volunteers	Conduct public policy forums	10/78–10/79
Anchorage	VISTA	2 volunteers	Advisory personnel	6/78–6/79
Oregon	VISTA	10 volunteers	Economic-development projects	12/78
National	VISTA	1,286,903	NA	1978–81

SOURCE: Freedom of Information Act requests.
*Figures represent dollars except where volunteers are indicated.

413

Table A5.2

FEDERAL TRADE COMMISSION FUNDING OF INTEREST GROUP TESTIMONY AND LEGAL FEES, 1975–79

Intervenor Group	FTC-Authorized Amount ($)	Rule-making Proceedings
Consumer Action—San Francisco	29,263	Vocational schools
National Consumer Law Center	2,474	Vocational schools
Illinois Governor's Consumer Advocate Office	5,460	Vocational Schools
National Council of Senior Citizens	2,070	Prescription drugs
National Consumer Law Center	3,093	Holder-in-due course
National Council of Senior Citizens	46,734	Hearing aids
National Hearing Aid Society	83,511	Hearing aids
Americans for Democratic Action—Consumer Affairs Committee	5,747	Funeral practices
Arkansas Consumer Research Center	7,775	Funeral practices
California Citizens Action Group	26,888	Funeral practices
Consumer Federation of America	11,329	Funeral practices
Consumer Union of United States, Inc.	3,980	Funeral practices
New York Public Interest Research Group	11,740	Funeral practices
Consumer Action—San Francisco	15,507	Protein supplements
Consumer Action Now—Council on Environmental Alternatives	13,956	Protein supplements
Americans for Democratic Action—Consumer Affairs Committee	30,202	Ophthalmic goods
Arkansas Community Organizations for Reform Now	2,813	Ophthalmic goods
California Citizen Action Group	38,285	Ophthalmic goods
Consumer Action—San Francisco	43,545	Ophthalmic goods
New York Public Interest Research Group	12,575	Ophthalmic goods
Consumer Action—Washington, D.C.	46,844	Food advertising
Consumer Union of United States, Inc.	7,360	Food advertising

Organization	Amount	Subject
Council on Children—Media and Merchandising	62,435	Food advertising
National Consumers Congress	9,295	Food advertising
National Consumers Congress	47,353	Care labeling
California Public Interest Research Group	46,354	Used cars
Center for Auto Safety	9,305	Used cars
Consumer Action—San Francisco	19,522	Used cars
Americans for Democratic Action—Consumer Affairs Committee	24,471	OTC drugs
California Citizen Action Group—Consumer Affairs Committee	43,683	OTC drugs
Council on Children—Media and Merchandising	25,249	OTC drugs
National Consumer Law Center	132,256	Credit practices
Americans for Democratic Action—Consumer Affairs Committee	47,780	Health spas
Consumer Union of United States, Inc.	47,991	Health spas
Center for Auto Safety	48,657	Mobile homes
California Public Interest Research Group	27,521	Thermal insulation
Sierra Club/Friends of the Earth/Natural Resources Defense Council	30,241	Thermal insulation
Consumer Federation of America	2,141	Thermal insulation
National Consumers League	42,484	Thermal insulation
Americans for Democratic Action—Consumer Affairs Committee	21,592	OTC antacids
California Citizen Action Group	64,228	OTC antacids
Council on Children—Media and Merchandising	41,065	OTC antacids
Action for Children's Television	77,016	Children's advertising
Community Nutrition Institute	40,666	Children's advertising
Consumer Union of United States, Inc.	73,916	Children's advertising
Council on Children—Media and Merchandising	58,392	Children's advertising

SOURCE: Barry Boyer, "Funding Political Participation in Aging Proceedings: The Federal Trade Commission Experience," *Georgetown Law Journal* (October 1981).

Table A6.1

ORGANIZATIONS REPRESENTED ON C/LEC's BOARD OF DIRECTORS

Association of Community Organizations for Reform Now
Amalgamated Clothing and Textile Workers Union
American Federation of State, County and Municipal Employees
Campaign for Economic Democracy
Citizens Action Coalition of Indiana
Citizens Action League
Connecticut C/LEC
Consumer Energy Council of America
Energy Action Project
Illinois Public Action Council
Iowa C/LEC
Kansas City C/LEC
Massachusetts Fair Share
Mountain Plains Congress of Senior Organizations
National Clients Council

National Community Action Agency Executive Directors Association
National Education Association
New Jersey Federation of Seniors
Northern Plains Resource Council
Ohio Public Interest Campaign
Oil, Chemical and Atomic Workers International Union
Operation PUSH
Oregon Fair Share
Public Citizen
Rural America
Service Employees International Union
Sheet Metal Workers' International Association
Solar Lobby
State and Local Leadership Project
United Automobile Workers
United Electrical, Radio and Machine Workers of America
West Virginia Citizens Action Group
Wisconsin Action Coalition

SOURCE: *Citizen Power*, June 9, 1983, p. 7.

Table A6.2
RECENT FEDERAL FUNDING OF C/LEC AFFILIATES

Organization	Taxpayer Subsidy ($)	Dates
AFL-CIO	12,539,962	1981–82
Amalgamated Clothing and Textile Workers Union	3,707,287	1977–83
American Federation of Government Employees	100,000	1981–82
American Federation of State, County and Municipal Employees	710,860	1979–83
Association of Community Organizations for Reform Now	801,215[a]	1979–81
Campaign for Economic Democracy	743,998	1978–80
Citizen/Labor Energy Coalition	288,490[b]	1979–81
Conference on Alternative State and Local Policies	68,492	1981
Environmental Action Foundation	358,822	1979–81
Gray Panthers	144,000[c]	1979–81
International Association of Machinists Union	1,515,024	1979–83
International Longshoremen's and Warehousemen's Union	126,419	1981–82
League of Women Voters	2,476,738	1977–82
Massachusetts Fair Share	521,631[d]	1979–81
National Council of Churches	438,000	1979–81
National Council of La Raza	5,850,000	1979–81
National Council of Senior Citizens	212,643,857	1979–83
National Education Association	855,282	1981
Ohio Public Interest Campaign	49,680[e]	1981
People United to Save Humanity	5,000,000	1979–82
Rural America	999,093	1979–81
Rural America	1,531,548	1979–82
United Automobile Workers Union	7,431,792	1979–82
United Electrical, Radio and Machine Workers of America	55,800	1981–82
United Food and Commercial Workers International Union	888,510	1980–81
United Steelworkers of America	300,000	1980–81

SOURCE: Freedom of Information Act requests.
[a]Plus numerous VISTA volunteers.
[b]Plus 8 VISTA volunteers.
[c]Plus 17 VISTA volunteers.
[d]Plus 34 VISTA volunteers.
[e]Plus 12 VISTA volunteers.

Table A7.1

SELECTED FEDERAL GRANTS TO ENVIRONMENTAL INTEREST GROUPS

Recipient	Awarding Agency	Grant*	Stated Purpose	Date
Audubon Society— Fairfield, Conn.	Dept. of Education	23,179	Museum operation	9/81
—Fairfield	Education	25,000	As above	9/80
—Maitland, Fla.	Environmental Protection Agency (EPA)	10,000	NA	10/78–4/79
—Massachusetts	EPA	7,000	NA	7/78–7/79
—Massachusetts	EPA	9,000	NA	7/80–5/81
—Freeport, Maine	National Endowment for the Humanities (NEH)	24,853	Consultant fees for a historical investigation	FY 1981
—Massachusetts	NEH	13,100	Exhibition history of land use in Mass. Regional Education Program	FY 1981
—Massachusetts	Dept. of Energy	1,000	Regional Education Program	12/80–3/81
—Concord, N.H.	Energy	150	Earth Day 1980	4/80
—Falmouth, Maine	Energy	25,000	Firewood study	9/77–9/78
—New York	National Science Foundation (NSF)	23,400	Evaluation of alternative energy approaches	6/80–11/82

—Fairfield	Education	Museum operation	25,000	9/80
—Maitland	EPA	NA	10,000	10/78–4/79
—Massachusetts	EPA	NA	7,000	7/78–7/79
—Falmouth	NSF	Farm and energy forums	41,800	10/78–12/79
—Falmouth	NSF	Ecological values of inland wetlands	18,000	7/78–1/80
—Falmouth	Energy	Maine firewood study	25,000	9/77–9/78
—Black Hills Alliance, S. Dak.	Energy	"1980 International Gathering for Survival"	10,000	4/80–1/81
Center for Renewable Resources (CRR)	Energy	Information packets on existing solar legislation	787,510	6/81–9/81
CRR	Energy	Participation in Earth Day	67,000	6/80–1/81
CRR	Dept. of Housing and Urban Development (HUD)	Outreach program on solar energy	25,000	6/80–1/81
CRR	Energy	Survey of solar-energy projects	402,060	1/79–2/80
CRR	Energy	Litigation	20,000	4/79–10/79
CRR	Education	Technical writings	8,000	7/79
Citizen/Labor Energy Coalition (C/LEC)	ACTION	NA	30,000	1980–81
C/LEC	Energy	NA	57,640	1979–81

Table A7.1 (continued)

Recipient	Awarding Agency	Grant*	Stated Purpose	Date
C/LEC	VISTA	8 volunteers	NA	1979–81
C/LEC	Community Services Administration (CSA)	200,000	NA	1980
Citizens Environmental Coalition Education Fund (CECEF)	EPA	28,000	NA	11/80–10/81
CECEF	EPA	28,500	NA	10/79–9/80
CECEF	Federal Trade Commission (FTC)	20,074	NA	1/78–9/79
Energy Task Force Inc.	CSA	150,000	NA	12/80
Environmental Action Foundation (EAF)	Energy	179,644	Utility clearing	6/81
EAF	EPA	50,000	NA	11/80–9/81
EAF	EPA	50,000	NA	1/79–1/82
EAF	EPA	62,000	NA	1/79–1/82
EAF	EPA	71,093	NA	1/79–1/82
EAF	EPA	25,000	NA	10/79–11/80

Organization	Agency	Amount	Purpose	Date
EAF	EPA	25,000	NA	10/79–11/80
EAF	EPA	9,000	NA	12/79–4/80
EAF	EPA	49,979	NA	12/79–4/79
EAF	EPA	6,931	NA	8/77–5/79
EAF	EPA	9,819	NA	9/77–5/79
Environmental Defense Fund (EDF)	Energy	19,999	National energy	3/81–5/81
EDF	FTC	2,332	NA	9/78–9/79
EDF	EPA	39,203	NA	10/80–9/82
EDF	EPA	11,999	NA	9/80–7/81
EDF	EPA	5,249	NA	9/80–7/81
EDF	Dept. of the Interior	17,350	Study of wildlife law	4/81
Friends of the Earth (FOE)	EPA	1,345	NA	2/81–4/81
FOE	Energy	30,000	Soft-energy project	10/79–9/80
Institute for Environmental Action	HUD	12,000	Pamphlets	2/80–6/81
International Solar Energy Society (ISES)	Energy	14,500	Solar conference	12/79–3/80
ISES	Energy	50,000	As above	10/80–7/81
ISES	Energy	60,000	Passive cooling	1/81–1/82

Table A7.1 (continued)

Recipient	Awarding Agency	Grant*	Stated Purpose	Date
National Center for Appropriate Technology (NCAT)	VISTA	30 volunteers	Community energy survey	9/80–12/81
NCAT	Energy	119,685	Technical assistance	8/81–9/81
NCAT	Energy	4,200	Review of energy technology	1/78–2/78
NCAT	CSA	3,700,000	NA	10/80
National Wildlife Federation (NWF)—Washington office	Energy	43,437	Symposium on synthetic fuels	8/81–11/81
NWF	EPA	60,000	NA	1/79–1/82
NWF	EPA	10,000	NA	11/76–11/79
NWF	EPA	66,000	NA	1/78–12/80
NWF	EPA	10,000	NA	1/78–12/80
NWF	EPA	7,500	NA	1/78–12/80
NWF	EPA	39,527	NA	11/78–3/80
NWF	EPA	5,000	NA	11/78–3/80
NWF	EPA	700	NA	11/78–3/80
NWF	EPA	90,065	NA	1/79–1/82

422

Organization	Agency	Amount	Description	Date
NWF	EPA	74,508	NA	1/79–1/82
NWF	EPA	7,040	NA	9/79–8/80
NWF	EPA	50,000	NA	10/80–5/83
NWF	EPA	451,600	NA	10/80–10/82
Natural Resources Defense Council—Augusta, Maine	EPA	200	NA	3/80–4/80
—Hampton, Va.	EPA	816,382	Training program	10/80–10/82
—Washington, D.C.	EPA	200,000	NA	10/80–10/82
—Washington	EPA	4,810	Ground water	9/80–2/81
—Washington	EPA	145,566	NA	4/80–8/81
—Washington	EPA	14,886	Ground water	9/80–4/81
—Washington	Energy	25,000	Alternative-energy study	4/80–8/81
—Washington	EPA	178	Pollution regulation	12/81
—Washington	EPA	13,310	NA	1/79–4/79
—Washington	EPA	127,613	NA	10/78–4/80
—Washington	EPA	20,000	NA	10/78–4/80
Northern California Solar Energy	Energy	27,018	"Third National Passive Solar Conference"	1/79–6/79
Ohio Public Interest Campaign	ACTION	14,478	NA	9/80–9/81
Sierra Club—San Francisco	National Endowment for the Arts (NEA)	15,000	NA	FY 1981

Table A7.1 (continued)

Recipient	Awarding Agency	Grant*	Stated Purpose	Date
—San Francisco	Energy	1,200	NA	4/80
—San Francisco	NEH	87,493	Taped interviews of environmental leaders	FY 1980
—San Francisco	EPA	30,000	NA	1/80–3/81
—San Francisco	EPA	14,250	NA	9/80–3/81
—San Francisco	EPA	6,852	NA	9/80–3/81
—San Francisco	EPA	4,917	NA	7/79–9/79
—San Francisco	EPA	46,894	NA	10/79–9/81
—San Francisco	EPA	48,328	NA	10/79–10/80
—Boston	EPA	129,819	NA	FY 1979–81
—San Francisco	EPA	128,411	NA	2/78–1/81
—New York	EPA	5,000	NA	10/78–7/79
—New York	EPA	3,500	NA	6/78–2/79
—San Francisco	EPA	200,000	NA	2/78–8/81
—Seattle	EPA	7,000	NA	9/78–9/80
—San Francisco	EPA	44,282	NA	2/78–1/81
—Lander, Wyo.	NSF	18,000	Groundwater study	7/78–6/79
Solar Action Inc.	EPA	5,000	NA	6/78–8/78
Solar Action Inc.	Education	17,000	Catalog of energy proposals	9/78

424

Organization	Agency	Purpose	Amount	Date
Solar America	CSA	Solar research	49,460	FY 1978
Solar America	Dept. of Health and Human Services	Aging program	72,718	FY 1980
Solar America	Dept. of Labor	CETA, national emphasis	455,570	11/80–11/81
Solar America	Labor	As above	785,217	9/80–1/81
Solar America	Labor	CETA	620,529	12/70–10/80
Solar America	Labor	National emphasis	291,900	12/79–10/80
Solar America	Labor	National OJT contract	96,413	5/80–10/80
World Wildlife Fund (WWF)	Dept. of the Interior	Ecosystem studies	6,000	4/81
WWF	Interior	Research study	93,000	9/81
WWF	Interior	Support services	30,000	10/80
WWF	Agency for International Development	As above	32,000	9/80–4/81

SOURCE: Freedom of Information Act requests.
*Figures represent dollars except where volunteers are indicated.

Table A7.2

SELECTED ENVIRONMENTAL LEGISLATION SINCE 1969

1969	National Environmental Policy Act
1970	Environmental Protection Agency Reorganization
1970	Poison Prevention Packaging Act
1970	Amended Federal Hazardous Substances Act
1970	Clean Air Act Amendments
1970	Resource Recovery Act
1970	Occupational Safety and Health Act
1971	Federal Boat Safety Act
1972	Amended National Traffic and Motor Vehicle Safety Act
1972	Technology Assessment Act
1972	Amended Federal Water Pollution Control Act
1972	Marine Protection, Research, and Sanctuaries Act
1972	Noise Control Act
1972	Drug Listing Act (Amended Federal Food, Drug, and Cosmetic Act)
1972	Federal Insecticide, Fungicide, and Rodenticide Act
1972	Consumer Product Safety Act
1973	Endangered Species Act
1974	Safe Drinking Water Act
1975	Federal Coal Leasing Act
1975	Amended Federal Insecticide, Fungicide, and Rodenticide Act
1976	National Science and Technology Policy, Organization, and Priorities Act
1976	Amended Federal Food, Drug, and Cosmetic Act
1976	Amended Public Health Services Act
1976	National Consumer Health Information and Health Promotion Act
1976	Medical Device Amendments
1976	Toxic Substances Control Act
1976	Resource Conservation and Recovery Act
1976	Amended Solid Waste Disposal Act
1976	Environmental Research and Development Demonstration Act
1977	Amended Clean Air Act
1977	Amended Federal Water Pollution Control Act
1977	Amended Federal Mine Safety and Health Act
1977	Surface Mining Control and Reclamation Act

SOURCE: As cited in Edith Efron, *The Apocalyptics* (New York: Simon & Schuster, 1984), pp. 62–66.

Table A7.3

ENVIRONMENTAL LEGISLATION AUTHORIZING ATTORNEY'S FEES

Alaska Native Claims Settlement Act, 43 U.S.C. 1619

Alien Owners of Land, 48 U.S.C. 1506

Clean Air Act (as amended by Pub. L. 95-95), 42 U.S.C. 7413(b), 7604(d), 7607(f), 7622(b)(2)(B), (e)(2)

Coal Mine Safety Act 30 U.S.C. 938(c)

Consumer Product Safety Act 15 U.S.C. 2059(e)(4), 2060(c), 2072(a), 2073

Deepwater Ports Act, 33 U.S.C. 1515(d)

Endangered Species Act, 16 U.S.C. 1540(g)(4)

Energy Policy and Conservation Act, 42 U.S.C. 6305(d)

Energy Reorganization Act of 1974 (as amended by Pub. L. 95-601), 42 U.S.C. 5351(b)(2)(B), (e)(2)

Federal Mine Safety and Health Act, 30 U.S.C. 815(c)(3) (added by Pub. L. 95-164), 30 U.S.C. 935(c)

Federal Power Act (as amended by Pub. L. 95-617, 212), 16 U.S.C. 825ql-(b)(2)

Federal Water Pollution Control Act Amendment of 1972, 33 U.S.C. 1365(d)

Marine Protection, Research, and Sanctuaries Act, 33 U.S.C. 1415(g)(4)

Natural Gas Pipeline Safety Act, 49 U.S.C. 1686

Noise Control Act of 1972, 42 U.S.C. 4911(d)

Outer Continental Shelf Lands Act (as amended by Pub. L. 95-372), 43 U.S.C. 1349(a)(5), (b)(2)

Safe Drinking Water Act, 42 U.S.C. 300j-8(d), 9(i)(2)(B)(ii)

Solid Waste Disposal Act, 42 U.S.C. 6971(c), 6972(e)

Surface Mining Control and Reclamation Act (Pub. L. 95-87), 30 U.S.C. 1270(d), (f) 1275(e), 1293(c)

Toxic Substances Control Act, 15 U.S.C. 2605(c)(4)(A), 2618(d), 2619(c)(2), 2620(b)(4)(C), 2622(b)(2)(B)

War Hazards Compensation Act, 42 U.S.C. 1714

Water Pollution Prevention and Control Act, 33 U.S.C. 1365(d), 1367(c)

SOURCE: *Federal Attorney Fee Awards Reporter*, July 8, 1981.

Table A8.1

SELECTED FEDERAL GRANTS TO "WELFARE RIGHTS" ORGANIZATIONS

Recipient	Awarding Agency	Grant*	Stated Purpose	Date
American Friends Service Committee (AFSC)	ACTION	5,000	Mini-grant	4/81–3/82
AFSC	ACTION	87,282	Volunteer program	12/79–11/80
AFSC	Dept. of Labor	183,804	CETA	9/78–4/81
AFSC	Administration for Children, Youth, and Families	40,000	Volunteers	3/80–2/81
AFSC	Dept. of Education	149,553	NA	6/81
AFSC	Education	84,630	NA	8/80
AFSC	Dept. of Health and Human Services (HHS)	40,000	Domestic violence	FY 1980
AFSC	HHS	5,307	NA	FY 1980
Bridgeport Neighborhood Housing Service	ACTION	3 volunteers	Housing referral and assistance	2/79–2/81
Center for National Housing Law Reform	ACTION	6 volunteers	Tenants rights	8/79–8/80
Children's Defense Fund	Education	200	Conference participation	6/79
Citizens for Better Nursing Home Care	ACTION	3 volunteers	Senior citizens advocacy	1/80–1/81
Coalition for Economic Justice	VISTA	5 volunteers	Expand membership in the coalition	10/79–10/80

Organization	Agency/Department	Program	Amount	Date
Community Nutrition Institute (CNI)	Education	Community education program	60,757	9/80
CNI	Federal Trade Commission (FTC)	Public participation in rule making	40,666	9/78–9/79
CNI	HHS	Program for the aging	184,900	FY 1980
CNI	Community Services Administration (CSA)	NA	320,000	FY 1981
Eastern Oklahoma Human Development	ACTION	NA	19,432	10/79–10/80
Federation of Southern Cooperatives (FSC)	ACTION	VISTA grant	300,000	2/81–3/82
FSC	ACTION	As above	641,759	2/80–1/81
FSC	Labor	NA	33,375	12/79–1/81
FSC	Labor	NA	133,500	12/79–1/81
FSC	CSA	NA	450,000	1/81–12/81
FSC	Education	Improvement of post-secondary education	23,656	9/81
FSC	Labor	NA	124,766	12/78–11/79
FSC	Labor	NA	130,625	11/77–12/78
FSC	CSA	Credit union assistance	36,000	9/80–7/81
FSC	ACTION/VISTA	Farmworkers program	126,978	9/80–7/81
FSC	CETA	As above	231,706	9/80–7/81
FSC	CETA	Development program	44,000	9/80–7/81
FSC	Rural America	Co-op housing program	76,550	9/80–7/81

Table A8.1 (continued)

Recipient	Awarding Agency	Grant*	Stated Purpose	Date
FSC	Dept. of Housing and Urban Development (HUD)	118,000	Neighborhood self-help	9/80–7/81
FSC	CETA—Ala.	184,000	Title VI project	9/80–7/81
FSC	Delta Housing—Ala.	29,897	NA	9/80–7/81
FSC	Delta Housing—Ala.	28,443	NA	9/80–7/81
FSC	ORA—Mo.	26,195	NA	9/80–7/81
FSC	ORA—Mo.	66,644	NA	9/80–7/81
FSC	Minnesota Migrant Council	41,197	NA	9/80–7/81
FSC	Dept. of Agriculture	65,000	Day-care program	9/80–7/81
FSC	National Endowment for the Arts (NEA)	17,500	NA	9/80–7/81
FSC	Dept. of State	7,200	NA	9/80–7/81
Food Research and Action Council (FRAC)	CSA	645,000	Newsletter	12/80–12/81
FRAC	Legal Services Corporation (LSC)	25,000	NA	1/83–6/83
FRAC	CSA	60,000	NA	FY 1981

Organization	Agency	Purpose	Amount	Date
Housing Action Council	ACTION	Housing referral	8 volunteers	9/80–9/81
Housing Assistance Council (HAC)	ACTION	NA	184,850	2/81–2/82
HAC	ACTION	NA	23,489	12/79–2/81
Institute for Social Justice (ISJ)	National Endowment for the Humanities (NEH)	History of social movements program	201,558	2/81–1/83
ISJ	NEH	As above	60,000	FY 1980
ISJ	National Science Foundation (NSF)	Mortgage research of low-income neighborhoods	25,274	6/80–11/82
League of United Latin American Citizens (LULAC)	Education	Talent search	1,237,600	5/81
LULAC	Labor	Job corps	64,723	2/81–3/82
LULAC	Labor	As above	51,195	2/81–9/81
LULAC	Dept. of Energy	Appropriate technology center	13,063	2/81–9/81
LULAC	Energy	Energy task force	9,880	2/81–3/81
LULAC	Energy	To construct a solar greenhouse	13,063	FY 1981
LULAC	Education	Improvement of post-secondary education	62,192	5/80
LULAC	Education	Talent search	1,190,000	6/80
LULAC	Education	As above	81,918	8/79
LULAC	Education	Improvement of post-secondary education	60,397	10/79

Table A8.1 (continued)

Recipient	Awarding Agency	Grant*	Stated Purpose	Date
LULAC—Corpus Christi, Tex.	Labor	88,848	Job Corps	1/80–1/81
—Corpus Christi	Labor	11,171	As above	10/80–1/81
—Corpus Christi	Labor	22,797	As above	1/80–9/80
Legal Research Services for the Elderly	Labor	79,970	National conference	7/80–6/81
Massachusetts Fair Share (MFS)	ACTION	310,000	NA	11/80–11/81
MFS	ACTION	215,331	NA	11/79–11/80
MFS	VISTA	34 volunteers	NA	FY 1981
National Association of Neighborhoods	ACTION	249,691	NA	7/79–10/81
National Center for Urban and Ethnic Affairs	ACTION	27,231	NA	2/80–4/80
National Citizen Coalition for Nursing Home Reform	ACTION	26,757	NA	1/80–1/81
National Council of Churches of Christ (NCCC)	Energy	10,000	Energy planning program	1/81–3/81
NCCC	Labor	435,775	CETA—national emphasis	3/80–4/81
NCCC	NEA	15,000	NA	FY 1980
NCCC	Energy	428,000	Energy-education project	9/79–9/80
NCCC	Labor	500,000	NA	9/78–3/80

Organization	Agency	Amount	Program	Date
National Council of La Raza (NCLR)	Various agencies	1,872,000 (78% of budget)	NA	FY 1979
NCLR	As above	3,978,000	NA	FY 1981
Ozark Institute	ACTION	192,000	NA	10/79–6/81
Residential Tenants Council	ACTION	3 volunteers	NA	4/78–6/79
Rural America (RA)	Labor	160,000	CETA	9/80–9/81
RA	Labor	358,948	As above	1/81–6/81
RA	Energy	185,000	Energy development	7/80–1/81
RA	Energy	21,379	National energy plan	3/81–5/81
RA	HUD	10,500	NA	8/80–11/81
RA	EPA	101,494	NA	3/80–5/81
RA	EPA	40,000	NA	3/80–5/80
RA	NEH	29,227	Rural humanities program	FY 1979
RA	Energy	20,115	Appropriation data	5/79–12/79
RA	Energy	72,430	Energy-standards program	3/80–5/80
Southside United Housing Development Fund Corporation	ACTION	15 volunteers	Housing education	5/80–8/81
Tenant Organizing Project	ACTION	10 volunteers	Housing referral/relocation	10/80–10/81
Tenants Union Project	ACTION	4 volunteers	Housing rehabilitation	10/80–10/81
Youth Project	ACTION	366,072		12/80–10/81
Youth Project	ACTION	6 volunteers	Community organizations	5/78–7/79

SOURCE: Freedom of Information Act requests.
*Figures represent dollars except where volunteers are indicated.

Table A9.1
SOCIAL PROGRAM FUNDS RECEIVED BY TELACU
OCTOBER 1, 1976–SEPTEMBER 30, 1979

Federal Funds

Department of Commerce

Economic Planning I: Grant to aid TELACU in economic planning to eliminate unemployment, increase incomes, and assist the underemployed by providing training opportunities.

Economic Planning II: Continuation of Economic Planning I.

Economic Planning III: Continuation of Economic Planning I.

TELACU Industrial Park: Grant authorizing the development of a 46.2 acre site, formerly the B.F. Goodrich tire plant, into an industrial park. The strategy was to create approximately 2,500 jobs for East Los Angeles residents.

Handbook Phase I: Grant authorizing the development of a handbook for national distribution that would develop methods and techniques for describing and analyzing subregional economics at the area and neighborhood levels. The underlying intent was to build the capacity and expertise of local organizations to effectively implement economic development projects that would result in reduced unemployment and improved economic stability.

Handbook Phase II: Continuation of Handbook Phase I.

TELACU Resource/Commercial Centers: Grant authorizing the construction of a 5-story, 100,000-square-foot resource commercial center in the City of Commerce to provide space for comprehensive business development services in the greater East Los Angeles special impact area.

Hacer Economic Technical Assistance: Grant for a technical assistance interchange program that would assist community economic development organizations to formulate and implement ongoing technical transfers among themselves with the intent of bolstering each organization's capabilities in functional areas to allow an increased ability to conduct major development projects from start to finish. Finally, to translate the *Handbook for Community Economic Development* into a series of 35mm audio-visual slide presentations.

Whittier Blvd. Commercial Revitalization Project: Grant to conduct final feasibility analysis and develop comprehensive plan for establishing the Whittier Blvd. area as a comprehensive commercial center, stimulate reinvestment in the area and in surrounding areas, increase secondary employment for local residents, and serve as a model and catalyst for initiating similar commercial revitalization efforts in greater East Los Angeles.

TELACU: Grant to increase the number of minority business starts, strengthen existing minority businesses, and improve opportunities for socially or economically disadvantaged persons to own successful businesses.

434

TELACU: Grant providing for management and technical assistance to the entire minority business community in its area as a means of aiding the minority business community in its pursuit of procurement opportunities with the railroad industry.

Department of Health and Human Services (HHS) (DHEW)

Planning for Community Health Center: Grant for "development of community health needs for local special impact residence [sic].

Department of Housing and Urban Development (HUD)

North Broadway: Grant to improve, through the provision of technical assistance services, the capability of neighborhood development organizations to participate in community development programs by cooperating with and extending the neighborhood revitalization activities of local governments.

National Endowment for the Arts (NEA)

Historical Preservation: Grant to support a survey in the East Los Angeles area for sites of cultural and historical significance.

Zocalo Implementation Studies: Grant to support the design and detailed planning of pedestrian areas in conjunction with the El Zocalo community center concept.

Zocalo Community Design Project: Grant to support documentation of the ethnic and folk history of Boyle Heights.

State Funds

Employment Development Department (EDD)

CETA Title III (YETP): Grant to provide youths aged 14 through 21 a broad range of employment and training services designed locally and adapted to local needs.

CETA Governor's 4%: Grant for fiscal years 1977, 1978, and 1979 to provide supplemental vocational education assistance in areas served by prime sponsors; encourage, coordinate, and establish linkages between prime sponsors and appropriate educational agencies and institutions; conduct governor's coordination and special services within the state and provide support to state employment and training councils.

Weatherization: Grant to implement a weatherization program to assist in insulating the dwellings of low-income persons, particularly the elderly and the handicapped.

California Access: Grant to serve the mentally and physically handicapped populations of the greater Los Angeles community.

Crisis Intervention: Grant to authorize the implementation of a crisis intervention program to financially assist low-income individuals and families affected by substantially higher energy costs, hardship, or danger due to a winter energy crisis.

Emergency Energy Assistance: See "Crisis Intervention" above.

Table A9.1 *(continued)*

California Department of Parks and Recreation

Historical Preservation: See listing under *National Endowment for the Arts* above.

California Office of Aging

Grant to pay for part of the costs of acquiring, altering, and renovating existing facilities to serve as multi-purpose senior centers.

County of Los Angeles Funds

Community Development Department

CETA Title I: Grant authorizing comprehensive manpower services, such as counseling, work experience, classroom training, and on-the-job training.

CETA Title III (YETP): See listing under state *Employment Development Department* above.

CETA Title III (HIRE II): Grant to encourage the development of additional employment and training opportunities for unemployed veterans and "persons for veterans placement" [*sic*].

CETA Title II: Grant for transitional public service employment (PSE) in areas of substantial unemployment.

CETA Title VI: Grant for additional public service employment jobs.

Housing Community Development Act

Whittier Blvd.: See listing under federal *Department of Commerce* above.

Historical Preservation: See listing under *National Endowment for the Arts* above.

Handyman: Contract to provide free minor house repairs and maintenance services for low-income households.

Agency on Aging

Senior Citizens Food Coop: Contract to provide social services for elderly persons.

Senior Citizens Transportation: Contract to provide transportation services for the elderly.

Road Department

Dial-A-Ride Handicapped: Contract to provide pre-reserved dial-a-ride transportation exclusive to the "transportationally handicapped" [*sic*] residents of the unincorporated East Los Angeles area.

Revenue Sharing

Senior Citizens Transportation: Grant authorizing the use of funds to increase the use of existing social, health, governmental, and nongovernmental services to senior citizens in East Los Angeles by providing an outreach transportation program.

West San Gabriel

CETA Title I: See listing under county *Community Development Department* above.

City of Montebello

CETA Title I: See listing under county *Community Development Department* above.

Southern California Association of Governments

East Los Angeles Transit Needs Study: Contract for the gathering of primary data, assessment of the performance of existing transit systems, evaluation of transportation alternatives, and evaluation of the primary data in terms of existing transit systems and transportation alternatives in the unincorporated East Los Angeles area.

City of Los Angeles Funds

Community Development Department

CETA Title I: See listing under county *Community Development Department* above.

CETA Title III (YETP): See listing under state *Employment Development Department* above.

CETA Title III (YCCIP): Grant to provide youths aged 16 through 19 with jobs and employment experience in community-betterment projects.

CETA Title IV (YSS): Grant to determine the relative effectiveness of three approaches to preparing disadvantaged youths for employment: work experience, classroom training, and work experience/classroom training.

Housing Community Development Act

Handyman: See listing under county *Housing Community Development Act* above.

Personnel Department

CETA Title VI: See listing under county *Community Development Department* above.

Private Nonprofit Funds

Community Health Foundation

Health Needs Assessment: Grant for developing an alternative-use feasibility study for the County of Los Angeles Comprehensive Health Center and for developing a long-range, overall development plan.

National Educational Institute for Economic Development (NEIED)

CRG Handbook for Regional Economic Development: Contract to develop a study design for a guide for district economic development.

SOURCE: *Report of Audit: The East Los Angeles Community Union (TELACU) Los Angeles, California, January 1, 1976—December 31, 1979*, vol. 1 (Washington: Department of Labor, 1982), app. 1, pp. 1–8.

Table A9.2

THE EAST LOS ANGELES COMMUNITY UNION, SUMMARY OF GRANTS AND QUESTIONED COSTS OCTOBER 1, 1976–SEPTEMBER 30, 1979

Funding Source	Contract Number	Budget ($)*		Total Questioned Costs ($)
CSA Special Impact	90115	11,818,690.00	(F)	3,192,670.95
		1,259,987.00	(NF)	—
Federal				
Department of Commerce—Economic Development Division				
Economic Planning I	07-05-15055	50,000.00	(F)	41,839.13
		16,667.00	(NF)	—
Economic Planning II	07-05-15055-01	75,000.00	(F)	26,813.24
		25,000.00	(NF)	—
Economic Planning III	07-05-15055-02	75,000.00	(F)	6,589.73
		25,000.00	(NF)	—
TELACU Industrial Park	07-19-01904.1	4,536,422.00		41,900.00
Handbook Phase I	OER-602-6-G-77-44	64,770.14		9,956.08
Handbook Phase II	OER-636-G-78-28	106,346.00		11,485.88
TELACU Resource/Commercial Centers	07-39-18008	100,000.00		—
Hacer Economic Technical Assistance	99-06-16006	100,000.00		17,799.08
—Office of Minority Business Enterprise				
Whittier Blvd.	90-30-65450-00	80,000.00		9,692.80
TELACU	5-36683	477,776.00		2,269.00

TELACU	R0-A01-78-00-5363	455,000.00	2,585.00
Department of Health and Human Services			
Planning Grant-CHC (Family Health Center)	09P-001260-5	249,402.00 (F) 91,612.00 (NF)	56,535.11 —
Department of Housing and Urban Development			
North Broadway	H-4367	167,440.00 (F) 293,036.00 (NF)	10,408.05 —
National Endowment for the Arts			
Historical Preservation	92-4233-067	20,000.00	—
Zocalo Implementation Studies	R60-42-175B	38,610.00 (F) 38,809.00 (NF)	24,576.81
Zocalo Community Design Project	R60-54-169BC	12,105.00 (F) 30,455.00 (NF)	12,105.00 —

State

Economic Development Department—
Employment and Training Advisory Office

CETA Title IV (YETP)	7900-63188	499,928.00	—
CETA Governor's 4%	7900-3989	261,842.00	—
CETA Governor's 4%	7800-3053	500,000.00	44,223.30
CETA Governor's 4%	7700-0793	850,000.00	32,163.42

—Office of Economic Opportunity

Weatherization	7901-0183	230,614.00	5,650.94
Weatherization	7800-1827	55,000.00	626.59
California Access	7800-8602	35,000.00	150.00
Crisis Intervention	7900-7706	45,000.00	—
Emergency Energy Assistance	7900-4778	42,980.00	8,020.00

439

Table A9.2 (continued)

Funding Source	Contract Number	Budget ($)*		Total Questioned Costs ($)
California Department of Parks and Recreation				
Historical Survey Project	36-09-009	15,000.00	(F)	—
		15,000.00	(NF)	—
California Office of Aging				
Senior Citizens Renovation Project	1959-1B10	14,372.00	(F)	7,672.78
		4,850.00	(NF)	—
County				
Community Development Department				
CETA Title I	27022	412,646.00		10,528.65
CETA Title I	29073	443,954.00		42,634.36
CETA Title I	30974	338,677.00		10,999.19
CETA Title II-B	33102	338,677.00		55,049.30
CETA Title III (YETP)	31789	100,000.00		2,214.00
CETA Title III (Hire II)	34200	100,000.00		11,165.00
CETA Title IV (YETP)	33181	100,000.00		10,695.00
CETA Title VI (Regular)	30957	313,023.00		79,411.54
CETA Title VI (Projects-Stimulus)	30957	977,840.00		81,624.15
CETA Title II-D	33969	176,550.00		40,402.27
CETA Title VI (Projects)	33969	461,796.00		52,295.00
Housing Community Development Act				
Whittier Blvd.	33946	80,000.00		—
Historical Preservation	32981	15,000.00	(F)	5,936.38
		1,123.00	(NF)	—

		Amount		Expended
Handyman	30957	135,000.00		28,616.99
Handyman	34089	105,000.00		4,800.00
Agency on Aging				
Senior Citizens Transportation	34803	37,100.00	(F)	2,400.00
		82,472.00	(NF)	—
Senior Citizens Food Coop	28825	74,999.00	(F)	4,543.90
		8,519.00	(NF)	—
Senior Citizens Transportation	32921	35,000.00	(F)	2,136.20
		4,220.00	(NF)	—
Road Department				
Dial-A-Ride Handicapped	4937	101,730.00		18,362.73
Dial-A-Ride Handicapped	3192	112,000.00		11,400.00
Revenue Sharing				
Senior Citizens Transportation	30673	35,000.00	(F)	5,671.63
Senior Citizens Transportation	29085	63,342.00	(NF)	24,573.42
		4,770.00	(F)	—
Senior Citizens Transportation	27863	63,342.00	(NF)	6,612.00
		4,770.00	(F)	—
West San Gabriel Consortium				
CETA Title I (11/76–9/77)	—	61,441.00		3,447.80
CETA Title I (10/77–9/78)	—	61,500.00		598.55
CETA Title II-B (10/78–9/79)	—	58,006.00		250.00
City of Montebello				
CETA Title I (12/76–9/77)	—	20,974.00		3,064.56
CETA Title I (10/77–9/78)	—	27,635.00		1,200.00
CETA Title II-B (10/78–9/79)	—	50,000.00		1,368.00
Southern California Association of Governments				
East L.A. Transit Needs Study	Project 052	144,740.00		144,555.00

441

Table A9.2 (continued)

Funding Source	Contract Number	Budget ($)*	Total Questioned Costs ($)
City			
Community Development Department			
CETA Title I	325-2-1	230,400.00	16,394.38
CETA Title I	325-2-1 (46588)	301,360.00	—
CETA Title II-B	557-2-13AD (49470)	419,843.00	1,120.00
CETA Title III (YETP)	523-3-IYE (48488)	393,600.00	118.20
CETA Title III (YETP)	557-3-IYE (49471)	384,971.00	—
CETA Title IV (YCCIP)	557-3-IYC (49943)	203,102.00	—
CETA Title IV (YSS)	557-1-13YS (50466)	270,000.00	—
Personnel Department			
CETA Title VI	47653	1,885,218.00	29,762.35
Housing Division			
Handyman	49931	495,490.00	360.00
Handyman	557-2-1YC (49943)	10,600.00	—
Private Nonprofit			
Community Health Foundation			
Health Needs Assessment	—	50,000.00	2,289.10
National Educational Institute for Economic Development			
Handbook for Regional Economic Development	EDR-711-G-79-46 (99-7-13519)	6,000.00	1,636.00

Undeterminable

WIN-PSE (state)	NA		NA	42,057.00
CETA Governor's 4% (state)	See above		See above	433.00
Senior Citizens Food Coop (county)	NA		NA	1,269.86
Senior Citizens Program (city, county)	NA		NA	5,239.26
CETA I (city)	025-020-1		NA	400.00
Project Heavy	NA		NA	468.00
Nuestro	NA		NA	573.50
TELACU/CETA brick account	NA		NA	18,042.80
Federal funds deposited directly to venture company	—		—	60,892.86
Cost Allocation Plan	—		—	79,155.00
Private pension plan improperly used	—		—	—
Program income not reported	—		—	43,388.32
Refund of FICA taxes	—		—	27,269.10
Total federal	—		30,527,113.14	4,564,157.24
Total nonfederal	—		1,906,290.00	—
Grand total	—		32,433,403.14	4,564,157.24

SOURCE: *Report of Audit: The East Los Angeles Community Union (TELACU) Los Angeles, California, January 1, 1976–December 31, 1979*, vol. 2 (Washington: Department of Labor, 1982) pp. 1–6.

* "F" indicates federal funds; "NF" indicates funds from nonfederal sources.

Table A10.1

Selected Federal Funding of "Civil Rights" and "Feminist" Organizations

Interest Group	Awarding Agency	Grant*	Stated Purpose	Date
Bay Area Bilingual Education (BABEL)	Dept. of Education	248,186	Hispanic center	1/82
BABEL	Education	1,950,107	As above	12/81
BABEL	Education	278,046	Civil rights training	5/82
BABEL	Education	87,067	Training in citizen advocacy	NA
BABEL	Education	975,000	Bilingual-education centers	4/81
BABEL	Education	82,378	As above	3/81
BABEL	Education	36,521	Metric education	3/81
BABEL	Education	290,650	Civil rights assistance	6/81
BABEL	Education	52,354	Improvement of post-secondary education	9/81
BABEL	Education	88,665	Career education	8/80
BABEL	Education	51,526	Metric education	9/80
BABEL	Education	526,953	Bilingual-education centers	12/81–6/82
BABEL	Education	144,104	Bilingual education	7/80
BABEL	Education	684,252	As above	9/80
BABEL	Education	236,098	As above	9/80
BABEL	Education	486,415	Civil rights assistance	6/80

Organization	Department	Amount	Purpose	Date
BABEL	Education	117,470	Bilingual education	9/79
BABEL	Education	660,451	As above	8/79
BABEL	Education	416,804	Civil rights assistance	7/79
Center for Independent Living	Education	239,588	As above	NA
Council on Interracial Books for Children (CIBC)	Education	103,025	"Feminist" readers for third graders	FY 1980
CIBC	Education	141,087	As above	FY 1981
Educational Development Center	Education	807,653	Publish Women's Educational Equity Act material	FY 1980
Feminist Press (FP)	Education	20,638	Women's/minority studies	11/81
FP	Education	64,635	As above	7/81
FP	Education	131,114	College guides	7/81
FP	Education	118,475	Improve post-secondary education	8/80
FP	Education	13,600	Black women's studies	4/79
FP	Education	69,996	College-level texts	1/82
Health Equity Project (HEP)	Education	91,000	Post-secondary manuals	8/81
HEP	Education	77,752	Title IX and health services	8/80
League of Women Voters (LWV)	Environmental Protection Agency (EPA)	8,000	NA	12/79–5/81

Table A10.1 (continued)

Interest Group	Awarding Agency	Grant*	Stated Purpose	Date
LWV	EPA	1,605	NA	9/80–2/81
LWV	EPA	13,989	Education fund	9/80–12/80
LWV	EPA	99,631	As above	2/79–4/81
LWV	EPA	124,671	As above	2/77–12/78
LWV	EPA	9,933	As above	10/77–12/79
LWV	EPA	65,310	As above	2/79–4/81
LWV	EPA	4,412	As above	2/79–3/82
LWV	EPA	59,596	As above	9/79–12/80
LWV	EPA	40,000	NA	8/81–8/82
LWV	EPA	18,000	NA	1/81–12/81
LWV	EPA	19,744	NA	10/79–12/80
LWV	EPA	15,000	NA	1/81–12/81
LWV	EPA	20,000	NA	10/79–12/80
LWV	Dept. of Energy	429,263	Nuclear-energy education project	6/80–5/81
LWV	National Endowment for the Humanities (NEH)	300,000	Education fund	FY 1979
LWV	NEH	10,000	As above	FY 1980
LWV—Phoenix	National Science Foundation (NSF)	40,766	Workshops on power consumption	5/80–10/81

—Glenmont, N.Y.	Education	10,000	Environmental education	8/79
—Oakland, Calif.	NSF	11,900	As above	1/79–6/79
—Salt Lake City	NSF	21,218	Conference on water policies	8/79–12/80
—Hamden, Conn.	NSF	21,350	Hazardous-waste management	8/79–11/81
—Overseas Education Fund (OEF)	Agency for International Development (AID)	174,175	NA	6/81–6/83
—OEF	Dept. of State	30,988	International exchange program	FY 1980
—OEF	State	15,000	NA	5/80
—OEF	AID	163,034	NA	4/80–12/80
—OEF	State	13,500	International exchange program	FY 1979
—OEF	State	101,700	As above	FY 1979
—OEF	AID	365,797	NA	8/79–3/82
—OEF	AID	210,140	NA	9/79–12/81
—OEF	AID	47,426	NA	9/79–5/80
National Association for the Advancement of Colored People (NAACP)	Dept. of Housing and Urban Development	82,500	To promote low-income housing	9/80–2/81
NAACP	Dept. of Justice	381,642	Advocacy on deadly force issue	7/80–2/82
NAACP	NEH	2,500	Black youth project	FY 1979

Table A10.1 (continued)

Interest Group	Awarding Agency	Grant*	Stated Purpose	Date
National Council of Negro Women (NCNW)	Education	132,363	NA	FY 1979
NCNW	Education	189,197	NA	FY 1980
National Organization for Women (NOW)	Education	160,004	Promote sex equity	FY 1980
NOW	Education	170,178	As above	FY 1981
NOW—Legal Defense Fund	Education	105,577	Television spots concerning equity	FY 1981
National Student Education Fund (NSEF)	Education	114,776	National conference	FY 1979
NSEF	Education	117,411	As above	FY 1980
National Urban League	Various agencies	108,730,000	NA	11/77–8/82
National Women's Law Center (NWLC)	Education	29,400	Women's rights project	6/81
NWLC	Education	152,000	As above	7/81
NWLC	Education	150,000	As above	9/80
NWLC	Education	150,000	As above	5/80
NWLC	Education	36,445	Consumer education	6/79
Planned Parenthood—New Haven, Conn.	Dept. of Health and Human Services (HHS)	158,196	Health services	1/82–3/82

Location	Agency	Amount	Service	Date
—Lebanon, N.H.	HHS	17,726	As above	1/82–3/82
—Tucson	HHS	17,726	As above	1/82–3/82
—Fresno, Calif.	HHS	130,735	Contraceptive services	1/82–12/82
—Rolla, Mo.	HHS	27,562	Family-planning services	1/82–7/82
—Lebanon	HHS	58,355	As above	1/82–12/82
—New Haven	HHS	580,011	As above	1/82–12/82
—Columbus, Ohio	HHS	571,957	As above	3/82–12/82
—Madison, Wis.	HHS	1,580,015	As above	3/82–12/82
—San Rafael, Calif.	HHS	43,001	As above	4/81–12/82
—Woodland, Calif.	HHS	122,472	As above	1/82–12/82
—Eureka, Calif.	HHS	86,409	As above	4/81–12/82
—Las Vegas	HHS	79,579	As above	1/81–12/82
—Phoenix	HHS	525,326	As above	4/82–12/82
—San Antonio, Tex.	HHS	131,770	As above	4/81–7/82
—Kansas City, Mo.	HHS	106,281	As above	1/81–7/82
—Columbia, Mo.	HHS	35,256	As above	6/81–8/82
—Kirksville, Mo.	HHS	24,435	As above	5/81–8/82
—Madison	HHS	2,422,739	As above	3/81–2/82
—Salt Lake City	HHS	360,176	As above	7/81–6/82
—Phoenix	HHS	689,912	As above	4/81–3/82
—Odessa, Tex.	HHS	13,160	As above	5/81–7/82
—Eureka	HHS	120,287	As above	4/81–3/82
—St. Paul, Minn.	HHS	1,587,365	As above	1/81–12/81

Table A10.1 (continued)

Interest Group	Awarding Agency	Grant*	Stated Purpose	Date
—Akron, Ohio	HHS	395,206	As above	7/81–6/82
—Santa Cruz, Calif.	HHS	118,500	As above	4/81–12/82
—Santa Barbara, Calif.	HHS	128,765	As above	4/81–12/82
—Santa Cruz	HHS	52,305	Title X patient education	9/81–9/82
—Santa Barbara	HHS	172,035	Family-Planning medical services	4/81–3/82
—Fresno	HHS	120,212	Contraceptive services	1/81–12/81
—Columbus, Ohio	HHS	711,688	Family-planning services	3/81–2/82
—Milwaukee	HHS	204,350	As above	7/81–6/82
—San Antonio	HHS	398,351	As above	4/81–3/82
—Lubbock, Tex.	HHS	56,245	As above	8/81–7/82
—Kansas City	HHS	295,272	As above	1/81–12/81
—Rolla	HHS	105,948	As above	1/81–12/81
—Columbia	HHS	47,797	As above	9/81–8/82
—Columbia	HHS	170,692	As above	6/81–5/82
—Kirksville	HHS	125,371	As above	5/81–4/82
—Waco, Tex.	HHS	456,708	As above	6/81–5/82
—Odessa	HHS	296,966	As above	5/81–4/82
—Lebanon	HHS	77,806	As above	1/81–12/81

City	Agency	Amount	Description	Date
—Denver	HHS	92,810	As above	3/81–2/82
—Salt Lake City	HHS	360,176	As above	7/81–6/82
—Tucson	HHS	360,250	As above	1/81–12/81
—San Rafael	HHS	75,000	As above	4/81–3/82
—Woodland	HHS	140,000	As above	1/81–12/81
—Santa Cruz	HHS	365,299	As above	4/81–3/82
—Las Vegas	HHS	55,009	As above	1/81–12/81
—Portland, Oreg.	HHS	541,211	As above	7/81–6/82
—New York	HHS	494,640	As above	7/81–6/82
—Franklin, Ohio	HHS	771,688	As above	FY 1981
—Utica, N.Y.	HHS	400,738	As above	FY 1981
—New Haven	HHS	694,414	As above	1/81–12/81
—Fort Worth	HHS	291,600	As above	12/80–5/82
—New York	HHS	296,700	Family nurse program	7/81–6/82
—Plainfield, N.J.	Dept. of Labor	15 volunteers	Job Corps	9/81
—Plainfield	Labor	82 volunteers	As above	9/81
—Plainfield	Labor	55 volunteers	As above	3/81–4/81
—San Francisco	Education	110,364	Research for handicapped	8/81
—Washington	HHS	198,239	Unwanted fertility	9/80–12/81
—Chicago	HHS	15,000	Interactive process among never-married partners	11/80–1/81
—Austin, Tex.	HHS	85,050	Family-planning services	11/80–5/82

Table A10.1 *(continued)*

Interest Group	Awarding Agency	Grant*	Stated Purpose	Date
—Ft. Worth	HHS	814,675	As above	12/80–11/81
—Lebanon	HHS	71,722	As above	FY 1980
—Phoenix	HHS	674,744	As above	FY 1980
—San Rafael	HHS	59,000	As above	FY 1980
—New York	HHS	592,000	As above	FY 1980
—New Haven	HHS	773,347	As above	FY 1980
—St. Paul	HHS	1,433,962	As above	FY 1980
—Milwaukee	HHS	2,269,818	As above	FY 1980
—Milwaukee	HHS	191,766	As above	FY 1980
—Davis, Calif.	HHS	140,000	As above	FY 1980
—Clark, Nev.	HHS	45,260	As above	FY 1980
—Clark	HHS	507,002	As above	FY 1980
—San Antonio	HHS	389,630	As above	FY 1980
—Lubbock	HHS	50,000	As above	FY 1980
—Ft. Worth	HHS	859,000	As above	FY 1980
—Washington	HHS	449,680	As above	FY 1980
—Baltimore	HHS	11,087	As above	7/79–6/80
—Lebanon	HHS	77,806	As above	1/78–12/81
—San Francisco	Education	107,668	Research for handicapped	7/79

—San Francisco	Education	110,364	As above	8/80
—Philadelphia	Education	24,991	Racism/sexism education	9/80
—Sacramento	HHS	5,309	Population research	FY 1980
—Sacramento	HHS	14,881	Centers for Disease Control	FY 1980
—San Francisco	Education	328,390	Research for handicapped	8/81
Project on the Status and Education of Women	Education	119,816	NA	FY 1979
People United to Save Humanity (PUSH)	Labor	1,999,968	CETA	1/81–12/83
PUSH	Education	656,664	CFDA program	9/81
PUSH	Education	1,000,000	As above	3/80
PUSH	Dept. of Commerce	250,000	Business education ownership program	9/77–8/80
PUSH	Education	700,000	To promote excellence in inner-city schools	4/79
PUSH	Education	45,037	Peer-counseling program	9/79
PUSH	Labor	550,000	NA	9/78–12/80
PUSH	Education	825,000	Education programs in inner-city schools	FY 1981
Women's Action Alliance, Inc. (WAA)	Education	143,893	Women's educational equity	8/80

Table A10.1 (continued)

Interest Group	Awarding Agency	Grant*	Stated Purpose	Date
WAA	Education	280,700	As above	6/81
WAA	Education	143,893	Non-sexist child-development project	8/80
WAA	Education	136,807	As above	3/80
Women's Educational Center, Inc.	Education	1,200	College library resources	8/81
Women's International League for Peace and Freedom	NEH	15,000	Historical documentary of the league	2/82

SOURCE: Freedom of Information Act requests.
*Figures represent dollars except where volunteers are indicated.

Table A11.1
Selected Federal Grants to "Senior Citizen" Organizations

Recipient	Awarding Agency	Grant*	Stated Purpose	Date
Gray Panthers (GP)	VISTA	4 volunteers	Nursing-home program	9/78–11/79
GP	VISTA	4 volunteers	Solar energy to benefit low-income senior citizens	9/78–11/79
GP	VISTA	4 volunteers	To organize for GP	11/80–10/81
GP	VISTA	5 volunteers	To develop GP network	7/80–7/81
GP	Administrator of Aging (AOA)	61,491	Training conference	8/79–2/80
GP	AOA	22,992	Media conference	11/80–10/81
GP–Pa.	Environmental Protection Agency (EPA)	30,000	NA	12/80–11/81
GP—Project Fund	AOA	29,992	NA	11/80–10/81
National Council of Senior Citizens (NCSC)	Dept. of Labor	58,506,670	NA	6/81–9/82
NCSC	Dept. of Health and Human Services (HHS)	74,307	Aging program	FY 1981

Table A11.1 (continued)

Recipient	Awarding Agency	Grant*	Stated Purpose	Date
NCSC	Community Services Administration (CSA)	3,000,000	SOS—Independent Living	10/80
NCSC	Labor	44,709,595	CETA	7/80–6/81
NCSC	AOA	39,860	Needs of the elderly	8/80–7/82
NCSC	AOA	224,000	To analyze key elderly issues	7/80–3/82
NCSC	HHS	112,500	Aging program (Title III)	FY 1980
NCSC	HHS	152,360	Aging program (Title IV)	FY 1980
NCSC	Dept. of Justice	198,680	Reducing crime in elderly communities	8/78–8/79
NCSC	Justice	49,041	Crime/citizen volunteer corps	9/80–8/81
NCSC	Justice	223,839	Research and technical assistance	8/79–8/80
NCSC	Labor	353,917	CETA—older workers	11/79–6/81
NCSC	Labor	28,109,000	NA	7/77–9/78
NCSC	Labor	36,157,000	NA	7/78–9/79
NCSC	Labor	40,597,472	NA	7/79–9/80
NCSC	CSA	12,248	Newsletter subscription	FY 1978

NCSC	Federal Trade Commission (FTC)	Public participation in rule making	2,010	1/76–2/76
NCSC	FTC	As above	8,100	5/76–3/77
NCSC	FTC	As above	41,933	7/76–9/81
NCSC	FTC	As above	52,323	
NCSC	FTC	As above	17,445	
NCSC	FTC	As above	560	
National Council on Aging (NCA)	AOA	Education center	133,000	6/80–6/81
NCA	AOA	Group-based program	93,074	10/79–9/81
NCA	AOA	Community organization	172,587	10/80–9/82
NCA	AOA	Aging conference	183,279	9/80–9/82
NCA	AOA	As above	34,754	11/83
NCA	AOA	Research on community support	124,913	10/81–9/82
NCA	AOA	Senior centers	348,959	9/78–9/80
NCA	AOA	Independent-living services	288,077	8/77–7/80
NCA	AOA	NA	162,250	8/79–11/81
NCA	Labor	NA	1,003,800	11/79–11/81
NCA	Labor	NA	23,787,109	7/80–7/81
NCA	Labor	NA	500,000	9/80–12/81
NCA	Labor	NA	210,000	12/80–11/81

Table A11.1 (continued)

Recipient	Awarding Agency	Grant*	Stated Purpose	Date
NCA	Labor	70,000	NA	1/81–12/81
NCA	Labor	70,000	NA	1/80–12/80
NCA	CSA	29,528	NA	1/81–6/81
NCA	Dept. of Education	38,620	CFDA program	8/81
NCA	Education	41,289	CFDA program	7/80
NCA	National Endowment for the Humanities (NEH)	760,907	Senior centers	FY 1979
NCA	NEH	150,000	As above	FY 1979
NCA	Labor	13,190,500	NA	7/77–9/78
NCA	Labor	18,208,000	NA	7/78–9/79
NCA	Labor	2,267,000	NA	10/77–9/79
NCA	Labor	21,130,676	NA	7/79–9/80
NCA	HHS	153,952	Senior program (Title IVC)	FY 1980
NCA	HHS	135,230	Senior program (Title IVA)	FY 1980
NCA	HHS	159,976	Senior program (Title IVG)	FY 1980
National Retired Teachers Association (NRTA)	Labor	79,366,585	CETA	7/80–7/81

Organization	Agency	Amount	Purpose	Date
NRTA	Labor	36,272,183	CETA	7/81–6/82
NRTA	EPA	544,640	NA	7/81–6/82
NRTA	EPA	70,000	NA	1/80–1/82
NRTA	EPA	122,716	NA	11/80–1/82
NRTA	EPA	381,938	NA	1/80–7/81
NRTA	EPA	7,947	NA	1/80–7/81
NRTA	EPA	147,500	NA	1/80–1/81
NRTA	EPA	18,277	NA	1/80–1/81
NRTA	EPA	89,635	NA	1/80–1/81
NRTA	EPA	71,765	NA	11/80–10/81
NRTA	EPA	100,000	NA	7/81–6/82
NRTA	Legal Services Corporation (LSC)	107,015	Pro bono legal work	FY 1980
National Senior Citizens Law Center (NSCLC)	LSC	609,079	NA	FY 1980
NSCLC	AOA	4,000	Legal services mini-conference	9/81–9/82
Nursing Home Ombudsmen Committee on Aging	ACTION	7 volunteers	Community service—legal rights	5/79–5/80

SOURCE: Freedom of Information Act requests.
*Figures represent dollars except where volunteers are indicated.

Table A11.2
National Council of Senior Citizens
Board of Directors

Congressman Claude Pepper
U.S. House of Representatives

E. G. Marshall
Movie Star

Lane Kirkland
President, AFL-CIO

Douglas A. Fraser
Past President, United Auto Workers

William Winpisinger
President, International Association of Machinists and Aerospace Workers

J. C. Turner
President, International Union of Operating Engineers

Charles Pillard
President, International Brotherhood of Electrical Workers

George Hardy
President emeritus, Service Employees International Union

David J. Fitzmaurice
President, International Union of Electrical, Radio, and Machine Workers

S. Frank Raftery
President, International Brotherhood of Painters and Allied Trades

Murray H. Finley
President, Amalgamated Clothing and Textile Workers Union

Thomas F. Miechur
President, United Cement, Lime, and Gypsum Workers International Union

Carl W. Studenroth
President, International Molders and Allied Workers Union

Source: Letterhead, 1983 NCSC fundraising letter.

460

Table A12.1

LEGAL SERVICES CORPORATION PROGRAM FUNDING LEVELS FY 1983

Program	Location	Funding ($)
Connecticut Legal Services, Inc.	Cromwell, Conn.	1,333,624
Community Renewal Team of Greater Hartford	Hartford	313,604
South Central Connecticut Legal Services	New Haven	543,892
Pine Tree Legal Assistance Association	Portland, Maine	1,099,574
Boston Bar Association— Volunteer Lawyers Project	Boston, Mass.	127,141
Greater Boston Legal Services, Inc.	Boston	1,842,952
National Consumer Law Center	Boston	539,961
Voluntary Defenders Committee, Inc.	Boston	370,091
Cambridge and Somerville Legal Services	Cambridge	342,371
Center for Law and Education	Cambridge	480,693
South Middlesex Legal Services, Inc.	Framingham	161,625
Legal Services for Cape Cod and Islands	Hyannis	209,005
Merrimack Valley Legal Services, Inc.	Lowell	332,951
Neighborhood Legal Services, Inc.	Lynn	241,266
Southeastern Mass. Legal Assistance Corporation	New Bedford	395,763
Western Massachusetts Legal Services	Northampton	499,839
Legal Assistance Corporation of Central Massachusetts	Worcester	404,040
New Hampshire Pro Bono Referral System	Concord, N.H.	70,367
New Hampshire Legal Assistance Inc.	Manchester	543,496
Rhode Island Legal Services, Inc.	Providence, R.I.	723,420

Table A12.1 *(continued)*

Program	Location	Funding ($)
Vermont Legal Aid, Inc.	Burlington, Vt.	594,465
Legal Aid Society of Northeastern New York	Albany, N.Y.	704,251
Oak Orchard Legal Services, Inc.	Albion	127,903
Mid Mohawk Legal Services, Inc.	Amsterdam	92,610
Southern Tier Legal Services	Bath	256,502
Broome Legal Assistance Corporation	Birmingham	153,518
Neighborhood Legal Services Inc.	Buffalo	624,440
Chautauqua County Legal Services, Inc.	Dunkirk	105,100
Chemung County Neighborhood Legal Services, Inc.	Elmira	193,788
Nassau/Suffolk Company Law Services	Hempstead	852,844
Legal Aid Society of Rockland County	New City	122,811
Center on Social Welfare Policy and Law	New York	522,449
Community Action for Legal Services	New York	8,652,988
Legal Aid Society Volunteer Division	New York	39,957
National Center on Women and Family Law	New York	202,174
National Employment Law Project	New York	416,189
Niagara County Legal Aid Society, Inc.	Niagara Falls	119,896
North County Legal Services	Plattsburg	244,835
Mid-Hudson Legal Services, Inc.	Poughkeepsie	472,004
Farmworker Legal Services of New York, Inc.	Riverhead	223,951
Monroe County Legal Assistance Corporation	Rochester	798,054

Legal Services of Central New York, Inc.	Syracuse	583,450
Legal Aid Society of Oneida County, Inc.	Utica	375,289
Westchester Legal Services, Inc.	White Plains	568,458
Inter-American University of Puerto Rico—San Juan C.L.O.	Santurce, P.R.	256,921
Puerto Rico Legal Services, Inc.	Santurce	10,908,786
Legal Services of the Virgin Islands	Christiansted, V.I.	401,903
Delaware Legal Services Corporation	Wilmington, Del.	382,007
Antioch School of Law/ Urban Law Institute	Washington, D.C.	353,025
Food Research and Action Center	Washington	50,000
Mental Health Law Project	Washington	75,396
Migrant Legal Action Program, Inc.	Washington	452,206
National Clients Council	Washington	524,700
NRTA/AARP Legal Counsel for Elderly	Washington	85,517
National Social Science Law Center	Washington	253,416
National Veteran's Legal Services Project	Washington	75,396
Neighborhood Legal Service Program	Washington	1,399,254
Legal Aid Bureau, Inc.	Baltimore, Md.	2,559,961
Cape-Atlantic Legal Services, Inc.	Atlantic City, N.J.	191,878
Warren County Legal Services Corporation	Belvedere	37,773
Camden Regional Legal Services, Inc.	Camden	856,960
Union County Legal Services Corporation	Elizabeth	227,569
Hunterdon County Legal Service Corporation	Flemington	34,967
Bergen County Legal Services Association	Hackensack	225,683
Hudson County Legal Services Corporation	Jersey City	466,330
Legal Aid Society of Morris County	Morristown	88,936

Program	Location	Funding ($)
Essex-Newark Legal Services Project Inc.	Newark	919,224
Middlesex County Legal Services Corporation	New Brunswick	251,196
Legal Services of New Jersey, Inc.	New Brunswick	161,439
Passaic County Legal Aid Society	Paterson	306,191
Somerset-Sussex Legal Services	Somerset	144,200
Ocean-Monmouth Legal Services	Toms River	335,127
Legal Aid Society of Mercer County	Trenton	277,880
Blair County Legal Services	Altoona, Pa.	99,142
Lehigh Valley Legal Services	Bethlehem	216,535
Bucks County Legal Aid Society	Bristol	160,450
Legal Services, Inc.	Carlisle	169,646
Delaware County Legal Assist Association	Chester	409,356
Northwestern Legal Services	Erie	448,798
Laurel Legal Services, Inc.	Greensburg	402,529
Southern Alleghenys Legal Aid, Inc.	Johnstown	239,182
Central Pennsylvania Legal Services	Lancaster	739,752
Montgomery County Legal Aid Services	Norristown	182,970
Community Legal Services, Inc.	Philadelphia	1,831,864
Neighborhood Legal Services Association	Pittsburgh	1,210,700
Schuykill County Legal Services	Pottsville	137,878
Northern Pennsylvania Legal Services	Scranton	277,600
Keystone Legal Services, Inc.	State College	263,765
Southwestern Pennsylvania Legal Aid Society	Washington	395,703

Legal Aid of Chester County, Inc.	West Chester	117,006
Legal Services of Northeastern Pennsylvania, Inc.	Wilkes-Barre	310,449
Susquehanna Legal Services	Williamsport	312,947
Legal Services of Southeastern Michigan	Ann Arbor, Mich.	335,086
Legal Services Organization of South Central Michigan	Battle Creek	164,685
Michigan Migrant Legal Assistance Program	Berrien Springs	353,820
Michigan Legal Services	Detroit	337,422
Wayne County Neighborhood Legal Services	Detroit	1,732,293
Legal Services of Eastern Michigan	Flint	590,586
Legal Aid of Western Michigan	Grand Rapids	644,280
Legal Aid Bureau of Southwestern Michigan	Kalamazoo	212,916
Legal Services of Central Michigan	Lansing	248,902
Lakeshore Legal Services	Mt. Clemens	337,945
Oakland Livingston Legal Aid	Pontiac	311,658
Berrien County Legal Services Bureau	St. Joseph	120,203
Upper Peninsula Legal Services, Inc.	Sault Ste. Marie	680,660
Summit County Legal Aid Society	Akron, Ohio	389,778
Stark County Legal Aid Society	Canton	180,812
Legal Aid Society of Cincinnati	Cincinnati	705,141
Council for Economic Opportunities	Cleveland	1,364,955
Legal Aid Society of Columbus	Columbus	632,347
Ohio State Legal Services Association of Southeast Ohio	Columbus	1,210,090
Legal Aid Society of Dayton	Dayton	301,961
Legal Aid Society of Lorain County, Inc.	Elyria	115,673

465

Table A12.1 (continued)

Program	Location	Funding ($)
Butler Warren Legal Assistance	Hamilton	161,766
Allen County Legal Services Association	Lima	211,004
Central Ohio Legal Aid Society	Newark	199,022
Rural Legal Aid Society of West Central Ohio	Springfield	335,857
Advocates for Basic Legal Equality, Inc.	Toledo	659,764
Toledo Legal Aid Society	Toledo	168,604
Wooster-Wayne Legal Aid Society	Wooster	45,036
Northeast Ohio Legal Services	Youngstown	396,651
Legal Services of Northern Virginia	Arlington, Va.	310,361
Client Centered Legal Services of Southwest Virginia	Castlewood	379,580
Charlottesville-Albemarle Legal Aid Society	Charlottesville	147,540
Legal Aid Society of New River Valley	Christiansburg	101,134
Rappahannock Legal Services, Inc.	Fredericksburg	274,104
Peninsula Legal Aid Center, Inc.	Hampton	420,050
Blue Ridge Legal Services, Inc.	Harrisonburg	218,755
Virginia Legal Aid Society	Lynchburg	824,374
Southwest Virginia Legal Aid Society	Marion	203,050
Tidewater Legal Aid Society	Norfolk	637,064
Petersburg Legal Aid Society, Inc.	Petersburg	131,940
Neighborhood Legal Aid Society, Inc.	Richmond	412,596
Virginia Poverty Law Center, Inc.	Richmond	181,243
Legal Aid Society of Roanoke Valley	Roanoke	294,498

Appalachian Research and Defense Fund, Inc.	Charleston, W.Va.	722,424
Legal Aid Society of Charleston	Charleston	347,116
West Virginia Legal Services Plan	Charleston	1,170,127
North Central West Virginia Legal Aid Society	Morgantown	255,963
Land of Lincoln Legal Assistance Foundation	Alton, Ill.	2,118,773
Cook County Legal Assistance Foundation	Chicago	556,931
Legal Assistance Foundation of Chicago	Chicago	3,255,061
West Central Illinois Legal Assistance	Galesburg	128,210
Prairie State Legal Services, Inc.	Rockford	1,349,286
Legal Services of Maumee Valley, Inc.	Fort Wayne, Ind.	226,402
Legal Aid Society of Gary, Inc.	Gary	341,194
Legal Services Organization of Indiana	Indianapolis	2,211,546
Legal Services Program of Northern Indiana	South Bend	645,513
Legal Aid Society of Polk County	Des Moines, Iowa	345,220
Legal Services Corporation of Iowa	Des Moines	1,992,448
Kansas Legal Services	Topeka, Kans.	1,809,957
Judicare of Anoka County	Anoka, Minn.	37,803
Anishinabe Legal Services	Cass Lake	150,657
Legal Aid Services of Northeast Minnesota	Duluth	325,419
Central Minnesota Legal Services	Minneapolis	927,896
Northwest Minnesota Legal Services,Inc.	Moorhead	386,036
Southern Minnesota Regional Legal Services	St. Paul	1,285,003
Southeast Missouri Legal Services	Caruthersville, Mo.	507,628
Mid-Missouri Legal Services Corporation	Columbia	270,603
Meramec Area Legal Aid Corporation	Farmington	234,817

Program	Location	Funding ($)
Legal Services of Northeast Missouri, Inc.	Hannibal	193,790
Legal Aid of Western Missouri	Kansas City	1,387,756
Legal Services of Eastern Missouri	St. Louis	1,234,893
Legal Aid Association of Southwest Missouri	Springfield	530,912
Legal Services of Southeast Nebraska	Lincoln, Nebr.	315,638
Legal Aid Society of Omaha	Omaha	541,712
Western Nebraska Legal Services, Inc.	Scottsbluff	487,934
Legal Assistance of North Dakota	Bismarck, N. Dak.	735,629
North Dakota Legal Services	New Town	98,036
Dakota Plains Legal Services	Mission, S. Dak.	729,775
Black Hills Legal Services, Inc.	Rapid City	160,613
East River Legal Services Corporation	Sioux Falls	422,238
Legal Services of Northeast Wisconsin	Green Bay, Wis.	444,353
Western Wisconsin Legal Services, Inc.	La Crosse	314,552
Legal Action of Wisconsin, Inc.	Milwaukee	1,472,940
Wisconsin Judicare,Inc.	Wausau	834,524
Birmingham Area Legal Services Corporation	Birmingham, Ala.	794,460
Legal Services of North Central Alabama	Huntsville	449,492
Legal Services Corporation of Alabama	Montgomery	4,290,521
Ozark Legal Services	Fayetteville, Ark.	393,096
Western Arkansas Legal Services	Fort Smith	275,069
Central Arkansas Legal Services, Inc.	Little Rock	752,757
Legal Services of Arkansas	Little Rock	824,654

Legal Services of Northeast Arkansas	Newport	396,867
East Arkansas Legal Services	West Memphis	605,274
Withlacoochee Area Legal Services	Brookville, Fla.	185,729
Central Florida Legal Services	Daytona Beach	561,579
Legal Aid Service of Broward County, Inc.	Ft. Lauderdale	453,686
Three Rivers Legal Services	Gainesville	377,348
Jacksonville Area Legal Aid	Jacksonville	790,122
Florida Rural Legal Services, Inc.	Lakeland	1,739,411
Legal Services of Greater Miami	Miami	1,232,028
Greater Orlando Area Legal Services	Orlando	421,851
Northwest Florida Legal Services	Pensacola	270,023
Gulfcoast Legal Services, Inc.	St. Petersburg	626,346
Legal Services of North Florida, Inc.	Tallahassee	642,076
Bay Area Legal Services, Inc.	Tampa	585,528
Atlanta Legal Aid Society	Atlanta, Ga.	1,142,407
Georgia Legal Services Program	Atlanta	5,263,733
Cumberland Trace Legal Services	Bowling Green, Ky.	340,388
Northern Kentucky Legal Services	Covington	241,506
Central Kentucky Legal Services, Inc.	Lexington	411,760
Legal Aid Society of Louisville	Louisville	848,303
Western Kentucky Legal Services	Madisonville	691,526
Northeast Kentucky Legal Services, Inc.	Morehead	382,360
Appalachian Research and Defense Fund, Ky.	Prestonsburg	1,796,005
Central Louisiana Legal Services, Inc.	Alexandria, La.	327,585
Capital Area Legal Services Corporation	Baton Rouge	846,341
Southeast Louisiana Legal Service	Hammond	518,810

Program	Location	Funding ($)
Acadiana Legal Services	Lafayette	977,815
Southwest Louisiana Legal Services Society	Lake Charles	323,958
North Louisiana Legal Assistance Corporation	Monroe	709,417
Kisatchie Legal Services Corporation	Natchitoches	290,756
New Orleans Legal Assistance Corporation	New Orleans	1,276,206
Northwest Louisiana Legal Services, Inc.	Shreveport	564,156
South Mississippi Legal Services Corporation	Biloxi, Miss.	495,056
Judicare of Mississippi	Columbus	105,219
East Mississippi Legal Services	Forest	494,605
Southeast Mississippi Legal Services	Hattiesburg	428,945
Central Mississippi Legal Services	Jackson	789,347
Southwest Mississippi Legal Services	McComb	439,013
North Mississippi Rural Legal Services	Oxford	2,323,417
Legal Services of Southern Piedmont	Charlotte, N.C.	540,254
North Central Legal Assistance Program	Durham	456,254
Legal Services of North Carolina, Inc.	Raleigh	5,028,037
Legal Aid Society of Northwest North Carolina	Winston-Salem	418,146
Neighborhood Legal Assistance Program	Charleston, S.C.	1,164,699
Palmetto Legal Services	Columbia	1,065,457
Carolina Regional Legal Services Corporation	Florence	226,695
Legal Services of Western Carolina	Greenville	535,112
Legal Services of the Fourth Judicial Circuit	Hartsville	388,901
Piedmont Legal Services, Inc.	Spartanburg	542,838

Southeast Tennessee Legal Services, Inc.	Chattanooga, Tenn.	517,747
Legal Services of South Central Tennessee	Columbia	447,288
West Tennessee Legal Services	Jackson	677,936
Legal Services of Upper East Tennessee	Johnson City	626,053
University of Tennessee Legal Aid Clinic/ Knoxville	Knoxville	467,526
Memphis Area Legal Services	Memphis	1,089,649
Legal Services of Nashville and Middle Tennessee	Nashville	1,062,958
Rural Legal Services of Tennessee	Oak Ridge	626,547
Pinal and Gila County Legal Aid Society	Coolidge, Ariz.	181,219
Coconino County Legal Aid	Flagstaff	85,341
Community Legal Services	Phoenix	1,083,049
Papago Legal Services	Sells	139,398
Southern Arizona Legal Aid, Inc.	Tucson	808,966
DNA-People's Legal Services, Inc.	Window Rock	1,767,407
Native Rights Fund Indian Law Center	Boulder, Colo.	205,694
Pikes Peak Legal Services	Colorado Springs	208,857
Colorado Rural Legal Services, Inc.	Denver	1,135,741
Legal Aid Society of Metropolitan Denver	Denver	821,292
Pueblo County Legal Services, Inc.	Pueblo	146,201
Legal Aid Society of Albuquerque, Inc.	Albuquerque, N. Mex.	413,381
Indian Pueblo Legal Services	Laguna	274,294
Southern New Mexico Legal Services, Inc.	Las Cruces	623,923
Northern New Mexico Legal Services	Taos	607,616
Oklahoma Indian Legal Services, Inc.	Oklahoma City, Okla.	228,744
Western Oklahoma Legal Services	Oklahoma City	1,670,888
Legal Services of Eastern Oklahoma	Tulsa	1,319,715

471

Program	Location	Funding ($)
Legal Aid Society of Central Texas	Austin, Tex.	1,129,407
Coastal Bend Legal Services	Corpus Christi	706,309
North Central Texas Legal Services Foundation	Dallas	1,094,422
El Paso Legal Assistance Society	El Paso	477,251
West Texas Legal Services	Fort Worth	2,353,272
Gulf Coast Legal Foundation	Houston	2,045,957
Laredo Legal Aid Society, Inc.	Laredo	198,750
East Texas Legal Services, Inc.	Nacogdoches	1,877,648
Bexar County Legal Aid Association	San Antonio	981,770
Heart of Texas Legal Services Corporation	Waco	344,455
Texas Rural Legal Aid, Inc.	Weslaco	3,348,209
Utah Legal Services, Inc.	Salt Lake City, Utah	841,866
Greater Bakersfield Legal Assistance, Inc.	Bakersfield, Calif.	321,805
National Economic Development Law Project	Berkeley	338,594
National Housing and Law Project	Berkeley	591,591
Southeast Legal Aid Center	Compton	487,606
Redwood Legal Services	Eureka	302,609
Fresno-Merced Counties Legal Services,Inc.	Fresno	604,993
Legal Aid Foundation of Long Beach	Long Beach	549,799
Bet Tzedek Legal Services	Los Angeles	79,472
Legal Aid Foundation of Los Angeles	Los Angeles	2,425,824
National Center for Immigrants Rights	Los Angeles	135,757
National Senior Citizens Center	Los Angeles	486,773
Western Center on Law and Poverty, Inc.	Los Angeles	860,026

472

Legal Aid Society of Monterey County	Monterey	171,769
California Indian Legal Services	Oakland	569,888
Charles Houston Bar Association	Oakland	113,578
Legal Aid Society of Alameda County	Oakland	1,287,515
Channel Counties Legal Services Association	Oxnard	320,148
San Fernando Valley Neighborhood Legal Society	Pacoima	737,105
Legal Aid Society of Pasadena	Pasadena	650,031
Legal Aid Society of San Mateo County	Redwood City	428,874
Contra Costa Legal Services Foundation	Richmond	376,518
Inland Counties Legal Services	Riverside	878,957
Legal Services of Northern California	Sacramento	938,048
Legal Aid Society of San Diego, Inc.	San Diego	844,672
Bar Association of San Francisco Volunteer Legal Services Program	San Francisco	15,744
California Rural Legal Assistance	San Francisco	3,978,641
National Center for Youth Law	San Francisco	499,622
San Francisco Neighborhood Legal Assistance	San Francisco	1,294,429
Legal Aid Society of Santa Clara County	San Jose	506,928
Legal Aid Society of Marin County	San Rafael	82,459
Legal Aid Society of Orange County	Santa Ana	586,642
National Health Law Program	Santa Monica	503,542
Solano County Legal Assistance Agency	Vallejo	163,558
Tulare County Legal Service Association	Visalia	321,597
Legal Aid Society of Santa Cruz County	Watsonville	135,511

473

Table A12.1 (continued)

Program	Location	Funding ($)
Nevada Legal Services	Carson City, Nev.	359,663
Washoe Legal Services	Reno	111,027
Alaska Legal Services Corporation	Anchorage, Alaska	1,325,118
Legal Aid Society of Hawaii	Honolulu, Hawaii	580,863
Native Hawaiian Legal Corporation	Honolulu	80,547
Idaho Legal Aid Services, Inc.	Boise, Idaho	868,778
Montana Legal Services Association	Helena, Mont.	852,932
Lake County Legal Aid Service, Inc.	Eugene, Oreg.	163,360
Legal Aid Service Multnomah Bar Association	Portland	408,278
Oregon Legal Services Corporation	Portland	1,497,311
Marion-Polk Legal Aid Service, Inc.	Salem	144,751
Evergreen Legal Services	Seattle, Wash.	2,690,643
Spokane Legal Services Center	Spokane	265,456
Puget Sound Legal Assistance Foundation	Tacoma	302,680
Legal Aid Services	Casper, Wyo.	201,783
Legal Services for Southeastern Wyoming	Cheyenne	159,602
Wind River Legal Services	Fort Washakie	133,856
Guam Legal Services Corporation	Agana, Guam	150,220
Micronesian Legal Services Corporation	Saipan Marina Island	712,300

SOURCE: Freedom of Information Act requests.

Table A12.2

LEGAL FEE AWARDS AND FUND BALANCES FOR LEGAL SERVICES CORPORATION GRANTEES, 1980–82

State or Territory	Legal Fee Awards ($)			Fund Balances ($)		
	1980	1981	1982	1980	1981	1982
Alabama	13,294	73,562	53,865	2,833,947	3,537,815	1,160,749
Alaska	38,638	22,254	439,704	–0–	138,435	–0–
Arizona	41,315	61,905	30,201	524,660	829,091	163,633
Arkansas	1,544	4,218	12,085	1,941,443	2,321,158	1,305,530
California	242,846	566,355	580,981	3,641,155	3,574,156	2,314,621
Colorado	96,393	101,657	119,769	358,258	556,586	687,157
Connecticut	4,850	1,115	336	111,829	131,373	36,645
Delaware	–0–	–0–	–0–	43,014	51,137	84,638
Florida	18,278	68,119	53,612	1,271,494	2,148,885	1,067,842
Georgia	19,031	56,820	169,129	1,119,102	1,423,315	629,245
Hawaii	–0–	–0–	–0–	8,861	72,571	61,375
Idaho	–0–	–0–	–0–	30,103	86,841	59,411
Illinois	298,064	425,065	440,779	1,114,088	1,737,483	770,298
Indiana	26,980	14,575	40,652	253,411	538,911	550,127
Iowa	–0–	–0–	1,500	296,459	558,637	149,054
Kansas	–0–	–0–	–0–	351,236	265,989	193,015
Kentucky	30,593	125,660	108,984	586,321	1,008,825	772,712
Louisiana	4,713	6,040	22,266	2,061,168	2,427,605	1,508,548
Maine	–0–	–0–	–0–	53,647	67,643	91,281
Maryland	–0–	–0–	–0–	309,108	40,354	8,435
Massachusetts	566,175	196,964	398,291	730,943	770,056	536,406
Michigan	71,223	52,907	96,751	799,886	1,099,068	506,542
Minnesota	1,477	2,232	64,850	531,323	417,646	304,815

Table A12.2 (continued)

State or Territory	Legal Fee Awards ($)			Fund Balances ($)		
	1980	1981	1982	1980	1981	1982
Mississippi	12,829	14,384	13,665	886,299	1,303,910	676,915
Missouri	40,018	62,017	73,188	829,299	1,688,263	1,120,057
Montana	200	239	100	51,835	125,849	122,729
Nebraska	28,391	18,560	16,800	298,114	346,615	136,674
Nevada	-0-	9,544	78,564	117,804	298,948	44,986
New Hampshire	7,562	35,186	10,818	73,580	83,473	13,156
New Jersey	7,610	13,118	9,309	388,402	742,777	595,149
New Mexico	354	4,352	5,861	176,756	319,986	276,954
New York	76,149	327,967	599,752	2,880,041	3,763,096	1,575,543
North Carolina	11,746	-0-	-0-	1,853,473	2,802,223	1,589,851
North Dakota	1,337	115	5,838	280,785	357,280	360,809
Ohio	30,969	39,711	93,128	1,697,749	2,186,697	745,353
Oklahoma	6,614	5,501	3,055	960,099	1,506,237	1,008,579
Oregon	19,351	26,276	32,501	155,978	-0-	13,924
Pennsylvania	15,068	5,325	149,373	1,521,834	1,467,948	1,802,585
Rhode Island	1,857	5,362	5,205	8,620	39,676	91,038
South Carolina	7,058	6,413	1,979	1,706,386	2,204,876	1,161,036
South Dakota	283	6,784	2,205	171,946	338,718	280,657
Tennessee	12,848	27,501	103,108	1,970,360	1,582,865	1,261,291
Texas	70,995	128,957	95,382	3,046,341	4,092,387	1,996,207
Utah	21,350	21,672	60,996	63,377	68,756	16,249
Vermont	-0-	200	333	23,714	24,401	39,258
Virginia	12,814	12,857	19,046	1,845,631	1,907,826	767,538
Washington	28,458	94,543	41,433	425,265	455,968	146,167

West Virginia	12,481	7,017	152,837	120,046	184,156	336,306
Wisconsin	38,160	168,998	62,196	253,338	550,344	448,633
Wyoming	–0–	–0–	350	107,098	193,113	80,429
District of Columbia	–0–	22,564	19,399	1,072,706	1,215,676	1,949,105
Guam	–0–	–0–	–0–	–0–	33,039	7,449
Micronesia	–0–	–0–	–0–	2,205	91,754	38,575
Puerto Rico	11,385	12,542	12,542	3,830,951	6,150,643	2,272,699
Virgin Islands	–0–	–0–	–0–	106,607	129,291	85,343
Total	1,951,301	2,857,153	4,302,718	44,898,095	60,060,371	34,023,323

SOURCE: Senate Committee on Labor and Human Resources, *Oversight of the Legal Services Corporation, 1983 Hearings before the Committee on Labor and Human Resources*, 98th Cong., 1st sess., 1983, pp. 476–505.

A12.3

Selected Federal Grants and Contracts to the American Bar Association

Contract No.	Awarding Agency	Grant ($)	Stated Purpose	Date
EMWG0872	Federal Emergency Management Agency (FEMA)	4,655	Arson task force assistance program	5/82–5/83
EMWK0577	FEMA	10,000	Arson for Profit: The Insurer's Defense	4/81–9/81
EMWK0605	FEMA	143,917	Alternatives for effective code enforcement and compliance programs	6/81–9/81
EMWG0033	FEMA	14,643	ABA Young Lawyers Division arson project	7/81–7/82
90CW631	Dept. of Health and Human Services (HHS)	100,000	Public education to encourage enactment of the Uniform Child Custody Jurisdiction Act	9/81–9/82
21-11-79-13	Dept. of Labor	99,930	Study of offender programs under CETA	FY 1981
13.637	HHS	85,003	Special program for aging (training)	FY 1981
90C1690	HHS	150,600	National Legal Resource Center for Child Advocacy and Protection	9/81–9/82
NA	National Endowment for the Humanities (NEH)	28,477	To support the planning of a program to increase the public's understanding of fundamental principles of the U.S. legal and judicial system	FY 1981
T901291010	Environmental Protection Agency (EPA)	3,000	Fund for public education	2/81–9/81
G008100688	Dept. of Education	1,000,000	Law school fellowships for the disadvantaged	6/81

FG01-81EV10524	Dept. of Energy	9,998	Joint conference between Canadian bar and ABA on common boundary, common problems: energy production and environmental consequences	5/81–10/81
NA	NEH	76,000	To support continuing preparation of vol. 2 of three-volume study on the war powers of the president and Congress in a debate about the use of these powers in American history	FY 1981
81IJCX0011	Dept. of Justice	79,978	To implement and study the effects of telephone conferencing to conduct court business in criminal cases	2/81–1/83
80CJAX0099	Justice	44,971	Continuation of a FY 1979 discretionary grant concerning victim/witness problems from the perspective of the ABA	10/80–10/81
80DFAX0029	Justice	75,000	Continuing education for appellate judiciary and staff (eight seminars)	10/80–9/81
NA	NEH	70,000	Program in undergraduate education in law and the humanities	FY 1980
NA	NEH	119,701	A design for elementary education in law and the humanities	FY 1980
NA	NEH	24,986	To support research, papers, and a symposium in which lawyers, scientists, and ethical analysts explore the dilemmas and options involved in maintaining the traditional values of individual privacy and autonomy in a society of rapidly expanding information technology	FY 1980

A12.3 *(continued)*

Contract No.	Awarding Agency	Grant ($)	Stated Purpose	Date
90-06-1690	Children, Youth and Families	259,806	National legal-resource center for child advocacy and protection	4/80–9/81
90-CW-631	Children, Youth and Families	75,067	The first year of a two-year grant for a public education project to encourage the enactment of the Uniform Child Custody Jurisdiction Act	9/80–9/81
13.608	HHS	75,067	Child-welfare research and demonstration grants	FY 1980
13.634	HHS	80,083	Special program for aging (Title IVC)	FY 1980
13.628	HHS	259,806	Child abuse and neglect—prevention and treatment	FY 1980
13.631	HHS	123,806	Developmental disabilities—special projects	FY 1980
79DFAX0198	Justice	51,125	Drafting of the Bar Leadership Manual on victim/witness assistance, providing specific information on start-up, operations, network coordination, and activities sponsored by and operating both within and without the criminal justice system	10/79–10/80
79DFAX0224	Justice	100,000	To keep the appellate judiciary abreast of new developments in the law and to make them better decision makers (six seminars)	10/79–10/80

Number	Agency	Amount	Description	Dates
21-11-79-13	Labor	80,000	NA	5/79–11/81
21-11-79-13	Labor	24,308	NA	5/79–11/81
21-11-79-13	Labor	190,928	NA	10/79–11/81
79DFAX0032	Justice	297,977	To find solutions, through research and exemplary projects, to the problems of court delay and excessive costs in litigation	2/79–11/80
NA	Dept. of State	46,260	To enable the ABA to arrange and conduct a seminar entitled "A Study of Citizen Access to Justice in U.S. and Selected Countries of Latin America and the Caribbean" for members of the legal profession from other countries	FY 1979
NA	State	6,547	To assist the ABA in sending American lawyers to the USSR to participate in a series of seminars sponsored by the Association of Soviet Lawyers	FY 1979
78TAAX0049	Justice	92,516	To provide seminars in regional locations for a large percentage of the nation's appellate judges, including lectures and workshops on topics in judicial philosophy, court decisions, having state and federal impact, etc.	9/78–9/79
G008200550	Education	960,000	Council on Legal Education Opportunity	2/82
78NIAX0023	Justice	35,055	To analyze the process by which the state and local pilot jurisdictions consider the model procurement code	3/78–2/79

A12.3 (continued)

Contract No.	Awarding Agency	Grant ($)	Stated Purpose	Date
79NAX0006	Justice	1,038,364	One of six projects constituting program on law-related education whose objective is to prepare long-range blueprint for law and juvenile education and to ensure coordinated activities among programs	11/78–11/81
78DFAX0054	Justice	174,938	To provide funding for a second and final 12-month phase of a project to update ABA standards relating to the administration of criminal justice	3/78–6/79
78DFAX0077	Justice	210,000	Core support to allow the National Judicial College to conduct 38 resident sessions, representing 55 weeks of judicial training for 1,325 participants	2/78–12/78
78JNAX0002	Justice	124,897	To develop legal and administrative standards to improve the effectiveness, efficiency, and fairness of the juvenile justice system	11/77–3/79
99-7-581-42-12	Labor	199,961	NA	12/76–2/79

SOURCE: Freedom of Information Act requests.

Table A13.1
Selected Federal Grants to Labor Unions and Union Organizations

Recipient	Awarding Agency	Grant ($)	Stated Purpose	Date
Amalgamated Clothing and Textile Workers Union (ACTWU)	Dept. of Health and Human Services (HHS)	176,188	Alcoholism project	11/81–9/82
ACTWU	HHS	163,144	Alcoholism treatment	FY 1980
ACTWU	Dept. of Labor	710,910	Job training	5/80–9/81
ACTWU	Labor	230,000	NA	7/80–12/81
ACTWU	National Endowment for the Humanities (NEH)	317,316	Seminars to help members see themselves and their work in broader historical and cultural contexts	FY 1979
ACTWU	NEH	15,000	Humanities program	FY 1979
ACTWU	Labor	493,384	Job training	5/79–5/80
ACTWU	Labor	571,676	NA	5/78–5/79
ACTWU	Labor	478,369	NA	5/77–5/78
ACTWU	Labor	276,300	Occupational safety and health training	5/77–5/78
ACTWU	Labor	275,000	As above	9/80–9/81

Table A13.1 (continued)

Recipient	Awarding Agency	Grant ($)	Stated Purpose	Date
American Federation of Government Employees	Labor	100,000	As above	8/81–7/82
AFL-CIO	Dept. of Transportation	2,762,956	Program to organize transit workers	5/81
AFL-CIO	Labor	23,543	Research	6/79–4/80
AFL-CIO—Appalachian Council (AC)	Labor	800,000	National OJT contract	2/82–1/83
—AC	Alcohol, Drug Abuse, and Mental Health Administration	500,000	Alcoholism program	3/81–2/82
—AC	Dept. of Education	25,652	Metric education	9/80
—AC	Labor	500,000	NA	5/80–12/80
—AC	Labor	1,349,000	NA	1/80–12/80
—AC	Labor	2,413,000	NA	1/80–11/81
—AC	Labor	1,125,000	Job Corps	4/80–12/80
—AC	Labor	1,125,000	As above	4/80–12/80
—AC	Labor	10,582,236	As above	10/80–9/81
—AC	Labor	1,049,083	As above	10/80–9/81

—AC	Labor	155,173	As above	10/80–3/82
—AC	Labor	199,770	As above	10/80–9/81
—AC	Labor	499,828	As above	10/80–3/82
—AC	Labor	80,003	As above	3/80–9/80
—AC	Labor	1,230,962	National OJT contract	1/79–12/79
—AC	Labor	203,790	As above	3/79–2/80
—AC	Labor	1,835,000	As above	10/79–9/80
—AC	Labor	99,327	As above	11/79–9/80
—AC	Labor	780	As above	9/79
—AC	Labor	897,133	As above	10/79–9/80
—AC	Labor	86,600	As above	11/79–11/80
—AC	Labor	905,415	As above	10/79–5/80
—AC	Labor	6,240,014	NA	1/78–12/81
—AC	Labor	75,000	OSHA training project	8/81–7/82
—AC	Labor	820,000	Job Corps	2/83–9/84
—AC	Labor	46,308	As above	10/82–1/83
—Philadelphia Council (PC)	HHS	210,000	Health-care project	9/81
—PC	HHS	657,675	As above	9/80
—Washington Council (WC)	ACTION	228,545	Foster-grandparent program	1/81–12/81
—WC	ACTION	215,848	As above	1/80–12/80
—WC	ACTION	4,290	NA	1/79–12/79

Table A13.1 (continued)

Recipient	Awarding Agency	Grant ($)	Stated Purpose	Date
—Akron Council (AKC)	HHS	84,025	Alcoholism program	10/81–3/82
—AKC	HHS	84,025	Employee assistance	4/81–9/81
—AKC	HHS	168,050	Alcoholism treatment	FY 1980
—West Virginia Council	Labor	191,704	NA	9/80–9/81
—St. Louis Council (SLC)	Labor	104,597	Job Corps	10/80–9/82
—SLC	Labor	32,727	As above	12/79–9/80
—SLC	Labor	73,351	OSHA safety program	8/81–7/82
—SLC	Labor	209,000	Job Corps	2/83–9/84
—Great Lakes Council (GLC)	Labor	474,732	NA	11/79–3/81
—GLC	Labor	75,000	Employee training	8/81–7/82
—Hawaii	Labor	219,939	NA	9/77–9/78
—Building and Construction Dept.	Labor	300,000	Health training	5/82–4/83
—Public Employee Dept.	Labor	75,000	As above	8/81–7/82
—Food and Beverage Dept.	Labor	100,000	Health and Safety	10/81–10/82

Organization	Category	Amount	Project	Date
Communications Workers of America	Labor	NA	OSHA project	NA
American Federation of State, County, and Municipal Employees—District 37	Labor	50,000	As above	10/81–10/82
—Career Development	Labor	320,608	NA	9/80–10/81
—Career Development	Labor	112,140	NA	7/79–10/80
—Career Development	Labor	278,118	National OJT contract	5/79–10/80
American Federation of Teachers (AFT)	Education	560,000	Research/dissemination project	1/81–12/82
AFT	Education	98,000	Resource exchange	1/81
AFT	Education	98,000	As above	2/81–5/82
AFT	Education	107,000	Handicapped-personnel preparation	2/81
AFT	Education	52,000	Citizen education	9/80
AFT	Education	107,000	Handicapped-personnel preparation	5/75
American Labor Education Center, Inc.	Labor	45,000	Job safety and health service	10/80–10/81

Table A13.1 (continued)

Recipient	Awarding Agency	Grant ($)	Stated Purpose	Date
Brown Lung Association	Labor	93,554	OSHA project	10/80–10/81
Chicago Teachers Union	HHS	135,161	Mental health service	4/81–3/82
Florida Farmworkers Council, Inc. (FFC)	HHS	403,252	Services to handicapped	FY 1981
FFC	Community Services Administration (CSA)	13,262	NA	1/81
FFC	CSA	10,000	NA	1/81
FFC	CSA	25,000	NA	9/81
FFC	Education	64,300	CFDA program	6/80
George Meany Center for Labor Studies (GMCLS)	NEH	99,008	AFL-CIO archives	2/82
GMCLS	Labor	82,699	National OJT contract	8/80–7/81
GMCLS	National Endowment for the Arts (NEA)	15,000	Performing arts activities for Washington labor representatives	FY 1980
GMCLS	Transportation	402,100	Research program	10/80

GMCLS	Labor	243,442	NA	2/78–7/80
Graphic Arts International Union (GAIU)	Labor	382,550	National OJT contract	12/79–11/81
GAIU	Labor	198,550	NA	12/79–11/81
GAIU	Labor	166,374	National OJT contract	12/78–11/79
GAIU	Labor	100,000	OSHA program	9/81–9/82
GAIU	Labor	225,000	As above	9/80–9/81
Institute for Labor Education and Research (ILER)	Education	99,933	Improvement of post-secondary education	7/81
ILER	Education	16,624	As above	3/81
ILER	Education	95,435	As above	7/80
ILER	NEH	140,220	Historical research	FY 1980
ILER	Education	85,876	Improvement of post-secondary education	6/79
ILER	Education	45,980	As above	FY 1978
International Association of Machinists and Aerospace Workers (IAM)	Labor	40,000	Training and education program	10/81–4/82
IAM	Labor	201,802	NA	7/80–7/81
IAM	Labor	149,522	NA	5/79–7/80
IAM	Labor	295,000	Training and education program	9/80–9/81

Table A13.1 (continued)

Recipient	Awarding Agency	Grant ($)	Stated Purpose	Date
International Brotherhood of Printers and Allied Workers (IBPAW)	Labor	3,811,087	NA	10/78–9/81
IBPAW	Labor	3,297,448	NA	10/78–9/81
IBPAW	Labor	5,069,867	Job Corps	10/78–3/82
International Brotherhood of Police Officers (IBPO)	Labor	375,000	As above	10/79–5/81
IBPO	Labor	272,285	NA	1/79–10/79
International Ladies Garment Workers Union (ILGWU)	Education	95,673	Organizer project	4/82
ILGWU	HHS	172,654	Occupational alcoholism	10/81–9/82
ILGWU	Education	137,267	Improvement of post-secondary education	7/81
ILGWU	Education	80,000	As above	8/80
ILGWU	HHS	143,461	Alcoholism treatment	FY 1980
ILGWU	Labor	120,000	OSHA training assistance	1/81–7/82

Organization	Source	Amount	Description	Date
International Longshoremen's and Warehousemen's Union (ILWU)	Labor	59,165	Health and training program	10/81–10/82
ILWU	Labor	67,254	As above	10/80–10/81
International Masonry Union Apprentice Trust (IMUAT)	Labor	1,127,000	National OJT contract	9/80–11/81
IMUAT	Labor	646,451	As above	9/79–12/80
International Union of Electrical and Radio Mechanics (IUERM)	Labor	937,478	As above	11/79–11/81
IUERM	Labor	539,000	NA	11/79–12/80
IUERM	Labor	138,000	Health and safety program	8/81–1/82
International Union of Electrical Radio and Machine Workers	National Science Foundation (NSF)	18,000	Psychological study	12/78–8/79
International Union of Operating Engineers (IUOE)	Labor	500,000	National OJT contract	2/82–1/83
IUOE	Labor	1,380,000	As above	8/80–11/81
IUOE	Labor	266,950	NA	3/80–8/81

491

Table A13.1 (continued)

Recipient	Awarding Agency	Grant ($)	Stated Purpose	Date
IUOE	Labor	1,200,000	NA	9/80–9/81
IUOE	Labor	2,286,555	NA	7/78–9/81
IUOE	Labor	1,922,082	NA	7/78–9/80
IUOE	Labor	2,509,089	NA	7/78–9/81
IUOE	Labor	275,000	OSHA program	8/81–7/82
International Union of Tile Marble Finishers (IUTMF)	Labor	611,844	National OJT contract	2/80–11/81
IUTMF	Labor	380,844	NA	2/80–3/81
International Union of United Auto Workers (UAW)	Labor	40,077	Occupational safety and health education	11/80–11/81
UAW	Labor	299,370	Reemployment opportunity	FY 1982
UAW	Education	7,686	Retired-worker project	1/81
UAW	Labor	33,500	Health research	2/81–9/81
UAW	NEA	10,000	To support the labor theater company	FY 1980
UAW	Education	71,267	Retirement project	FY 1980
UAW	Labor	2,934,000	NA	12/79–9/81

Organization	Agency	Program	Amount	Dates
UAW	Labor	National OJT contract	3,226,000	12/79–11/81
UAW	Education	Retirement project	69,942	FY 1979
—Bell County	Labor	Job Corps	297,893	10/79–3/82
—District 65	Labor	Occupational safety and health education	40,000	11/80–10/81
—Hazelwood, Mont.	HHS	Assistance program	102,687	12/80–11/81
Labor Education Film Center (LEFC)	Education	"Working Women Past and Present" movies	63,000	9/81
LEFC	NEA	NA	20,000	FY 1981
LEFC	NEH	Historical film	40,080	FY 1980
Migrant and Seasonal Farmworkers Association—W. Va.	Labor	Migrant farmworkers (Title III)	282,985	3/82–9/82
—N.C.	Labor	As above	1,994,522	3/82–9/82
—Va.	Labor	As above	614,547	3/82–9/82
—Del.	Labor	As above	106,127	3/82–9/82
—Md.	Labor	As above	266,524	3/82–9/82
—Ga.	Labor	As above	750,121	3/82–9/82
—Wheat Ridge County	Labor	Youth program (Title IV)	49,000	7/81–6/82
—Ala.	Labor	Migrant farmworkers (Title III)	837,000	12/81–9/82

Table A13.1 (continued)

Recipient	Awarding Agency	Grant ($)	Stated Purpose	Date
—N.C.	Labor	1,681,732	Youth program (Title IV)	7/81–6/82
—N.C.	CSA	411,184	NA	7/81
—N.C.	Dept. of Agriculture	125,000	NA	2/81
—N.C.	Education	16,383	Community education program	9/80
—N.C.	Labor	6,710,498	CETA	10/79–8/81
—Md.	Labor	864,066	CETA	10/79–8/81
—Del.	Labor	320,935	CETA	10/79–9/81
—Va.	Labor	2,325,450	CETA	10/79–9/81
—Ga.	Labor	2,469,402	CETA	10/79–9/81
—N.C.	Labor	1,328,000	CETA	12/79–9/81
—Ala.	Labor	2,091,320	CETA	10/79–9/81
National Association of Farmworkers Organization (NAFO)	ACTION	175,106	VISTA grant	4/80–4/81
NAFO	ACTION	9,923	NA	5/78–4/80
NAFO	NA	225,000	Occupational safety and health program	NA

—Research and Public Affairs	NA	20,000	OSHA grant	NA
—Ark.	Labor	1,448,748	NA	1/82–9/82
—Ky.	Labor	668,000	NA	1/82–9/82
—New England	HHS	58,871	Farm-worker health	7/81–6/82
—Mont.	Labor	635,400	NA	11/81–9/82
—Mont.	Labor	710,630	NA	3/82–9/82
—New England	CSA	12,500	NA	7/81
—New England	CSA	50,000	NA	1/81
—Midwest	Labor	83,161	NA	9/80–10/81
—New England	CSA	100,000	NA	10/80
—New England	Labor	997,383	NA	10/79–9/81
—New England	Labor	7,500	Job Corps	10/79–10/80
National Association of Social Workers	U.S. Information Agency	40,000	Trip to China	1/81–1/82
National Farmers Union (NFU)	NEH	226,983	Humanities program on rural life	FY 1980
NFU	NEH	199,546	Historical program on rural life	FY 1979
National Ironworkers Training Program (NITP)	Labor	837,833	National OJT contract	2/82–11/82
NITP	Labor	3,722,000	As above	6/80–11/81

Table A13.1 (continued)

Recipient	Awarding Agency	Grant ($)	Stated Purpose	Date
NITP	Labor	2,567,000	NA	6/80–5/81
NITP	Labor	2,037,564	National OJT contract	11/81–9/82
National Maritime Union Pension and Welfare Plan	HHS	151,578	Alcoholism program	11/81–9/82
National Steelworkers Foundation (NSW)	Labor	500,000	NA	9/80–9/81
NSW	Labor	500,000	NA	9/80–9/81
NSW	NSF	5,000	Research on health hazards	9/77–3/79
National Union of Hospital and Health Care Employees	Labor	113,593	Occupational-hazard recognition training	8/81–7/82
Teamsters Joint Council (TJC)	Labor	308,525	NA	6/80–6/81
TJC	Labor	447,525	National OJT contract	6/80–11/81
TJC	Labor	285,867	As above	6/79–6/80
United Brotherhood of Carpenters and Joiners of America (UBCJA)	Labor	750,000	As above	2/82–1/83

Organization	Agency	Amount	Purpose	Date
UBCJA	Labor	202,800	Historical presentation	2/81–6/82
UBCJA	Labor	2,339,000	National OJT contract	2/81–6/82
UBCJA	Labor	1,537,000	NA	4/80–4/81
UBCJA	Labor	1,140,062	National OJT contract	4/79–4/80
UBCJA	Labor	8,090,002	NA	10/78–12/80
UBCJA	Labor	1,727,383	NA	3/78–4/79
UBCJA	Labor	6,922,183	NA	10/78–12/80
UBCJA	Labor	10,583,045	Job Corps	10/78–3/82
UBCJA	Labor	225,000	Health and safety training	8/81–7/82
United Electrical Radio and Machine Workers of America	Labor	55,800	Occupational safety and health program	8/81–7/82
United Federation of Teachers (UFT)	Education	55,919	Parent participation program	8/81
UFT	Education	62,831	As above	9/80
United Food and Commercial Workers (UFCW)	Labor	750,000	National OJT contract	1/81–1/83
UFCW	NEH	14,070	Historical research	FY 1980
UFCW	Labor	100,000	Occupational safety and health program	8/81–7/82
—Mediation and Conciliation Service	NA	24,400	Training for union stewards	9/81

Table A13.1 (continued)

Recipient	Awarding Agency	Grant ($)	Stated Purpose	Date
United Furniture Workers (UFW)	Labor	519,000	National OJT contract	8/80–11/81
UFW	Labor	316,600	As above	8/79–8/80
UFW	Labor	114,668	Occupational safety and training program	8/79–8/80
United Mine Workers of America (UMW)	HHS	104,000	Effect of cost sharing	5/81
UMW	HHS	164,641	Health-care survey	FY 1980
United Paperworkers International Union	Labor	127,385	OSHA training	8/81–7/82
United Rubber, Cork, Linoleum, and Plastic Workers of America	Labor	120,000	As above	9/81–9/82
United Steelworkers of America	Labor	300,000	Occupational safety and health training	9/80–9/81
United Union of Roofers (UUR)	Labor	198,554	NA	3/79–8/80
UUR	Labor	199,304	NA	8/80–7/81
Utility Workers Union of America	Labor	75,000	Occupational and health training	7/81–8/81

SOURCE: Freedom of Information Act requests.

Table A14.1
NATIONAL ENDOWMENT FOR DEMOCRACY GRANTS, FY 1984

Recipient	Grant ($)	Purpose
Free Trade Union Institute	11,000,000	To conduct a broad range of programs aimed at promoting the development of free and independent democratic trade unions
National Chamber Foundation	1,700,000	For the work of the Center for International Private Enterprise
National Republican Institute for International Affairs	1,500,000	For programs designed to support the development of democratic political systems and institutions, especially political parties, around the world
National Democratic Institute for International Affairs	1,500,000	For programs to foster and support democratic institutions and pluralistic values, with special emphasis on Third World countries
Afghanistan Relief Committee	50,000	To provide aid to reopen schools in an area in central Afghanistan controlled by the Afghan resistance
Caribbean Central American Action	127,500	To support the work of the Centro de Estudios Politicos, a nonpartisan center for political studies in Guatemala City
Chinese International	200,000	To establish a Chinese-language quarterly magazine for distribution to more than 15,000 students from mainland China currently studying in the United States, Western Europe, and Japan
Columbia University	200,000	To establish a series of International Human

Recipient	Grant ($)	Purpose
		Rights Law Student Internships and Exchanges
Committee in Support of Solidarity	91,825	To support the organization's Eastern European Democracy Project
Committee for a Community of Democracies	75,000	To hold a conference bringing together representatives of the world's democracies to plan for the establishment of a new association of democracies
Cuban American National Foundation	60,000	To establish citizen committees in six European countries to gather and disseminate information about the human-rights situation in Cuba in order to encourage pluralism and respect for human rights in Cuba
Freedom House	50,000	To establish a network of democratic opinion leaders in both the developing and developed worlds in order to facilitate a free exchange of ideas and end the isolation of democratic intellectuals and journalists
International Freedom to Publish Committee (IFPC)	50,000	To mount "America through American Eyes," an exhibit for the 1985 Moscow International Book Fair
IFPC	6,000	To support the publication of *Zeszyty Literackie*, a Paris-based Polish-language quarterly

Overseas Education Fund (OEF)	187,500	To establish a Democracy in Action training program in Francophone Africa
OEF	135,000	To support Conciencia, a nonpartisan Argentine women's organization similar to the League of Women Voters, which has been established to provide civic education to Argentine voters
Partners of the Americas	90,000	To enable Partners to establish a partnership between Chile and the state of Washington
Polish Institute for Arts and Sciences of America	90,000	To provide assistance to Polish political prisoners and to assist in maintaining independent cultural, educational, and scholarly activities in Poland
Andrei Sakharov Institute	50,000	To conduct a feasibility study on establishing a Center for Human Rights and Peace at the institute
Stanford University	100,625	To conduct a comparative, multi-authored study on the democratic experience in selected Third World nations
U.S. Committee for the Fifth Sakharov Hearings	45,000	To support the planning and execution of the next series of Sakharov hearings to be held in London in spring 1985
United States Overseas Cooperative Development Committee	90,000	To establish a program of exchanges and "sister co-op" relationships between U.S. cooperatives and their counterparts in Chile
YMCA of the USA International Division	41,500	To establish a training program for Panamanian youth

SOURCE: National Endowment for Democracy, October 1984.

Table A14.2

NATIONAL ENDOWMENT FOR DEMOCRACY GRANTS
FY 1985–MARCH 31, 1985

Recipient	Grant ($)	Purpose
Free Trade Union Institute	11,560,788	To continue the broad range of programs for the development of the free independent trade unions that were begun with the support the institute received from NED in FY 1984
National Chamber Foundation	1,438,326	For the work of the Center for International Private Enterprise
American Friends of Afghanistan	180,845	For a pilot project to provide educational opportunities for Afghans living in areas controlled by the Afghan resistance
Association for Education in Journalism and Mass Communication	25,000	For an exploratory program to assess the potential role of regional bodies in providing training, information, and other resources to African journalism educators
Caribbean/Central American Action (CCAA)	15,700	To design an education-for-democracy program for youth in the Eastern Caribbean
CCAA	211,250	To administer two projects to be conducted by the Centro de Estudios Politicos in Guatemala City
Jamaica-World Relief	106,940	To provide planning assistance to the International Conference of Youth and the World Youth Festival of Arts to be held in Jamaica in April 1985 to celebrate the UN International Youth Year

National Council of Negro Women, Inc.	155,830	For a one-year project to train women leaders in Guinea, Botswana, Swaziland, and Lesotho in democratic principles, organization building, constituency outreach, private-sector development, and making women's concerns known to government
Overseas Education Fund	25,000	To work with Uruguayan women to design a program to increase their contribution to national economic efforts and to the consolidation of democracy
Phelps-Stokes Fund	10,000	To convene a series of three day-long meetings of African professionals
Friends of the Democratic Center in Central America (PRODEMCA)	100,000	To support *La Prensa*, the only major independent newspaper in Nicaragua
PRODEMCA	200,000	To support the Nicaraguan Center for Democratic Studies, which is being established by the Coordinadora Democratica, a broadly based alliance of democratic political, civic, and economic groups in Nicaragua, and the Nicaraguan Permanent Commission on Human Rights
Time and We and *Problems of Eastern Europe*	50,000	To enable the editors of these Russian-language journals to put their publications on a more secure financial footing by providing funds for publishing costs

SOURCE: National Endowment for Democracy, March 1985.

Notes

Chapter 1. Introduction

1. Matthew Lesko, *Getting Yours: The Complete Guide to Government Money* (New York: Penguin Books, 1982), pp. 8–9.

2. 18 USC Sec. 1913. The law provides for termination of employment or removal from office, a $500 fine, and one-year imprisonment for violations.

3. *Galda* v. *Bloustein*, 686 F.2d. 159 (3d. Cir. 1982).

4. See "Regulatory Report—Lobbyists Unite to Lobby Against OMB's Proposed Curbs on Lobbying," *National Journal*, February 19, 1983, p. 371.

5. *Oklahoma* v. *Civil Service*, 330 U.S. 127, 132 (1947).

6. For a more detailed discussion of the issue of political speech, see Marshall J. Breger, *Halting Taxpayer Subsidy of Partisan Activity*, Heritage Foundation Lectures no. 26 (Washington, 1983).

7. Alexander Hamilton, James Madison, and John Jay, *The Federalist Papers* (New York: New American Library, 1961), p. 77.

8. For a discussion of how the courts and legislators have subverted constitutional safeguards of both civil and economic liberties over the past decades see Bernard Siegan, *Economic Liberties and the Constitution* (Chicago: University of Chicago Press, 1980). Siegan also discusses the economic consequences of these actions, as do Terry L. Anderson and Peter J. Hill, *The Birth of a Transfer Society* (Stanford University: Hoover Institution Press, 1980).

9. For a more detailed discussion of this phenomenon, which economists call "rent seeking," see James Buchanan, Gordon Tullock, and Robert Tollison, eds., *Toward A Theory of the Rent-Seeking Society* (College Station: Texas A&M University Press, 1979). Empirical estimates of the effects of interest-group activity on economic growth are found in Mancur Olson, *The Rise and Decline of Nations* (New Haven: Yale University Press, 1982).

Chapter 2. The Tax-Funded Political Network

1. As cited in Rael Isaac and Erich Isaac, "The Utopian Think Tanks," *New York Tribune*, March 20, 1984, p. 2B.

2. Rael Isaac and Erich Isaac, "The Utopian Think Tanks," *New York Tribune*, March 19, 1984, p. 1B. A more detailed description of IPS's economic policy perspective is found in chapter 3.

3. As cited in "Institute for Policy Studies," Heritage Foundation Institution Analysis no. 2 (Washington, May 1977).

4. Ibid.

5. Ibid.

6. Ibid.

7. Ibid., p.5.

8. Ibid.

9. Ibid.

10. Ibid.

11. Martin Carnoy and Derek Shearer, *Economic Democracy* (New York: M. E. Sharpe, 1979), as cited in William T. Poole, "The Attack on the Corporation," Heritage Foundation Institution Analysis no. 5 (Washington, September 1981), p. 23.

12. *Public Interest Profiles* (Washington, Foundation for Public Affairs, 1982), p. B29.

13. Ibid.

14. Isaac and Isaac, March 20, 1984, p. 2B.

15. As cited in Poole, p. 23.

16. Ibid., p. 24.

17. *America's Cities and Counties: A Citizen's Agenda* (Washington: Conference on Alternative State and Local Policies, 1983). Copies may be obtained from CASLP, 2000 Florida Ave., N.W., Washington, D.C. 20009.

18. William T. Poole, "The New Left in Government," Heritage Foundation Institution Analysis no. 9 (Washington, November 1978), p. 17.

19. "IPS Finds the Message Meant for Nicaragua," *Washington Times*, January 13, 1984, p. A5.

20. Ibid.

21. Ibid.

22. *Information Digest*, May 19, 1978, as cited in Rael Isaac and Erich Isaac, *The Coercive Utopians: Social Deception by America's Power Players* (Chicago: Regnery Gateway, 1984), p. 14.

23. Ibid.

24. As cited in Harry C. Boyte, *The Backyard Revolution: Understanding the New Citizen Movement* (Philadelphia: Temple University Press, 1980), p. 39.

25. Ibid., p. 109.

26. Youth Project Annual Report (Washington, 1977).

27. Data obtained from Freedom of Information Act requests. Also see Poole, "The New Left in Government," p. A15.

28. *Information Digest*, August 20, 1979, as cited in Poole, "The New Left in Government," p. 7.

29. As cited in Robert Goralski, "Front-Door Tactics, Back-Door Objectives," *Washington Times*, November 10, 1983, p. 2C.

30. Ibid. How they intend to do this is discussed in chapter 3.

31. *In These Times*, June 1982, as cited in Milton Copulos, "Inflationary Rhetoric," *Reason*, July 1983, p. 24.

32. Ibid.

33. Boyte, p. 110.

34. Taken from Midwest Academy "Direct Action" training manuals, as cited in Poole, "The New Left in Government," pp. 9–10.

35. John Herbers, "Grass-Roots Groups Go National," *New York Times Magazine*, September 4, 1983, p. 42.

36. Ibid.

37. *In These Times*, April 1982, p. 10, cited in Copulos.

38. *Working Papers for a New Society*, March/April 1978, as cited in Poole, "The New Left in Government," p. 8.

39. Poole, "The New Left in Government," p. 10.

40. Ibid., p. 11.

41. David Moberg, "Midwest Academy Looks Beyond 1984," *In These Times*, August 10, 1983, p. 8.

42. *Public Interest Profiles* (Washington: Foundation for Public Affairs, 1982), p. B35.

43. Ibid., p. B36.

44. "NPA Conference 83." Obtained from National People's Action, 954 W. Washington Blvd., Chicago, Illinois 60607.

45. *Public Interest Profiles*, p. B37.

46. Ibid.

47. *Disclosure*, November/December 1983, p. 1. Available from *Disclosure*, NTIC, 954 W. Washington Blvd., Chicago, Illinois 60607.

48. Ibid., p. 7.

49. *Policy Networks*, vol. 2 (Washington: Foundation for Public Affairs, September 1982), p. 1.

50. Ibid.

51. *In These Times*, September 8, 1982, as cited in *Information Digest*, vol. 15, October 1, 1982, p. 298.

52. Ibid.

53. Herbers, p. 22.

54. Poole, "The New Left in Government," p. 12.

55. Ibid.

56. Herbers, p. 46.

57. Ibid., p. 48.

58. Boyte, p. 93.

59. *Public Interest Profiles*, p. B1.

60. *ACORN Members Handbook, 1983*. Obtained from ACORN, 1638 R St., N.W., Washington, D.C. 20009.

61. ACORN *Community Organizing Handbook*.

62. Rochelle L. Stanfield, "Social Lobbies—Battered But Stronger After Round Two With Reagan," *National Journal*, October 2, 1982, p. 1673.

63. "Budget Cuts and the Poor," *Congressional Quarterly*, April 18, 1981, p. 660.

64. "A Loyal Bureaucracy?" *Richmond Times Dispatch*, January 24, 1981, p. 12.

65. Ibid.

66. Tom Diaz, "Barnes Casts Eye on #2 Slot in '84," *Washington Times*, December 7, 1982, p. 4A.

67. Ibid.

68. Jessica Lipnack and Jeffrey Stamps, *Networking: The First Report and Directory* (Garden City, N.Y.: Doubleday & Co., 1982).

69. Ibid., p. 1.

70. Ibid., p. 3.

71. Felicity Barringer, "Keeping Track of Budgeteers," *Washington Post*, December 21, 1984, p. A21.

72. Ibid.
73. Ibid.

Chapter 3. The Anti-Industry Coalition

1. William T. Poole, "The Attack on the Corporation," Heritage Foundation Institution Analysis no. 5 (Washington, September 1981), p. 1.

2. Richard Barnet, *The Crisis of the Corporation* (Washington: Institute for Policy Studies, 1975).

3. Poole, p. 3.

4. Herman Nickel, "The Corporation Haters," *Fortune*, June 16, 1980, pp. 126–36.

5. In 1981 it received at least $50,000 in federal tax funds. See *Public Interest Profiles* (Washington: Foundation for Public Affairs, 1982), p. B32.

6. As quoted in Justin Raimondo, "Inside the CED," *Reason*, February 1982, p. 20.

7. Ibid., p. 21.

8. Justin Raimondo, "The CED Syndrome: The Politics of the New Class," *Libertarian Review*, January 1980, as cited in William T. Poole, "Campaign for Economic Democracy, Part I: The New Left in Politics," Heritage Foundation Institution Analyis no. 13 (Washington, September 1980), p. 3.

9. Martin Carnoy and Derek Shearer, *Economic Democracy: The Challenge of the 1980s* (White Plains, N.Y.: M. E. Sharpe, Inc., 1980).

10. Ibid.

11. Poole, "The Attack on the Corporation," p. 6.

12. Ibid., p. 8.

13. For example, see *America's Cities and Counties: A Citizen's Agenda* (Washington: Conference on Alternative State and Local Policies, 1983).

14. Poole, "The Attack on the Corporation," p. 11.

15. Ibid.

16. Ibid.

17. Ibid., p. 13.

18. Ibid., p. 14.

19. Ibid.

20. Ibid., p. 15.

21. Ibid., p. 19.

22. Ibid., p. 2.

23. John Kenneth Galbraith, *The New Industrial State* (Boston: Houghton-Mifflin, 1967), p. 206.

24. See, for example, Robert Hessen, *In Defense of the Corporation* (Stanford: Hoover Institution Press, 1979).

25. Adam Smith, *An Inquiry into the Nature and Causes of the Wealth of Nations* (New York: Modern Library, 1937), p. 128.

26. Domenick Armentano, *Antitrust and Monopoly: Anatomy of a Policy Failure* (New York: John Wiley and Sons, 1982).

27. Yale Brozen, *Is Government the Source of Monopoly?* (Washington: Cato Institute, 1980), p. 29.

28. Ibid., p. 30.

29. Ibid., p. 32.

30. Yale Brozen, *Concentration, Mergers, and Public Policy* (New York: Macmillan, 1980).

31. Address of Benjamin Fairless before the Baltimore Association of Commerce, April 1950, as cited in Brozen, *Concentration, Mergers, and Public Policy*, p. 9.

32. John Kenneth Galbraith, "What Comes after General Motors?" *New Republic*, November 2, 1974, p. 16.

33. For an examination of Ralph Nader's legislative approach, see Hessen.

34. Henry Manne, "Mergers and the Market for Corporate Control," *Journal of Political Economy* (March/April 1965): 110–20.

35. See, for example, Armen Alchian and Harold Demsetz, "Production, Information Costs, and Economic Organization," *American Economic Review* (December 1972): 777–95.

36. Eugene F. Fama, "Agency Problems and the Theory of the Firm," *Journal of Political Economy* (June 1980): 288–307.

37. Joe Klein, "Ralph Nader: The Man in the Class Action Suit," *Rolling Stone*, November 20, 1975.

38. Ralph Nader, Mark Green, and Joel Seligman, *Constitutionalizing the Corporation: The Case for Federal Chartering of Giant Corporations* (Washington: Corporate Accountability Research Group, 1976), p. 353.

39. Ibid., p. 32.

40. Ludwig von Mises, *Bureaucracy* (New Haven: Yale University Press, 1944), p. 1.

41. See Gordon Tullock, *The Politics of Bureaucracy* (Washington: Public Affairs Press, 1965).

42. James T. Bennett and Manuel H. Johnson, *Better Government at Half the Price: Private Production of Public Services* (Ottawa, Ill.: Caroline House, 1981); and E. S. Savas, *Privatizing the Public Sector* (Chatham, N.J.: Chatham House, 1982).

43. Thomas E. Borcherding, "The Sources of Growth in Public Expenditures in the U.S.: 1902–1970," in *Budgets and Bureaucrats: The Sources of Government Growth* (Durham: Duke University Press, 1977), p. 62.

44. Carnoy and Shearer, as cited in Poole, "The Attack on the Corporation," p. 14.

45. E. Bastone, "Industrial Democracy and Worker Representation at Board Level: A Review of the European Experience," *Industrial Democracy Committee Research Report* (London: Her Majesty's Stationery Office, 1976), as cited in Steve Pejovich, "Codetermination: Labor Participation in Management," *Modern Age* (Winter 1978): 34.

46. Michael Jensen and William Meckling, "Rights and Production Functions: An Application to Labor-Managed Firms and Codetermination," *Journal of Business* 52 (1979): 472–73.

47. See Pejovich; and E. Furobotn, "The Long-Run Analysis of the Labor-Managed Firm: An Alternative Interpretation," *American Economic Review* (March 1976): 104–23.

48. Pejovich.

49. Ibid., p. 36.

50. Ibid.

51. Jensen and Meckling.

52. The following data are found in Milton Friedman and Rose Friedman, *Free to Choose: A Personal Statement* (New York: Harcourt Brace Jovanovich, 1979), pp. 190–91.

53. Murray Weidenbaum, *The Future of Business Regulation* (New York: Amacom Books, 1979), p. 13.

54. Ibid.

55. W. K. Viscusi, "The Impact of Occupational Safety and Health Regulation," *Bell Journal of Economics* (Spring 1979): 136.

56. Sam Peltzman, *Regulation of Pharmaceutical Innovation: The 1962 Amendments* (Washington: American Enterprise Institute, 1974).

57. Ronald Coase, "Economists and Public Policy," in *Large Corporations in a Changing Society*, ed. J. F. Weston (New York: New York University Press, 1975), pp. 182–84.

58. U.S. Commission on Federal Paperwork, *Final Summary Report* (Washington: Government Printing Office, 1977), p. 5.

Chapter 4. The Campaign for Economic Democracy

1. John Herbers, "Grass Roots Groups Go National," *New York Times Magazine*, September 4, 1983, pp. 22–23, 46–48.

2. *Public Interest Profiles* (Washington: Foundation for Public Affairs, 1982), p. B32.

3. As cited in John H. Bunzel, *New Force on the Left: Tom Hayden and the Campaign Against Corporate America* (Stanford: Hoover Institution Press, 1983), p. 47.

4. William T. Poole, "Campaign for Economic Democracy, Part 1: The New Left in Government," Heritage Foundation Institution Analysis, no. 13 (Washington, September 1980), p. 3.

5. Ibid., p. 47.

6. Bunzel, p. 46.

7. Ibid.

8. Ibid., p. 94.

9. Poole, p. 8.

10. Justin Raimondo, "Inside the CED," *Reason*, February 1982, p. 21.

11. Bunzel, p. 43.

12. Ibid., p. 80.

13. John Boland, "Nader Crusade: The Anti-Business Lobby is Alive and Kicking," *Barron's*, October 12, 1981, p. 20.

14. Robert Bleiberg, "Rotten Boroughs: New York City Has Been Undermined by Rent Control," *Barron's*, October 27, 1976, p. 7.

15. Eric Hemel, "What Does Rent Control Control?" *Taxing and Spending* (Fall 1979): 85.

16. Ibid.

17. Ibid.

18. Ibid., p. 84.

19. Ken Auletta, *The Streets Were Paved with Gold* (New York: Random House, 1979).

20. Hemel, p. 87.

21. Ibid.

22. As cited in Poole, p. 22.
23. Ibid.
24. Ibid.
25. Ibid., p. 14.
26. Ibid., p. 20
27. Ibid.

Chapter 5. Consumer Activists

1. H. L. Mencken, *Prejudices,* ed. James T. Farrell (New York: Vintage Books, 1958), p. 172.

2. S. Robert Lichter and Stanley Rothman, "What Interests the Public and What Interests the Public Interests," *Public Opinion* (April/May 1983): 44–48.

3. Ibid., p. 46.

4. Department of Transportation, National Highway Traffic Safety Administration, *Evaluation of the 1960–63 Corvair Handling and Stability* (Washington: Government Printing Office, 1972), p. ii.

5. Earl S. Holt, "Social Regulation: The New Interventionism," *Human Events,* September 19, 1981.

6. *Washington Post,* October 6, 1979, p. D9, as cited in Barry Boyer, "Funding Public Participation in Agency Proceedings: The Federal Trade Commission Experience," *Georgetown Law Journal* (October 1981): 62.

7. "Interview: Ralph Nader," *Rolling Stone,* September 20, 1975, p. 57.

8. Tom Diaz, "Nader Group's Fee System Opposed," *Washington Times,* August 9, 1983, p. 3A.

9. A listing of VISTA 1979 program grants is available from Program Grants Manager, VISTA, 806 Connecticut Ave., N.W., Suite 1100, Washington, D.C. 20525.

10. William M. Wardell and Louis Lasagna, *Regulation and Drug Development* (Washington: American Enterprise Institute, 1975).

11. Ibid., p. 193.

12. See Sam Peltzman, *Regulation of Pharmaceutical Innovation* (Washington: American Enterprise Institute: 1974).

13. Murray Weidenbaum, *The Costs of Government Regulation* (St. Louis: Washington University, Center for the Study of American Business, 1977).

14. Ibid.

15. Marcia B. Wallace and Ronald J. Penoyer, "Directory of Federal Regulatory Agencies," Working Paper no. 36, Center for the Study of American Business, Washington University (St. Louis, September 1978).

16. Frank Van Der Linden, "Consumerists Move in on Banking Field," *Sacramento Union,* December 16, 1979, p. B11.

17. Kathy McPhail, "Ralph Nader on Co-ops," *Co-op Magazine,* March/April 1980, p. 34.

18. Michael Schaff, *Cooperatives at the Crossroads: The Potential for a Major New Economic and Social Role,* (Cambridge, Mass.: Exploratory Project for Economic Alternatives, 1977), p. 29, cited in "The National Consumer Co-op Bank," Republican Study Committee Fact Sheet, House, June 20, 1980.

19. Ibid.

20. As cited in Van Der Linden, p. 11.

21. These data were obtained through a request to the NCCB.

22. As cited in William Poole, "Campaign for Economic Democracy, Part I: The New Left In Politics," Heritage Foundation Institution Analysis no. 2 (Washington, May 1977), p. 9.

23. Comptroller General, *The National Consumer Cooperative Bank: An Institution in Transition* (Washington: General Accounting Office, December 15, 1983).

24. Ibid., p. 68.

25. Ibid., p. 70.

26. Ibid., p. 71.

27. Charles R. Babcock, "U.S. Co-op Bank Fails to Live up to Projections," *Washington Post*, May 6, 1983, p. A11.

28. Philip Kreitner, "Abandoned Theories: The Cooperative Commonwealth," *Co-op Magazine*, March/April 1980, p. 44.

29. Ibid., p. 31.

30. "The National Consumer Co-op Bank," p. 162.

31. Babcock, p. A11.

32. Ibid.

33. "How Budget Cuts Hurt Nonprofit Groups," *Washington Post*, August 18, 1983, p. A27.

34. See *Grocery Manufacturers of America* v. *Carol Tucker Foreman et al.*, Civil Action no. 2245-78, U.S. District Court, Washington, D.C., as cited in H. Peter Metzger, *The Coercive Utopians: Their Hidden Agenda* (Denver: Public Service Company of Colorado, 1979), p. 13.

35. As cited in Metzger, p. 14.

36. *Public Interest Profiles* (Washington: Foundation for Public Affairs, 1983), p. C28.

37. This publication can be obtained from National Consumers League, 1522 K Street, N.W., Suite 406, Washington, D.C. 20005.

38. "Consumer Groups Plan Assault on Reagan's Policies," *National Review*, January 30, 1982, p. 214.

39. A copy of the booklet can be obtained for $5.00 from the National Consumers League.

40. Data were obtained from Freedom of Information Act requests. See chapter 12.

41. *Public Interest Profiles*, p. C44.

42. Ibid.

43. Senate bill 2145, introduced November 18, 1983. See Peter Germanis, "Why Not Let Americans Work at Home?" Heritage Foundation Backgrounder no. 325 (Washington, January 30, 1984).

44. In a letter to the authors dated July 18, 1983, Susan Phillips, NCC's Public Affairs Director, stated that the NCC "depends on membership dues, . . . subscriptions, and contributions from labor unions . . . to sustain our programs."

45. *Public Interest Profiles*, p. C45.

46. Ibid., p. C27.

47. Ibid., p. C29.

48. Ibid., p. C28.

49. Harry C. Boyte, *The Backyard Revolution: Understanding the New Citizen Movement* (Philadelphia: Temple University Press, 1980), p. 34.

50. Herman Nickel, "The Corporation Haters," *Fortune*, June 16, 1980, p. 128.

51. *The Presbyterian Layman*, November/December 1975, as cited in Rael Isaac and Erich Isaac, *The Coercive Utopians: Social Deception by America's Power Players* (Chicago: Regnery Gateway, 1983), p. 26.

52. Ibid.

53. Ibid., p. 24.

54. Ibid., p. 31.

55. Data were obtained from Freedom of Information Act requests.

56. "The National Council of Churches," in *Eye on Bureaucracy* (Vienna, Va.: Conservative Caucus Research, Analysis and Education Foundation, April 1983).

57. Data were obtained from these agencies through Freedom of Information Act requests. For an indication of one of the roles played by the League, see Karen DeWitt, "Infant Formula Drive is Assailed," *New York Times*, June 18, 1981, p. A26.

58. Nickel, p. 130.

59. Ibid., p. 126.

60. As reported in Carol Adelman, "Infant Formula, Science, and Politics," *Policy Review* (Winter 1983): 110.

61. Ibid.

62. Ibid., p. 111.

63. Ibid. The following studies are based on Adelman.

64. Ibid., p. 123.

65. Nickel, p. 130.

66. Adelman, p. 123.

67. Nickel, p. 134.

68. Ibid., p. 136.

69. Ibid., p. 132.

70. Ibid.

71. Consumer Affairs Letter, March 1981, as cited in Isaac and Isaac.

72. Such federal statutes are listed in *Federal Attorney Fee Awards Reporter* 4, no. 4 (June 1981): 2.

73. Dawn Jackson, "Paying Lawyers to Sue the Government," *National Journal*, April 17, 1982, p. 680.

74. Donald Lambro, "Government Pays Fat Fees to Leftist Lawyers," *Washington Inquirer*, July 30, 1982, p. 7.

75. Ibid.

76. Ibid.

77. Jackson, p. 682.

78. "Paying Public Interest Law Fees," *BusinessWeek*, August 4, 1980, p. 53.

79. "Transcript of Proceedings—President's Commission on the Accident at Three Mile Island," August 23, 1979, p. 243, as cited in Metzger, p. 23.

80. Ibid.

81. Ibid.

82. Ibid., p. 24.

83. Boyer, p. 124.

84. Ibid., p. 56.

85. Ibid., p. 131.

86. Ibid., p. 79.

87. Ibid., p. 90.

88. Ophthalmic Goods Proceedings, Transcript 6401–02, Federal Trade Commission, as cited in Boyer, p. 96.

89. Lee Benham, "The Effects of Advertising on the Price of Eyeglasses," *Journal of Law and Economics* (October 1972): 337.

90. See Yale Brozen, *Concentration, Mergers, and Public Policy* (New York: Macmillan, 1982).

91. Public Law 96-481. See Ruth Marcus, "To Some Victors Go the Legal Fees," *Washington Post*, July 20, 1982, p. A15.

92. Ibid.

Chapter 6. The Anti-Energy Industry

1. As cited in Robert Goralski, "Front-Door Tactics, Back-Door Objectives," *Washington Times*, October 10, 1983, p. 2C.

2. Petr Beckmann, *The Health Hazards of Not Going Nuclear* (New York: Golem Press, 1976), p. 178.

3. As cited in Milton Copulos, "CLEC: Hidden Agenda, Hidden Danger," Heritage Foundation Institution Analysis no. 26, (Washington, February 9, 1984).

4. David Moberg, "Activists Regroup for Reagan Years," *In These Times*, March 1981.

5. Michael Harrington, "Toward a Socialist Presence in America," *Social Policy* (January/February 1974): 8.

6. Goralski.

7. *Public Interest Profiles* (Washington: Foundation for Public Affairs, 1982), p. F13.

8. Moberg.

9. Department of Energy grant contractor computer printouts, 1980.

10. Ibid.

11. *Public Interest Profiles*, p. B30.

12. Testimony of William Schroer before the Colorado Public Utility Commission, November 28, 1979, as cited in Peter Metzger and Richard Westfall, *Government Activists: How They Rip Off the Poor* (Denver: Public Service Company of Colorado, 1981), p. 21.

13. Ibid.

14. Ibid.

15. Energy Advocates meeting, sponsored by the Community Services Administration (Denver, April 22, 1978), as cited in Metzger and Westfall, p. 22.

16. League of Women Voters, *Final Report, Solar Energy Project* (Washington, November 23, 1981), p. 1.

17. League of Women Voters 1980 Annual Report.

18. "The National Council of Churches," in *Eye on Bureaucracy* (Vienna,

Va.: Conservative Caucus Research, Analysis and Education Foundation, April 1983).

19. Don Wiener and Robert Brandon, *Energy Policy: Challenge of the '80s* (Washington: Citizen/Labor Energy Coalition, 1980), p. 49.

20. See Harry C. Boyte, *The Backyard Revolution: Understanding the New Citizen Movement* (Philadelphia: Temple University Press, 1980), p. 202.

21. *Public Interest Profiles*, p. F14.

22. James Carberry, "Red Tape Entangles Big Petroleum Firms in Complying with Federal Regulations," *Wall Street Journal*, September 3, 1975, p. 32.

23. Irving Kristol, "The Mugging of Con Ed," *Wall Street Journal*, May 17, 1974, p. 10.

24. Copulos, p. 10.

25. William Nordhaus, Robert Rusch, and Fredrich Sturdevent, "Turmoil and Competition in the Gasoline Marketing Industry" (Cambridge, Mass.: Management and Analysis Center, Inc., May 1983).

26. Ibid., p. 95.

27. John Barron and John Umbeck, "A Dubious Bill of Divorcement," *Regulation*, January/February 1983.

28. Nordhaus, Rusch, and Sturdevent; and Philip E. Sorenson, "Additional Evidence on the Economic Impact of Refiner Divorcement from Retail Gasoline Marketing in Maryland," Department of Economics, Florida State University, Tallahassee, Fla., September 1983.

29. Nordhaus, Rusch, and Sturdevent, p. 97.

30. *Congressional Quarterly*, April 23, 1983, p. 793.

31. C/LEC press release, September 15, 1983.

32. *Citizen Power*, June 1983, p. 1.

33. *Citizen Power*, June 1981, p. 2.

34. Nolan Clark, "Natural Gas Regulation: Throwing Out Supply and Demand," Cato Institute Policy Analysis no. 20 (Washington, December 1, 1982).

35. "Friends of the Millionaires," *Wall Street Journal*, August 24, 1984, p. 24.

36. See Milton Copulos, "Ammo for Decontrol," *Washington Times*, October 31, 1983, p. 1C.

37. It has long been recognized that the media have a "liberal bias." See, for example, Allan Brownfeld, "Is the Liberal Media Bias Real or Imagined?" *Washington Times*, September 21, 1982, p. 11A.

38. As cited in Milton Copulos, "Inflammatory Rhetoric," *Reason*, July 1983, p. 27.

39. Ibid., p. 29.

40. Ibid.

41. Ibid., p. 30.

42. Ibid.

43. Ibid.

44. Ibid.

45. Michael C. Jensen and William H. Meckling, "Can the Corporation Survive?" *Financial Analysts Journal* (January/February 1978): 36.

46. *Washington Times*, July 2, 1984, p. 7B.

47. Jensen and Meckling, p. 37.

48. The tax-funded activities of "environmentalist" groups, such as the Sierra Club and Friends of the Earth, are discussed in chapter 7. Data were obtained through Freedom of Information Act requests.

49. Amory B. Lovins, *Soft Energy Paths* (Cambridge, Mass.: Ballinger, 1977).

50. Nuclear Information and Resource Service, *Groundswell* (Washington, October 1982).

51. Ibid.

52. Barry Commoner, "A Reporter at Large: Energy III," *New Yorker*, February 16, 1976.

53. "The No-Nukes Court," *Wall Street Journal*, May 2, 1983, p. 30.

54. Ibid.

55. "The Anti-Nuclear Age," *Wall Street Journal*, January 23, 1984, p. 22.

56. Charles Alexander, "Pulling the Nuclear Plug," *Time*, February 13, 1984, p. 36.

57. M. Stanton Evans, "The $200 Million Delay," *National Review*, February 2, 1979, p. 174.

58. Alexander, p. 34.

59. Matthew Wald, "Utilities Chapter 11 Prospects," *New York Times*, June 26, 1985, p. D1.

60. Alexander, p. 39.

61. Wald, p. D4.

62. Alexander, p. 39.

63. Barry L. Brownstein, "The Price-Anderson Act: Is It Consistent with a Sound Energy Policy?" Cato Institute Policy Analysis no. 36 (Washington, April 17, 1984).

Chapter 7. Politics and the Environment

1. Robert J. Smith, "Privatizing the Environment," *Policy Review* (Spring 1982): 11–50.

2. John Baden, "Conservatives Need to Get Conservation Act Together," *Washington Times*, November 6, 1984, p. 8D.

3. Ibid.

4. Rachel Carson, *Silent Spring* (Greenwich, Conn.: Fawcett Press, 1962).

5. Ibid., as quoted from Albert Schweitzer.

6. As quoted in Robert Blieberg, "Bring Back DDT," *Barron's*, June 29, 1981.

7. As discussed in George Claus and Karen Bolander, *Ecological Sanity* (New York: David McKay Co., 1977), p. 541.

8. Paul Erlich, *The Population Bomb* (New York: Ballantine, 1968).

9. Ibid., pp. 66–67.

10. Ibid.

11. Edith Efron, *The Apocalyptics*, (New York: Macmillan, 1984), p. 35.

12. Rae Goodell, *The Visible Scientists* (Boston: Little, Brown & Co. 1977), p. 60.

13. As cited in Efron, p. 36.

14. Ibid.

15. Ibid., p. 37.

516

16. Barry Commoner, *The Poverty of Power: Energy and the Economic Crisis* (New York: Alfred A. Knopf, 1976), p. 262.

17. Rene Dubos and Barbara Ward, *Only One Earth: The Care and Maintenance of a Small Planet* (New York: Norton, 1972), p. 28.

18. Donella Meadows, Dennis Meadows, Jorgen Randers, and William Behrens, *The Limits to Growth* (New York: Potomac Associates Books, 1974).

19. Ibid., p. 29.

20. As cited in Efron, p. 48.

21. Lord Zuckerman, "Science, Technology, and Environmental Management," in *Who Speaks for the Earth*, ed. Maurice Strong (New York: Norton, 1973), p. 70.

22. *Time*, April 26, 1976, p. 56, as cited in Julian Simon, "Global Confusion, 1980: A Hard Look at the Global 2000 Report," *Public Interest* (Winter 1981): 7.

23. *New York Times*, April 13, 1976, as cited in Herman Kahn and Ernest Schneider, "Globaloney 2000," *Policy Review* (Spring 1981): 129.

24. As cited in Kahn and Schneider, p. 129.

25. Ibid.

26. Julian Simon, "False News is Truly Bad News," *Public Interest* (Fall 1981): 81.

27. Simon, "Global Confusion," p. 4.

28. Paul Ehrlich et al., *Ecoscience* (San Francisco: Freeman, 1977), p. 170.

29. Study Group on Environmental Problems, *Man's Impact on the Global Environment* (Cambridge: MIT Press, 1970), p. 13.

30. *Public Interest Profiles* (Washington: Foundation for Public Affairs, 1982), p. F31.

31. Ibid.

32. As described in William T. Poole, "The Environmental Complex, Part III," Heritage Foundation Institution Analysis no. 19 (Washington, June 1982).

33. Ibid.

34. Ibid.

35. Ibid.

36. Environmental Action 1983 Annual Report.

37. As cited in Poole, p. 2.

38. Sierra Club, "Conservation Priority: Budget and Appropriations," (Washington, 1984).

39. Sierra Club 1982–83 Annual Report.

40. John Hooper, "Privatization: Master Plan for Government Giveaways," *Sierra*, November/December 1982.

41. As quoted in James Weber, *Power Grab: The Conserver Cult and the Coming Energy Catastrophe* (New York: Arlington House, 1979), p. 46.

42. Statements by Michael McClosky, executive director of the Sierra Club, as reported in *Public Interest Profiles* (Washington: Foundation for Public Affairs, 1983), p. F-93.

43. Form letter issued by Friends of the Earth, 530 7th St., S.E., Washington, D.C. 20003.

44. Hugh Nash, ed., *Progress As If Survival Mattered* (Washington: Friends of the Earth, 1977), p. 40.

45. As cited in a 1981 fundraising letter.

46. "Congress Considers a Policy on Population," *Not Man Apart*, July/ August 1983, p. 4.

47. *Not Man Apart*, April 1984, p. 2.

48. William Symonds, "Washington in the Grip of the Green Giants," *Fortune*, October 4, 1982, p. 139.

49. As cited in H. Peter Metzger, *The Coercive Utopians: Their Hidden Agenda* (Denver: Public Service Company of Colorado, 1979), p. 24.

50. Ibid.

51. Ibid.

52. Ibid., p. 22.

53. As cited in Rael Isaac and Erich Isaac, *The Coercive Utopians: Social Deception by America's Power Players* (Chicago: Regnery Gateway, 1983), p. 55.

54. Claus and Bolander.

55. *NCAT's Best*. Available from NCAT, Box 3838, Butte, Montana 59702.

56. E. F. Schumacher, *Small is Beautiful* (New York: Harper & Row, 1973).

57. Ibid., p. 152.

58. Ibid., p. 30.

59. Ibid., p. 159.

60. "Capability Statement." Available from NCAT, 815 15th St., N.W., Suite 627, Washington, D.C. 20005. The statement lists NCAT's governmental funding sources as the Department of Energy, Department of the Interior, Department of State, Department of Housing and Urban Development, Community Services Administration, Department of Labor, ACTION, National Alcohol Fuels Commission, National Consumer Co-op Bank, and state and local governments.

61. *NCAT's Best*, p. 18.

62. Amory Lovins, "Energy Strategy: The Road Not Taken," *Foreign Affairs* (October 1976).

63. Data obtained from EPA grant documents.

64. Data obtained from Department of Energy grant documents.

65. Garrett Hardin, "The Tragedy of the Commons," *Science*, December 13, 1968, pp. 1244–45.

66. Smith, p. 32.

67. Ibid., p. 31.

68. Ibid., p. 35.

69. John Baden and Richard Stroup, "The Environmental Costs of Governmental Action," *Policy Review* (Spring 1978): 31.

70. Smith.

71. *Statement of David Alberswerth for the National Wildlife Federation before the Senate Subcommittee on Energy and Mineral Resources*, October 18, 1983, pp. 5–6.

72. Bruce Ackerman and William Hassler, *Clean Coal, Dirty Air* (New Haven: Yale University Press, 1981), p. 62.

73. See "Deep-Sixing Debate," *Wall Street Journal*, June 28, 1984, p. 28.

74. *Should Offshore Oil Be Put Off Limits?* (Washington: American Petroleum Institute, April 1, 1984), p. 4.

75. Ibid., p. 26.

76. Ibid., p. 29.

77. From the inside cover of Efron.

78. As cited in ibid., p. 21.

79. Ibid., p. 433.

80. Ibid., p. 434.

81. Ibid.

82. As cited in Mary Douglas and Aaron Wildavsky, *Risk and Culture* (Berkeley: University of California Press, 1982), pp. 55–56.

83. Efron, p. 478.

84. Russell Wild, "Fluoride: Miracle Cure or Public Menace," *Environmental Action*, July/August 1984, p. 19.

85. For a discussion of "free-market environmentalism" see Richard Stroup and John Baden, *Natural Resources: Bureaucratic Myths and Environmental Management* (San Francisco: Pacific Institute for Public Policy Research, 1984).

Chapter 8. Poverty, Politics, and Social Programs

1. "Why There's No Welfare Fat Left to Trim," *BusinessWeek*, March 26, 1984, p. 84.

2. Ibid., p. 81.

3. Lawrence D. Maloney, "The Desperate World of America's Underclass," *U.S. News and World Report*, March 26, 1984, p. 55.

4. Ibid.

5. J. Peter Grace, "Little Things Mean a Lot, Grace Panel Found," *Wall Street Journal*, January 12, 1984, p. 24.

6. William E. Simon, *A Time for Action* (New York: Reader's Digest Press, 1980), p. 91.

7. Ibid.

8. "Relief Is No Solution," *New York Times*, February 2, 1962, p. 28.

9. Charles A. Murray, *Safety Nets and the Truly Needy: Rethinking the Welfare System* (Washington: Heritage Foundation, 1982), p. 18. Also see Murray's book, *Losing Ground: American Social Policy, 1950–1980* (New York: Basic Books, 1984).

10. Jonathan R. Hobbs, "Welfare Need and Welfare Spending," Heritage Foundation Backgrounder no. 219 (Washington, October 13, 1982), p. 4.

11. "Welfare and Poverty" (Dallas: National Center for Policy Analysis, 1983), p. 7.

12. See Martin Anderson, *Welfare* (Stanford: Hoover Institution Press, 1978), especially chap. 5.

13. Edgar K. Browning and William R. Johnson, *The Distribution of the Tax Burden* (Washington: American Enterprise Institute, 1979), p. 70, table 17.

14. Henry J. Aaron, *Why Is Welfare So Hard to Reform?* (Washington: Brookings Institution, 1973), pp. 33–34.

15. George Gilder, *Wealth and Poverty* (New York: Basic Books, 1981), p. 122.

16. Ibid., pp. 124 and 278n.

17. "How Budget Cuts Hurt Nonprofit Groups," *Washington Post*, August 18, 1983, p. A27.

18. Gordon Tullock, *Economics of Income Distribution* (Boston: Kluwer-Nijhoff, 1983), p. 91.

19. *The Food Stamp Program: Income or Food Supplementation?* (Washington: Congressional Budget Office, 1977), p. 2.

20. Ibid.

21. Ibid.

22. This point has been discussed in detail elsewhere and will not be treated at length here. For a full discussion, see Dan C. Heldman, James T. Bennett, and Manuel H. Johnson, *Deregulating Labor Relations* (Dallas: Fisher Institute, 1981).

23. Doug Bandow, "Reagan Yields to the Kiwi Lobby?" *New York Times*, July 3, 1984, p. A15.

24. Ward Sinclair, "Costly Farm Supports Make GOP Nervous About Toll on '84 Vote," *Washington Post*, August 14, 1983, p. A3.

25. H. L. Mencken, "The Husbandman," in *A Mencken Chrestomathy* (New York: Alfred A. Knopf, 1949), p. 360.

26. Teachers are in many ways similar to farmers in terms of political sophistication. It is no accident that teachers as an interest group were able to pressure Congress and the Carter administration into creating a cabinet-level department to represent the education lobby.

27. James Bovard, "How Federal Food Programs Grew and Grew," *Policy Review* 26 (Fall 1983): 45.

28. As reported in *Food and Nutrition Issues in the Food Stamp Program* (Washington: Food Research and Action Center, 1981), p. 1n.

29. *FRAC's Guide to the Food Stamp Program*, 7th ed. (Washington: Food Research and Action Center, 1983), p. 7. The example begins as follows: "The Branchwaters are a family of six, including Uncle Bourbon, who is 78. They have four cars."

30. *The Food Stamp Program*, p. xiv. There is no way of knowing with certainty, but it is possible that food stamps do *not* stimulate food consumption at all. Recipients may spend so much less of their own income on food that total food expenditures may not increase or may increase only very slightly. As evidence of this effect, Bovard cited a Department of Agriculture study showing that "each additional dollar of food stamp payments increased food consumption by only 14 cents." See Bovard, p. 47.

31. *The Food Stamp Program—Overissued Benefits Not Recovered and Fraud Not Punished* (Washington: General Accounting Office, 1977), p. i.

32. *Need for Greater Efforts to Recover Costs of Food Stamps Obtained Through Fraud or Error* (Washington: General Accounting Office, 1983), p. i.

33. *The Food Stamp Program*, p. 17. By 1976, about half the population of Puerto Rico was receiving food stamps.

34. *Food Stamp Work Requirements—Ineffective Paperwork or Effective Tool?* (Washington: General Accounting Office, 1978), p. i.

35. *Insights Gained in Workfare Demonstration Project* (Washington: General Accounting Office, 1981), p. 4.

36. *World Food Nutrition Study: Enhancement of Food Production for the United States*, Report of the Board of Agriculture and Renewable Resources (Washington: National Academy of Sciences, 1975), p. 61.

37. *Feeding Children: Federal Child Nutrition Policies in the 1980's* (Washington: Congressional Budget Office, 1980), p. 61.

38. Ibid.

39. J. Patrick Madden and Marion D. Yoder, *Program Evaluation: Food Stamps and Commodity Distribution in Rural Areas of Central Pennsylvania,* Agricultural Experiment Station Bulletin no. 780 (University Park: Pennsylvania State University Press, 1972).

40. Bovard, p. 48.

41. *Feeding Children,* p. xx.

42. *Informing the Public About Food—A Strategy Is Needed for Improving Communication* (Washington: General Accounting Office, 1982), pp. i, 5–6.

43. Ibid.

44. Ibid., p. 11.

45. *How Good Are School Lunches?* (Washington: General Accounting Office, 1978), p. i.

46. *Child Care Food Program: Better Management Will Yield Better Nutrition and Fiscal Integrity* (Washington: General Accounting Office, 1979), p. ii.

47. *Efforts to Improve School Lunch Program—Are They Paying Off?* (Washington: General Accounting Office, 1981), p. i.

48. *Feeding Children,* p. 58.

49. For a discussion of this episode and for further references, see Bovard, pp. 43–44.

50. Quoted in *Food and Nutrition Issues in the Food Stamp Program* (Washington: Food Research and Action Center, 1981), p. 16. Members of food advocacy and lobbying groups have a tendency to overstate. Consider the following paragraph on page 7 of the *Findings and Recommendations of the Nutrition Watch Committee.* The NWC was appointed by Governor Hugh Carey to study the extent of hunger in the State of New York in January 1982:

> Through [sic] life, nutrition affects everyone's health, regardless of age, race, sex or economic status. Since the adage "you are what you eat" is true, *New Yorkers are in serious trouble.* Lifelong improper food choices and appetites insensitive to reasonable limits *have significantly undermined* the health of New York State residents. For the *majority,* their productivity and quality of life have been negatively affected. Ignorance of and disinterest in the consequences of poor nutrition appear to be the major hindrances to improving New Yorkers' nutritional habits. Although the steps to correct the problems of ignorance and disinterest are longer term than the steps to alleviate hunger, the necessity of addressing both problems is equally compelling [emphasis added].

In the absence of additional information, a visitor to New York State might expect to find a majority of its population in the same condition that often prevails in the drought-plagued countries of Sub-Saharan Africa where hunger is all too real. But the phrase "appetites insensitive to reasonable limits," whatever it might actually mean, seems to imply that New York State's population is, on average, obese. How does that square with the suggestion that vast numbers of people are hungry? Apparently, food advocates wish to dictate not only how much individuals eat, but also what is consumed. The notion that "New Yorkers are in serious trouble" must be taken with a grain of salt.

51. Federal regulations prohibit food stamps from being used to pur-

chase imported food. The Department of Agriculture is not interested in reducing the agricultural surpluses of other nations.

52. For a discussion of administrative lobbying, see Peter Woll, *American Bureaucracy*, 2d ed. (New York: W. W. Norton, 1977), pp. 194–205.

53. Bovard, p. 45.

54. *Food and Nutrition Issues,* inside front cover. Credit for printing this publication is given to the Playboy Foundation.

55. "Government-Supported Groups Help Liberals Fleece Taxpayers," *Conservative Digest* (April 1983): 26.

56. "Defund the Left—The 10 Worst Agencies: Legal Services Corporation," *Conservative Digest* (April 1983): 22.

57. "Sources Identified for New Revenues," *Foodlines,* June 1983, p. 10.

58. "Action Corner," *Foodlines,* June 1983, p. 10.

59. Lisa Schwartz, "National Let Eat Cake Sale," *Foodlines,* June 1983, p. 8.

60. Ibid.

61. "Soviet Attack: The Exaggerated Threat," *Foodlines,* June 1983, p. 12.

62. "F.A.C.T. Feed America's Communities Today" (Washington: Food Research and Action Center, n.d.), p.1.

63. Ibid., p. 2.

64. "Working to End Hunger in America" (Washington: Food Research and Action Center, n.d.).

65. Ibid.

66. *Need for Greater Efforts,* p. 29.

67. Bovard, p. 47.

68. *An Organizer's Manual,* 2d ed., part 2 (Washington: Fair Budget Action Campaign, n.d.), p. 1.

69. Ibid., part 3, "How to Lobby."

70. Ibid.

71. Ibid., part 1, "Reaganomics."

72. Ibid., part 3, "Voter Registration and Education," pp. 1–2.

73. Ibid., p. 2.

74. Ibid., part 3, "Public Demonstrations," p. 2.

75. *Guide to Quality School Lunch and Breakfast Programs* (Washington: Food Research and Action Center, 1981), p. 2.

76. Ibid., p. 9.

77. Ibid., p. 12.

78. Ibid., pp. 35–49.

79. *Guide to State Legislation* (Washington: Food Research and Action Center, 1983).

80. Ibid., p. II-1.

81. Ibid., chap. 5.

82. Ibid., p. V-7.

83. Ibid.

84. Ibid., p. V-11.

85. *Public Interest Profiles* (Washington: Foundation for Public Affairs, 1982), pp. B1ff.

86. *ACORN Members Handbook: 1983* (Washington: Association of Community Organizations for Reform Now, 1983), p. 1.

87. Ibid., p. 5.

88. William T. Poole, "The New Left in Government, Part II: The VISTA Program as 'Institution Building,' " Heritage Foundation Institution Analysis no. 17 (Washington, 1982), p. 4.

89. Ibid.

90. *ACORN Members Handbook*, p. 16.

91. Ibid., pp. 17–28.

92. Ibid., p. 4.

93. Paul R. Wieck, "Citizens at Work," *New Republic*, September 28, 1974, p. 8.

94. Poole, p. 4.

95. Austin Scott, "Citizens' Reform Scores Quite a Success in Arkansas County," *Washington Post*, June 3, 1973, p. A2.

96. *Public Interest Profiles*, p. B3.

97. *Acorn Members Handbook*, p. 1.

98. *Public Interest Profiles*, p. B3.

99. See, for example, Jonathan Wolman, "ACORN Moving Its Front-Porch Democracy into National Politics," Baton Rouge *State Times*, July 2, 1979, p. 14A; Don McLeod, "ACORN Clout Grows in Delegate Selection," *Times Picayune*, April 23, 1980, p. 8B; Tom Limmer, "Inner-City Could Have Big Say in Democratic Party Caucus," *Grand Rapids Press*, March 21, 1980, p. 1; and Hugh McDiarmid, "League of Poor People Could Pack Dem Caucuses," *Detroit Free Press*, February 28, 1980, p. A3.

100. "Picking a President," *ACORN USA* (Spring 1983): 8.

101. *Acorn Members Handbook*, p. 15.

102. Roy Reed, "Lobby of Have-Nots Nettles the Southern Establishment," *New York Times*, October 6, 1976, p. 20.

103. Will Collette, "Going to Court: A Research Guide," *Organizer* 9 (Spring 1982): 23.

104. Lee Staples, "The Seven D's of Defense," *Organizer* 9 (Winter 1983): 13.

105. Richard A. Cloward and Frances Fox Piven, "Realigning the Democrats," *Organizer* 9 (Winter 1983): 21.

106. Ibid., p. 132.

107. *Rural America* (Washington: Rural America, n.d.), p. 3.

108. See *The 1981 Platform for Rural America* (Washington: Rural America, 1981).

109. Barbara Swaczy, *Getting People Together in Rural America—A Beginner's Guide to Consumer Organizing* (Helena, Mont.: Northern Rockies Action Group, n.d.).

110. Linda A. Svoboda, *Making Democracy Real in Rural America—A Guide to Organizing and Advocacy in Rural Areas* (Washington: Rural America, 1982), p. ii.

111. Swaboda, p. 1.

112. Swaczy, p. 5.

113. Murray, *Losing Ground*.

Chapter 9. The Antipoverty Industry

1. *Report of Audit: The East Los Angeles Community Union (TELACU) Los Angeles, California, January 1, 1976–December 31, 1979*, vol. 1 (Washington: U.S. Department of Labor, 1982), pp. 11–12.

2. Robert Welkos and Claire Spiegel, "Politicking: Another Murky Area for TELACU," *Los Angeles Times*, March 28, 1982, pp. 1–19.

3. Claire Spiegel and Robert Welkos, "Giant Anti-Poverty Agency Did Little to Create Jobs," *Los Angeles Times*, March 30, 1982, p. 1.

4. Claire Spiegel and Robert Welkos, "Anti-Poverty Agency: Leaving Barrio Behind," *Los Angeles Times*, March 28, 1982, p. 1.

5. *Report of Audit.* The audit covers the calendar years 1976 through 1979, but financial data on grants and contracts cover the three fiscal years October 1, 1976 through September 30, 1979. Federal grants and contracts are typically made on a fiscal-year basis.

6. Ibid., p. 19.

7. Ibid., p. 25.

8. Ibid., p. 20.

9. The discussion in this section is taken from ibid., pp. 36–38.

10. Ibid., p. 38.

11. Robert Welkos and Claire Spiegel, "Far-Flung Empire Is Built on Federal Grants," *Los Angeles Times*, March 29, 1982, p. 8.

12. Ibid.

13. Ibid., p. 3.

14. *Report of Audit*, p. 47.

15. Spiegel and Welkos, "Leaving Barrio Behind," p. 3.

16. Howie Kurtz, "Audit Says Anti-Poverty Agency and Subsidiaries Misused Funds," *Washington Post*, August 12, 1982, pp. A2 ff.

17. Spiegel and Welkos, "Giant Anti-Poverty Agency," p. 18.

18. The discussion of InterAmerican Entertainment is based on Welkos and Spiegel, "Far-Flung Empire," pp. 3, 8.

19. Ibid.

20. There is one exception. Community Development and Planning Corporation, with 83.7 percent of its gross revenues from government sources, sustained a loss of about $250,000.

21. The material on Aqua-Pet is based on Welkos and Spiegel, "Far-Flung Empire," p. 9.

22. Ibid.

23. Spiegel and Welkos, "Giant Anti-Poverty Agency," p. 18.

24. Robert Welkos, "Supervisors Place Lien on TELACU Industrial Park," *Los Angeles Times*, June 15, 1983, p. II-1.

25. *Report of Audit*, p. 39.

26. Ibid., p. 40.

27. Ibid., p. 54.

28. Ibid., p. 41.

29. Claire Spiegel, "TELACU Invested Money Given for Needy, Audit Says," *Los Angeles Times*, September 18, 1982, p. 1.

30. Claire Spiegel, "TELACU Ordered to Pay Back $1 Million," *Los Angeles Times*, April 17, 1983. p. 1.

31. Ibid.
32. *Report of Audit*, pp. 43–44.
33. Welkos and Spiegel, "Far-Flung Empire," p. 3.
34. *Report of Audit*, p. 44.
35. Ibid., pp. 57–58.
36. Ibid., p. 59.
37. Ibid., pp. 59–61.
38. Ibid., pp. 61–62.
39. Ibid., pp. 61–67.
40. Spiegel and Welkos, "Giant Anti-Poverty Agency," p. 10.
41. *Report of Audit*, pp. 106–9.
42. Claire Spiegel and Robert Welkos, "Poverty Agency Largely Immune from Corruption Probe," *Los Angeles Times*, November 12, 1982, p. II-5.
43. *Report of Audit*, p. 108.
44. Spiegel and Welkos, "Giant Anti-Poverty Agency," p. 18.
45. Ibid.
46. *Report of Audit*, p. 75.
47. Ibid., p. 84.
48. Spiegel and Welkos, "Leaving Barrio Behind," p. 11.
49. Ibid., p. 14.
50. Ibid., pp. 11–12.
51. *Report of Audit*, p. 96.
52. Ibid., pp. 96–98.
53. Spiegel and Welkos, "Giant Anti-Poverty Agency," p. 18.
54. *Report of Audit*, p. 98–99.
55. Ibid.
56. Spiegel and Welkos, "Giant Anti-Poverty Agency," p. 18.
57. Ibid.
58. Claire Spiegel, "TELACU Dedicates Offices Financed by Federal Funds," *Los Angeles Times*, July 9, 1983, p. 1.
59. Kurtz, p. A2.
60. Lewis M. Simons and Ron Shaffer, "Pride Firm Tied to $600,000 Theft," *Washington Post*, October 21, 1979, p. A1.
61. Lewis M. Simons and Ron Shaffer, "How HUD Gave Project to Pride," *Washington Post*, October 23, 1979, p. A15.
62. Simons and Shaffer, "$600,000 Theft," p. A1.
63. Ibid., p. A15.
64. Ibid.
65. Ibid.
66. Joe Pichirallo, "Homes of City Aides, Developers Repaired by Crews from Project," *Washington Post*, March 18, 1984, p. A10.
67. Ibid.
68. Ibid.
69. "Auditors Question Memphis Ventures," *New York Times*, April 29, 1984, p. 31.
70. Howard Kurtz, "How Cities Profited on HUD," *Washington Post*, April 12, 1984, p. A14.
71. Ibid.
72. Ibid.

73. As an example of an exposé written for a popular audience, see Patty Newman and Joyce Wenger, *Pass the Poverty Please!*(Whittier, Calif.: Constructive Action, 1966). This work is now nearly 20 years old, but its message is as current as if it had been published today.

74. *Report of Audit*, p. 68.

75. Ibid., p. 71.

76. Ibid., pp. 191–92.

77. Ibid., pp. 193–94.

78. Ibid., p. 194.

79. Welkos and Spiegel, "Politicking," p. 3.

80. "Councilman Pays $14,000 Political Fine," Los Angeles *Daily News*, December 8, 1982, p. 10.

81. Welkos and Spiegel, "Politicking," p. 3.

82. Spiegel and Welkos, "Leaving Barrio Behind," p. 12.

83. Alan Ehrenhalt, ed., *Politics in America: Members of Congress in Washington and at Home* (Washington: Congressional Quarterly Press, 1983), p. 189.

84. Spiegel and Welkos, "Leaving Barrio Behind," p. 13.

85. Ehrenhalt, p. 189.

86. Welkos and Spiegel, "Politicking," pp. 19–20.

87. Ibid., p. 20.

88. Spiegel and Welkos, "Leaving Barrio Behind," p. 14.

89. Kurtz, "How Cities Profited," p. A14.

90. Ronald D. White, "Judge Is Urged to Sentence Treadwell," *Washington Post*, April 12, 1984, p. C3.

91. Ron Shaffer and Lewis M. Simons, "How HUD Watched the Thefts at Clifton Terrace," *Washington Post*, October 24, 1979, p. 1.

Chapter 10. Politics and the Redefinition of "Civil Rights"

1. In our discussion of the civil rights movement, we will be concerned primarily with the activities of organizations in the movement, rather than with specific individuals.

2. See, for instance, Bernard Siegan, *Economic Liberties and the Constitution* (Chicago: University of Chicago Press, 1980).

3. By the "federal government" we mean member of Congress and the bureaucrats who serve them.

4. As cited in Joseph Perkins, "Are Black Leaders Listening to Black America?" *Wall Street Journal*, October 10, 1984, p. 28. See also Walter E. Williams, *The State Against Blacks* (New York: McGraw-Hill, 1982); and Thomas Sowell, *Civil Rights: Rhetoric or Reality?* (New York: William Morrow & Co., 1984).

5. Perkins.

6. Gallup Opinion Index, Report 143, June 1977, p. 23.

7. Everett C. Ladd, "Traditional Values Regant," *Public Opinion* (March–April 1978): 48.

8. Herbert H. Denton, "Civil Rights Groups Strive to Keep Federal Grants," *Washington Post*, April 12, 1981, p. 10.

9. For a review of the failures of federal job training programs, see Thomas J. DiLorenzo, "The Myth of Government Job Creation," Cato

Institute Policy Analysis no. 48 (Washington, February 19, 1985). Also see chapter 13.

10. Information provided to the Department of Labor through Freedom of Information Act requests.

11. Ibid.

12. Ibid.

13. The League's 1982 Annual Report stated that of $12,096,000 in revenues for "specific projects," 85 percent, or $10.2 million, came from the government.

14. Tom Joe, "Gutting the Great Society," *Urban League Review* (Winter 1982–83): 23.

15. Charles Murray, *Losing Ground: American Social Policy, 1950–1980* (New York: Basic Books, 1984).

16. Joe, p. 51.

17. See Sowell, p. 39.

18. Ibid., p. 43.

19. Ibid., p. 49.

20. Ibid., p. 51.

21. Ibid., p. 52.

22. Ibid., p. 53.

23. See any economics text.

24. See Jacob Mincer, "Unemployment Effects of Minimum Wages," *Journal of Political Economy* (August 1976): 87–105; and Simon Rottenberg, ed., *The Economics of Legal Minimum Wages* (Washington: American Enterprise Institute, 1981).

25. Williams.

26. Ibid.

27. In a documentary on *The State Against Blacks* produced by the Public Broadcasting System in 1984.

28. As cited in Sowell, p. 92.

29. Ibid.

30. Ibid., p. 93.

31. Ibid.

32. Ibid., p. 96.

33. Ibid., p. 108. For a more detailed examination of this issue, see Deborah Walker, "Value and Opportunity: The Issue of Comparable Pay for Comparable Worth," Cato Institute Policy Analysis no. 38 (Washington, May 31, 1984).

34. Jeff Gerth, "Questions Arise on Jackson Group's Finances," *New York Times*, January 29, 1984, p. 1.

35. Ibid., p. 18.

36. Howard Hurwitz, "Jackson's PUSH Over the Brink," *Washington Times*, September 6, 1983, p. 2C.

37. The audits can be obtained from the Inspector General's Office, U.S. Department of Education. For a discussion of these and other Department of Education grants, see John Fund and Martin Wooster, "An Education in Empire Building," *Reason*, May 1984, pp. 42–48.

38. Ibid., p. 46.

39. Ibid.

40. "2 Jesse Jackson Groups Misused $1.7 million, U.S. Auditors Say," *New York Times,* August 20, 1983, p. 6.

41. Ibid.

42. Gerth, p. 18.

43. Freedom of Information Act requests. See also Ron Cordray, "Massive Abuses of Funds Charged," *Washington Times,* December 6, 1982, p. 3.

44. Council on Interracial Books for Children, *Guidelines for Selecting Bias-Free Textbooks,* as cited in David Asman, "The Council on Interracial Books for Children," Heritage Foundation Institution Analysis no. 18 (Washington, June 10, 1982), p. 1.

45. Ibid.

46. Ibid.

47. Ibid.

48. Ibid.

49. Ibid. These include Hollie Nox of NOW's Legal Defense Fund, which received $300,000 in 1981; Leslie Hergert of The Network, Inc., which received $1,000,000 from the Department of Education; and members of Feminist Press Collective, which received over $300,000.

50. Asman, p. 5.

51. Ibid.

52. Ibid.

53. The following is based on David Asman, "The National Student Educational Fund," Heritage Foundation Institution Analysis no. 20 (Washington, June 24, 1982).

54. Ibid., p. 3.

55. Ibid., p. 4.

56. Taken from grant proposal obtained from Freedom of Information Act request.

57. Ibid.

58. Data obtained from Freedom of Information Act request.

59. Ibid.

60. June 1983 letter to the authors.

61. Copies of the report can be obtained from WEAL, 805 15th St., N.W., Washington, D.C. 20005.

62. *WEAL Washington Report,* June 1983, p. 5.

63. *PEER Perspective,* March 14, 1983. Copies are available from PEER, 1413 K St., N.W., Washington, D.C. 20005.

64. *Education Funding News,* March 15, 1983, p. 15.

65. League of Women Voters, "Facts About the League of Women Voters," 1982. This can be obtained from 1730 M St., N.W., Washington, D.C. 20036.

66. The following examples are taken from *Impact on Issues 1982–84* (Washington: League of Women Voters 1982).

67. Ibid., p. 40.

68. League of Women Voters Education Fund, "Going to Court in the Public Interest," April 1983.

69. Ibid.

70. "Restrictions on Abortion and Lobbying Activities in Family Plan-

ning Programs Needs Clarification," GAO Report no. HRD-82-106 (Washington: General Accounting Office, September 24, 1982).

Chapter 11. The Senior Citizen Lobby

1. *A Progress Report: January, 1984* (Washington: National Council of Senior Citizens, 1984), p. 48.

2. *Senior Citizen News,* July 1983, p. 1.

3. Ibid.

4. Ibid.

5. Ibid., p. 3.

6. *A Progress Report,* p. 8.

7. Ibid., p. 20.

8. Ibid., p. 23.

9. Ibid.

10. Ibid. How the Legal Services Corporation used taxpayer funds for partisan political purposes is the topic of chapter 12.

11. Ibid., p. 32.

12. Ibid., p. 30.

13. Ibid.

14. Donald Lambro, *Fat City: How Washington Wastes Your Taxes* (Chicago: Regnery Gateway, 1980), p. 121.

15. Ibid., pp. 128–32.

16. Ibid., p. 132.

17. *A Progress Report,* pp. 37–43.

18. Ibid., p. 37.

19. Ibid., p. 41.

20. Ibid., p. 42.

21. The following is found in *Public Interest Profiles* (Washington: Foundation for Public Affairs, 1982), pp. A21–A25.

22. Ibid., p. A24.

23. Ibid., p. A21.

24. Ibid.

25. Ibid.

26. Ibid.

27. *Age and Youth in Action,* April/May 1984. Copies of this publication can be obtained from Gray Panthers, 755 8th St., N.W., Washington, D.C. 20001.

28. Ibid.

29. Ibid.

30. Ibid.

31. *Monthly Tax Features* (Washington: Tax Foundation, June/July 1980 and June/July 1984).

32. *Age and Youth in Action,* March 1984.

33. Ibid.

34. *Shelterforce* 7, no. 3 (1982). Published at 380 Main St., East Orange, N.J. 07018.

35. Thomas Hazlett, "Rent Controls and the Housing Crisis," in *Resolving the Housing Crisis,* ed. M. Bruce Johnson (San Francisco: Pacific Institute for Public Policy Research, 1982), p. 282.

36. Ibid.

37. Ibid.

38. Comptroller General, *Rental Housing: A National Problem that Needs Immediate Attention*, report no. CED-80-11 (Washington: General Accounting Office, 1979), p. ii.

39. The Davis-Bacon Act mandates that "prevailing wages" in a geographic area, usually union-scale wages, be paid to all workers on federally subsidized construction projects. Sometimes the "prevailing wage," which is determined by the Department of Labor, is the union wage paid hundreds of miles from the construction site. This tactic is used to artificially raise wages. See James T. Bennett, Dan C. Heldman, and Manuel Johnson, *Deregulating Labor Relations* (Dallas: Fisher Institute, 1981).

40. Joseph Pechman, Henry J. Aaron, and Michael Taussig, *Social Security: Perspectives for Reform* (Washington: Brookings Institution, 1981), p. 1.

41. For a review of these studies see Peter J. Ferrara, *Social Security: The Inherent Contradiction* (Washington: Cato Institute, 1980).

42. Ibid., p. 8.

43. A. Haeworth Robertson, "The National Commission's Failure to Achieve Real Reform," *Cato Journal* 3, no. 2 (Fall 1983): 403.

44. Ibid.

45. John C. Goodman, "Private Alternatives to Social Security: The Experience of Other Countries," *Cato Journal* 3, no. 2 (Fall 1983): 563–74.

46. *A Progress Report*, p. 21.

47. 1978 Annual Report of the Social Security Board of Trustees (Washington, May 15, 1978), p. 3.

48. 1980 Annual Report of the Social Security Board of Trustees (Washington, June 17, 1980), p. 5.

49. Peter J. Ferrara, "The Prospect of Real Reform," *Cato Journal* 3, no. 2 (Fall 1983): 612.

50. *1984 Federal and State Legislative Policy* (Washington: American Association of Retired Persons, 1984), p. 23.

51. Ferrara, "The Prospect of Real Reform," p. 609.

52. Richard S. Foster, "Short-Range Financial Status of the Social Security Problem Under the Social Security Amendments of 1983," 1983 Annual Report of the Social Security Board of Trustees as cited in Ferrara, "The Prospect of Real Reform," p. 610.

53. Paul Craig Roberts, "Social Security: Myths and Realties," *Cato Journal* 3, no. 2 (Fall 1983): 400.

54. Ibid., p. 401.

55. "Report to the Presidential Candidates," *Age and Youth in Action*, April/May 1984, pp. 5–7.

56. Edgar K. Browning and Jacqueline M. Browning, *Public Finance and the Price System* (New York: Macmillan, 1983), p. 175.

57. Ibid.

58. Ibid. While the quality of hospital care has increased in many ways, it is important to note that this improvement has come about partly because of the increase in third-party payments. Because net out-of-pocket costs are so low, doctors and patients are more apt to choose "Cadillac-quality" health care.

530

59. John C. Goodman, "N.H.S.: An Ill for All Cures," *Policy Review* (Fall 1980): 117.

60. Richard Zeckhauser and Christopher Zook, "Failure to Control Health Costs: Departures from First Principles," in *National Health Insurance Proposals*, Legislative Analysis no. 19 (Washington: American Enterprise Institute, 1974), p. 87, as cited in Browning and Browning, p. 178.

Chapter 12. Poverty, Politics, and Jurisprudence

1. For an extensive discussion of the theory and practice behind civil legal services for the poor, see Marshall Breger, "Legal Aid for the Poor: A Conceptual Analysis," *North Carolina Law Review* 60 (1982): 282–363.

2. *Report to the President of the Legal Services Corporation: Review of Legal Services Corporation's Activities Concerning Program Evaluation and Expansion* (Washington: General Accounting Office, 1980), p. 12.

3. Senate Committee on Labor and Human Resources, *Oversight of the Legal Services Corporation, 1983 Hearings before the Committee on Labor and Human Resources*, 98th Cong., 1st sess., 1983, p. 506.

4. Senate Committee on Labor and Human Resources, *Legal Services Corporation Act Amendments of 1983, Hearings before the Committee on Labor and Human Resources*, 98th Cong., 1st sess., 1983, p. 3.

5. *Oversight of the Legal Services Corporation*, p. 140.

6. "City Asked to Pay Bill for Man's Sex Change," *Washington Post*, January 15, 1981, p. B3.

7. "Two Complaints," *New Republic*, February 3, 1979, p. 5.

8. See Reginald Stewart, "Court to Decide if Black English Is a Learning Barrier," *New York Times*, June 12, 1979, p. A12.

9. Stewart Taylor, "Indians on the Lawpath," *New Republic*, April 30, 1977, pp. 16–21.

10. Shirley Scheibla, "Bar Sinister: The Legal Services Corporation Stretches Its Mandate," *Barron's*, January 24, 1977, pp. 5, 12.

11. *Clearinghouse Review*, March 1980, p. 878.

12. The discussion of *Simer* v. *Olivarez* is based on Heather Stuart Richardson, "A Sweetheart of a Lawsuit?" *Wall Street Journal*, August 20, 1980, p. 18.

13. Ibid.

14. "Memorandum Opinion," *Elsie Simer, et al.* v. *Graceila Olivarez, et al.*, Northern District of Illinois, Eastern Division, Civil Action no. 79 C 3960, October 29, 1980.

15. Richardson.

16. Ibid.

17. Heather Stuart Richardson, "How to Beat Congress by Losing a Lawsuit," *Washington Post*, August 31, 1980, pp. D1, D2. Reprinted from the *Wall Street Journal*, August 20, 1980.

18. H. Peter Metzger and Richard A. Westfall, *Government Activists: How They Rip Off the Poor* (Denver: Public Service Company of Colorado, 1981), p. 15. Fortunately for the taxpayer, the judge in the *Simer* case saw through the ploy being used by CSA and LSC and refused to accept the settlement arranged out of court. The funds were returned to the Treasury.

19. Breger, p. 302.

20. Rael Isaac and Erich Isaac, *The Coercive Utopians: Social Deception by America's Power Players* (Chicago: Regnery Gateway, 1983), p. 238. Even the *New York Times* has described legal aid attorneys as "liberal" and "activist." See Stuart Taylor, "Conservatives Press Fight to Curb Legal Aid," *New York Times*, July 31, 1983, p. E5.

21. *Oversight of the Legal Services Corporation*, pp. 87–88.

22. Ibid., p. 90.

23. Ibid., p. 93.

24. Ibid., p. 109.

25. Ibid., p. 112.

26. Ibid., p. 115.

27. Ibid., p. 118.

28. Ibid., p. 120.

29. Ibid., p. 101.

30. Ibid., p. 102.

31. Ibid., p. 103.

32. Ibid., p. 100.

33. Ibid., pp. 105–6.

34. House Committee on Appropriations, *Departments of State, Justice, and Commerce, the Judiciary, and Related Agencies Appropriations for 1980, Hearings before a Subcommittee on the Departments of State, Justice, and Commerce, the Judiciary, and Related Agencies (Part 6)*, 96th Cong., 1st sess., 1979, pp. 477–78.

35. Mary Thornton, "Former Employees of Legal Services Faulted," *Washington Post*, September 21, 1983, p. A6. For further information on LSC involvement in Proposition 9, see Tom Diaz, "Probe Sought of Legal Services Campaign Activity in California," *Washington Times*, October 21, 1983, p. 5A; idem, "Jarvis Plans to Sue California Legal Services," *Washington Times*, December 20, 1983, p. 3A; and "Illegal Services," *Wall Street Journal*, September 29, 1983, p. 30.

36. Alan Houseman, LSC memorandum, December 9, 1980, reprinted in *Oversight of the Legal Services Corporation*, p. 50. For further details on the LSC Survival Campaign, see Tom Diaz, "Video Reveals Legal Services Corp. Drew 'Survival Plans,' " *Washington Times*, August 29, 1983, p. 5A; George Lardner, "Legal Services Agency Lobbied Hard to Save It," *Washington Post*, July 13, 1983, p. A17; "Survivalists at Legal Services," *Washington Times*, July 21, 1983, p. 11A; Tom Diaz, "Misuse of Legal Aid Fund Revealed," *Washington Times*, July 12, 1983, pp. 1A, 12A.

37. Alan Houseman, LSC memorandum, December 1, 1980, reprinted in *Oversight of the Legal Services Corporation*, p. 39.

38. Alan Houseman, LSC memorandum, December 29, 1980, reprinted in *Oversight of the Legal Services Corporation*, p. 67.

39. Ibid., p. 73.

40. Coalition for Legal Services, letter, February 20, 1981, reprinted in *Oversight of the Legal Services Corporation*, p. 84.

41. Ibid., p. 551. Also, see Tom Diaz, "Legal Aid Unit Said Barring U.S. from Monitoring Grant," *Washington Times*, April 12, 1984, p. 5A. NLADA officials refused to permit Reagan appointees to audit the association's

expenditures, claiming that the LSC has "no right" to information from its grantees.

42. Houseman, December 29, 1980, reprinted in *Oversight of the Legal Services Corporation*, p. 75.

43. Joseph Lipofsky of Legal Services of Eastern Missouri to Rhonda Roberson of Legal Services Corporation, letter, April 29, 1981, reprinted in *Oversight of the Legal Services Corporation*, p. 121. Also see "Legal Services Corporation: Limits Sought on Lobbying Funds," *Washington Post*, July 16, 1983, p. A4.

44. *Oversight of the Legal Services Corporation*, p. 123.

45. Ibid.

46. Ibid.

47. LSC payment approval form, account no. 14-1160-000004, July 17, 1981, reprinted in *Oversight of the Legal Services Corporation*, p. 633.

48. Coalition for Sensible and Humane Solutions, "Community Based Training Agenda, July 2, 1981, St. Louis, Missouri," reprinted in *Oversight of the Legal Services Corporation*, p. 631.

49. Joseph Lipofsky to Lilian Johnson, attachment to letter, July 8, 1981, reprinted in *Oversight of the Legal Services Corporation*, p. 630.

50. For information on activities in Arizona, Colorado, New Mexico, and Texas, see *Statement of Franklin A. Curtis, Associate Director of the Human Services Division, before the Senate Committee on Labor and Human Resources, April 11, 1984*, General Accounting Office, mimeo.

51. Alan Houseman, LSC memorandum, December 8, 1980, reprinted in *Oversight of the Legal Services Corporation*, pp. 46–47.

52. Hulett H. Askew, LSC memorandum, December 4, 1980, reprinted in *Oversight of the Legal Services Corporation*, pp. 60–61.

53. Acting Comptroller General Milton J. Socolar to Rep. F. James Sensenbrenner, Jr., letter (B-202116), May 1, 1981, reprinted in *Oversight of the Legal Services Corporation*, pp. 24–25.

54. *Oversight of the Legal Services Corporation*, pp. 25–26.

55. Ibid., p. 27.

56. Ibid.

57. Ibid., p. 28.

58. *Review of Legal Service Corporation's Activities Concerning Program Evaluation and Expansion* (Washington: General Accounting Office, 1980), p. 17.

59. Socolar to Sensenbrenner, p. 33.

60. Breger, pp. 308–10.

61. Ibid., pp. 304–7.

62. Dan J. Bradley to Milton J. Socolar, letter, May 11, 1981, reprinted in *Oversight of the Legal Services Corporation*, pp. 18, 21.

63. Friends of Advocacy, Inc., to the executive committee of the board of directors of Connecticut Legal Services, memorandum, in files of Senate Commitee on Labor and Human Resources.

64. Calvin C. McCants, Jr., *A Proposal for a Management Training Curriculum and Manual* (Washington: Institute for Non-Profit Management Training, 1981), p. 1, reprinted in *Oversight of the Legal Services Corporation*, p. 385.

65. Ibid., pp. 390–91.

66. Gregg Krech, *Alternatives to Retrenchment* (Washington: Legal Services Corporation, 1982), p. 2.

67. These are described in *Oversight of the Legal Services Corporation*, pp. 400–410.

68. Krech, pp. 4, 23.

69. Paul Newman, *LSC Program Report for South Central Connecticut Legal Services Corporation, October 13, 1982* (Washington, Legal Services Corporation 1982), p. 8.

70. *Oversight of the Legal Services Corporation*, p. 413.

71. Ibid., p. 436. Texas Rural Legal Aid aggressively pursued its advocacy projects. The organization placed the following classified advertisement in the Austin *American-Statesman* on November 5, 1980:

WANTED: PROJECT coordinator for Legislative Advocacy Project for farm workers, job includes proposal writing, reports, staff supervision; coordination with advocacy groups. Must have experience with governmental agencies and knowledge of problems of farm workers; bilingual preferred. Salary $18,000–$28,000; commensurate with experience and skills. Submit resume to Texas Rural Legal Aid.

72. Ibid., p. 301.

73. Ibid., p. 401.

74. Iris Rothman, ed., *The Law and Direct Citizen Action* (Washington: Legal Services Corporation, 1981), p. i. Also see Tom Diaz, "Legal Services Manuals Press Political Advocacy," *Washington Times*, July 26, 1983, p. 3A.

75. Rothman, p. 1.

76. Ibid.

77. Ibid., p. 2.

78. Ibid., pp. 2–3.

79. Ibid., p. 3.

80. Ibid., p. 4.

81. Ibid., p. 11.

82. Ibid., p. 95.

83. Emma Jones, *Communication Skills, Community Advocacy and Leadership/Community Development, Vol. I, Trainer Guide* (Washington: Legal Services Corporation, 1981), p. 73.

84. Ibid., p. 87.

85. *Oversight of the Legal Services Corporation*, pp. 582–619 passim; *Legal Services Corporation Act Amendments of 1983*, pp. 282–542 passim.

86. See William Rusher, "A Legal Fiefdom Fighting the Law," *Washington Times*, August 31, 1983, p. 2C; Tom Diaz, "Funds Held Misused for Lobbying," *Washington Times*, July 15, 1983, p. 3A; idem, "Conservatives Press Fight on Legal Services Abuses," *Washington Times*, July 14, 1983, p. 3A; and idem, "Official Denies Legal Aid Fund Used for 'Survival,'" *Washington Times*, July 13, 1983, pp. 1A, 12A.

87. *Oversight of the Legal Services Corporation*, p. 169.

88. *Legal Services Corporation Act Amendments of 1983*, pp. 392–97.

89. Ibid., pp. 256–58.

90. Jack Anderson, "Legal Services Mismanagement Is Uncovered," *Washington Post*, April 11, 1984, p. F16.

91. William Kucewicz, "A Little Larceny in Legal Services?" *Wall Street

Journal, August 19, 1983, p. 18; also see Tom Diaz, "Shredding of Files in LSC Probe Disclosed," *Washington Times*, September 23, 1983, p. 2A.

92. For example, the *Washington Post* published a number of articles on the board members' travel and consulting fees: "Legal Services Appointees Get Fat Fees," December 15, 1982, pp. A1, A11; "Legal Services Head's Contract Is Sweet," December 16, 1982, pp. A1, A8; "Sabotaging Legal Services," December 16, 1982, p. A22; "Reagan Outlines Inquiry on Legal Services," December 17, 1982, p. A2; "Recovery of Legal Fees Paid Legal Officials Demanded," December 18, 1982, pp. A1, A5; "Legal Disservice," December 19, 1982, p. C6; "Hill Group Asks GAO Inquiry Into Legal Services Board Fees," December 21, 1982, p. A3; "Legal Board Members Avoid Joining 'Em by Representing 'Em," December 21, 1982, p. A2; "Reagan Aide Meese Defends Members of Legal Services Panel on Fee Charge," December 24, 1982, p. A2; "July Memo Warned Legal Services Officials on Fees," December 31, 1982, p. A5; and "The Dubious Deals of Reagan's Crowd," January 2, 1983, p. A1.

93. Comptroller general to Rep. Robert Kastenmeier, letter (B-210338), August 31, 1982, p. 1. In light of the flood of articles published by the *Washington Post* on the payment "scandal," it is interesting to note that it took eight days for the newspaper to report on the GAO investigative report: Howard Kurtz, "No Violations Found in Legal Services Fees," *Washington Post*, September 8, 1983, p. A6; also see Tom Diaz, "LSC to Stop Funds for Clients Council," *Washington Times*, January 4, 1984, p. 4A.

94. See Tom Diaz, "Press Held 'Used' in Legal Services Ploy," *Washington Times*, August 4, 1983, p. 2A; and idem, "Story Behind the Story on 'Smokescreen' Attack in Legal Service Hassle," *Washington Times*, September 12, 1983, p. 4A.

95. Tom Diaz, "Legal Services Flap Produces Charges of Death Threats," *Washington Times*, July 20, 1983, p. 2A.

96. Pete Early, "Legal Aid Board Votes to Request Budget Increase," *Washington Post*, January 7, 1984, p. A5.

97. Ibid.

98. Sen. Orrin Hatch, "Opening Statement," in *Legal Services Corporation Act Amendments of 1983*, p. 1.

99. Michael S. Serrill, "An Organization at War with Itself," *Time*, October 3, 1983, p. 83.

100. "Gifts Support Bar's Social Budget," *Washington Post*, November 16, 1981, Washington Business section, p. 15; also see "A.B.A. Grants Rejected," *New York Times*, September 27, 1982, p. A12.

101. "Whom Can You Trust?" *Wall Street Journal*, January 29, 1985, p. 32.

102. Ibid.

Chapter 13. Tax-Funded Unionism

1. See C. J. Parsley, "Labor Unions and Wages: A Survey," *Journal of Economic Literature* 18 (March 1980): 1–31.

2. James T. Bennett and Thomas J. DiLorenzo, "Unions, Politics, and Protectionism, *Journal of Labor Research* 5 (Summer 1984): 287–307.

3. See, for example, Dan C. Heldman and Deborah L. Knight, *Unions*

and Lobbying: The Representation Function (Washington: Foundation for the Advancement of the Public Trust, 1980); Dan C. Heldman, *American Labor Unions: Political Values and Financial Structure* (Washington: Council on American Affairs, 1977); and J. David Greenstone, *Labor in American Politics* (New York: Alfred Knopf, 1969). This list is by no means exhaustive. For an account of union political activity at the local level of government, see Randolph H. Boehm and Dan C. Heldman, *Public Employees, Unions, and the Erosion of Civic Trust* (Frederick, Md.: University Publications of America, 1982).

4. Oscar W. Cooley, *Paying Men Not to Work* (Caldwell, Idaho: Caxton Printers, 1964), p. 98.

5. Ibid., p. 99.

6. James Bovard, "Busy Doing Nothing: The Story of Government Job Creation," *Policy Review* 24 (Spring 1983): 88.

7. All professional economists recognize the disemployment effects of the minimum wage. Virtually no other economic phenomenon has been so carefully documented and widely accepted. For a summary of this literature, see Dan C. Heldman, James T. Bennett, and Manuel H. Johnson, *Deregulating Labor Relations* (Dallas: Fisher Institute, 1981), pp. 86–98.

8. John M. Berry and Art Pine, "19 Years of Job Programs—Question Still is 'What Works,' " *Washington Post,* April 24, 1979, p. E1.

9. John M. Berry and Art Pine, "Jobs Goals Consensus Seen," *Washington Post,* April 26, 1979, p. D2.

10. Many of these reports are referenced in Bovard.

11. Ibid., pp. 91–92.

12. Helen Dewar, "Labor Dept. Overhauling Jobs Program," *Washington Post,* February 2, 1979, p. A4.

13. "Unmasking CETA," *Wall Street Journal,* May 24, 1978, p. 22.

14. James J. Kilpatrick, "The CETA Boondoggle Should Be Stopped," *Washington Star,* August 8, 1978, p. A9.

15. Edward M. Gramlich, "The Effect of Federal Grants on State and Local Expenditures: A Review of the Econometric Literature," in *Proceedings of the Sixty-second Conference on Taxation* (Cambridge, Mass.: National Tax Association, 1969), p. 11.

16. Ronald Ehrenberg, "The Demand for State and Local Government Employees," *American Economic Review* 63 (June 1973): 366–79.

17. George E. Johnson and James D. Tomola, *An Impact Evaluation of the Public Employment Program,* Technical Analysis Paper no. 17 (Washington: Department of Labor, Office of the Assistant Secretary for Policy Evaluation and Research, Office of Evaluation, April 1974), pp. 8ff; Orley Ashenfelter and Ronald Ehrenberg, "The Demand for Labor in the Public Sector," in *Labor in the Public and Non-Profit Sectors,* ed. Daniel S. Hamermesh (Princeton: Princeton University Press, 1976).

18. Much of the material on the Human Resources Development Institute was provided by the Center on National Labor Policy of Springfield, Va., which obtained it through the legal process of discovery. We gratefully acknowledge the assistance of Steve Antosh and Michael Arif at the center.

19. "Arnold Appointed as HRDI's New Director," *HRDI Manpower Advisory,* April 1979, pp. 1ff.

20. *Human Resources Development Institute: Manpower Arm of the AFL-CIO* (Washington: Human Resources Development Institute, n.d.).

21. *Report of the Executive Council of the AFL-CIO Fifteenth Convention* (Washington: AFL-CIO, 1983), p. 65.

22. *Proceedings of the Thirteenth Constitutional Convention of the AFL-CIO* (Washington: AFL-CIO, 1979), p. 57.

23. *Proceedings and Executive Council Reports of the AFL-CIO* (Washington: AFL-CIO, 1981), p. 67.

24. *CETA and Organized Labor* (Washington: Human Resources Development Institute, n.d.), p. 6.

25. Ibid., p. 1.

26. *Report of the Executive Council*, p. 64.

27. *Proceedings of the Thirteenth Constitutional Convention*, p. 57.

28. *Proceedings and Executive Council Reports*, p. 66.

29. *Report of the Executive Council*, p. 63.

30. Ibid., p. 64.

31. *Human Resources Development Institute: Job Development, Job Placement, Job Training and Upgrading* (Washington: Human Resources Development Institute, n.d.), p. 4.

32. *Opening Doors for the Disabled . . . to Good Union Jobs* (Washington: Human Resources Development Institute, n.d.), front cover.

33. Ibid., p. 3.

34. Ibid.

35. *A Proposal to Provide the Severely Disabled with On-The-Job-Training* (Washington: Human Resources Development Institute, 1979), p. 7.

36. Ibid., p. 4.

37. Coordinator of Handicapped Programs, Vince Moretti, HRDI memorandum no. 162, August 21, 1978.

38. Vince Moretti, HRDI memorandum no. 630, June 30, 1980.

39. *HRDI Helping Youth* (Washington: Human Resources Development Institute, n.d.), p. 2.

40. Ben Stahl, HRDI memorandum on "Norfolk Youth Program," April 15, 1980.

41. "New HRDI Program Will Test Youth Services," *HRDI Manpower Advisory*, May 1979, p. 1.

42. Ibid., p. 3.

43. *Murphy* v. *Human Resources Development Institute, et al.*, June 13, 1984, p. 6.

44. *Human Resources Development Institute: Job Development, Job Placement, Job Training and Upgrading*, p. 4.

45. Ibid.; also see *HRDI Helping Performing Artists* (Washington: Human Resources Development Institute, n.d.).

46. Rachel Cowan, "A Labor of Love," *Village Voice*, October 15, 1979, p. 1.

47. Ibid.

48. Georgeen Comerford, *1199: A Family Portrait—Photographs of Hospital Workers* (New York: District 1199 Cultural Center, n.d.).

49. Ibid., p. ii.

50. Susan Reverby, *One Strong Voice . . . Or an Out of Tune Chorus?* (New York: District 1199 Cultural Project, n.d.).

51. Ibid., pp. 22–23.

52. Ibid., pp. 23.

53. William Cahn, *Lawrence 1912: The Bread and Roses Strike* (New York: Pilgrim Press, 1980), p. iv.

54. Ibid., pp. 14–17 passim.

55. *The Working American* (Washington: Smithsonian Institution, 1979), p. vii.

56. *Bread and Roses: A Special Report* (New York: District 1199 Cultural Center, n.d.), p. 10.

57. Ibid., p. 7.

58. *Bread and Roses: Books, Posters and Records* (New York: District 1199 Cultural Center, n.d.), front cover.

59. Discussion guide and fact sheet for *Rise Gonna Rise: Portraits of Southern Textile Workers* (New York: District 1199 Bread and Roses Project, n.d.), mimeo., p. 1.

60. Ibid., p. 3.

61. See Morgan O. Reynolds, "Union Violence: A Review Article," *Journal of Labor Research* 5 (Summer 1984): 240; also see Armand J. Thieblot, Jr., and Thomas R. Haggard, *Union Violence: The Record and the Response by Courts, Legislatures, and the NLRB* (Philadelphia: Industrial Research Unit, Wharton School, University of Pennsylvania, 1983).

62. *Bread and Roses: A Special Report*, pp. 29, 31.

63. *Our Own Show: Organizing Cultural Programs for Working People* (New York: District 1199 Bread and Roses Project, n.d.), p. 2.

64. Ibid., p. 1.

65. Ibid., p. 20.

66. Ibid., p. 23.

67. Ibid., p. 20.

68. For a more detailed discussion of ACORN and its activities and personnel, see chapter 8.

69. William T. Poole, "The New Left in Government, Part 2: The VISTA Program as 'Institution Building,' " Heritage Foundation Institution Analysis no. 17 (Washington, 1982), pp. 3–5.

70. See Ralph Kinney Bennett, "CETA: $11-Billion Boondoggle," *Reader's Digest*, August 1978, pp. 72–76.

71. Armand J. Thieblot, Jr., and Ronald M. Cowin, *Welfare and Strikes: The Use of Public Funds to Support Strikes* (Philadelphia: Wharton School, University of Pennsylvania, 1972), p. 263.

72. Ibid., p. 216.

Chapter 14. Funding the Right

1. There is no universally accepted definition of "right-wing" groups. For the purposes here, we focus on groups discussed in two books purporting to describe conservative organizations and their agendas: Richard A. Viguerie, *The New Right: We're Ready to Lead* (Falls Church, Va.: Viguerie Company, 1980) and Alan Crawford, *Thunder on the Right: The "New Right" and the Politics of Resentment* (New York: Pantheon Books, 1980). An excel-

lent summary of the conservative agenda is given in Stuart M. Butler, Michael Sanera, and W. Bruce Weinrod, eds., *Mandate for Leadership II: Continuing the Conservative Revolution* (Washington: Heritage Foundation, 1984).

2. Connie Paige, *The Right to Lifers: Who They Are, How They Operate, and Where They Get Their Money* (New York: Summit Books, 1983). The descriptions of some of the personalities involved in the right-to-life movement are frequently unflattering. For example, Howard Phillips of the Conservative Caucus is described as "a great hulk of a man, . . . [who] always looks as if he could use a trip to the cleaners. With his rumpled clothes and his oily hair hanging limp on his forehead, he seems to have no time for appearances" (p. 141).

3. Ibid., pp. 249–50.

4. Ibid., pp. 251–62.

5. Ibid., p. 138.

6. Mary Thornton, "Conservatives Get Grants: Legal Services' Award of $1 Million Questioned," *Washington Post*, October 29, 1984, p. A3.

7. Ibid.

8. Ibid.

9. Ibid.

10. *Legal Services Corporation Grants to Establish National Support Centers*, HRD 85-54 (Washington, General Accounting Office, March 29, 1985).

11. Thornton, p. A3. Frank himself is not opposed to tax-funded politics as a matter of principle. With an approval rating of 100 percent from the liberal Americans for Democratic Action, he is merely opposed to the funding of the right. He is a strong supporter of funding the left through the Legal Services Corporation.

12. Jack Anderson, "USIA Counters Propaganda with More of It," *Washington Post*, February 28, 1983, p. C11.

13. Christopher Hitchens, "Do We Really Need to Sell Democracy?" *Washington Post*, February 27, 1983, p. B3.

14. Ibid.

15. Jack Anderson, "USIA Teaching Foreign Powers to Sway Media," *Washington Post*, February 23, 1983, p. C13.

16. Howard Kurtz and Pete Early, "Hollywood-Style Diplomacy: Wick Adds Flair to U.S. Story," *Washington Post*, July 13, 1983, p. A1.

17. Kathy Sawyer, "Abortion Foes Urged to Seek Vista Funding," *Washington Post*, January 24, 1985, p. A4. Also see George Archibald, "VISTA Defends Grant Used to Halt Abortions," *Washington Times*, January 24, 1985, p. 4A.

18. "How Budget Cuts Hurt Nonprofit Groups," *Washington Post*, August 18, 1983, p. A27.

19. "Commerce Funds Technology Study," American Enterprise Institute Memorandum no. 40 (Washington, Fall 1983), p. 6.

20. "Grant to Health Policy Center to Study Incentives-Based Reforms," American Enterprise Institute Memorandum no. 40 (Washington: Fall 1983), p. 7.

21. "NEH Grant Supports Study of Constitution," American Enterprise Institute Memorandum no. 40 (Washington, Fall 1983), p. 8.

22. " 'Fraternity of Founders' Share Ideas at Conference on Constitutions," *American Enterprise Institute Memorandum* no. 40 (Washington, Fall 1983), p. 3.

23. This discussion is based on Martin Wooster, "Defunding the Left, But Then What?" *Wall Street Journal*, November 30, 1984, p. 30. A detailed treatment may be found in House Committee on Education and Labor, Subcommittee on Human Resources, *Oversight Hearing on the Office of Juvenile Justice and Delinquency Prevention*, 98th Cong., 2d sess., 1984.

24. Wooster.

25. John S. Friedman and Eric Nadler, "The Culture Wars: Hard Right Rudder at the N.E.H.," *Nation*, April 14, 1984, front cover.

26. Ibid. and p. 448.

27. Peter W. Kaplan, "U.S. Aids Study of Vietnam Film," *New York Times*, June 14, 1984, p. C22.

28. "Grant Information—Awards as of 08/84," (Washington: National Endowment for the Humanities, n.d.).

29. Friedman and Nadler, p. 450. The distinction between Public Research, Syndicated and the Claremont Institute is questionable—they share the same address.

30. Ibid.

31. Ibid., p. 451.

32. Ibid.

33. Ibid.

34. Milton Friedman, *Capitalism and Freedom* (Chicago: University of Chicago Press, 1962), p. 18.

35. Florence Graves, "The High and the Mighty," *Common Cause*, August 1981, pp. 16–17.

36. Ibid., p. 17.

37. Florence Graves, "Lookin' Good," *Common Cause*, March/April 1984, pp. 12–21.

38. Graves, "The High and the Mighty," p. 17.

39. National Alliance of Business Annual Report, 1983 (Washington, 1983), p. 6.

40. Ibid.

41. Ibid., p. 41.

42. Ibid., pp. 29–31.

43. Joel M. Woldman, "Project Democracy and the National Endowment for Democracy: Issue Brief Number IB83107," (Washington: Library of Congress, Congressional Research Service, Foreign Affairs and National Defense Division, 1983), p. 2.

44. House Committee on Appropriations, Subcommittee on the Departments of Commerce, Justice, and State, the Judiciary, and Related Agencies, *Hearings on Departments of Commerce, Justice, and State, the Judiciary, and Related Agencies Appropriations for 1985, Part 5*, 98th Cong., 2d sess., 1984, p. 12.

45. *Events Leading to the Establishment of The National Endowment for Democracy* (Washington: General Accounting Office, 1984), p. 1.

46. For a discussion of these foundations *(stiftungen)*, see Alan J. Watson,

The Political Foundation in West Germany (London: Anglo-German Foundation for the Study of Industrial Democracy, 1976).

47. *Events Leading to the Establishment*, p. 6.

48. Ibid., p. 7.

49. Ibid., p. 8.

50. Ibid., p. 10.

51. Ibid., p. 12.

52. Ibid., p. 13.

53. Ibid., p. 14.

54. *Congressional Record-House*, May 31, 1984, p. H5017.

55. Ibid., p. H5019.

56. *Hearings on Departments of Commerce, Justice, and State, the Judiciary, and Related Agencies*, p. 496.

57. "Prepared Statement of Hon. Michael A. Samuels," ibid., p. 269–70.

58. "Prepared Statement of Lane Kirkland, President, AFL-CIO," in ibid., p. 263. Kirkland claims a commitment to democracy abroad, which is quite odd since it is rarely practiced in American labor unions. As the *New York Times* observed, "Only a handful of some 130 major American labor unions . . . elect major officers by rank and file vote. . . . The lack of . . . elections in most American unions has some people concerned." See William Serrin, "Democracy by Unions: Few Let Members Elect Top Officers," *New York Times*, November 15, 1982, p. A17.

59. Jack Anderson, "GAO Doubtful on Endowment for Democracy," *Washington Post*, July 9, 1984, p. C14.

60. *Congressional Record-House*, May 31, 1984, p. H5025.

61. Ibid., p. H5019.

62. Ibid., p. H5022.

63. Ibid., p. H5019.

64. Ibid., p. H5020.

65. Ibid., p. H5024.

66. Ibid., p. H5025.

67. *Events Leading to the Establishment*, p. 18.

68. Ibid., p. 30.

69. Ibid.

70. Norman D. Atkins, "Endowment for Democracy Fights to Live," *Washington Post*, June 28, 1984, p. A13.

71. Ibid.

72. *Events Leading to the Establishment*, p. 28.

73. Atkins.

74. *Events Leading to the Establishment*, p. 27.

75. Woldman, p. 11.

76. See Michael Kinsley, "Conservatives Meet to Dine on Red Herrings," *Wall Street Journal*, May 9, 1985, p. 29; and David Aikman, "Conservative Conclaves," *Time*, May 13, 1985, p. 27.

Chapter 15. Ideas Have Consequences

1. Milton Friedman, *Capitalism and Freedom* (Chicago: University of Chicago Press, 1962), p. 16.

2. Richard M. Weaver, *Ideas Have Consequences* (Chicago: University of Chicago Press, 1948).

3. Friedman, p. 18.

4. See Joseph R. Wright, Jr., *Testimony before the House Committee on Government Operations*, March 1, 1983, p. 2.

5. Ibid.

6. Section 7 of Public Law 95-435, the Bretton Woods Agreements Act approved on October 10, 1978, states, "Beginning with fiscal year 1981, the total budget outlays of the Federal Government shall not exceed its receipts." Public Law 96-5, approved in 1979, also mandates a balanced budget. See James T. Bennett and Thomas J. DiLorenzo, *Underground Government: The Off-Budget Public Sector* (Washington: Cato Institute, 1983), especially p. 176.

7. In effect, members of Congress do not believe that what is good for the goose is also good for the gander. See James T. Bennett and Manuel H. Johnson, *The Political Economy of Federal Government Growth: 1959–1978* (College Station, Tex.: Center for Education and Research in Free Enterprise, Texas A&M University, 1981), p. 140. The laws passed by Congress might be considerably different if members of Congress were also subject to them.

8. Marshall Breger, "Partisan Subsidies: Democracy Undone," *Washington Times*, December 6, 1983, p. 2C.

9. Bureau of the Census, *Statistical Abstract of the U.S.* (Washington: Government Printing Office, 1984), p. 268.

10. "Only Business PACs a Concern," *Wall Street Journal*, November 15, 1983, p. 34.

11. Terry L. Anderson and Peter J. Hill, *The Birth of a Transfer Society* (Stanford: Hoover Institution Press, 1980).

12. Murray L. Weidenbaum, *The Future of Business Regulation* (New York: Amacom Books, 1979).

13. Ibid., pp. 22–23.

14. See Dan C. Heldman, James T. Bennett, and Manuel H. Johnson, *Deregulating Labor Relations* (Dallas: Fisher Institute, 1981), pp. 13–39.

15. For a discussion of the "political economy of deregulation," see James T. Bennett and Thomas J. DiLorenzo, *Labor Unions and the State* (Dallas: Fisher Institute, forthcoming), especially chap. 2.

16. We conjecture that few who advertise themselves as "environmentalists" have ever worked in the nation's coal mines. To regard coal as a safe alternative to nuclear power is to ignore the accident and death rates for workers in the coal industry relative to those in the nuclear power industry. Moreover, whether coal can reasonably be regarded as "clean" and nonpolluting in comparison with nuclear power is highly debatable.

17. Peter Woll, *American Bureaucracy* (New York: W. W. Norton & Co., 1977), p. 194.

18. Tom Palmer, "Uncle Sam's Ever-Expanding P.R. Machine," *Wall Street Journal*, January 10, 1985, p. 26.

19. Thomas B. Edsall, "Unspent Funds for Campaign Lift Eyebrows: Defeated Lawmaker Can Pocket $270,000," *Washington Post*, December 19, 1984, p. A3.

20. Ibid.

21. Ibid.

22. Bill Hogan, Diane Kiesel, and Alan Green, "The Senate's Secret Slush Funds," *New Republic*, June 20, 1983, pp. 13–20 passim.

23. Ibid., p. 13.

24. Gordon Tullock, *Welfare for the Well-To-Do* (Dallas: Fisher Institute, 1983), p. 71.

25. Recall from chapter 14, in the discussion of the National Endowment for Democracy, that West German taxpayers were supporting private, nonprofit foundations established by the country's major political parties.

26. James Pawsey, *The Tringo Phenomenon* (London: Adam Smith Institute, 1983), pp. 15–46.

27. Ibid., pp. 9–10.

28. 48 *Federal Register* 3348 (January 24, 1983).

29. Marshall J. Breger, "Halting Taxpayer Subsidy of Partisan Advocacy," Heritage Foundation Lectures no. 26 (Washington, 1983), p. 3.

30. 48 *Federal Register* 18260 (April 27, 1984).

31. Bill Kling, "Fight Grows on Curbs in Politicking Funds," *Washington Times*, March 15, 1983, p. 1A.

32. 48 *Federal Register* 50860 (November 3, 1983).

33. 48 *Federal Register* 18261 (April 27, 1984).

34. Breger, p. 4.

35. Friedman, pp. 190–95.

36. Ibid., p. 192.

Index

Aaron, Henry, 174, 184
ABA. *See* American Bar Association
Accuracy in Media, 367
Acid rain, 163
ACORN. *See* Association of
Community Organizations for Reform
Now
ACORN USA, 209
ACTION
  antipoverty industry, funding for,
    428–29, 431–33
  CED, funding for, 407, 408
  environmental movement, funding
    for, 419, 423
  PIRGs, funding for, 83, 412
  senior citizen lobby, funding for, 459
  unions, funding for, 355–56, 485, 494
Activist training centers, 16–25, 72–75,
  403
ACTWU. *See* Amalgamated Clothing
  and Textile Workers Union
Adelman, Carol, 101
Administration on Aging, 278, 455–56,
  457, 459
Advertising, regulation of, 108
Advocacy group network
  activist training centers, 16–25, 72–
    75, 403
  functioning of, 32–34
  grass-roots organizations, 25–30
  national coalitions, 28–30
  planners' network, 14
  political agenda, 9–10
  think tanks, 10–16
  unions and, 30–32
Aellife, Derick B., 100
Aetna Life and Casualty, 22
Affirmative action, 249–50, 252–56
AFL-CIO, 14, 26, 30, 39, 113, 256, 277,
  281, 372
  federal funding for, 355, 376, 377,
    380, 381, 417, 484–86
  HRDI, relation to, 343, 344–45, 346
AFL-CIO News, 126, 350
AFSCME. *See* American Federation of

State, County and Municipal
Employees
Agency for International Development
  (AID), 102, 145, 365, 372–73, 425, 447
Agriculture, U.S. Department of
  (USDA), 93, 145, 392
  antipoverty industry, funding for,
    430
  food assistance programs, 176, 187,
    189, 192, 193, 195–96, 199
  unions, funding for, 494
AID. *See* Agency for International
  Development
Aid to Families with Dependent
  Children, 174, 177
Alderson, George, 149
Ali, Tariq, 15
Alinsky, Saul, 17, 26
Alperovitz, Gar, 10, 14, 93
Alternative Business School, 89
Amalgamated Clothing and Textile
  Workers Union (ACTWU), 24, 25, 29,
  351–52, 353–54, 416, 417, 483
American Bar Association (ABA), 332–
  33, 478–83
American Cancer Society, 170
American Civil Liberties Union, 272
American Council on Nuclear Energy,
  132
American Enterprise Institute for Public
  Policy Research (AEI), 364–65
American Federation of Government
  Employees (AFGE), 28, 32, 405, 417,
  484
American Federation of State, County
  and Municipal Employees (AFSCME),
  14, 18, 24, 25, 28, 29, 39, 404, 405, 416,
  417, 487
American Federation of Teachers
  (AFT), 18, 404, 487
American Petroleum Institute, 23
American Political Foundation (APF),
  373, 374–75
Americans for Democratic Action, 78,
  98, 106, 107, 414, 415

545

Carolina Action, 17
Carolina Brown Lung Association, 21, 404
Carson, Rachel, 139
Cartels, 43–44
Carter, Jimmy, 124, 242, 243, 290
Carter administration, 188, 196
CASLP. *See* Conference on Alternative State and Local Policies
Castro, Fidel, 80
CDC. *See* Community development corporations
CED. *See* Campaign for Economic Democracy
CED News, 74
Cellophane industry, 43–44
Center for Community Change, 295, 405
Center for Cuban Studies, 16
Center for Investigative Reporting, 15
Center for New Corporate Priorities, 65, 408
Center for Public Policy, 75
Center for Renewable Resources, 146, 419
Center for Science in the Public Interest, 94, 280, 405
Center for Urban Encounter, 17, 403
Central Intelligence Agency, 145
CETA. *See* Comprehensive Employment and Training Act programs
CFA. *See* Consumer Federation of America
Chamber of Commerce, U.S., 372, 376–77
Champaign-Urbana Tenants Union, 25
Chavez, Cesar, 62, 74, 243
Child Care Food Program, 190
Child labor laws, 97
Children's Defense Fund, 14, 39, 405, 428
China, People's Republic of, 163
Christensen, Erling and Ethel, 227
Cincinnati Gas and Electric, 133
Citizen/Labor Energy Coalition (C/LEC), 17, 28, 36, 37, 100, 111, 135, 148, 155, 280, 282, 286
  board of directors, 113, 416
  congressional support for, 123–24
  federal funding for, 113–14, 407, 417, 419–20
  media, use of, 124, 126–28
  origins of, 29–30, 112

  political agenda, 116–17
  regulation, attitude toward, 112–13, 118–27
  unions, involvement of, 113
Citizens Against Nuclear War, 148
Citizens Against the Rate Increase, 25
Citizen's Energy Act, 116–17
Citizens Party, 141
Civil Aeronautics Board, 57, 390
Civil Rights: Rhetoric or Reality (Sowell), 247
Civil Rights Act of 1964, 247, 248, 253, 254, 274
Civil rights laws, 247–48
Civil rights movement (*see also specific groups*), 273–75
  federal funding for, 249, 250–51, 262–64, 271, 444–54
  political agenda, 249–50, 252–53, 256–58
Civil Works Administration, 339
Clamshell Alliance, 130
Claremont Institute, 362, 367
Clark, Nolan, 125
Claus, George, 155
Clayman, Jacob, 279
C/LEC. *See* Citizen/Labor Energy Coalition
Clergy and Laity Concerned, 98, 404, 405
Client's Council of Legal Services of Southeast Nebraska, 312
Clifton Terrace housing venture, 236–38
Cloward, Richard A., 211
Club of Rome, 142–44, 145
Coal industry, 153, 164–66
Coalition for Consumer Education, 93
Coalition for Legal Services, 315–16, 405
Coalition for Sensible and Humane Solutions (CSHS), 317–18
Coalition on Block Grants and Human Needs, 28
Coalition to Save Legal Services, 28
Coase, Ronald, 56
Coastal Barrier Resources Act, 152
Code of Federal Regulations, 217–18, 219, 228, 231
Codetermination, 51–54
Cohen, David, 225–26
Cohen, Wilbur J., 295
Collins, Mary Jean, 18
Collins, William, 343

Colorado Energy Advocacy Project, 114–16
Comerford, Georgeen, 351
Commerce, U.S. Department of, 116, 262, 339, 361, 364, 434–35, 438–39, 453
Commission on Federal Paperwork, U.S., 57
Committee for Full Employment, 148
Committee on Political Education, 329
Common Cause, 78, 98, 272, 369, 370
Common Cause, 359
Commoner, Barry, 131, 137, 141
Commonwealth Edison, 132
Communitas, 66, 407
Community action groups, 71
Community development corporations (CDC), 216, 219
Community Economics (Oakland), 10
Community Nutrition Institute, 92, 94, 281, 405, 415, 429
Community Organizations Research and Action Project (CORAP), 205–6
Community Services Act of 1964, 216, 240
Community Services Administration (CSA), 196, 198
  anti-energy industry, funding for, 114–15, 116
  antipoverty industry, funding for, 206, 429, 430
  CED, funding for, 407
  environmental movement, funding for, 156, 420, 422, 425
  LSC suit against, 307–9
  senior citizen lobby, funding for, 278, 289, 456, 458
  Special Impact Program, 216
  TELACU, funding for, 217, 223, 228, 229
  unions, funding for, 488, 494–95
Comparable worth, 260–61
Comprehensive Employment and Training Act of 1973 (CETA)
  programs, 66, 177, 231–32, 243, 340, 341, 345, 346, 429–30, 435–37, 439–42
Conference on Alternative State and Local Policies (CASLP), 10, 12–14, 17, 32, 36, 39, 61, 114, 417
Congregate Feeding Program for the Elderly, 190
Congress, 1–2
  campaign financing by, 389
  campaign funds, personal use of, 394–95

C/LEC, support for, 123–24
Legal Services Corporation, relations with, 331–32
tax-funded politics, awareness of, 386–87
Congressional Black Caucus, 249
Congressional Budget Office, 187, 191, 193–95
Congressional Quarterly, 30, 123
Congress Watch, 25, 28, 84, 94, 281, 286, 405
Conn, Jim, 66
Connecticut Legal Services (CLS), 321–22
Conservative groups (*see also* National Endowment for Democracy)
  corporate politics and, 368–71, 383
  federal funding for, 361–68, 381–82
  funding resources, 360–61
Conservatives, definition of, 360
Consolidated Edison, 120
Constitutional Law Center, 361–62
Consumer Action-San Francisco, 106–7, 108, 414, 415
Consumer Federation of America (CFA), 28, 78, 92, 93–94, 96, 97, 280, 286, 405, 414, 415
Consumer Product Safety Commission (CPSC), 57, 86–87
Consumer protection movement (*see also* Public interest movement), 77–78, 92–93
  church support for, 98–103
  consumer education, 94–96
  federal funding for, 89, 93–94, 96, 99–100
  intervenor funding, use of, 103–9
  lobbying by, 96–98
  Nestlé boycott, 100–103
  Reaganomics, criticism of, 94–96
Consumers Power Company of Michigan, 132
Consumers Union of the United States (CU), 92, 94, 106, 280, 414, 415
Cooperatives, 40–41, 51, 91–92
Cooperative Telecommunications Project, 88
Copeland v. *Marshall*, 104
Corbett, Judy, 71
Corporate control, market for, 46–47
Corporate Data Exchange, 14, 36, 42, 43, 98
Corporate democracy act, 117
Corporate Examiner, 36

549

National Alliance of Business (NAB), 370–71
National Anti-Hunger Coalition (NAHC), 28, 199, 405
National Association for the Advancement of Colored People (NAACP), 249, 253, 295, 447
National Association of Attorneys General, 104
National Association of Indian Legal Services, 316
National Association of Manufacturers, 23
National Association of Schools of Public Affairs and Administration, 283
National Association of Social Workers, 29, 405, 495
National Audubon Society, 139, 140, 145, 146, 418–19
National Budget Coalition, 30
National Bureau of Standards, 96
National Center for Appropriate Technology (NCAT), 130, 146, 156–59, 422
National Center for Economic Alternatives, 10, 14
National Center for Health Statistics, 169–70
National Center for Policy Alternatives, 10
National Center for the Medically Handicapped, 362
National Chamber Foundation, 376
National Citizen's Monitoring Project, 173
National Clients Council (NCC), 316, 416
National Coalition Against the Misuse of Pesticides, 148
National Consumer Co-op Bank (NCCB), 41, 87–92, 289
National Consumer Law Center, 14, 105, 106, 414, 415
National Consumers League (NCL), 92–93, 94, 96–97, 106, 295–96, 406, 415
National Council of Black Mayors, 257
National Council of Churches (NCC), 36, 98–103, 116, 296, 406, 417
National Council of La Raza, 296, 406, 417, 433
National Council of Senior Citizens (NCSC), 31, 92, 94, 106, 113, 126, 251, 296, 337, 406, 414
  board of directors, 460

federal funding for, 278–79, 280, 417, 455–57
health care, activities re, 297–98
lobbying activities, 280–86
networking activities, 286
political activities, 279, 285
Progress Report, 277, 280, 281
Social Security, activities re, 294
unions and, 31, 279–80, 286
National Council on Aging, 290, 296, 457–58
National Education Association, 18, 29, 404, 406, 416, 417, 496
National Endowment for Democracy (NED), 359, 371–81, 499–503
National Endowment for the Arts (NEA), 99, 100, 350, 423, 430, 432, 435, 439, 488, 492–93
National Endowment for the Humanities (NEH), 116, 206, 364, 366–68
  ABA, funding for, 478–79
  antipoverty industry, funding for, 431, 433
  civil rights movement, funding for, 271, 446–47, 454
  environmental movement, funding for, 418, 424
  senior citizen lobby, funding for, 458
  unions, funding for, 350, 355, 483, 488–89, 493, 495, 497
National Highway Transportation Safety Administration (NHTSA), 81
National Institute of Education, 263
National Journal, 29
National Lawyers Guild, 309
National Legal Aid and Defenders Association (NLADA), 316
National Let Them Eat Cake Sale, 198–99
National Low-Income Housing Coalition, 28, 289, 406
National Oceanic and Atmospheric Administration, 145
National Organization for Women (NOW), 17–18, 249, 250, 258, 265, 270–71, 272, 404, 448
National Organization of Legal Services Workers (NOLSW), 316
National People's Action, 22, 23
National Research Council, 170
National Retired Teachers Association, 290, 458–59

National Rural Housing Coalition, 28, 406
National School Lunch Program, 190
National School Safety Center, 365–66
National Science Foundation, 145, 418, 424, 431, 446, 447, 491, 496
National Senior Citizens Law Center, 296, 459
National Student Educational Fund (NSEF), 267–68, 448
National Taxpayers Union, 359–60
National Tenants Union, 289
National Training and Information Center (NTIC), 22–25, 403
National Union of Hospital and Health Care Employees, District 1199, 350–54
National Urban League, 29, 249, 250–52, 296, 406, 448
National Wildlife Federation, 130, 138, 139, 145, 151–52, 164–65
  federal funding for, 146, 160, 422–23
Natural gas, 123–26, 282
Natural Gas Policy Act of 1978, 124–25
Natural Gas Supply Association, 126
Natural Resources Defense Council (NRDC), 130, 139, 145, 146, 152–55, 159, 272, 415, 423
Natural Resources Defense Council v. *Hughes*, 153
NCAT. *See* National Center for Appropriate Technology
NCAT's Best, 156, 157
NCC. *See* National Council of Churches
NCCB. *See* National Consumer Co-op Bank
NCL. *See* National Consumers League
NCSC. *See* National Council of Senior Citizens
NEA. *See* National Endowment for the Arts
NED. *See* National Endowment for Democracy
NEH. *See* National Endowment for the Humanities
Neighborhood Development Agency (NDA), 244
Neighborhood Youth Corps, 339
Nestlé boycott, 100–103
Networking: The First Report and Directory, 33
New American Movement, 38, 406
New England Training Center for Community Organizers, 17, 403

New Haven Legal Assistance Association, 323
New Jersey Senior Citizens Coalition, 21
New Jersey Tenants Organization, 14, 39
Newman, Dan, 115
New Mexico Legal Support Project, 311
New Mexico Solar Energy Institute, 157
New Orleans Legal Assistance Corporation, 305
New Republic, 208, 394
New York Council for the Humanities, 350
New York State Council on the Arts, 350
New York Times, 11, 15, 25, 61, 65, 144, 169, 180, 198, 210
Nicaragua, 15
Nicholson, George, 365
Nine to Five, 18, 404
Nixon, Richard M., 190
North American Congress on Latin America, 15, 36, 75
NOW. *See* National Organization for Women
NRDC. *See* Natural Resources Defense Council
NTIC. *See* National Training and Information Center
Nuclear power industry, 131–34
Nuclear Regulatory Commission, 132
Nuestro Publications, 220
Nuila, Pablo, 363

Oakland Urban Legal Foundation, 362
Occupational licensing laws, 257–58, 261
Occupational Safety and Health Administration (OSHA), 56, 57
Office of Economic Opportunity (OEO), 303
Office of Juvenile Justice and Delinquency Prevention (OJJDP), 365
Office of Management and Budget (OMB), 33, 56, 104, 281, 307, 397–400
Offshore leasing, 166–67
Ohio Public Interest Campaign, 123, 280–81, 286, 404, 416, 417, 423
Oil, 94–95, 126–27, 143, 166–67
Oil, Chemical, and Atomic Workers International Union, 29, 416
OMB. *See* Office of Management and Budget

About the Authors

James T. Bennett is an Eminent Scholar at George Mason University and holds the William P. Snavely Chair of Political Economy and Public Policy in the Department of Economics. He received his Ph.D. from Case Western Reserve University in 1970 and has specialized in research related to public policy issues, the economics of government and bureaucracy, and labor unions. He is editor of the *Journal of Labor Research* and has published more than 50 articles in such professional journals as the *American Economic Review, Review of Economics and Statistics, Policy Review, Public Choice,* and *Cato Journal.* His books include *The Political Economy of Federal Government Growth* (1980), *Better Government at Half the Price* (1981), *Deregulating Labor Relations* (1981), *Underground Government: The Off-Budget Public Sector* (1983), and *Labor Unions and the State* (1985). He is an adjunct scholar of the Heritage Foundation, a member of the Mont Pelerin Society, and a member of the Philadelphia Society.

Thomas J. DiLorenzo is associate professor of economics at George Mason University. He received his Ph.D. from Virginia Polytechnic Institute and State University in 1979. His research interests include public choice, state and local public finance, labor economics, and industrial organization. He has published numerous articles in such professional journals as the *American Economic Review, Southern Economic Journal, Public Choice, Public Finance Quarterly, Quarterly Review of Economics and Business, Journal of Labor Research, Policy Review, Cato Journal,* and *International Review of Law and Economics.* His books include *Underground Government: The Off-Budget Public Sector* (1983) and *Labor Unions and the State* (1985). He is an adjunct scholar of the Cato Institute.

Cato Institute

Founded in 1977, the Cato Institute is a public policy research foundation dedicated to broadening the parameters of policy debate to allow consideration of more options that are consistent with the traditional American principles of limited government, individual liberty, and peace. Toward that goal, the Institute strives to achieve a greater involvement of the intelligent, concerned lay public in questions of policy and the proper role of government.

The Institute is named for *Cato's Letters*, pamphlets that were widely read in the American Colonies in the early eighteenth century and played a major role in laying the philosophical foundation for the revolution that followed. Since that revolution, civil and economic liberties have been eroded as the number and complexity of social problems have grown. Today virtually no aspect of human life is free from the domination of a governing class of politico-economic interests. A pervasive intolerance for individual rights is shown by government's arbitrary intrusions into private economic transactions and its disregard for civil liberties.

To counter this trend the Cato Institute undertakes an extensive publications program dealing with the complete spectrum of policy issues. Books, monographs, and shorter studies are commissioned to examine the federal budget, Social Security, regulation, NATO, international trade, and a myriad of other issues. Major policy conferences are held throughout the year, from which papers are published thrice yearly in the *Cato Journal*.

In order to maintain an independent posture, the Cato Institute accepts no government funding. Contributions are received from foundations, corporations, and individuals, and other revenue is generated from the sale of publications. The Institute is a nonprofit, tax-exempt, educational foundation under Section 501(c)3 of the Internal Revenue Code.

CATO INSTITUTE
224 Second St., S.E.
Washington, D.C. 20003